AF615896

A TASARIM MİMARLIK

THE ARCHITECTURE OF
ALİ OSMAN ÖZTÜRK

THE MASTER ARCHITECT SERIES

A TASARIM MİMARLIK

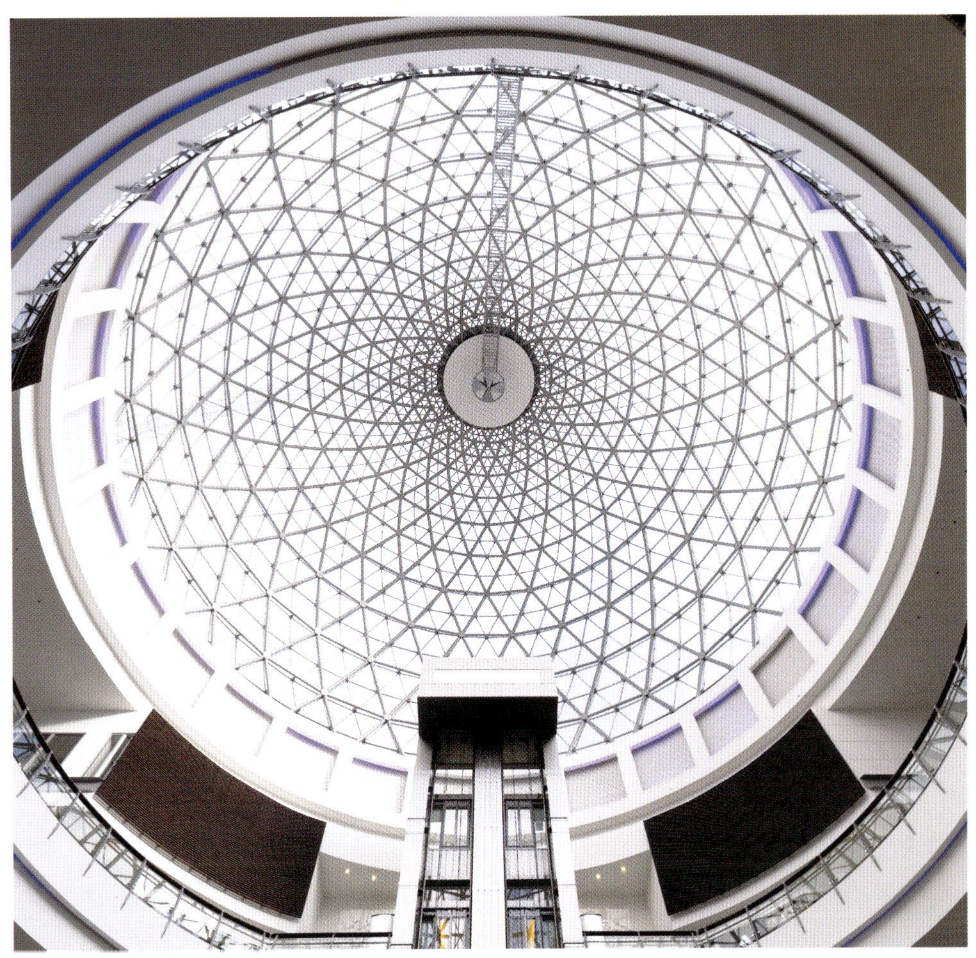

THE ARCHITECTURE OF ALİ OSMAN ÖZTÜRK

images
Publishing

Published in Australia in 2014 by
The Images Publishing Group Pty Ltd
ABN 89 059 734 431
6 Bastow Place, Mulgrave, Victoria 3170, Australia
Tel: +61 3 9561 5544 Fax: +61 3 9561 4860
books@imagespublishing.com
www.imagespublishing.com

The Images Publishing Group Reference Number: 1101

National Library of Australia Cataloguing-in-Publication entry:

Author:	Öztürk, Ali Osman, 1965–
Title:	A Tasarım Mimarlik : The Architecture of Ali Osman Öztürk
ISBN:	978 1 86470 565 2 (hardback)
Subjects:	Öztürk, Ali Osman, 1965–
	Architects—Turkey.
	Architecture—Turkey—20th century.
	Architecture, Modern—20th century.
Dewey Number:	720.9561

Edited by Mandy Herbet

Designed by The Graphic Image Studio Pty Ltd, Mulgrave, Australia
www.tgis.com.au

Pre-publishing services by United Graphic Pte Ltd, Singapore
Printed through Asia Pacific Offset/China on 140gsm GoldEast Matt Art paper

IMAGES has included on its website a page for special notices in relation to this and our other publications. Please visit www.imagespublishing.com.

To my mother, Melahat Öztürk, and father, Satılmış Öztürk, who have prepared me for life; to my sisters, Reyhan and Nazife; to my better-half, my wife İlgiz Öztürk, my daughter Zeynep, and my son Mehmet Ali; with love.

Contents

Profiles

Project Chronology

Foreword

When I graduated from the Faculty of Architecture in the Middle East Technical University in 1987 I was excited and just stepping into my professional life.

In 1997, after a variety of professional experiences and 10 years after my graduation, I established **A Tasarım Mimarlık** and started down the path to produce better buildings.

When I look back today, I realize how lucky I have been; so many beautiful things I could never have dreamed of have become real. With this in mind, I wanted to share our work and incorporate it into this book—a document to represent our work for perpetuity.

The work on this book—our first one, like a first child—began about five years ago. It all started with scanning the archives, with many among the team having had a hand in it. But since the very beginning, Süreyya Atalay has picked every single document and laid the groundwork. İlgiz Öztürk launched the project with our publisher, The Images Publishing Group, establishing the most important connection for the book's publication and she has shaped the working process. Funda Mehter then coordinated publication.

We approached our professor at METU, Professor Dr. Celal Abdi Güzer, with the concept for this book and we are grateful that he steered us in the right direction with his insightful comments and assistance.

Two prominent figures from my professional life to whom I have always looked up—Suha Özkan, Secretary General of the Aga Khan Award for Architecture and founder of the World Architecture Community, and Erkut Şahinbaş, one of the pillars of our profession—have both honored us with their valuable articles and I am grateful for their mentorship and input.

This endeavor means a lot to us, to our families, and I believe contributes much to other disciplines, employers, contractors, and to everyone with the love of architecture.

Thanks to my team and all who contributed to this book and, of course, to the projects in it.

Ali Osman Öztürk
Ankara

—yesille baglantı —su ögesi —sehir meydanı

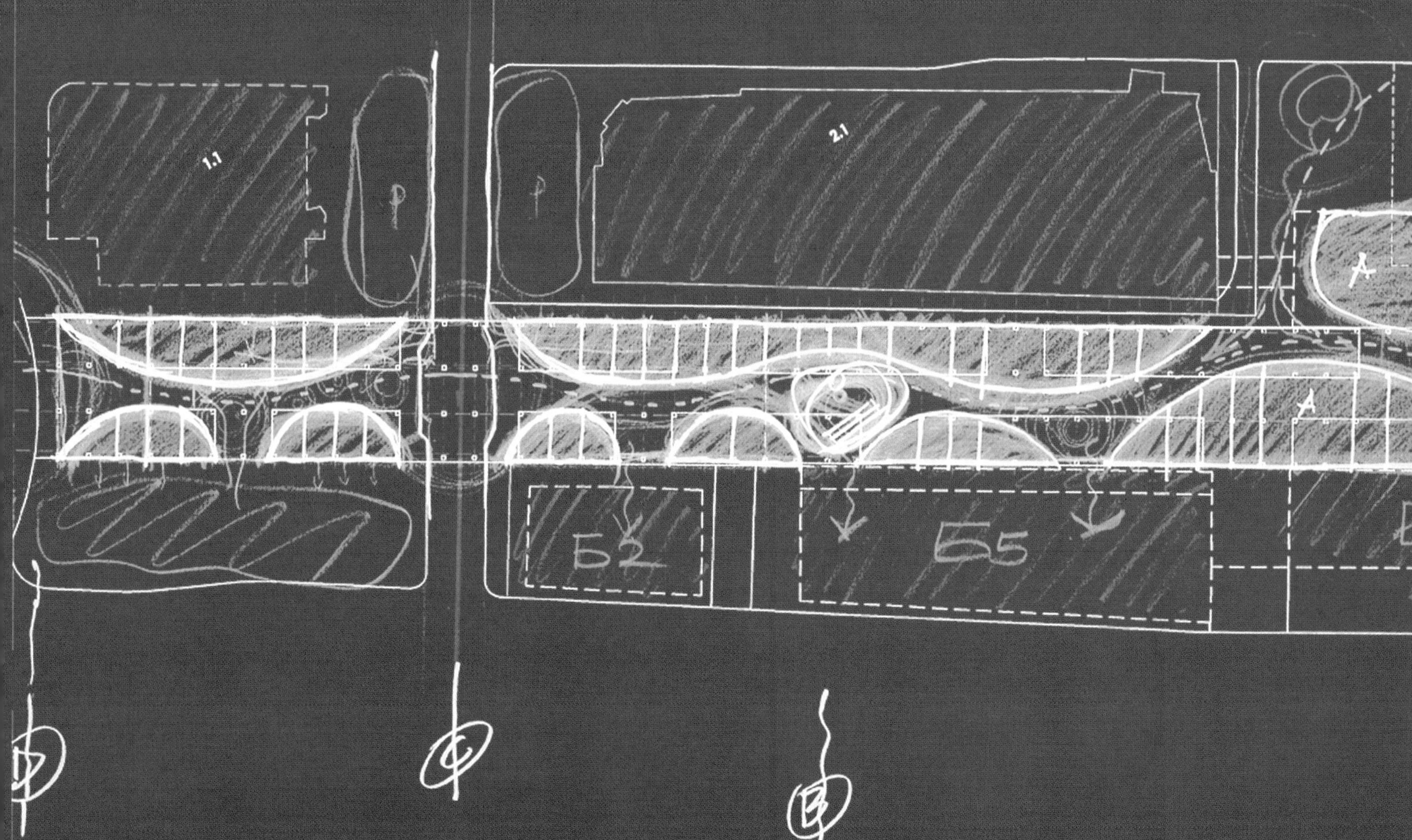

Essays

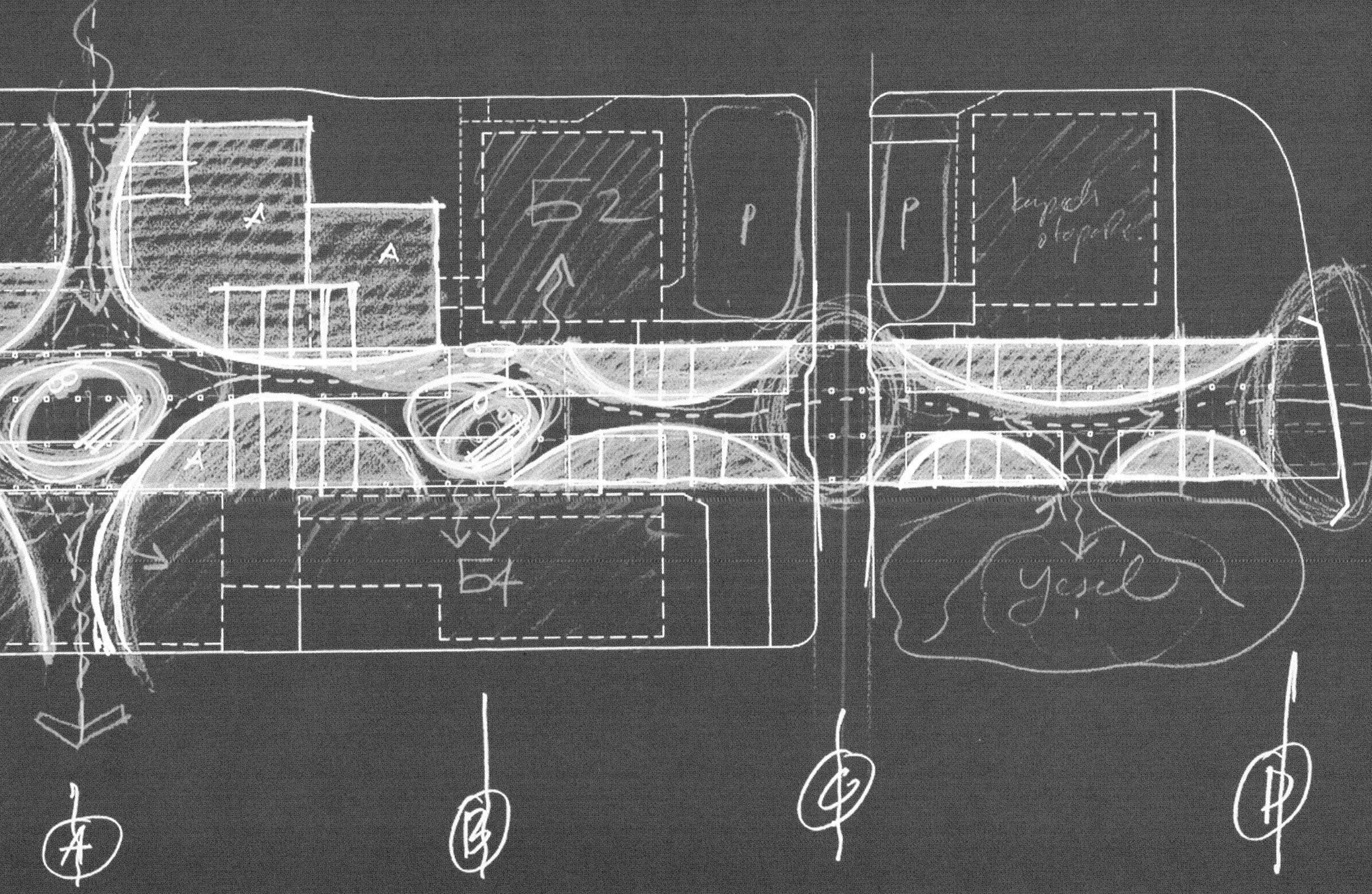

Ali Osman Öztürk: Quiet and Profound

Suha Özkan

For many years in Turkey, architectural design has been an artisanal mode of production. This was particularly the case in Ankara due to the limited scale of construction and architecture, as well as the fact that the public sector was the industry's most notable client. Urban planning and architecture have always been considered as separate disciplines and the "Urban Design" that creates urban life could not flourish as a discipline that brings architectural quality to urban areas.

The staff structure of most architects' offices rarely exceeded a handful of employees, and the organization of these offices was limited to the provision of architectural design services, and incapable of creating integrated projects. This has been the main reason that architecture as a profession in Turkey has not emerged onto the international arena. However, today we have an ambitious field of investments in place, with the employers and financial mechanisms that expect architectural services that create room for urban living over large patches of inefficiently used areas.

Architecture as a profession has redeemed itself, leaving its mark in the last two decades as a respected business with innate authority on and skills in urban design. Such an environment, where project production provides all engineering services, has allowed our profession to develop its "Design Corporations." A Tasarım Mimarlık-Ali Osman Öztürk, together with other groups such as Tabanlıoğlu, Arolat, and Öncüoğlu today enjoy designing grand projects in both hemispheres, and hopefully will go on doing so in the future.

A decade ago in the field of international construction, contractors enjoyed many successes as a sector, with an undisputable presence. However, the most crucial component and the creative engine of that very sector, namely "Design" could not, unfortunately, take on a considerable role. In Turkey, the absence of architecture and urban design as an integrated area of design has been diminished. Today, integrated urban design projects utilizing the most advanced levels of technology have almost become natural as the demands of the new generation of clients grow. Time has come for our architects to contribute universally with creativity and their professional expertise. Our profession has reached a level where it will become more visible and claim its international position. In such an environment, we have high expectations for Ali Osman Öztürk. As a group, A Tasarım Mimarlık has inserted urban life and quality architecture into large-scale construction and as such, the firm is ready and mature enough to compete with many international design groups.

I taught at METU for a total of 20 years and not having worked with Ali Osman during all that time for me is a loss. However, he had organized a tour of Europe and visited me in Geneva, where we met for the first time. A group of bright people, eager to learn, chasing after novel solutions and new buildings, and gathering exciting impressions was an encouraging experience for me. Amid those dynamic and young people, Ali Osman has fast become a good friend. His qualities as a leader, and his intimate, sympathetic personality have been remarkable. This friendship has always been based on love and respect and it will remain so.

The same professional brightness I witnessed in Ali Osman, I saw in Laurinda Spear, my student at Columbia University, New York. What Ali Osman created in A Tasarım in terms of integrated large-scale building design capacity, Laurinda has achieved with her husband Bernardo in their corporate practice: Arquitectonica. Today, the level of design quality that A Tasarım Mimarlık has accomplished can professionally be compared with that of Arquitectonica. Even though they have more than 100 international projects in their portfolio.

A close observation of A Tasarım Mimarlık's projects, reveals the presence of a serious training of their clients. Ali Osman in all his qualities is silent, modest, and personable. He gets along well in harmony, in both social and professional spheres. However, his struggle for perfection transpires all through his work. One feels proud in watching him as a "Trainer of Design"—never oppressive, never a source of conflict, or never dominating the entire process but with a focus on consensus and finding solutions through negotiations. It is all so natural when one considers the long range of his efforts: his clients and investors who have been opening themselves up to new concepts to execute. For the newly fledged circles of clients, working with him bears the hope of new horizons to explore.

Architecture, by its nature, has no room for growing old. The industry's longevity is the greatest resource for architects. Similarly, Ali Osman, who has carried out such great projects with success from such a young age, leaves us anticipating what is still to come. His quiet, tolerant, and harmonious attitude enchants his friends while his large-scale building designs are the sources of envy for all. His solutions, offering newer urban spatial experiences, become more profound in time.

I am sure that this book will share with the global public A Tasarım Mimarlık's prominent architectural achievements. As Ali Osman's career progresses and flourishes, there are sure to be more books showing the world the great works he is capable of producing.

Ali Osman, for all these years, I have been watching you. What I see is that you take your work seriously. Your approach deserves to be remembered as the deontology of our business.

Prof. Dr. Suha Özkan *is the founder of*
World Architecture Community

Creativity as a matter of self-discipline

Erkut Şahinbaş

Architecture is the union of aesthetic ideals and views; it is designing authentic inventions through imagination and creativity.

As much as I can keep track of him, and as much as I know and have gotten to know him during his school years, my colleague Ali Osman Öztürk has always been an outstanding and a noteworthy figure with his enthusiasm to learn about our profession and even more so, with his ardent belief in "I can"—which is the precondition of creativity. Now, after many years, I see that I was not mistaken. His passion to work, his connection with the material, his keen eye for technology, the richness of his expression that never oversees the human quality and that is never oblivious of the human scale, and his sensitivity for details are all integral to his work.

When designing, architects sometimes tend to steer their accumulated energies into chaos. Preventing chaos rising from creativity is a matter of self-discipline. Ali Osman Öztürk has that discipline when it comes to overcoming this challenge that surfaces in his multi-purpose buildings; and he overcomes those challenges with his logic.

When you consider successful architects, the talent called "creativity" that they have inbred in their character, the courage to take on responsibility, and the inflated freedom of spirit you see are accompanied by modesty and the ability to focus on the essence. These features, along with others, give way to trust, respect, and compromise. That is why these people can handle projects calmly and little details with gravity.

Frank Barron distills this out of his research on creativity: the scale to measure creativity operates on the traits of the created object and the social acceptance it receives. What attracts my attention in Ali Osman Öztürk's architecture is how intimately his buildings are accepted and internalized by their occupants, clients, and visitors.

All designs desire responsibility. The architect is free during design; yet there is no escape from responsibility—that is a fact. Because responsibility houses blame, punishment, and praise. Responsibility and freedom are always side-by-side. Ali Osman is worthy of praise as he lives up to his responsibilities. This is evident in the success he reaps from his recent large-scale assignments. This is evident in both quality and quantity.

As Ernest Hemingway says, "The secret to the power of being able lies in humility." Alex Rovira says, on the other hand, "Humility is not a weakness, but on the contrary an indication of inner strength. Humble people, their grandeur spares no one. There is always something to learn from them. There is always someone to find out in them. That is why humility goes hand in hand with conscience."

Ali Osman Öztürk, with his self-confidence and modesty, can complete his task through clinging to ideals that are—sometimes—much bigger than himself. As he matures and as, in the last decade, he adds to our country's architectural culture and environment, we are increasingly proud of him and my belief is firm and intimate that his contribution will become more and more valuable into the future.

__Erkut Şahinbaş__ is the winner of the Mimar Sinan Grand Award in 2012, awarded by The Chamber of Architects in Turkey.

The Architecture of A Tasarım Mimarlık: Between Mainstream Modernity and Contextual Reality

Celal Abdi Güzer

Contemporary architecture in Turkey demonstrates an "in-between" state, much like anything else in the geography. Turkey finds itself in-between east and west; in-between different cultures, religions, and languages; as well as being in-between wealth and poverty. As such, Turkey not only represents cultural plurality but also conflicts and contradictions. The urban image of Turkish cities, the architectural composition of buildings reflects this eclectic plurality and contradictions. In this cultural context, it is neither easy to engage with modern architecture in the western sense nor sustain local and vernacular values. However, during the republican period, there had always been a conscious effort to engage with the international tradition of architecture. Most of these efforts ended up as second-hand reproduction of mainstream architecture, where the production represented eclectic transformations due to cultural, economic, and social context. The early 21st century, in this sense, can be seen as a breaking point where, parallel to the liberation of economic policies, global transparency established a platform for an alternative architectural organization. Many architectural offices started to work on an international approach, especially in collaboration with Turkish construction firms in the Middle East and former republican countries of Soviet Union. New building types and large scale projects had been introduced to Turkey as a result of privatization projects. Many international architectural firms established offices and started projects in Turkey. In this context, some of the local architectural offices managed to establish a sustainable connection with the international market. **A Tasarım Mimarlık, Ali Osman Öztürk** is one of the first Turkish architectural firms that has successfully established a practice to international standards. Over the course of 25 years, the group not only realized major projects in metropolitan Turkish cities but also partnered with many well-known international architectural groups.

The work of **A Tasarım Mimarlık** can be analyzed in different titles and periods. However, independent from the stylistic approach, the common ground to understand its unique character is a critical sensitivity and awareness towards Turkey's cultural context. Most of the projects, while based on international typologies and prototypes, are adapted to the local context and requirements. Context in this definition stands not only for the limited understanding of the physical surroundings but rather a wider understanding inclusive of culture, tradition, available technologies, and bureaucracy. Such a contextual approach also forms the major legislative ground behind the form, language, and style-based differences between different projects. Freeing the design approach from a style-based identity also creates a sense of freedom to develop contextual solutions.

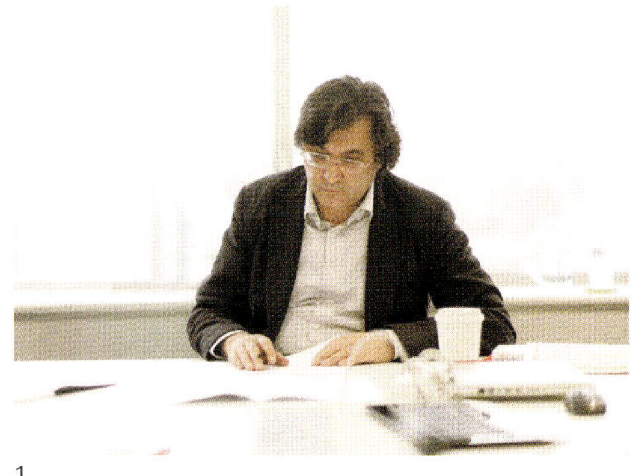

1

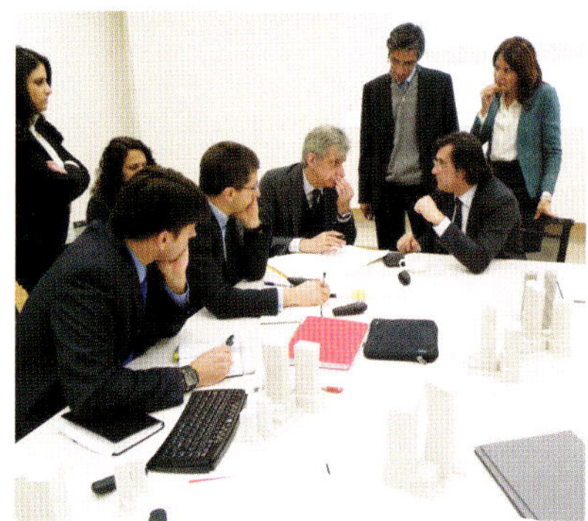

2

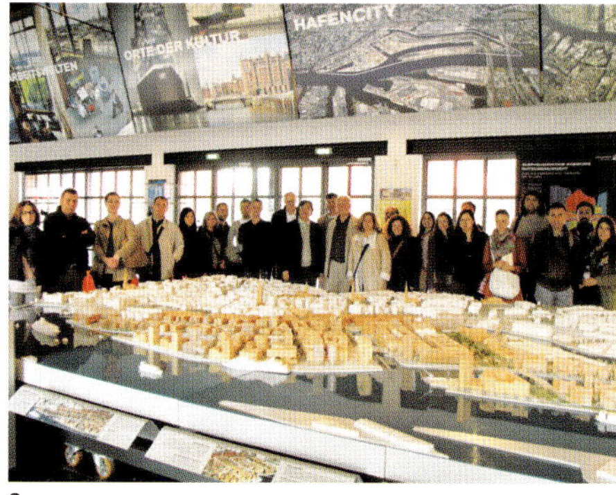

3

1 Ali Osman Öztürk
2 Ali Osman Öztürk, Paul Katz, Mustafa Chebabeddine, Dominic Dunn, and the Ziraat Bank team meeting in the KPF London Office
3 A Tasarım Mimarlık team with Prof. Volkwin Marg, Wolfgang Haux, and Yasemin Erkan in Hamburg

Ali Osman Öztürk is modest enough to adopt typological and conventional established values. In this sense, being unique is not reduced to an understanding of expression but rather an urban, contextual contribution of the building. As a graduate of one of the international architecture schools, and, after gaining teaching experience and working in different partnerships, Ali Osman Öztürk established **A Tasarım Mimarlık**, which quickly became one of Turkey's best-known architectural firms.

The Armada development is one of the first large-scale projects that helped make Ali Osman Öztürk and **A Tasarım Mimarlık** well known in Turkey. As one of the first shopping mall and office complexes in Ankara, Armada transformed the established typology of shopping malls into a more transparent building type. With multiple entrances in different levels and the potential to connect different parts of the city, the building becomes a major intersection point within the neighborhood. The annex of the building sustained this idea with an interior pedestrian path, a street where the urban character of the building had been underlined. Later, such an idea was carried out to an extreme in the Tepe Prime shopping and office complex where all composition is based upon continuity of an urban public space. In this project, ground level is reserved for public functions and

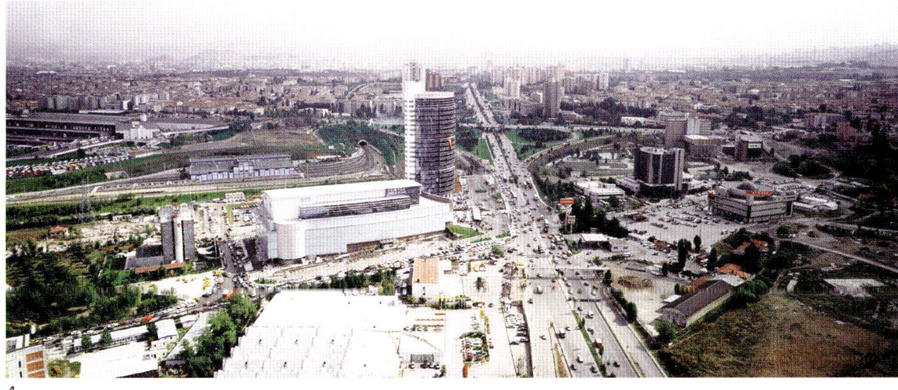
4

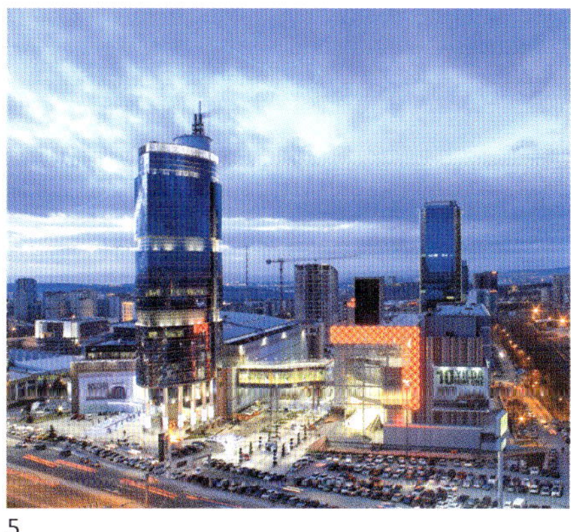
5

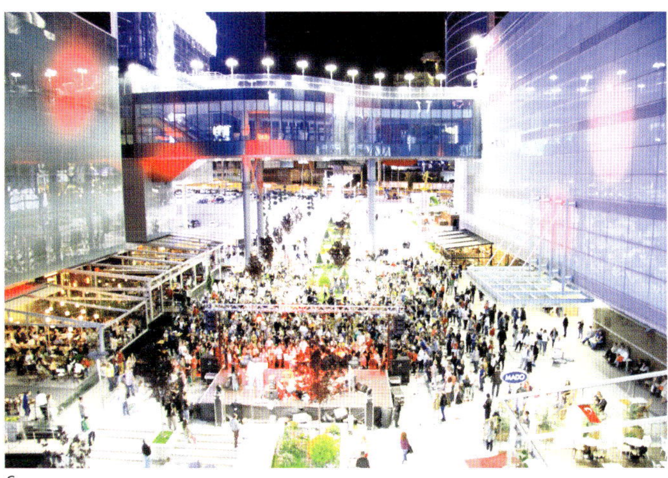
6

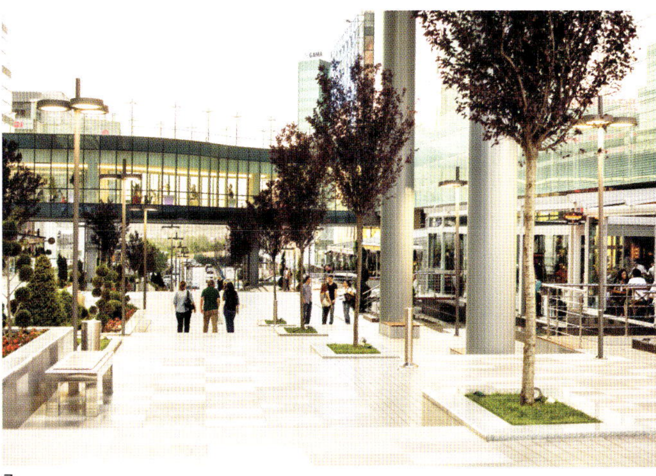
7

4 Armada, Söğütözü District, 2002
5 Armada Development Project
6 A concert being held in Armada
7 Armada pedestrian alley

gastronomical facilities, not only supporting the upper office spaces but also creating a public hub in the district city scale. With open urban qualities, Tepe Prime represents a unique project open to be utilized as an alternative to conventional shopping mall typologies.

Re-creation of the urban context is a major goal in many **A Tasarım Mimarlık** projects. The basic reason for such a starting point is the insufficiency of urban planning in most metropolitan Turkish cities. Under the pressure of accelerated urbanization and growth, planning had always been subject to an eclectic and non-comprehensive approach, where most of the large-scale projects tended to be developed as independent entities within gated borders and in separate parcels. In this context, architectural scale inevitably faces an additional difficulty of not only providing programmatic expectations but also providing services and facilities that are lacking due to planning shortfalls. The MIA, Central District of Business Project is a unique example where a single project had been utilized to transform the historical center of Ankara. In this project, **A Tasarım Mimarlık** was commissioned to realize a series of new office buildings, replacing the existing fabric of small industrial production ateliers in the central part of Ankara.

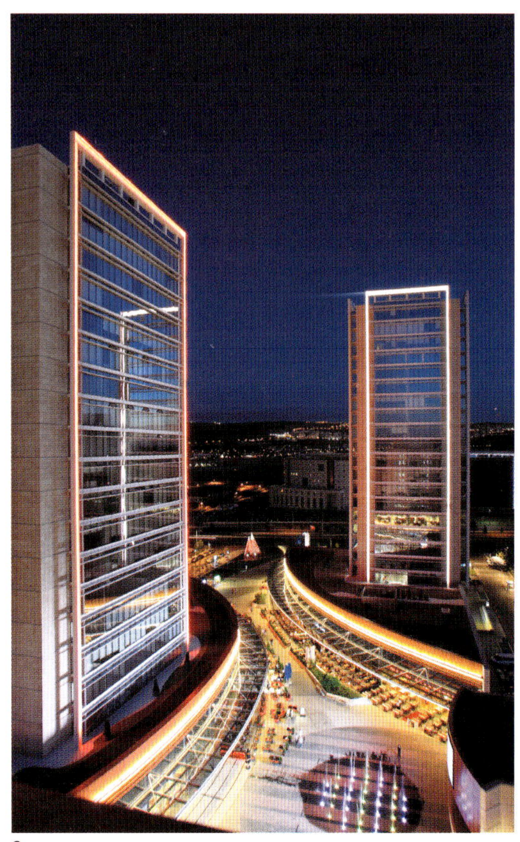
8

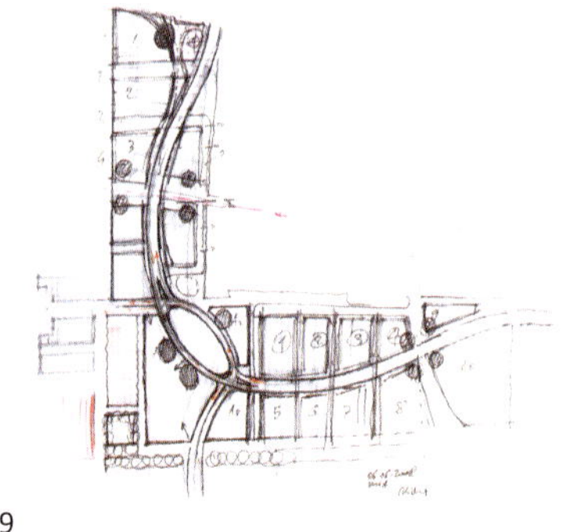
9

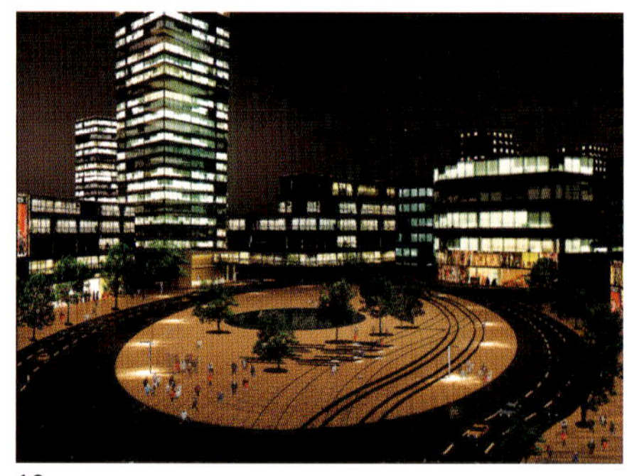
10

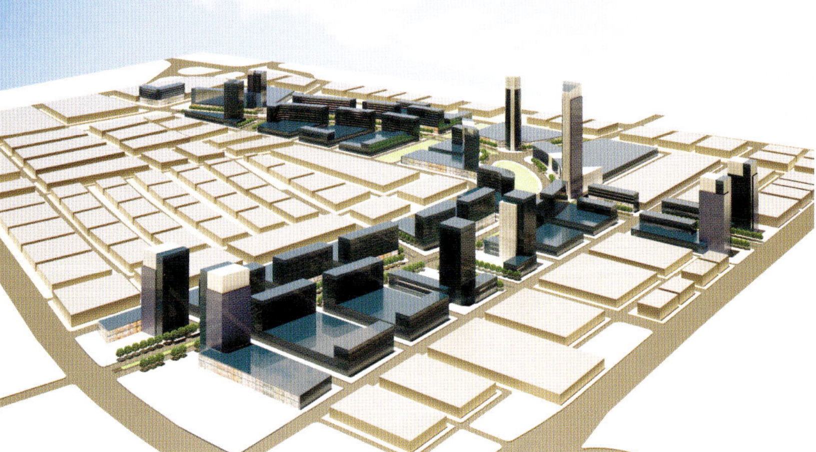
11

8 Tepe Prime
9 Central Business District Project sketch by Ali Osman Öztürk
10 Central Business District Project visualisation at night
11 Central Business District Project model

The site was composed of independent small parcels, which had been accidentally brought together due to ownership patterns. Rather than developing an architectural project directly, **A Tasarım Mimarlık** utilized a model whereby owners gathered to represent a more meaningful urban lot. Following that, a number of alternatives were presented to the municipality where, alongside the office buildings, a central urban area with urban facilities and open public spaces was introduced as an integrated part of the project. The end product is, once again, not only an urban transformation project but also a model to be adapted for similar developments.

Another project aiming to establish an urban sense and continuity beyond the projects borders is the TOBB University project. To establish a private University, the Union of Chambers of Commerce bought an old high-school building in Ankara. In addition to this main land, some additional building lots in the same area had also been bought due to availability. **A Tasarım Mimarlık** converted the existing building into a main university building, upgrading its existing structure with contemporary architectural language. A public atrium acted as a transitory space between the existing and additional building. This main campus later connected to sub-functional areas and a sense of urban continuity had been established.

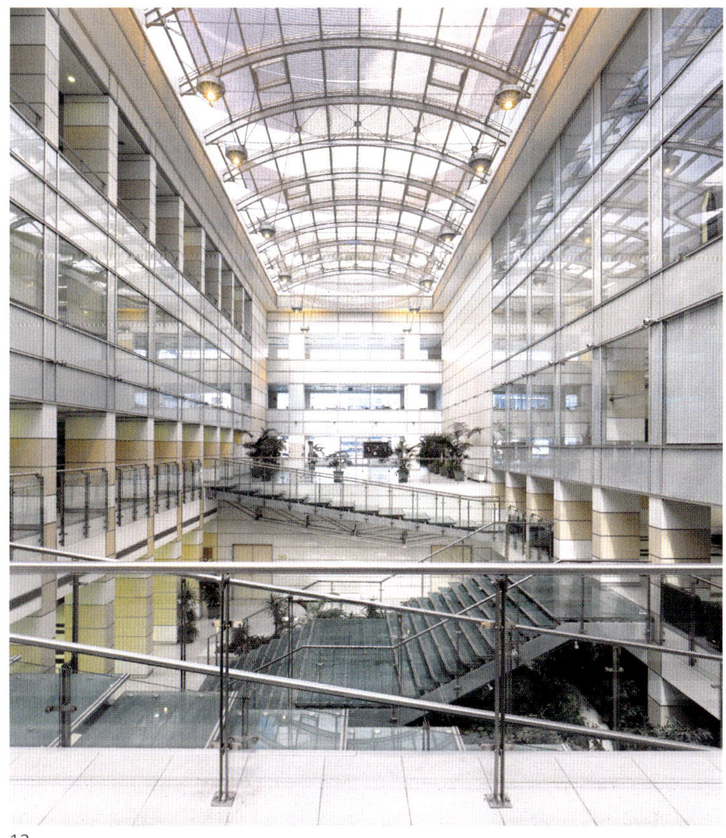

12

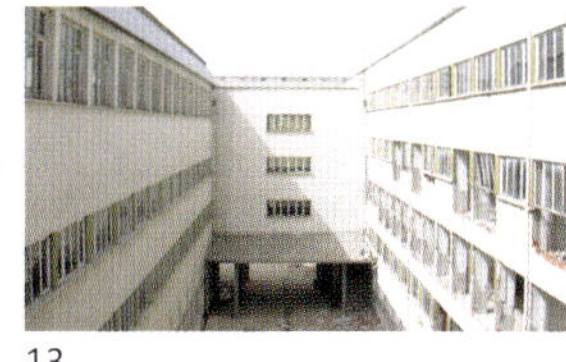

13

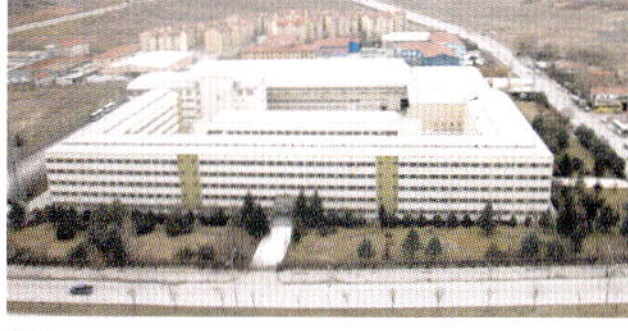

14

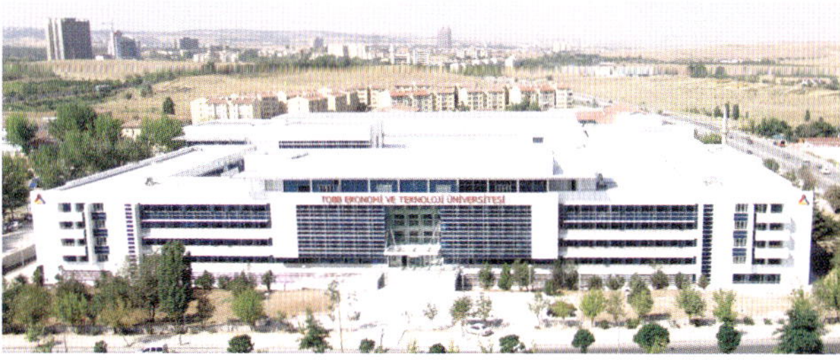

15

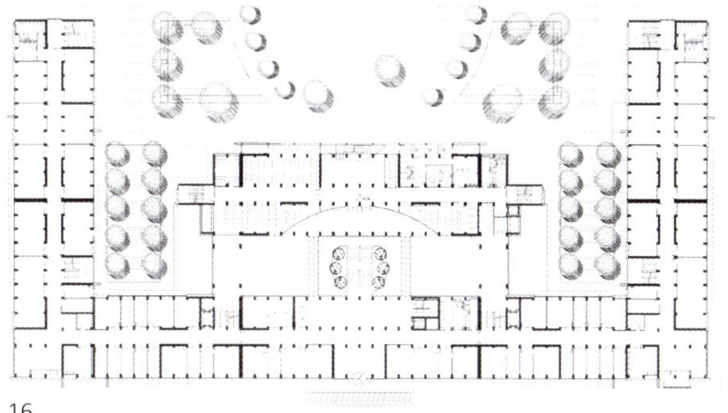

16

12 TOBB UET renovated atrium
13 Former TOBB UET atrium
14 General view of the former TOBB UET buildings
15 TOBB UET general view of renovated project
16 TOBB UET ground floor plan

The Panora shopping complex and Antares multi-functional complex, which include housing blocks as well as shopping facilities, are two other projects that attempt to emphasize the public and urban character of the settlements. Panora had sought to be integrated with an urban park where the classical box typology of the shopping mall had been converted to a semi-transparent building. The ground level facing the park and following floors on the same façade have been reserved for food and beverage facilities, encouraging an urban use independent from the building itself. In a similar way, in the Antares project, additional units were surrounded by the main shopping mass to provide a sense of the street pattern and to strengthen the definition of public spaces. Departing from these two experiences in the Skopje project, urban sensitivity became the major consideration. The upper borders of a proposed tram tunnel were assigned as a potential building lot in the central historical part of Skopje. Existing buildings, green areas, empty lots, and a historical and listed train station surrounded the site, with the intention to convert the station into a museum building. The site was at the end of the central pedestrian alley,

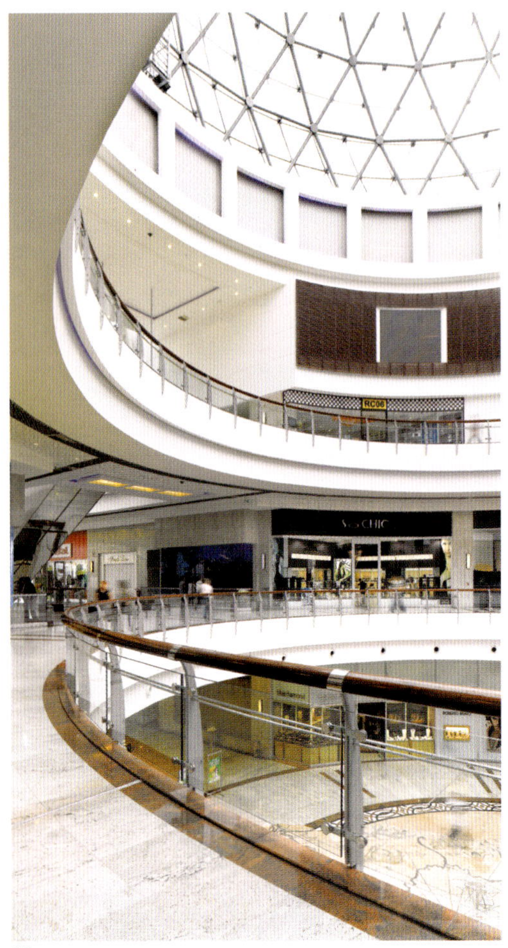

17

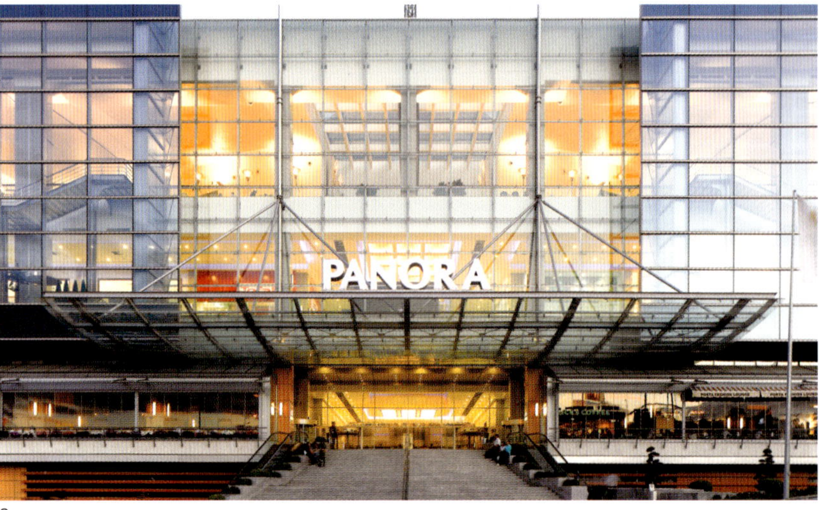

18

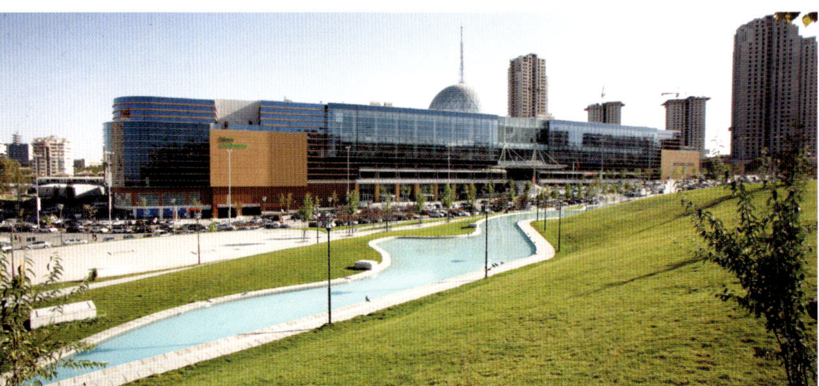

19

17 Interior view of Panora
18 Panora main entrance
19 Panora general view with park

connecting old city to the new development area, which is next to the district planned by Japanese architect and planner Kenzō Tange. The existing tram tunnel and the structure assigned by this tunnel as the bases of development were additional challenges. In this context, the project represented a potential transformation not limited to the site itself but rather affecting the whole historical center. The proposed ground level is an alternative pedestrian shopping arcade connecting different nodes of the neighborhood. The linear structure includes passages between different parts of the city, small public squares, green terraces, and links to the neighboring buildings. The museum, as well as the pedestrian axis, becomes an integral part of the project. The Skopje Multi-Functional Center aims to provide a sustainable pedestrian urban experience, blurring the differences between old and new. The project is a multilevel continuity of the existing city fabric rather than being a single and traceable building.

20 Antares general view
21 Antares upper level plan
22 Antares interior

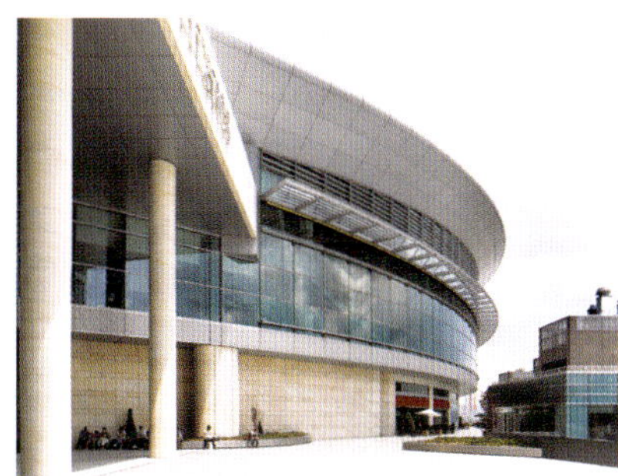

20

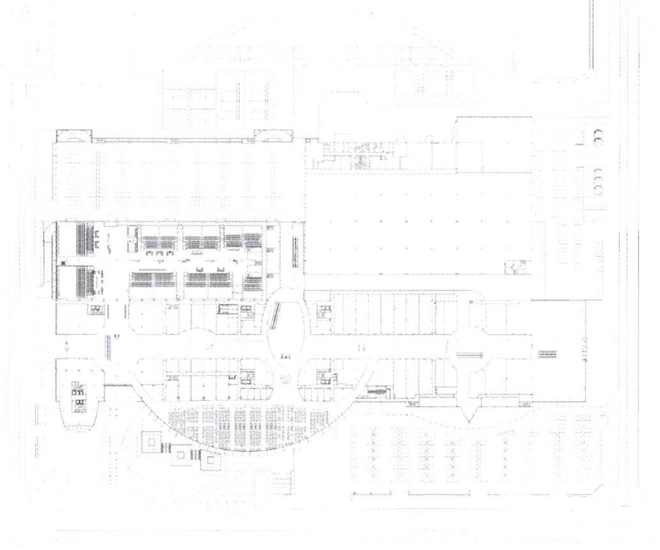

21

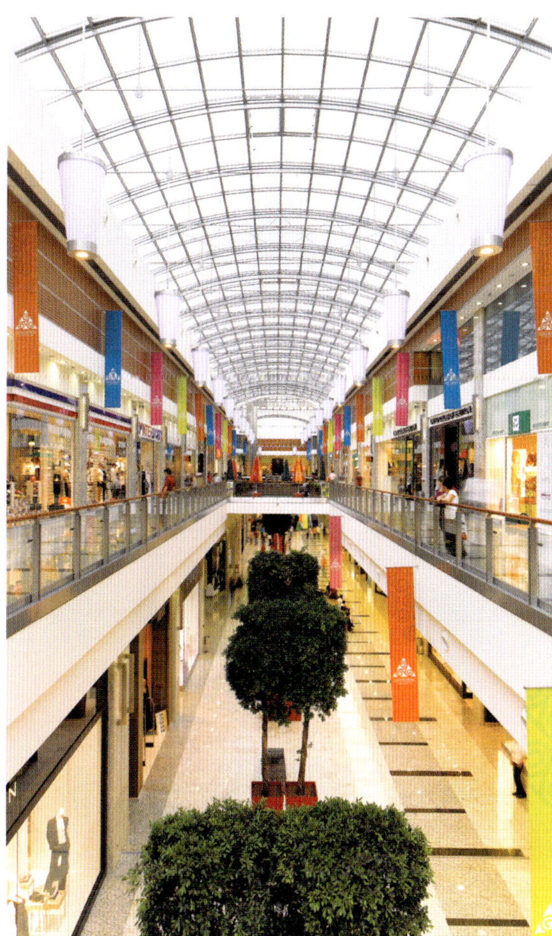

22

Representation of cultural diversity is a theme that is repeated in many **A Tasarım Mimarlık** projects. Among these, a contemporary mosque project is unique in terms of the abstract utilization of traditional architectural elements and conventional typologies. With its powerful and dominant iconography based upon tradition, mosque architecture is one of the most conservative building typologies in the Turkish context. On the other hand, referring to the traditional and local values and creating a sense of sustainability had always been a major challenge in modern understanding of mosque architecture. In Yaşamkent Mosque, the composition is based on freestanding parallel walls, not only defining the essence of interior space, but also creating a transitory medium for exterior and interior spaces. As a powerful traditional element, the walls and courtyard use glass and concrete as finishing elements. The use of abstract and solid geometries, modest simplicity, and minimalist architectural attitude refers to a contemporary architectural language whereas abstract *kufic* expressions of minaret as well as the abstract motives of fences refer to more familiar traditional elements. In the main prayer hall, a modest concrete dome has not only been used as a reference to tradition but also enhances the interior scale and allows light inside. With these characteristics, the Yaşamkent mosque must be seen as an experiment in blurring significant and ideological differences and popular architectural contradictions between tradition and modernity.

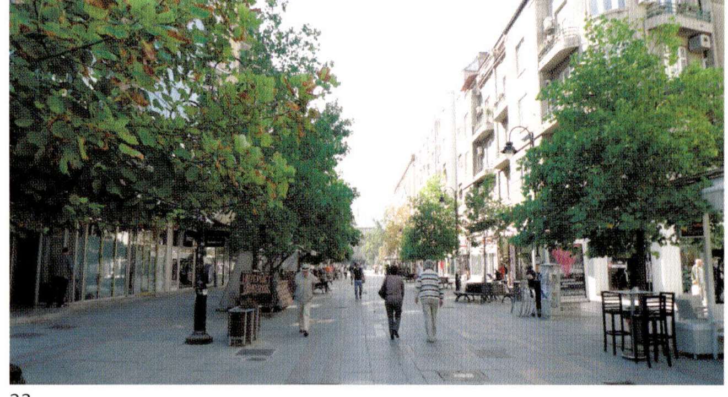

23

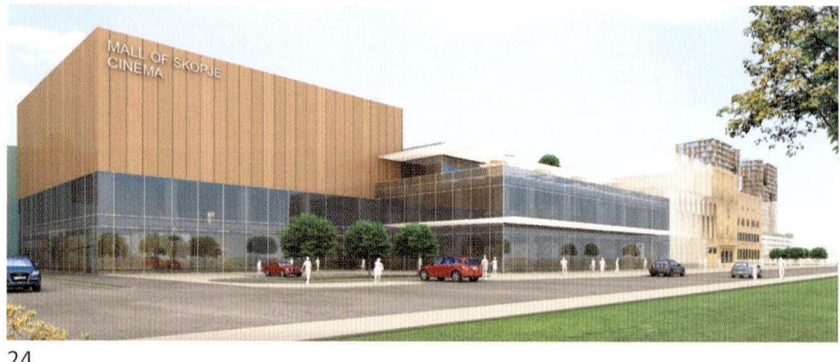

24

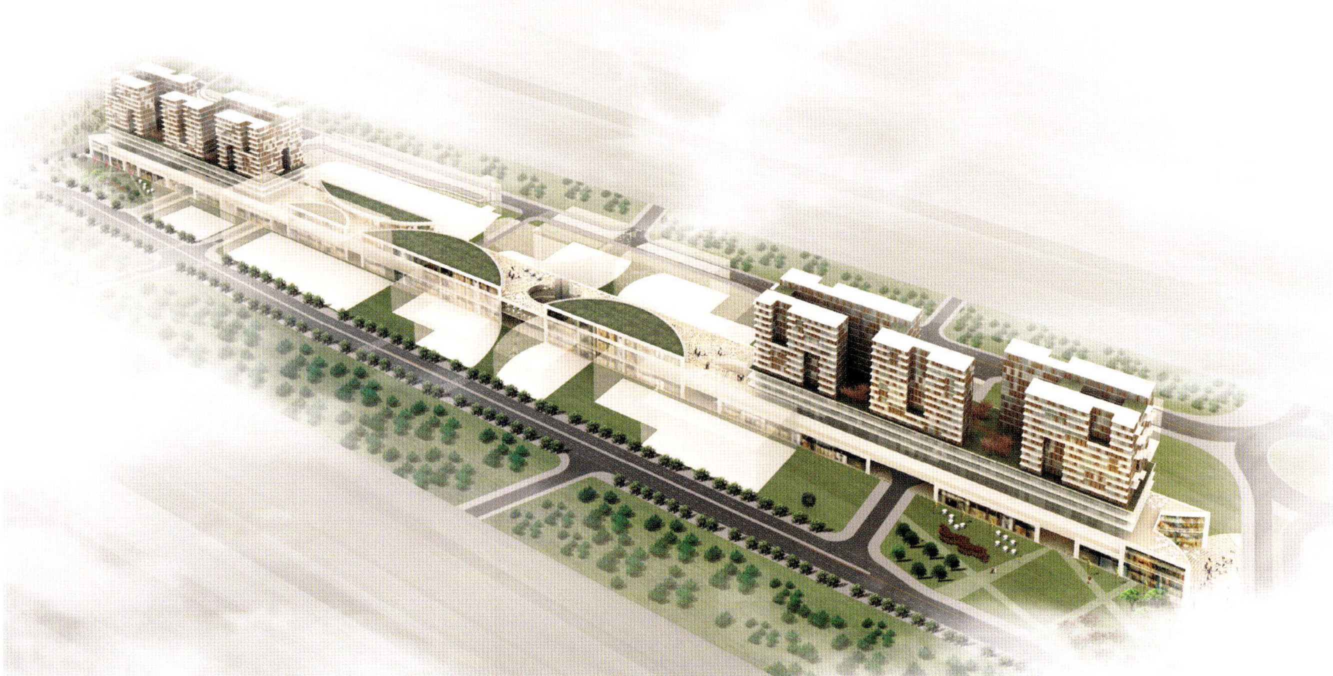

25

The Türk Telekom Headquarters high-rise tower is one of the first projects to use eco-friendly research in the high-rise typology. The use of a double façade, along with gardens on different floors and the use of recycled material and solar energy becomes the basis for developing original details and solutions. Despite the building's high-tech image, most of the elements and details are conventional. The use of conventional details, thereby eliminating complicated construction solutions, is common in most of **A Tasarım Mimarlık's** projects.

Ali Osman Öztürk prefers to highlight a project-specific challenge as the main impetus of each design process. This may vary from urban integration to cultural diversity, or environmental sustainability to language-based research. Such positional flexibility inevitably brings a variety of projects free from style-based continuity. In other words, **A Tasarım Mimarlık** aims to search for context and case-based solutions in every project, instead of seeking a continuity of language or style. This approach not only prepares the ground for research-based and unique solutions, but also allows for collaboration with different national and international partners, and the ability to work in different regions and programs. The production and unique effort of Ali Osman Öztürk is open to be read in multiple domains. However, the collection of projects in this book represents the plurality of a flexible and contextual approach more than anything else. For a sustainable architecture aiming to blur the conflicts between mainstream modernity and contextual reality, such flexibility is inevitable.

Celal Abdi Güzer *is a professor at Middle East Technical University*

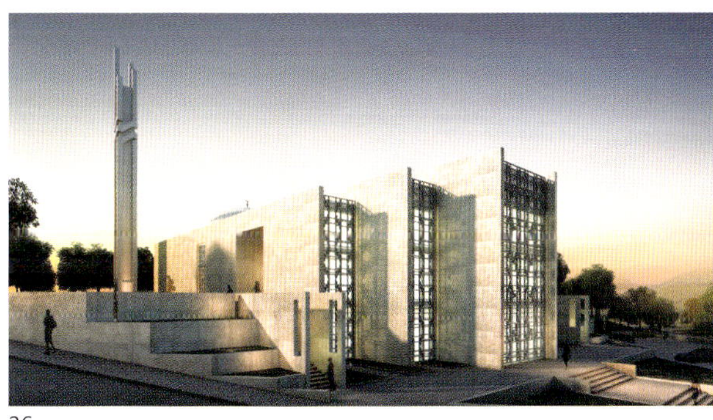

26

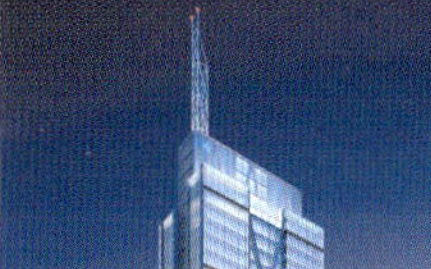

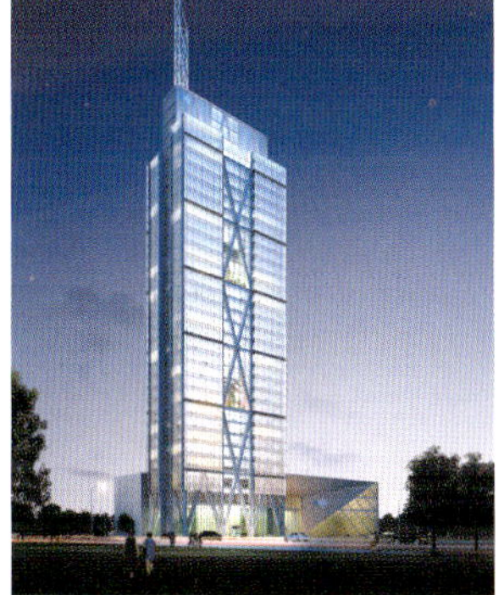

27

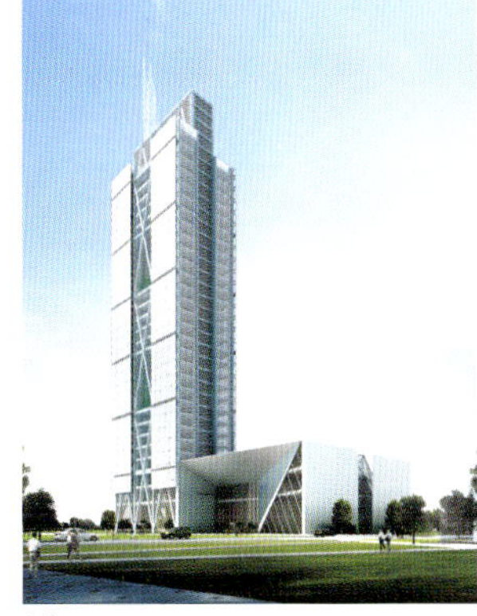

28

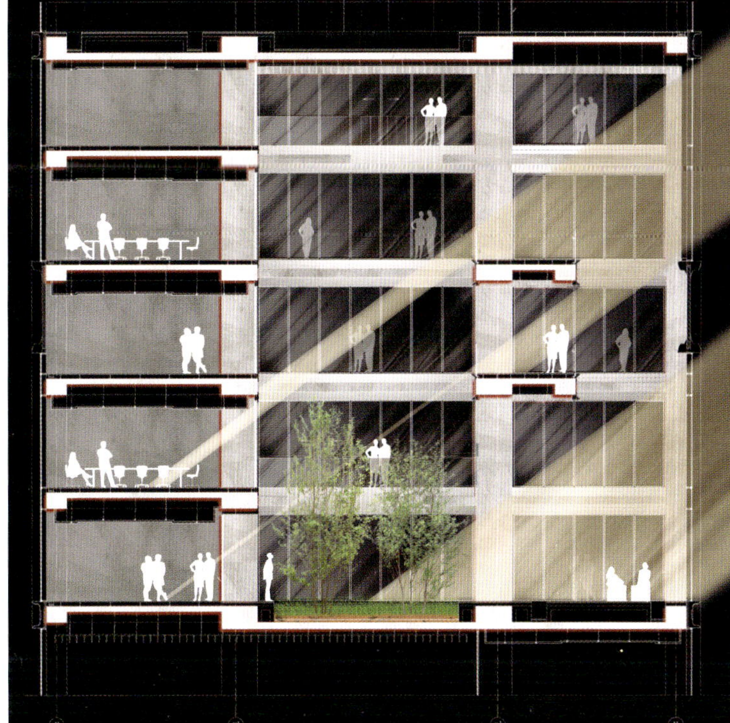

29

23 Pedestrian street towards the Skopje Mixed-Use Center
24 Skopje Mixed-Use Center project overview
25 Skopje Mixed-Use Center project entrance view
26 Yaşamkent Mosque
27 Türk Telekom Headquarters at night
28 Türk Telekom general view
29 Türk Telekom section detail

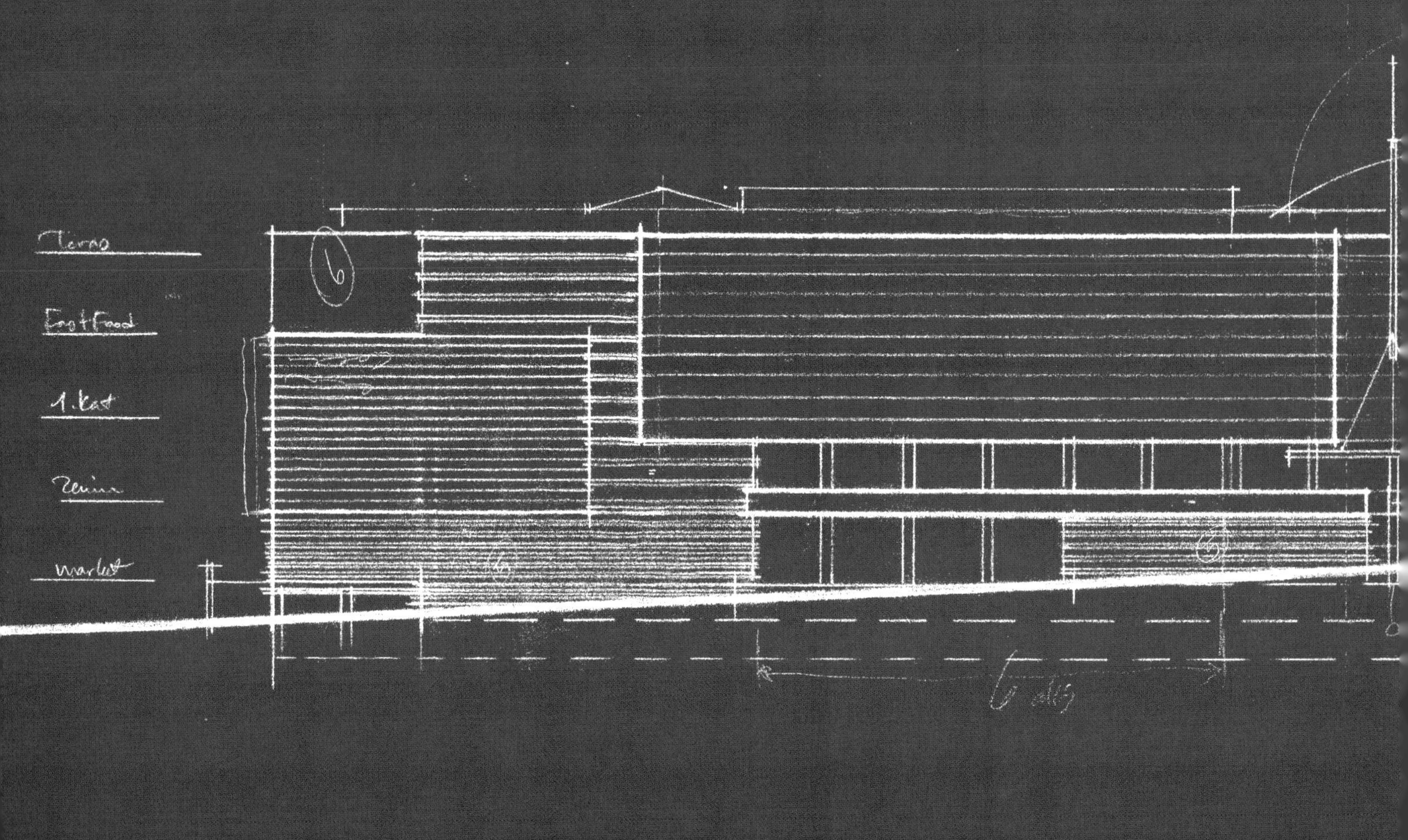
Teras
FastFood
1.kat
Zemin
market

Selected Projects

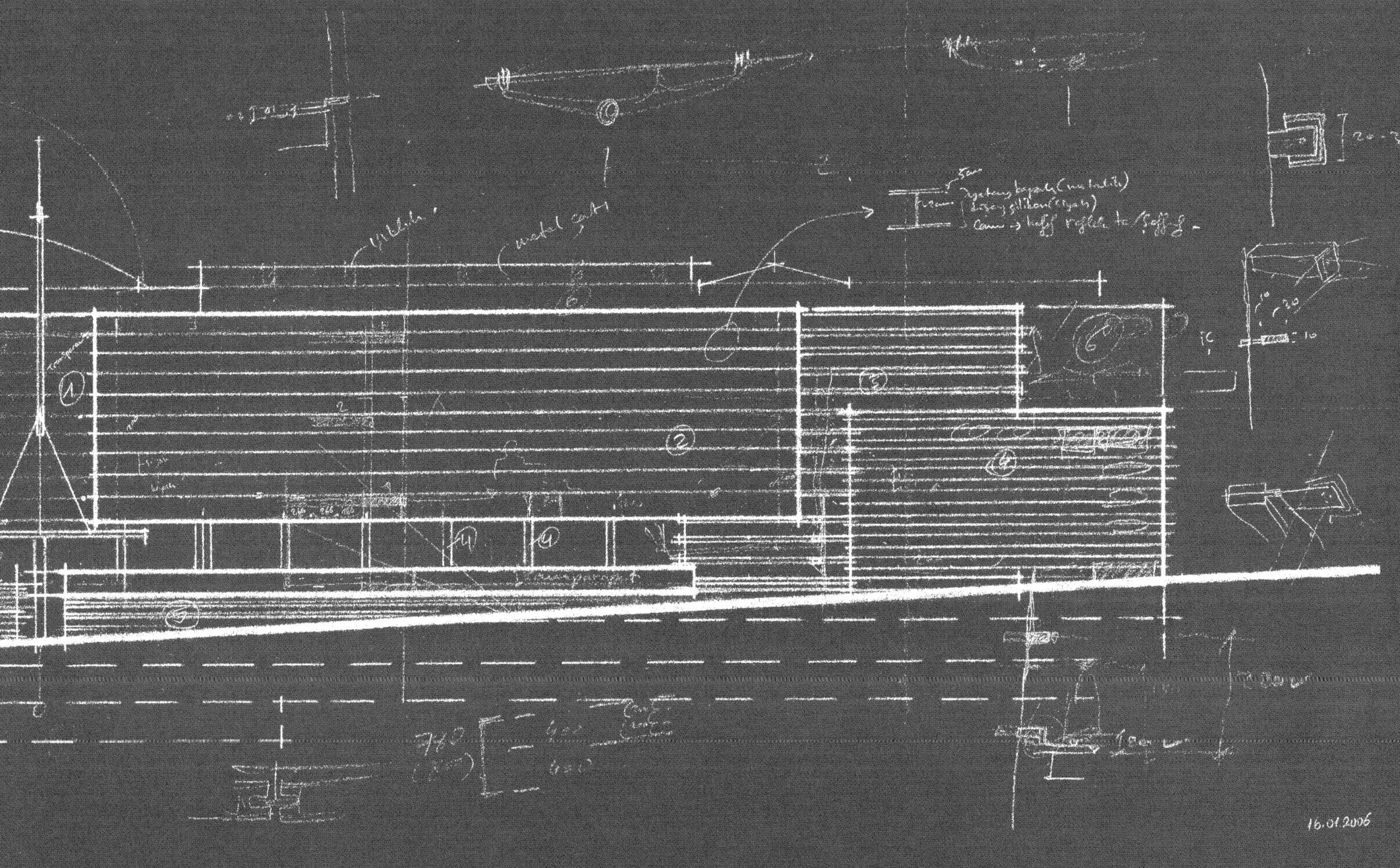

Armada

Client Söğütözü Construction and Management
Project Date 1998–2002
Area 125,000 m^2
Location Ankara
Design Consultant Salih Bezci, Vecihi Yıldız, and GMW Architectural Ltd.
Structural Engineer Yüksek Project
Mechanical Engineer Ünlü Engineering
Electrical Engineer Emak Engineering
Leasing Consultant Alkaş Consultancy, Avi Alkaş
Mechanical Consultant İhsan Önen
Construction Supervisor Ömer Genç, Sonay Özar
Contractor Söğütözü Construction and Management
2004 ICSC European Shopping Center Awards First Prize
2005 ICSC International Design and Development, Merit

The Armada Business and Commercial Center was one of the first high-rise buildings to be erected along the development strip on the west corridor of Ankara. Beyond being a business and commercial center, the building has functioned as an urban generator and has helped define the developments. The building, a business and commercial center, was inaugurated in September 2002, and was designed as a refined and appealing shopping center distinguished from buildings of similar function.

The building is composed of one horizontal and one vertical block. By taking advantage of the inclination of the site, the building has an entrance on each of its four façades, situated on three different levels. The main entrance, which opens to the Eskişehir Avenue, is through a hallway that rises three-stories high and is naturally lit. Following the entrance hall, circulation halls divide into two individual paths. These corridors connect at the atrium, creating an uninterrupted circulation route through the building.

The commercial center has a rentable area of approximately 32,000 square meters and includes around 150 stores and fast food counters of various sizes. There is a cinema hall with 11 theaters, a large supermarket, and a 3,100-vehicle car park, serving both the visitors and residents of the center.

The design of the office block is based on the intersection of two arches in panoramic relation with each other. The 21-story office tower has a trapezoidal plan and was designed to offer a series of different impressions of the block from various points of the city and from within the building itself. The main effort leading the design of the tower was to create a building with distinctive and original spatial quality that will hopefully take its place in the city silhouette.

Opposite:
View of the roof from west with the food-court terrace

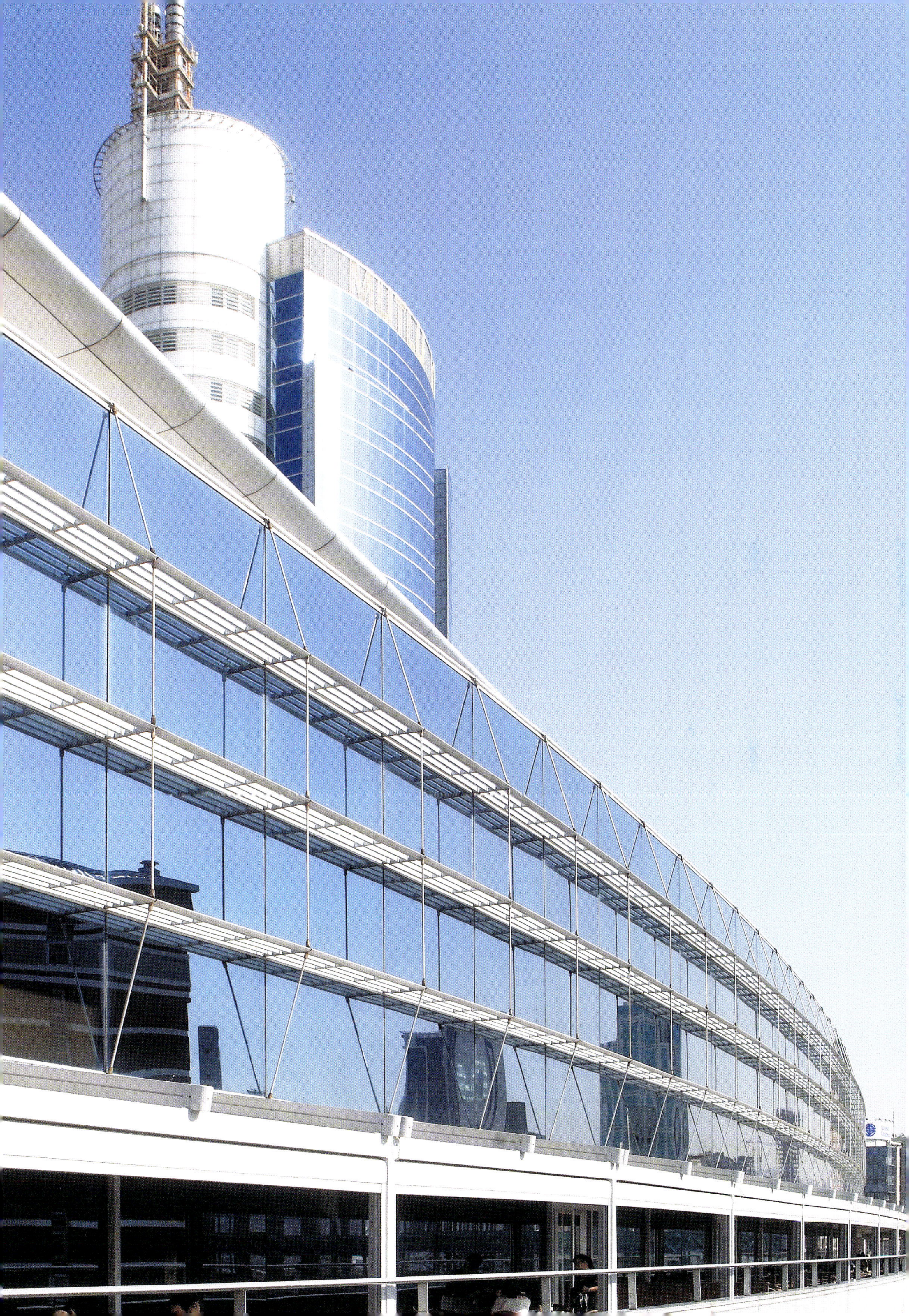

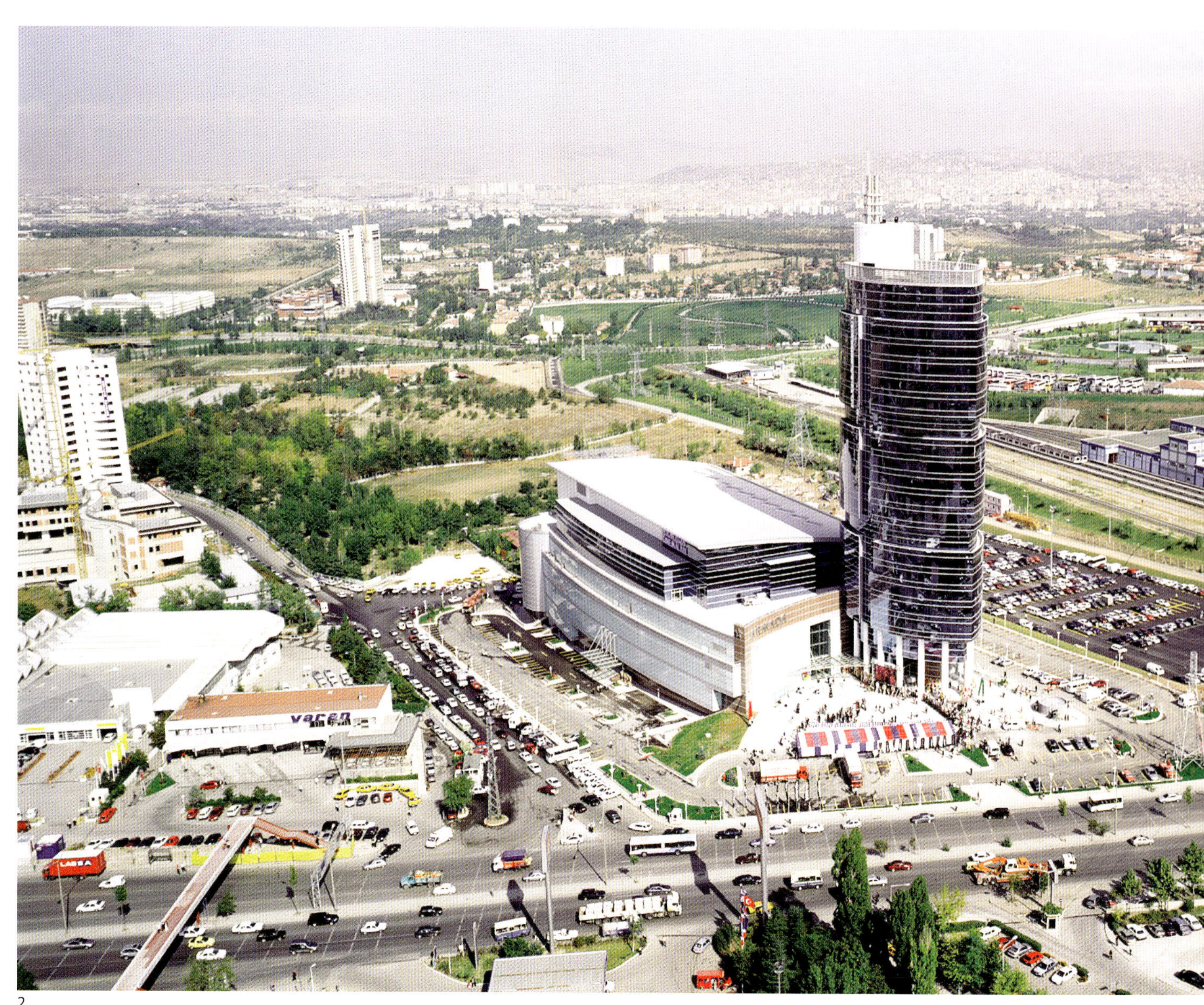

2

2 General view from Eskişehir Highway from 2002
3 The main entrance at night
4 Interior
5 View from the atrium and shops
6 Sketch by Ali Osman Öztürk
7 Detail from the glass façade articulation

3

4

galliano
CLASS
roberto cavalli
VERSACE
TRUSSARDI
VERSACE
D&G
JUNIOR
BEYMEN
5

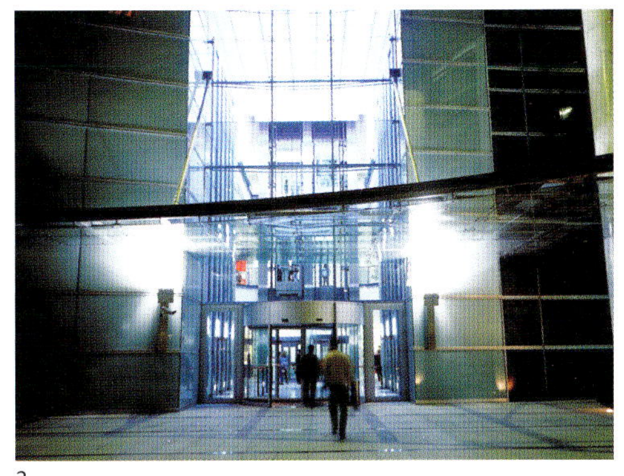

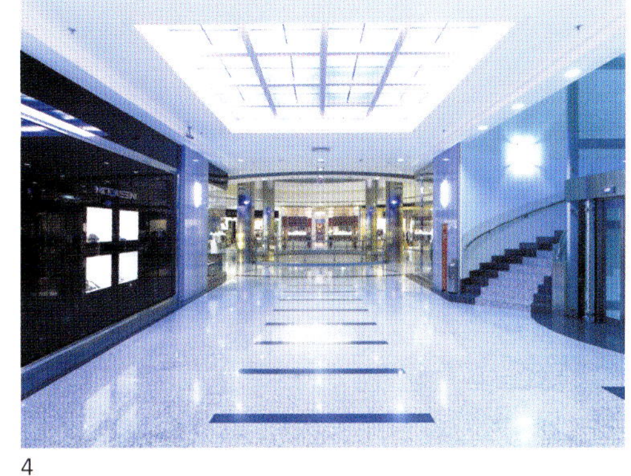

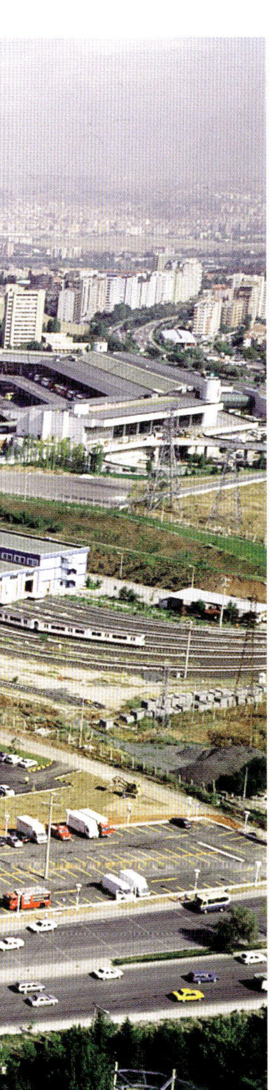

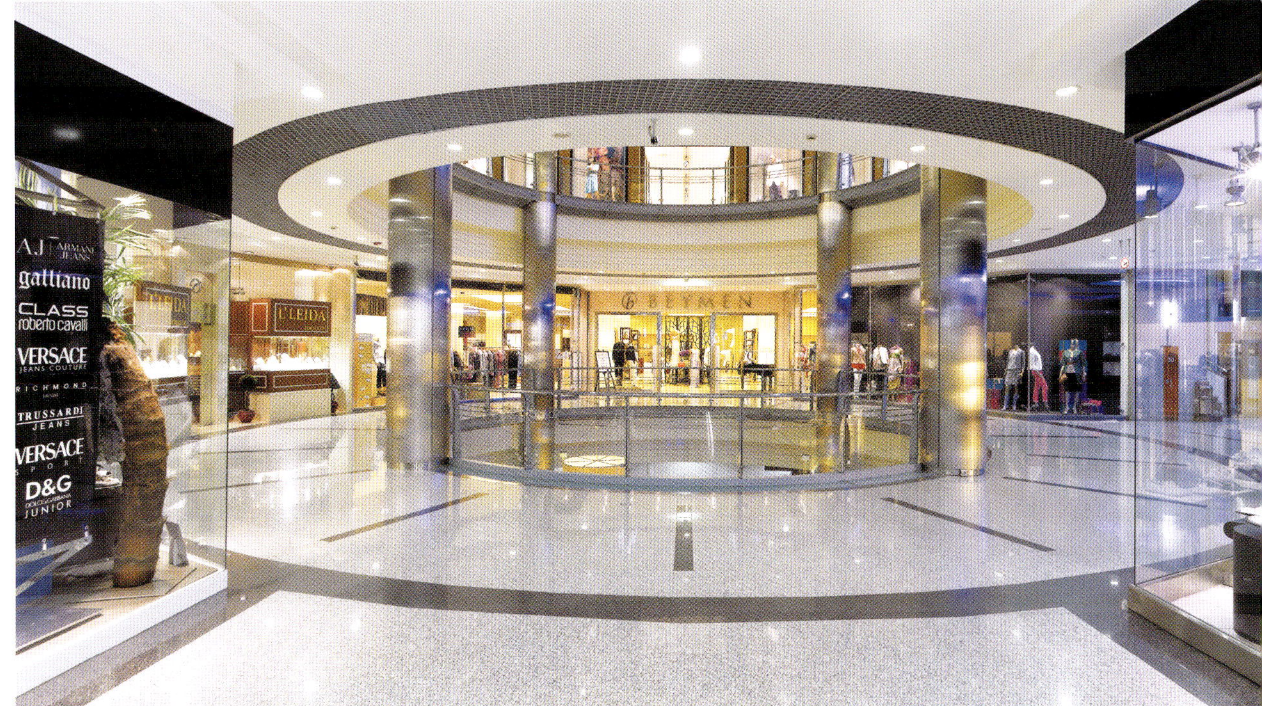

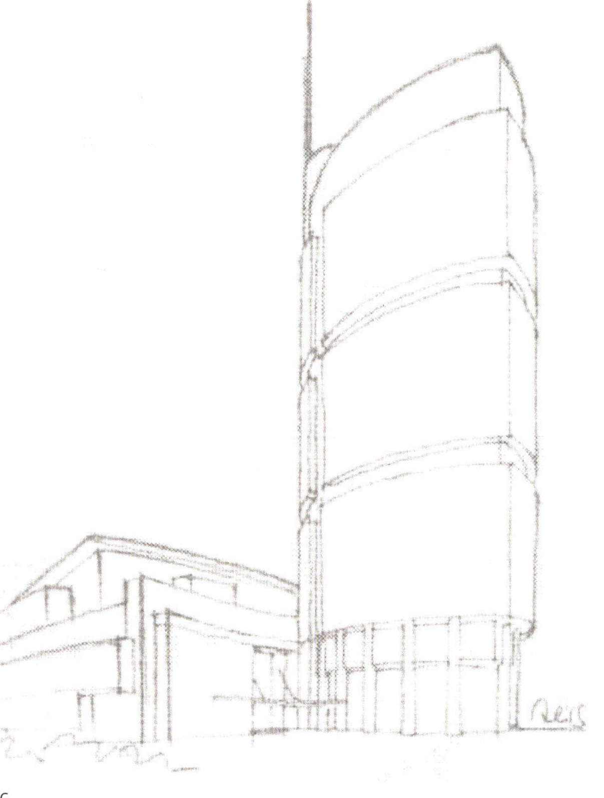

6

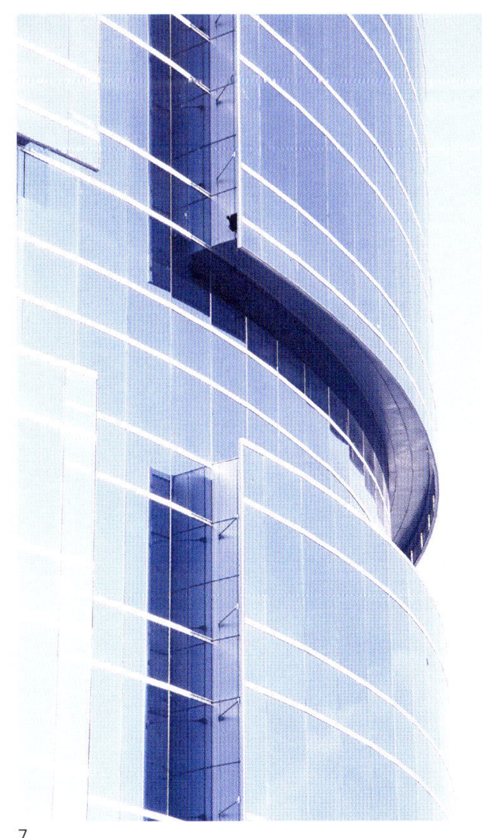

7

Armada Development Project

Client Söğütözü Construction Management Inc.

Project Date 2004–2010

Area 80,000 m^2

Location Ankara

Design Consultant Salih Bezci

Structural Engineer Yüksek Project

Mechanical Engineer Metta Engineering

Electrical Engineer Akay Engineering

Landscape Design Promim Urban & Environmental Design

Fire Consultant Karina

Leasing Consultant Jones Lang LaSalle Turkey

Construction Supervisor Sonay Ozar

Contractor Söğütözü Construction Management Inc.

Designed as a shopping center and office building, the Armada Business and Commercial Center was one of the first buildings in the Söğütözü area. The building, with its ship-like architectural form, soon became one of the city's urban landmarks and received the "Best Shopping Center of the Year Award" in 2004.

Construction began in 1999 and plans for its redevelopment were being discussed even prior to completion. Since then, alternatives to the conservative shopping center design have been explored. The Armada development project was considered as an opportunity to reconnect the introverted shopping center typology with its urban context and make the building a part of daily life in the city. Instead of merely increasing the building area, the development project adopted an approach that would join indoor and outdoor spaces and thus reunite the building's users with the street.

The most significant and complementary part of the development project is not the existing building and its annex, but more so the pedestrian alley in-between the low structures. While this alley connects the new building with the old, it also forms a small urban center and a sustainable pedestrian walkway for the Söğütözü area. The ground floor activities on both buildings were designed to interact with the street and outdoor spaces. The pedestrian alley between the existing building and the development project was evaluated as an urban space.

The Armada pedestrian axis was designed in collaboration with the landscape architect and city and regional planner Can Kubin. A public square and a set of stairs, which make use of the natural topography of the site, were designed on this pedestrian axis, at the entrance of the two buildings. According to the planning regulations of the time, the project aimed for the green outdoor areas and pedestrian axis to continue into the university campus, while crossing the Eskişehir Avenue from underground to carry on into the Konya highroad direction.

Another noteworthy aspect of the project is that it forecasted the expansion of the pedestrian area to include various other buildings in the Söğütözü area.

1,2 Sketches of the pedestrian alley showing Armada with the Development project, by Ali Osman Öztürk
3 Söğütözü area at night, with Armada and Development projects
4,5 Main entrance with glass cube structure

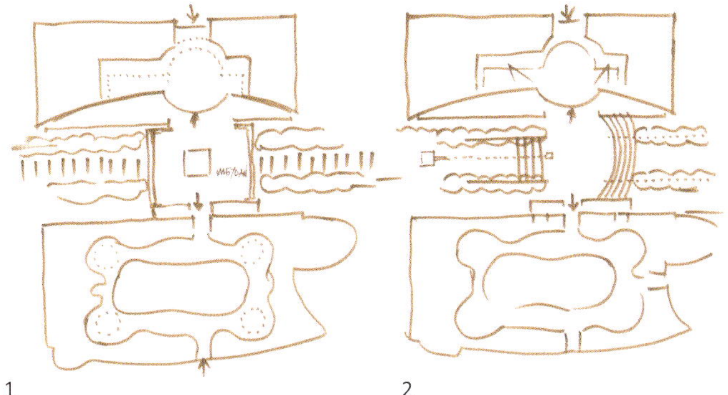

1 2

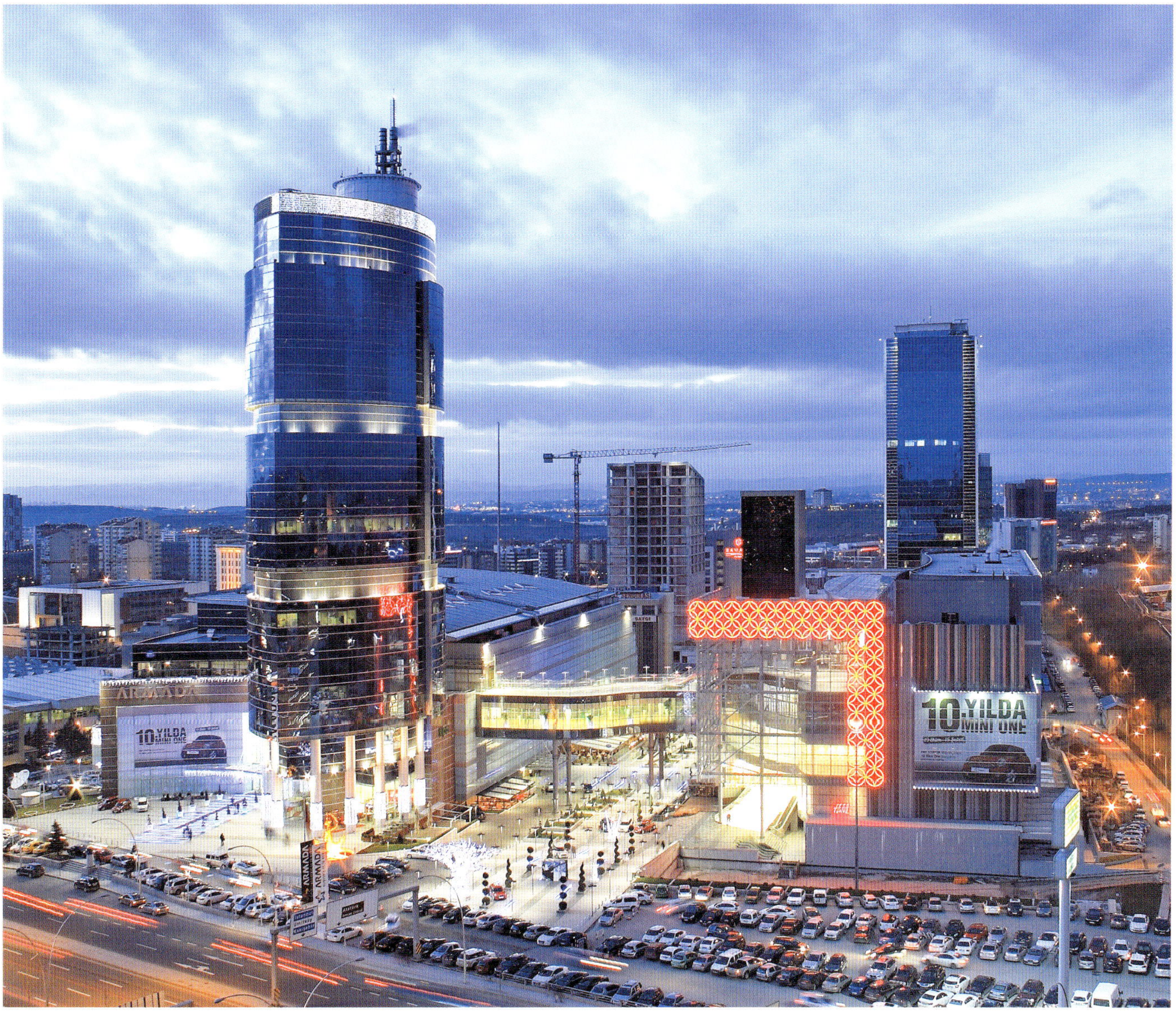

3

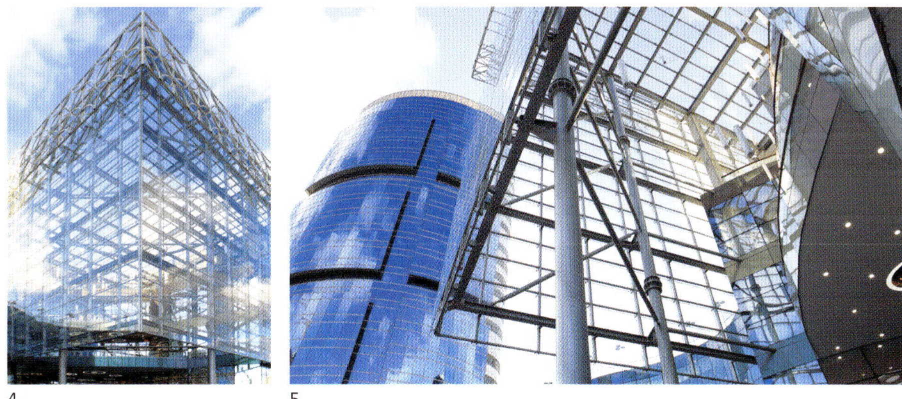

4 5

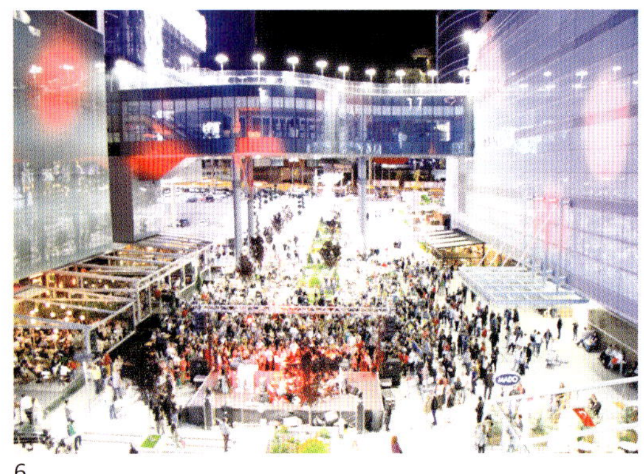
6

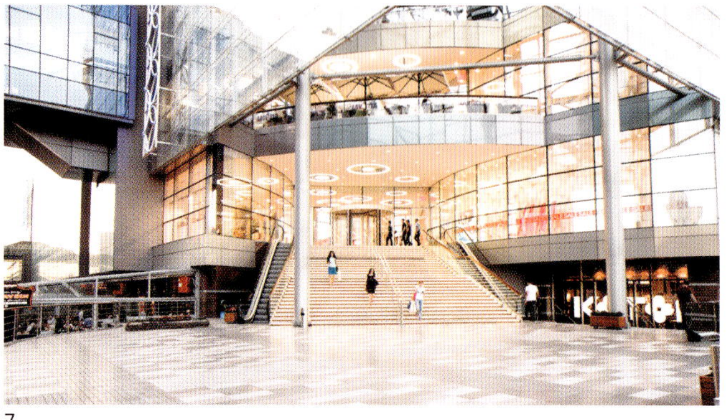
7

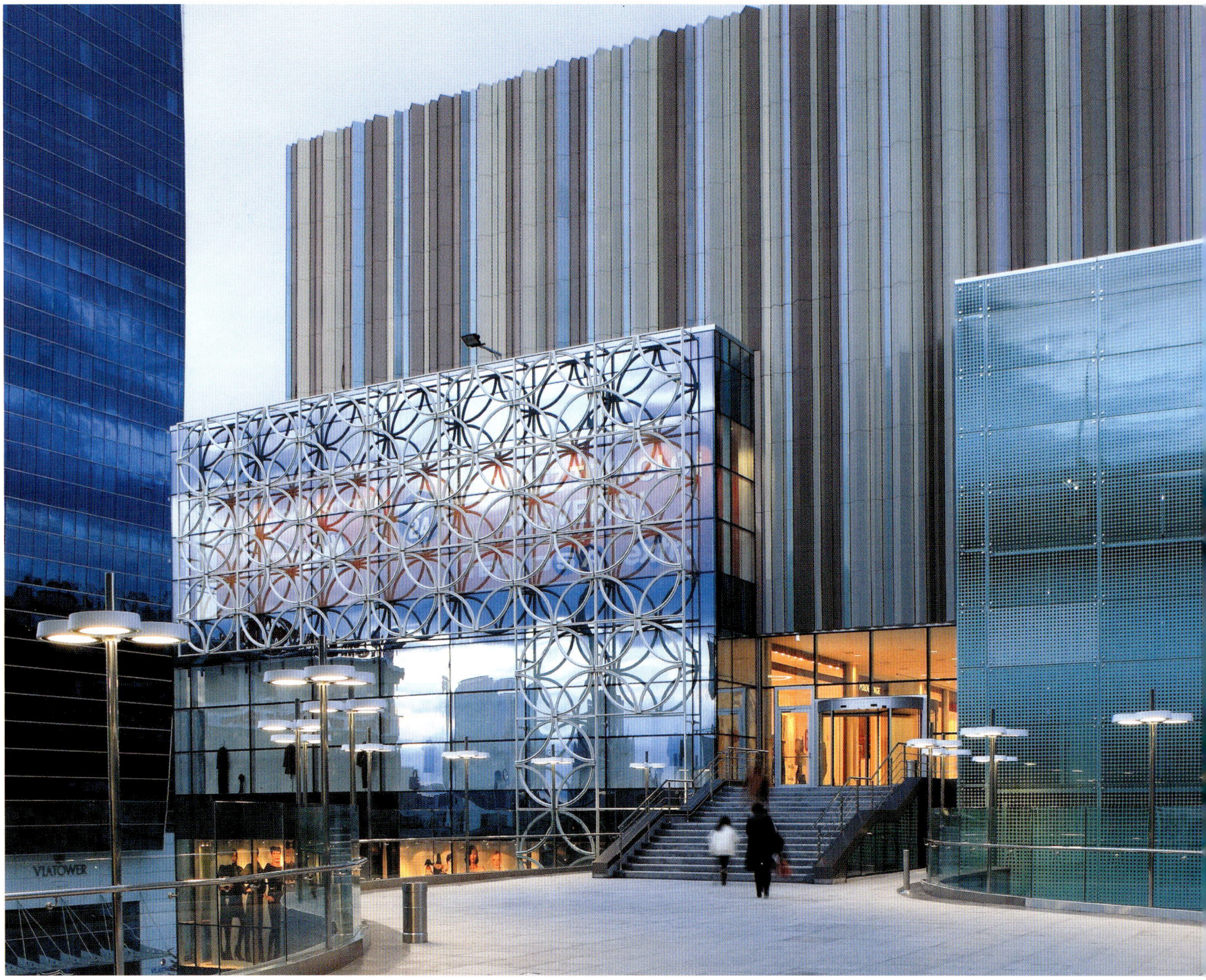

8

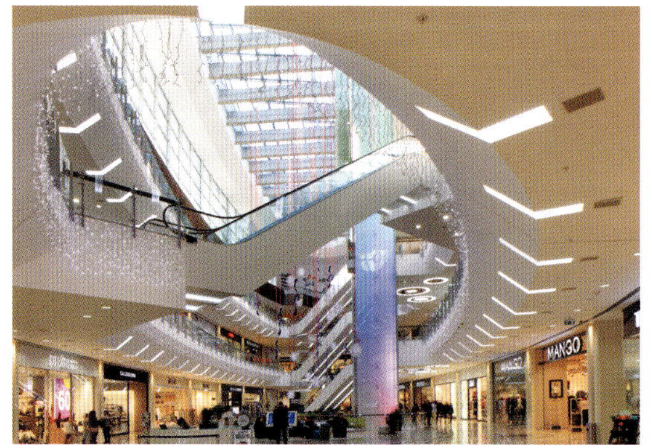

9

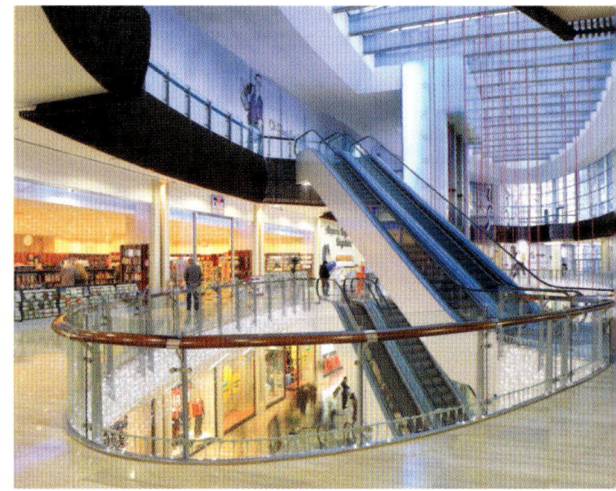
10

6 The alley at night during a jazz concert
7 Main entrance underneath the glass cube
8 Visitors walking on the bridge linking the Armada and Development projects
9 Ground floor view of the elliptical atrium and skylight
10 Interior
11 View of the alley with well-known Turkish restaurants and cafés
12 Site plan showing Armada and Development projects with the pedestrian alley
13 Cross section of the office tower, alley, Armada, and Development projects

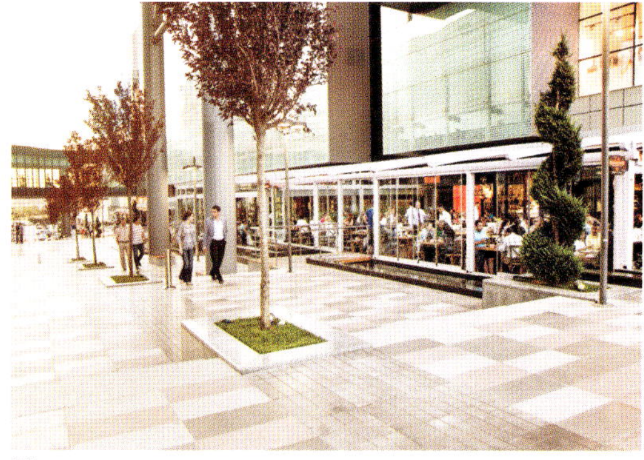
11

While the existing Armada building has a circulation system technically known as “a double mall,” meaning one in which both sides of a corridor are flanked with stores, the new block has a series of stores aligned along the void of an elliptic gallery, thus allowing visual access between all floors of the building. The gallery is roofed by an elliptical skylight, which provides the inner space with maximum use of daylight. Circulation within the two buildings is uninterrupted by way of bridges that connect both the buildings to each other, and the inner spaces with the outdoors.

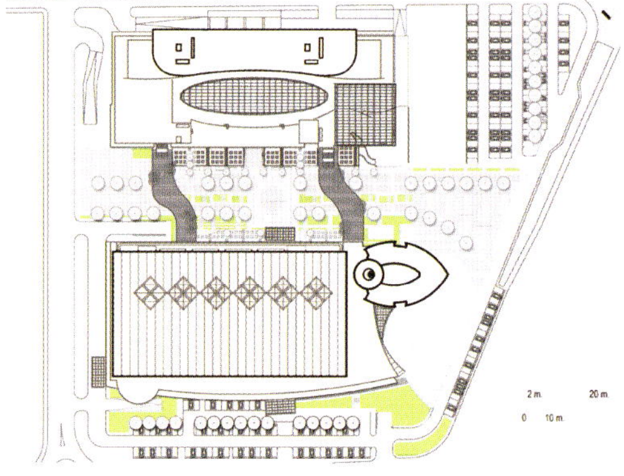
12

The choice of materials in the interior design and the building façade was conducted to complement the existing building. Light green sable glass and aluminum panels that change color throughout the day were used in the new building.

The glass cube defines a semi-outdoor space, providing natural air circulation to the terraces. The transparency of this architectural element allows inner and outer spaces to flow into each other. To prevent the cube from obstructing the building entrance, its steel structure was specially designed so that all loads concentrating on its corner would be redirected to both its sides. The multi-colored ring lighting fixtures on the cube are one of the most striking architectural features of the project.

The development project for the Armada building presents an original experience in urban planning, which may also act as a model for projects in the area with similar functions.

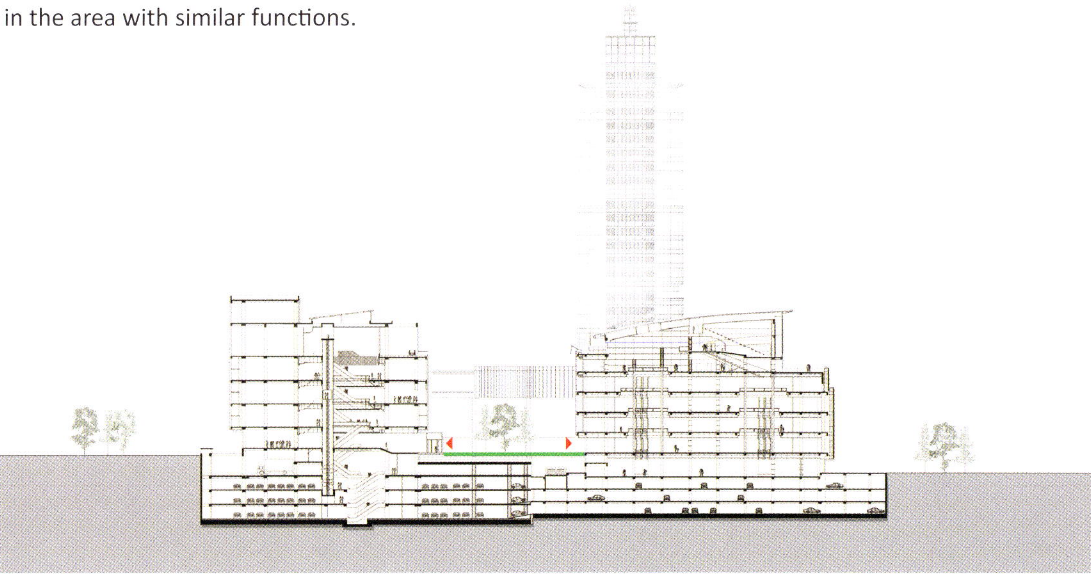
13

Tepe Prime

Client Tepe Construction Inc.
Project Date 2007
Area 92,750 m²
Location Ankara
Project Director Fehmi Çataltepe
Structural Engineer Yüksek Project
Mechanical Engineer GMD Engineering
Electrical Engineer Yurdakul Engineering
Landscape Design Dalokay Design Studio
Fire Consultant Alara Design and Engineering
Contractor Tepe Construction Inc.
Construction Supervisor Tepe Construction Team
2012 Arkiparc Mixed-Use Category Finalist, 2013 Global RLI Awards International Retail and Leisure Destination Category Finalist

Opposite:
Night view of the office buildings along with the public space

The Tepe Prime Project was designed with the objective of creating an alternative urban center on the newly developed western axis of Ankara, and, unlike most conventional shopping centers, offering an outdoor public space integrated with urban life. This public space consists of a square, which houses dining, shopping, and various other activities, together with a series of streets opening into the square. The building units define these outdoor spaces. The project stands as an architectural attempt to understand the tendencies and conventions of contemporary business life, and present an urban substructure without disconnecting itself from the city at large.

The project offers a variety of uses based on an assortment of public and private spaces. The residential blocks, which cohabit with the business world, form a significant part of the design. The project presents various architectural solutions that integrate the office spaces with various activities, thereby preventing them from having a limited span of use and being abandoned at night. There are a series of social spaces that appeal to both those working at the center and to those visiting the complex from the city.

The general design of the center consists of three separate building islands integrated with a series of outdoor spaces. These outdoor areas, beginning with the corner entrance, which is in direct contact with from the main road, are shaped in accordance to the design of the building blocks. Building activities generating outdoor spaces are located on the ground and lower levels. Independent commercial facilities and social areas take place along the circulation pattern that has direct outdoor access. Unlike most indoor shopping centers, the retail spaces and dining facilities of the Tepe Prime Center have direct access to outdoor public areas. These facilities include cafés, specialized stores, bookstores, banks, fast food counters, service stores, and restaurants of various sizes.

The project includes a total of 218 offices, 100 studio flats, and 37 retail stores within an arrangement of streets. The complex aims at being a lively urban center through all hours of the day, every day of the week with its indoor and outdoor car parks, office spaces, stores, studio flats, and outdoor facilities. The two separate office blocks rise 18 and 19 stories high. Each office block offers working areas of various sizes, arranged in

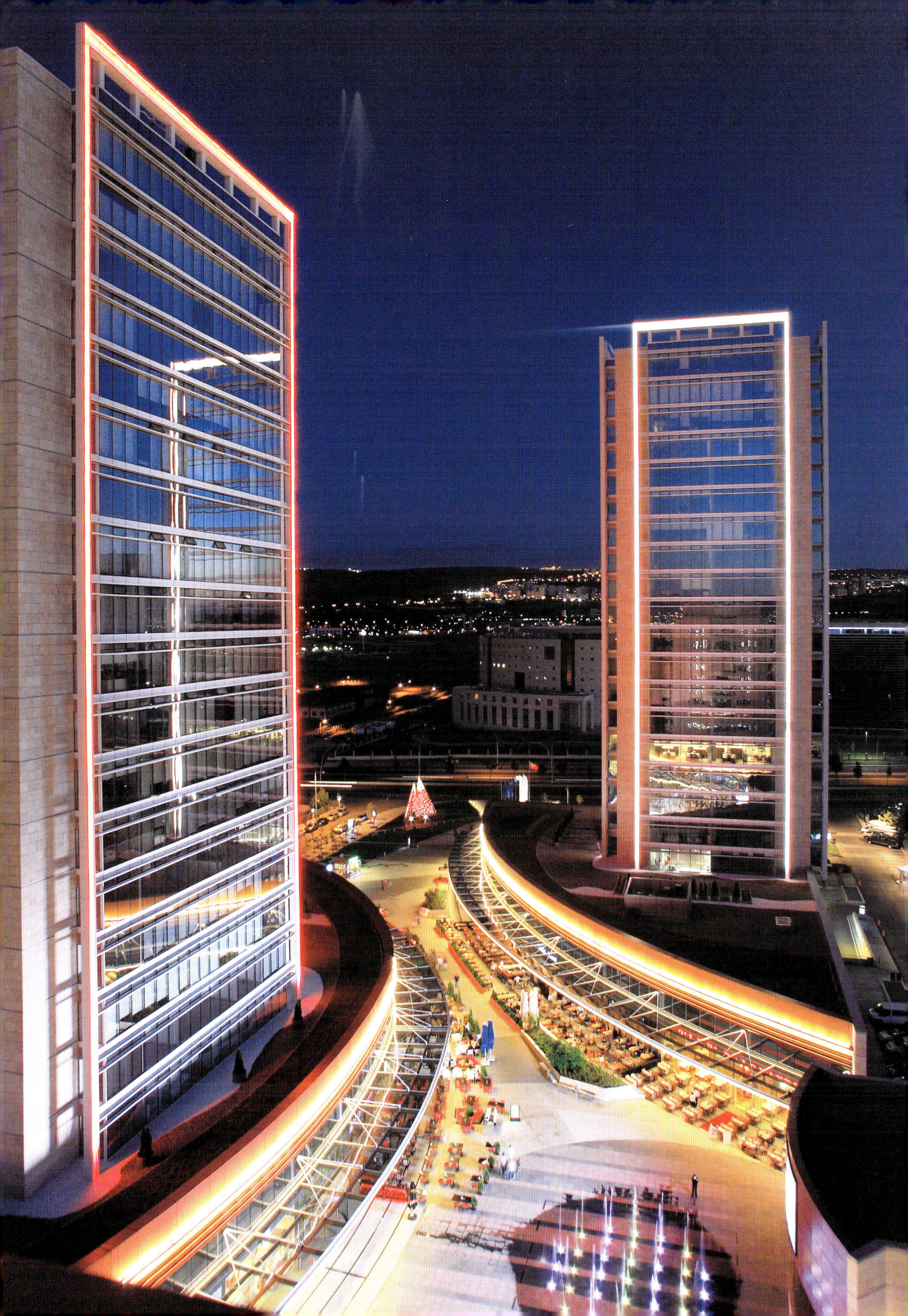

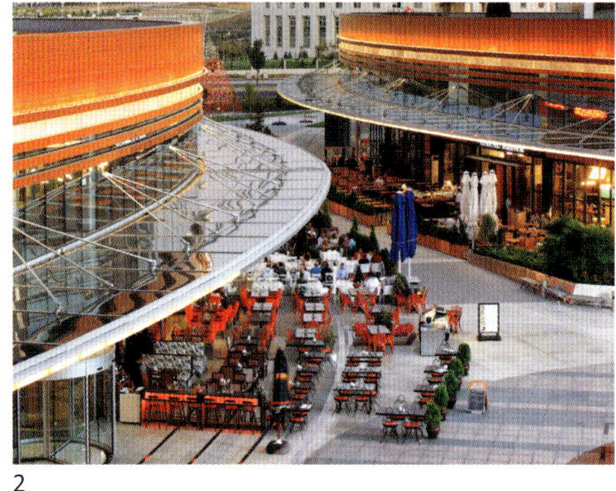
2

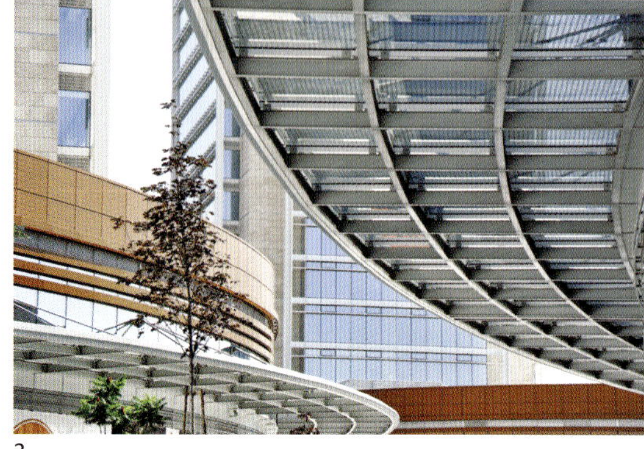
3

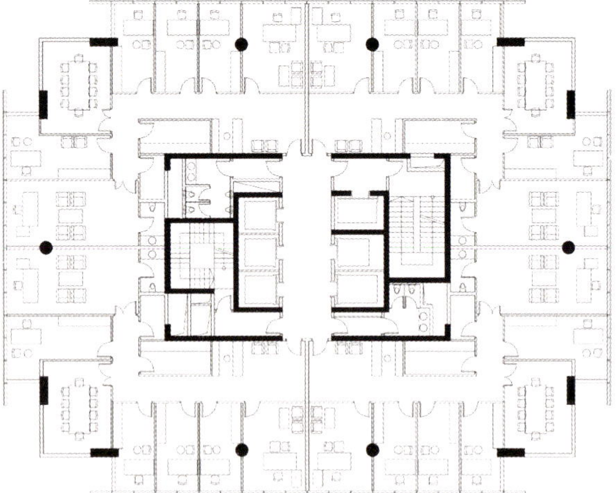
4

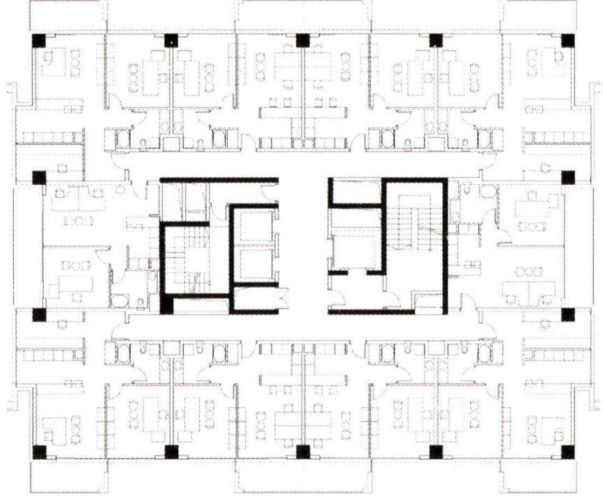
5

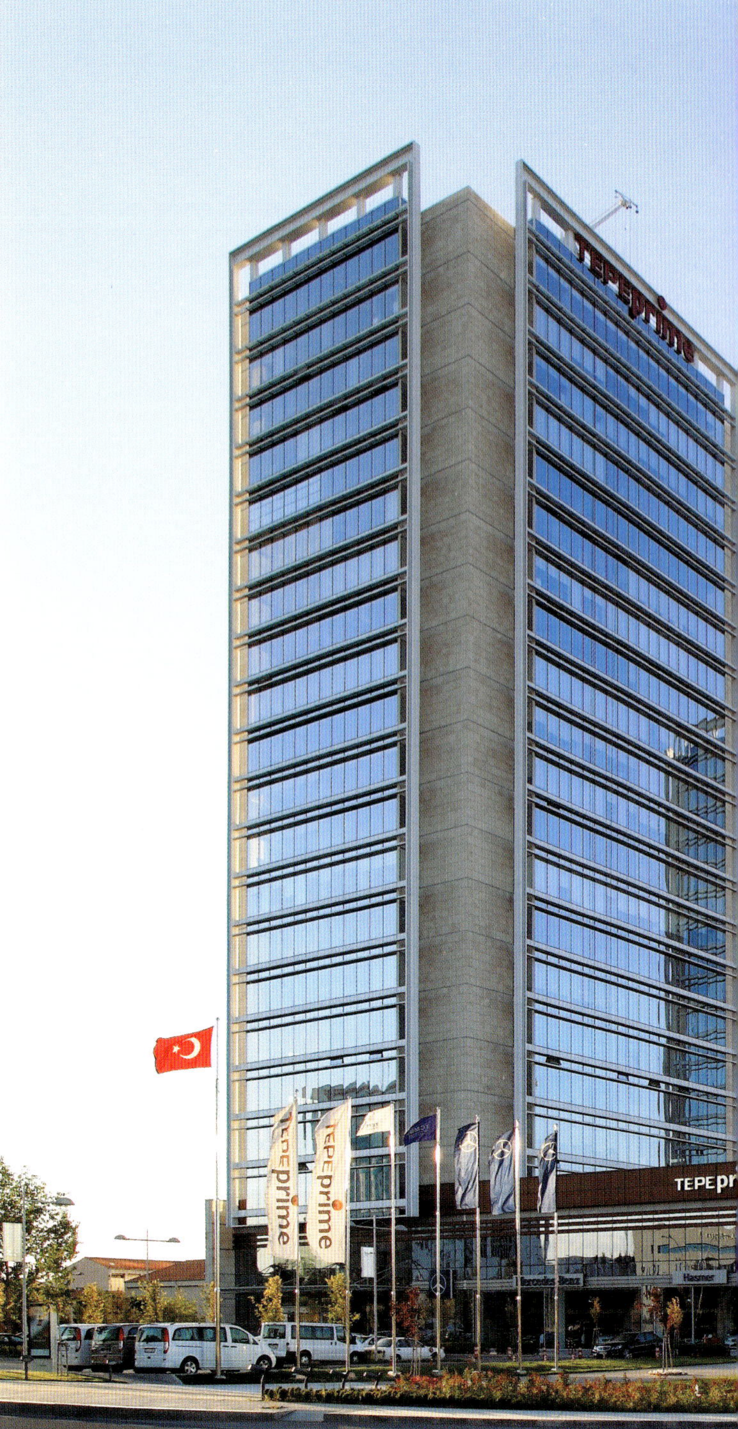

6

2 View of the cafés and restaurants in the public space
3 Detail of the circular canopies
4 Typical floor plan of Block A
5 Typical floor plan of Block C that is used mostly as home office
6 General view from the Eskişehir highway
7 Aerial view of the lighting details
8 Rendering of the general project area

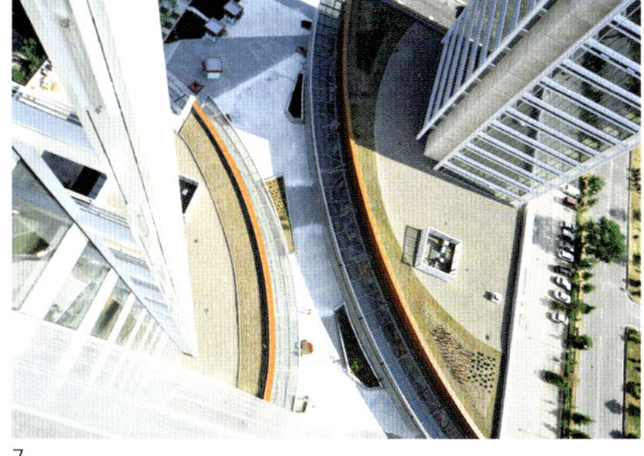

7

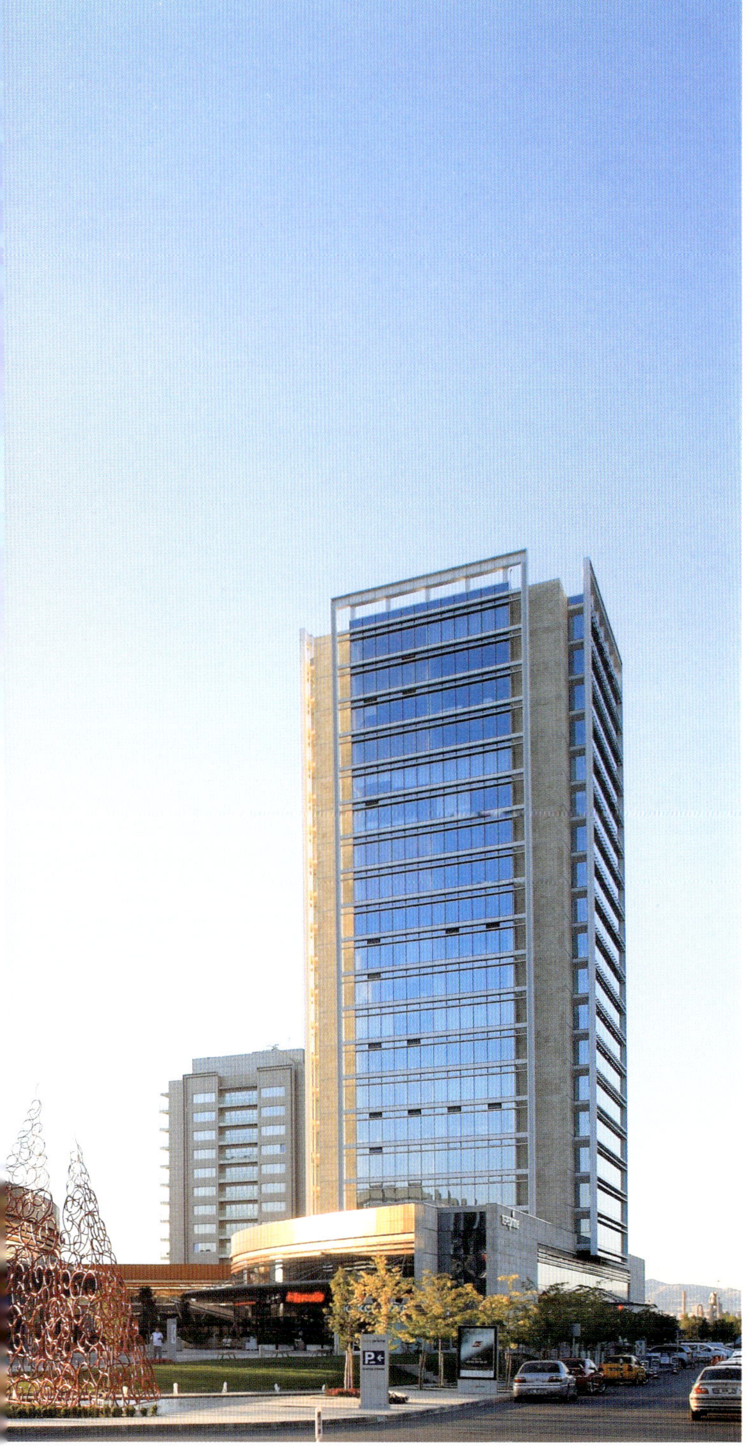

open plan arrangement to accommodate alternative office solutions. An interior design firm conceived the design for the entrance halls and lobbies on each floor. The office spaces have winged windows that permit natural ventilation and cladded façade systems. The residential block consists of a variety of flats ranging from 70 to 100 square meters in 1+1 and 2+1 room arrangements. Each story houses 10 independent spaces, which can be used as both offices and/or residential flats.

The variety of building material was kept to a minimum throughout the design, with the main materials being natural stone and glass. Stone cladding was used for the high-rise blocks while a clear-cut effect was obtained by the cladded planar surfaces of the building. Composite planes with a timber appearance were used on the lower levels. All the floors are composed of natural stone. The choice of material provides a natural and effortless effect throughout the building.

The center was completed and inaugurated in 2011, and has since presented an alternative urban space for Ankara.

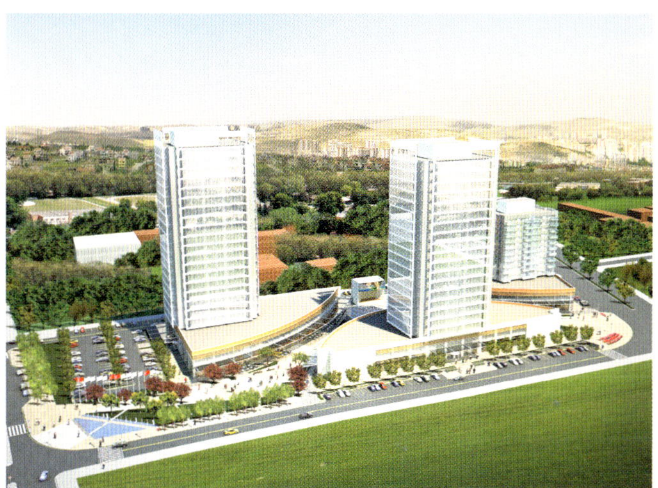

8

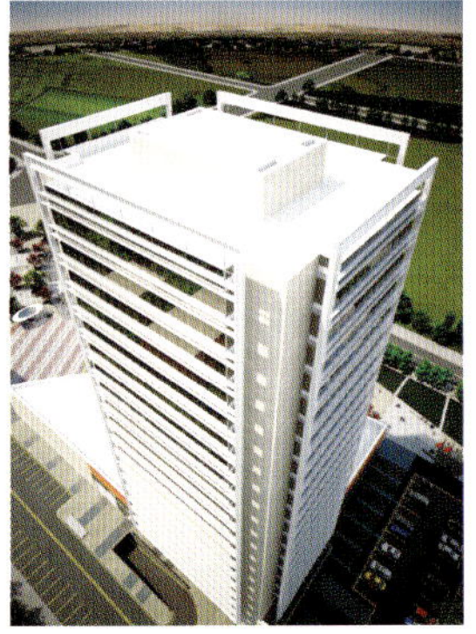
9

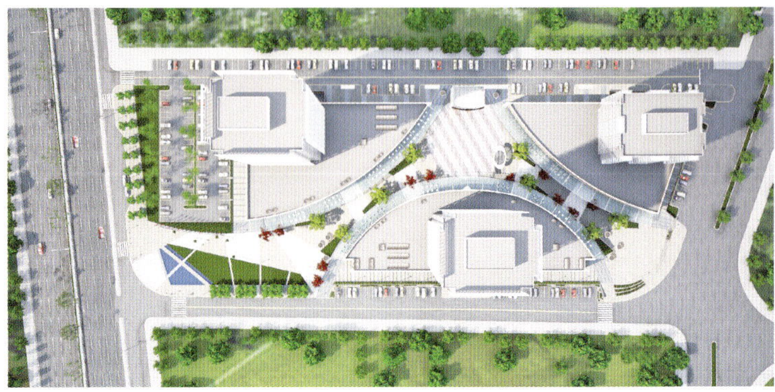
10

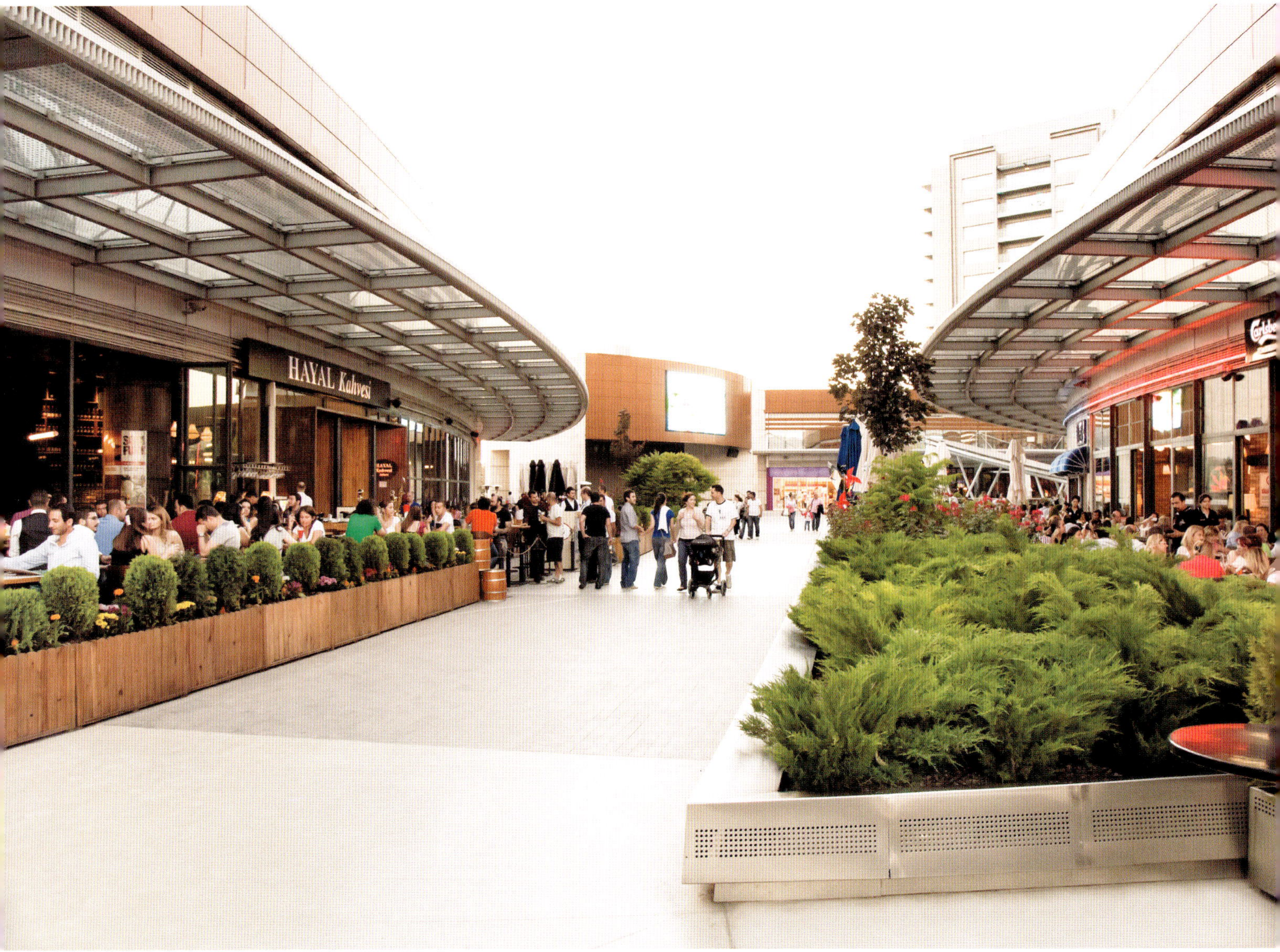

11

9 Rendering of the office block
10 Site plan of the buildings with the public space and landscape
11 The variety of the restaurants and cafés during the day
12 Façade detail
13,14 Perspective model sectional
15 Cross section of the office and studio apartments with parking
16 Visitors enjoying the open space at lunchtime
17 Multi-functional area with the pool and light show

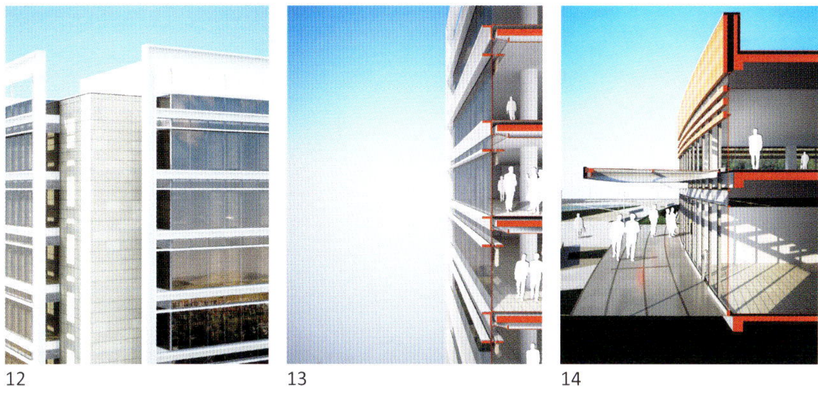
12 13 14

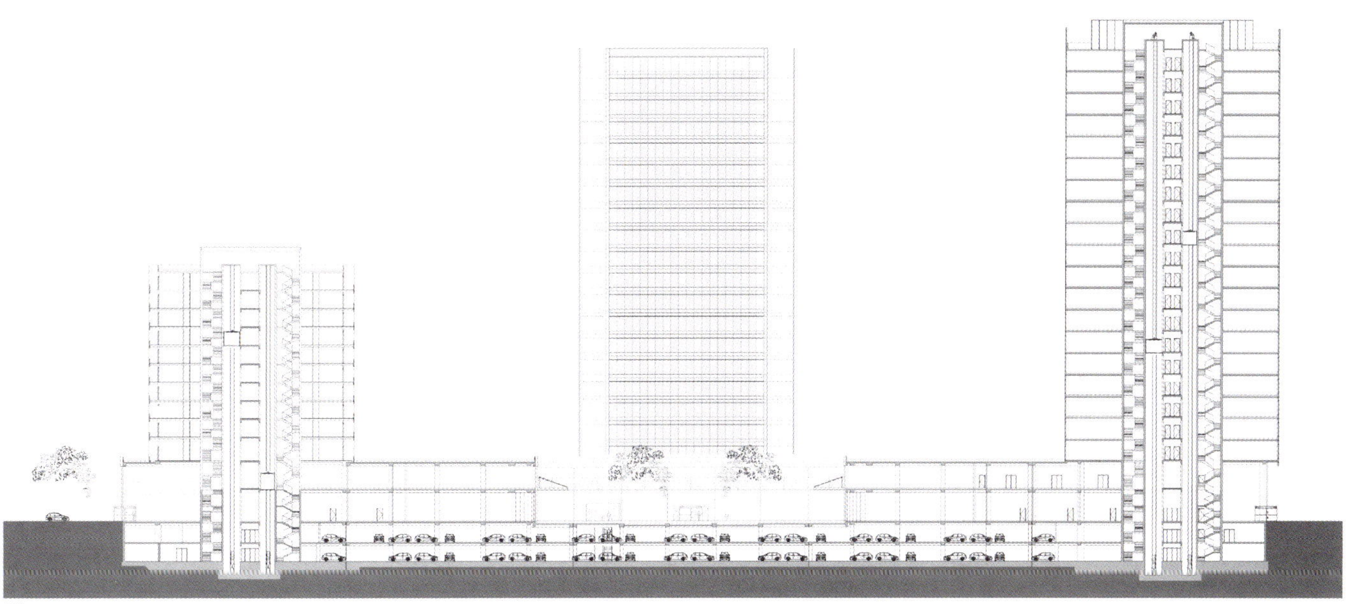
15

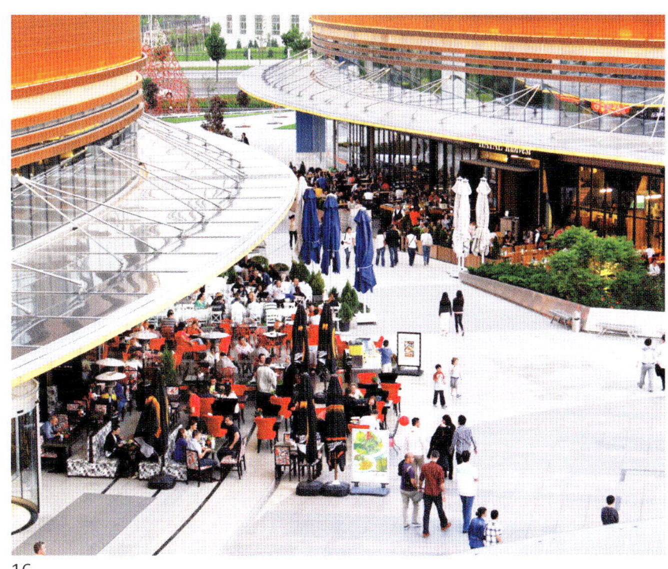
16

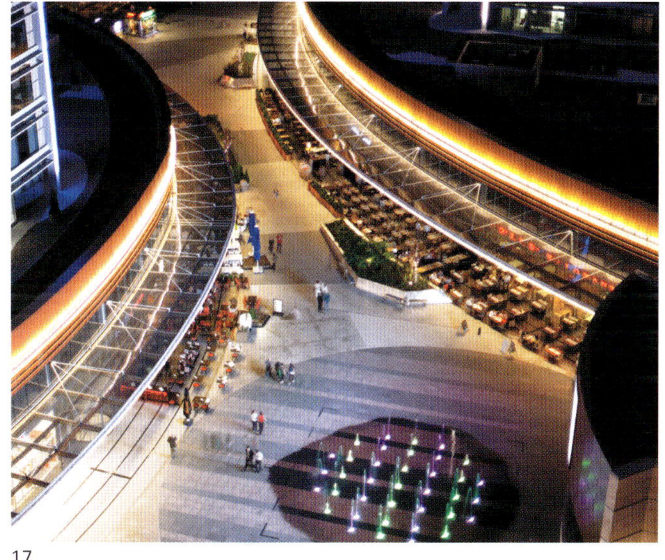
17

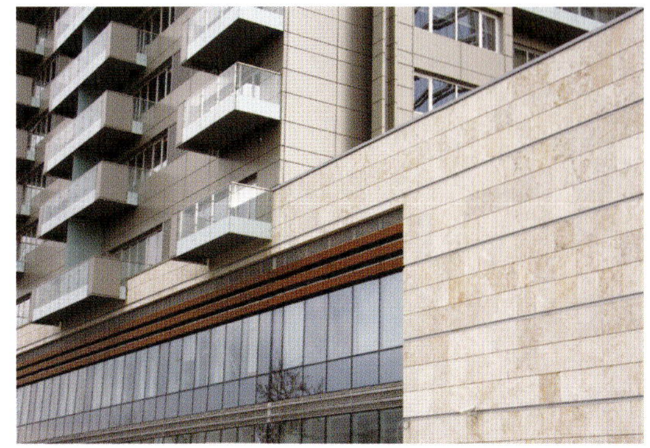
18

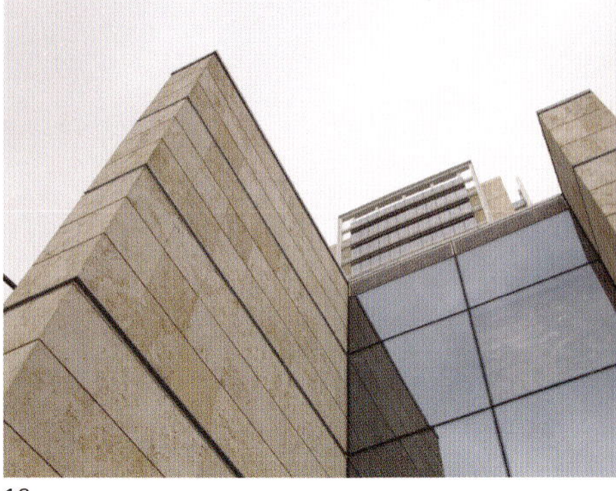
19

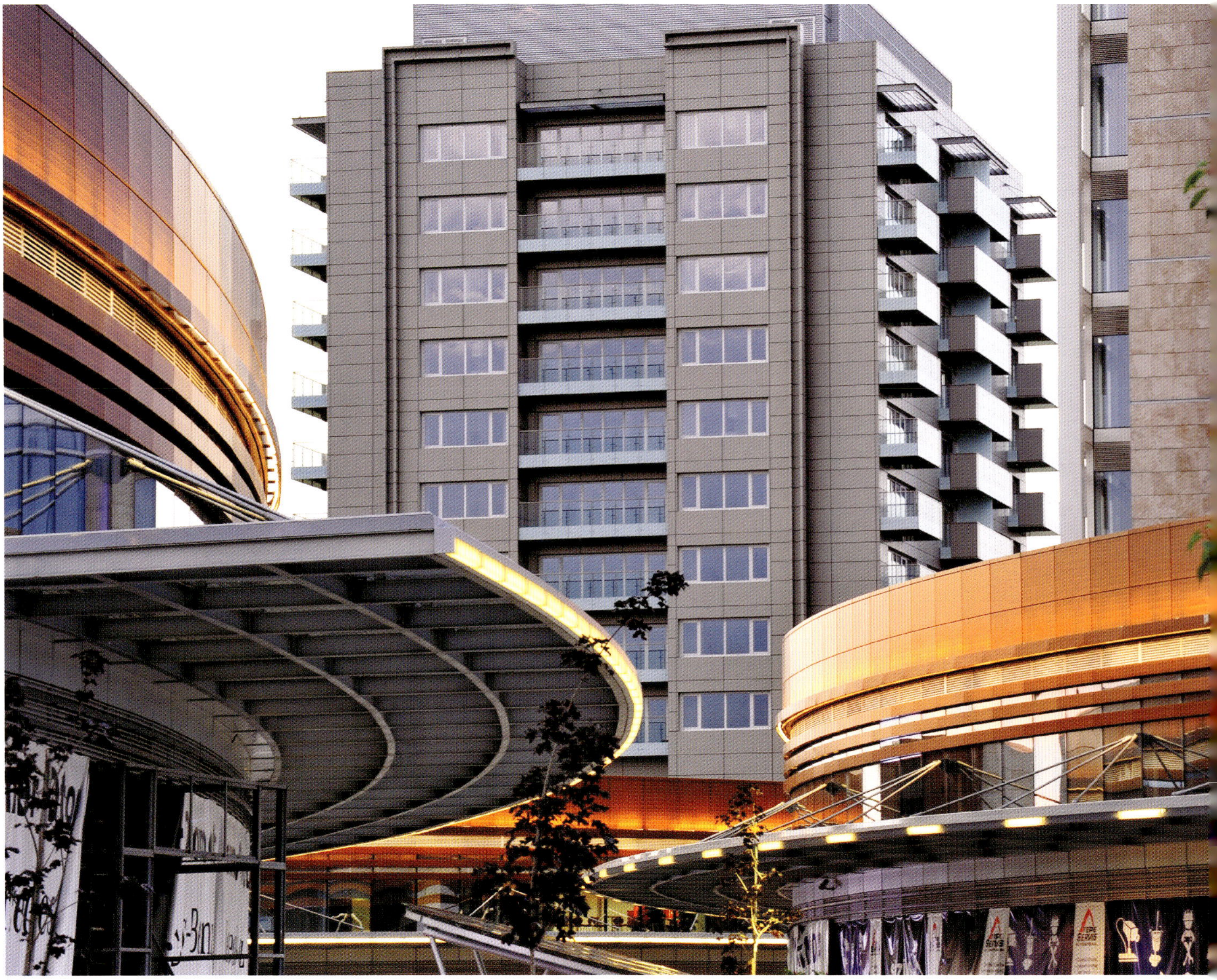

20

18,19 Natural stone cladding detail
20 View towards the studio apartments
21 Children playing in the multi-functional public area
22 General view at twilight
23,25 Detail from the balconies
24 Façade detail

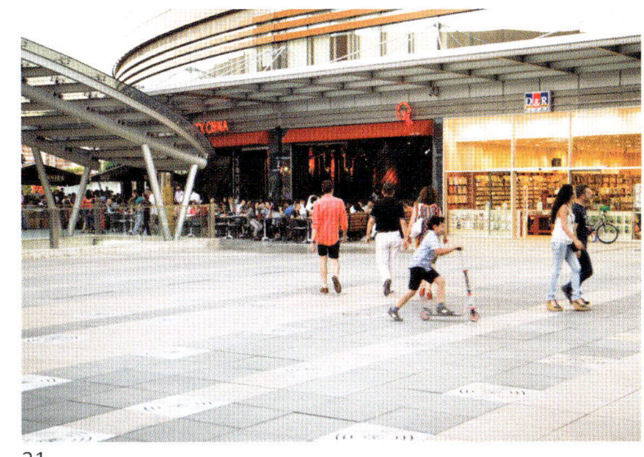
21

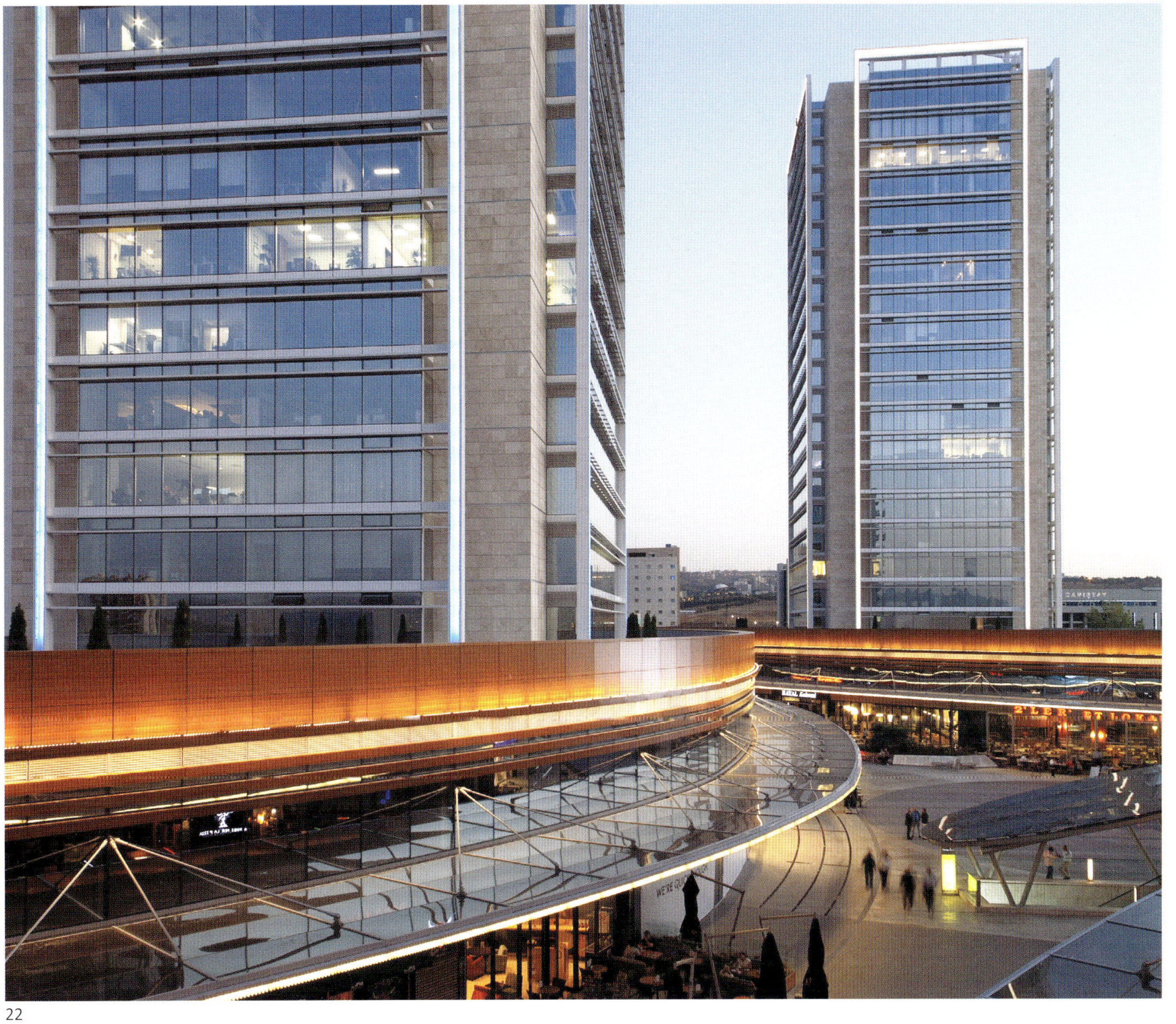

22

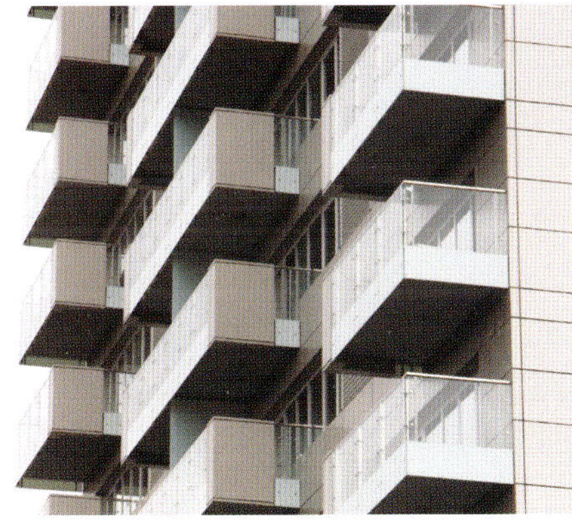
23

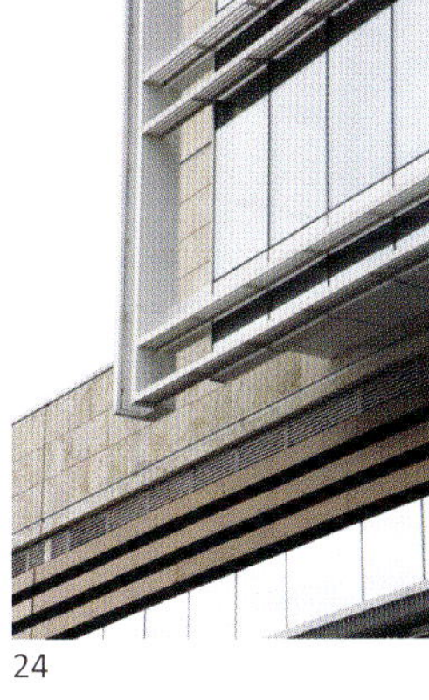
24

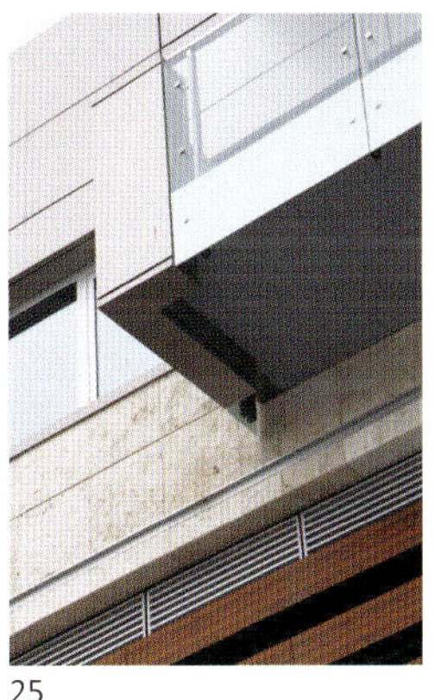
25

Türk Telekom

Client Türk Telekom
Project Date 2010
Area 54,000 m^2
Location Ankara
Structural Engineer Yüksek Project
Mechanical Engineer Metta Engineering
Electrical Engineer Yurdakul Engineering
Landscape Design Dalokay Design Studio
Fire Consultant Alara Design and Engineering
Façade Consultant Pridemann Building Envelope Consultants Kaan Kuran
Lighting Consultant Atilla Uysal
Acoustic Consultant Mezzo Studio, Prof. Dr. Mehmet Çalışkan
Contractor Burkay Construction

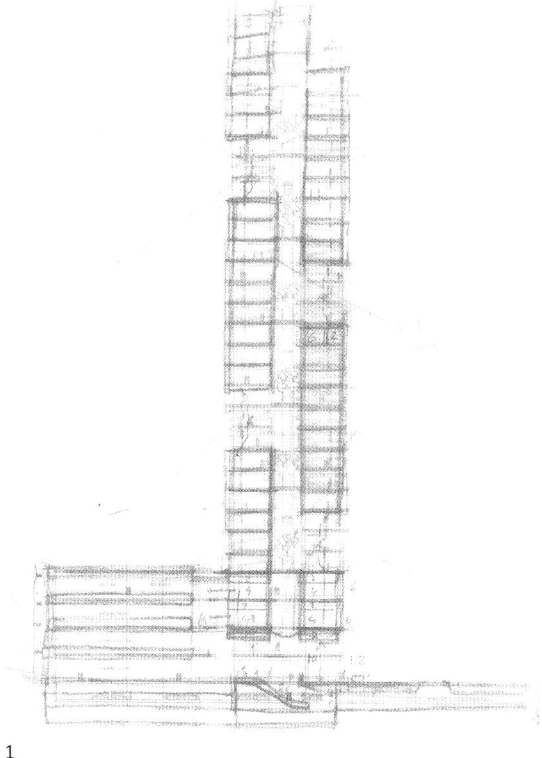

1

A Tasarım Mimarlık won the contract for the Türk Telekom general headquarters building through a limited architectural competition. It is located in a 94,000-square-meter campus in the Aydınlikevler district of Ankara. The design is fundamentally composed of a binary structure: the telecommunication units, such as the system halls of Türk Telekom, data centers, network tracking units, and crisis management offices as well as a conference hall, are all situated in a pedestal building named "the factory," while employee offices are located in the tower block. The pedestal building was designed in a more secluded architectural language due to the character and significance of the technological functions it houses, whereas the office tower is a completely transparent building, which corresponds with its outer environment.

One of the significant factors that shaped the design was the fact that this building, unlike most conventional office buildings today, would be used by a single company. By allocating the lifts, staircases, and service units to the corners of the plan, a central void was created, and this central space was embellished with different inner gardens and atriums that relate to the façade. The flexible working spaces, most of which have open plans, all have visual access to each other. The floors housing bridges and inner gardens are generally reserved as communal leisure areas and include meeting spaces and small alternative dining areas. From this perspective, the building provides an alternative working environment and aims to take place among the leading examples of contemporary office design.

The architectural approach shaping the design of the building lays emphasis on environmental issues and energy efficiency, adopting the concepts of green design and sustainability.

1 Sketch by Ali Osman Öztürk
Opposite:
Night view

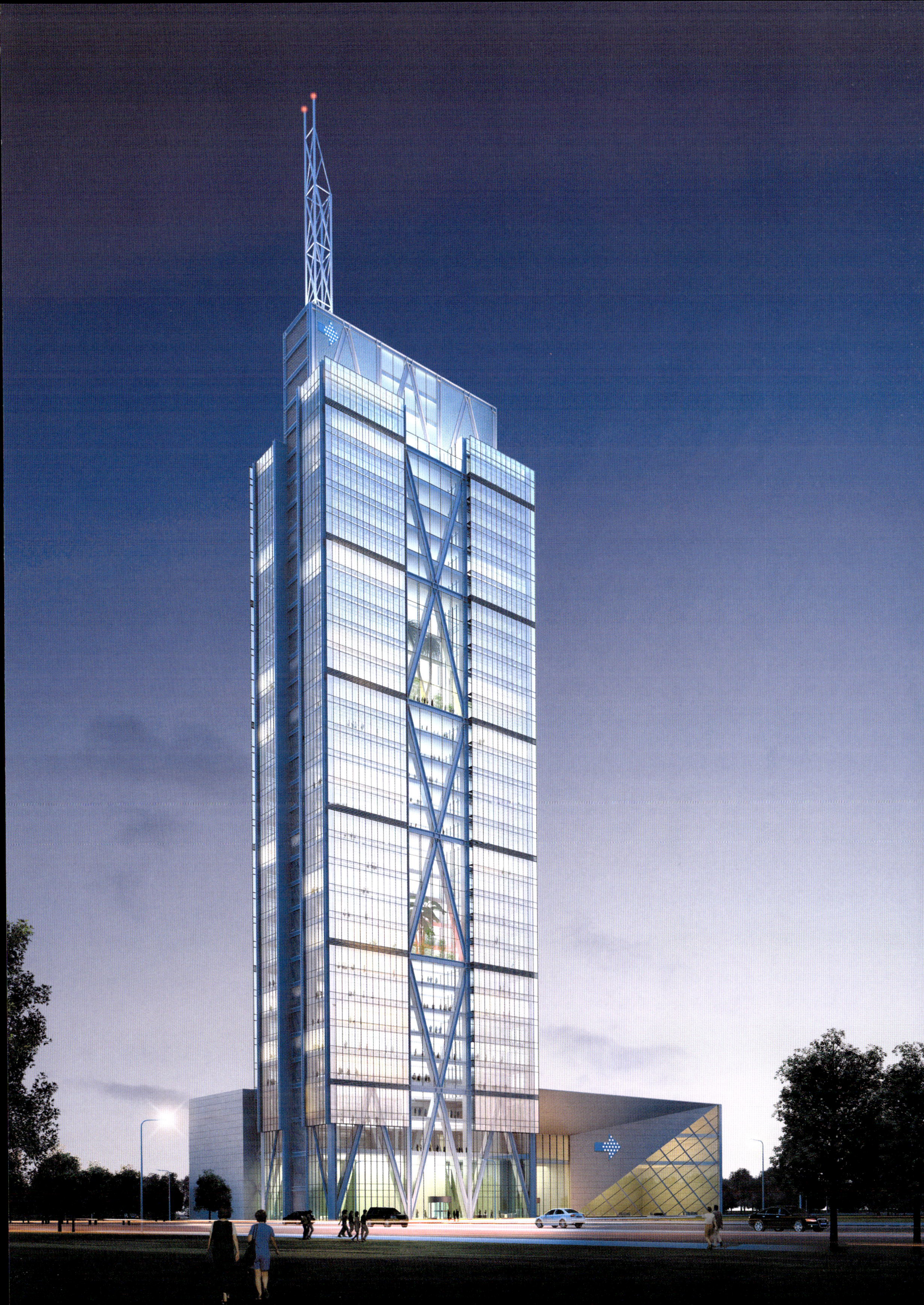

The design of inner gardens carries the outdoor green spaces inside the building, to the upper levels and working areas. All mechanical systems are environmentally friendly, with solar panels placed on the roof, and natural or recyclable materials used throughout the building. As a result, the building is in accordance to the standards defined by the LEED certificate. The office façades are glass from floor to ceiling and have maximum access to daylight, thereby providing a more efficient and pleasant atmosphere for productivity. The tower has been designed with a double-layered façade in order to facilitate indoor temperature, allow natural ventilation in suitable seasons, and provide a second skin-barrier against dust and noise pollution.

Due its location, the general headquarters building is likely to become one of the major landmarks of Ankara, and, with its specially designed illumination at night, it will certainly take its place in the city's skyline.

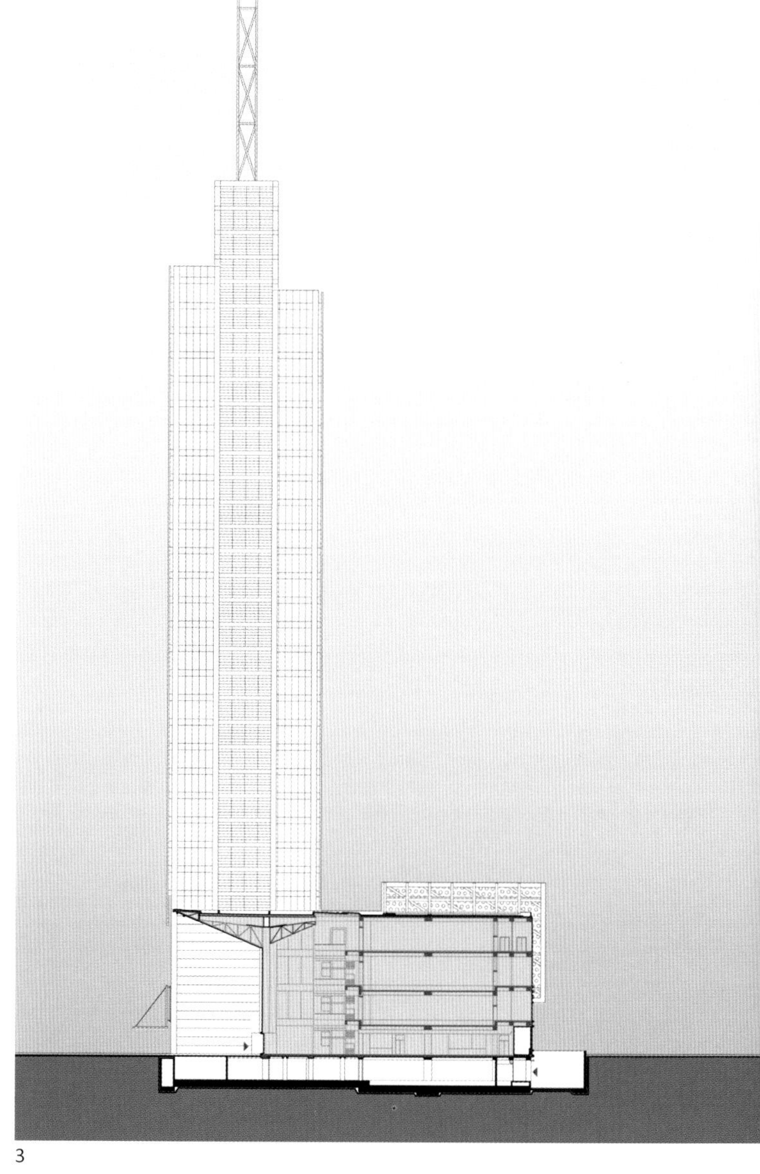

3

3 Section through podium
4 Ground floor plan
5 Rendering of the main entrance, showing the façade details
6,7 Construction

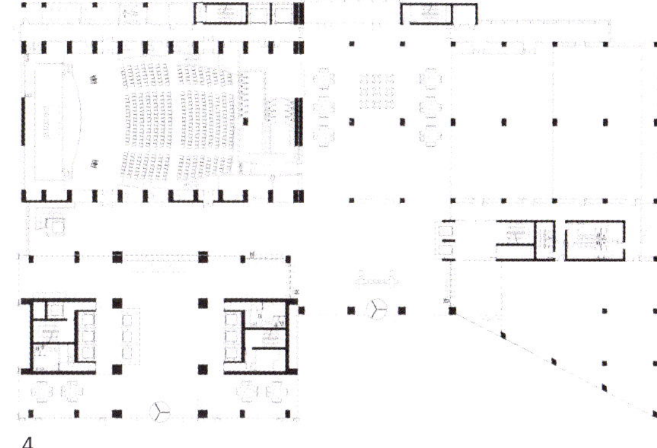

4

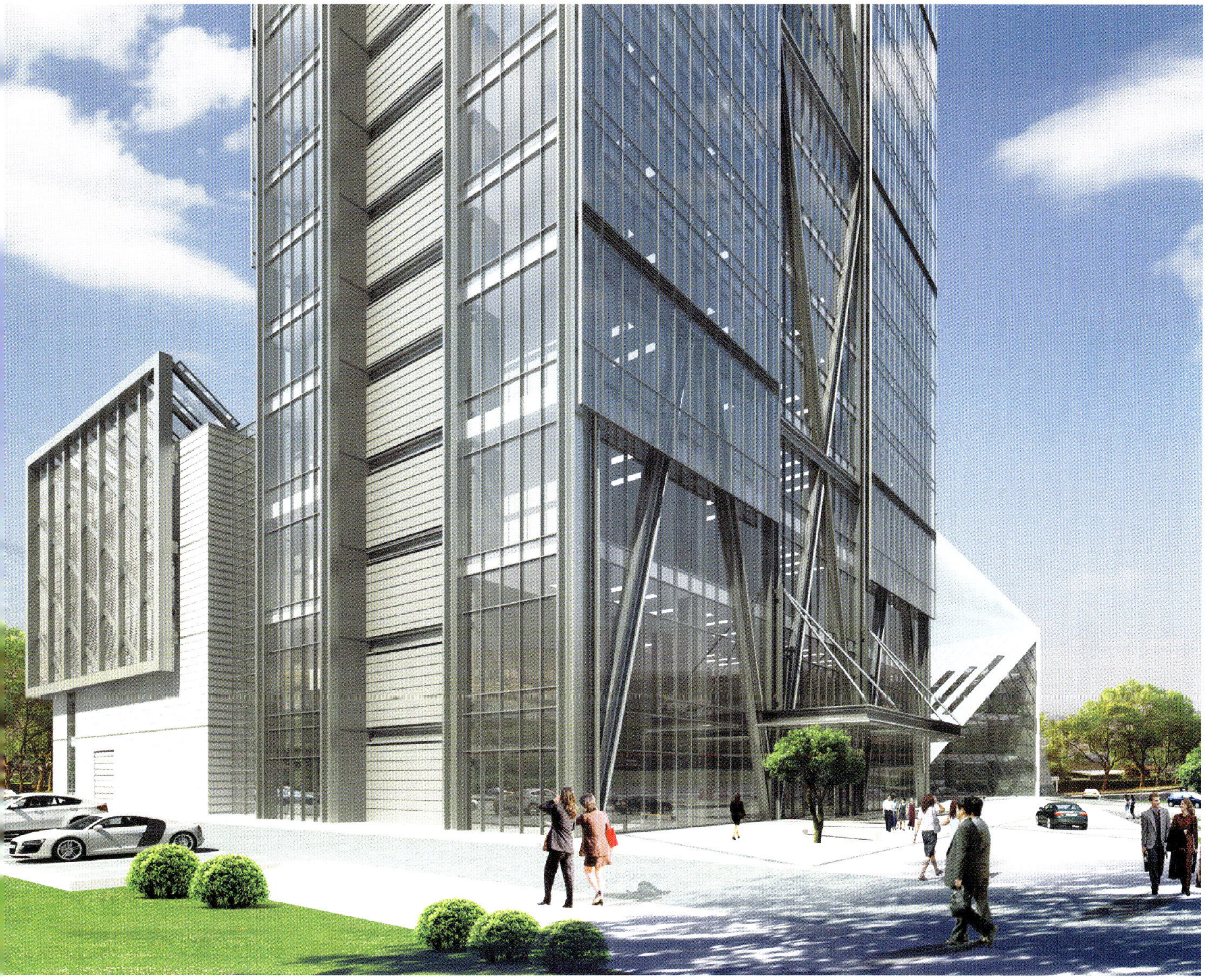

5

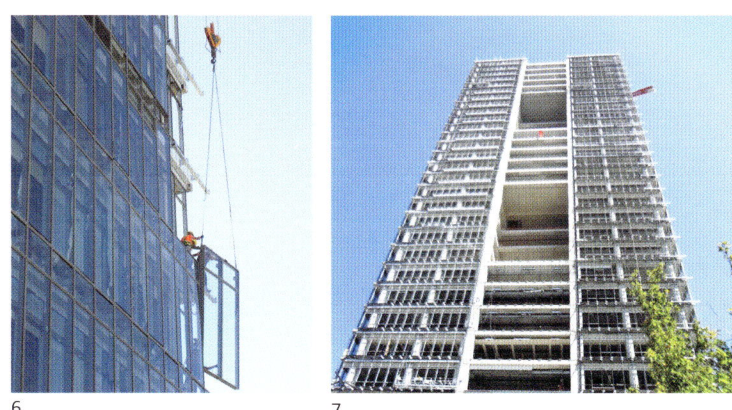

6

7

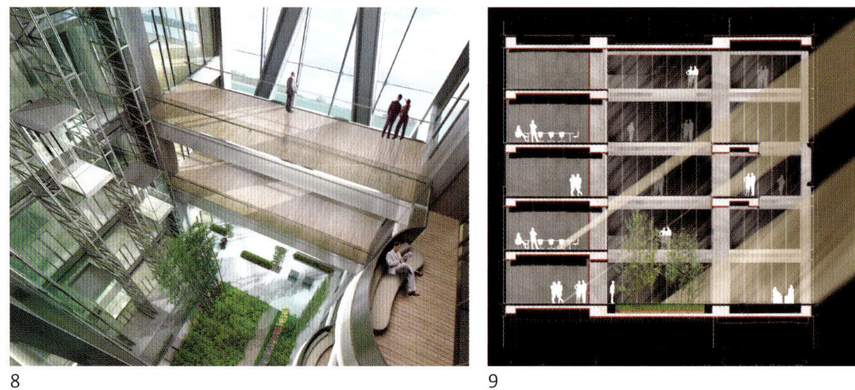

8

9

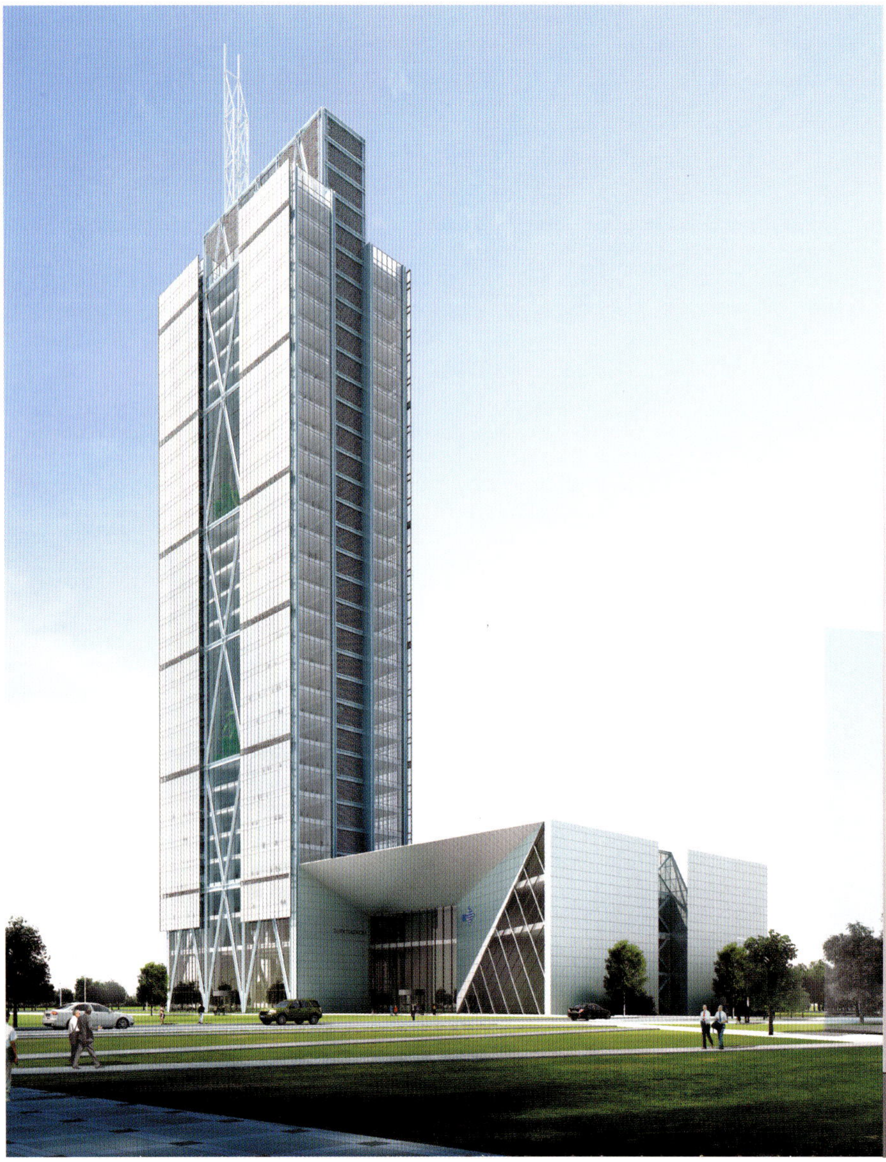

10

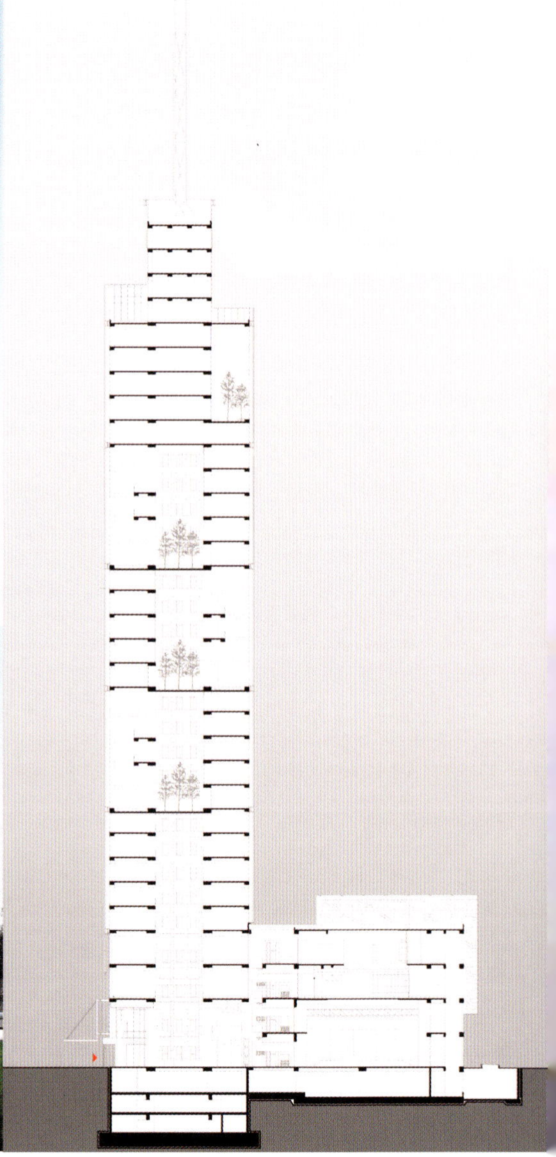

11

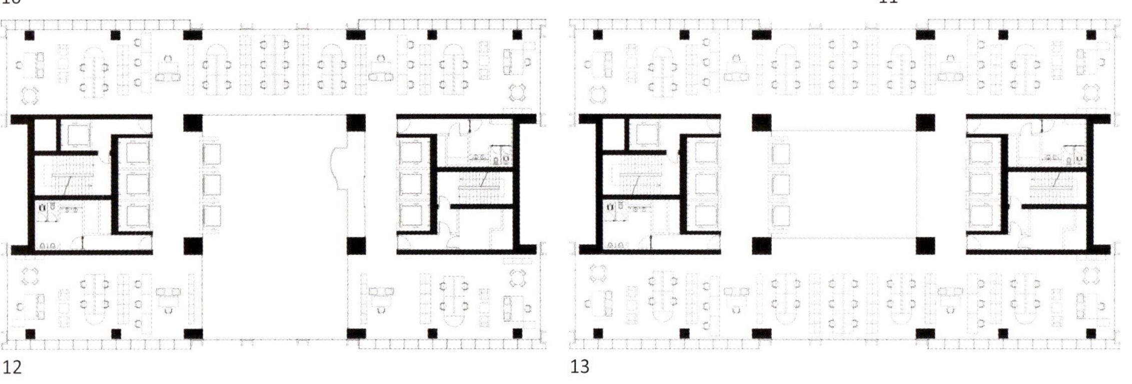

12

13

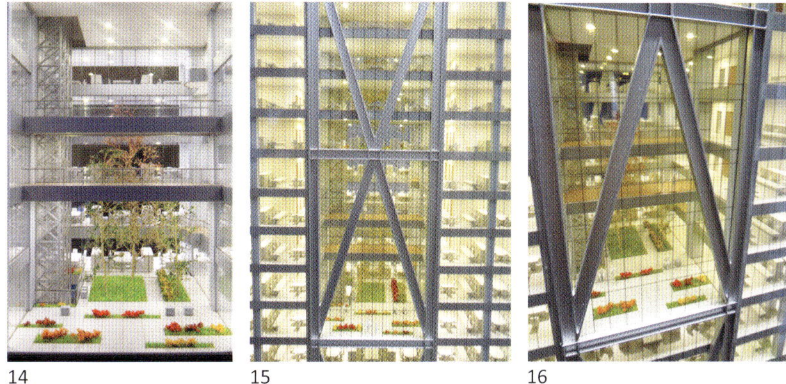

14 15 16

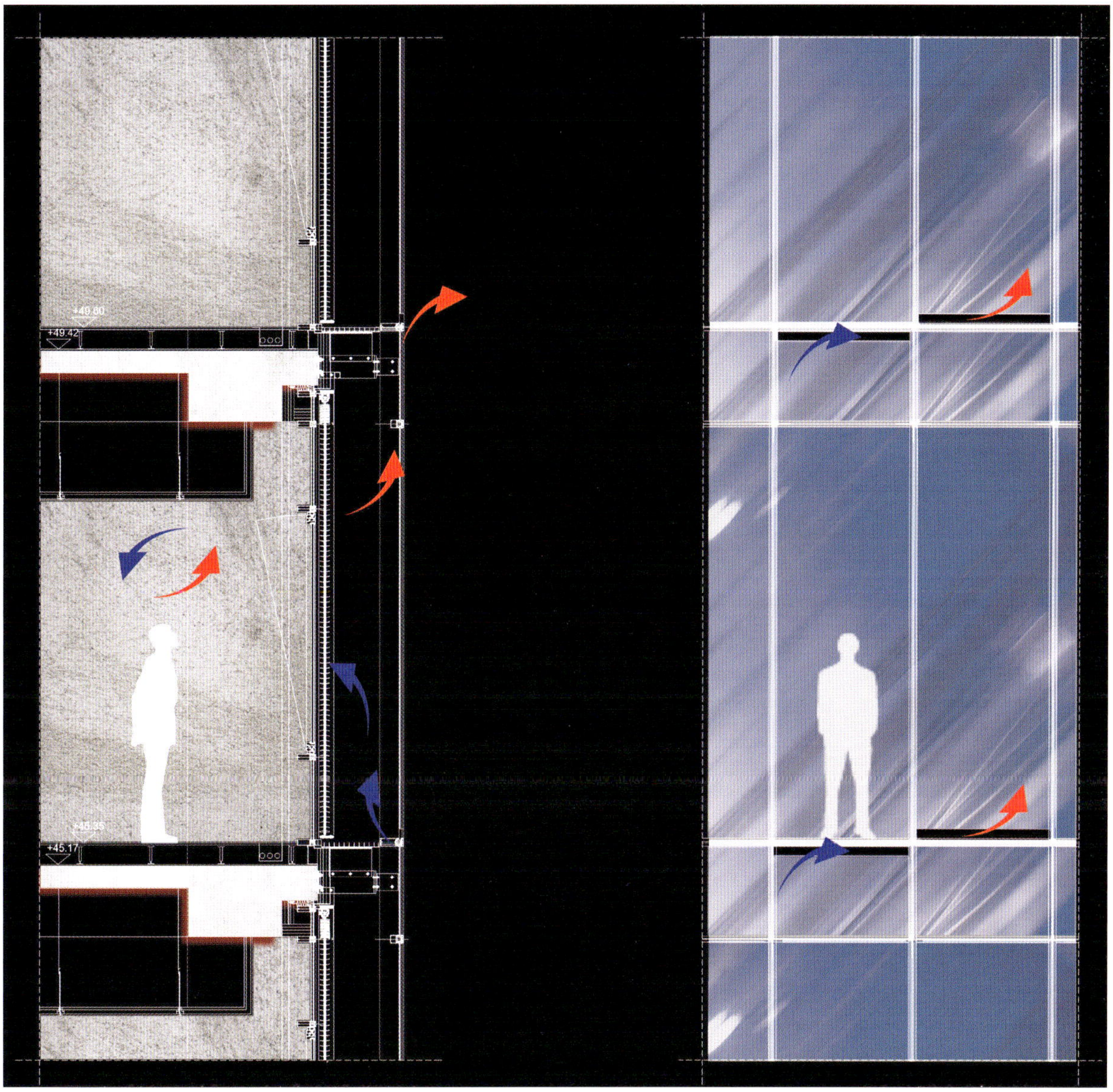

17

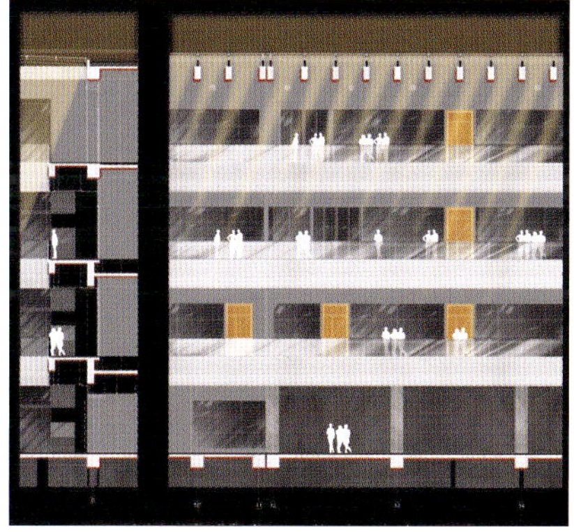

18

8 Atrium
9 Partial section through the tower atrium, showing inner gardens
10 General view
11 Section through the podium and tower
12 Type 1—typical floor plan with inner garden
13 Type 2—typical floor plan
14–16 Models
17 Double façade detail
18 Detail drawing showing the skylight from the podium

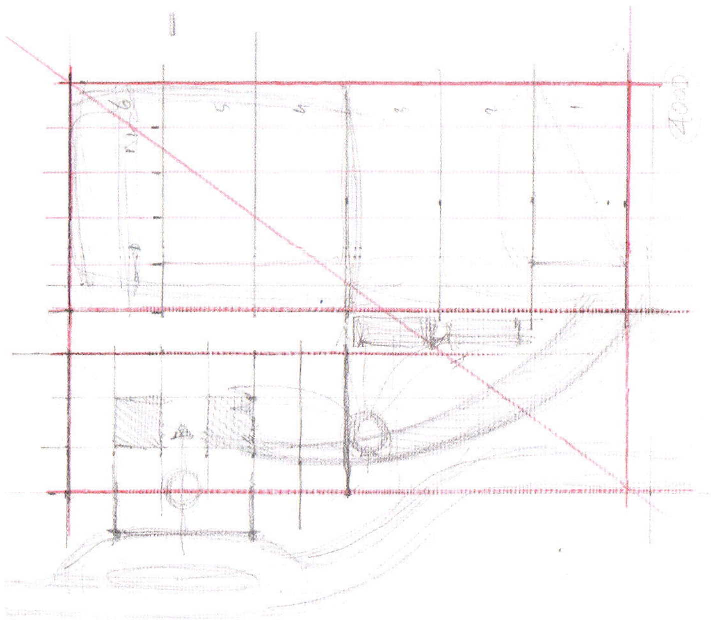

19

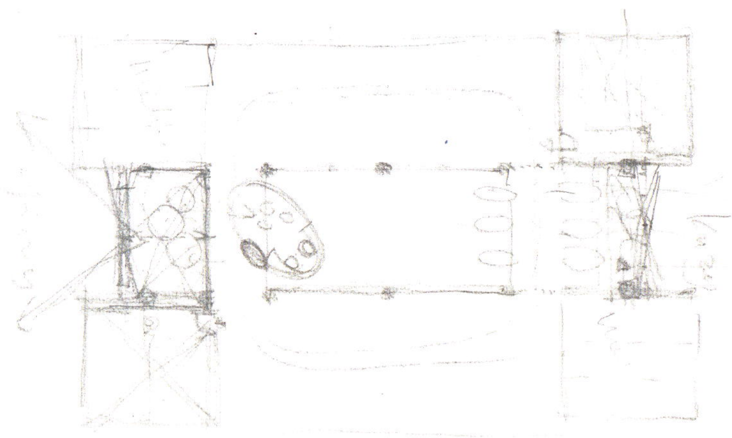

20

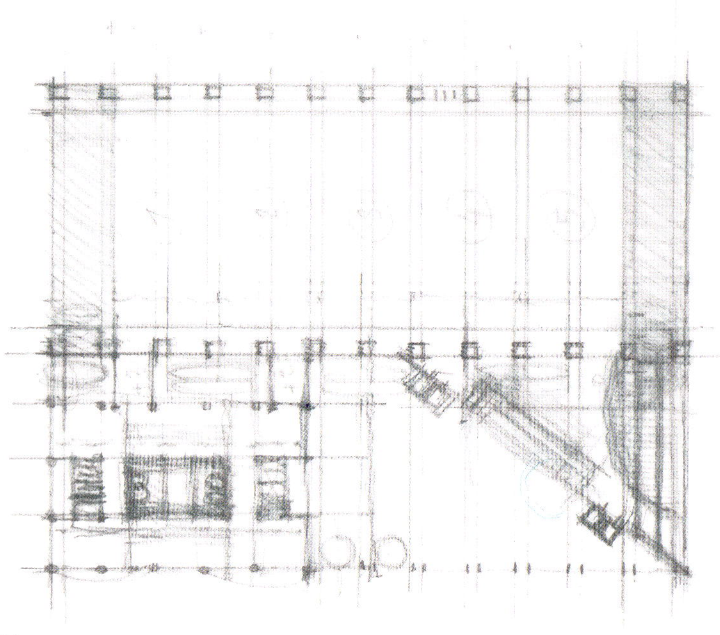

21

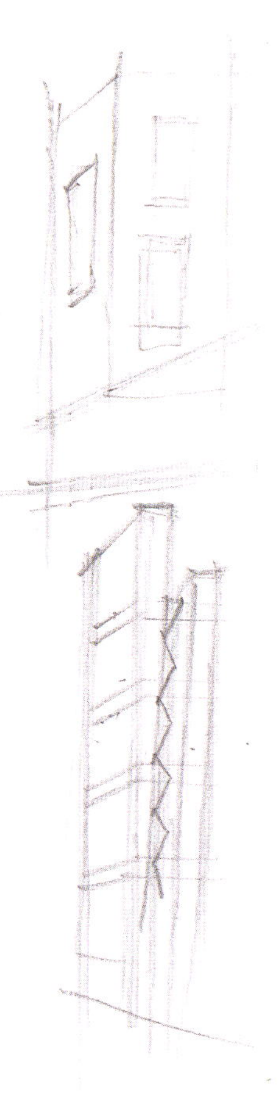

22

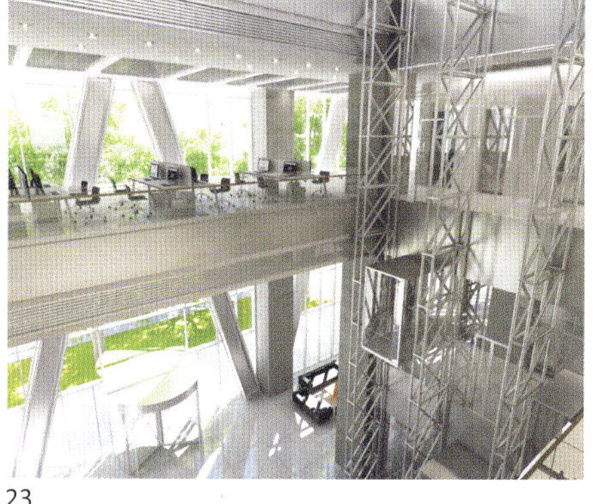
23

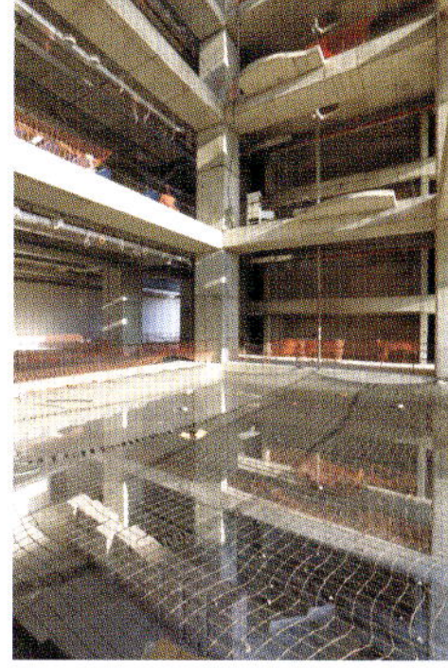
24

19–22 Sketches by Ali Osman Öztürk
23 Ground and first floor view
24 Construction
25 Rendering
26,27 View through the apartments during construction

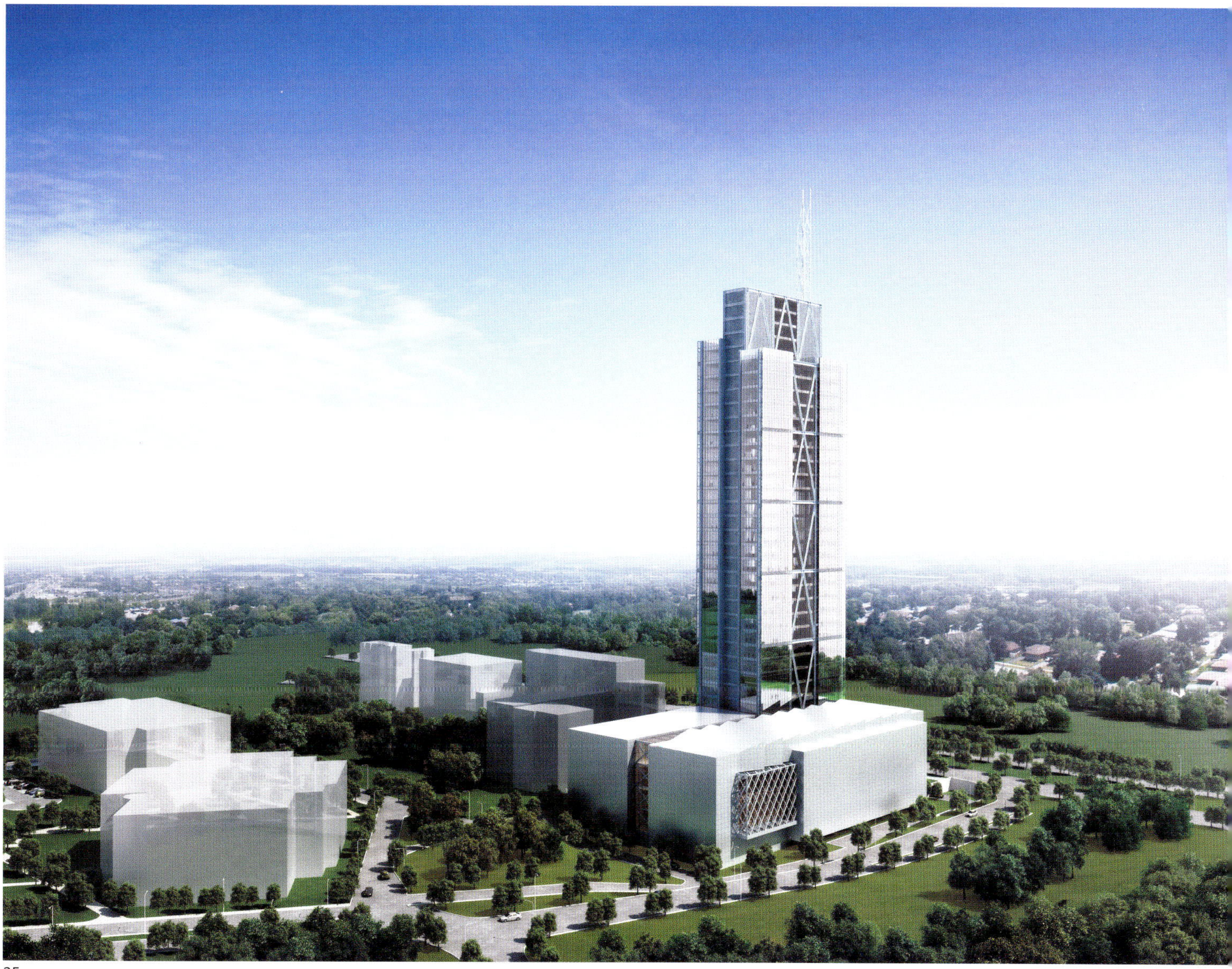

25

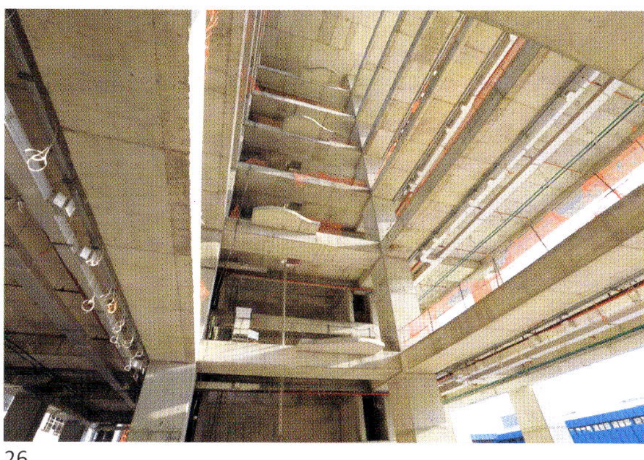
26

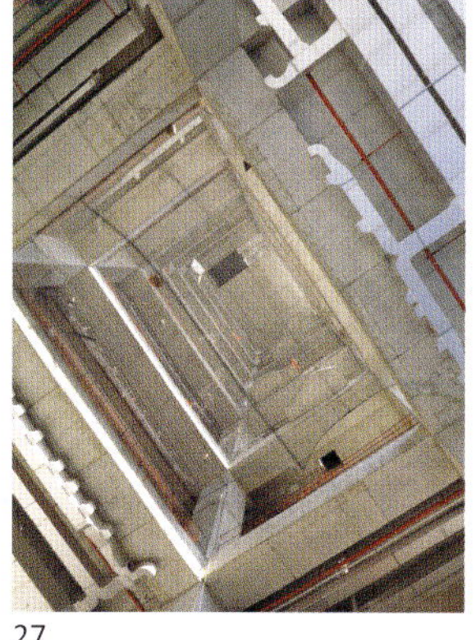
27

IFC Ziraat Bank

Client T.C. Ziraat Bank A.Ş.
Project Date 2013
Area 400,000 m^2
Location İstanbul
Architectural Design KPF
Local Architect A Tasarım Mimarlık
Structural/Mechanical/Electrical Engineer Arup London, Arup İstanbul
Workplace Interior Consultant KKS Strategy
Landscape Design Dalokay Design Studio
Fire Consultant Arup İstanbul
Acoustics Consultant Mezzo Studio
LEED Consultant Altensis
Façade Consultant ALT

The master plan studies for Istanbul's Financial Center were conducted by HOK and Arup and coordinated by the Ministry of Environment and Urbanism. The area designated for the General Headquarters of Ziraat Bank buildings is in the second planning zone. The architectural design for the site was prepared in collaboration by A Tasarım Mimarlık and KPF. The proposed towers aim to create a symbolic flagship structure in the silhouette of the Financial Center. The complex consists of a 7-story base with two towers that are 40 and 46 stories high. This mass was designed to form a foundation for the towers and to create a lively and dynamic public area around the buildings.

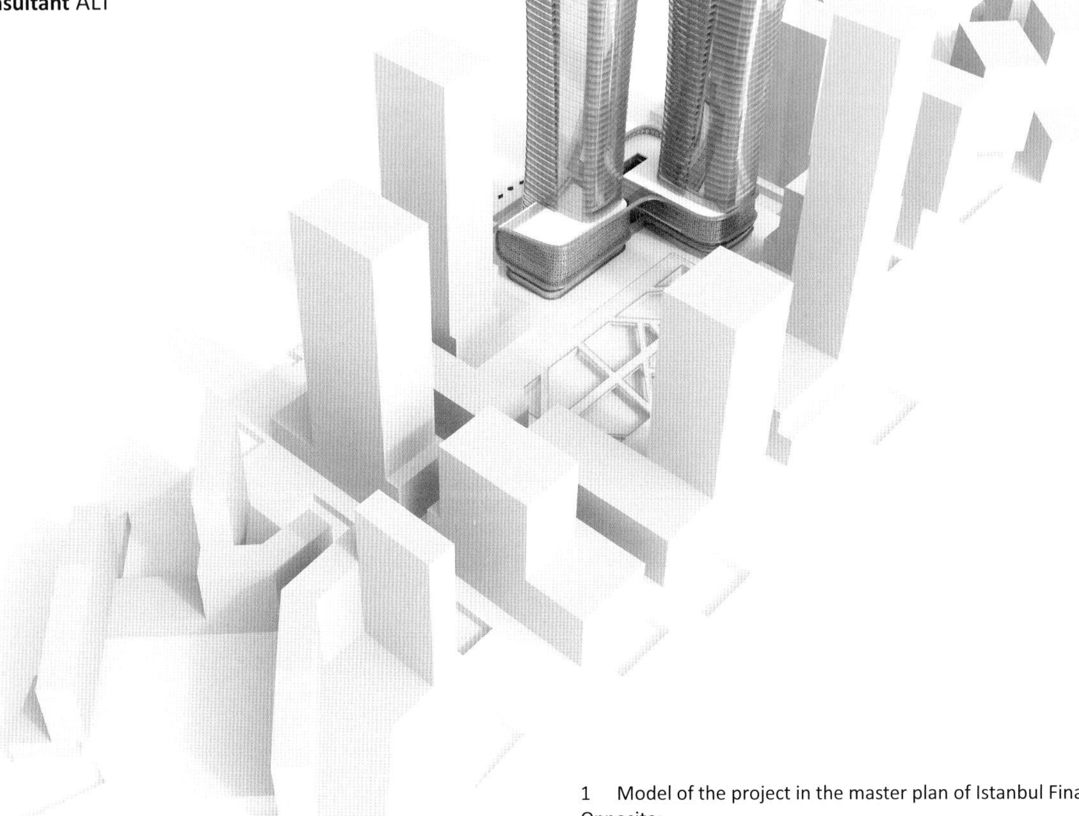

1

1 Model of the project in the master plan of Istanbul Financial Center
Opposite:
General view of the towers and the podium

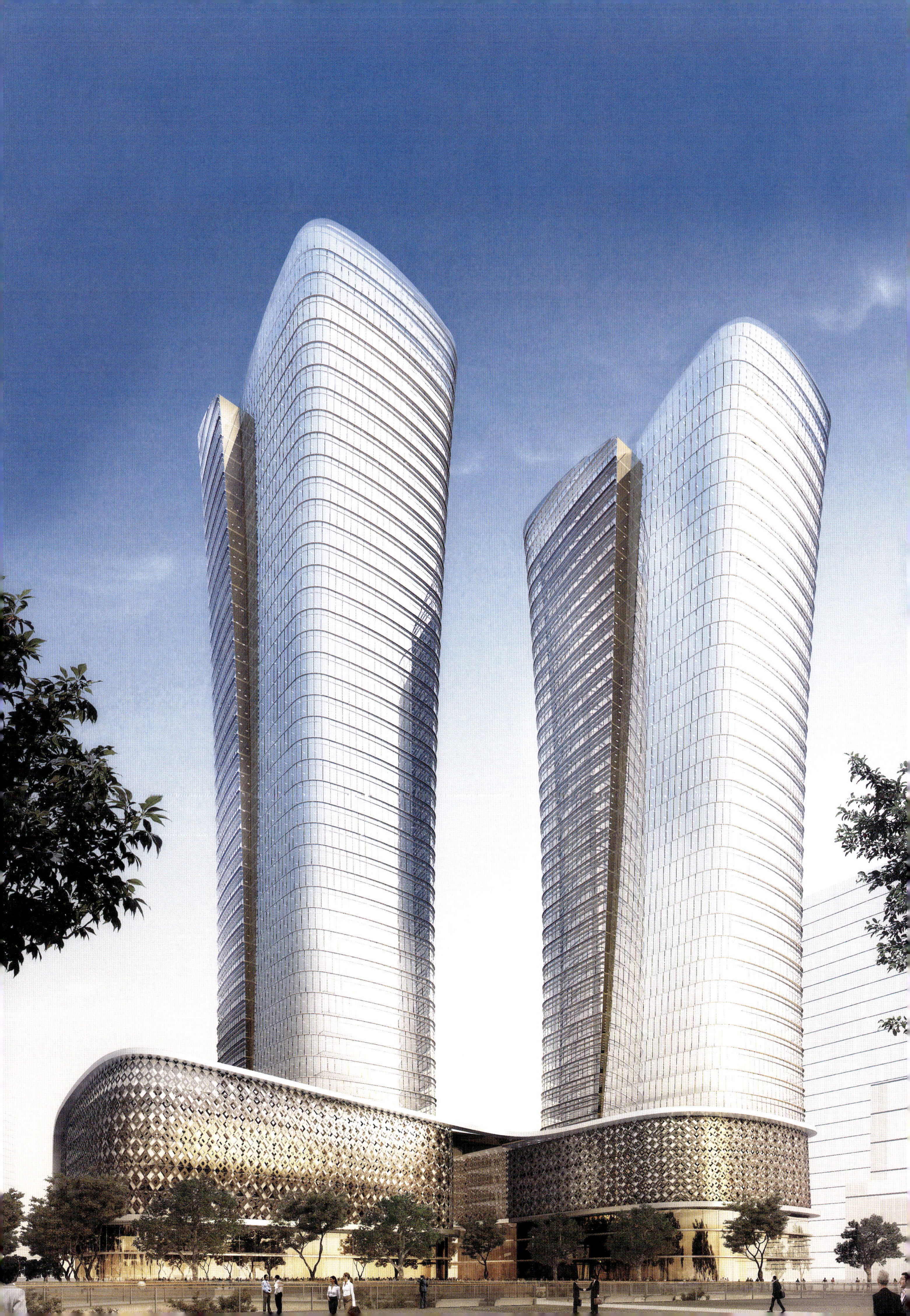

Skopje Mixed-Use Center

Client Limak

Project Date 2012

Area 213,156 m^2

Location Skopje

Architectural Design A Tasarım Mimarlık, CAG Architectural Workshop

Structural Engineer Prota Engineering

Mechanical Engineer Metta Engineering

Electrical Engineer Yurdakul Engineering

Fire Consultant Taru Engineering

This is a conservation and development project for a location in the historical center of the city of Skopje. The project site is in the planning area defined by Japanese architect Kenzō Tange. Tange's principles, especially on issues such as density and height, constitute the design's framework. The project site is located at the end of the pedestrian axis that begins at the river and ends at the old train station, connecting the historical fabric of Skopje to the new development areas. There is also a proposed underpass and tramline nearby. The most important constraints on the project are the long and narrow shape of the plot and the surrounding urban fabric.

The design is based on channeling pedestrian traffic to the 800-meter alley in the project site and creating an alternative pedestrian axis that contains functions that are integrated with the city on the ground level. This alley meets the perpendicular pedestrian movement from the city center and offers a new urban node—a secondary center that integrates with the city through open and semi-open spaces. It contains functions such as food and beverage and exhibition spaces, as well as commercial facilities. The structure is integrated with the former train station, now a museum, and other older structures around it. In this sense, the project can be considered an integration project, rather than a single building. The planned underpass and tramline determines the load-bearing system of the whole complex. The project constitutes an example of participatory planning processes, due to the collaboration with the conservation committee and local experts as well as the engineering and infrastructure groups.

1 Aerial view of Skopje showing the project in relation to the pedestrian path and city center
2 General view
3 Sketch by Ali Osman Öztürk, highlighting the multiple entrances and variety of functions

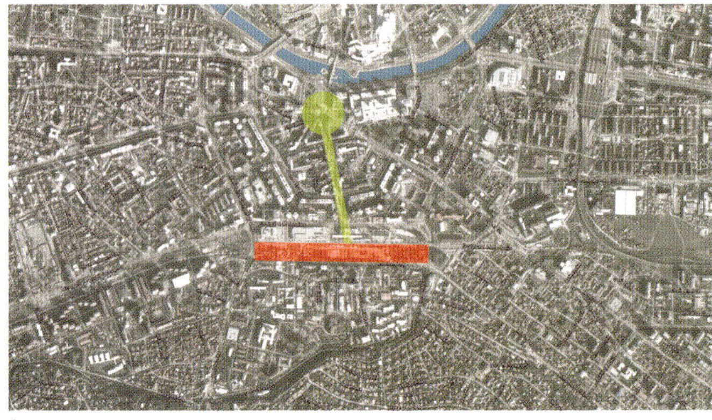

1

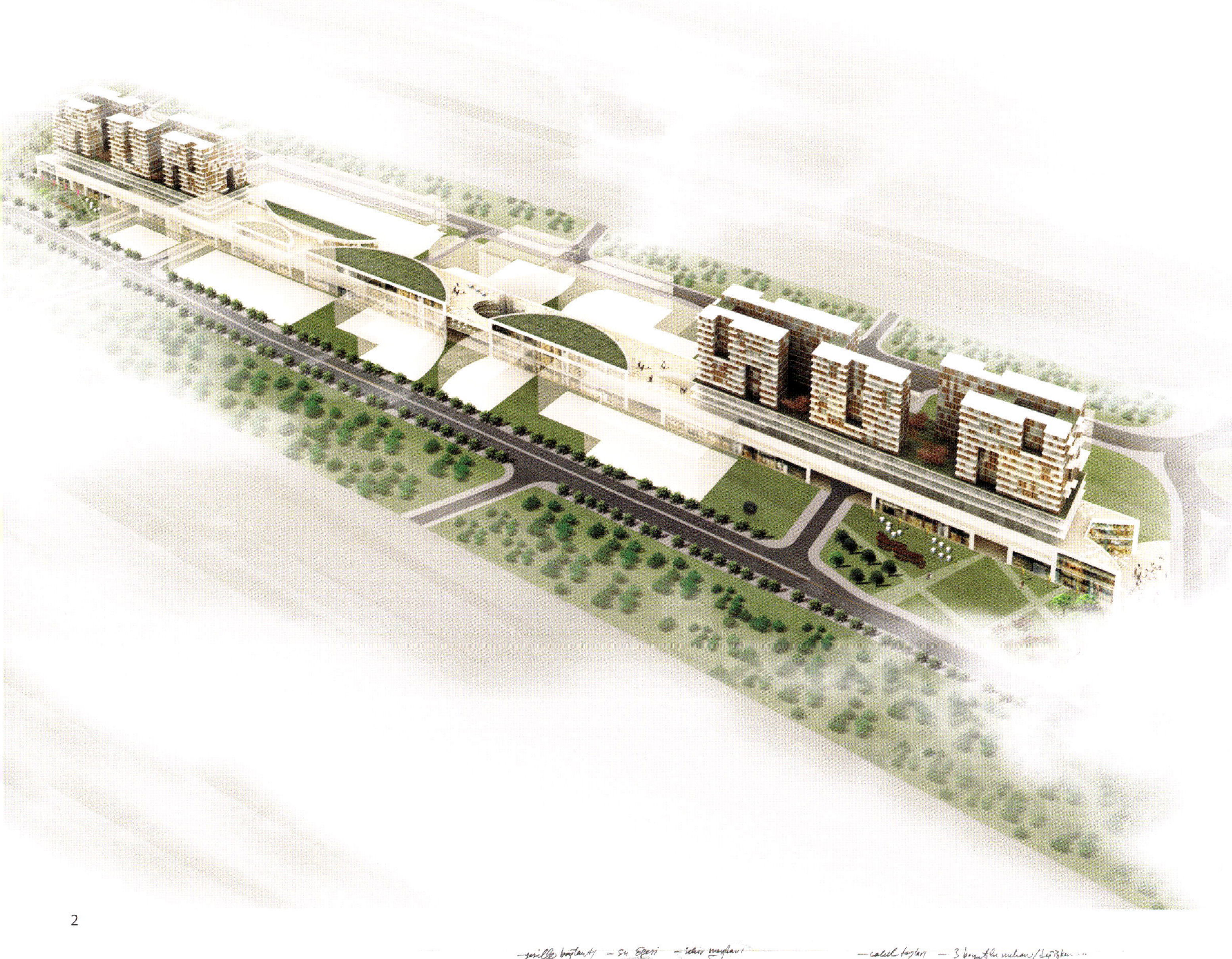

2

3

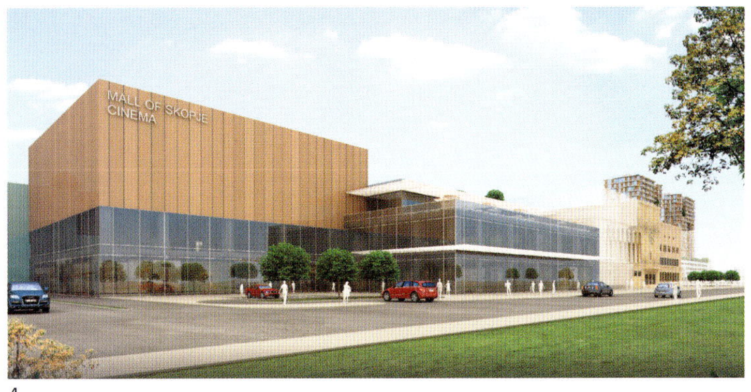

4

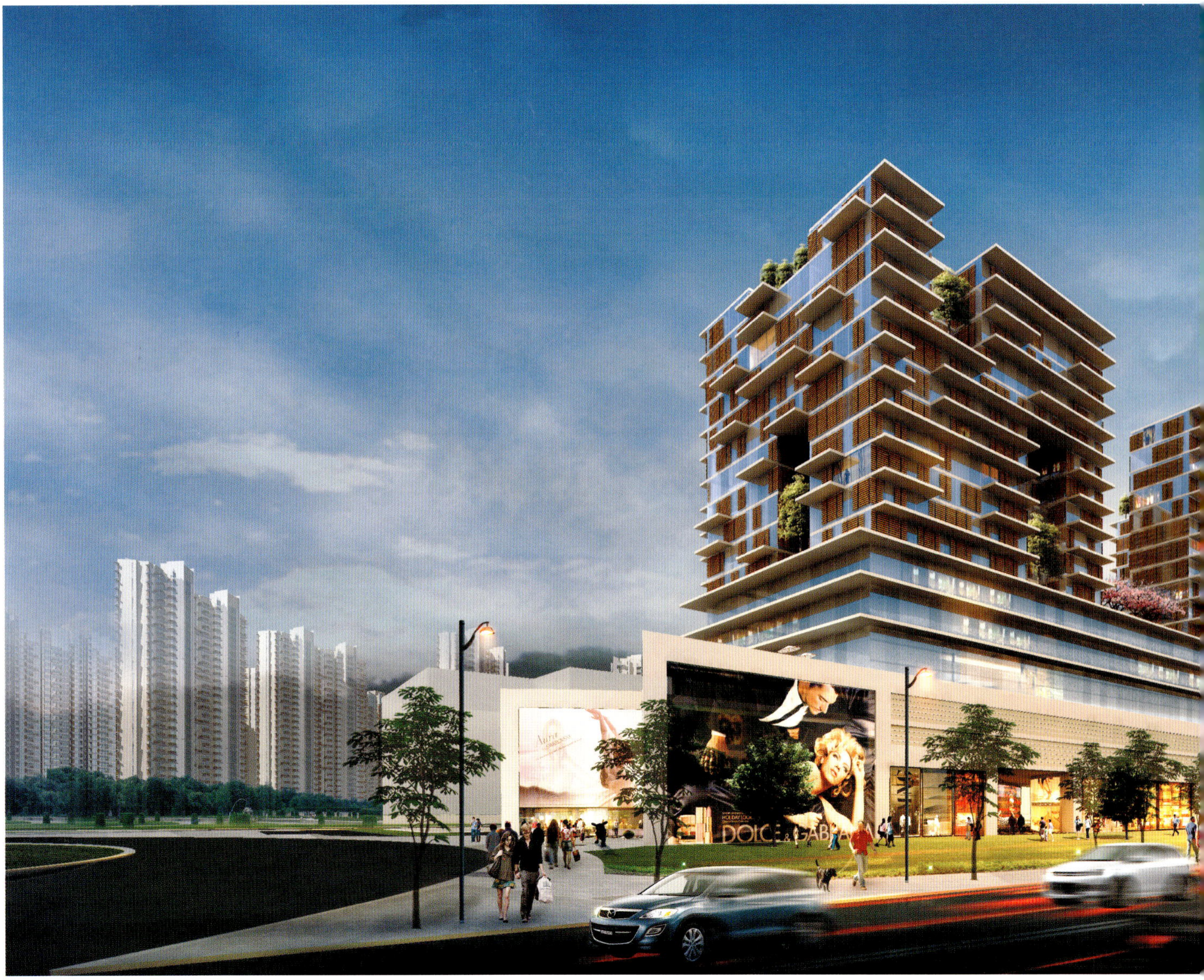

5

4 General view of the main entrance, highlighting the transparency of the project, located near the museum
5 General view showing the street life in front of the building
6 Typical floor plan of the residential apartments
7 Rendering of the museum near the Skopje Mixed-Use Center

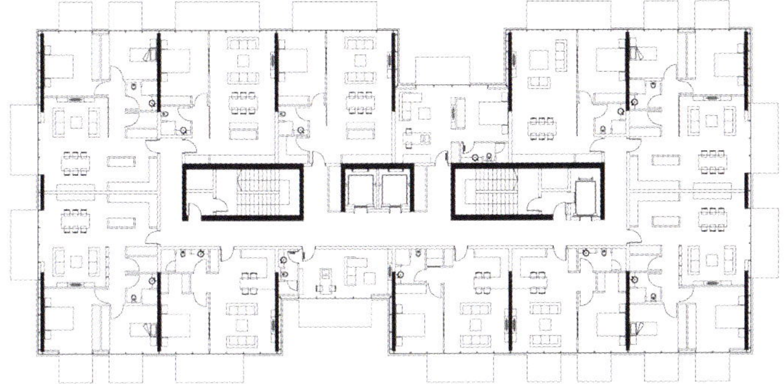

6

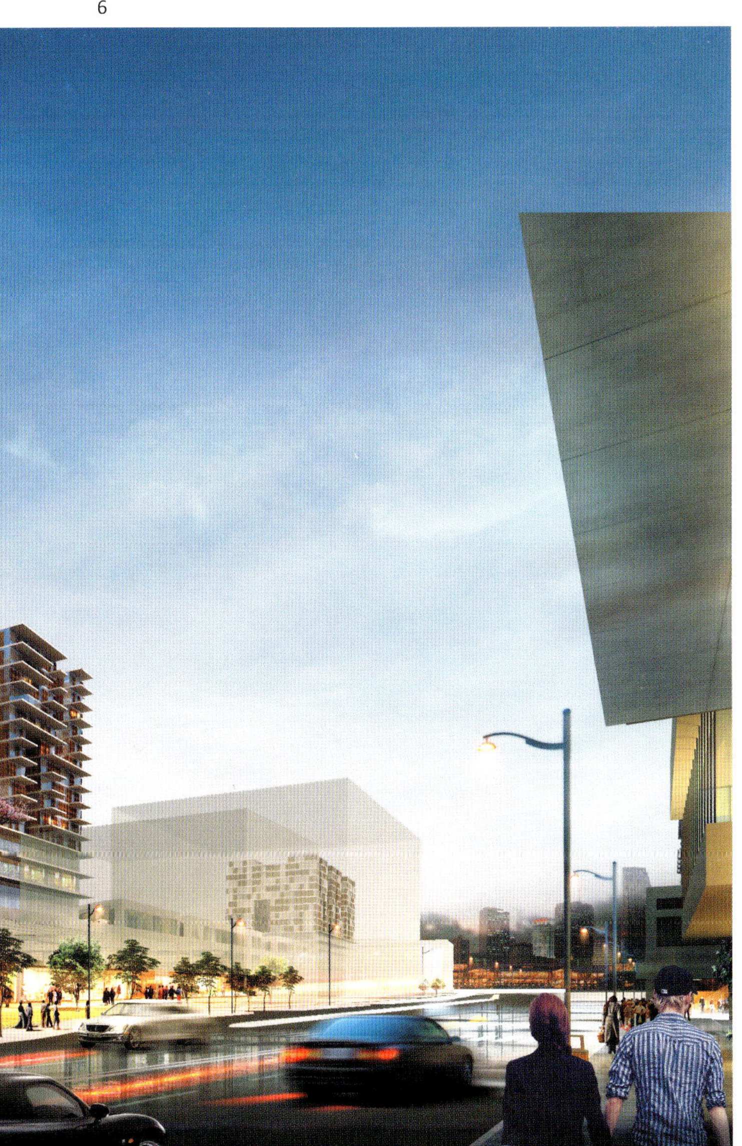

The Skopje Mixed-Use Center project proposes to renovate the existing museum building and add new surrounding structures that will revitalize and highlight this symbolic urban space. Open, semi-open, and closed spaces and passages proposed by the project connect the residential areas in the southern part of the city with business, accommodation, and other activities in the northern districts, reuniting an urban fabric formerly divided by the railway.

The main building defines the axis of the project and consists of a ground floor, two upper floors, and three basement floors. The ground floor is designated for cultural activities such as art galleries, art salesrooms, and open exhibition areas. The activities located near the museum are also culturally oriented. The main functions include open exhibition areas, an art gallery, a cultural center, cinema, theater, and food and beverage spaces. Technical services and indoor parking areas are designed below the ground floor. Other food and beverage patios open to the exterior and face towards the city center. These elements help integrate the complex with the urban fabric. The roof of this linear block is designed to be an urban park, bringing green elements to the higher levels. This greenery also constitutes a base for the four housing towers sitting above the linear block. The towers contain small apartments, and the blocks are designed according to Tange's planning approach.

The architectural language is minimalistic, given the diversity of the surrounding buildings and, especially, the museum's historical value. The ground floor is designed more or less as a background structure that allows interaction with the city via open and semi-open spaces.

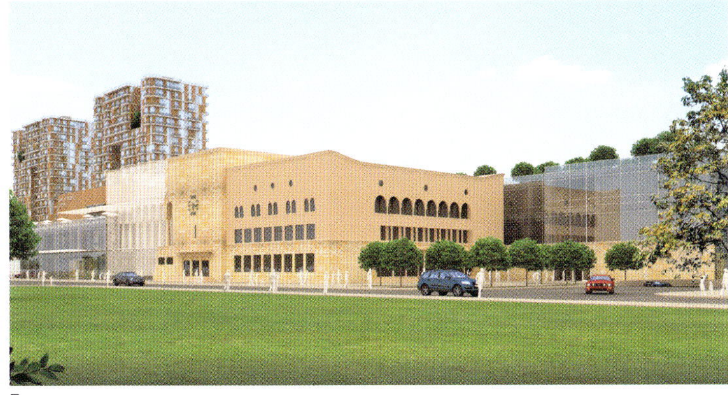

7

Ankara International Exhibition and Convention Center

Client Ankara International Exhibition and Convention Organization Inc.

Project Date 2011

Area 168,000 m^2

Location Ankara

Architectural Design gmp Architekten von Gerkan, Marg und Partner, A Tasarım Mimarlık

Structural Engineer Binnewies, Yüksek Project

Mechanical Engineer Protec, Metta Engineering

Electrical Engineer Protec, Yurdakul Engineering

Landscape Design Breimann & Bruun, Dalokay Design Studio

Signage Form Kombinat, Katharina Marg

Planned for a site in the new development area of Akyurt, near Esenboğa Airport, The Ankara International Exhibition and Convention Center is a project by the Ankara International Exhibition and Convention Organization in partnership with the Ankara Metropolitan Municipality, the Ankara Special Provincial Administration, the Turkish Union of Chambers and Commodity Exchanges, the Ankara Chamber of Commerce, the Ankara Chamber of Industry, the Ankara Commodity Exchange, the Akyurt Municipality, and the Ankara Union of Chambers of Merchants and Craftsmen.

The development plan for the Exhibition and Convention Center was completed in 2009. The project was prepared by a partnership of gmp and A Tasarım Mimarlık. gmp's proven experience in international fair structures and A Tasarım Mimarlık's experience in local culture and building technologies were combined. gmp and A Tasarım Mimarlık developed the project with workshops organized in collaboration with engineering teams and consultants in Ankara and Hamburg.

The new Exhibition and Convention Center is located in the Northern Ankara Akyurt development area. A rail system will connect the airport to the city center to make the new convention center accessible. There are three convention centers in the world—Dubai, Paris, and Berlin—where aerospace conventions can be organized due to their proximity to an airport. As a result of its strategic location, Ankara's fair center is a candidate to be the fourth. The Ankara International Exhibition and Convention Center with its square layout centered on a courtyard (serenity garden) is a unique project as opposed to usual convention buildings that contain exhibition rooms attached on a linear circulation area.

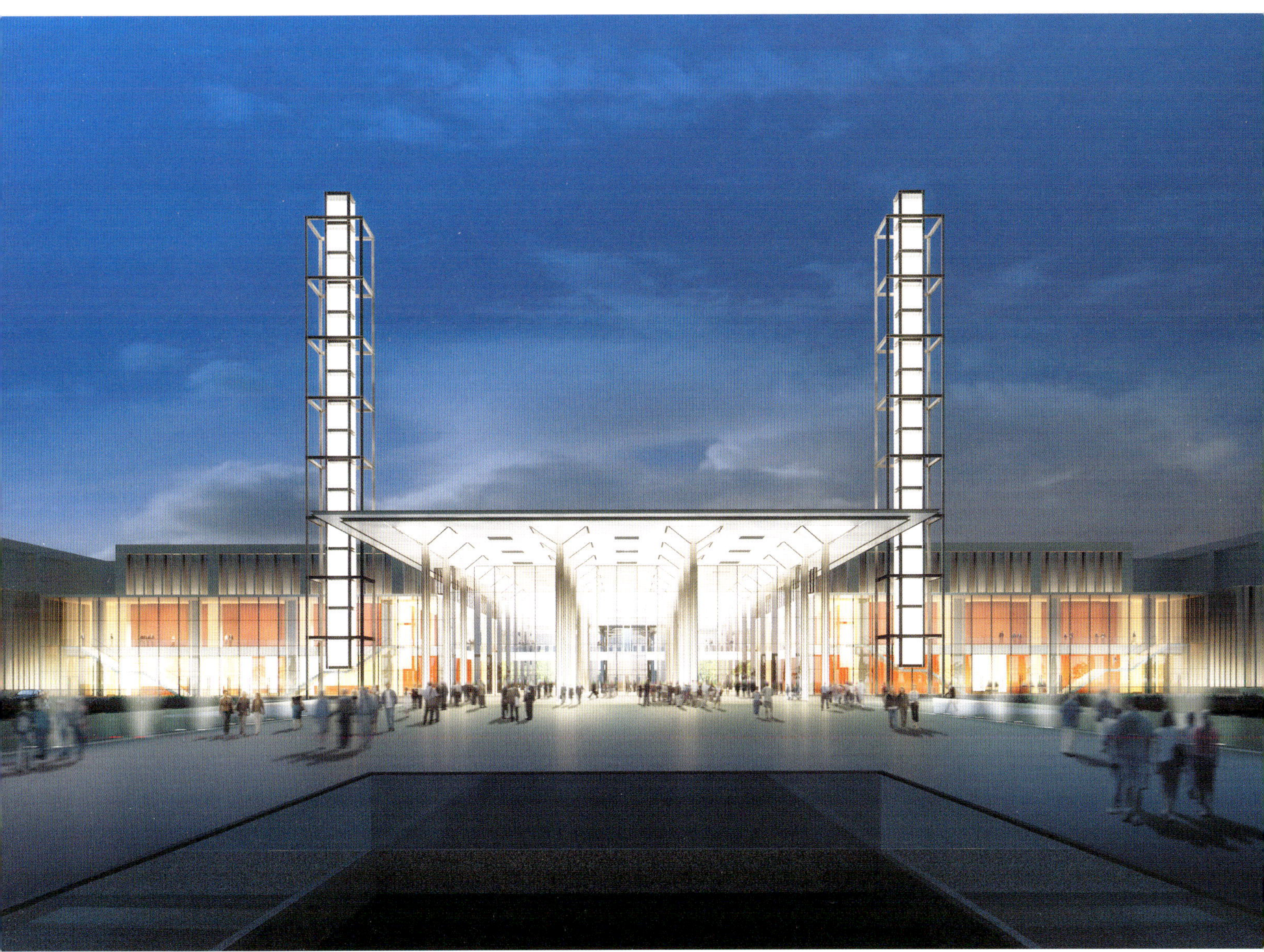

General view

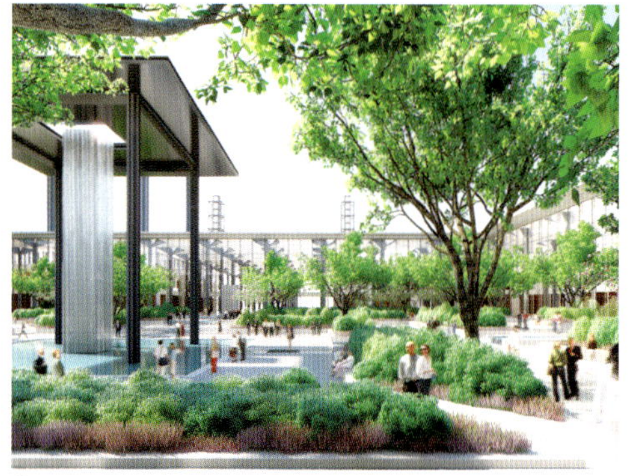
2

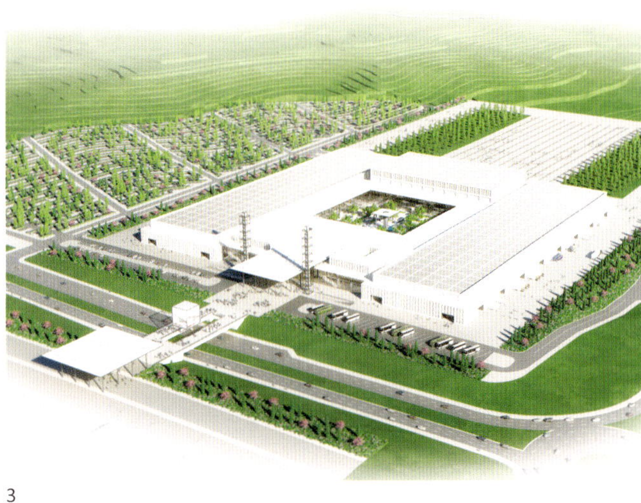
3

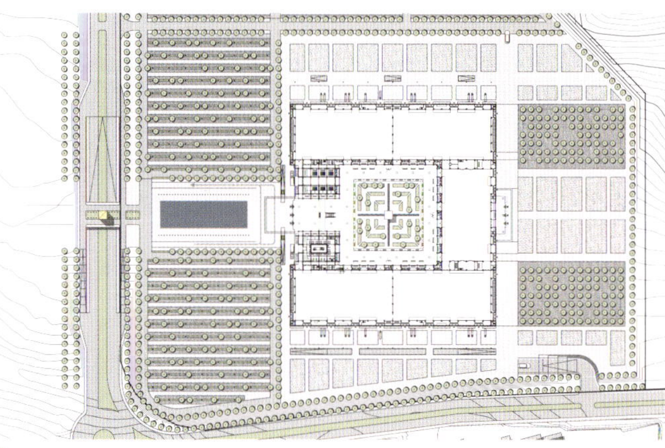
4

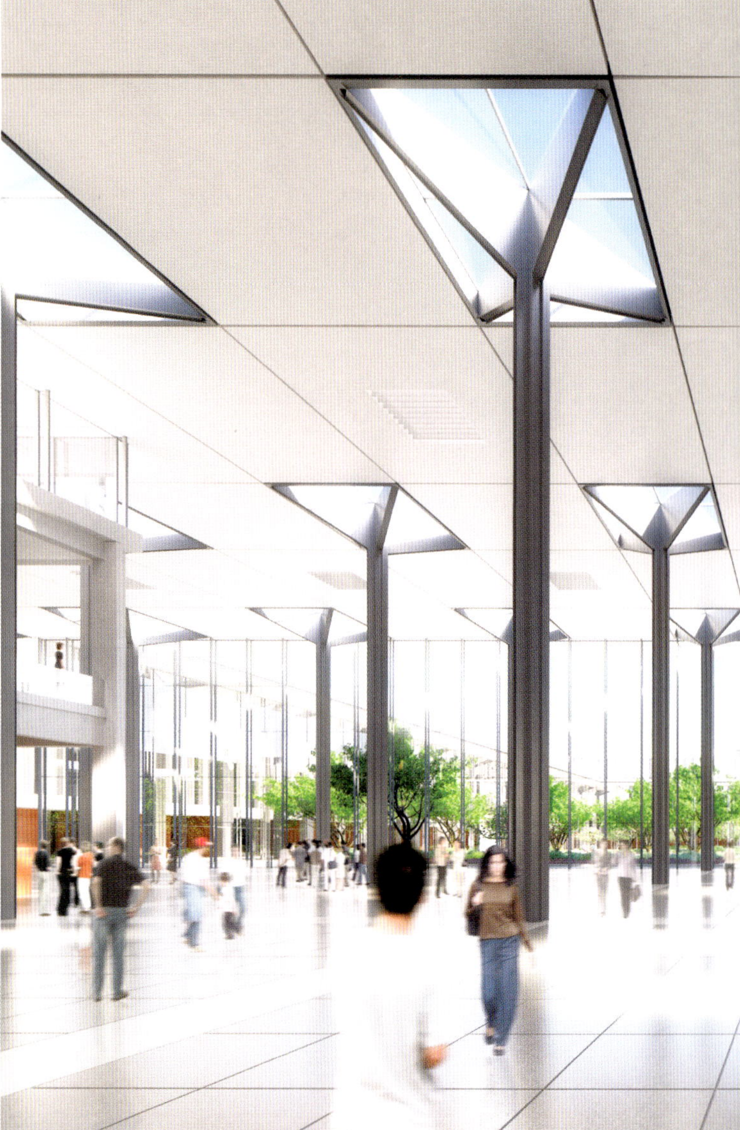
5

2 Rendering of the serenity garden
3 Bird's-eye view
4 Ground floor plan
5,6 Central hall

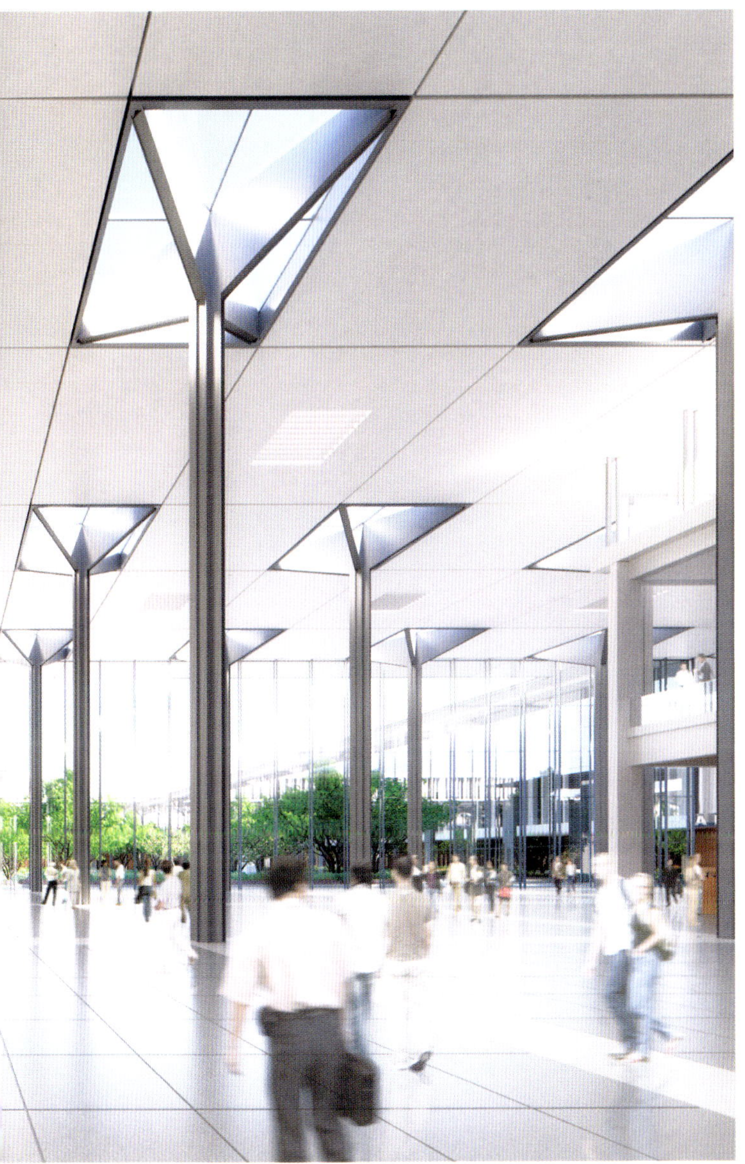

The first stage of the project consists of 50,000 square meters of exhibition and activity areas and 50,000 square meters of conference, food and beverage, and service spaces. The second stage of modular expansion will contain 100,000 square meters of closed exhibition space. The expansion area can be used as an open exhibition area. The proposed project includes a separate exhibition area designated for Air Expos in conjunction with the planned third runway of the airport.

There are highly visible media cubes and light towers located on the access route that will guide visitors. The first stage includes five exhibition and activity halls with an area of 10,000 square meters. The center of the design is the serenity garden. This section's design is inspired by Anatolian *caravanserais*, with water elements and multi-level pools in the middle of the courtyard. The courtyard aims to provide a serene atmosphere and offer visitors a respite from the business of the fair organizations.

The building will be built quickly and structural systems have been proposed for all functional, aesthetic, and conceptual needs of the building. The building system is based on U-modules that are integrated with each other in various ways. The façade design and the load-bearing systems were developed on the basis of the 120-centimeter axes of these modules.

The materials used in the building include concrete, steel, glass, wood, and natural stone. The flooring materials are travertine in the general-purpose spaces, parquet for the conference and meeting rooms, and carpet for the offices.

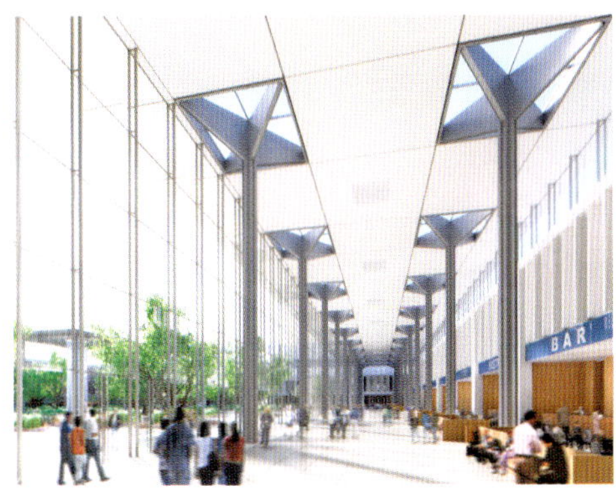

6

Yaşamkent Mosque

Client Association of Ankara Ataşehir Mosque
Project Date 2009
Area 2,685 m^2
Location Ankara
Structural Engineer Yüksek Project
Design Consultant Salih Bezci, Vecihi Yıldız
Project Manager Ömer Tunavelioğlu
Mechanical Engineer Metta Engineering
Contractor Besa Construction Inc.
Electrical Engineer Akay Engineering
2012 Cityscape Dubai Finalist
2012 WAF Finalist

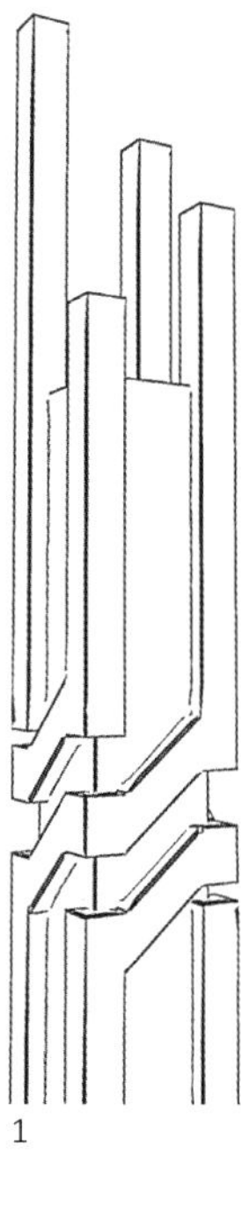

1

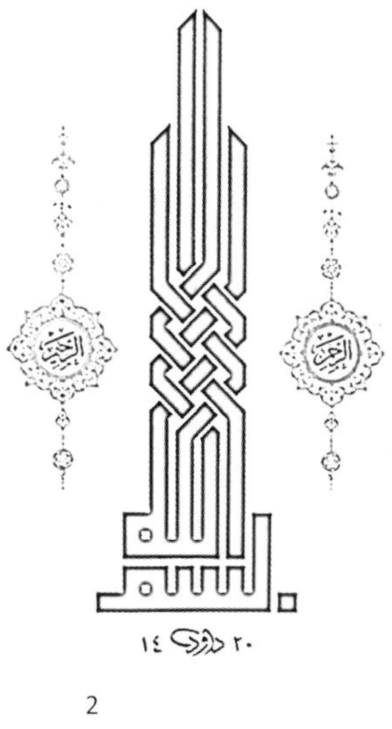

2

With its powerful and dominant iconography, based upon tradition, mosque architecture is one of the most conservative building typologies in Turkish context. On the other hand referring traditional and local values creating a sense of sustainability had always been a major challenge in modern understanding of mosque architecture. In this respect, Yaşamkent Mosque represents an investigation into creating a sense of consciousness and a peaceful continuity between traditional and modern values of cultural accumulation.

Located in a relatively small plot within the new development area of Ankara, which also gives its name to the complex, Yaşamkent Mosque is the search for balance between open and closed areas, modesty and expression, identity and convention as well as modernity and tradition.

The building is an outcome of topography where natural level difference is used to reorganize programmatic differences and create a hierarchy between public and private entrances. The composition is based upon freestanding parallel walls not only defining the essence of interior space, but also creating a transitory medium for exterior and interior spaces. As a powerful traditional element, the walls are major expressions of architectural language. As they come together, limit, and blur the boundaries, alternative spatial experiences are created. Similar to walls, the courtyard is a significant traditional element, which both unifies and separates the main praying area from the library and less public areas like lodging. The courtyard is utilized as an instrument to integrate exterior and interior as well as soft and hard landscapes. In the main praying hall a modest concrete dome is not only used as a reference of tradition but also upgrades the interior scale and provides significant mystical light quality.

3

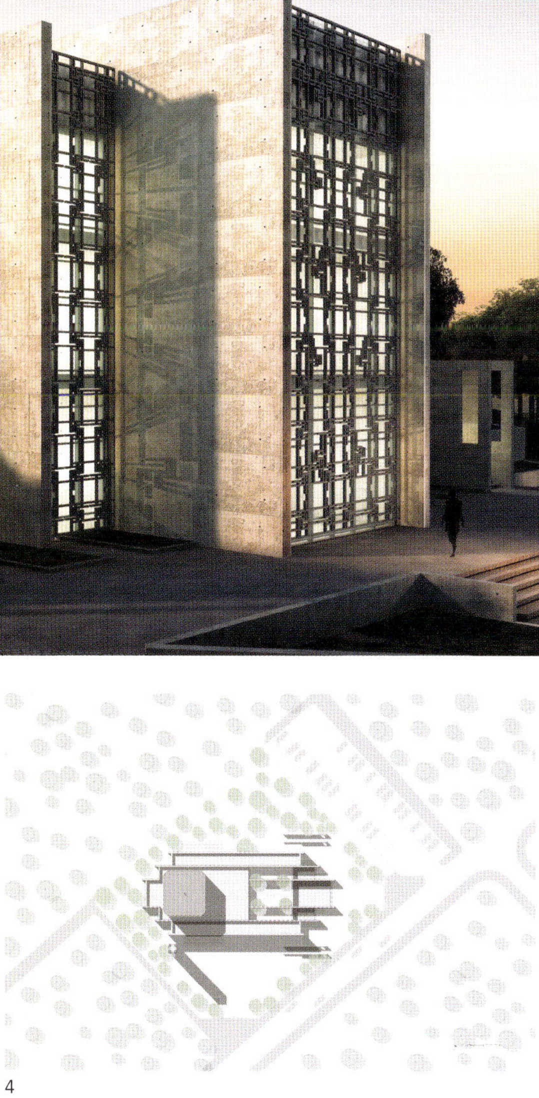

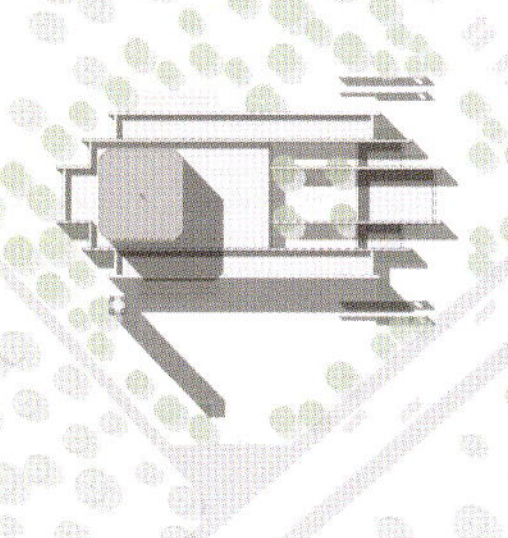
4

1 Sketch of the minaret
2 Kufic script written by Davut Bektaş
3 General view
4 Site plan

5 Bird's-eye view
6 Cross section
7 Longitudinal section
8 Lower level plan
9 Ground floor plan
10 Interior view towards the mihrab

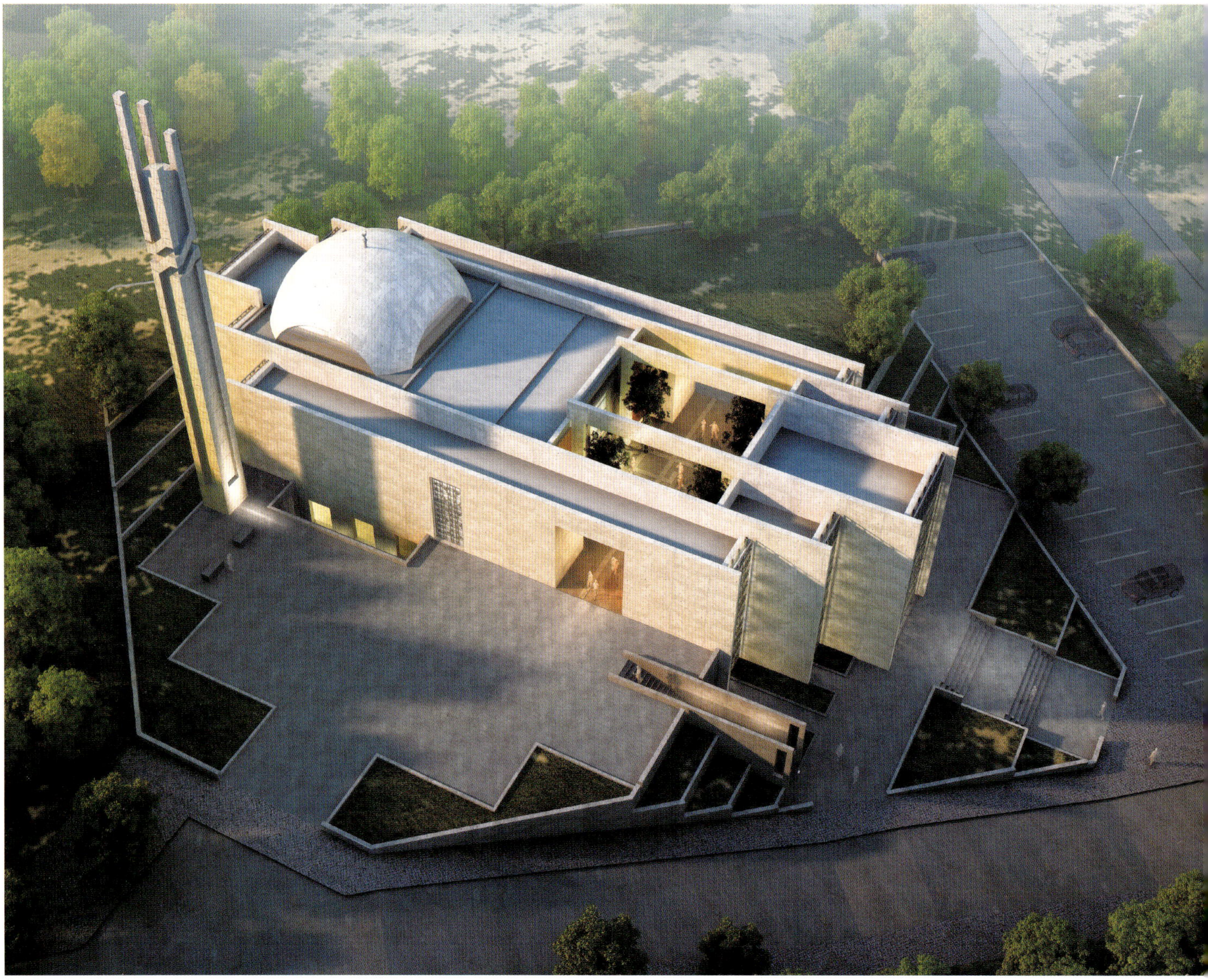

5

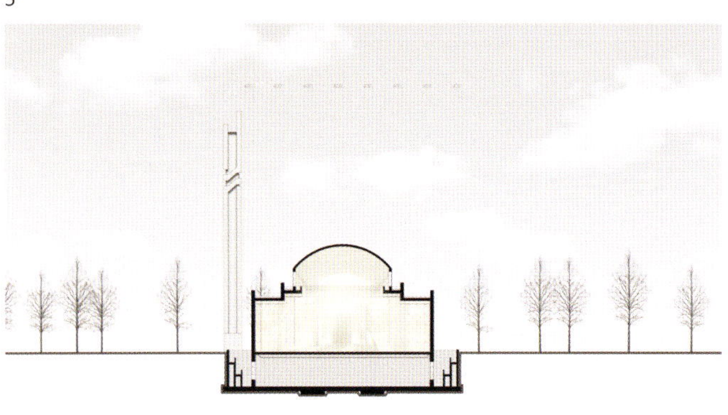

6

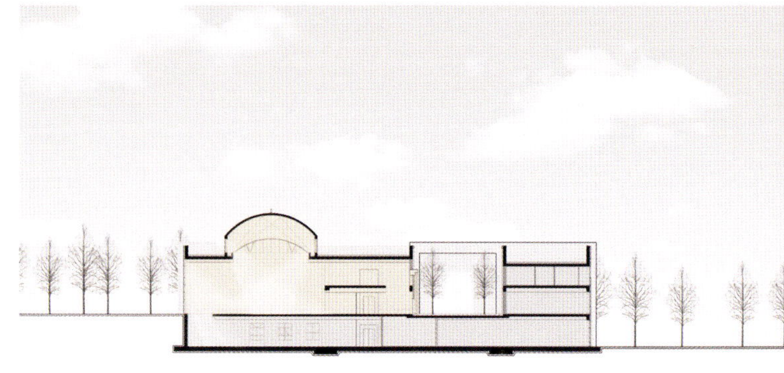

7

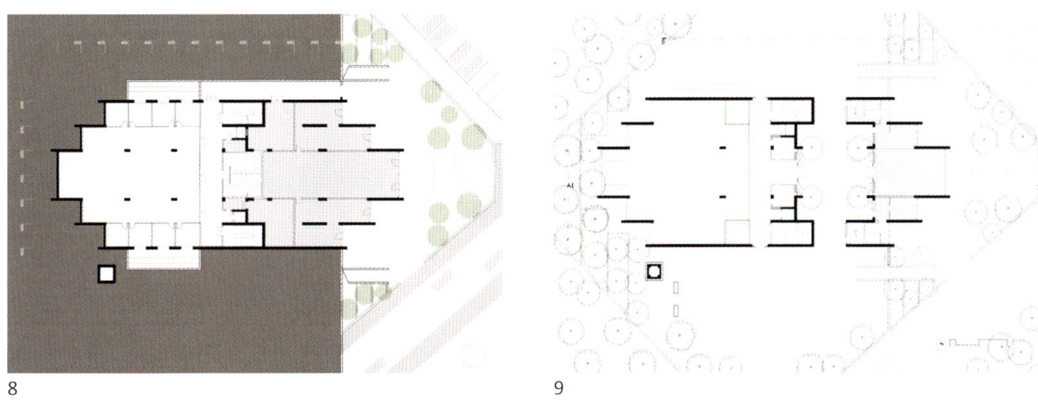
8 9

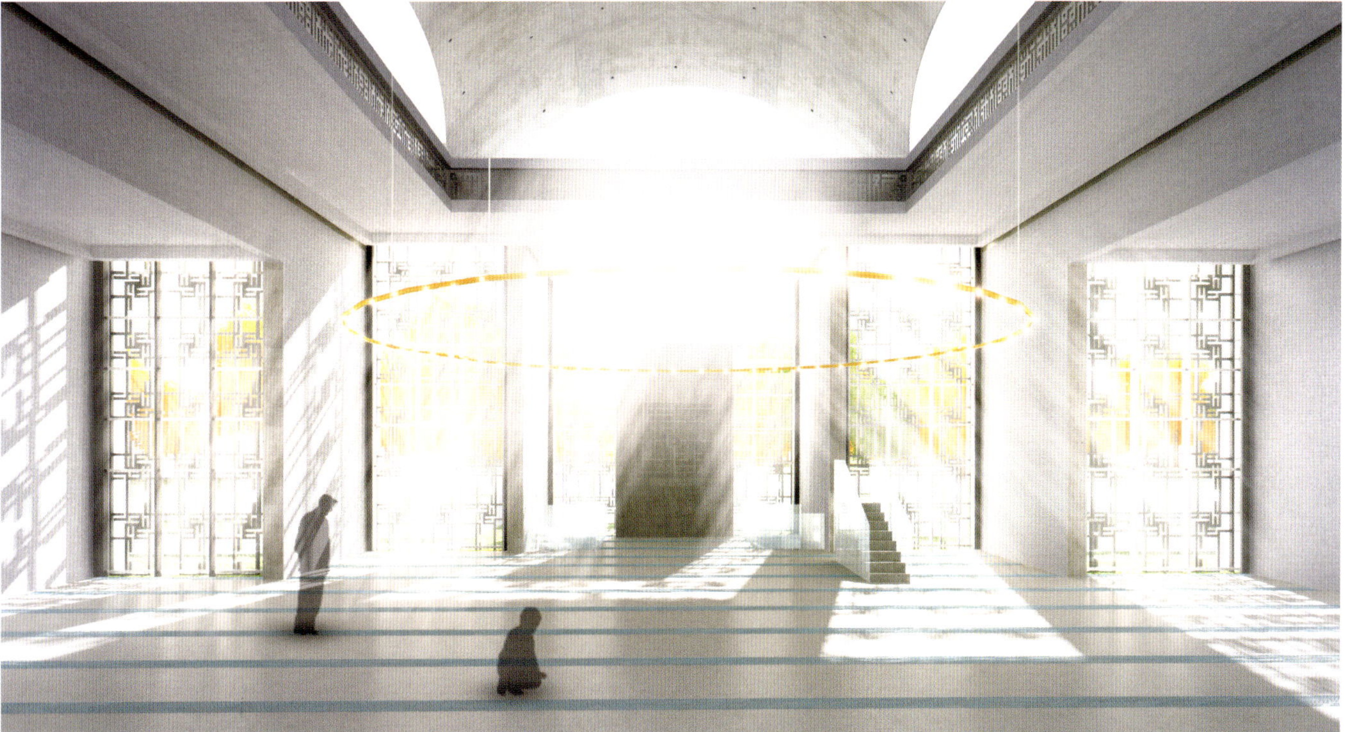
10

The use of reinforced concrete and glass as a finishing element, along with the use of abstract and solid geometries, modest simplicity, and minimalist architectural attitude directly refers to a contemporary architectural language whereas the abstract Kufic expression of the minaret as well as the abstract motives of fences refer to familiar traditional elements.

With all these characteristics Yaşamkent Mosque must be seen as a challenge towards blurring the significant and ideological differences and popular architectural contradictions between traditional and modern.

Mesa Plaza

Client MESA Housing Industries Inc.
Project Date 2004
Area 19,800 m^2
Location Ankara
Architectural Design A Architectural Design, MESA Design Group
Structural Engineer MESA Housing Industries, Yüksek Project
Mechanical Engineer MESA Mechanical Group, Beşeli Engineering
Electrical Engineer MESA Electrical Group
Contractor MESA Housing Industries Inc.

The oldest shopping mall on the Eskişehir Road, Mesa Plaza became an important social hub as soon as it was opened, filling an important gap in the area, and maintained this function for many years. However, the expansion of residential areas and the creation of new urban fabric on the rapidly developing western axis of Ankara changed the density and quality of commerce in this district. Mesa Plaza is considered an urban renewal project in the context of this transformation, which aimed to revise the existing mall in terms of architectural use and language.

The proposed design partially preserves the mall by retaining the elements that are used from the outside. Circulation is reestablished. Connections between floors are reorganized, and alternative solutions are proposed for the main corridors. According to the hierarchy of the mall spaces, the supermarket section is reduced, movie theaters are removed, and all floors are connected to the indoor parking area. The existing load-bearing system is protected while the façades are changed, in an attempt to give the structure a more modern architectural style. Together with the façade material, special lighting details were developed, emphasizing the perception of the building in its environment.

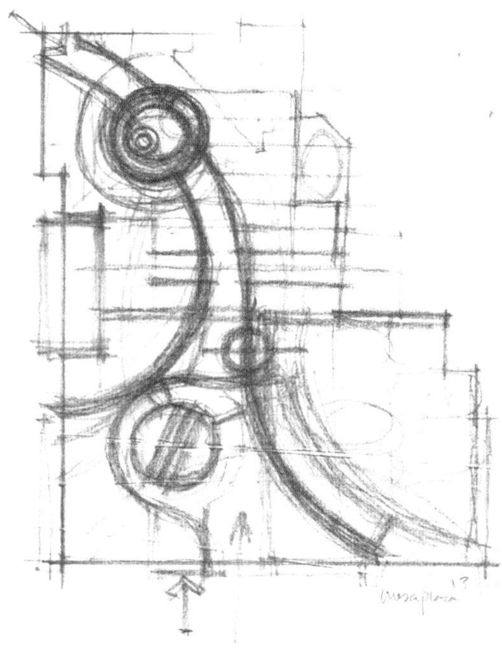

1

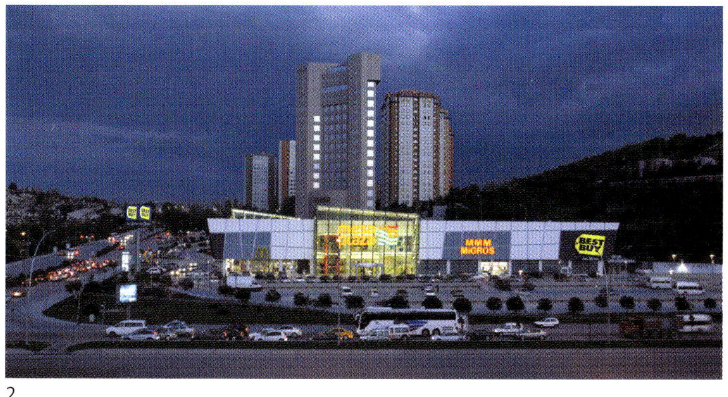

2

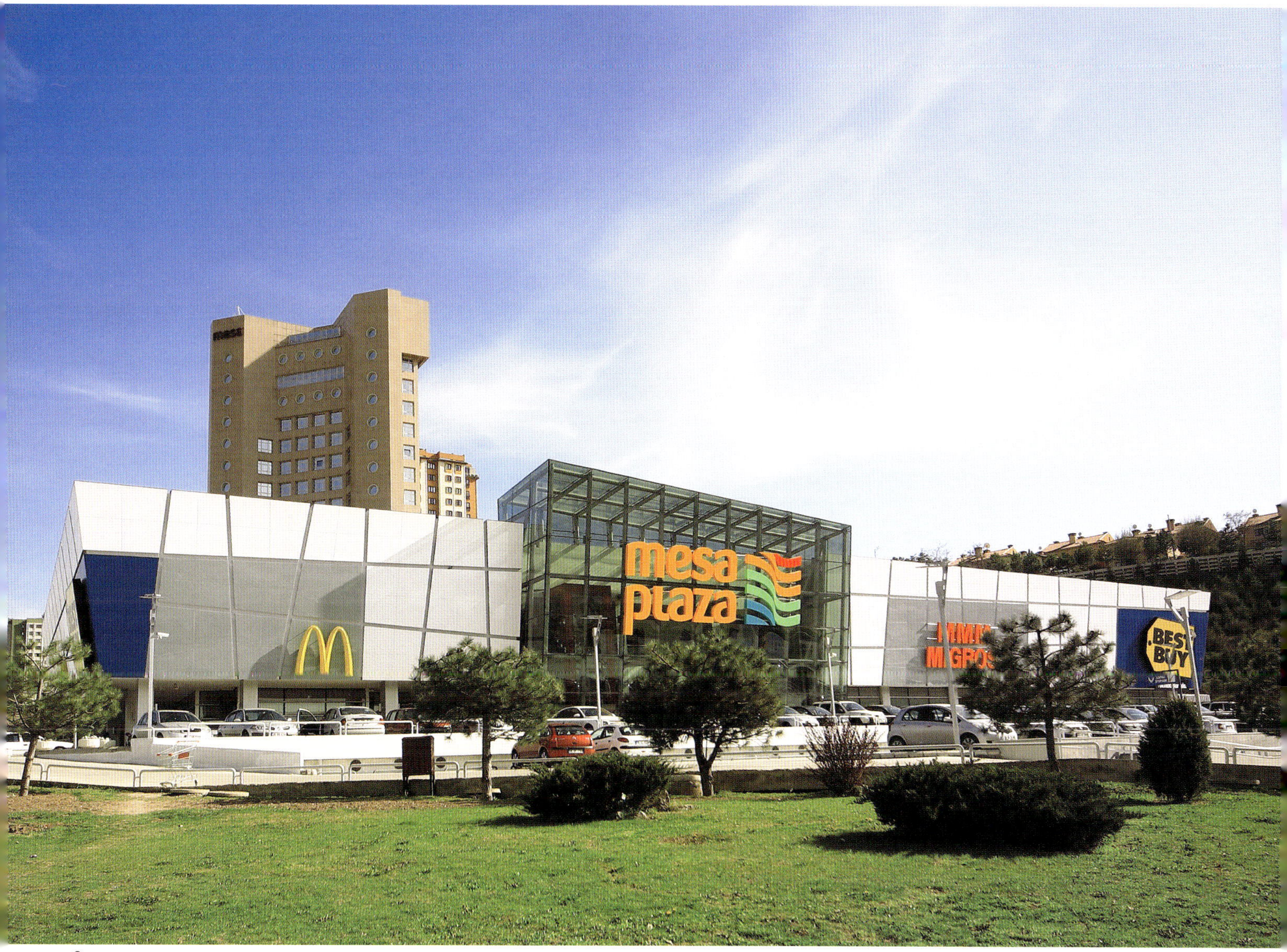

3

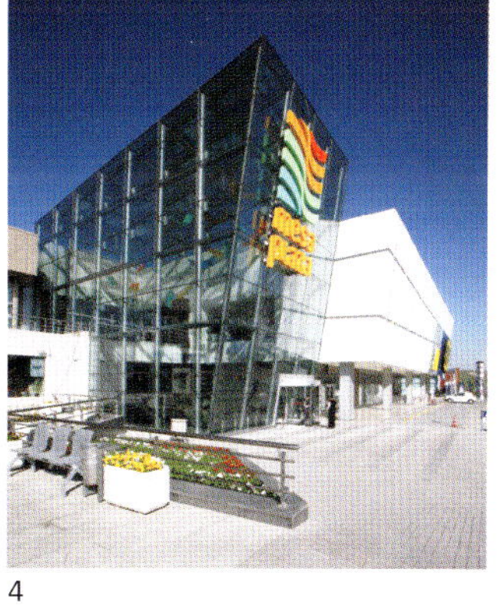

4

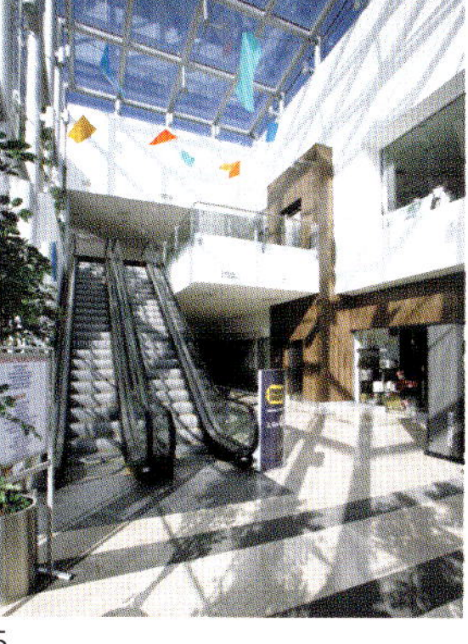

5

1 Sketch by Ali Osman Öztürk
2 View from Eskişehir Road at night
3 Northwest view
4 View of the exterior from the northeast entrance
5 Interior

Atakule

Client Alara Design and Engineering
Project Date 2010
Area 50,000 m^2
Location Ankara
Existing Tower Design Ragıp Buluç
Structural Engineer Yüksek Project
Mechanical Engineer Metta Engineering
Electrical Engineer Akay Engineering
Leasing Consultant Jones Lang LaSalle Turkey
Fire Consultant Alara Design and Engineering

Designed by architect Ragıp Buluç, this building was built at the end of the 1980s. A symbol for the capital city, Atakule—along with the connected shopping spaces—has long been abandoned. After the sale of the building, its new owner, Atakule Real Estate Investment Company, decided to modify and improve the structure with current needs in mind.

Alternative studies have been conducted in the context of the renovation project that began in 2010. Initial proposals preserved the structural system of the existing building. These studies maintained the revolving platform on the tower and modified the bottom of the mass. The starting point of these changes was the continuity to be created with the botanical park, as well as the new functional organization. At this stage, the circulation scheme, the botanical park view, the size and placement of the shops, and the efficiency of the parking garage were examined, and a new layout was proposed. However, the parking needs for this layout could not be met with the current number of basement floors.

The next alternative focused on maintaining the tower and its immediate surroundings while demolishing and reconstructing the surrounding mass. This proposal aimed to preserve the tower with special precautions and increase parking facilities. Circulation areas were reduced by locating the proposed central atrium on the botanical park axis, utilizing the existing tower as a part of the atrium. Continuity with the existing park was created by having the interior space opening upwards, thus providing a rich spatial experience that will add value to the building.

1 Sketch of the different levels by Ali Osman Öztürk
Opposite:
Rendering of Atakule at night

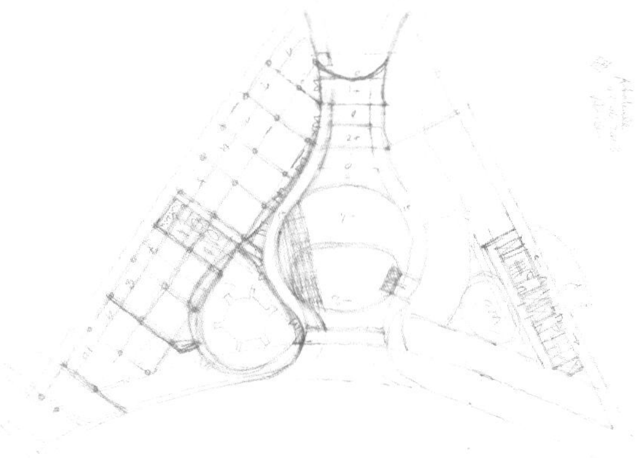

1

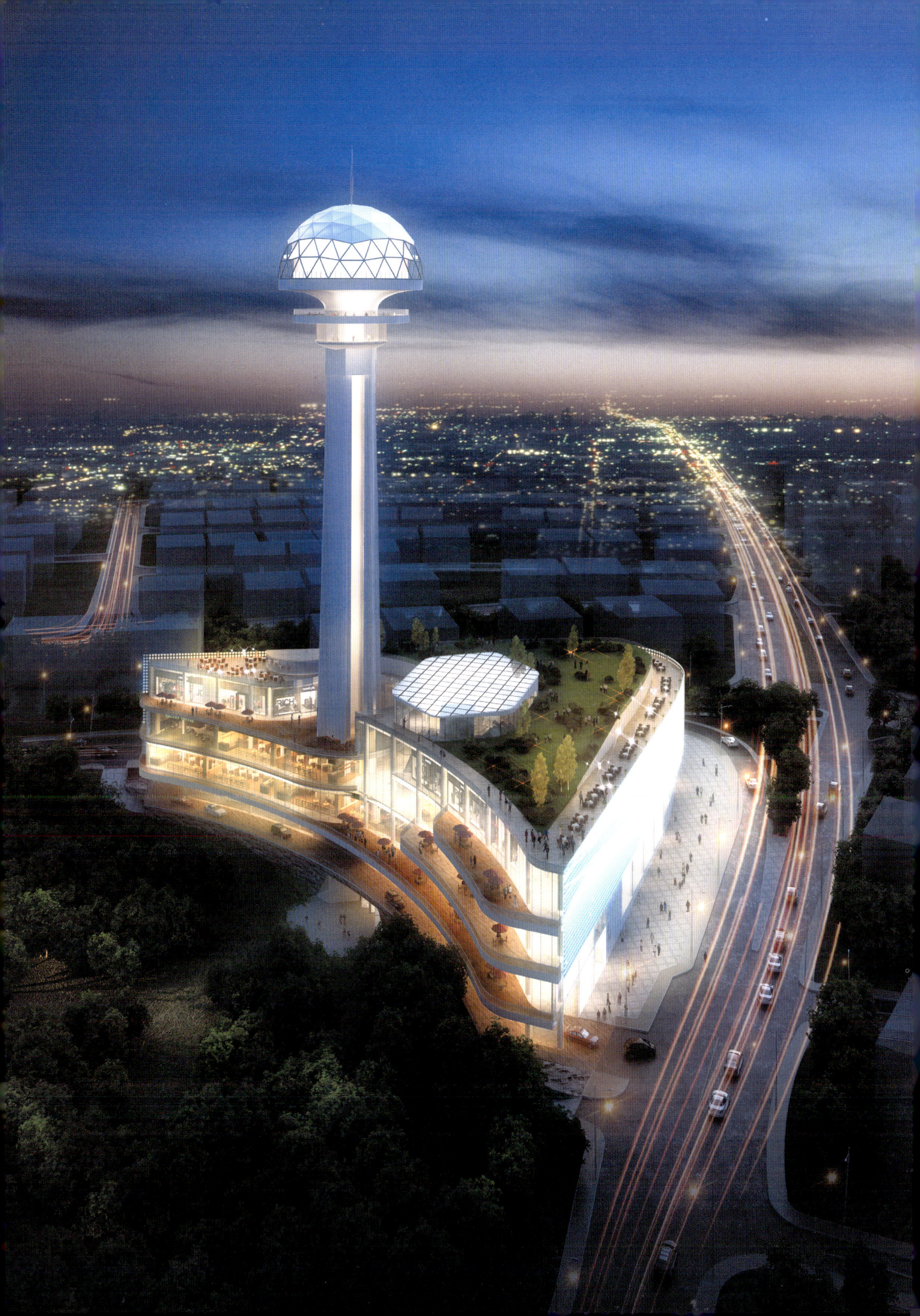
RICH

Ankara High Speed Train Station

Client Limak, Kolin & Cengiz Construction
Project Date 2013
Area 175,000 m^2
Location Ankara

Planned by German urban planner, Jansen, Ankara Train Station is located at the end of Cumhuriyet Avenue. Architectural products of the modernization movement of the Republican period are all located on this avenue and the train station was considered both a gateway to the city and its end point. Today, the station has lost its gateway character due to the expansion of the city, and it is now insufficient in terms of capacity. Moreover, the "speed train" infrastructure created the need for a new station to be integrated with the old station.

The importance of the building in the Republican period architecture and urban culture, as well as in the urban memory, requires the new (additional) station building design to create an asset that pursues and highlights urban and architectural values. The new train station was designed to connect to the historical station without marring its appearance, while expanding its functionality as an integral part of the new structure. In this sense, the new station building design takes the urban scale of the old station building into account.

The building starts from the overhang level of the old station's marquee and rises towards Celal Bayar Boulevard, reaches the maximum height that is allowed by the development plan there and presents its main entrance façade to the city. Entering the building from this main façade, visitors can observe the operations on every floor of the building and perceive the spatial organization from the entrance hall, which is a permeable and fluid gathering space—the heart of the building. Natural light reaches the main entrance level and even the platform level without interruption through roof elements and the atriums. The aim is to allow maximum use of natural light within the building and to generate high quality, lively spaces.

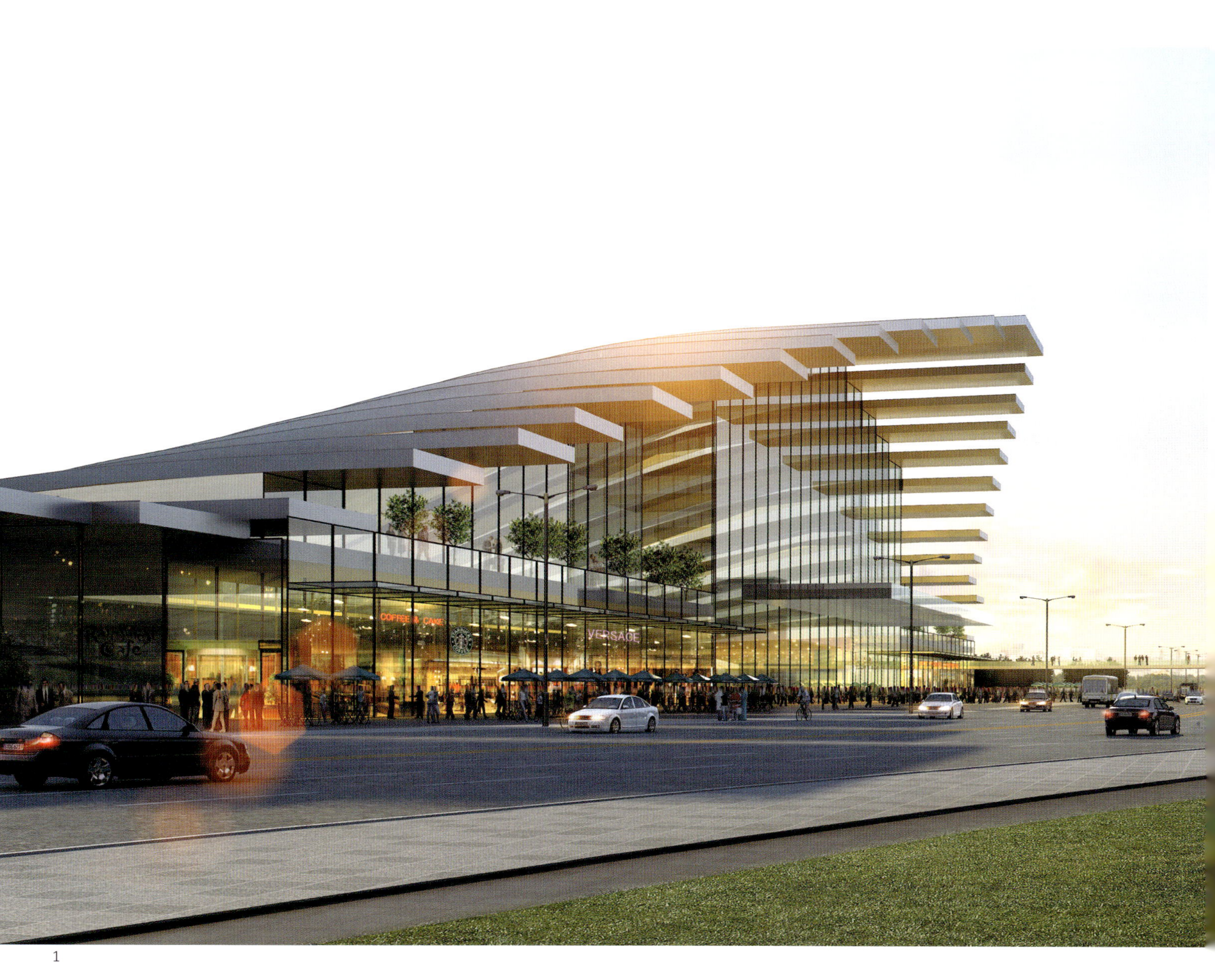

1

1 View of main entrance on Celal Bayar Boulevard

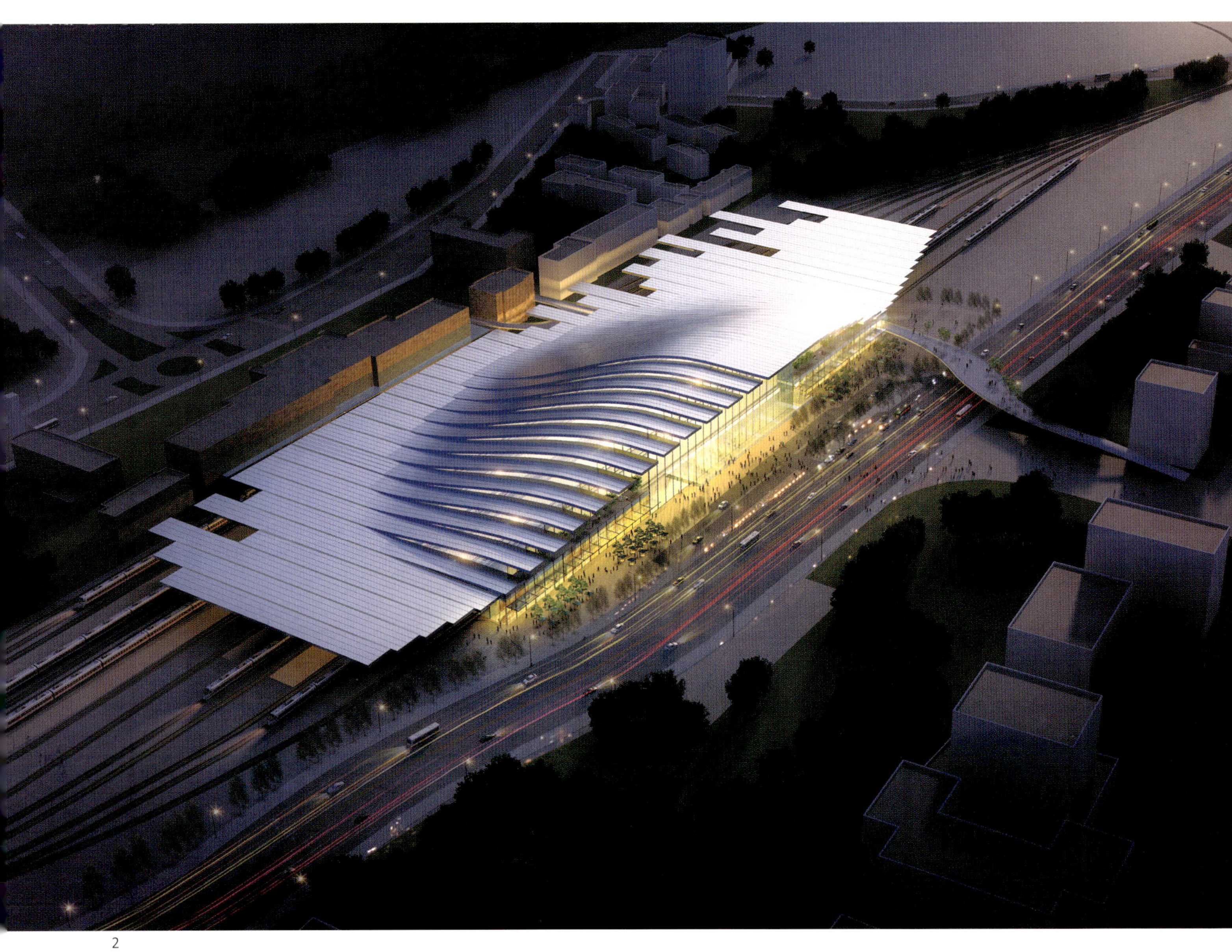

2

2 Bird's-eye view
3 Interior view of the visual connections between passengers, visitors, and trains
4 Sketch by Ali Osman Öztürk of the pedestrian passages connecting the cultural facilities on the northern side to the residential and commercial facilities on the southern side of the city

One of the most important problems of the existing building is that Celal Bayar Boulevard can be seen an obstacle between the residential and university area and the old city of Ulus. Today, the only connection between the two areas is the underground passage that is used as a Military Bazaar, which is problematic both in terms of natural light and security. The design for the new building offers a connection that starts at the Maltepe exit of the Ankara subway system, passes through Celal Bayar Boulevard, and connects to the new station building, ending at the old station's plaza. Thus the station will become a part of the city and have a strong connection with it once more. The new Ankara train station is not simply a transport structure— it also serves as an urban center, with commercial, food and beverage, and accommodation functions.

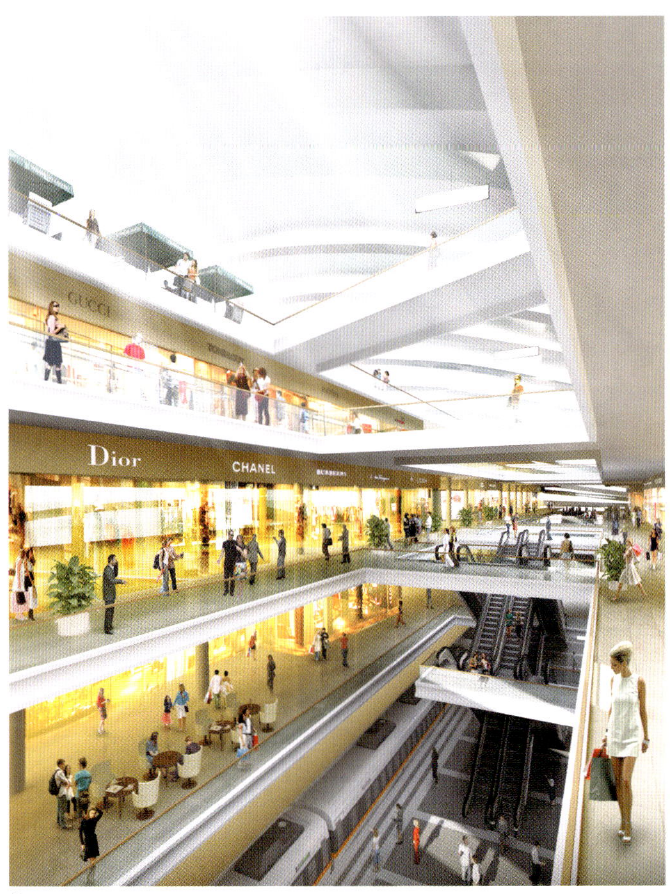

3

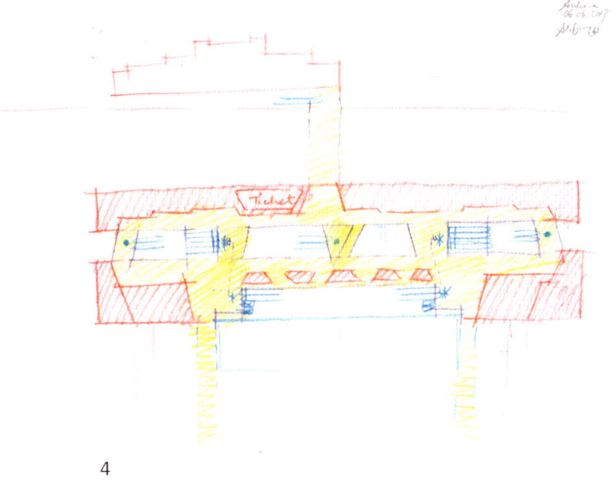

4

Yaşamkent Housing

Client Tepe Construction Inc., MESA Housing Industries Inc.
Project Date 2012
Area 215,000 m^2
Location Ankara
Structural Engineer Yüksek Project
Mechanical Engineer Metta Engineering
Electrical Engineer Yurdakul Engineering
Landscape Design Dalokay Design Studio
Fire Consultant Alara Design and Engineering

A new development area on Ankara's western axis, Yaşamkent relates to the surrounding housing areas with its low and high-rise housing fabric. The project site has a southeast orientation and is located on a connecting road. The 40-story block planned for the entrance will be a flagship structure, representing the entire complex. This block contains five apartments on each floor, while the rest of the fabric consists of a combination of low-rise and high-rise blocks.

Some of the 855 housing spaces designed within the complex are located in linear blocks. These blocks, laid out in accordance with the slope of the land, have seven floors including the ground floor, and they include a courtyard arrangement with housing spaces that have façades in two directions. There are two apartments on each floor, in either 3+1, 4+1, or 5+1 configurations. The dining areas constitute the main living spaces and are located in the middle, with living, dining, and cooking functions combined. Apartments with southeast and northwest orientations offer a wealth of alternatives within a single space. The living room arrangement that is used in traditional and modern housing design has been reconfigured for this proposal and opens to both the kitchen and living areas.

Creating a living environment and a secondary urban center on its own, this project won first place as a limited competition proposal.

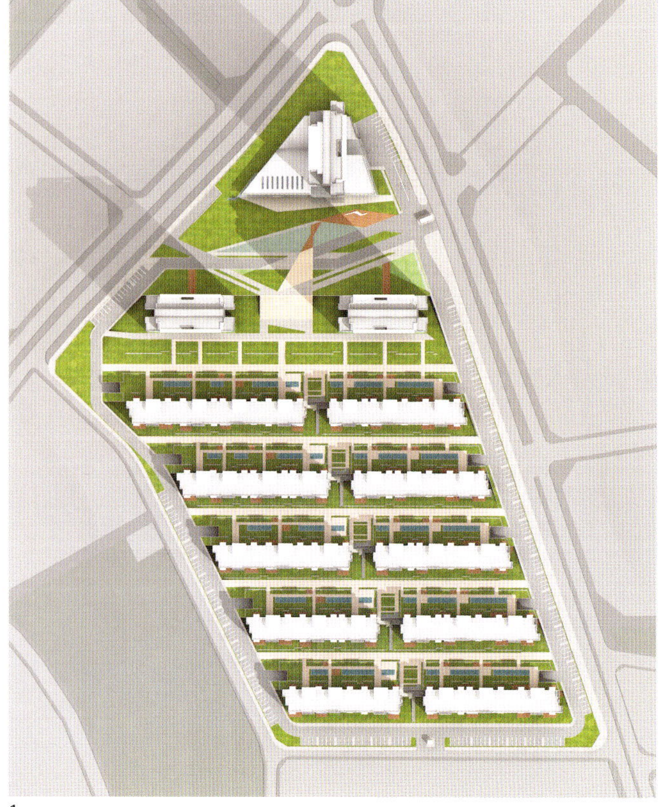
1

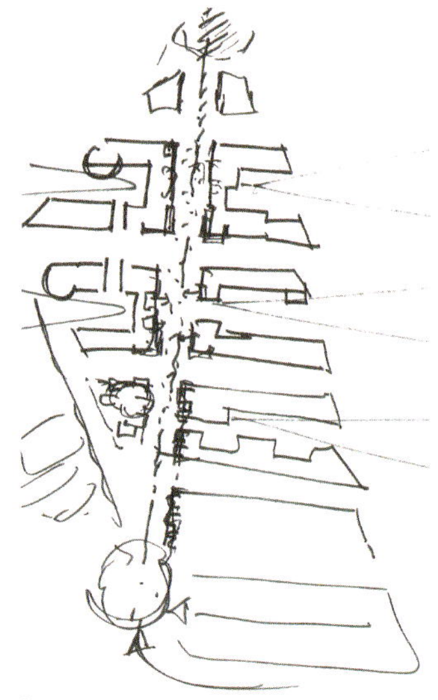
2

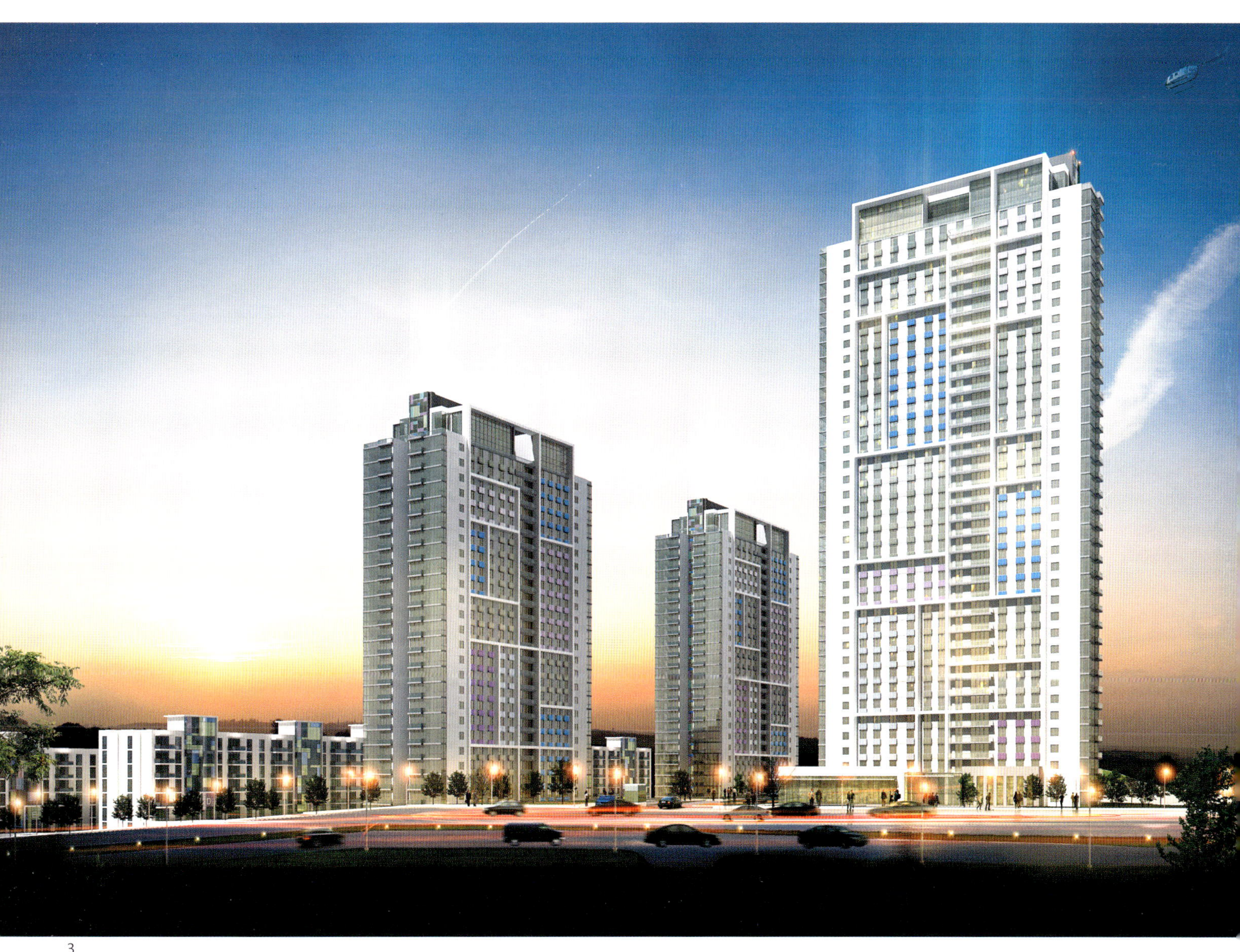

3

1 Site plan
2 Sketch by Ali Osman Öztürk
3 General view

4 General view from the residential units
5 Rendering of the outdoor living spaces
6–8 Rendering of the interior
9 Typical floor plan A type 3+1
10 Typical floor plan B type 3+1
11 Typical floor plan type 4+1
12 Typical floor plan type 4+1 and 5+1
13 Typical floor plan for Block A

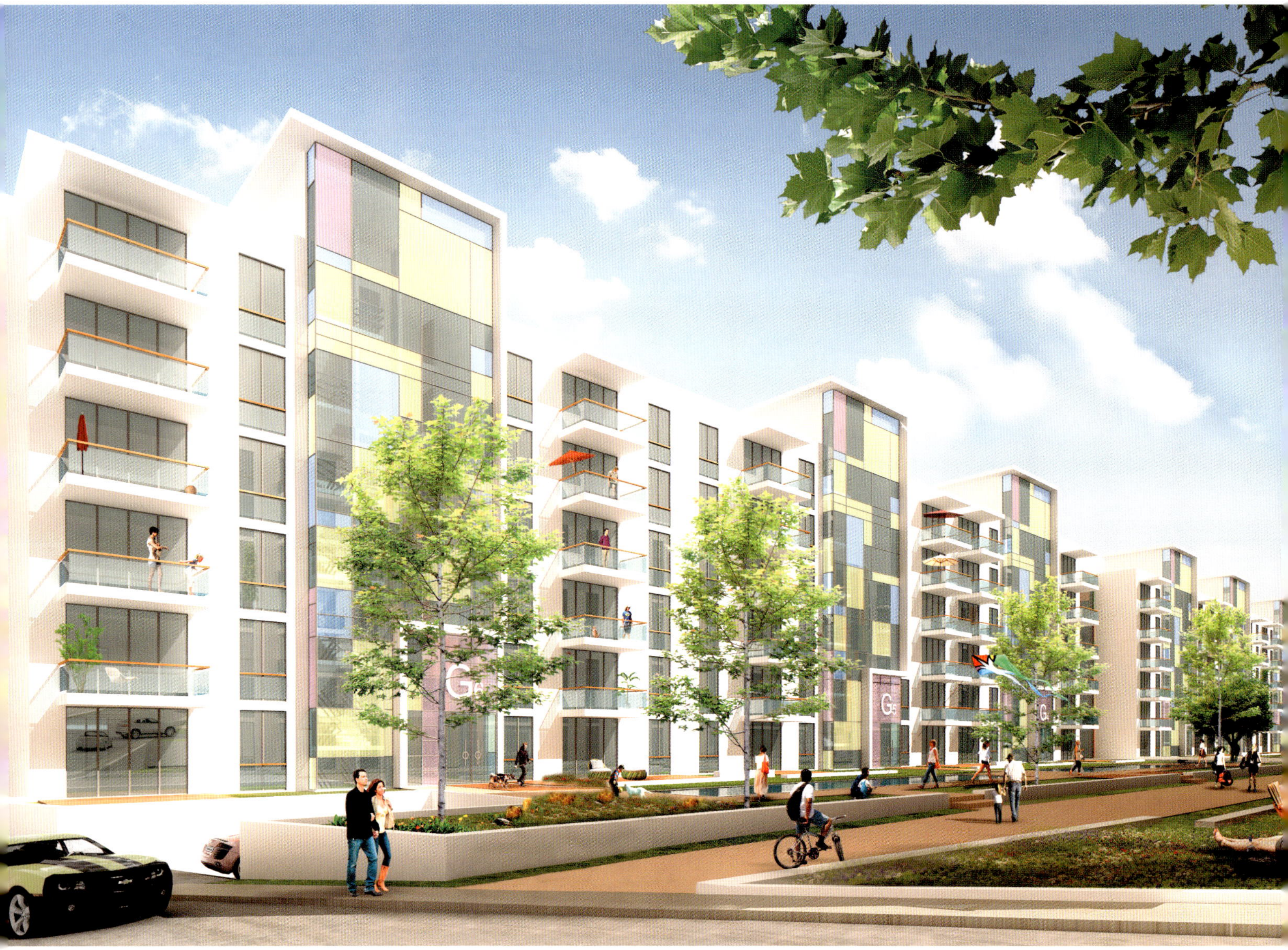

4

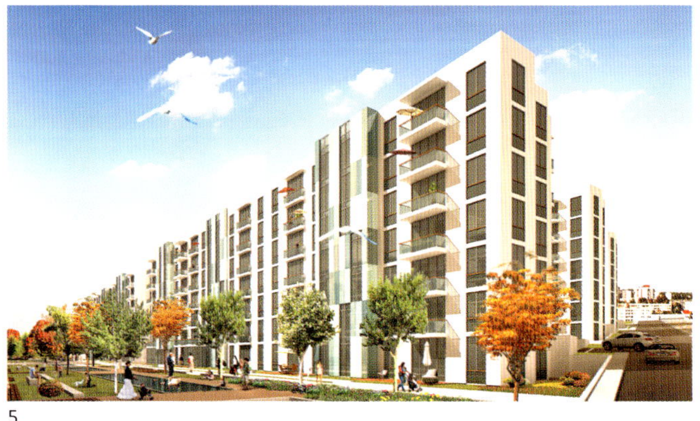

5

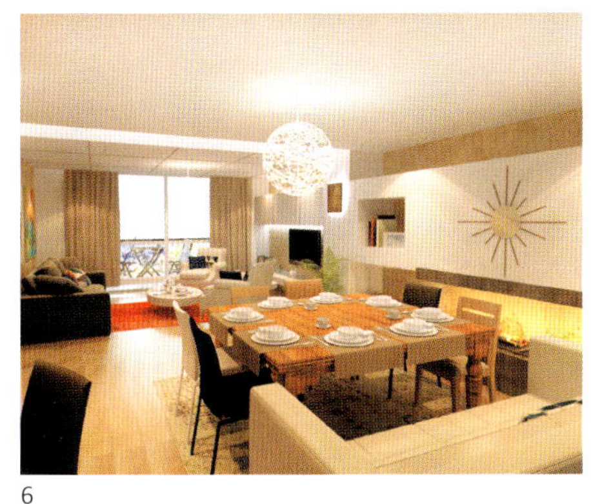
6

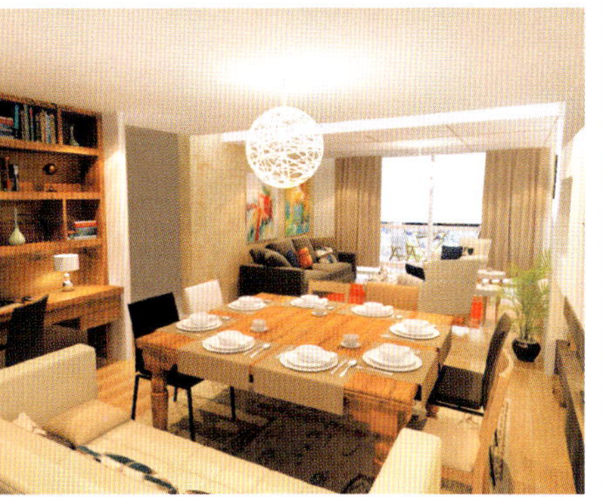
7

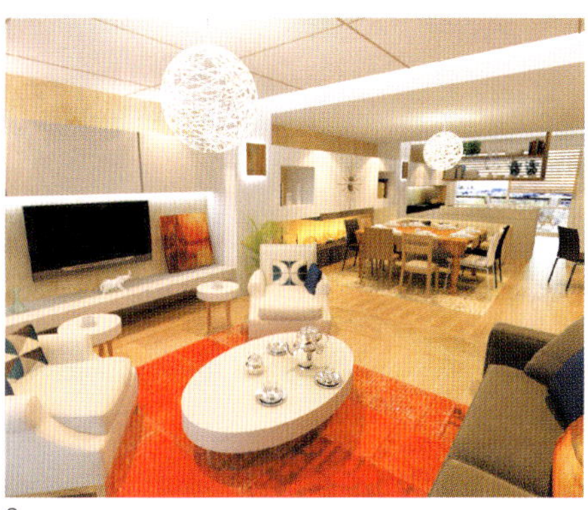
8

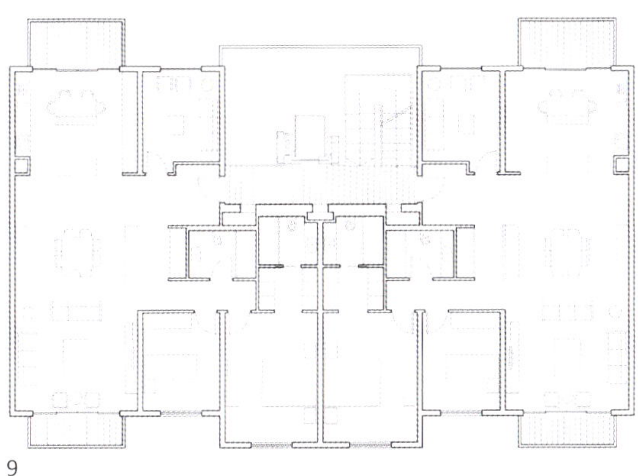
9

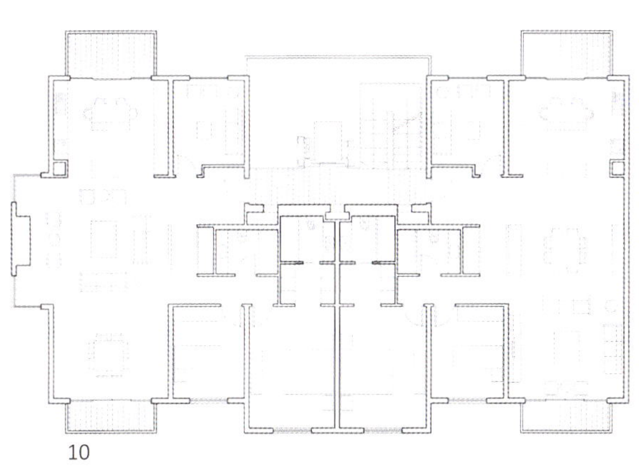
10

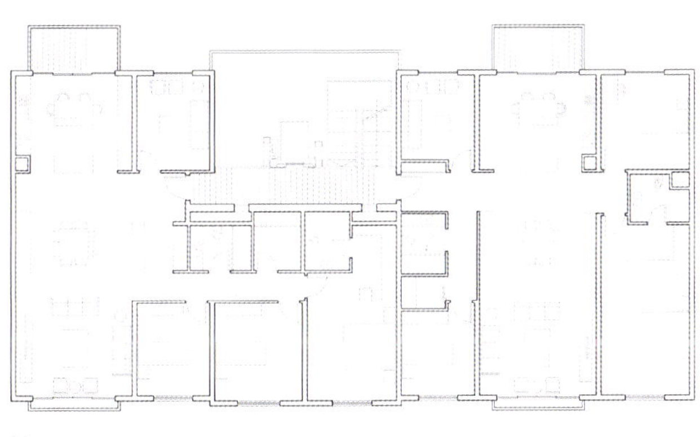
11

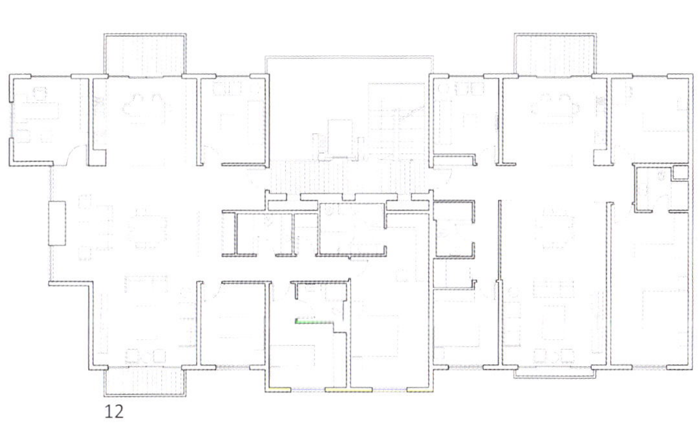
12

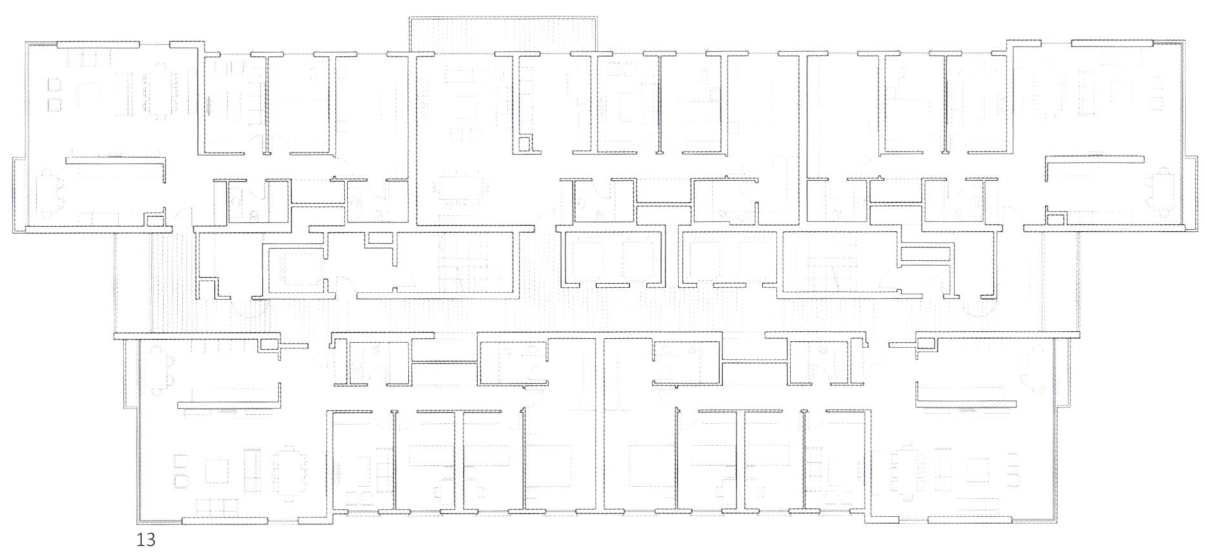
13

Sipopo Mall

Client SUMMA Inc.
Project Date 2011
Area 12,300 m^2
Location Malabo
Structural Engineer Yüksek Project and Meinhardt Engineering
Mechanical Engineer Metta Engineering
Electrical Engineer Yurdakul Engineering
Landscape Design Dalokay Design Studio
Fire Consultant Alara Design and Engineering

Located in the newly planned urban center of Malabo in Equatorial Guinea, this building has been designed to create an exquisite top-end shopping center. Designed parallel to the ocean, the wavy façade of the building integrates it both with the natural environment and the ocean.

The circulation areas in the complex, which contain roughly 8,500 square meters of leasable space, consist of plazas defined by curvilinear surfaces and interconnected for pedestrian flow. These plazas were designed to allow for a sufficiently wide variety of uses to accommodate the activities to be organized there. On the ground floor, there are approximately 40 shops of different sizes, cafés, and a supermarket. The first floor contains a high-tech entertainment center, casino, movie theater complex, and fast food counters.

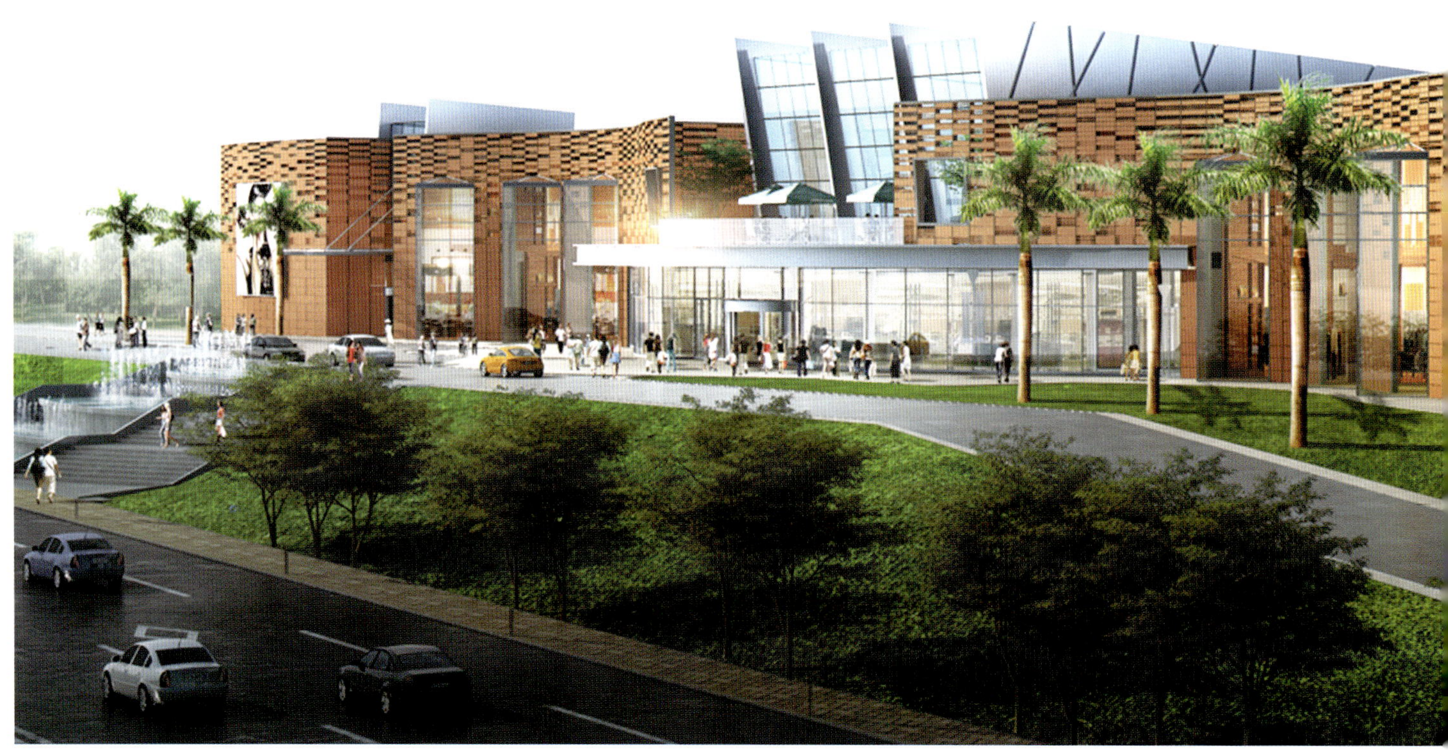

1

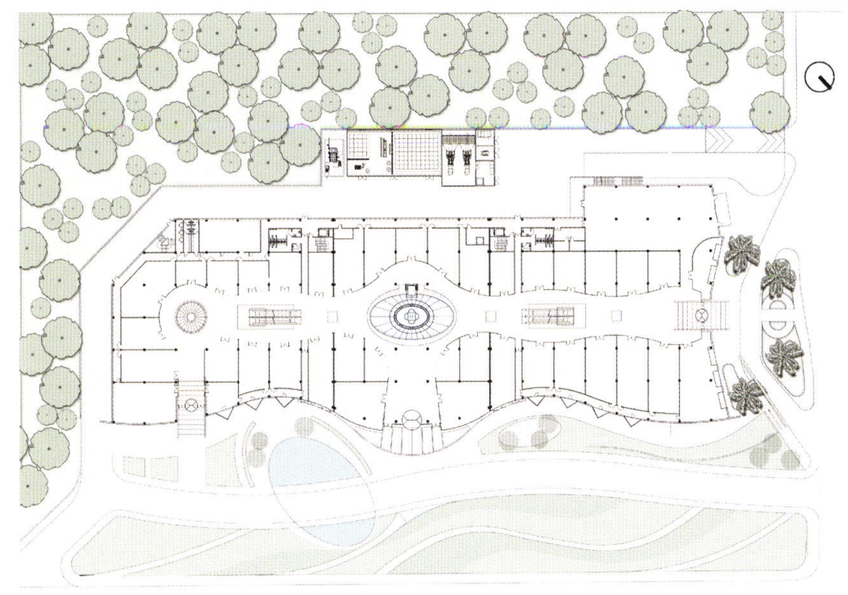

2

1 General view
2 Ground floor plan

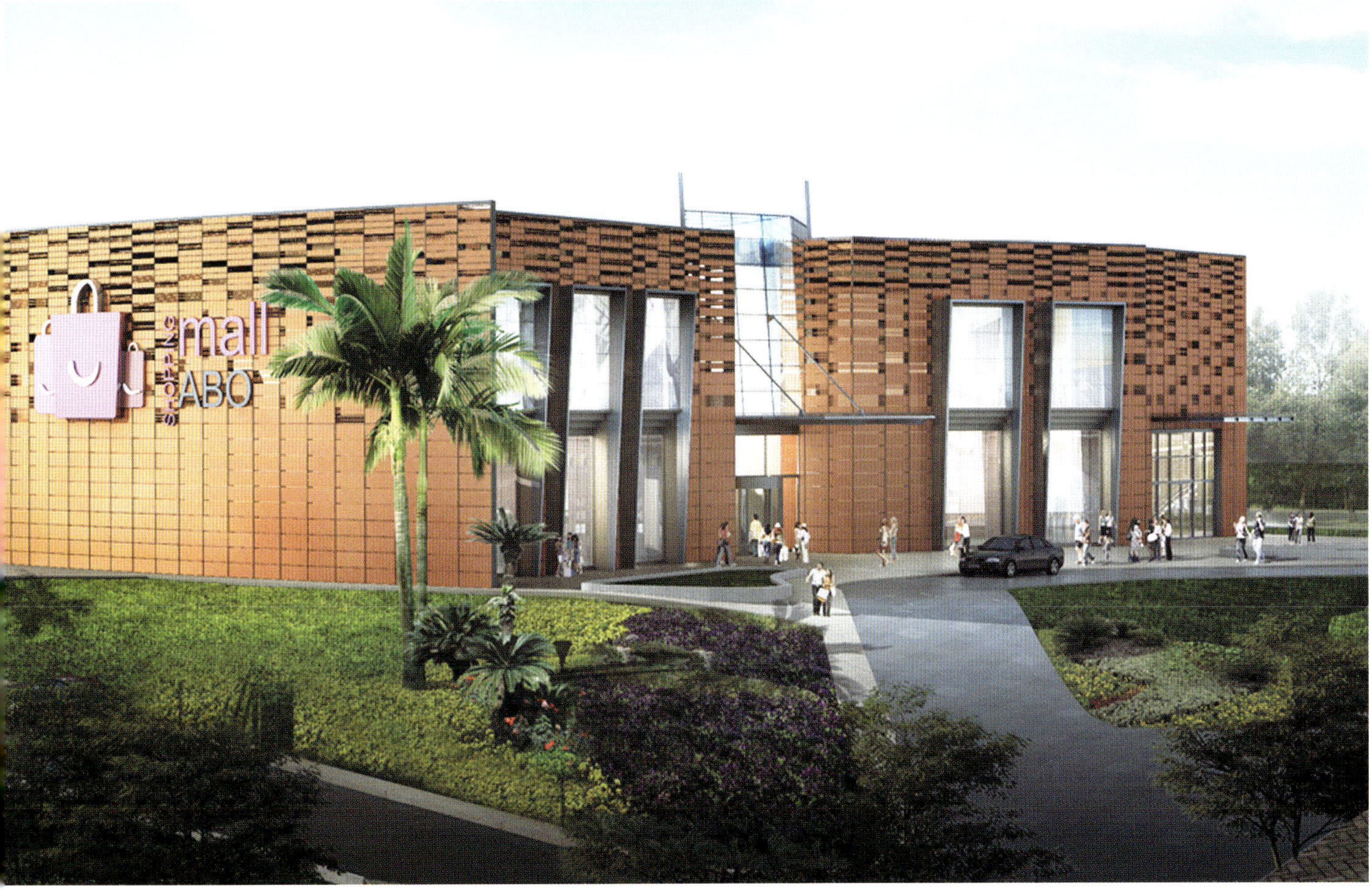

Taurus

Client Taurus Balgat Shopping Center Investment Inc.
Project Date 2010
Area 153,000 m^2
Location Ankara
Structural Engineer Yüksek Project
Mechanical Engineer Metta Engineering
Electrical Engineer Yurdakul Engineering
Landscape Design Çevre Landscaping
Fire Consultant Alara Design and Engineering
Acoustics Mezzo Studio
Contractor Tepe Construction Industry Inc.

The project area is on Konya Highway in Ankara, which is an important transportation axis. Considering the potential of the district, a mixed-use building program was proposed. Entrances on different levels are provided by utilizing the existing slopes of the site's topography, which reinforces the connections between the commercial floors. The commercial axis created on Konya Highway was brought into the building, giving the impression of a new commercial street within the outer shell.

Commercial floors that horizontally connect with the high-rise office block provide social facilities both for the complex as well as the neighboring residential areas.

The use of natural light and materials, as well as the natural air circulation within the building, works to make the shopping mall energy efficient and environmentally friendly, while minimizing the air-conditioning load in shared spaces.

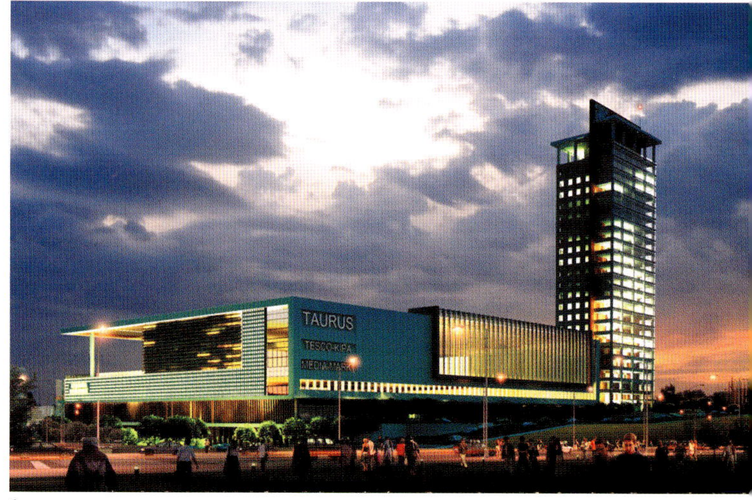

1

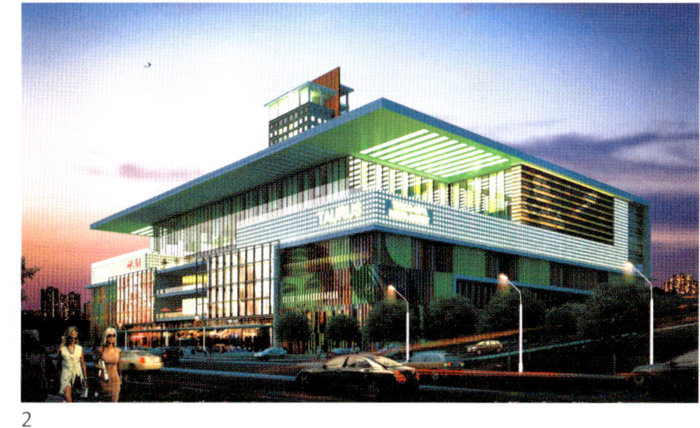
2

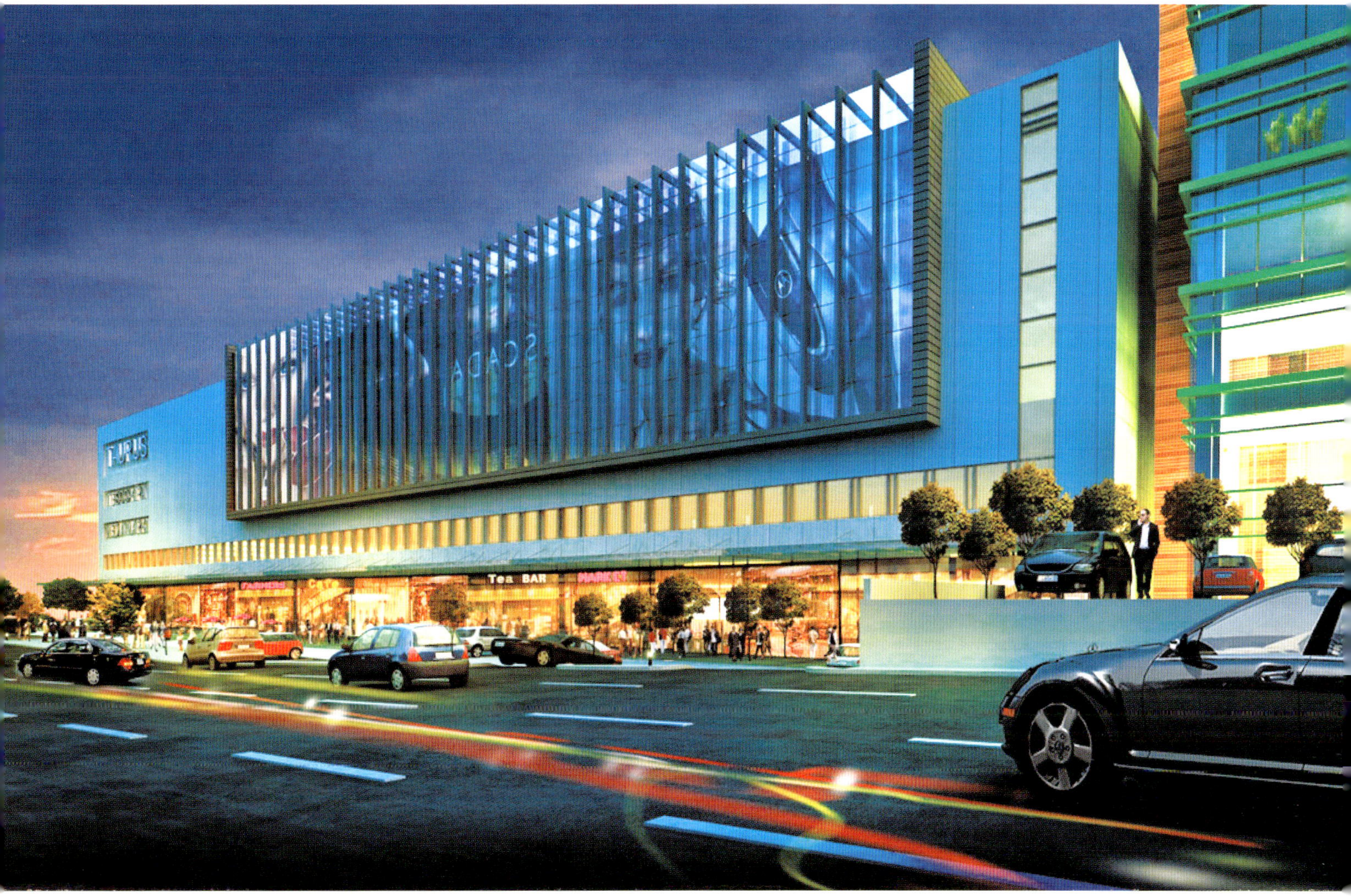

3

1 General view at night
2 Front view
3 View through the west façade

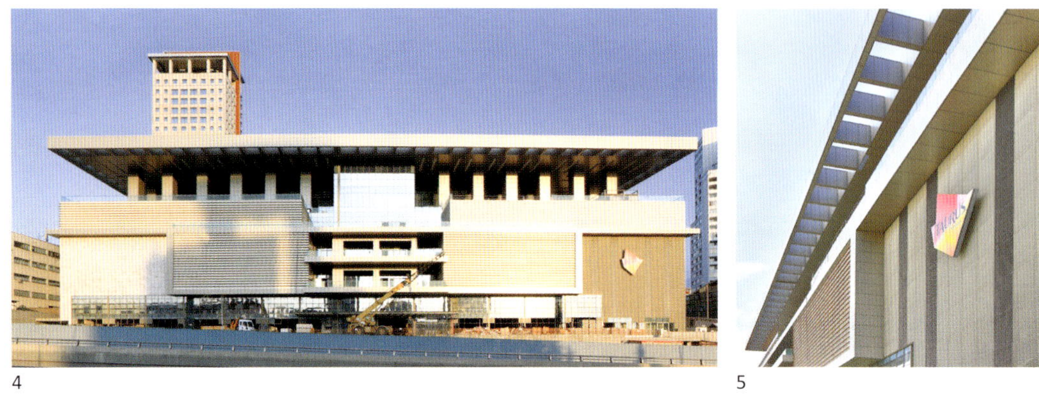

4

5

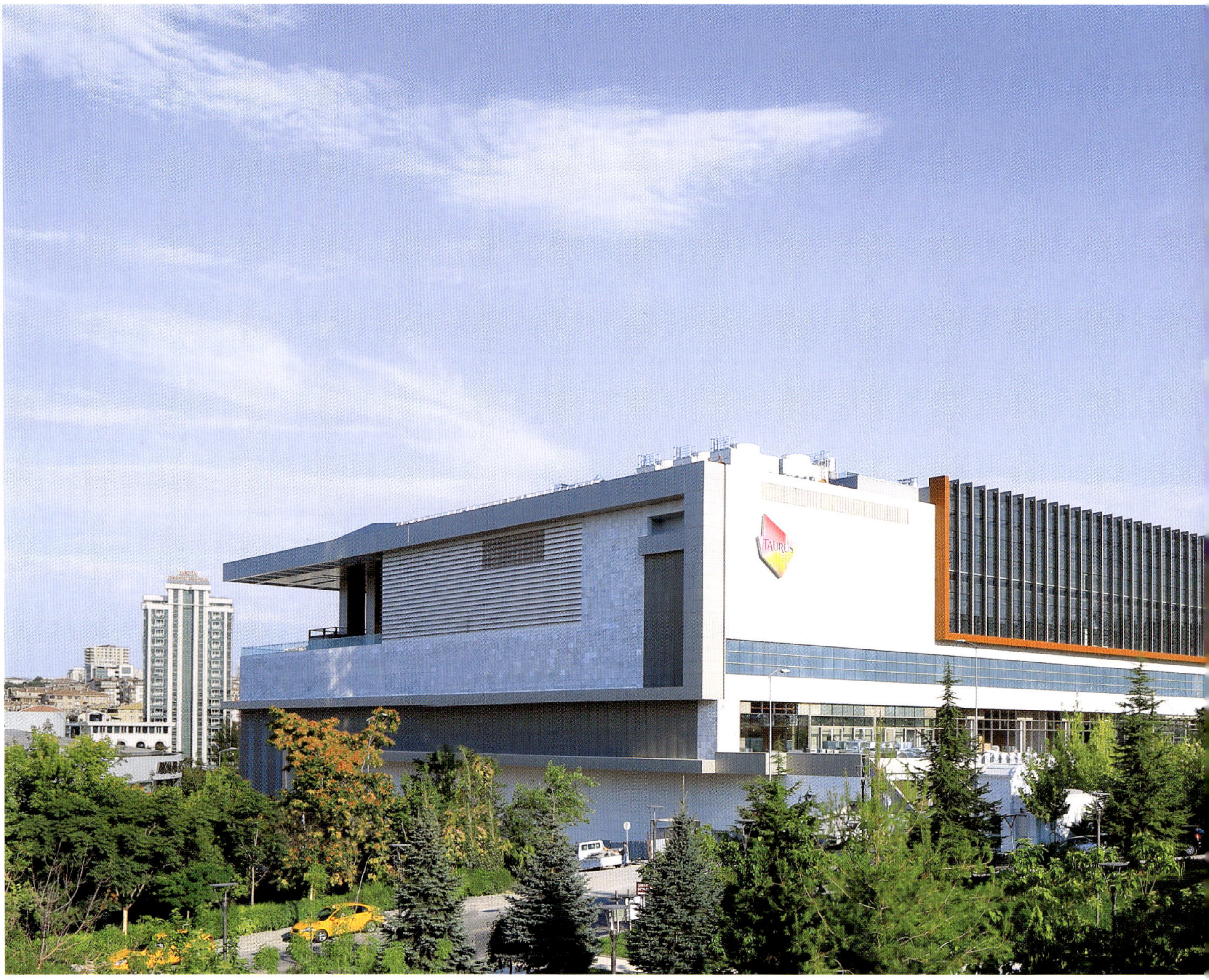

6

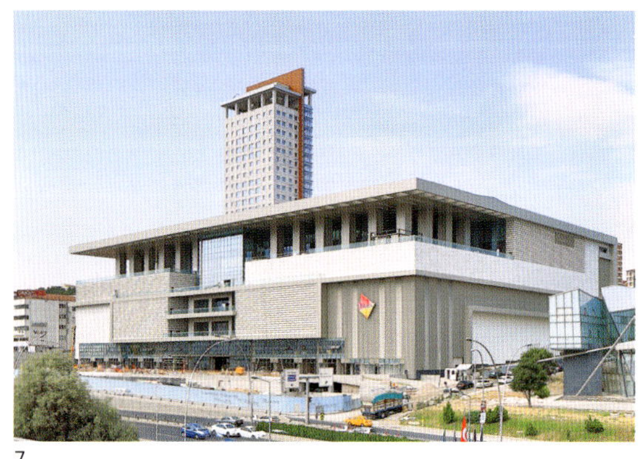

7

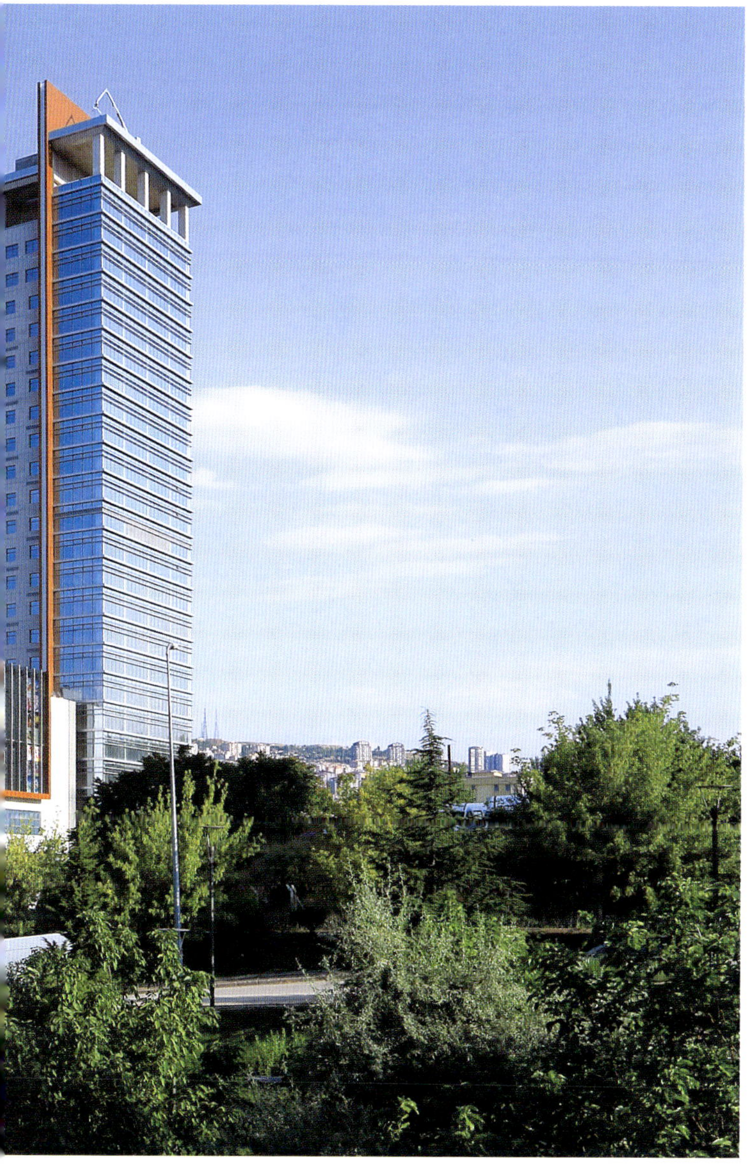

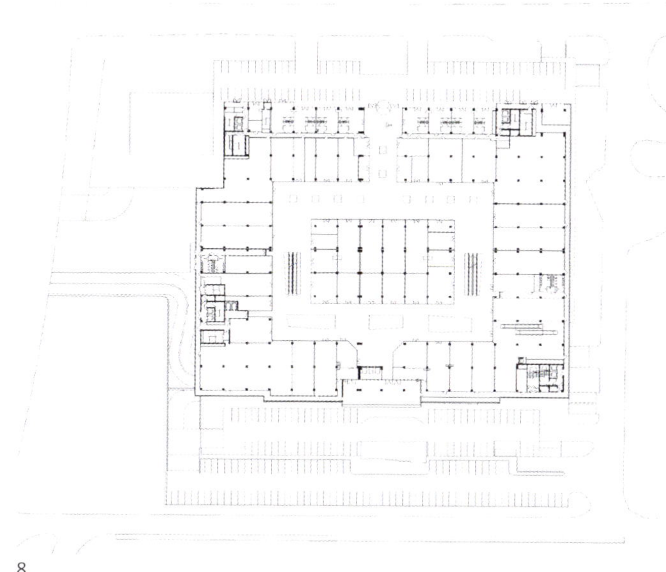

8

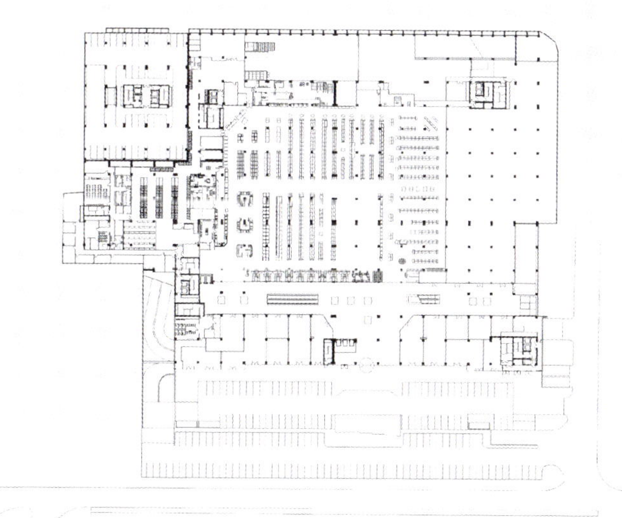

9

4 Façade view from Konya Highway
5 Façade detail
6 View through the complex from the northwest
7 View through the complex from the northeast
8 First floor plan
9 Ground floor plan

TOBB Brussels

Client TOBB
Project Date 2010
Area 2,700 m^2
Location Belgium
Architectural Design Willen Associates Architekten
Local Architect Pierre Accarain Architectes, Marc Bouillot Associés SA
Renovation Design A Tasarım Mimarlık
Structural Engineer Be Franz Dupont
Mechanical Engineer Crea-Tec S.P.R.L
Electrical Engineer Crea-Tec S.P.R.L
Consultants A.A.U. SA

This project repurposes a building for use as the TOBB Agency in Brussels. Various office and meeting spaces were created for TOBB member organizations.

All of the architectural characteristics of the exterior façade have been preserved, while the interior of the building is completely rearranged according to the needs of the agency and the building program.

Spatial arrangements use daylight more effectively in the attached building block. Mobile dividing walls offer flexible, divisible, and permeable spaces for meeting and exhibition areas as well as offices.

In terms of the representational value of the building, award-winning products designed by Turkish designers have been selected for interior design.

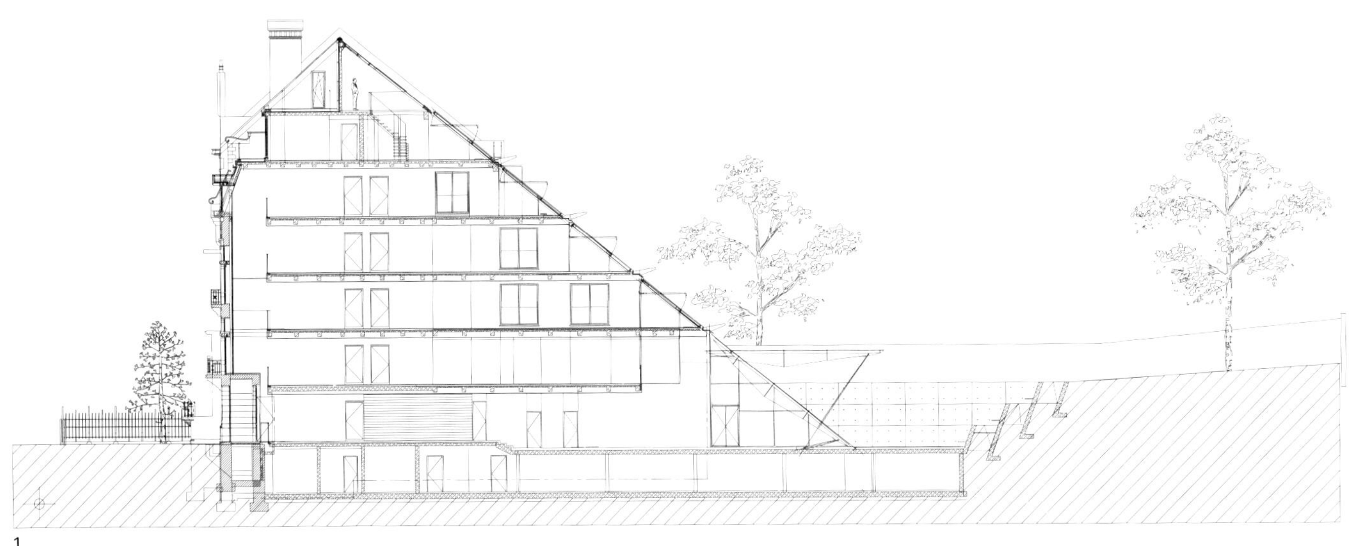

1

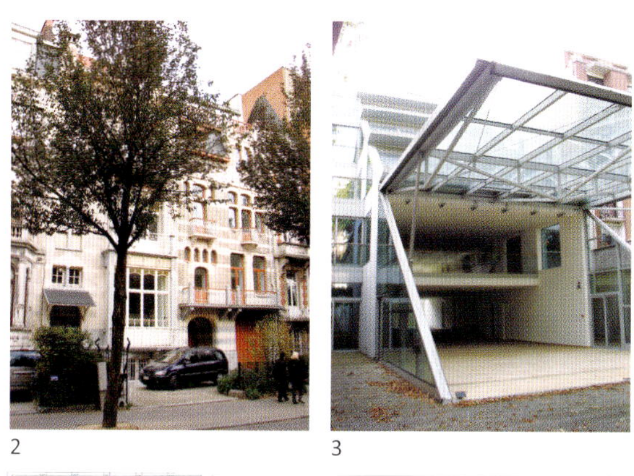

2 3

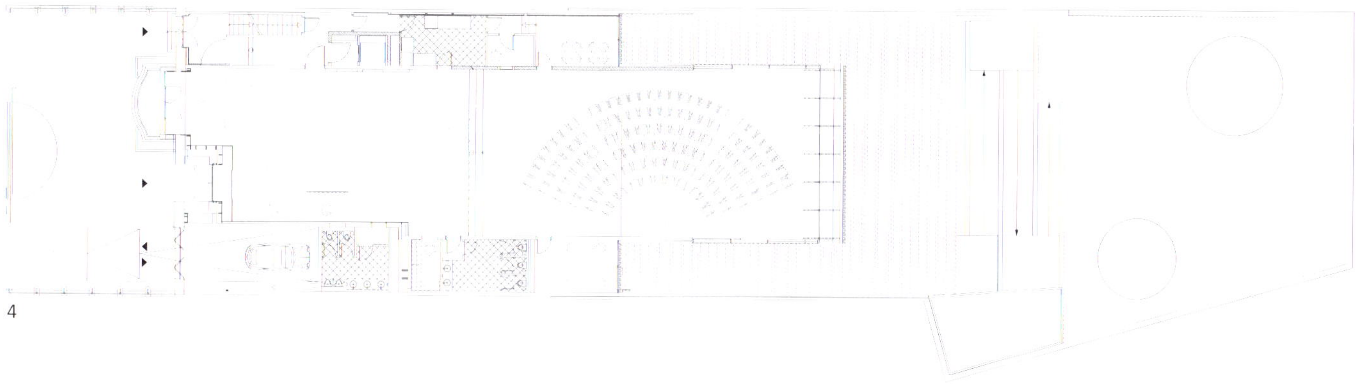

4

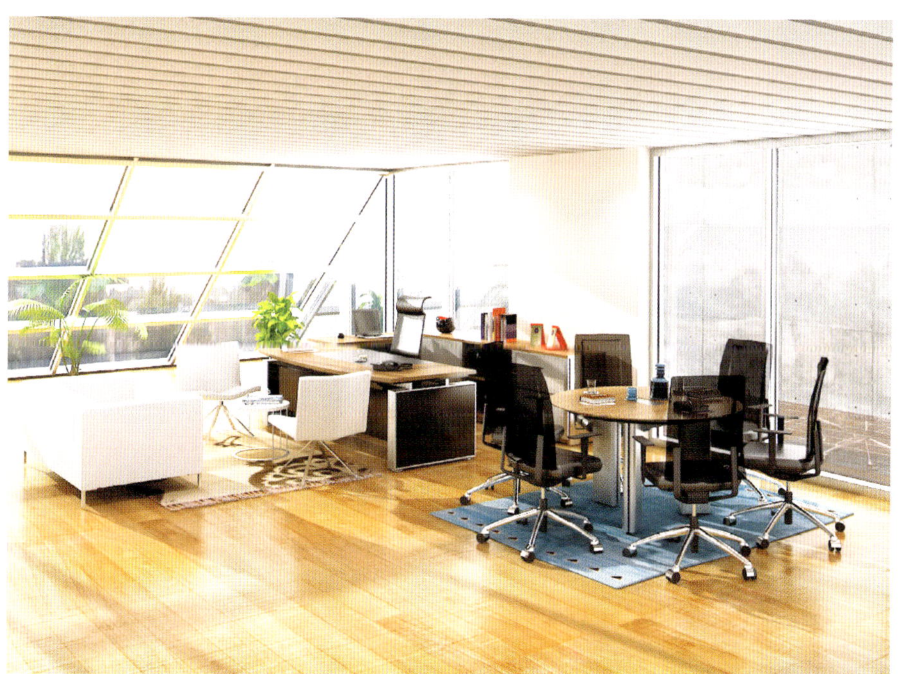

5

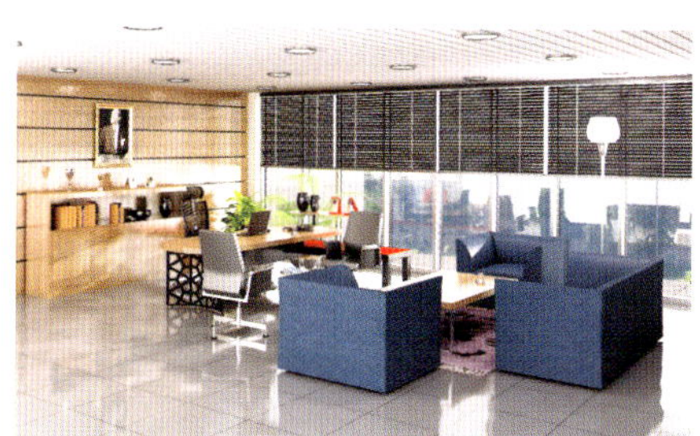

6

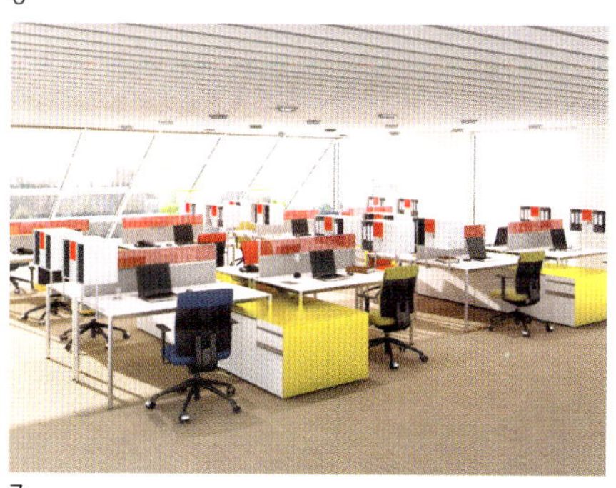

7

1 Longitudinal section
2 Front façade
3 Northeast façade
4 Ground floor plan
5–7 Office spaces

Ceylan Karavil Park

Client Ceylan Group, Karavil Group
Project Date 2008
Area 210,000 m^2
Location Diyarbakır
Structural Engineer Yüksek Project
Mechanical Engineer Setes Engineering
Electrical Engineer Akay Engineering
Landscape Design Dalokay Design Studio
Fire Consultant Alara Design and Engineering

This project area is located on Şanlıurfa Boulevard, one of the most important arteries of the rapidly developing western axis in the city of Diyarbakır. Arrangements have been made in order to allow the structure to be seen from the main intersection. A second entrance has been proposed for motorized access and pedestrian movement. Cafés are located on both sides of these entrances.

Streets of varying style and character with kiosks have been situated inside, aiming to simulate the urban atmosphere of an urban downtown area. The fast food courtyard is designed with a view of the plaza above the main entrance and the intersection. One of the structure's design features is the sense of flexibility between the outdoor spaces.

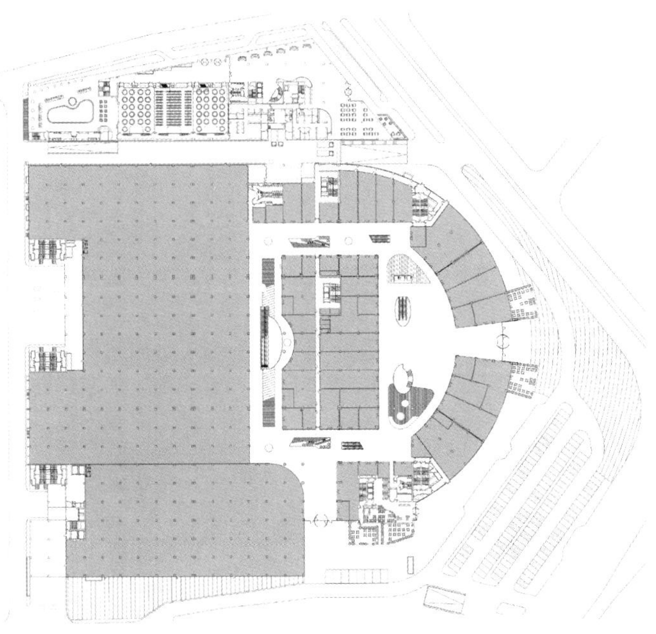

1

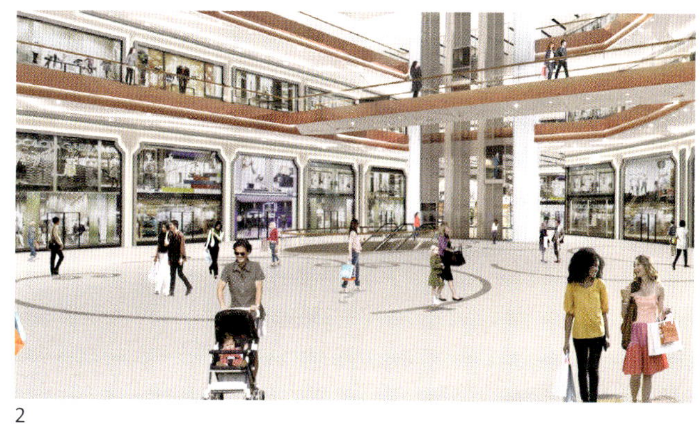

2

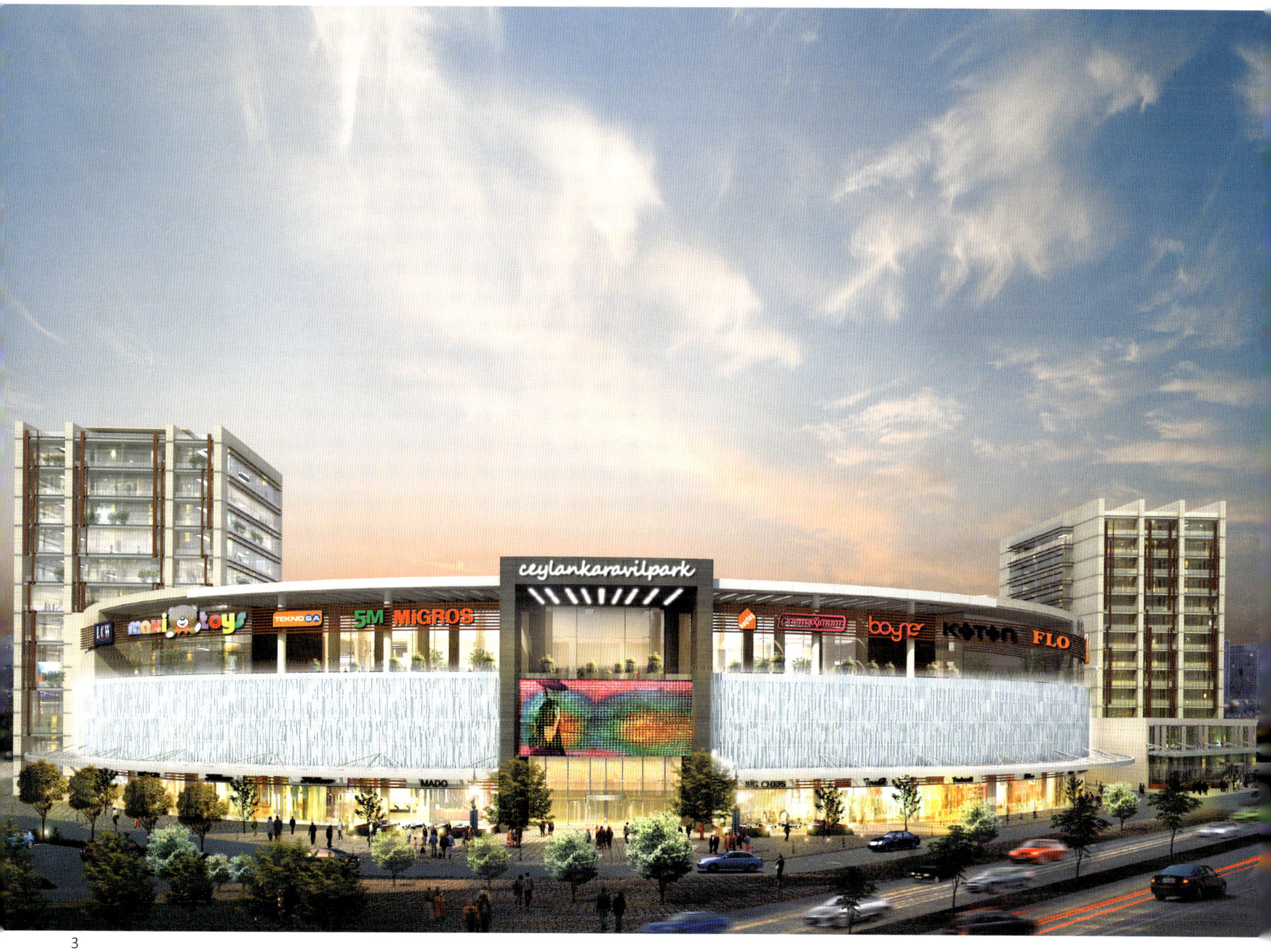

3

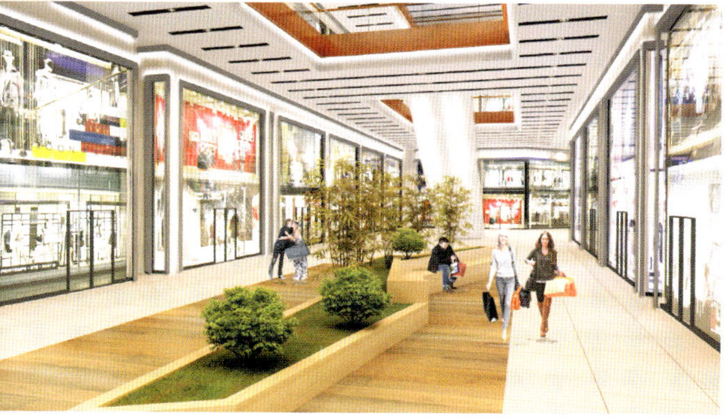

4

1 Ground floor plan
2 View of the interior
3 Rendering of the overall view
4 View through the shops and the circulation halls

Ankara Stadium

Client Ankara Municipality
Project Date 2012
Area 200,000 m^2
Location Ankara

This proposal was prepared for the concept competition by invitation from the Mass Housing Administration and the Ministry of Youth and Sports. The proposal is for a stadium with a 40,000-person capacity located at a major intersection on Eskişehir Road, an important development axis. It is easily accessible from the rest of the city.

Ankara Stadium is designed not merely as a stadium, but as a block that will host all types of sports-related activities. The building aims to connect with the city in all directions and play a symbolic role for the city of Ankara.

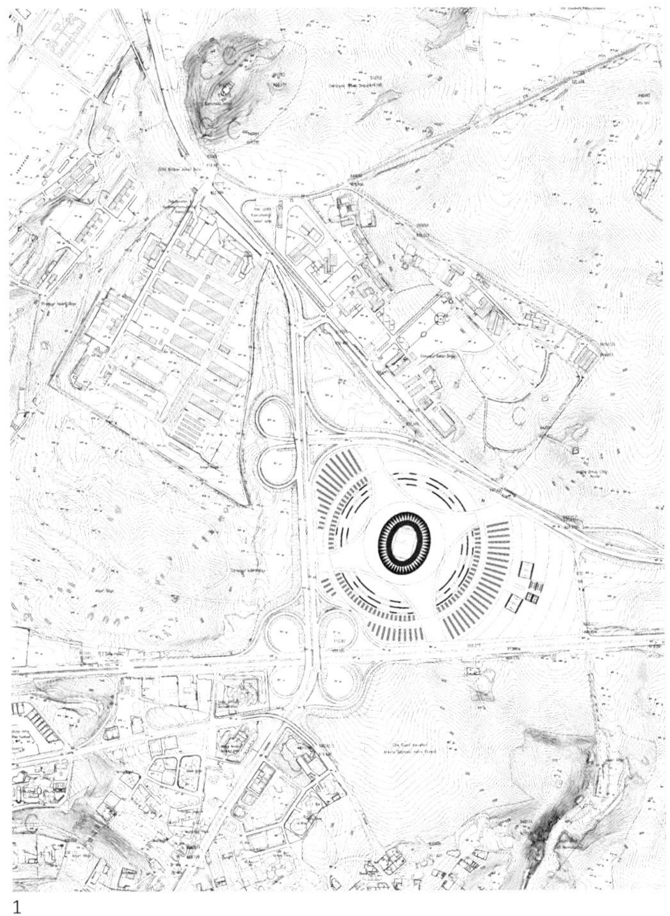

1

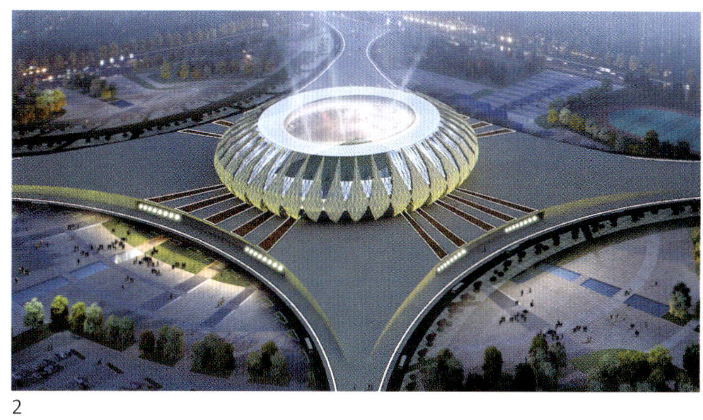

2

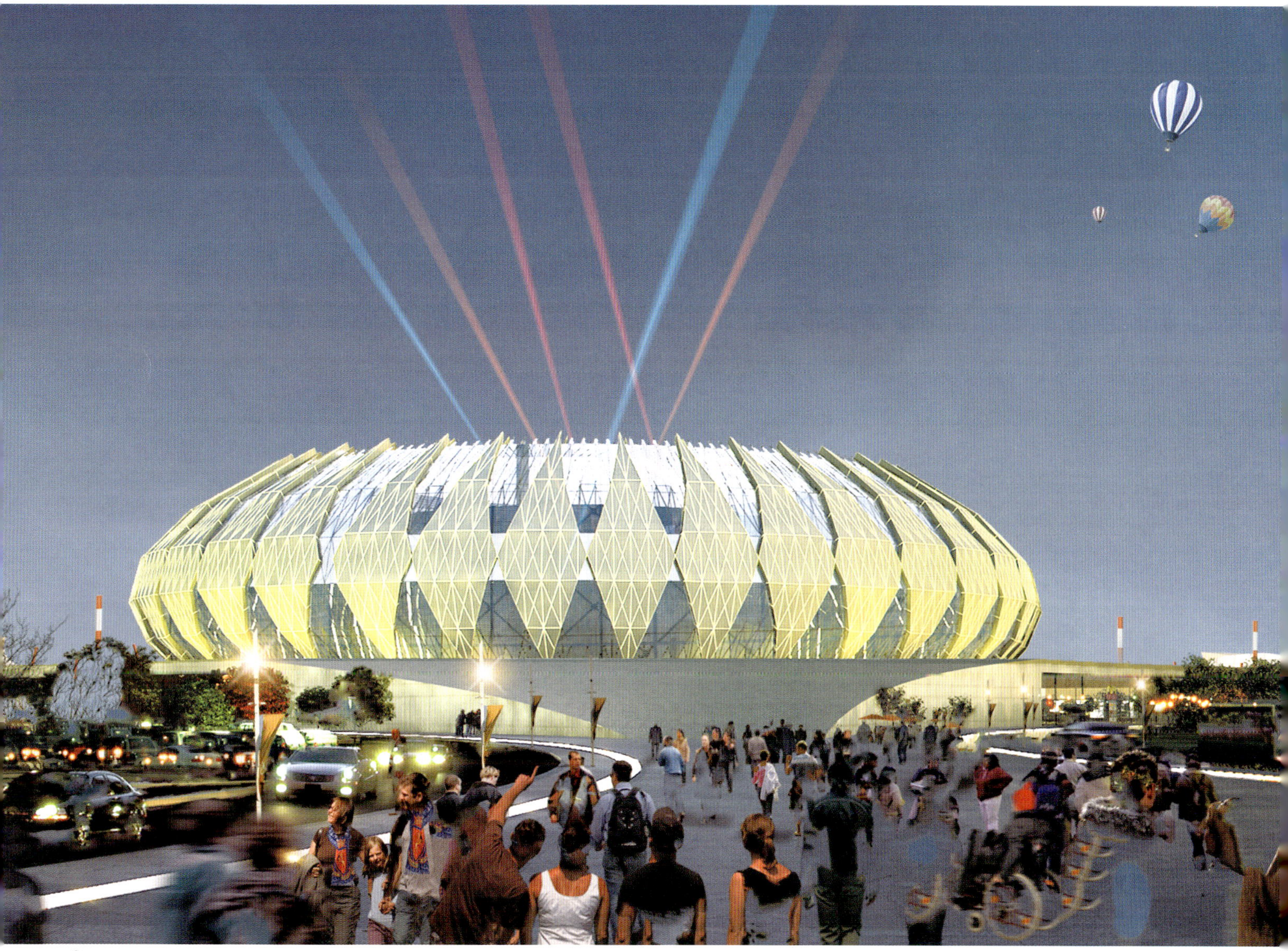

3

1 Site plan
2 Bird's-eye view
3 Rendering of the stadium and surrounds

Congresium

Client Ankara Chamber of Commerce
Project Date 2001–2007
Area 80,490 m^2
Location Ankara
Structural Engineer Yüksek Project
Design Consultant Salih Bezci
Mechanical Engineer Celal Okutan Engineering
Electrical Engineer Akay Engineering
Landscape Design Dalokay Design Studio
Project Manager Rüstem Gezen
Fire Consultant Alara Design and Engineering
Acoustic Consultant Prof. Dr. Mehmet Çalışkan
Audio, Lighting, and Video System Consultant Yesa Electronics Systems
Contractor Ankara Chamber of Commerce

The Söğütözü neighborhood has newly developed accommodation, education, healthcare, business, and commercial structures that give it the flavor of an urban center. Congresium is a multi-functional structure built by the Ankara Chamber of Commerce that offers spaces for conferences, fairs, exhibitions, demonstrations, and meetings.

Located at the junction of two major transportation axes, the structure is designed as a single mass that fills the property, while existing elevation differences were utilized in order to allow entrances to the building at different levels. With this approach, the highest level of the building and the roof becomes a rooftop garden, forming a continuum with the garden levels of the neighboring structures. The foyer of the building was designed as an attractive, transparent volume that integrates with the exterior along all its façades.

All the rooms in the building are designed to be multifunctional. Large and spacious exhibition areas were created by column-free openings. The dividing walls are moveable and, as a result, rooms can be reconfigured in various combinations, offering functional flexibility. The necessary service spaces are located on the lateral façades.

The mezzanine floors surrounding the rooms house technical utilities (air conditioning stations) and audio, lighting, and simultaneous translation rooms that serve the reconfigurable lower areas. This set-up allows the rooms to be entered from two different floors. The auditorium, ballroom, pressroom, and VIP areas are located on the convention floor. The auditorium seats 3,200 people—among the largest in Ankara—and it can be accessed from various floors. It can also be reconfigured for a variety of uses with a specially designed curtain system. The control platform is located in the middle of the room in order to allow this division.

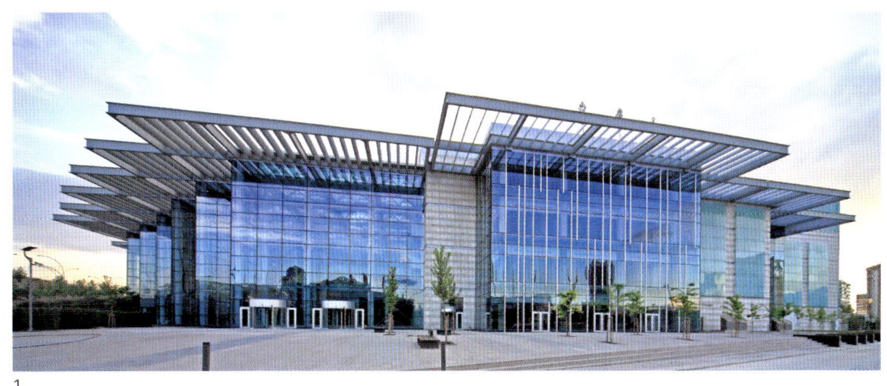

1

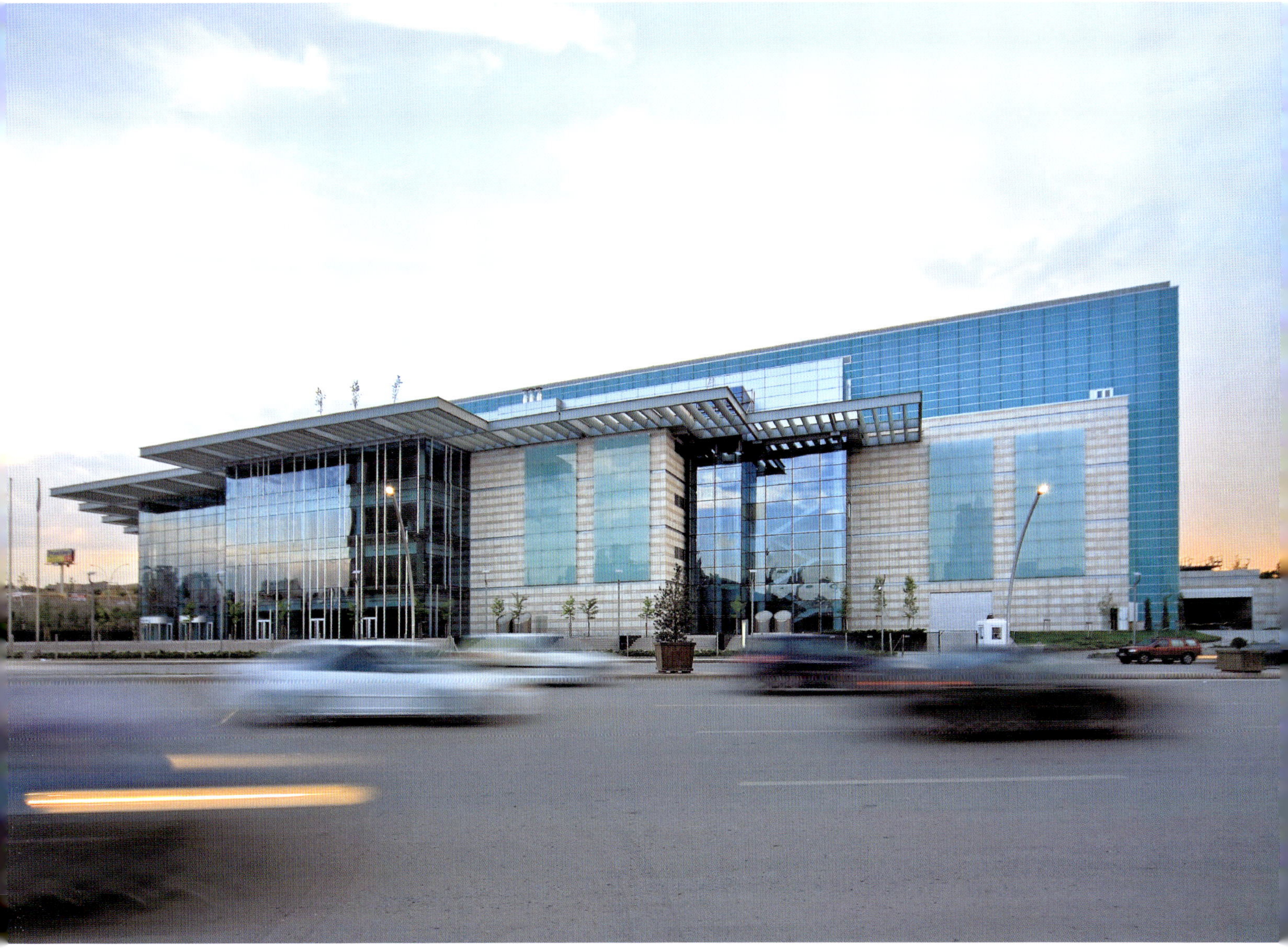

2

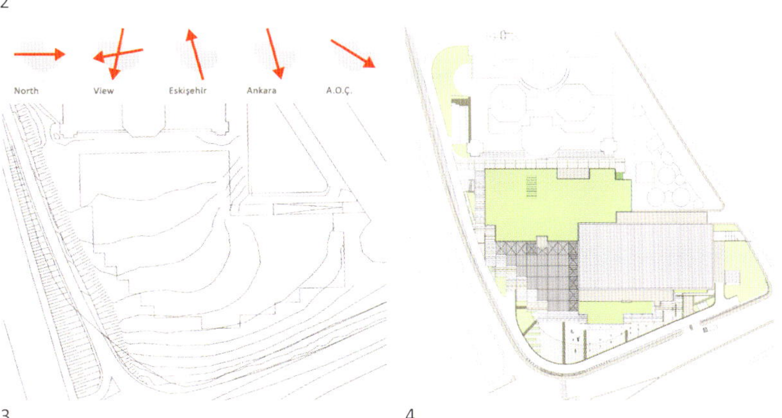

3

4

1 View of the main entrance
2 General view from Söğütözü Street
3 Site studies of directions, Eskişehir Highway, and the city view
4 Site plan

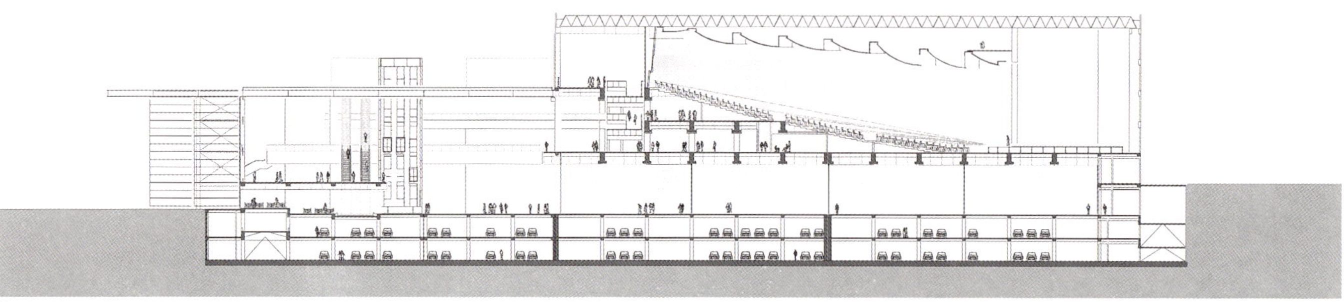
5

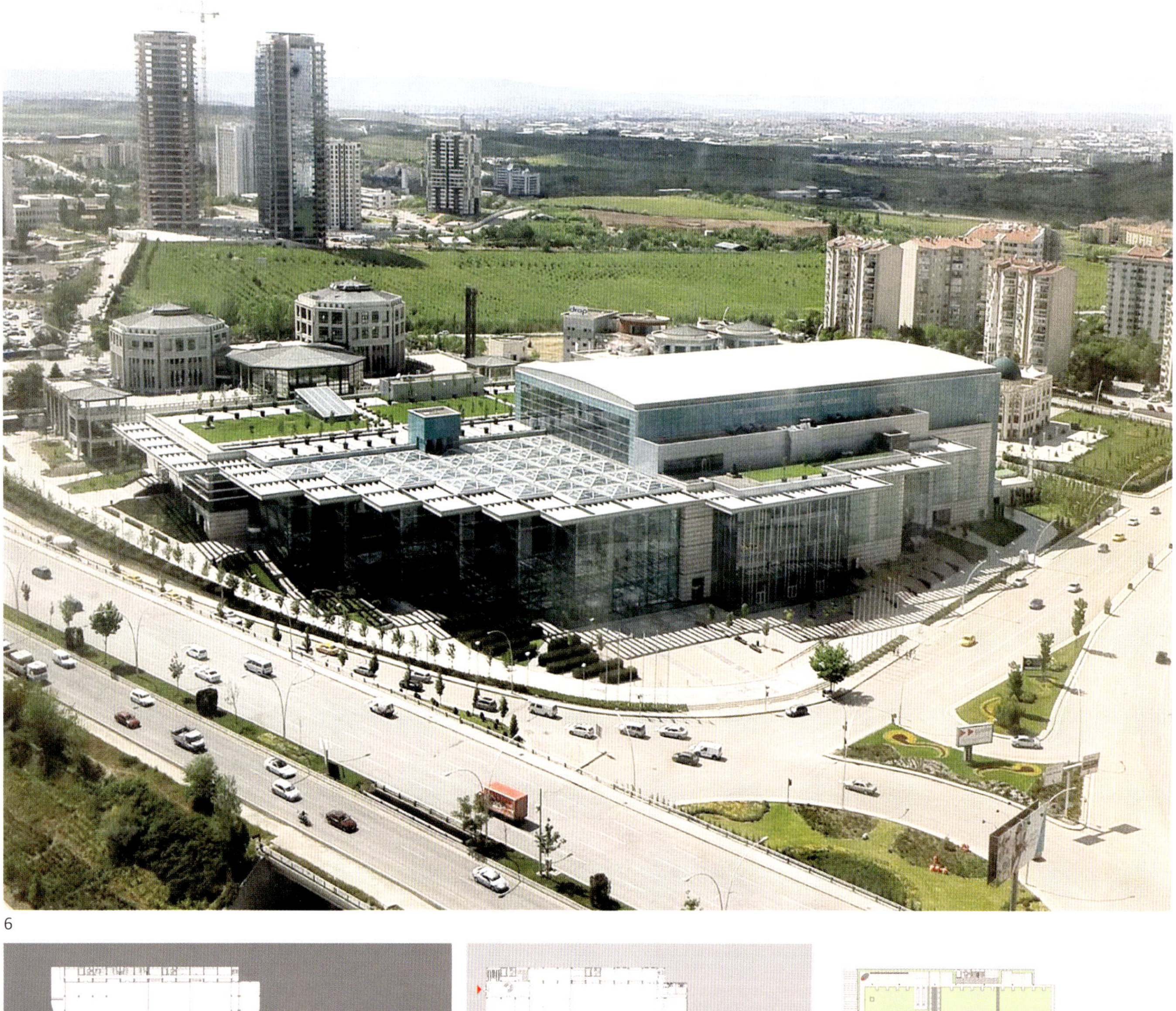

6

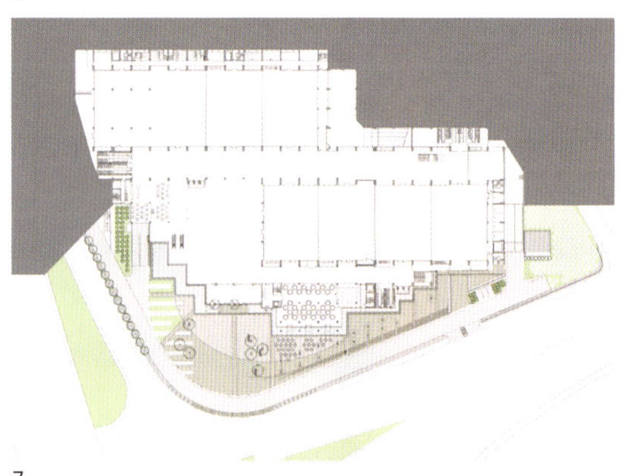
7

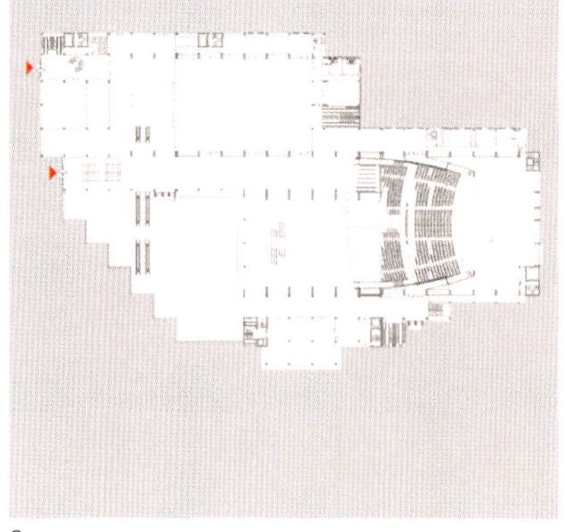
8

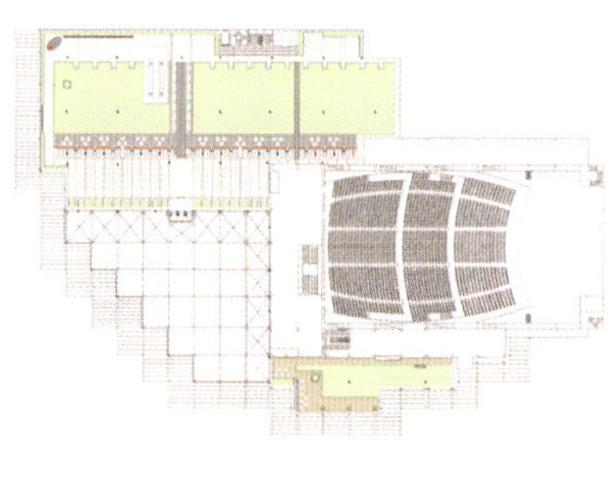
9

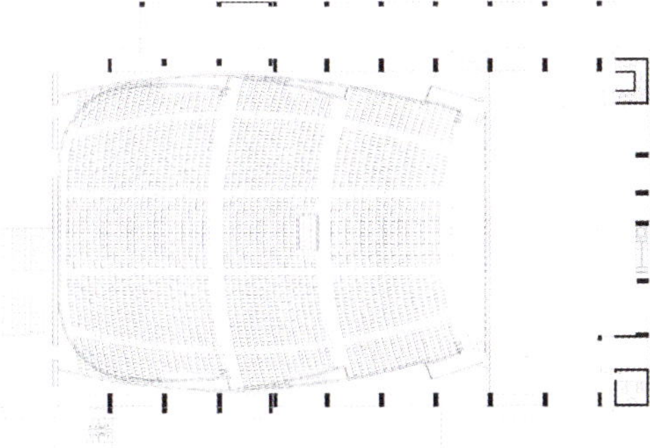

10

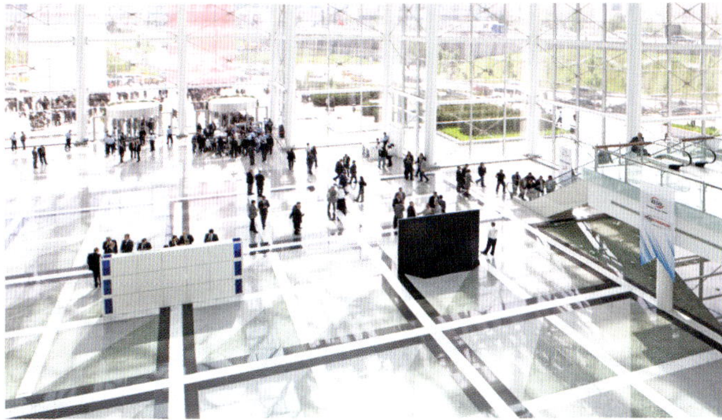

11

Escalators connect the convention floor to the rooftop on a linear axis. The rooftop design creates the effect of an upper plaza, offering an open space for use inside the building.

The structure is made up of natural stone, glass, and steel elements. The natural stone façade creates an orderly, repetitive continuum around the building with size and texture variations. Both transparent and painted glass have been used on the façades. The colored marble and the floor patterns used in the atrium reflect the ceiling's design.

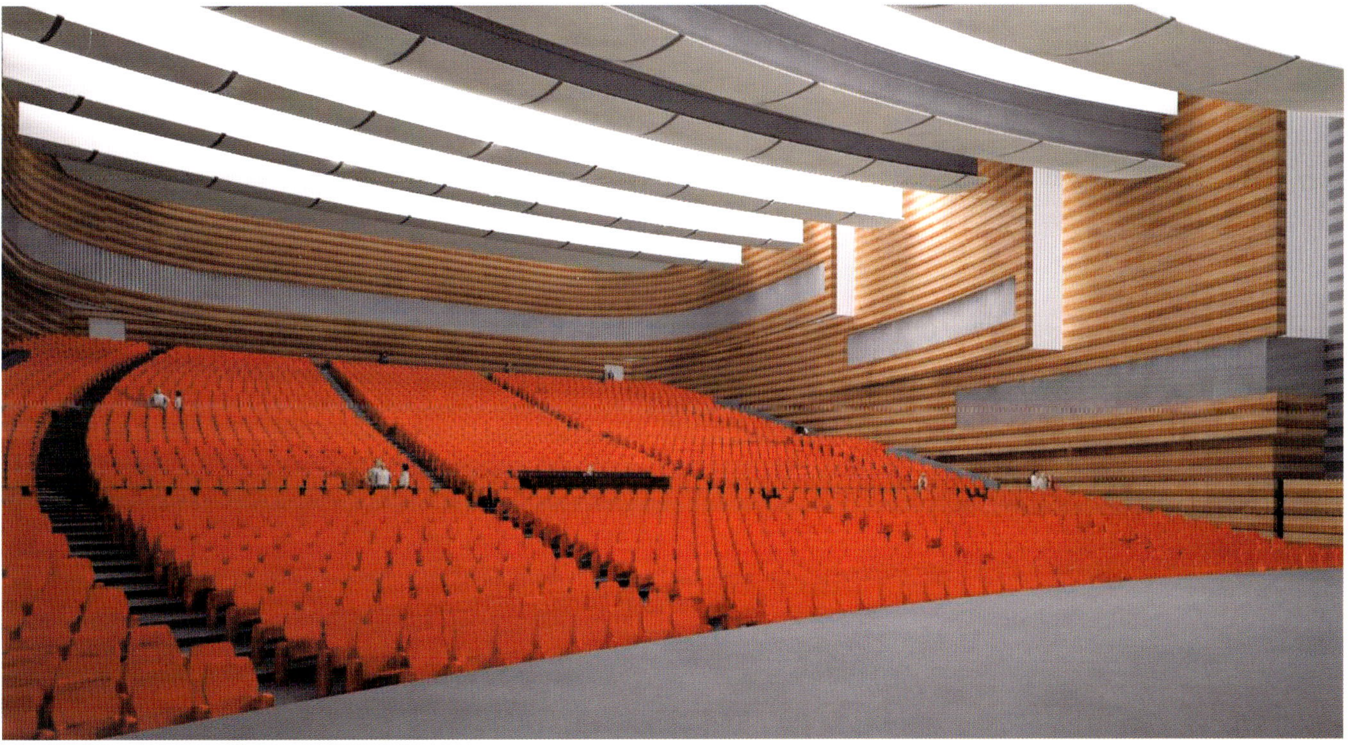

12

5 Longitudinal section
6 View of Congresium from one of the nearby towers
7 Ground floor plan
8 Upper level plan
9 Terrace floor plan
10 Auditorium plan
11 View of the entrance hall
12 Rendering of the auditorium
13 Interior view of the auditorium during an event

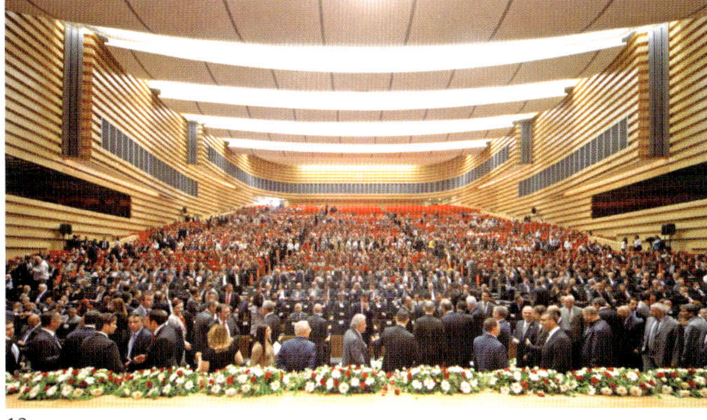

13

Panora

Client Merkez Construction, Tourism and Management Inc.
Project Date 2004–2007
Area 180,000 m^2
Location Ankara
Design Consultant Salih Bezci, Vecihi Yıldız
Construction Supervisor Sonay Ozar
Structural Engineer Yüksek Project
Mechanical Engineer GMD Engineering
Electrical Engineer Yurdakul Engineering
Landscape Design Dalokay Design Studio
Leasing Consultant Jones Lang Lasalle Turkey
Contractor Merkez Construction, Tourism and Management Inc.
2004 ICSC (International Council of Shopping Centres) European Shopping Center Awards Certificate of Merit

Panora was designed not only as a shopping center, but also as a building that would have urban impact and act as a meeting point for the area. On an urban scale, one of the main design objectives of the project was to create a transitional building that would direct the recreational and social activities on the Eymir Lake and METU Forest and flowing into the Dikmen Valley and the green areas nearby.

The building's indoor spaces were designed to take full advantage of the northern light and, as a result, create an inner atmosphere that emphasizes transparency, while the inner circulation halls flanked by double-story retail stores were designed to give the effect of an urban boulevard.

The inclination of the site provides access to the building from several different levels. The building offers a series of multi-functional spaces, which may accommodate several different activities at the same time. The three-story structure includes a series of shopping spaces, restaurants, and cafés, along with with a center for culture, arts, and sports. Both sides of the main entrance are reserved for independent restaurants, which have direct access to outdoor spaces and may be used beyond the center's opening hours.

The ground level consists of shopping spaces and activity areas. A hypermarket stretching over an area of 10,000 square meters, and which will actively appeal to the residential area, takes place on the lower ground floor. Cultural, artistic, and leisure activities are located on the second floor, which includes a complex of 12 cinema halls. The dining areas on the second floor overlook the outdoor parks through the building's transparent façade. A series of spatial alternatives are created by the use of different levels on the food court, which opens to the outdoors and to the building's view.

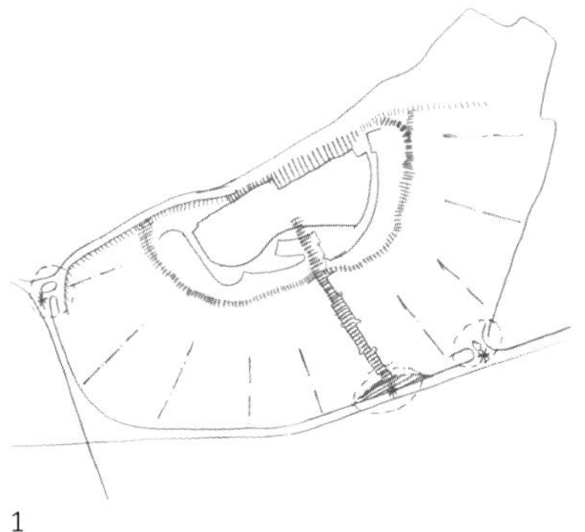

1

1 Sketch of the pedestrian connections by Ali Osman Öztürk
2 View of the main entrance
3 Aerial view of the park and residential blocks
4 Façade drawing of the main entrance
Following pages:
General view showing the transparency of the mall

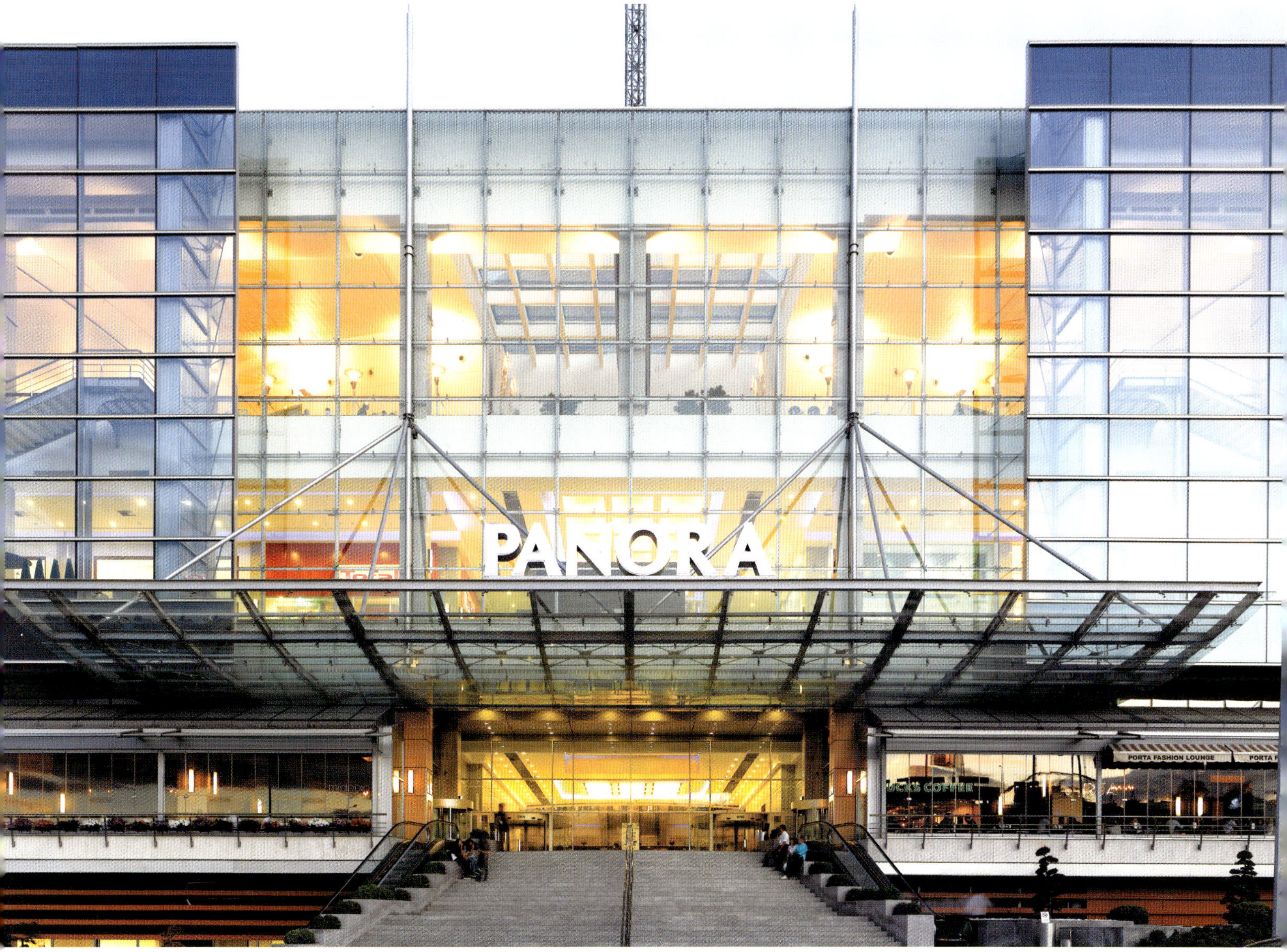

2

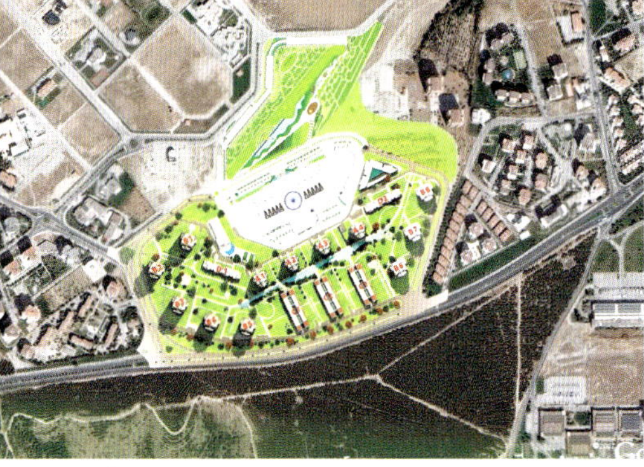

3

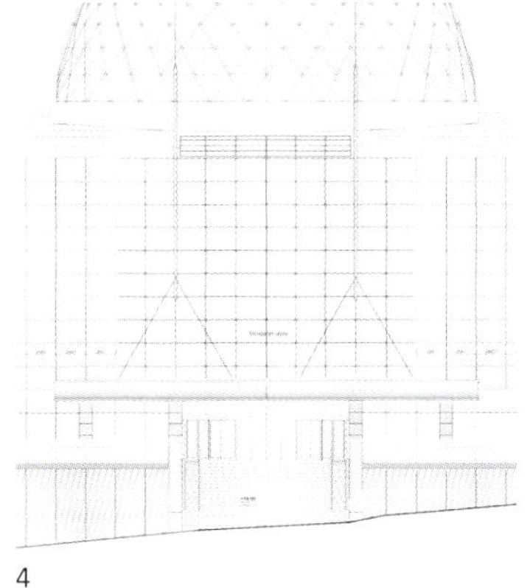

4

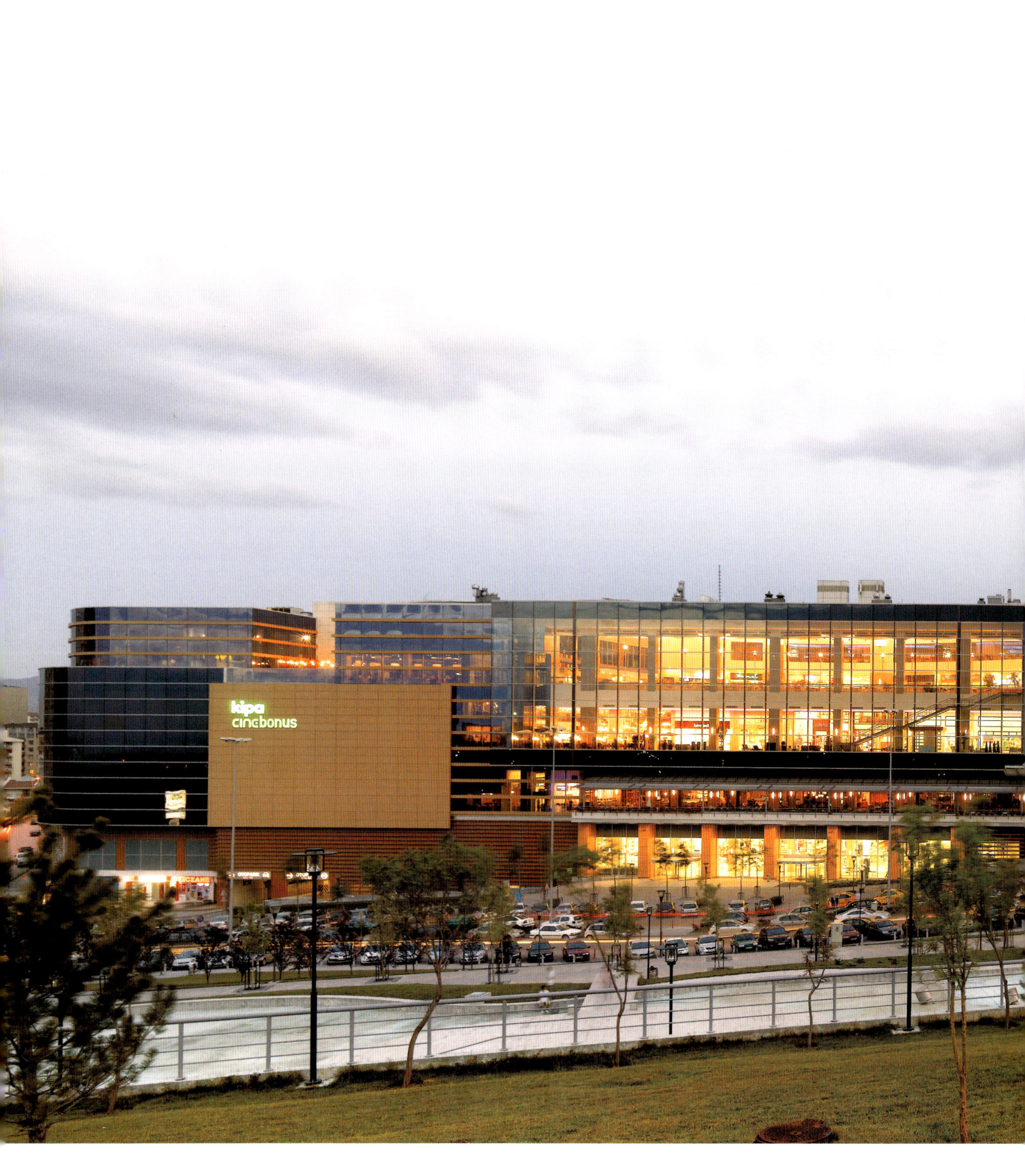
kipa
cinebonus

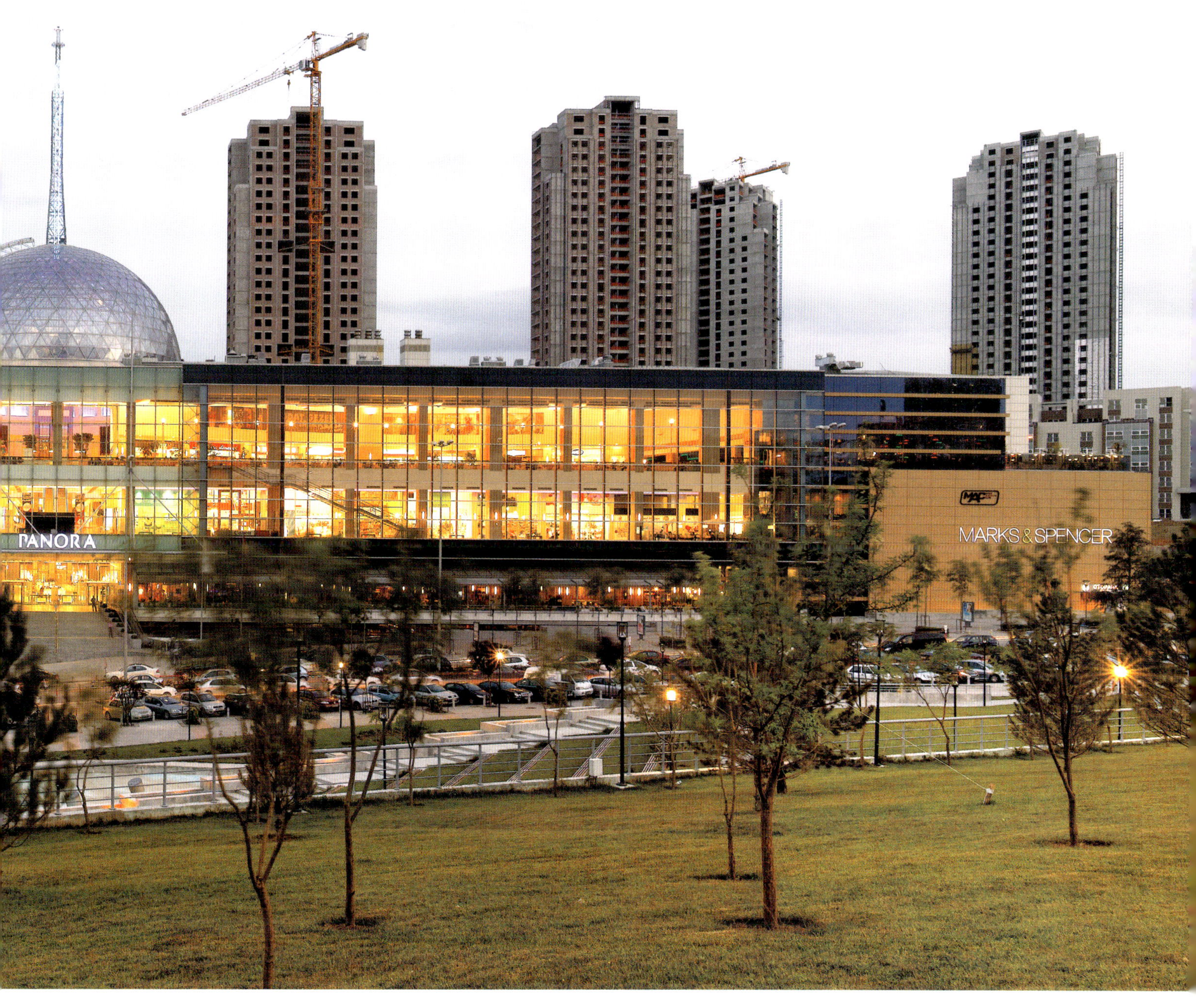
PANORA
MARKS & SPENCER

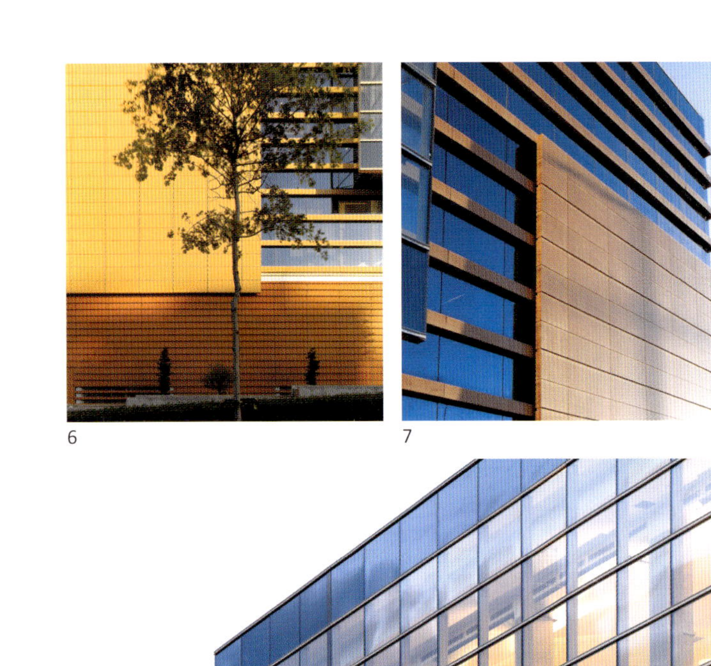

6

7

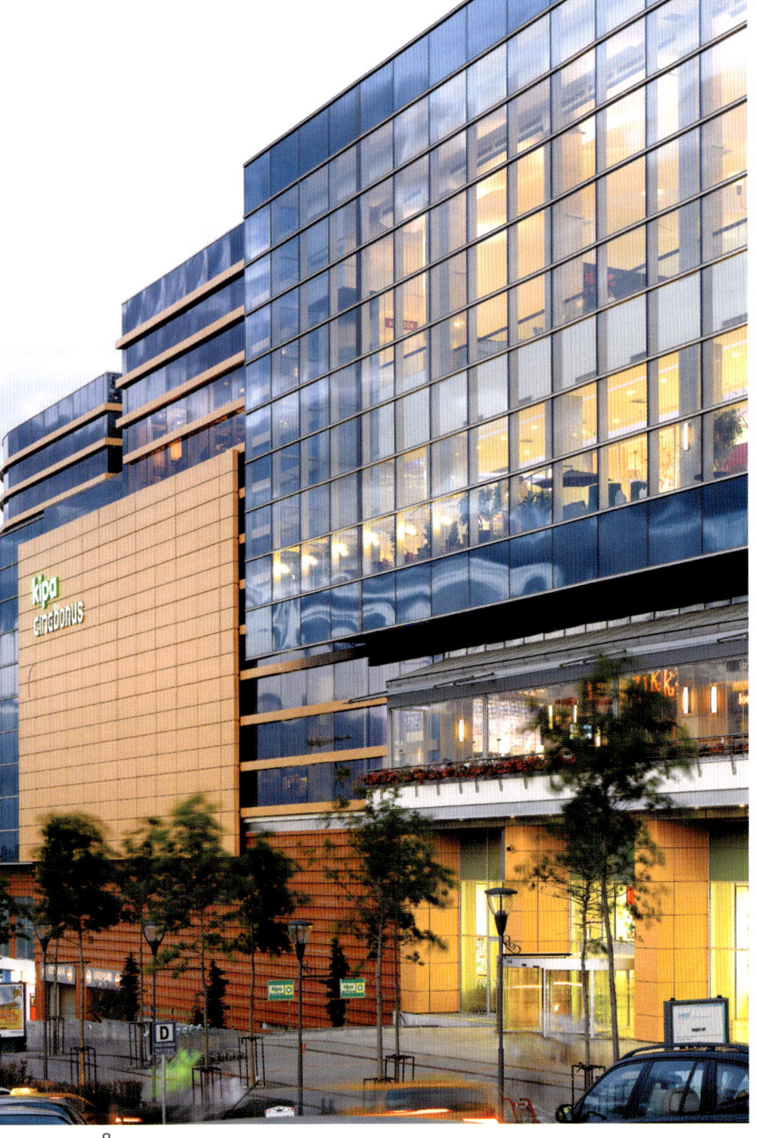

8

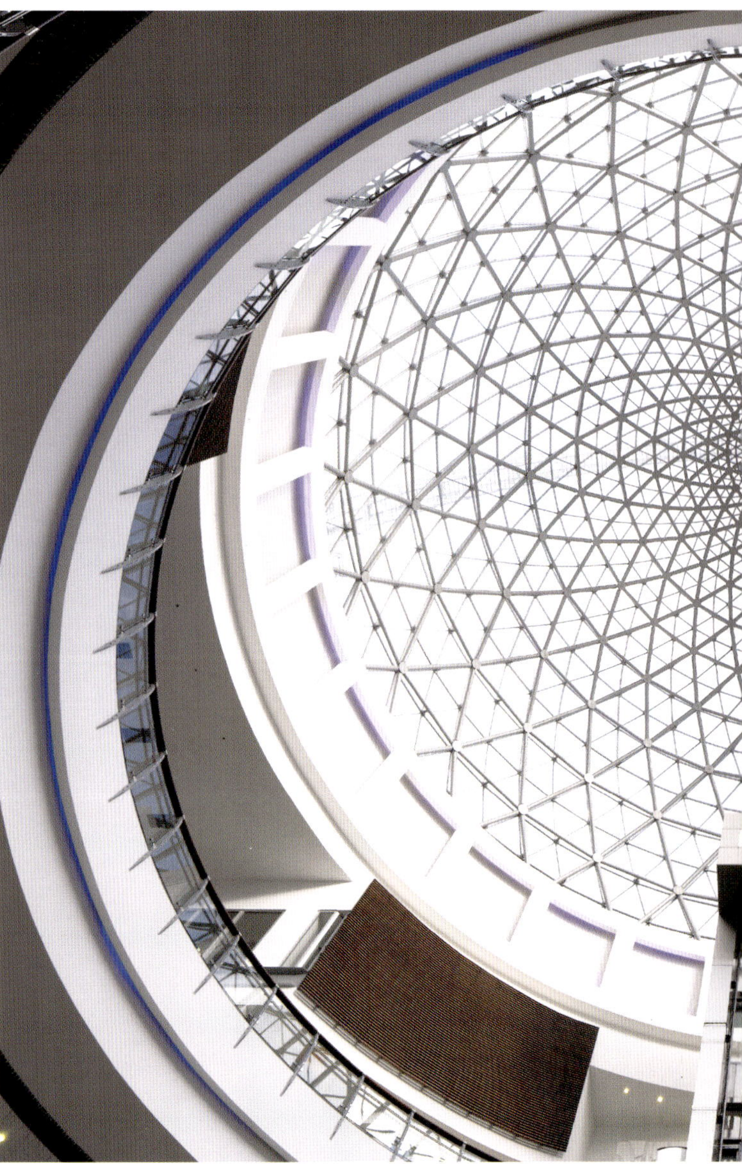

9

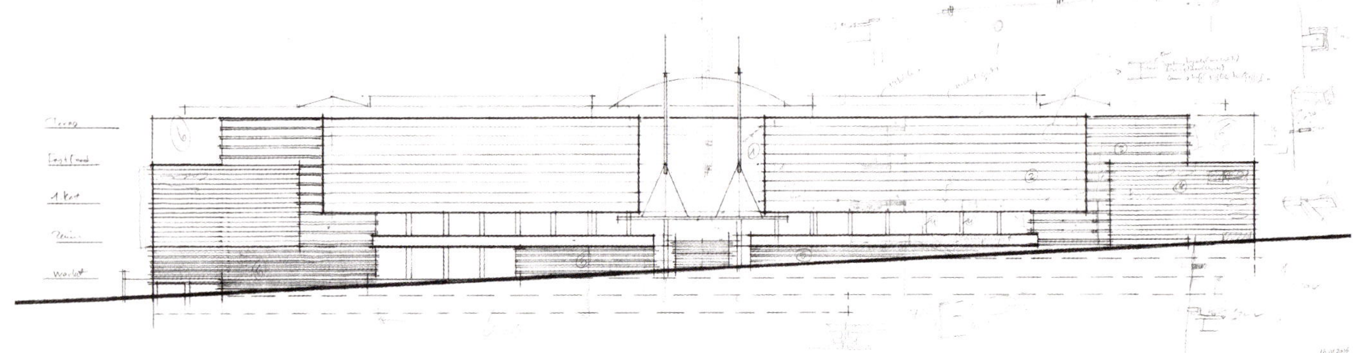

10

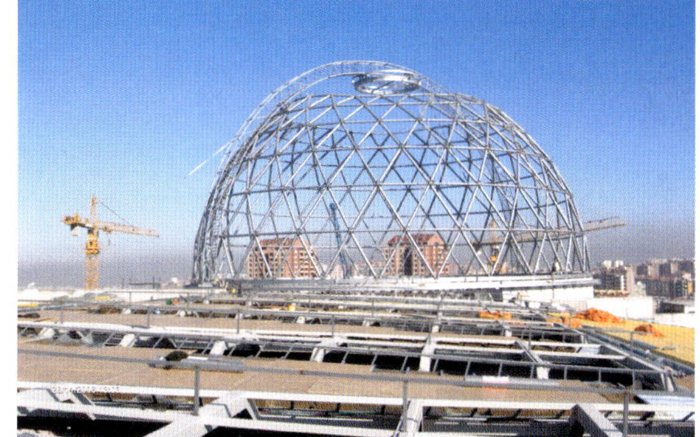

11

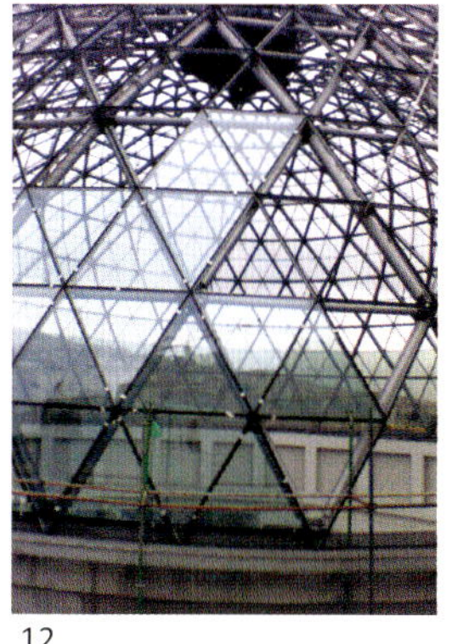

12

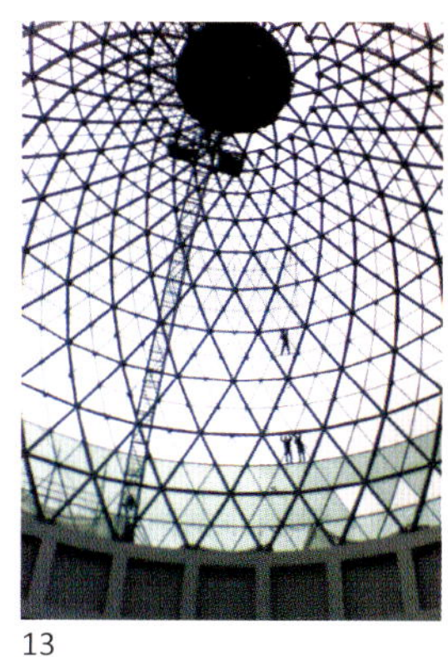

13

The domed area was designed to act as a multi-functional urban space, and is large enough to accommodate live activities such as shows and concerts. This dome spans 38 meters in diameter and its outer shell is covered with a steel system that brings light into the interior spaces. A giant mosaic made from 320,000 individual pieces in 49 different colors, which depicts the world map of the famous Ottoman admiral Piri Ries, lies on the floor of this central space.

Together with the use of its ground level and the outdoor use of its dining facilities, Panora presents an architectural alternative to conventional box-like shopping centers, functioning as an urban center integrated with its immediate environment and the city at large.

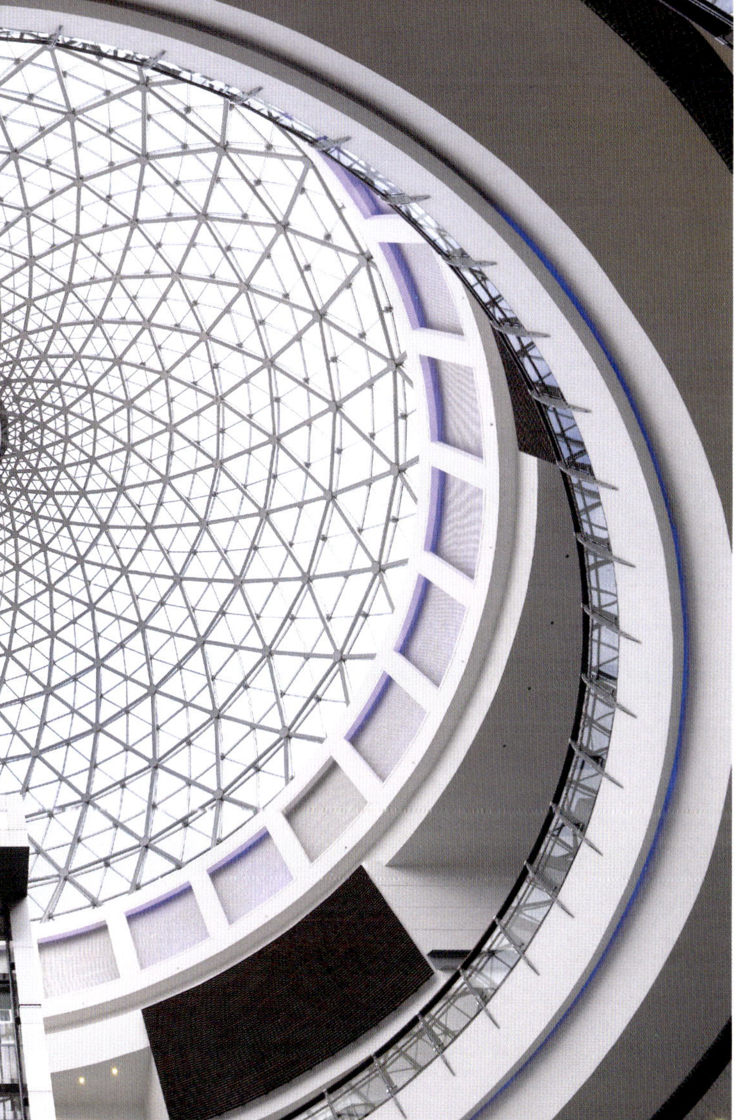

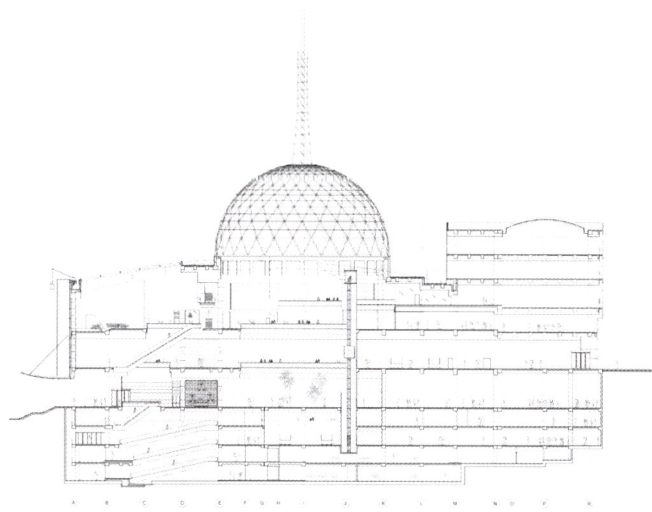

15

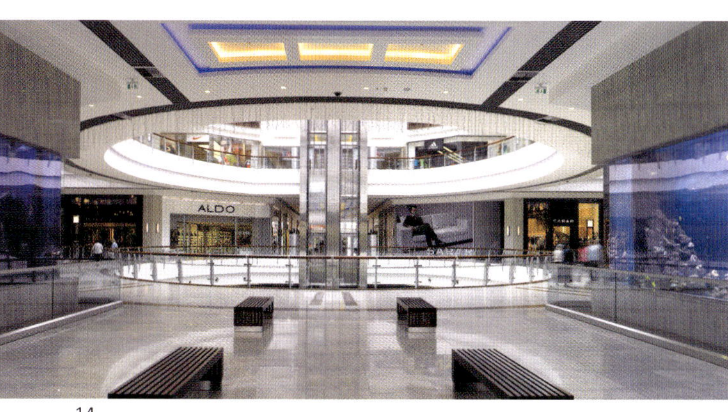

14

6,7 Detail of the façade
8 Entrance on supermarket floor level
9 View of the dome above the multi-functional area
10 Sketch of north elevation by Ali Osman Öztürk
11–13 Construction stages of the glass dome showing the triangular modules
14 Interior view of the symmetrical aquariums and circular atrium beneath the dome
15 Cross section showing the different levels, park side entrance and the south entrance

16 Interior view of the multi-functional area where exhibitions and concerts are held
17 Food court plan
18 Upper level floor plan
19 Entrance floor plan

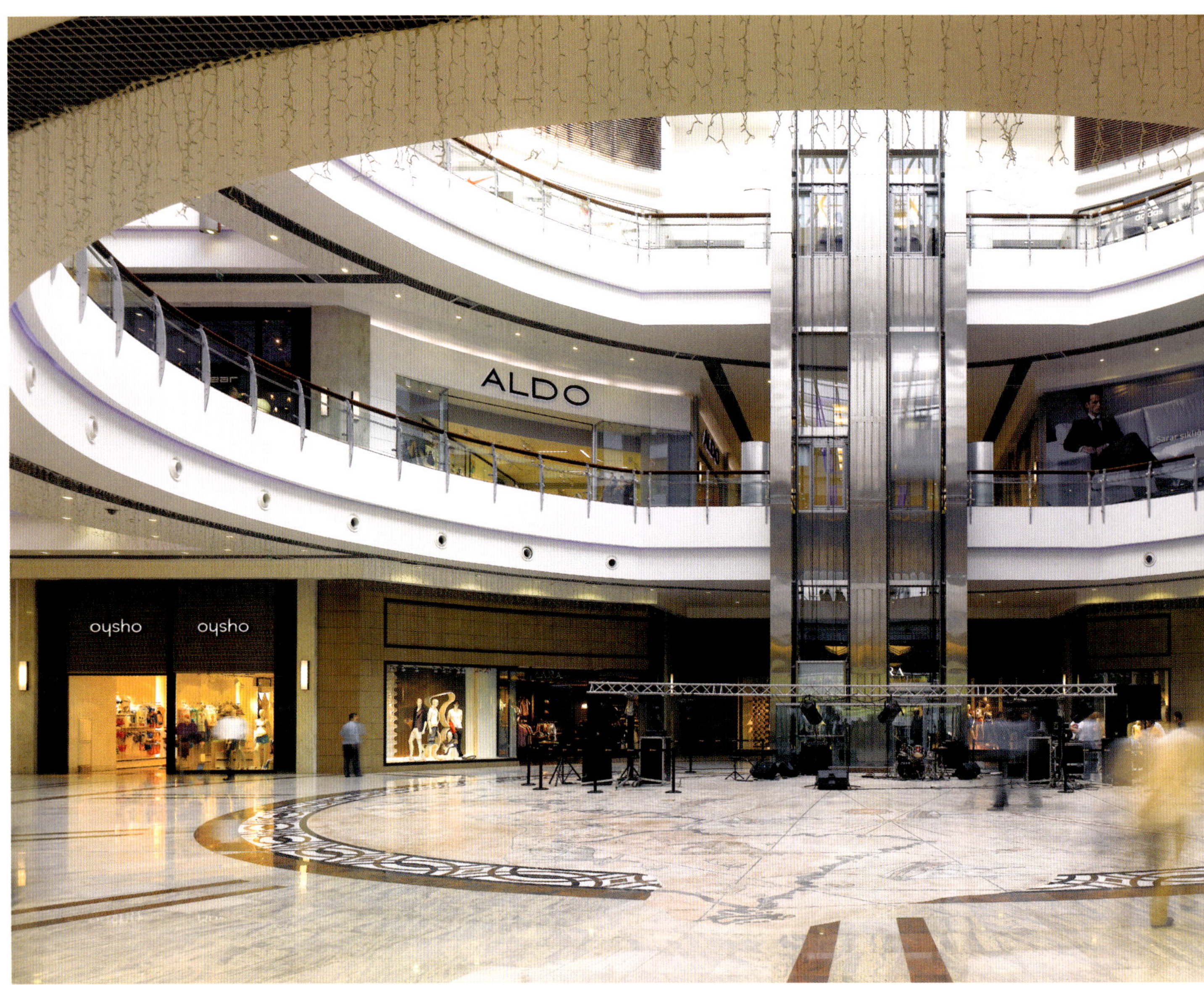

16

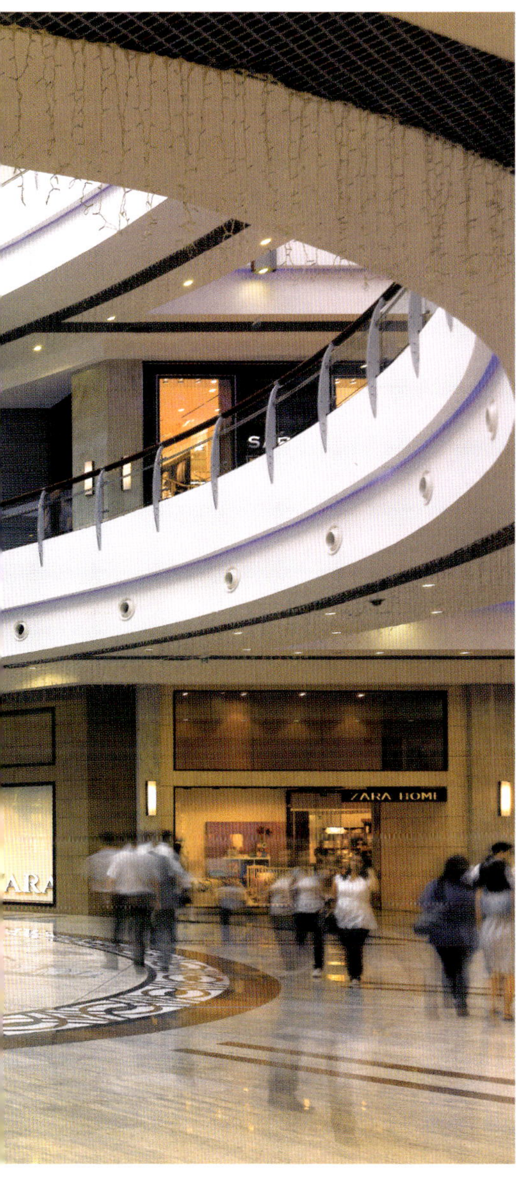

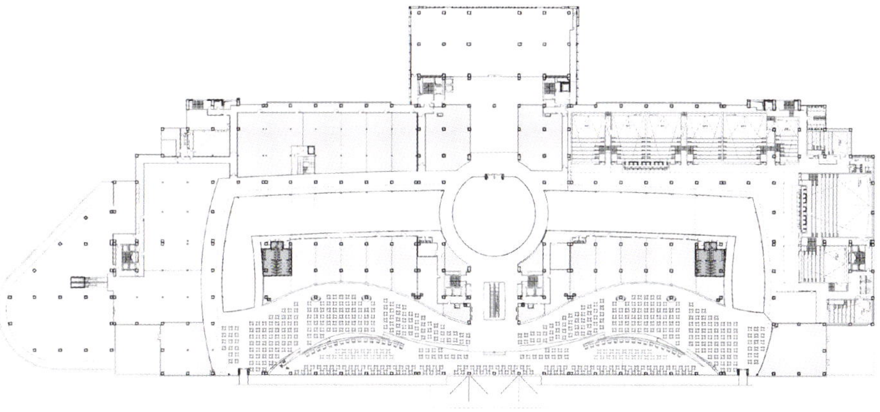

17

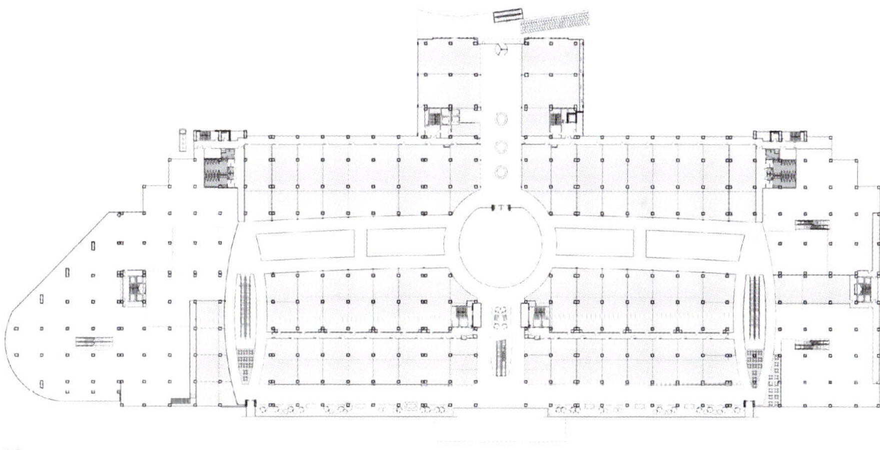

18

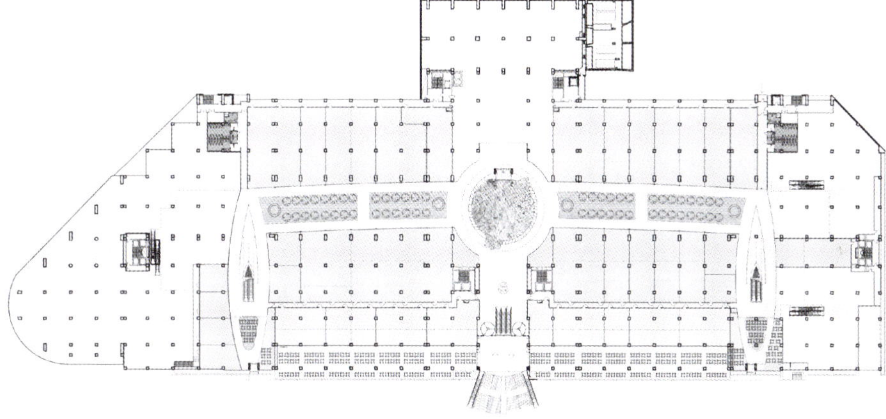

19

Liva City

Client Liva
Project Date 2013
Area 37,700 m^2
Location Ankara
Structural Engineer Yüksek Project
Mechanical Engineer Metta Engineering
Electrical Engineer Akay Engineering
Fire Consultant Alara Design and Engineering

Planned for Eskişehir Highway, Liva City was designed with environmental data, topography, and the functions and values represented by the Liva brand in mind.

The building program includes a museum and food and beverage spaces, along with a factory. The atrium designed above the main entrance connects these spaces and provides visual relationships between different levels and functions.

The 10-meter axial system that constitutes the factory structure expands to the rest of the building, allowing for wide open spaces and guiding the design of the ballrooms located on the upper level. The structural integrity of the fragmented masses is maintained by the vertical elements used on the façade.

1 View of the front façade
2 Model of the chocolate museum

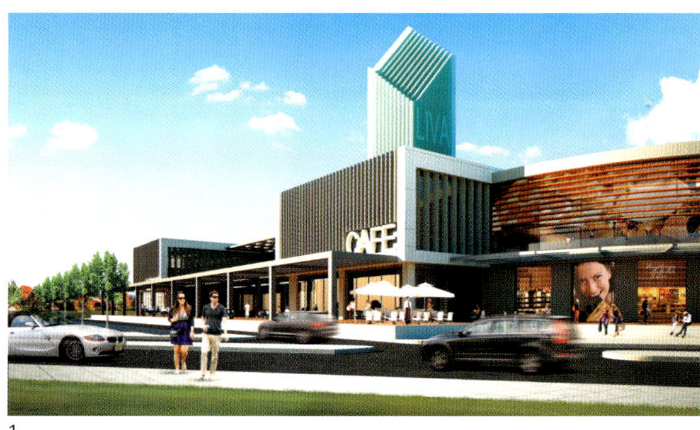

1

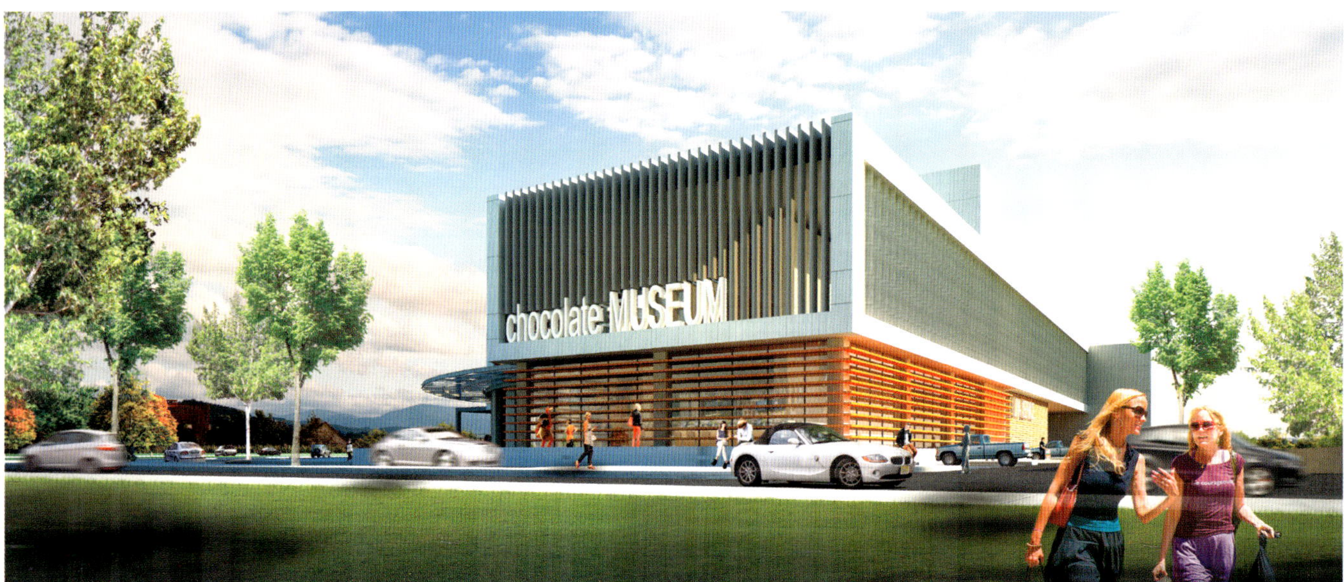

2

MFS Business Center

Client Alternatif Construction
Project Date 2011
Area 60 000 m^2
Location Ankara
Structural Engineer Yüksek Project
Mechanical Engineer Setes Engineering
Electrical Engineer Akay Engineering

The development of the central business area of southern Ankara continues on the Mevlana (Konya) Boulevard. This axis mainly compounds offices, shops, and showrooms. This building was built on the Mevlana Boulevard developed in parallel commercial urban texture, including commercial offices of different sizes. The slope of the land has allowed different arrangements on stories. The arrangements on the podium creates the impression of independent access points. Offices can be combined or divided if needed. An interior garden has been designed between the units in podium. On the surface of the façade, a sense of fragmental regulation is adopted within the prismatic structure of the building. Natural stone and glass is used.

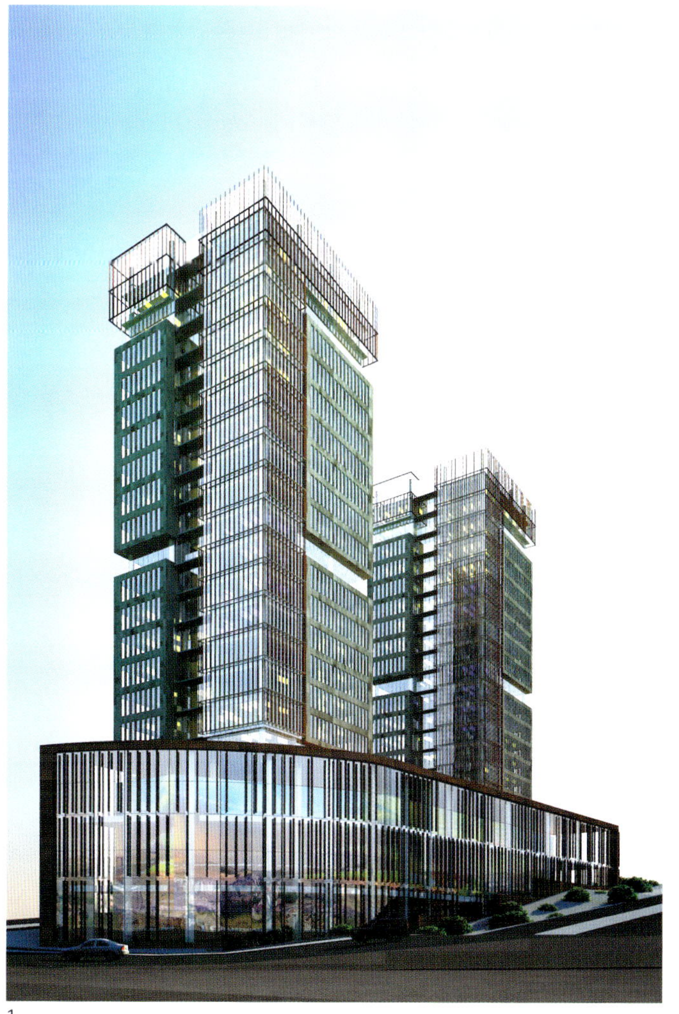

1

1 General view
2 Typical floor plan

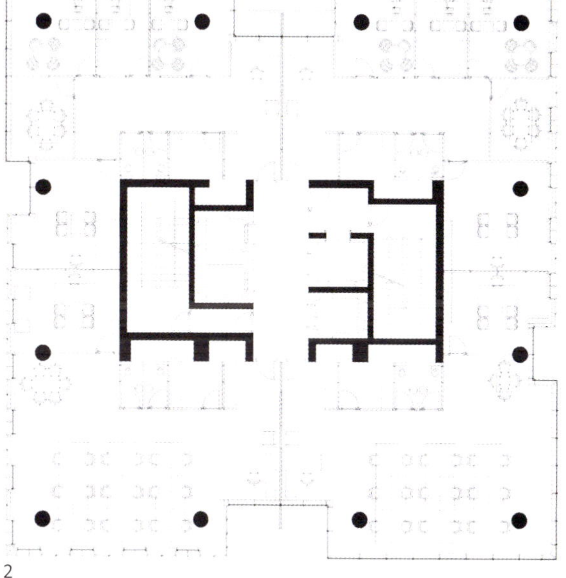

2

Antares

Client Dolunay Forest Trade Ltd.
Project Date 2005–2007
Area 222,205 m^2
Location Ankara
Structural Engineer Yüksek Project
Mechanical Engineer GMD Engineering
Electrical Engineer Yurdakul Engineering
Landscape Design Dalokay Design Studio
Fire Consultant Alara Design and Engineering
Leasing Consultant Metro, Jones Lang LaSalle Turkey
Contractor Dolunay Forest Trade Ltd.

Antares is a secondary urban center consisting of shopping and commercial areas as well as residential blocks. The campus is located in the primarily residential district of Etlik on an independent building block that is surrounded by roads. An urban fabric consisting of large commercial areas, housing, shared social areas, and an office structure was created and, as it is not self-enclosed, the complex will serve its immediate surroundings as well.

The elements of the campus that are connected to the main avenue are designated for supermarkets, shopping, and food and beverage spaces, while the residential towers are located behind these in a more private area. Utilizing the slope of the plot, separate entries and exits to and from the side and the front roads are available on almost every floor. The parking floors are directly connected to the shopping floors. As opposed to traditional malls, Antares has functions located outside the building, independent from the mall. This is an attempt to reinforce the outdoor functions and the urban quality of the complex.

The structure includes open spaces for both residents and visitors. In this context, a pond has been designed next to the plaza that connects the office block and the shopping mall. Some of the food and beverage spaces have been moved to the plaza as independent structures. Gradually, Antares has become a secondary urban center used by the whole city.

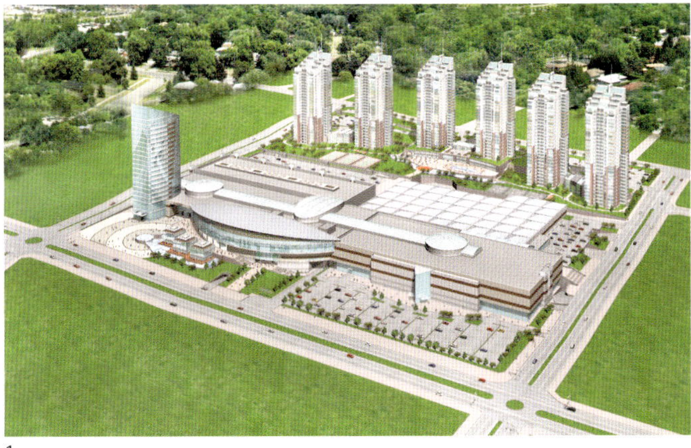
1

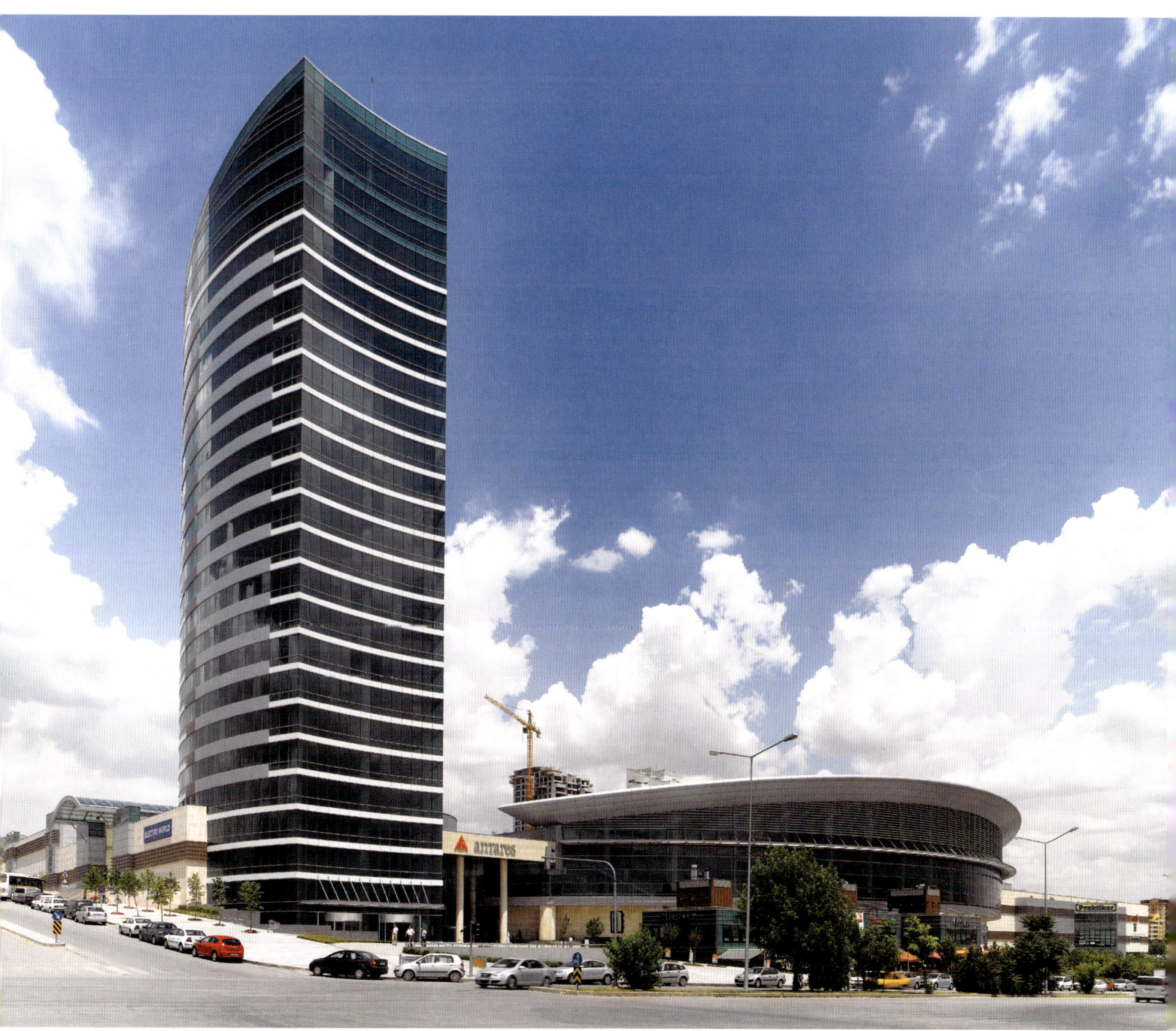

2

1 Model of the complex
2 General view showing the office tower and the mall
Following pages:
Panoramic view of the complex

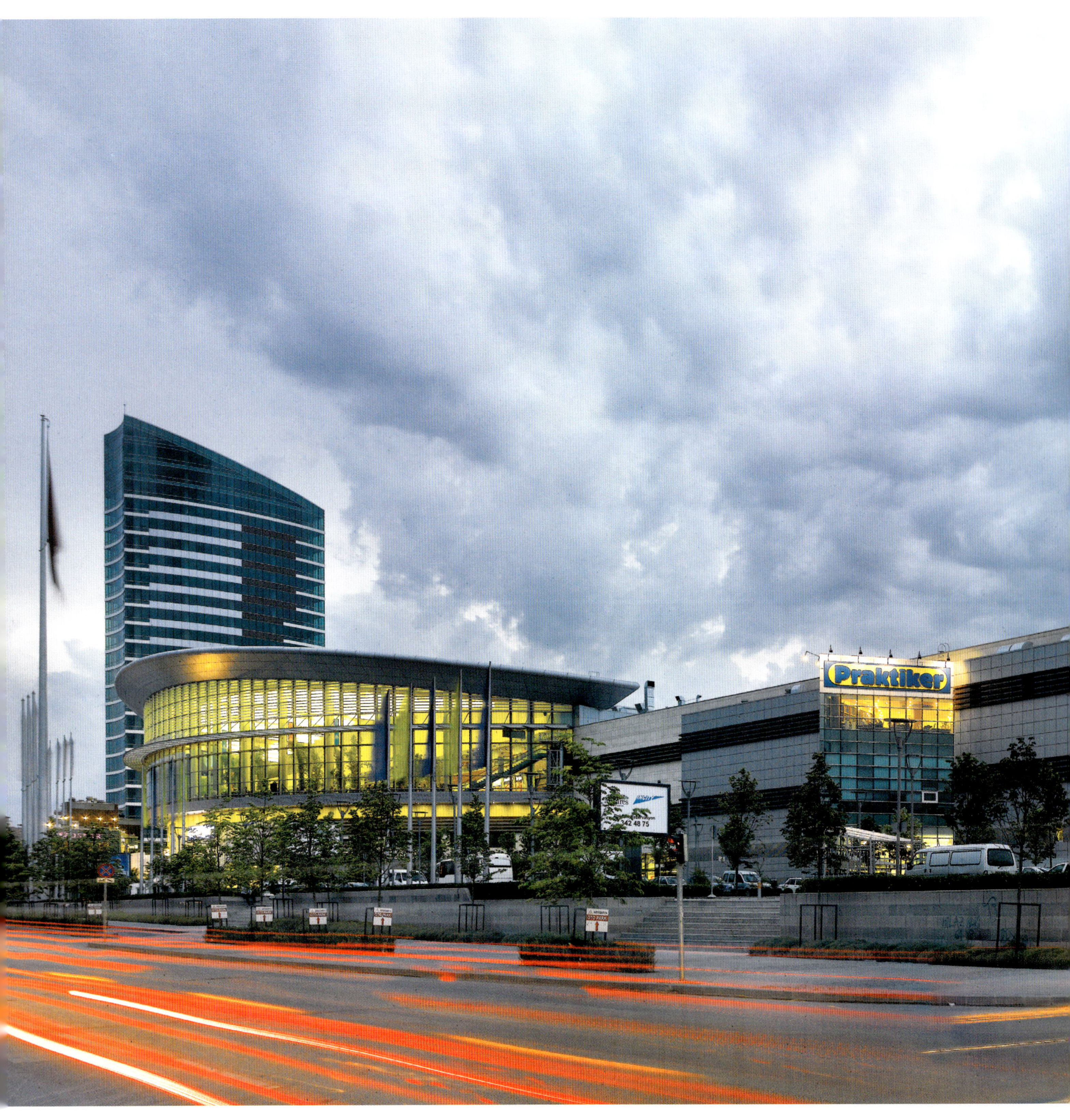
Praktiker

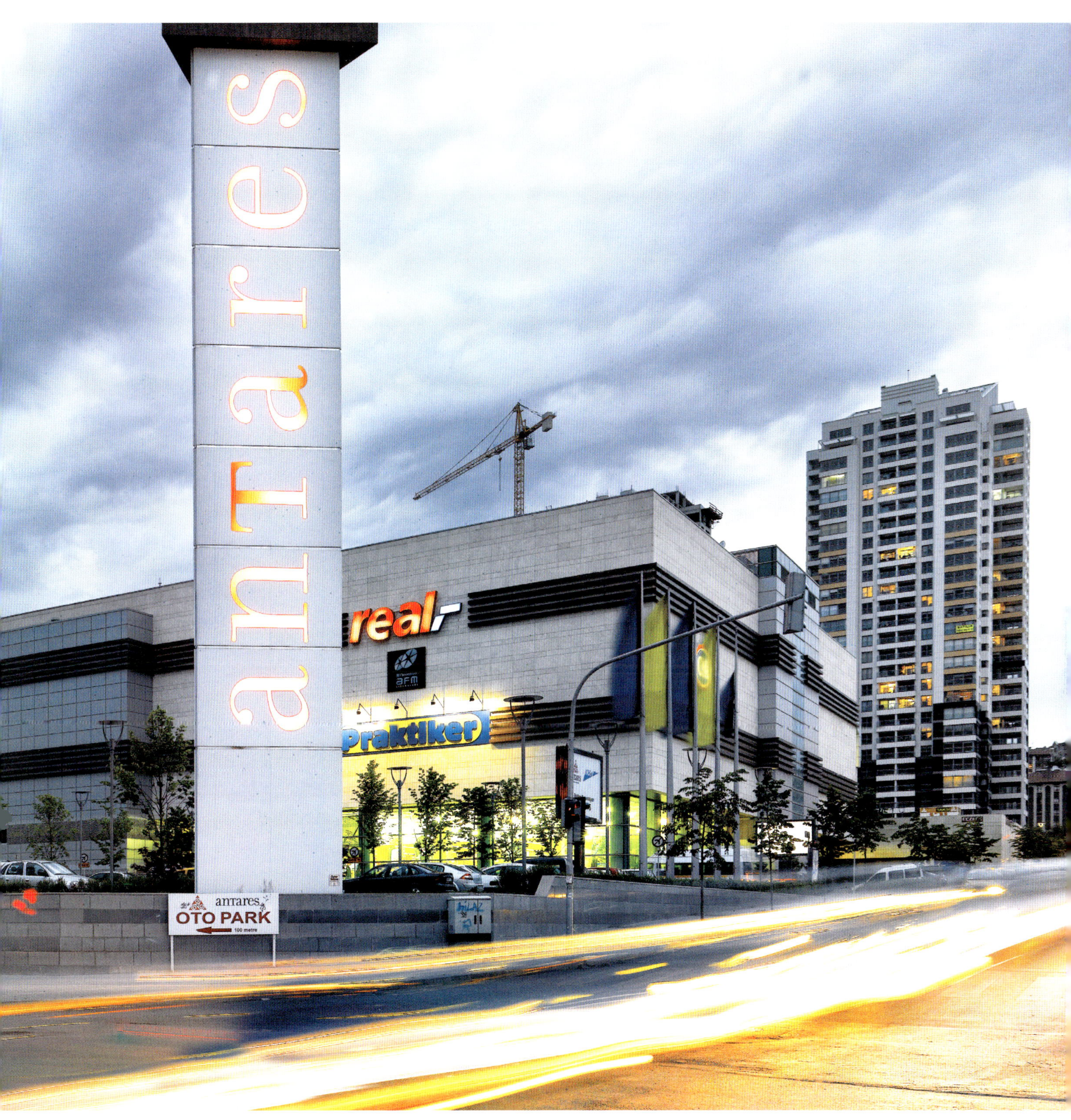
antares
real
Praktiker
antares
OTO PARK
100 metre

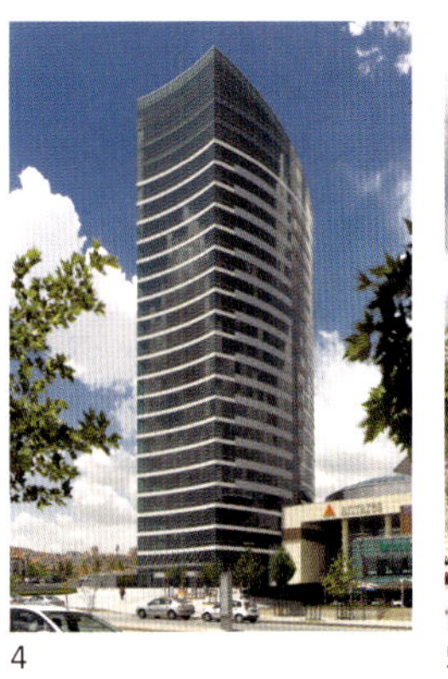
4

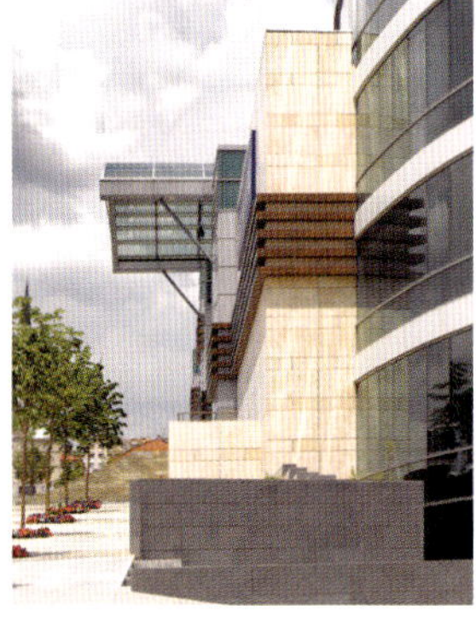
5

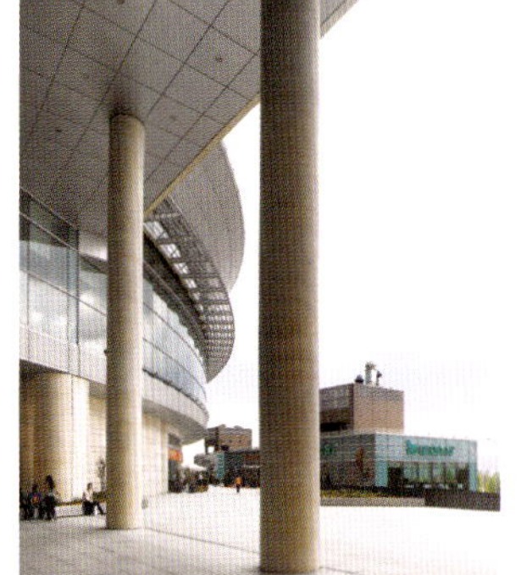
6

4 Office tower
5 Side entrance to the mall
6 Main entrance detail
7 Elliptical atrium
8 Lower level floor plan
9 Upper level floor plan
10 View along one of the circulation areas
11 Food court
12,13 View into the void

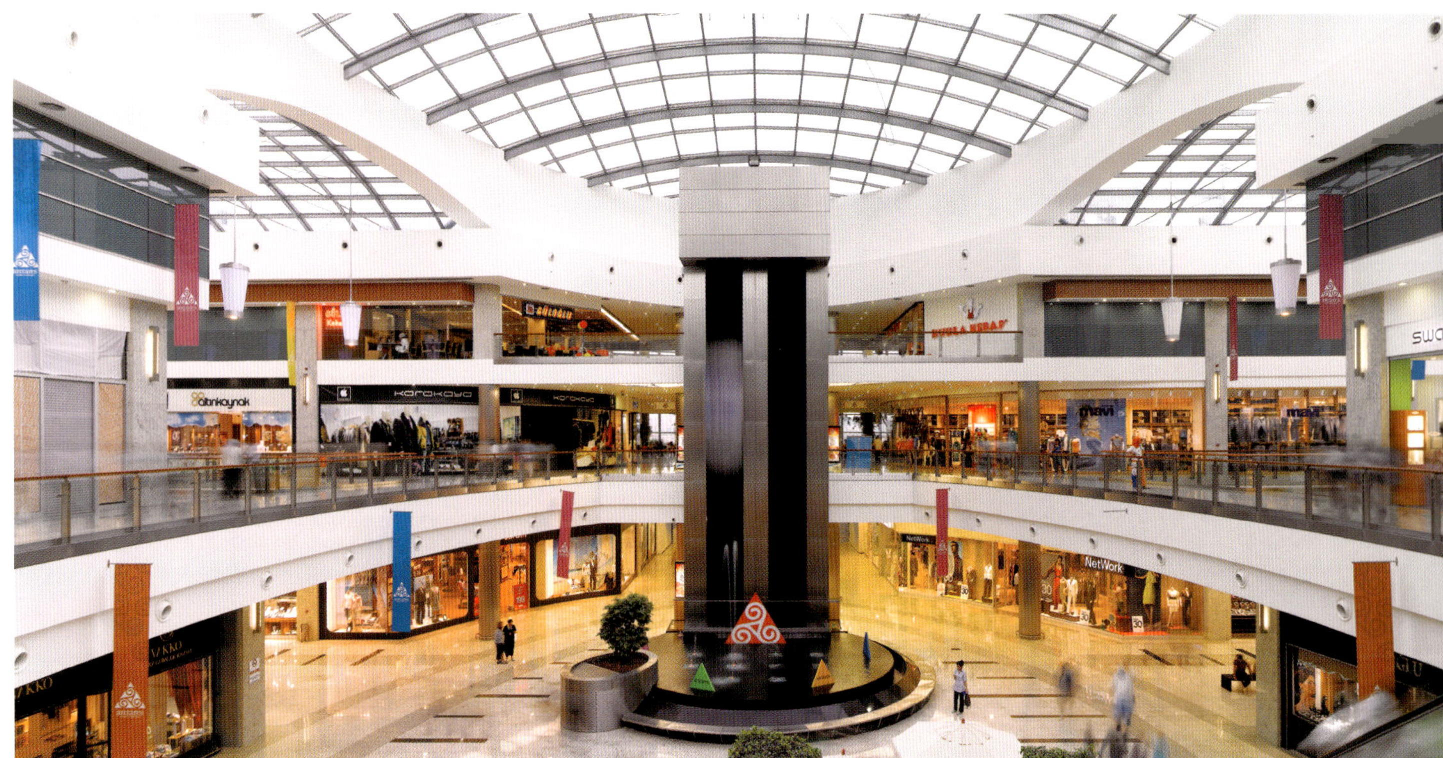

7

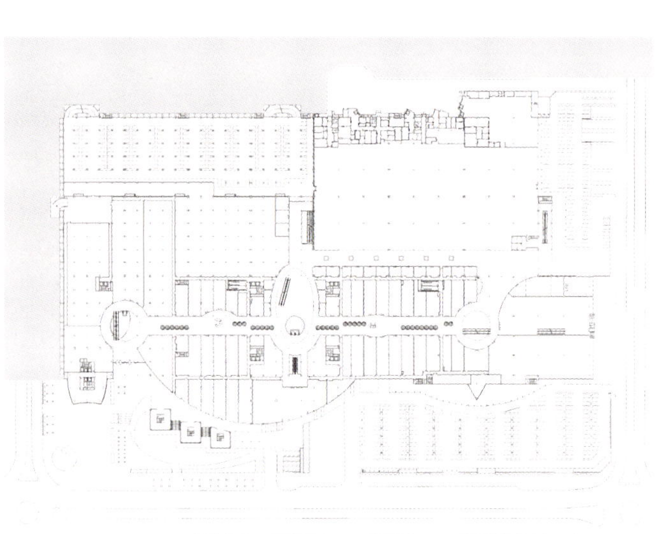
8

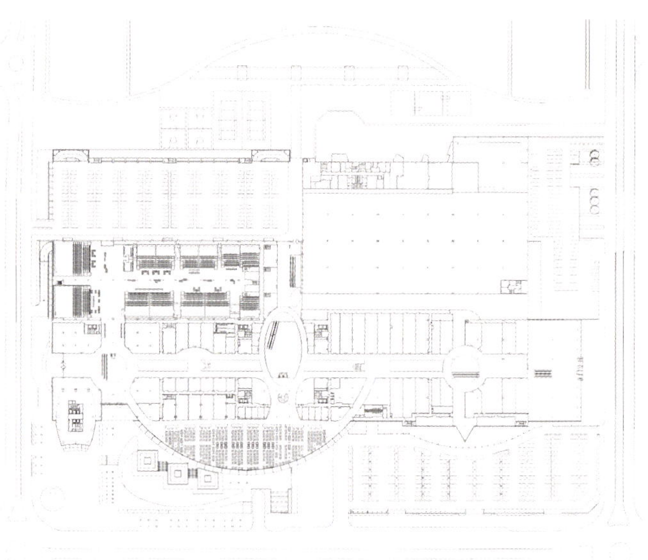
9

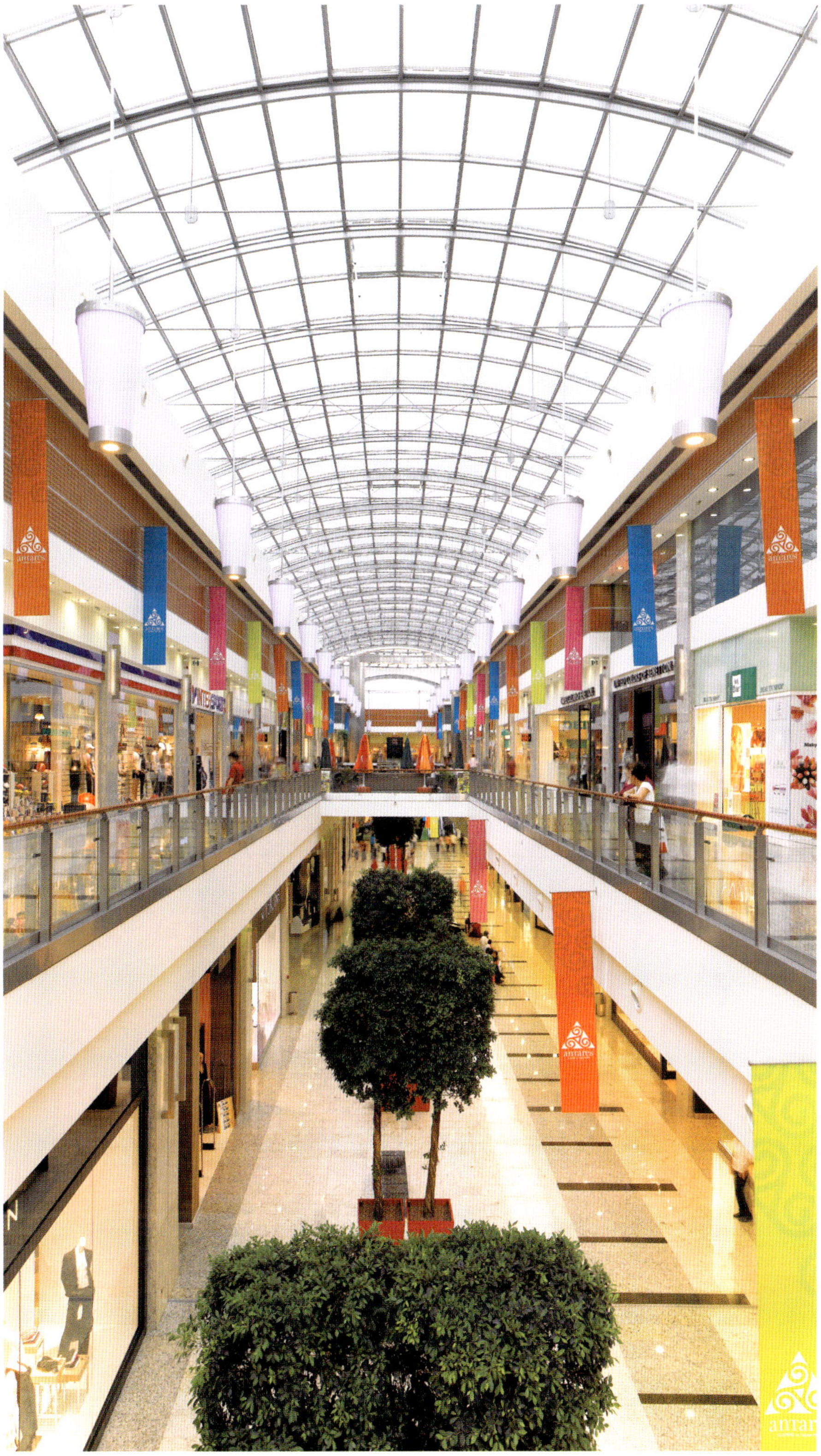

10

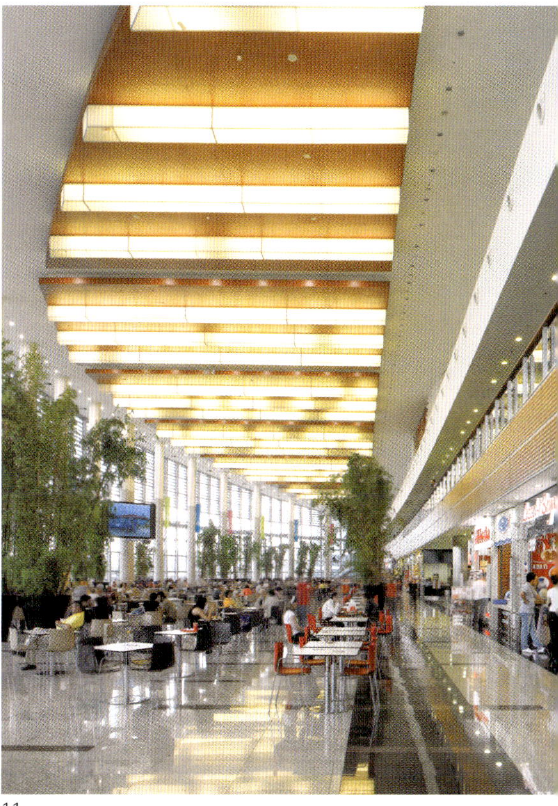

11

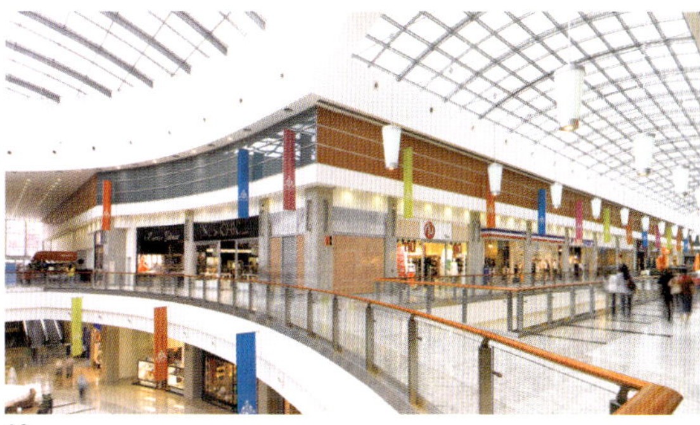

12

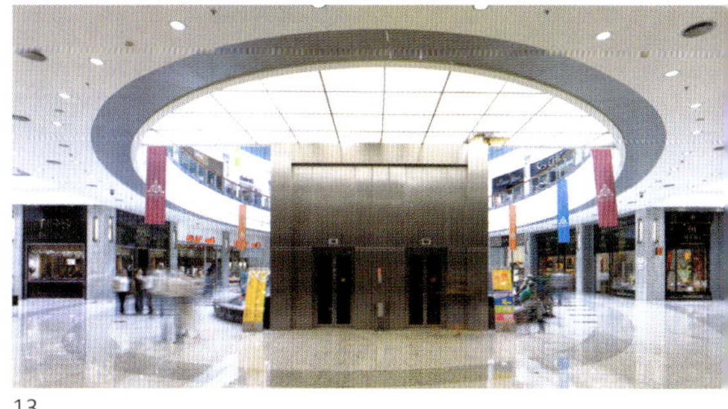

13

NATA Vega

Client NATA Group and MNM Eurasia Forest Foundation
Project Date 2008–2010
Area 184,510 m^2
Location Ankara
Structural Engineer Yüksek Project
Mechanical Engineer Metta Engineering
Electrical Engineer Akay Engineering
Landscaping Dalokay Design Studio
Leasing Consultant Jones Lang La Salle Turkey
Fire Consultant Alara Design and Engineering
Contractor NATA Group and MNM Eurasia Forest Foundation

This is a mixed-use, large-scale investment project on 50,000 square meters of land in Ankara's Mamak district. The first stage of the investment includes the NATA Vega and the Ankara Anatolium shopping mall buildings. These buildings are designed to include recreation areas, domestic and foreign commercial spaces, auto showrooms, food and beverage spaces, entertainment spaces, and movie theaters. Outdoor areas, parking spaces, green areas, and plazas unify the buildings within the complex.

Ankara Anatolium Shopping Mall will be home to the fifth Ikea in Turkey, a large home improvement and construction center, and other commercial spaces of various sizes.

NATA Vega contains exterior arrangements that create an avenue-like setting as well as indoor spaces. The shopping avenue can be accessed on various levels. The development includes an open bazaar designed for a variety of uses. A 360-degree aquarium and a restaurant have been designed for the section where the auto showroom is located. The fast-food level has outdoor patio areas and is also designed to be the cinema and entertainment floor. Natural stone, perforated aluminum composite plate, and glass are used in the construction.

1 Site model illustrating the complex including NATA Vega, Ankara Anatolium, IKEA, and the residential blocks
2 View from the main entrance showing the canopy and upper floor terrace

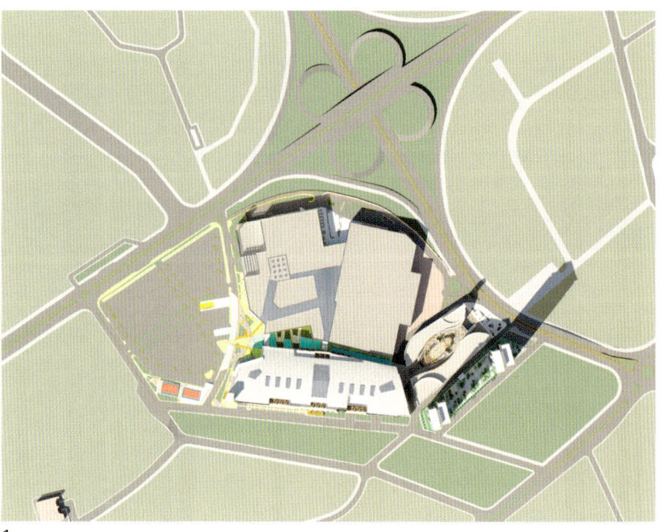

1

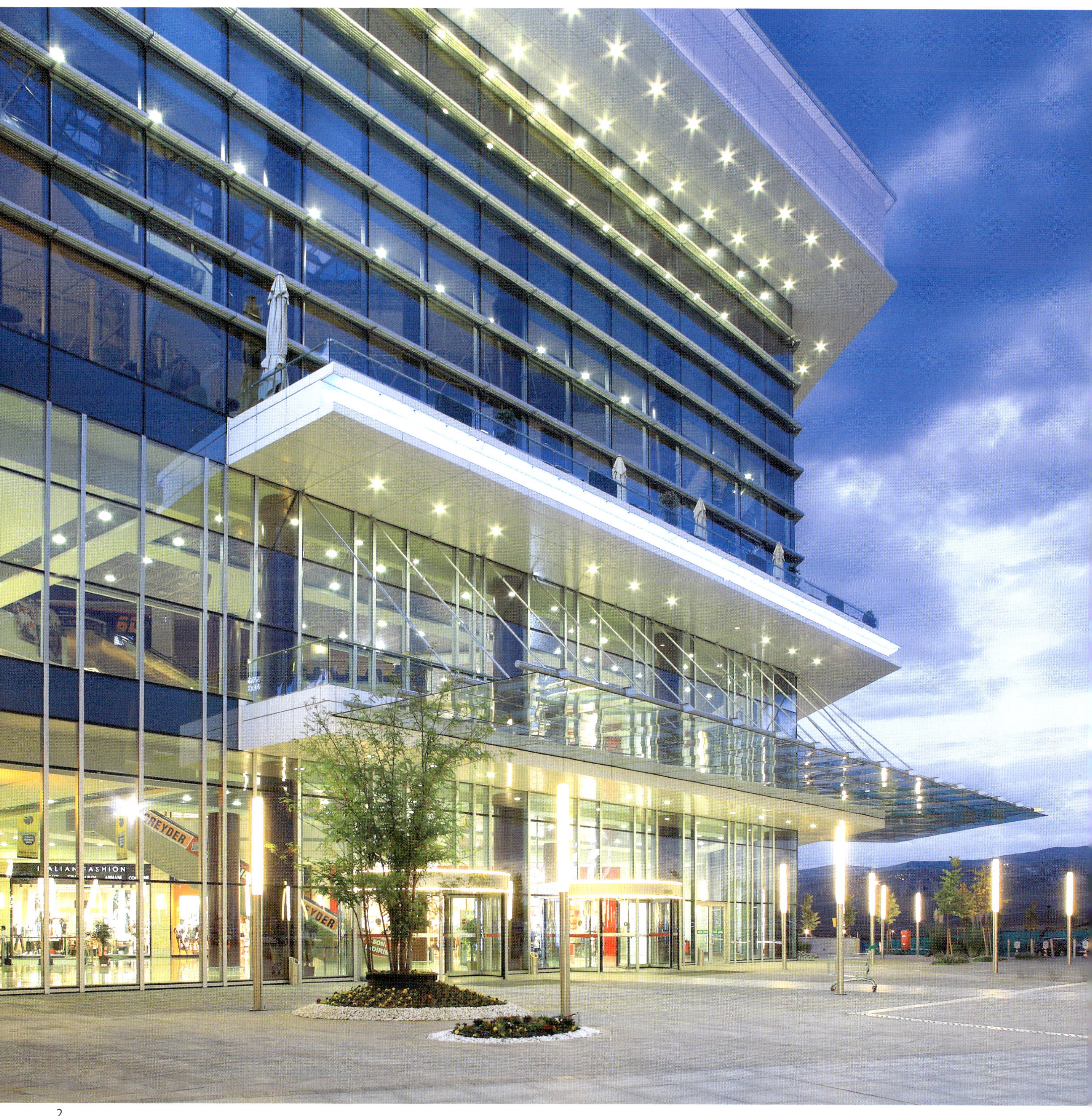

2

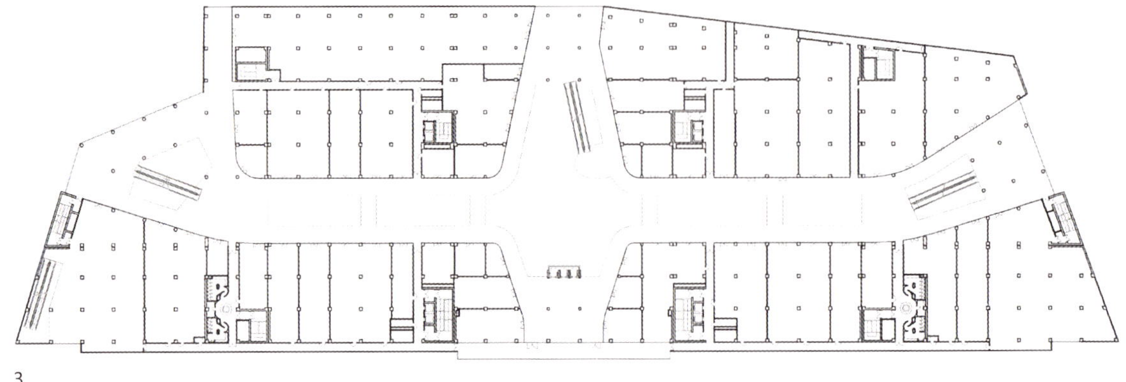

3

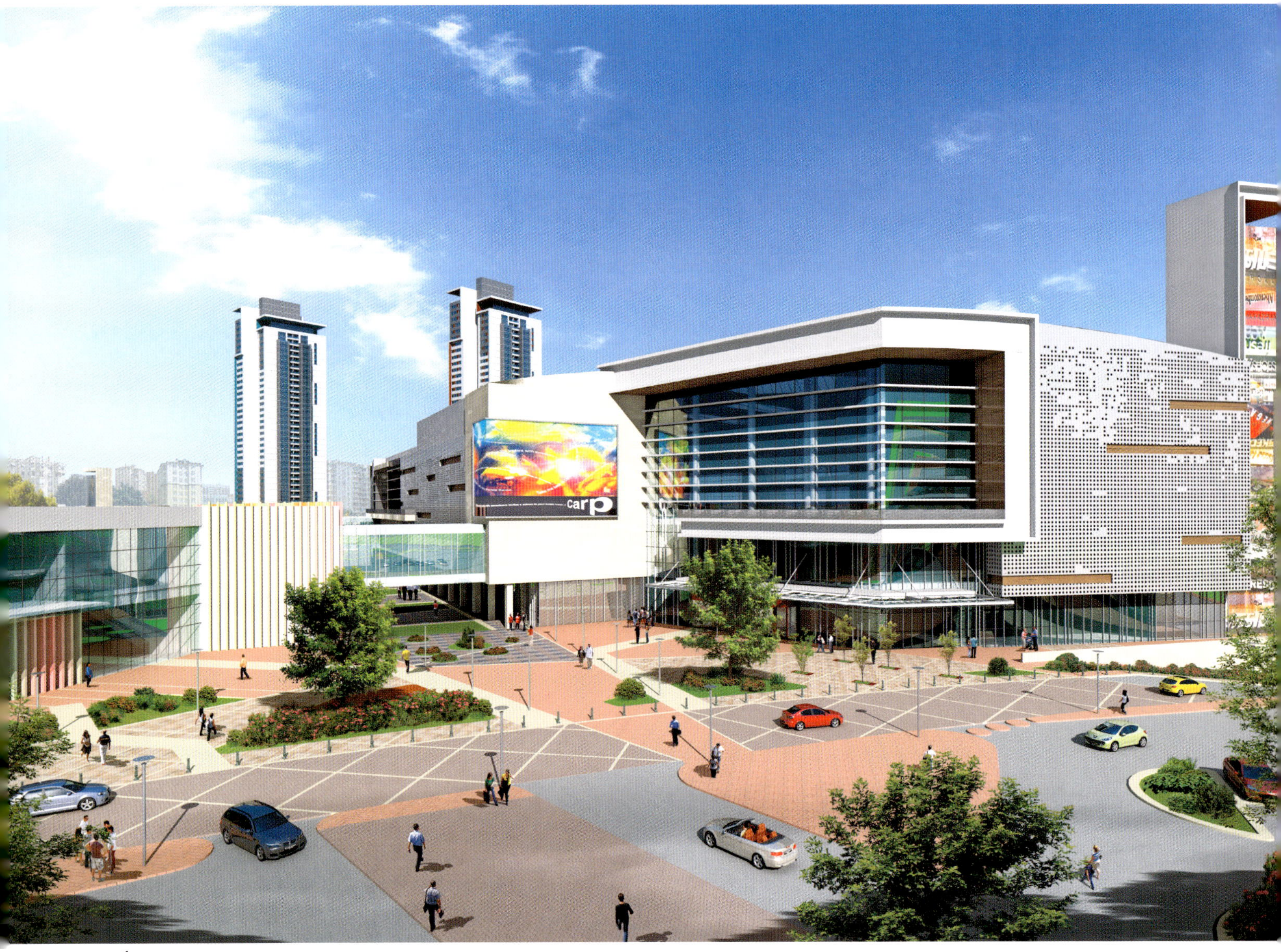

4

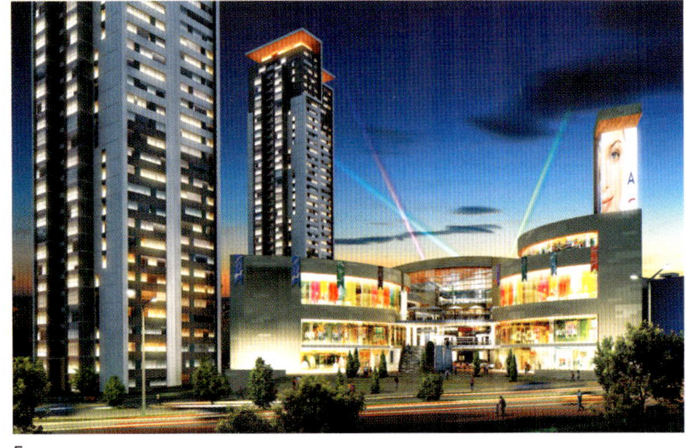

5

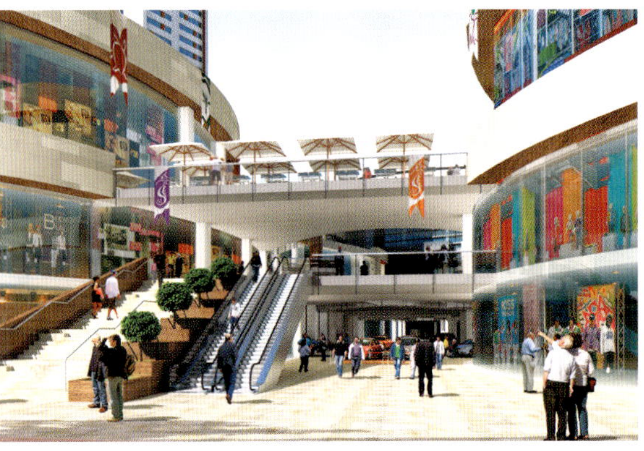

6

3 Floor plan
4 Model of the main entrance and the plaza
5 Rendering of the entrance and residential blocks at night
6 Model of the west entrance
7 Façade from the İmrahor Valley
8 Interior of the mall

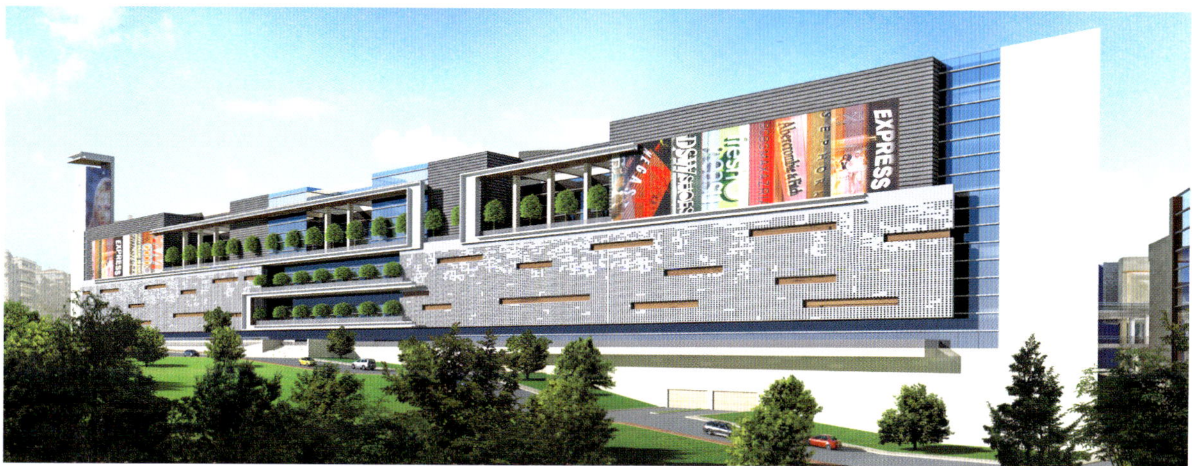

7

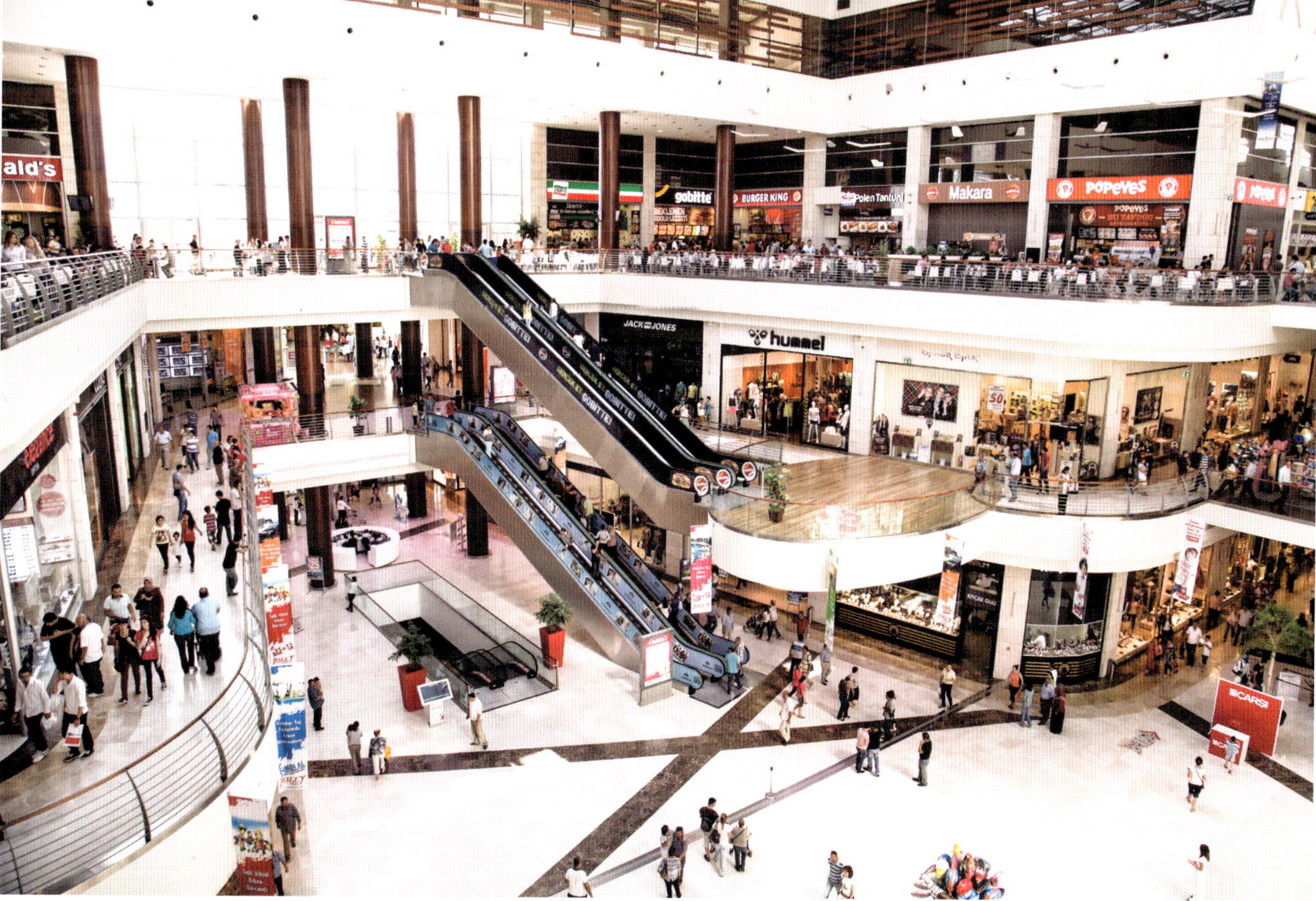

8

Kipaş Headquarters

Client Kipaş Holding
Project Date 2011
Area 12,840 m^2
Location Kahramanmaraş
Structural Engineer Yüksek Project
Mechanical Engineer Setes Engineering
Electrical Engineer Akay Engineering
Landscape Design Dalokay Design Studio

This proposal for a management building has been prepared for Kipaş Holding, a leading firm in the textile sector. The design's objective is to create a distinguished building among the factory buildings on the Maraş-Gaziantep road. The structure surrounding the building creates a symbolic empty space below—an urban balcony.

The main block has been designed with a showroom and a conference room on the ground floor, with offices and the management levels above. The showroom and the cafeteria open into the patio. The design of the building's façade takes the climate of Kahramanmaraş into consideration and, as a result, sunshades form the major elements of the façade's structure.

1 Site plan
2 Construction
3 Construction of the atrium
4 Rendering of the building at night
5 Typical floor plan
6 Detail of the steel structure

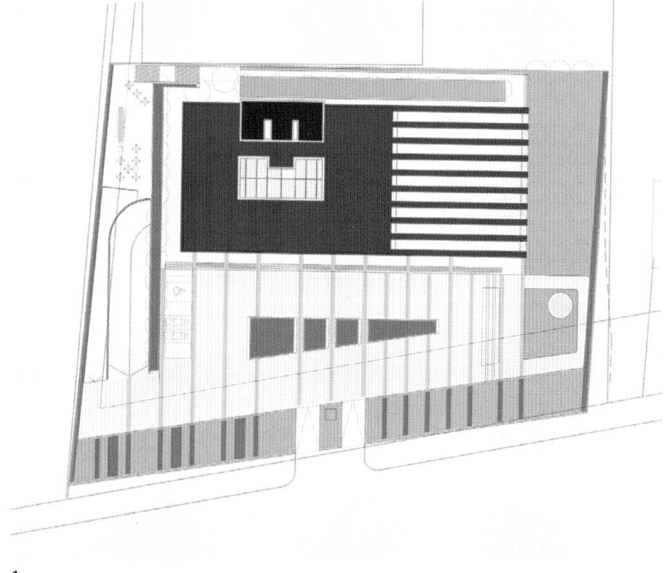

1

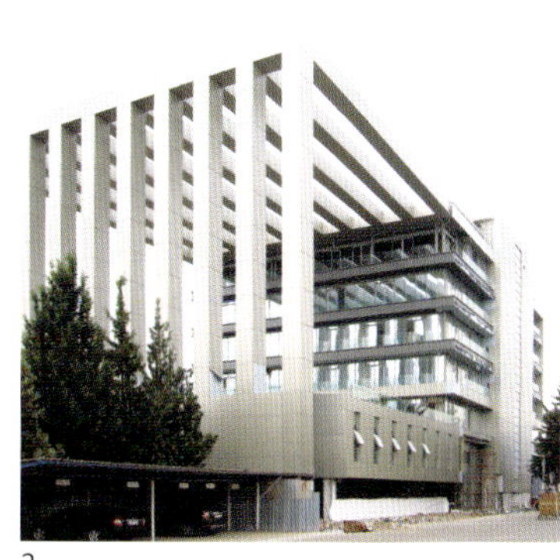
2

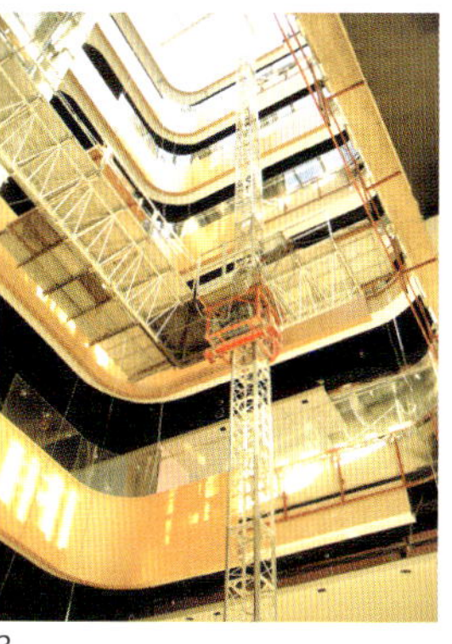
3

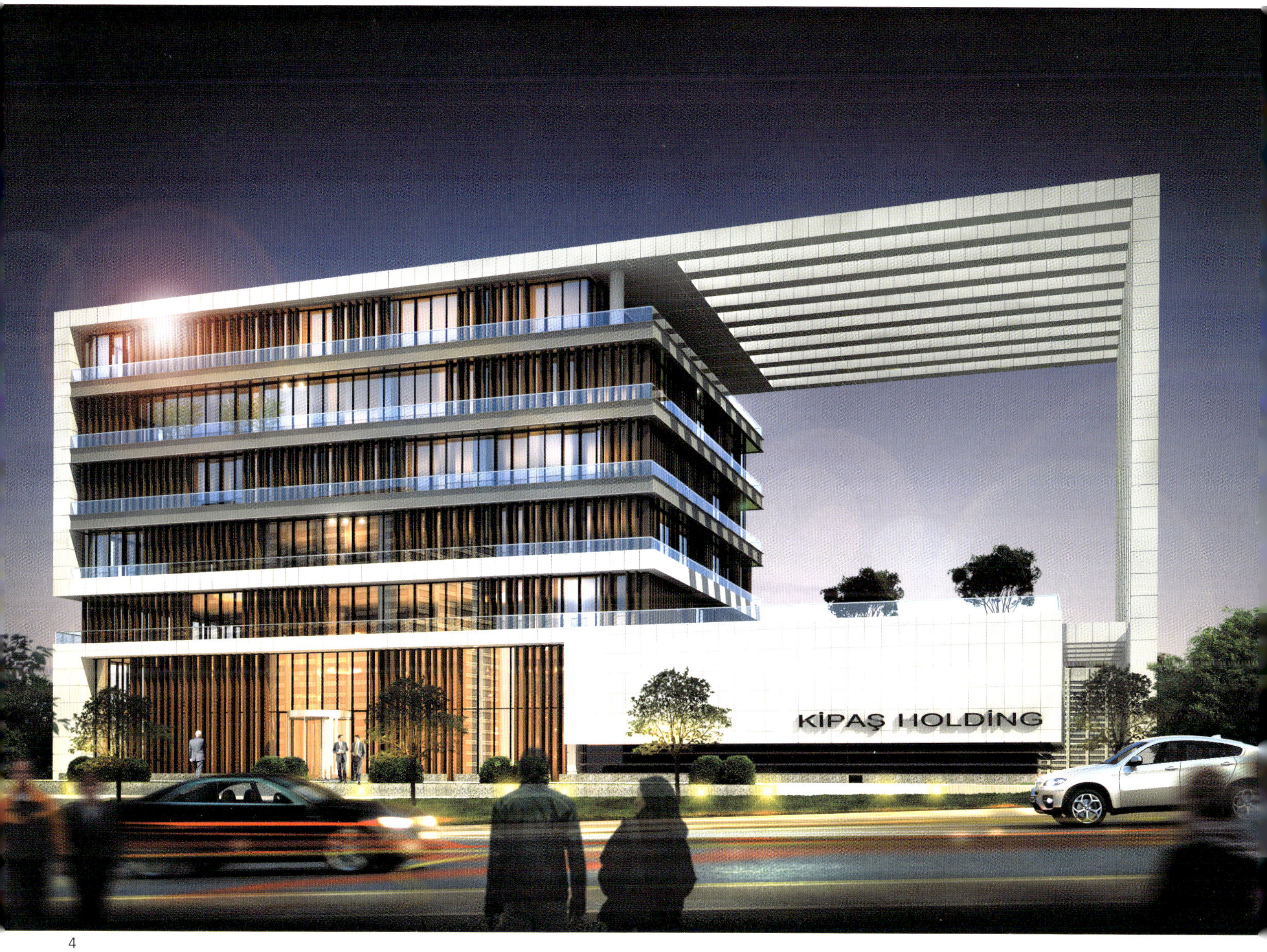

4

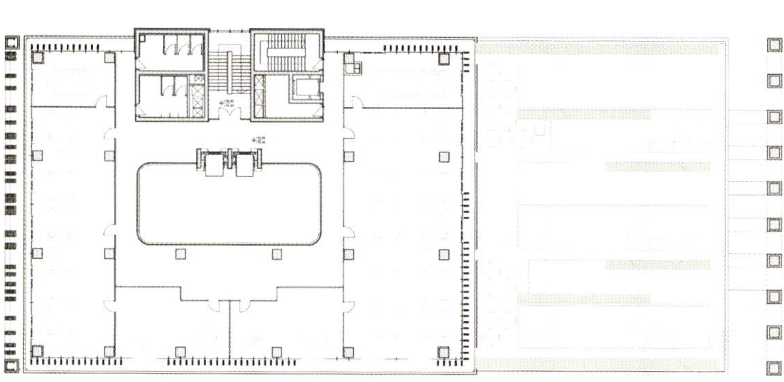
5

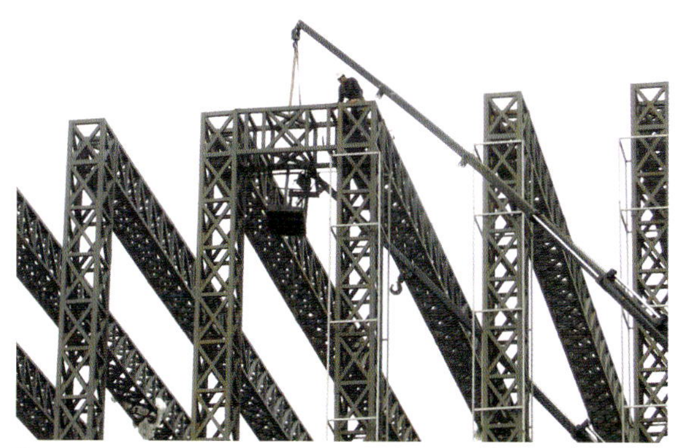
6

KOSGEB

Client KOSGEB (Republic of Turkey, Small and Medium Enterprises Development Organization)

Project Date 2010

Area 36,885 m^2

Location Ankara

Engineering Projects Aliş Project

Contractor Özoğuz Construction

The Administration for the Development Organization of Small and Medium Scale Enterprises (KOSGEB) Service Building project is located on the corner of Istanbul Avenue and Kazım Karabekir Avenue. The offices and service spaces and the social center, where the shared-use spaces are located, constitute the two major sections of the building.

The building program is categorized in order to simplify circulation. The official entrance is on Istanbul Avenue, while the staff and public entrances are on Kazım Karabekir Avenue. The conference room and meeting rooms can be accessed via the staff entrance.

The 20-story office and service building has a southwest and northeast orientation. Both façades provide daylight and airflow to the interior spaces and the service nodes are located on both sides of the building for a more efficient use of space. The office areas can be divided with mobile elements that are part of the façade system. Management offices are located on the top floors.

The low-rise block contains common areas such as the conference room, meeting rooms, library, cafeteria, and kindergarten. The cafeteria has a patio, allowing for outdoor dining. The indoor parking area and services are located below the ground level.

The materials used suit the simple and plain language of the design.

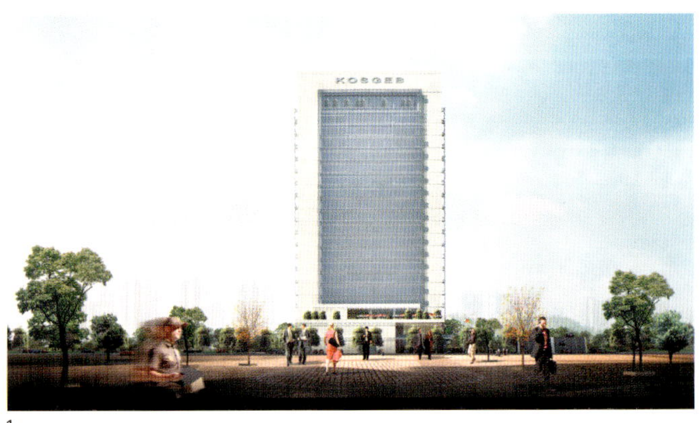

1

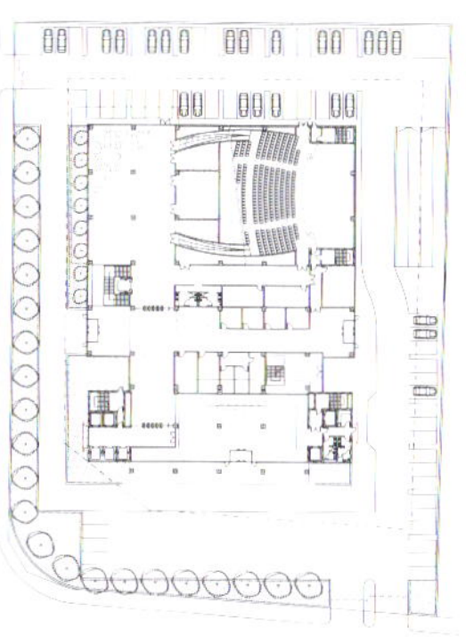

2

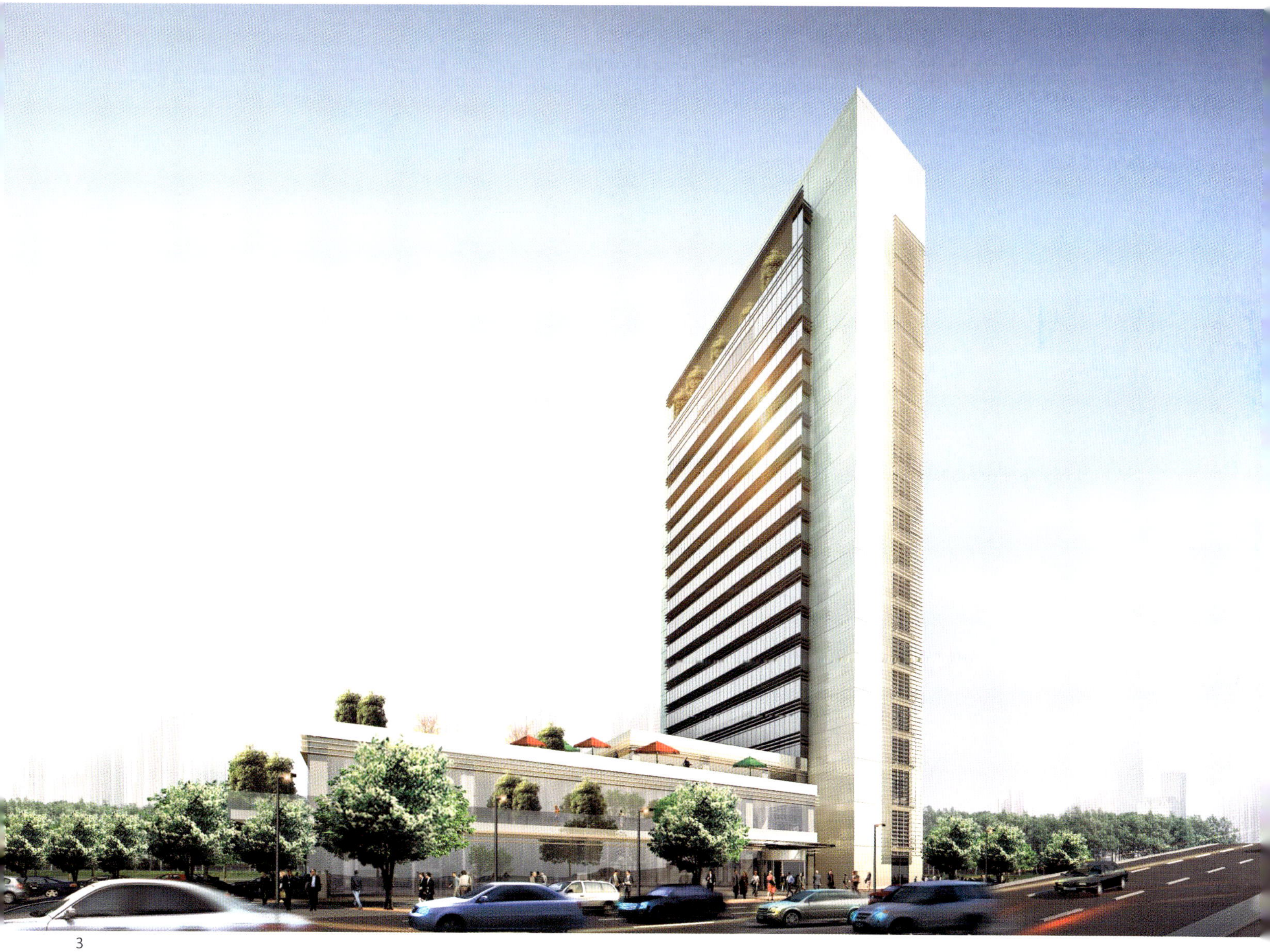

3

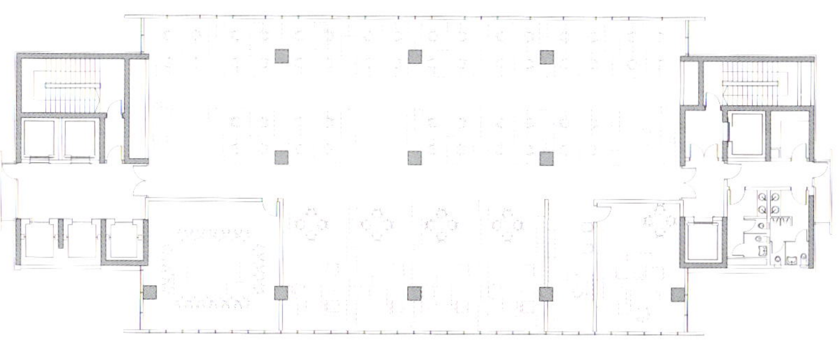

4

1 General view from Istanbul Avenue
2 Ground floor plan
3 General view from Kazım Karabekir Street
4 Typical floor plan

Kazıkiçi Bostanları Central Business District

Client İskitler Union of Building Cooperatives
Project Date 2008
Lot Area 640,000 m²
Location Ankara

The historical center of Ankara, Ulus, has deteriorated over time. Regenerating the historical identity and central quality of Ulus is one of Ankara's planning objectives. The Kazıkiçi Bostanları area located on the edge of the Ulus district will be transformed into a central business district. An urban design project has been created for the area, which will provide a framework for development plans and this was followed by the development of an organizational model. Property owners will be involved directly as investors in the project, with each building block designed to be developed by separate investor groups. Although the first stage of the project is restricted to the architectural scale, the fabric of the neighborhood and the development plan is designed comprehensively.

As opposed to the traditional urban fabric of small avenues and streets—a continuous main axis—an urban space has been constructed with the aim to define and enliven the space with horizontal and vertical variety among the blocks.

The client group is guided with suggestions concerning urban, social, cultural, and commercial functions to be located in the district. The overall plan includes not only business functions, but also cultural, social, and recreational uses, which are necessities of urban life. This project is experimenting with new building programs that combine private and public spaces and the building fabric and urban design will be open to uses such as office buildings, hotels, boulevard shops independently accessible from the outside, bookstores, cafés, and restaurants. Development in the area will be realized in stages. The circulation within the district is pedestrian oriented and supported with public transport facilities.

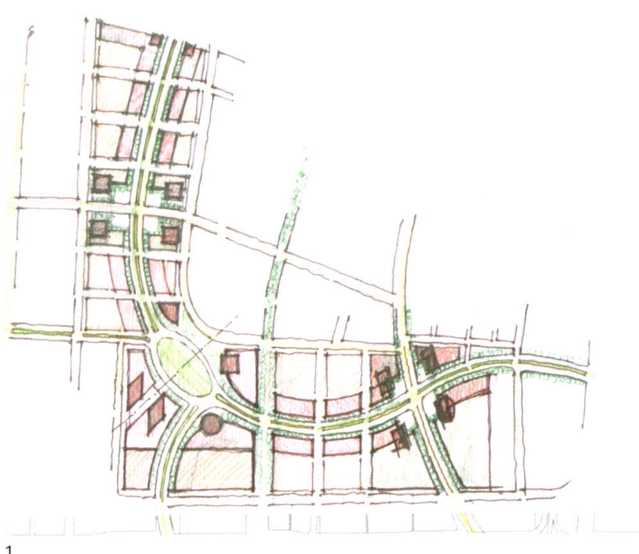

1

1 Sketch by Ali Osman Öztürk
2 Silhouette model of the buildings as seen from Kazım Karabekir Street
3 Rendering of the pedestrian street at night
4 Rendering of the pedestrian street during the day
5 Bird's-eye view of the settlement

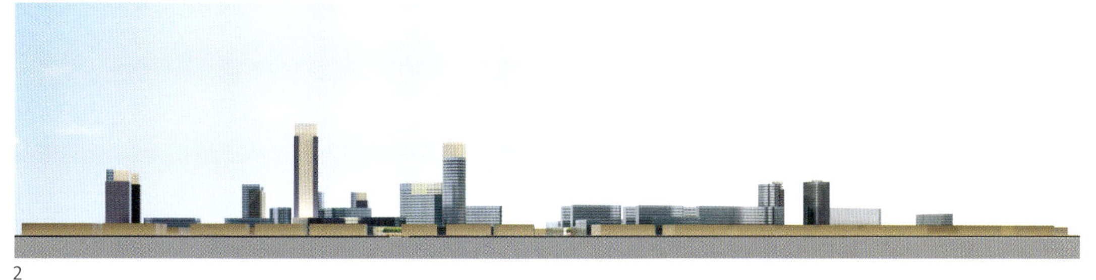
2

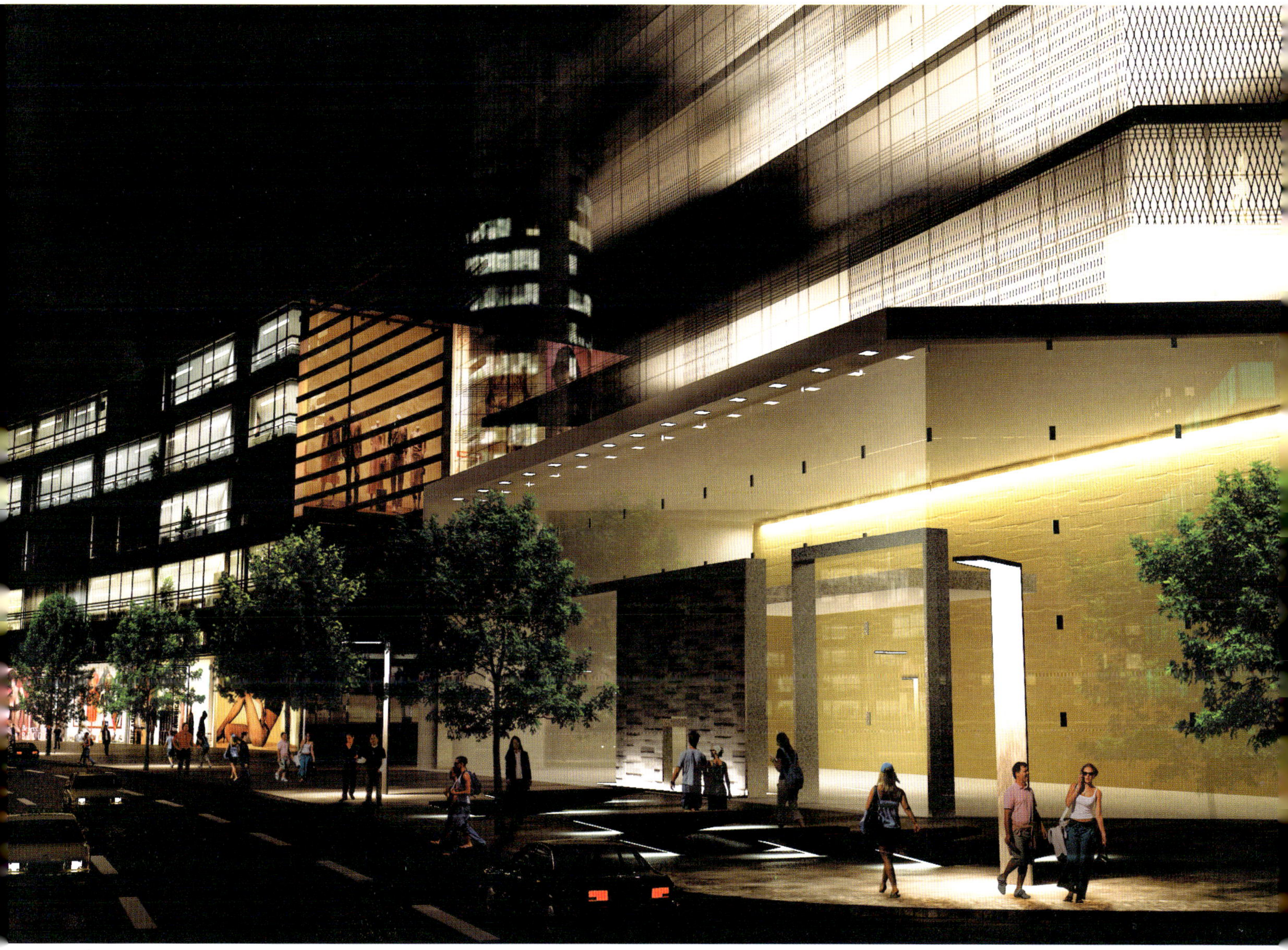

3

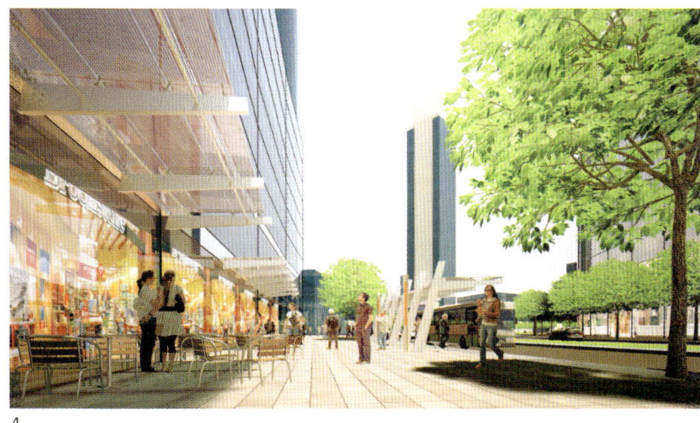
4

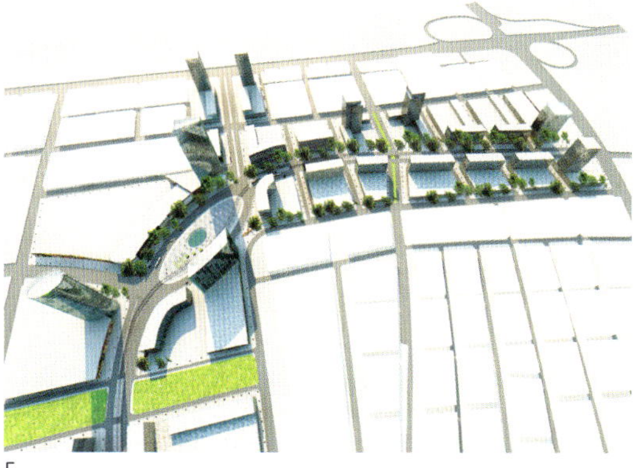
5

Metroport

Client Mutlu Evren Construction
Project Date 1998–2008
Area 100,000 m^2
Location İstanbul
Structural Engineer Yüksek Project
Mechanical Engineer Çilingiroğlu Engineering
Electrical Engineer Elsan Electricity
Interior Design Dara Kızıltoprak
Contractor Mutlu Evren Construction

Located in the Şirinevler neighborhood, Metroport Bakırkoy is a special station structure to be connected with the subway line. For this mixed-use building program, three separate blocks were designed for the shopping mall, residential units, and the hospital.

The purpose of the dominant arch used in the design is to create the perception of a dynamic structure from different points of view. The volumes created by the arches in the geometric arrangement of the masses located within the confines of the property form a mixed building group. Both its silhouette and its open spaces create a continuum with the urban fabric.

One of the high-rise blocks is a residential, while the other is a hospital and the shopping mall is situated between the two blocks. During the construction process, particular details unique to this structure were developed. Exclusive brick dimensions and horizontal and vertical aluminum elements were designed for the exterior façades.

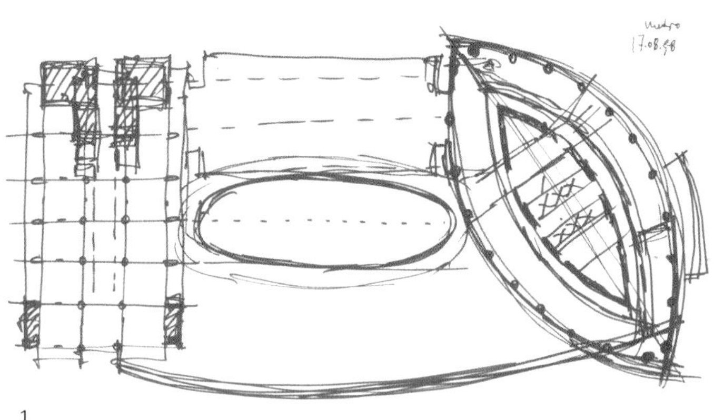

1

1 Sketch by Ali Osman Öztürk
Opposite:
View of the hospital

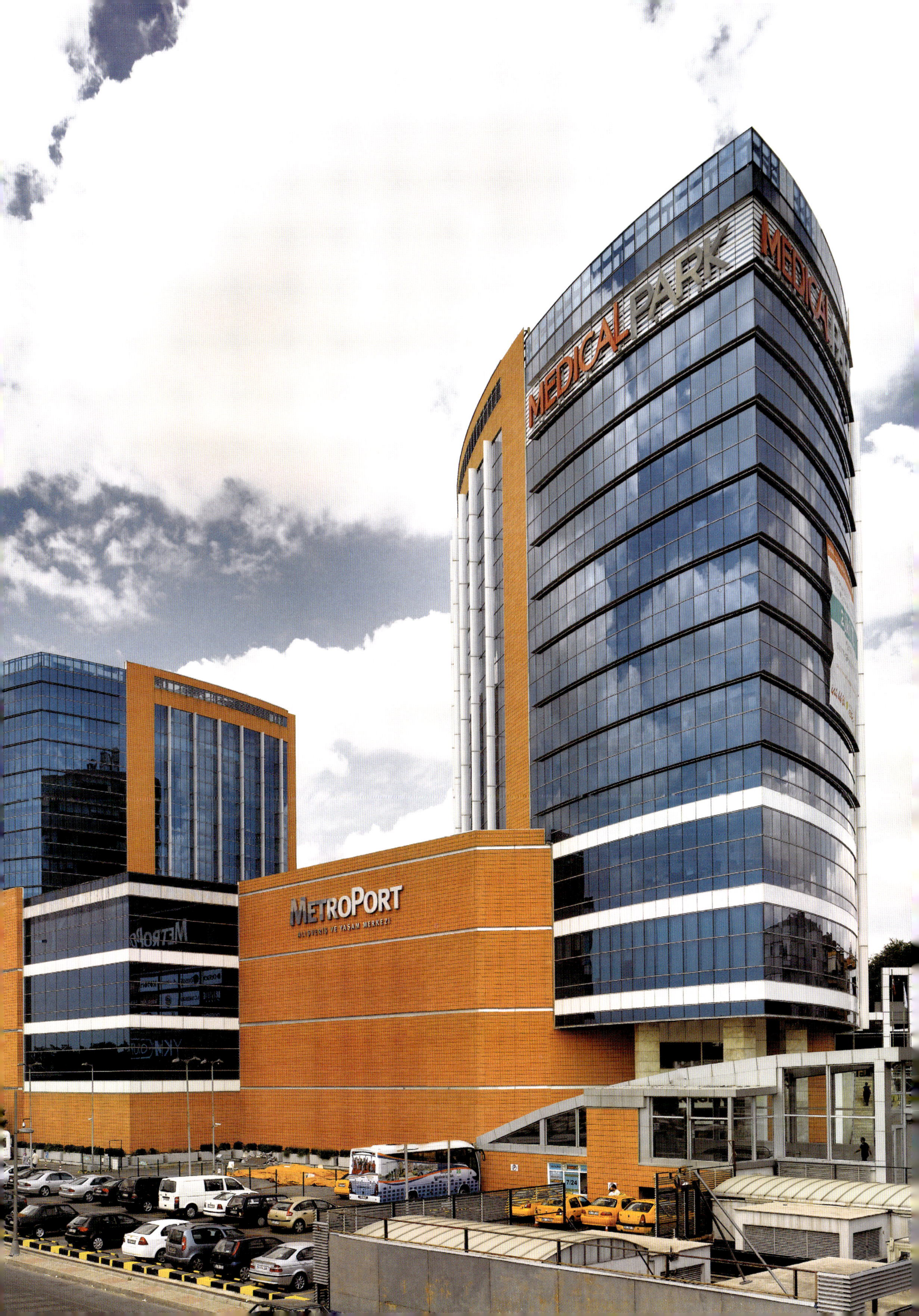
MEDICAL PARK
METROPORT
7/24

3 Sketch of the ground floor plan by Ali Osman Öztürk
4 General view
5 Main entrance
6 Façade detail
7,8 Alternative sketch of the fast food area and movie theater by Ali Osman Öztürk
9 Interior view of the mall
10 Entrance hall of the studio apartments
11 Interior view of the studio apartments
12 Interior view of the circulation halls
13 Interior view

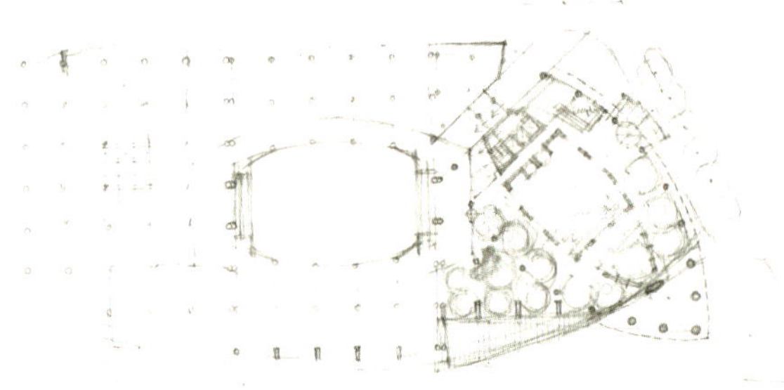

3

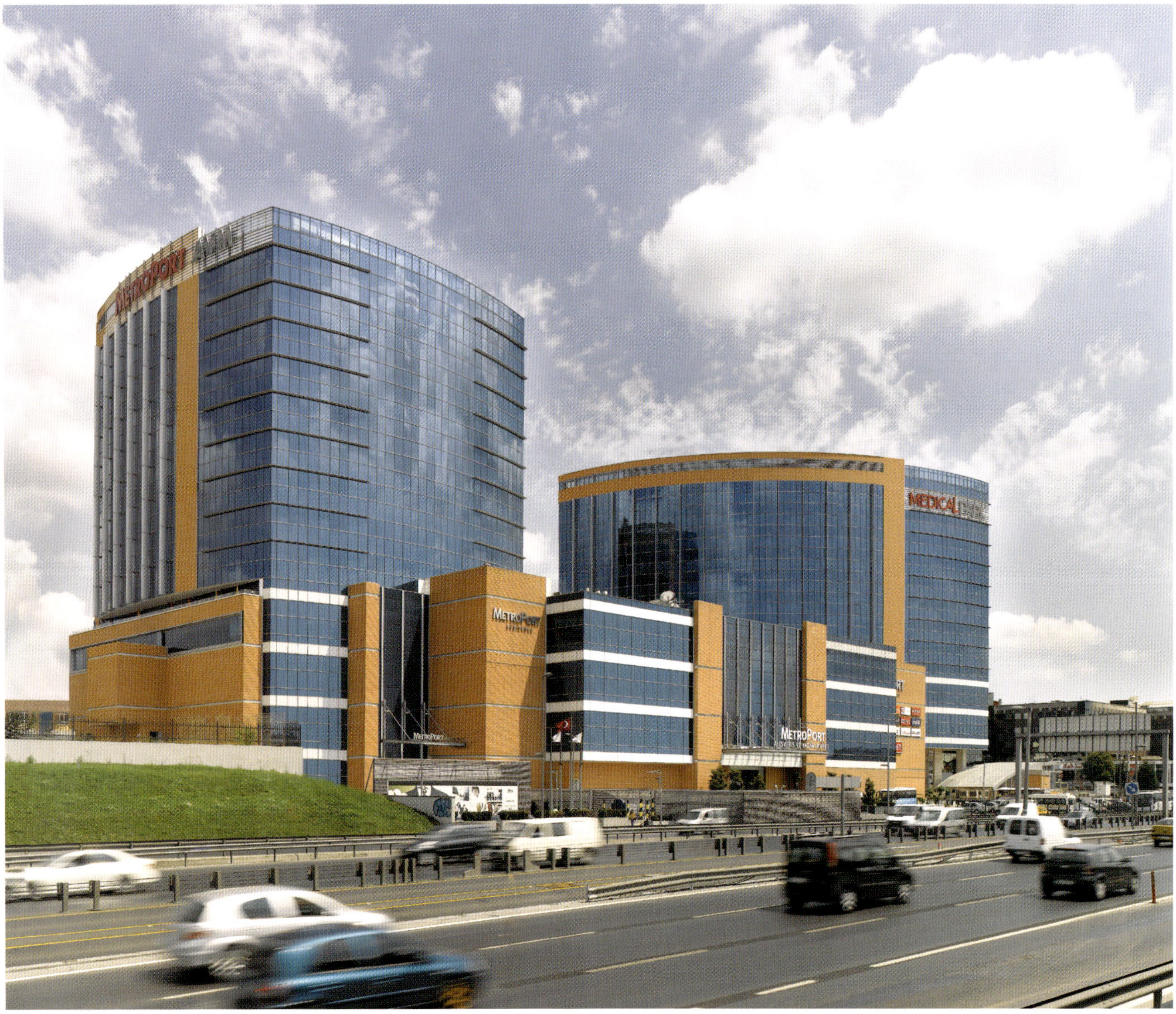

4

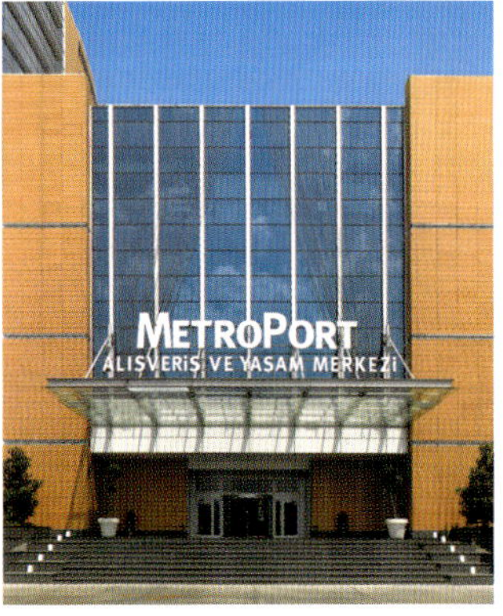

5

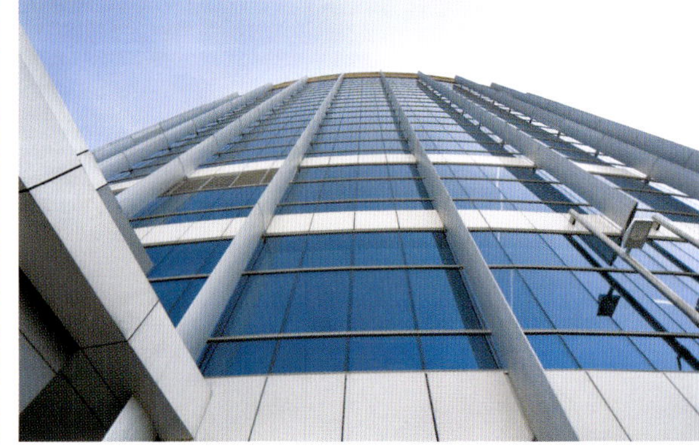

6

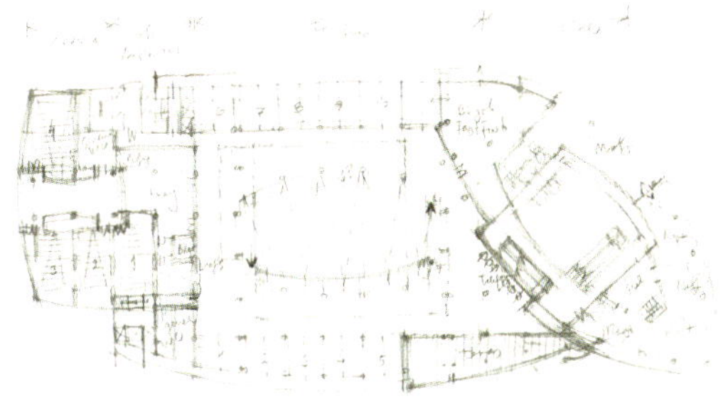
7

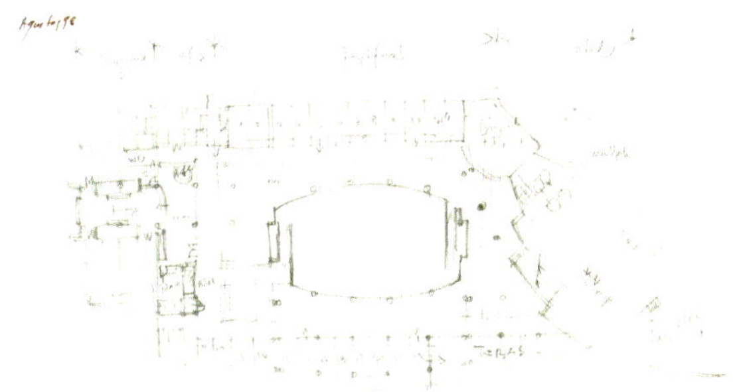
8

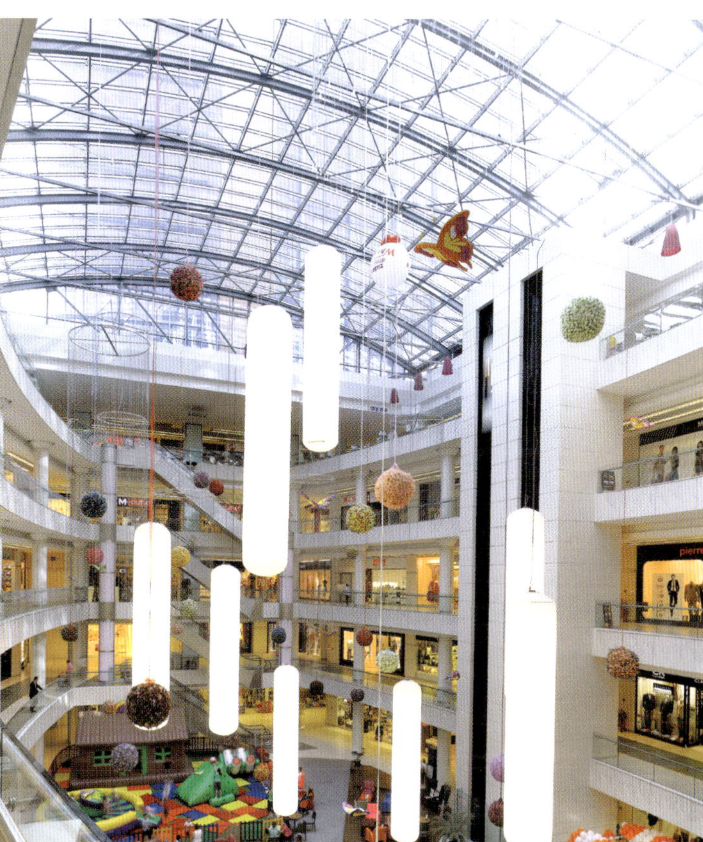
9

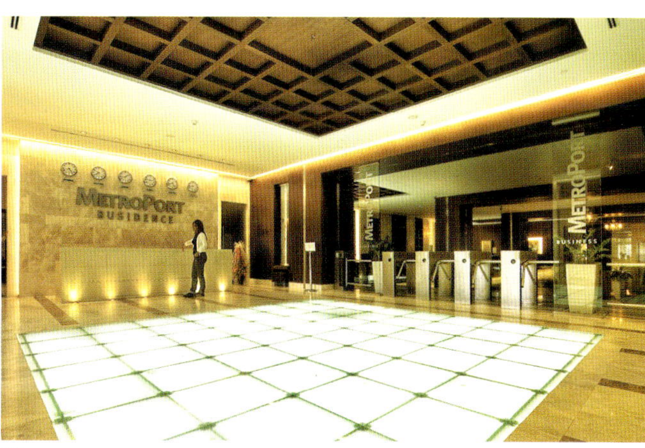

10

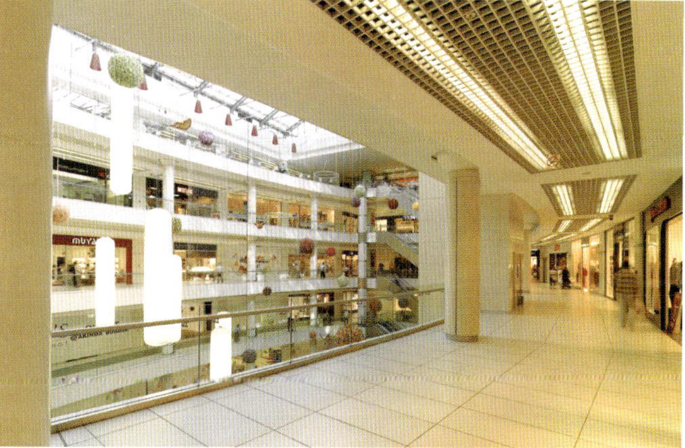
11

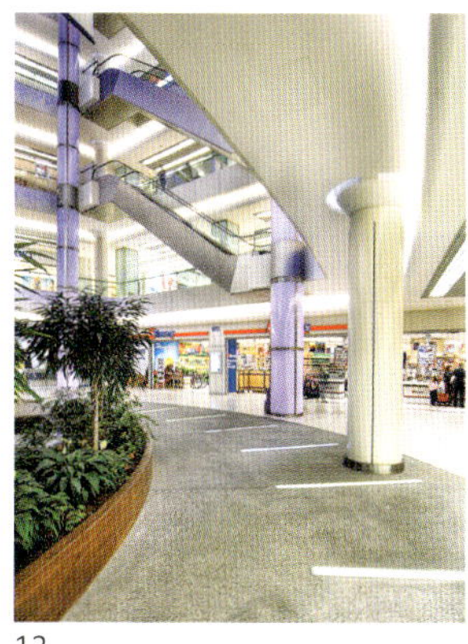
12

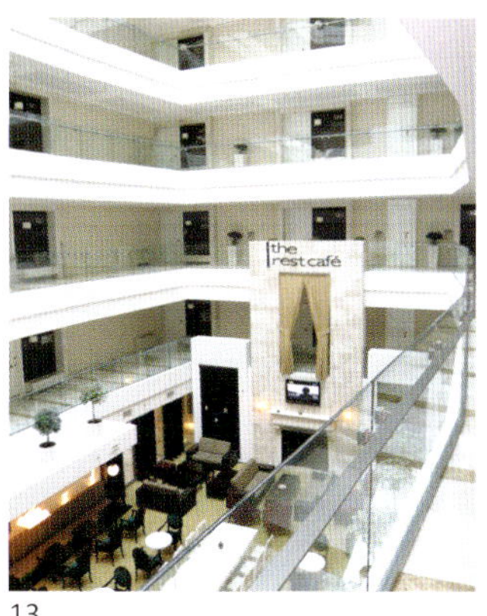

13

Via/Port

Client Bayraktar Construction

Project Date 2004–2007

Area Outlet 90,000 m^2, Convention and Exhibition Center 120,000 m^2, Hotel 42,000 m^2

Location İstanbul

Structural Engineer Yüksek Project

Mechanical Engineer BTC Engineering

Electrical Engineer BTC Engineering

Contractor Bayraktar Construction

2009 AMPD Foundation for Shopping Malls and Retailers Mall of the Year

2010 ICSC Finalist

2010 Cityscape Abu Dhabi Best Commercial/Retail Project Category Finalist

Via/Port is located on a plot that constitutes a virtual gateway in the Pendik-Kartal area, an increasingly important part of Istanbul. Via/Port is a multipurpose complex designed to appeal to a variety of groups. It contains facilities for exhibitions and conventions, a hotel, and an outlet center. Seen as a secondary urban center, the open spaces in the project have directly determined the overall design, and the commercial areas that constitute the majority of the design are located in a street setting. The largest outlet in Turkey and Europe at the time of its construction, Via/Port Outlet was designed as a multi-functional urban recreation area, able to accommodate visitors for long periods of time.

The open areas host elements such as a pond, green areas, playgrounds, fast food facilities, and restaurants. As a unique application, the outlet design includes a covered bazaar while the basement floor hosts a 12,000-square-meter food market and a 5,000-square-meter electronics market. The five-star hotel located within the complex is designed for conventions, fairs, as well as providing facilities for the shopping outlets.

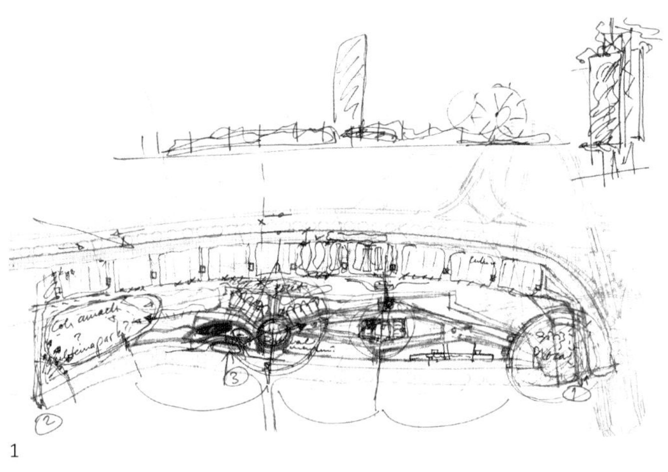

1

1 Sketch by Ali Osman Öztürk

Opposite:

General view of the pedestrian areas

Following pages:

Amusement park in front of Via/Port at night

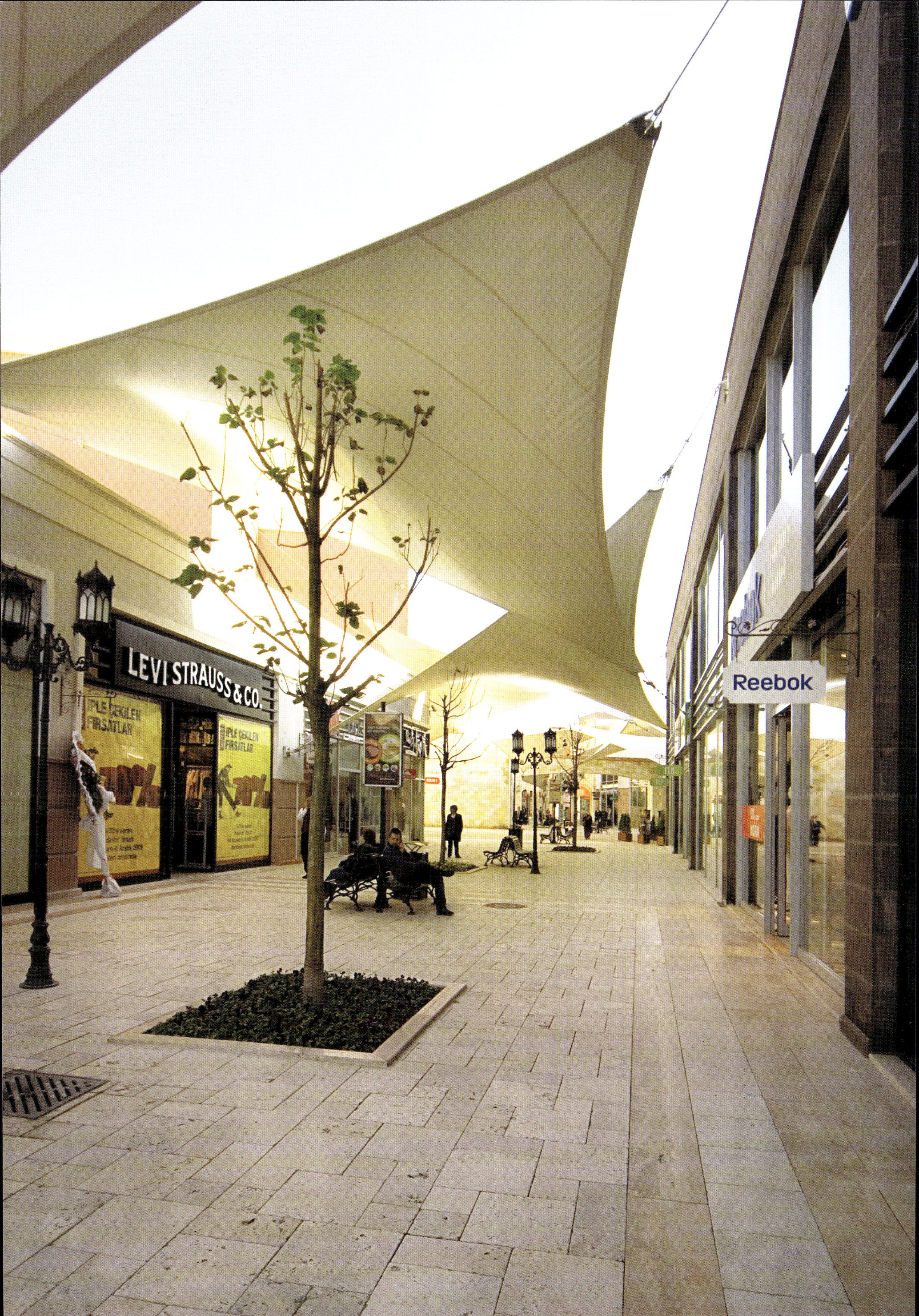
LEVI STRAUSS & CO.
İPLE ÇEKİLEN
FIRSATLAR
Reebok

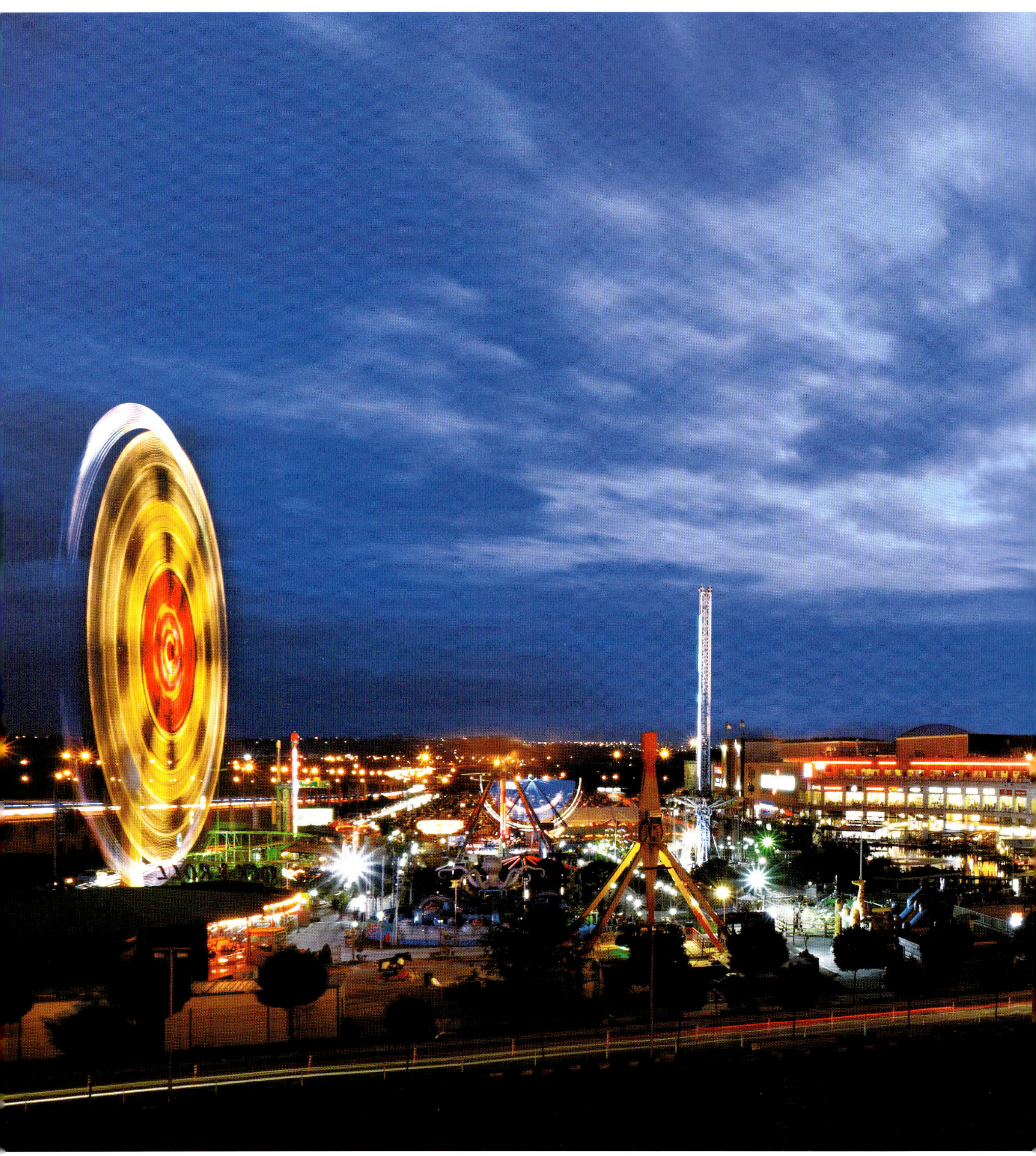

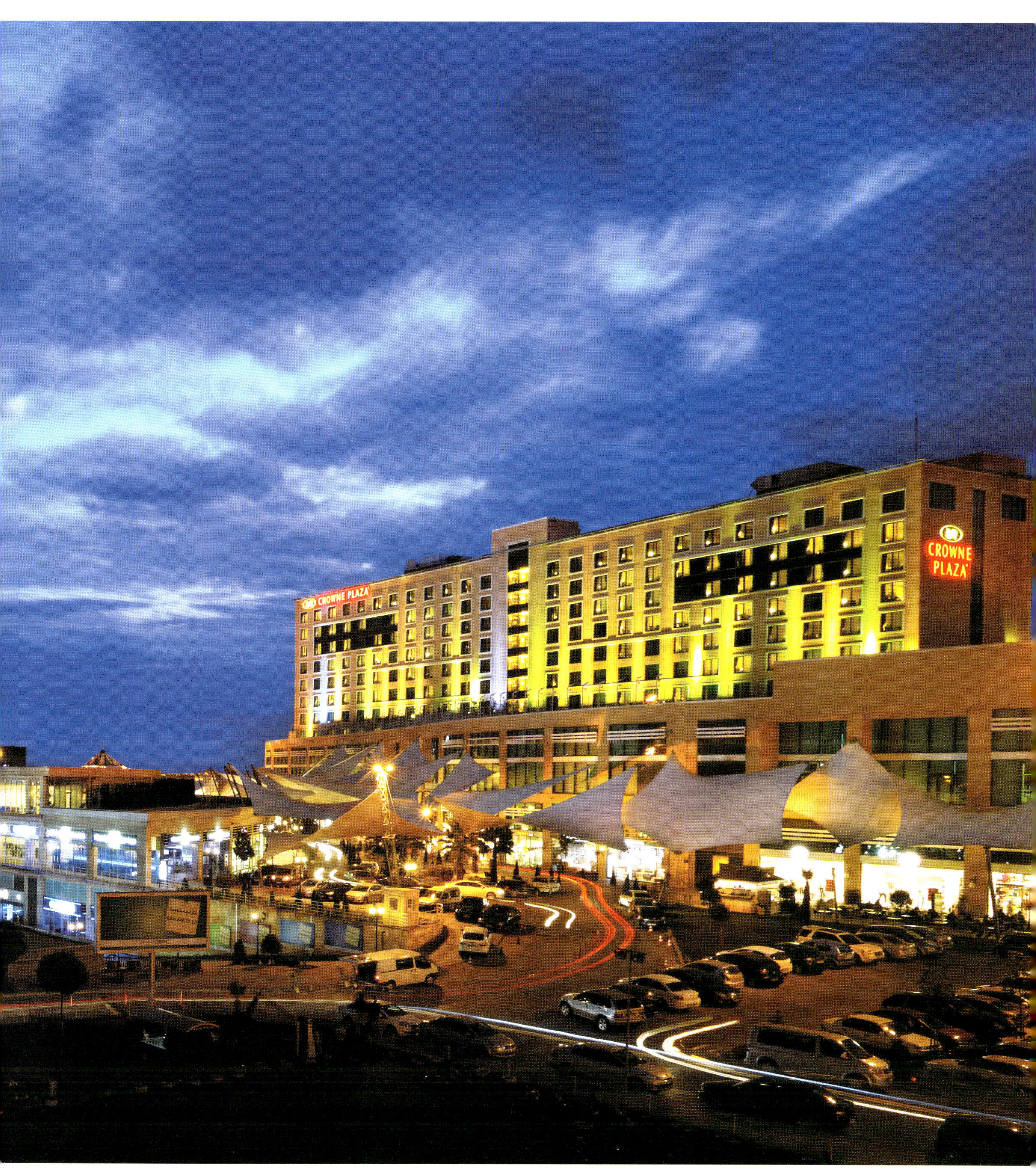
CROWNE PLAZA
CROWNE PLAZA

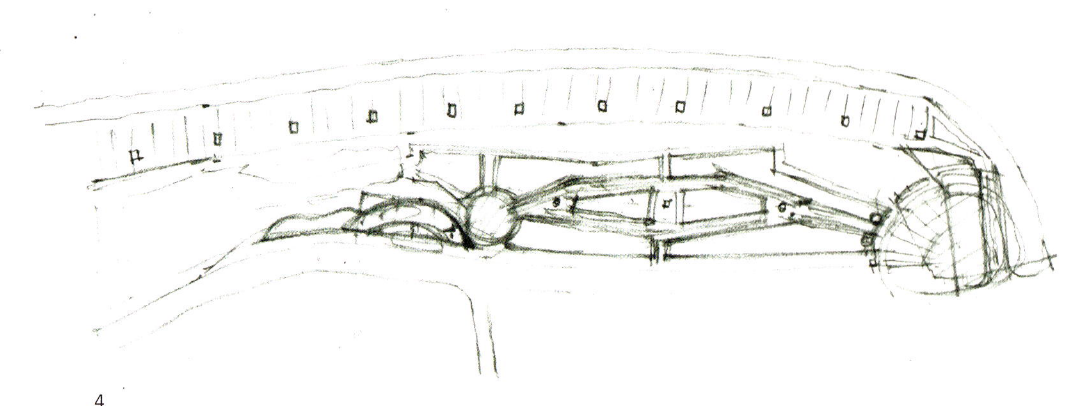

4

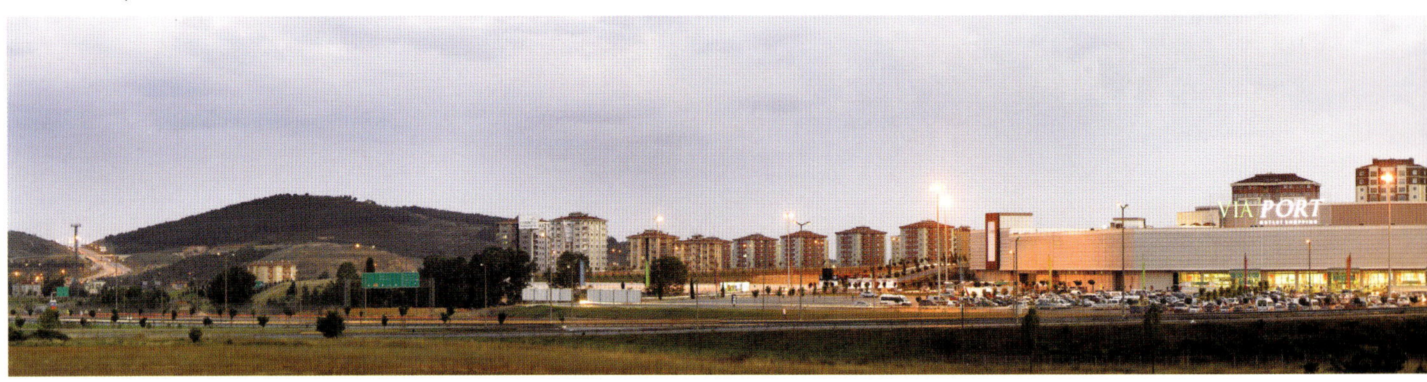

5

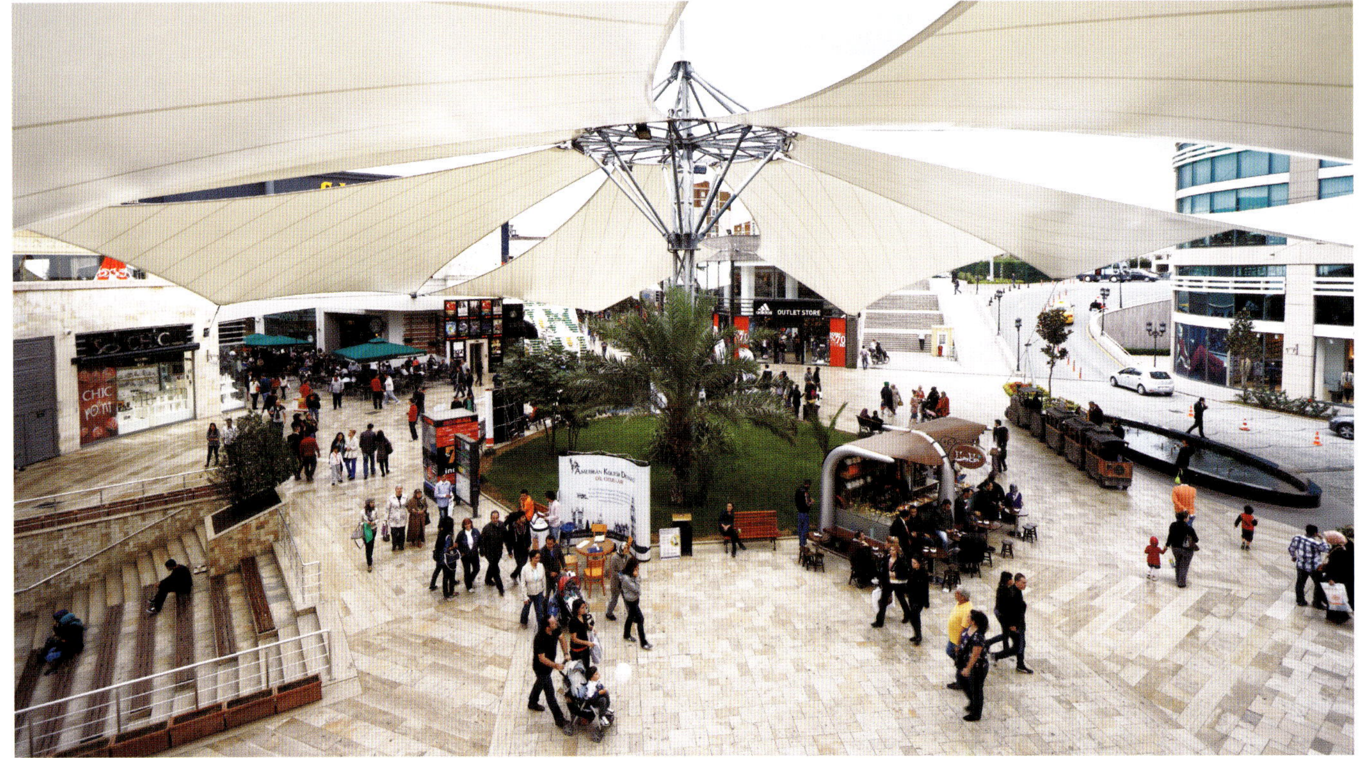

6

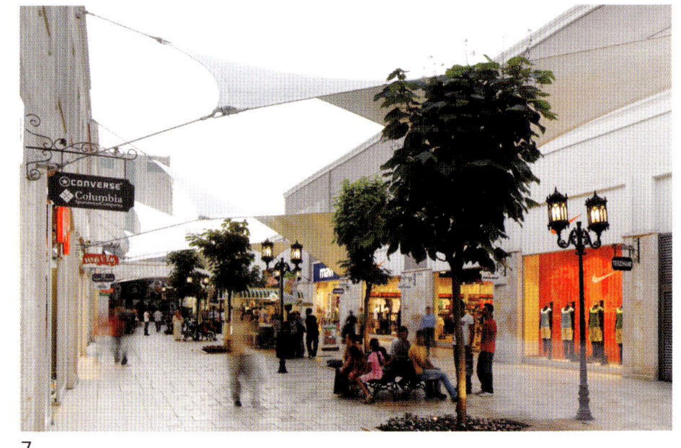

7

4 Concept sketch of the general layout by Ali Osman Öztürk
5 Panoramic view of the complex
6 The plaza in front of Via/Port Hotel
7 General view of one of the pedestrian streets with shops and rest areas
8 Detail of the outdoor aisle tents
9–11 View of the outdoor shopping areas

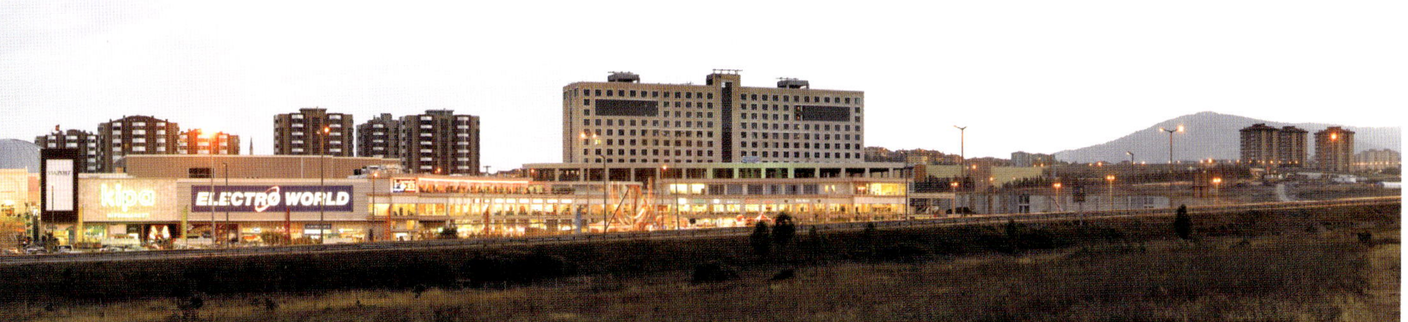

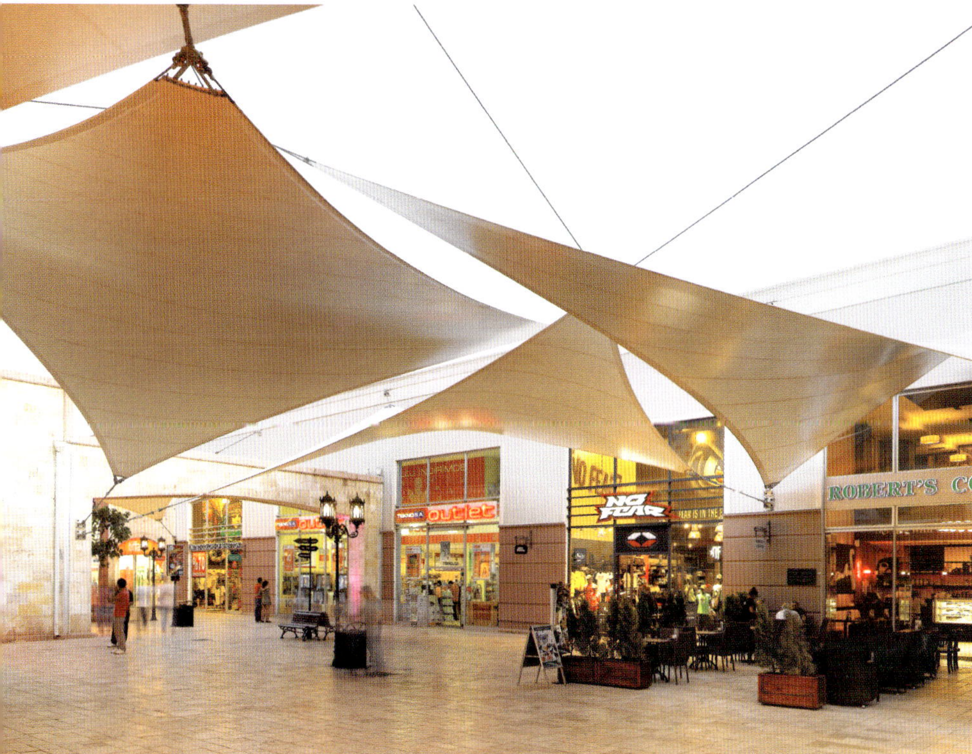

8

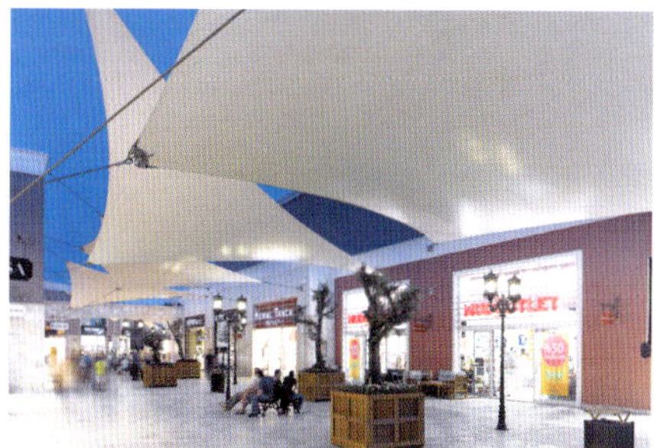

9

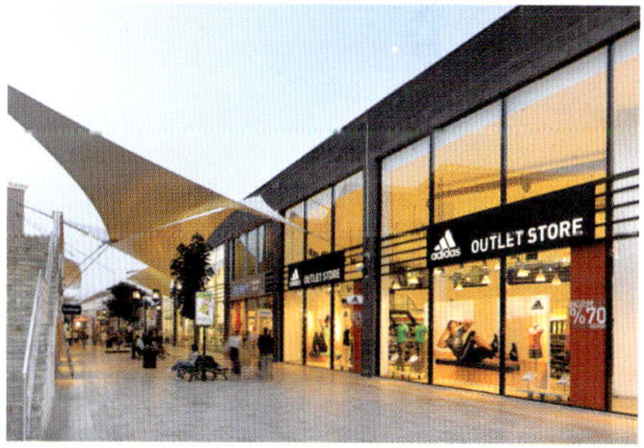

10

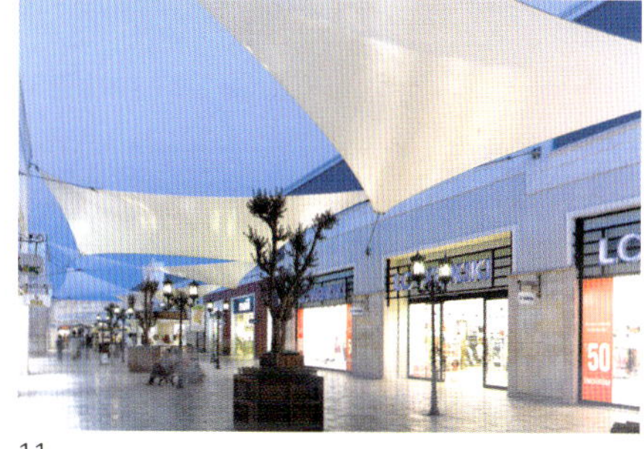

11

Ziraat Bank Kadıköy Branch

Client Ziraat Bank General Directorate
Project Date 2004
Area 4,000 m^2
Location İstanbul
Structural Engineer Yüksek Project
Mechanical Engineer Okutan Engineering
Electrical Engineer Akay Engineering

The Kadıköy branch of the Ziraat Bank is located on a corner site of adjacent buildings behind the Kadıköy pier, facing the Kadıköy coast and the view of the historic peninsula. The design work for the branch office began in May 2004 with an effort to renovate the branch according to contemporary requirements and bring together the dispersed units of the bank.

As per the building program, branch office units are located on the ground floor of the building and remaining offices are on the upper levels. Contrary to the conventional design of banks, which favor the use of solid, massive surfaces, this design emphasizes transparency. The aim was to achieve a building where the façade complements the existing urban fabric of Kadıköy and is not hostile to its environment without compromising its originality. The structural system, which shaped the design and forms the backbone of the building, continues along the existing arcade on the Rıhtım Avenue and alludes to conventional designs of bank buildings.

Building codes restricted the height of the building to 21 meters, and a maximum number of stories were required within this limit. To provide interior spaces with plenty of daylight and access to the panoramic view, the façade was clad with floor-to-ceiling glass panels on each level. All mechanical equipment was placed in suspended ceilings and elevated floors.

The design provides bank employees with the widest possible view of the Kadıköy pier, the historic peninsula, and the historic Haydarpaşa train station.

Various types of glass that change according to their color and lucidity were used on the different orientations of the façade, while the structural system that continues onto the façade was covered with white opaque glass. Unique details were developed on the columns to apply lighting fixtures to illuminate the façade at night.

This building represents an attempt to design a contemporary building within an authentic historical context.

Opposite:
View from Rıhtım Avenue

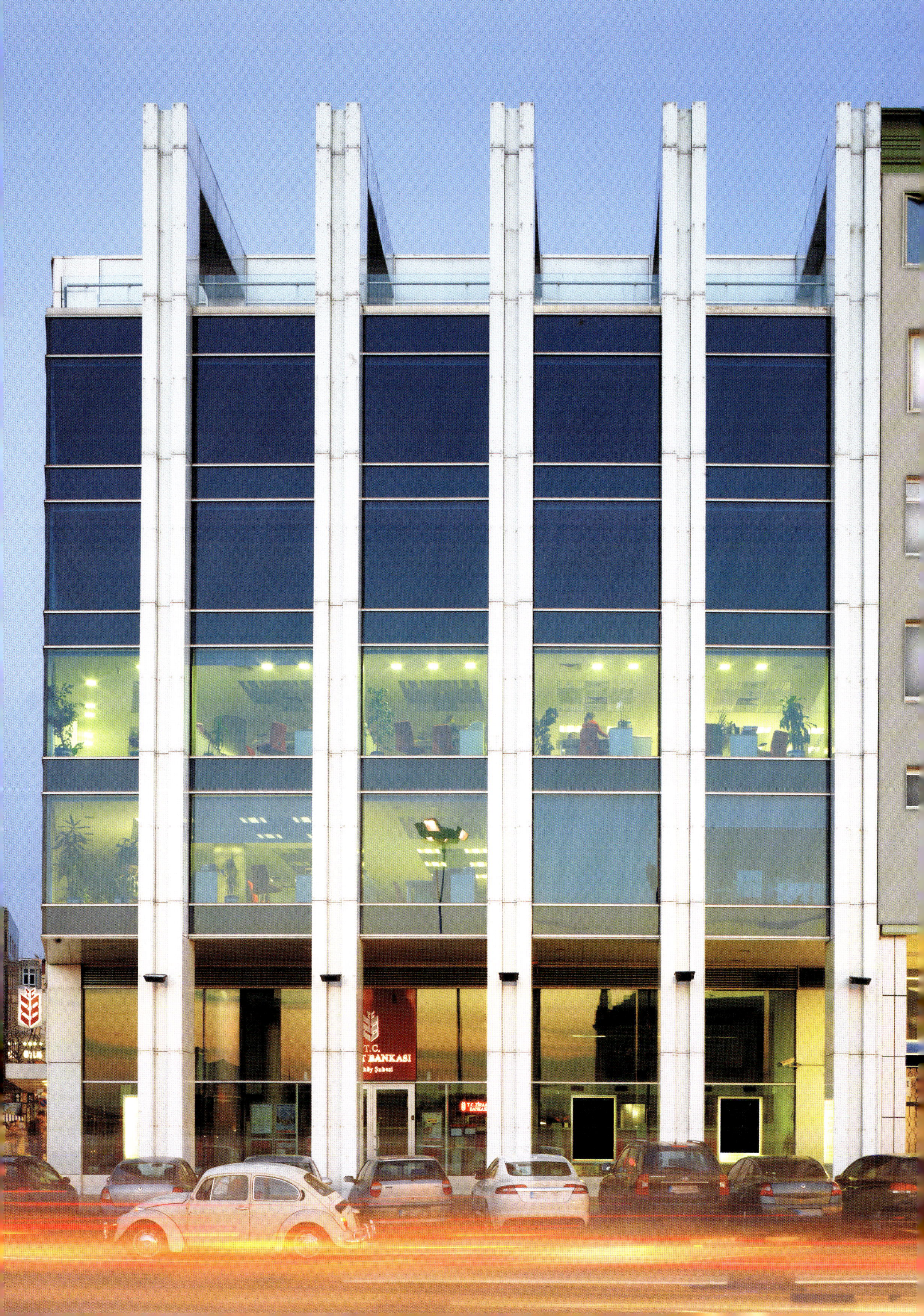
T.C.
BANKASI

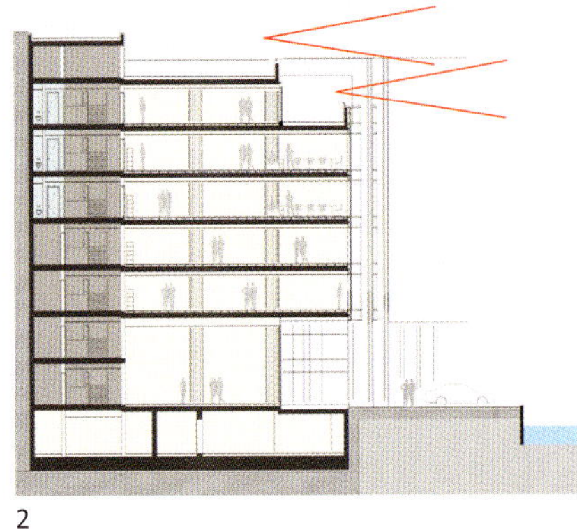
2

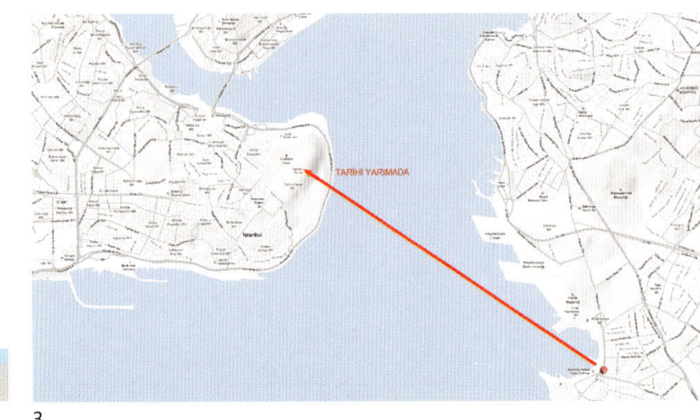

3

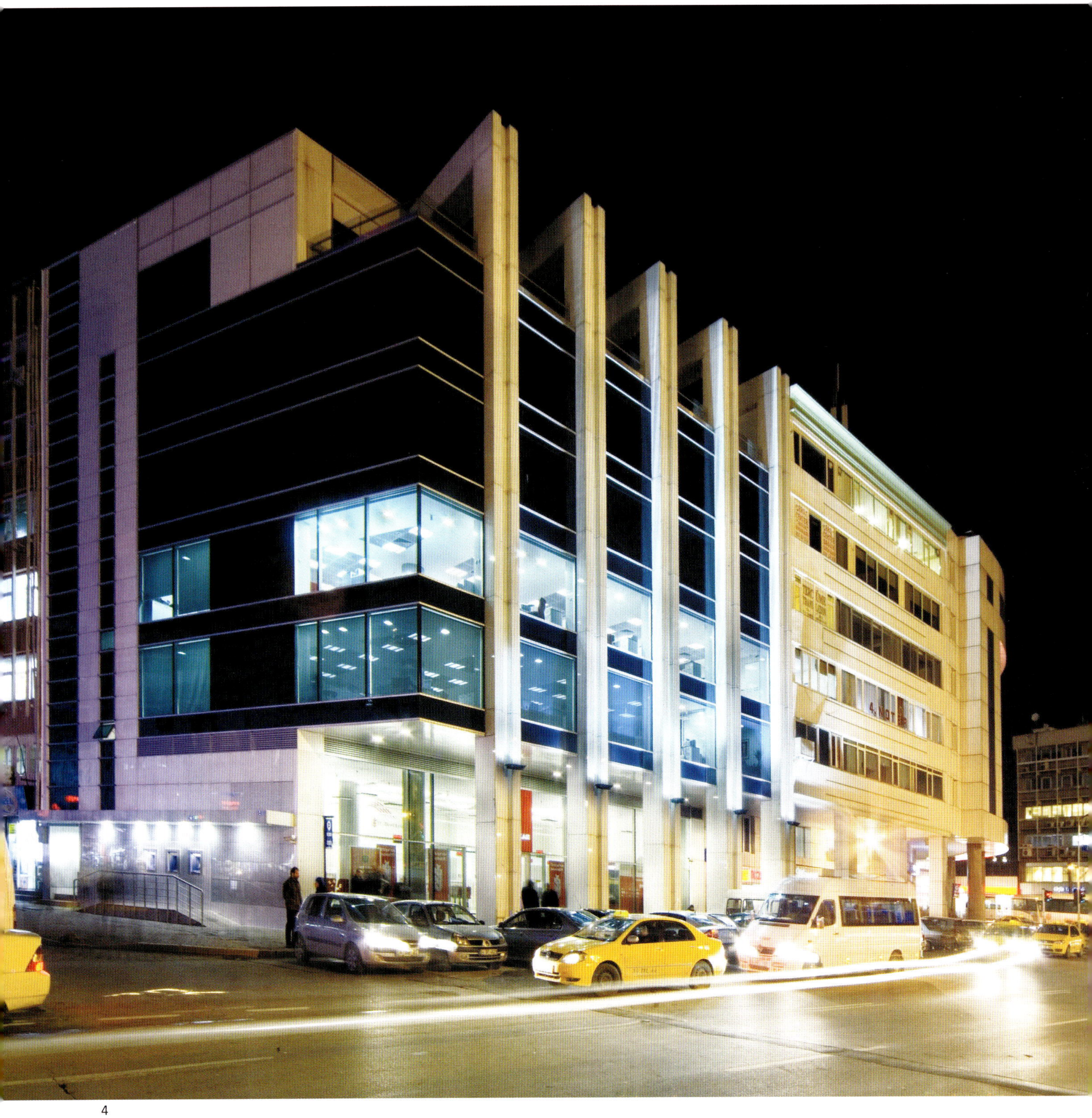

4

2 Section highlighting the maximum number of stories required within the height limitations
3 Map of the Kadıköy coast and historic peninsula
4 Night view of the lighting detail and the arcade on Rıhtım Avenue
5 Map of the historic peninsula and Haydarpaşa train station
6 The historic peninsula and the Haydarpaşa train station from the office flats
7 Section showing the floor-to-ceiling glass panels reaching each level
8 Ground floor plan
9 Typical floor plan

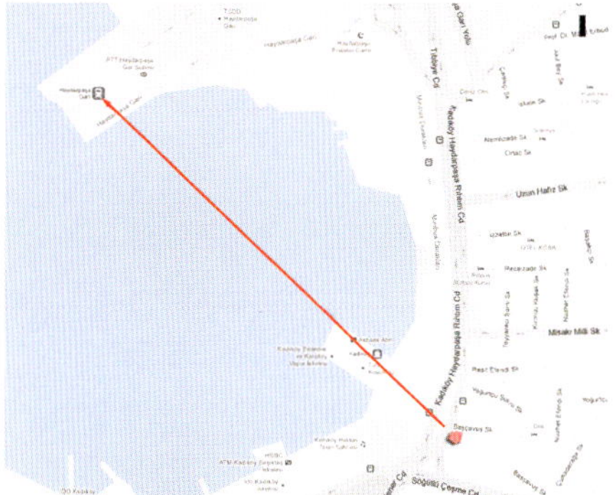

5

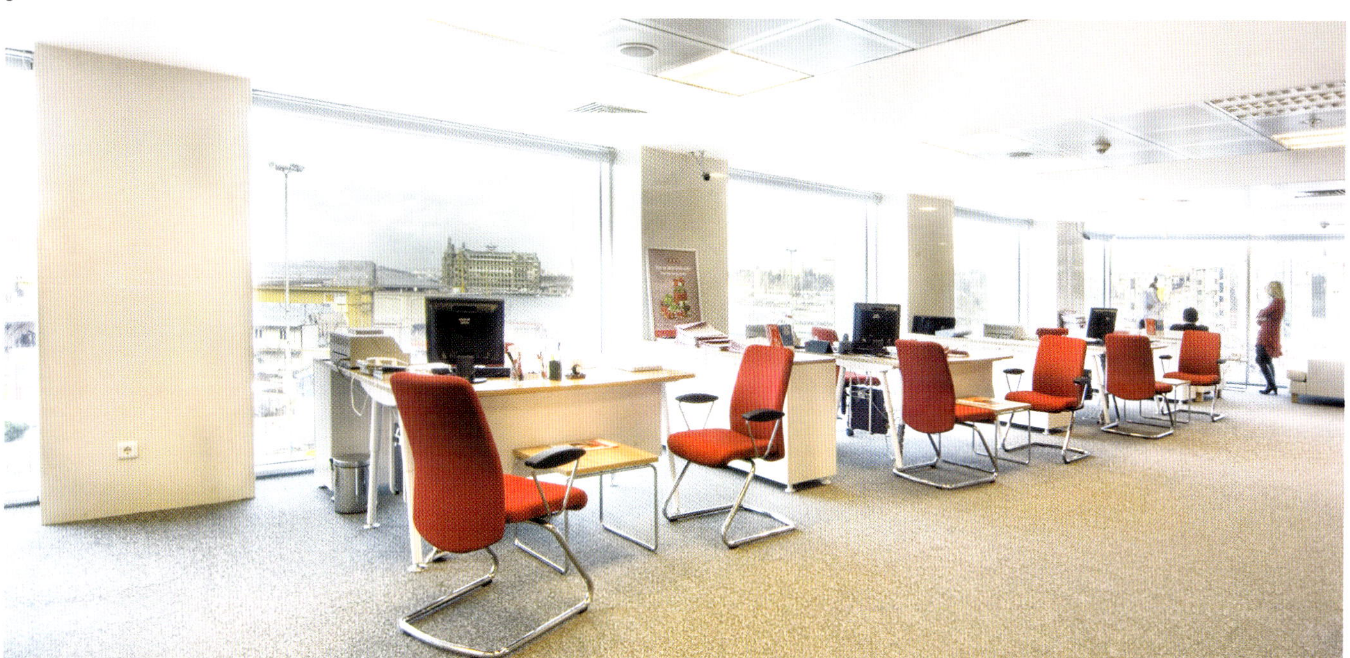

6

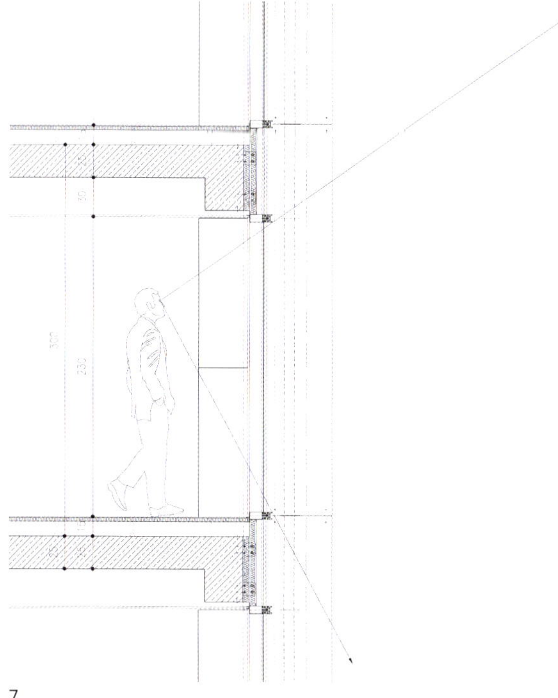

7

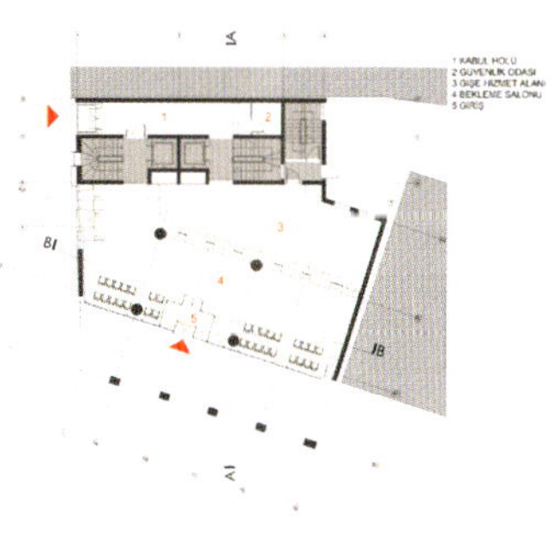

8

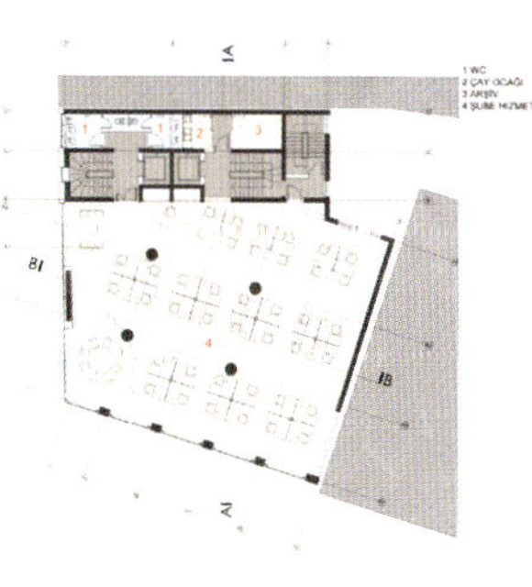

9

Küçükyalı Business Center

Client Bostancı Real Estate
Project Date 2011
Area 93,090 m^2
Location İstanbul
Structural Engineer Yüksek Project
Mechanical Engineer Okutan Engineering
Electrical Engineer RAM Engineering
Landscape Design Dalokay Design Studio
Contractor Renaissance Construction

Developed as an alternative to the recent development of typical "office plazas" of Istanbul, the Küçükyalı Business Park was created with the idea of being connected to nature. The main goal of the design is to provide a work environment that seamlessly connects with social activities and green spaces.

The project area consists of two parcels divided by a road. There are shopping malls, educational facilities, and housing structures around the area. To the southwest, the area looks out to the Prince Islands and the Marmara Sea, an asset that is enhanced by the slope of the site.

The fundamental constraint of the design is the topography of the land. Open spaces are determined by the vistas, and masses and open spaces that follow elevation differences offer alternative outdoor experiences. The design attempts to unify the two separate parcels, with a fluidity supported by angled forms and rich perspectives.

The northeast side is designated as the main entrance plaza and covered with a large overhang. This plaza is oriented towards the sea view, and the natural topography creates terraced gardens between the two blocks. Topographically dictated indentations in the structure create terraces and, along with the gardens, these create social spaces. All the open spaces and gardens are accessible from every floor, and the balconies are accessible from all the upper floors. The slope of the site was used to create added value by designating separate entry privileges for some of the offices. The terracing varies the style of offices and creates alternative workspaces.

The façades feature floor-to-ceiling glass joinery, which provides an affordable alternative to conventional curtain wall systems. The façade design aims to make optimum use of sunlight, and the sunshades are designed according to their solar orientation, offering both visual diversity and functionality. The design aims for maximum utilization of natural light everywhere in the building, especially in the indoor gardens.

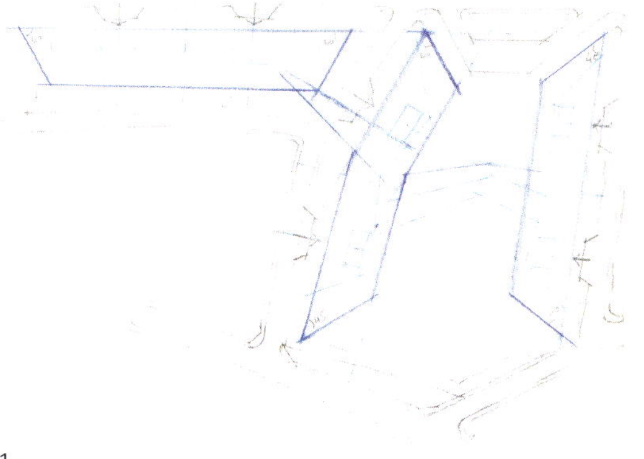

1

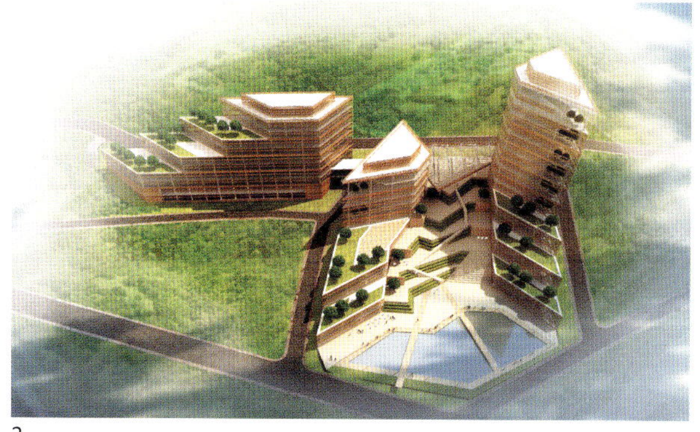

2

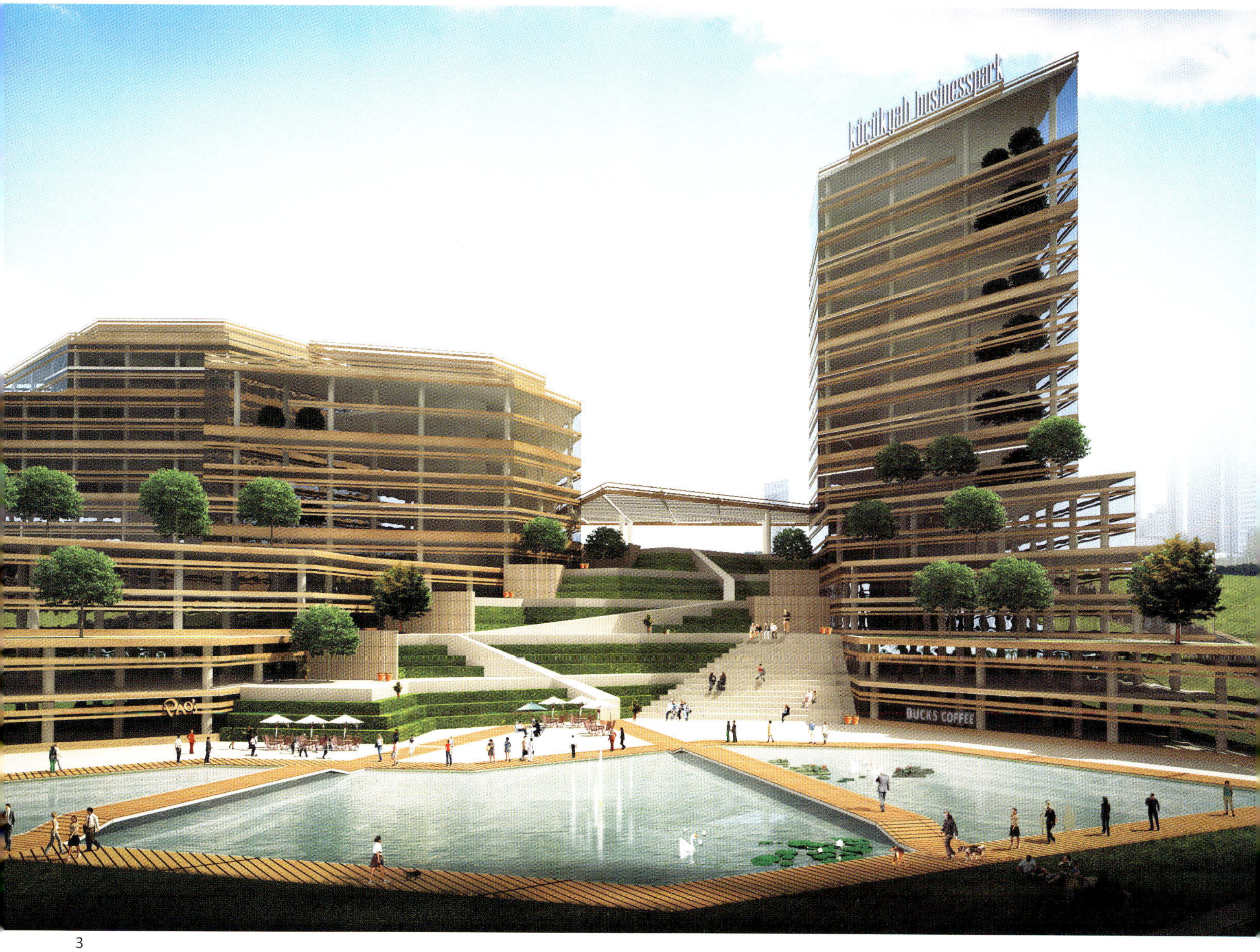

3

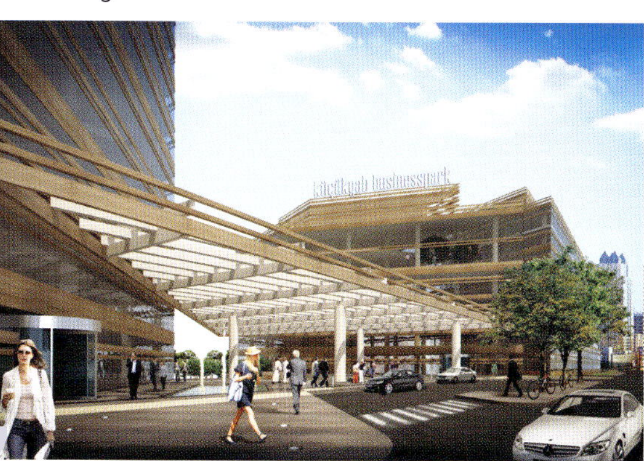

4

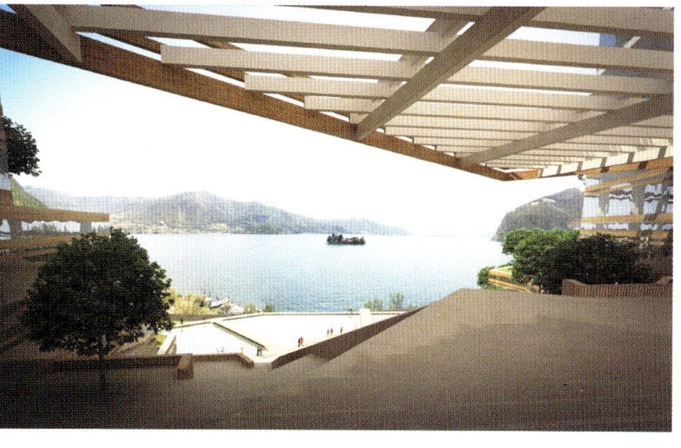

5

1 Sketch by Ali Osman Öztürk
2 Aerial view
3 Rendering of the buildings, plaza, and pool
4 Canopy detail
5 View from the terrace

TOBB World Trade-Business Center and Technopolis Master Plan

Client The Union of Chambers and Commodity Exchanges of Turkey (TOBB)

Project Date 2010

Lot Area 133,340 m^2

Location Ankara

This is the master plan proposal for TOBB University of Economics and Technology Technopolis buildings and TOBB Business Center. Office blocks have been arranged on a main road in order to define the urban space. The offices on the pond and the green area have been organized as high-rise flexible workspaces with atriums. Lower buildings are proposed for the Technocity section on the right side of the campus, while the business center contains masses of varied heights.

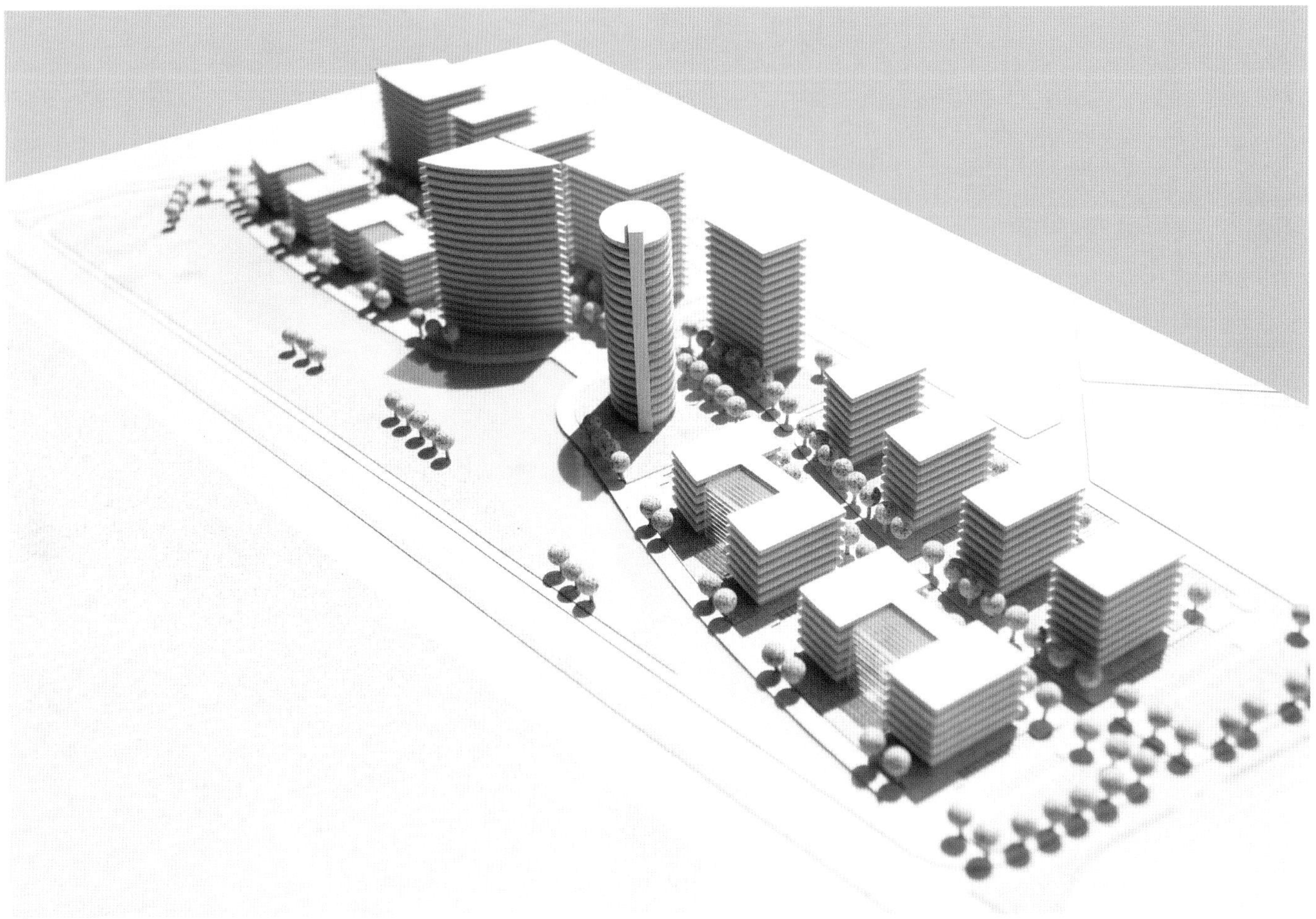

Model of the settlement

Balıkuyumcu

Client Besa Construction Inc.
Project Date 2011
Area 413,000 m^2
Location Ankara

Balıkuyumcu is on Eskişehir Road near Ankara's Temapark. The main objective of the project is to create a public space. The project proposes mixed-use functions on a main street that will take on central functions of the district. A flexible staging program was planned to diversify the functions that are part of the development project.

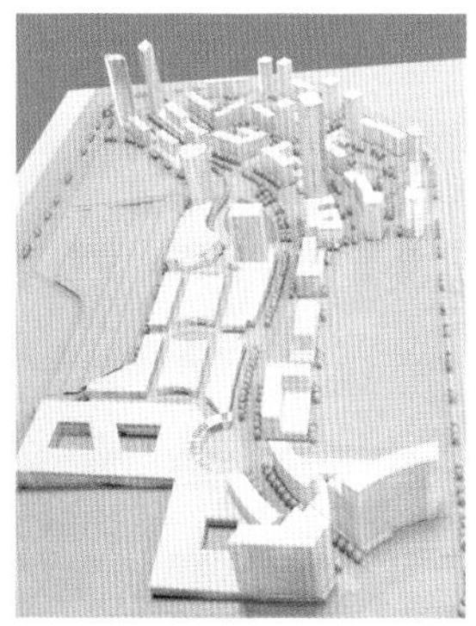

2

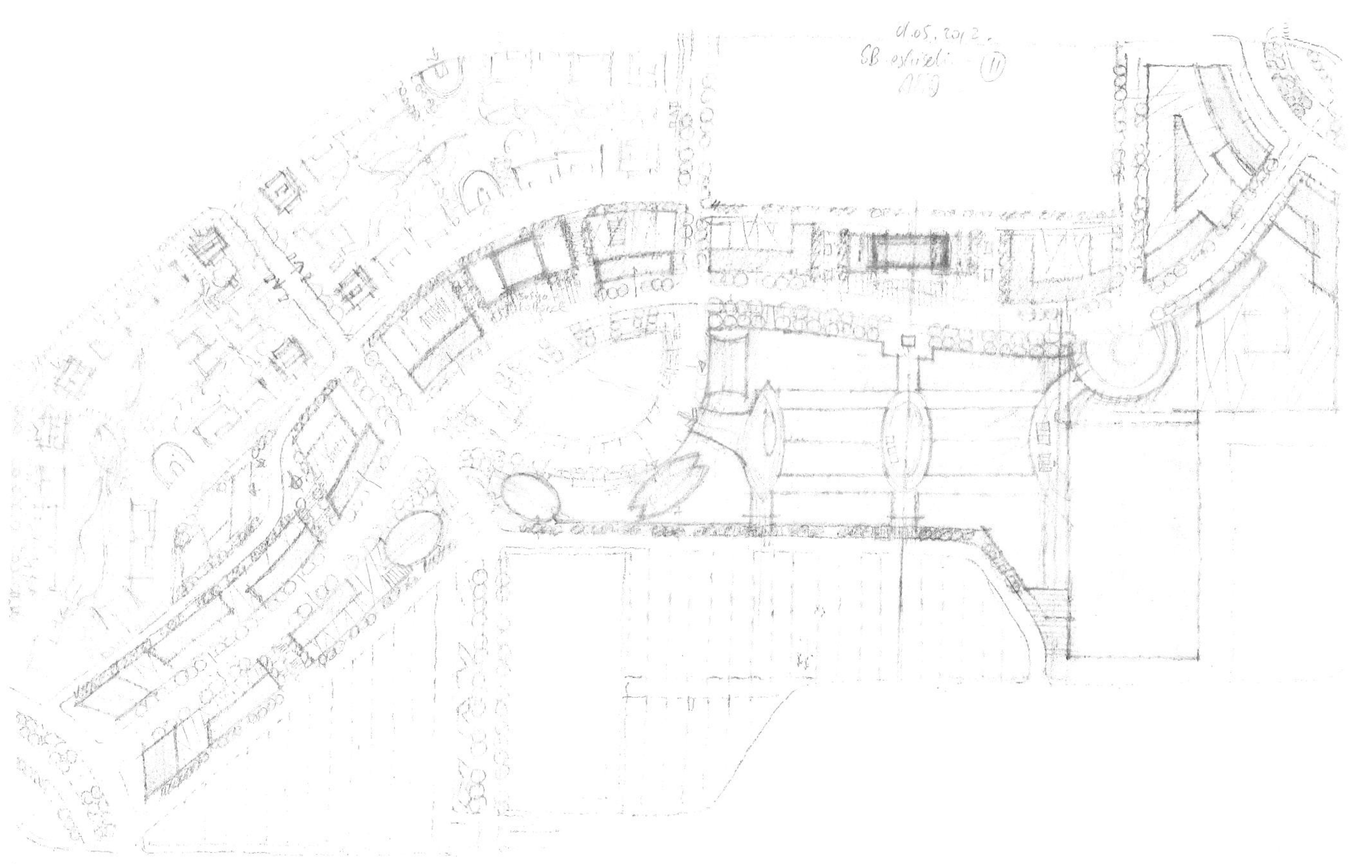

1

1 Sketch by Ali Osman Öztürk
2 Model of the master plan

Evo

Client Mutlu Construction and Tokur Construction
Project Date 2011
Area 44,000 m^2
Location Ankara
Structural Engineer MN Engineering
Mechanical Engineer Yapıtes Engineering
Electrical Engineer Denge Engineering
Contractor Mutlu Construction and Tokur Construction

The project will be built on the Eskişehir Highway and is designed as a social space containing housing, business, commerce, food, and sports facilities. The units in the horizontal block are located on two separate levels and the passage connecting these levels also provides access to the rooftop. The base mass generates spaces of various volumes. There are eight small apartments on each floor of the residential block and these apartments can also be used as home offices. The rooftop, which includes recreational sport facilities, is considered a special space.

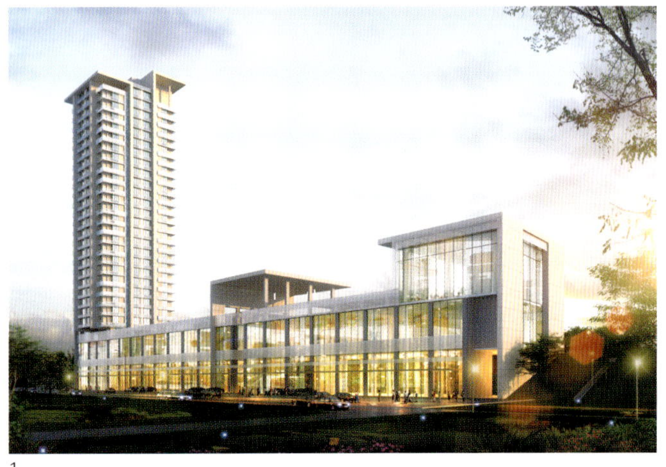

1

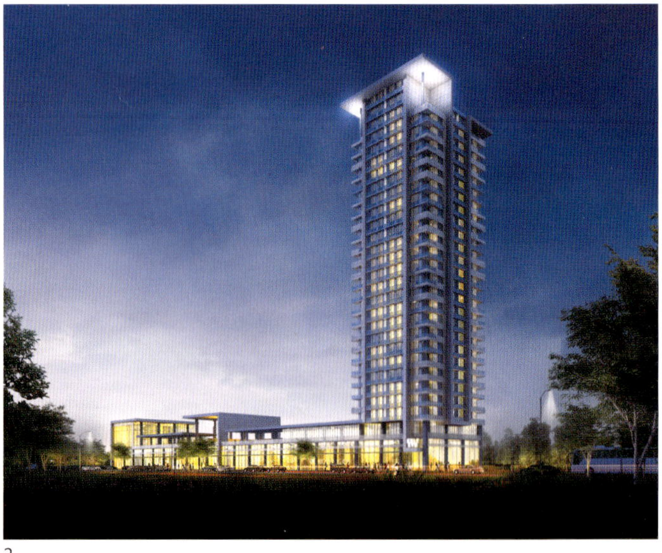

2

1 View of the southern façade
2 Rendering of the building at night
3 Urban activity in front of the building

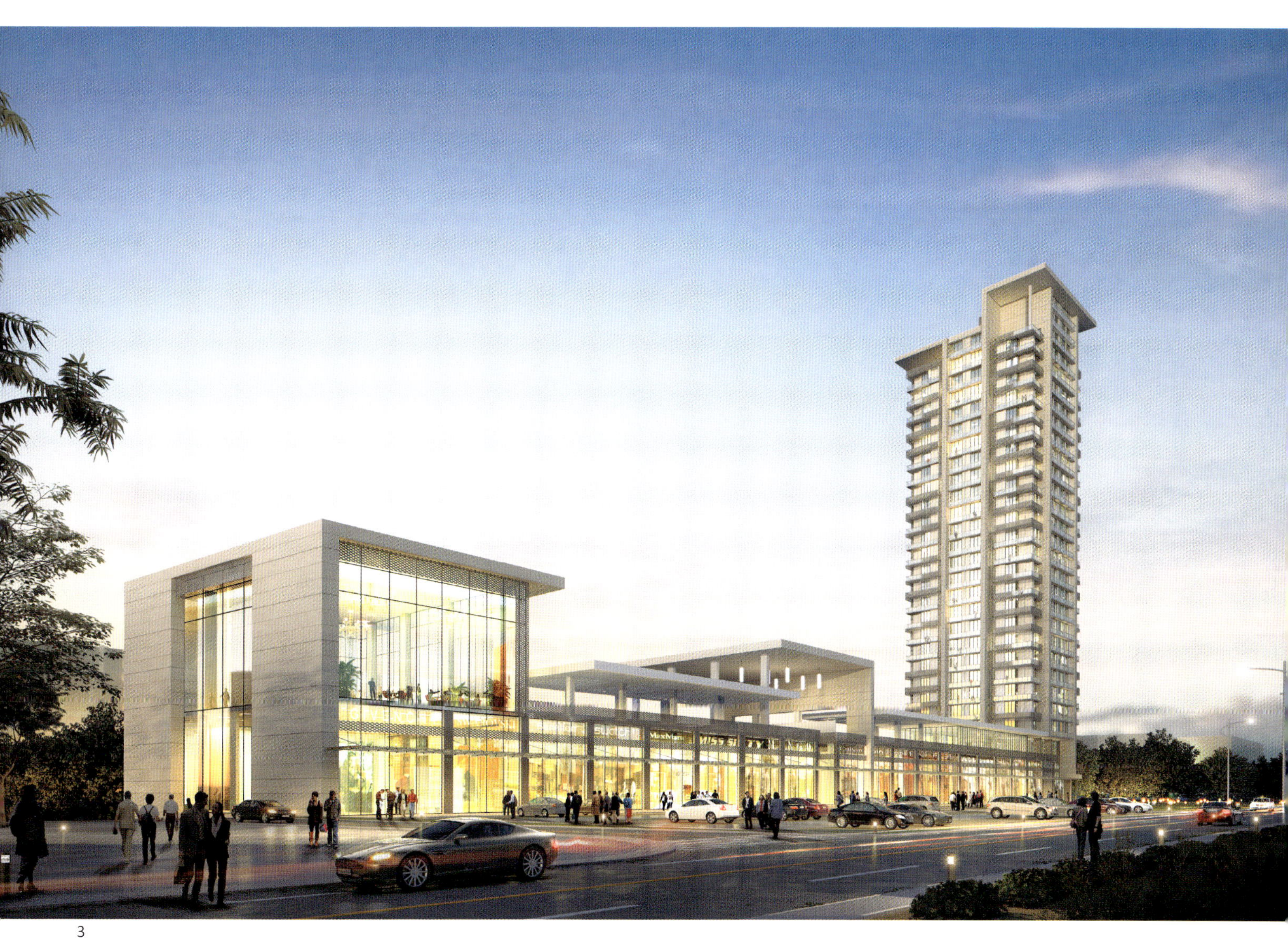

3

Turgut Plaza

Client Tepe Construction Inc.
Project Date 2008
Area 123,500 m^2
Location İstanbul

This project combines both office and residential units and, despite the constraints of the site, it was designed as an urban arrangement instead of a single building block. The office and residential units are located in a symbolic tower block that stands on Büyükdere Avenue, with a view of the Bosphorous. These units have direct access to the main space of the project—the atrium and its hanging gardens. Another group of residential units consists of low-rise blocks and is detached from the tower block to form another, more private living area at the rear of the site. The project stands as an architectural experiment in combining different sizes and types of living spaces in one site.

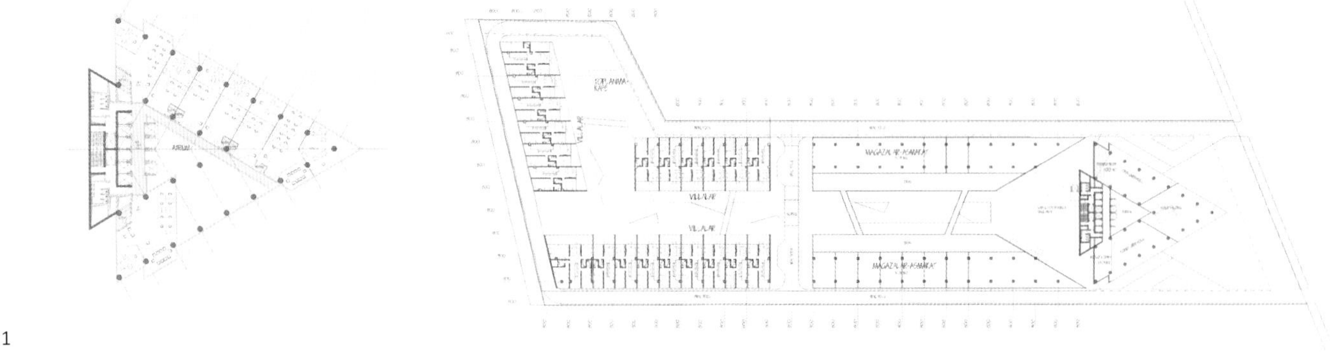

1

2

1 Typical floor plan
2 Ground floor plan showing the tower entrance and low-rise buildings
3 Rendering of the tower at night
4 View of the tower from Büyükdere Avenue
5 View of the city from the building's interior

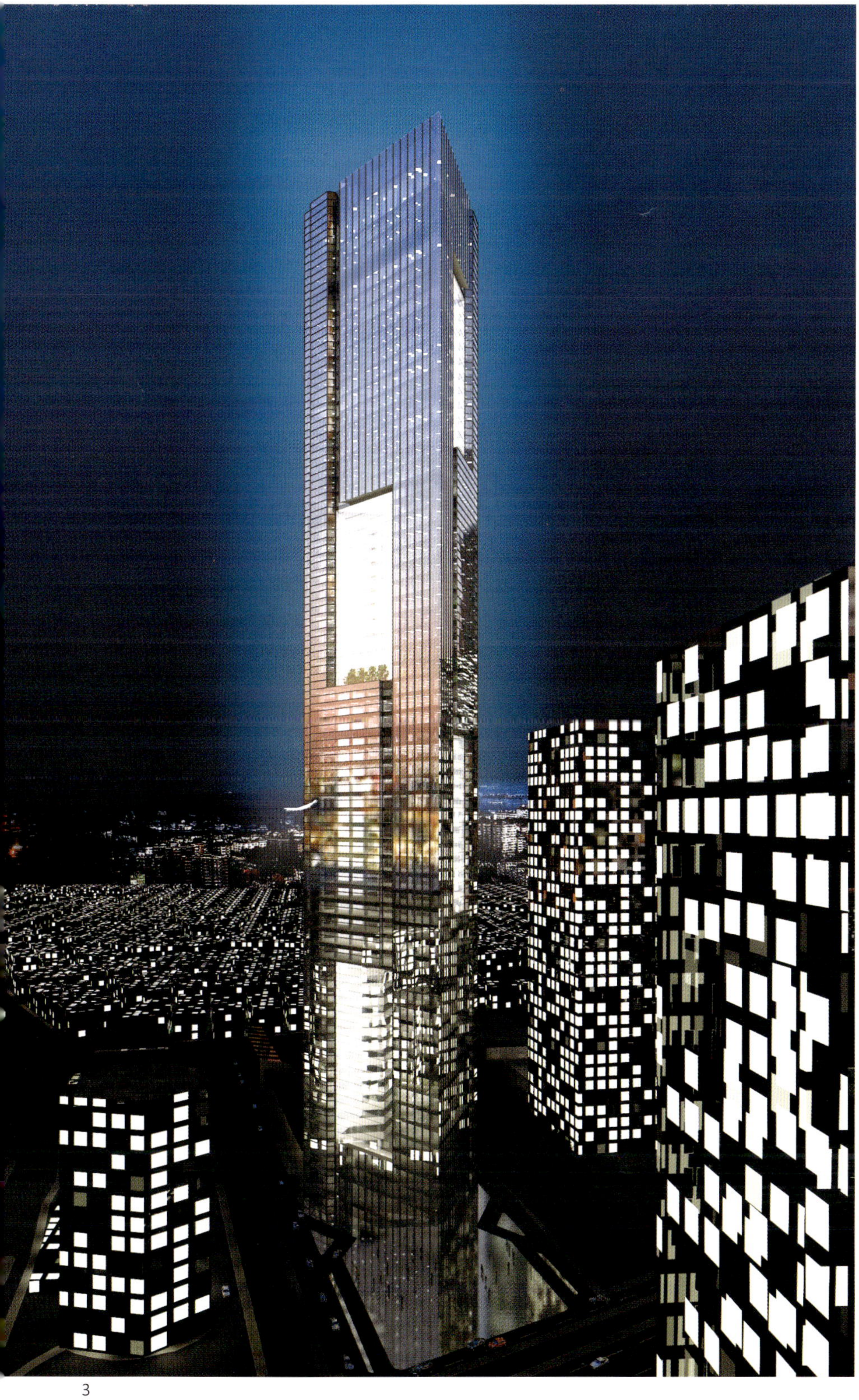

3

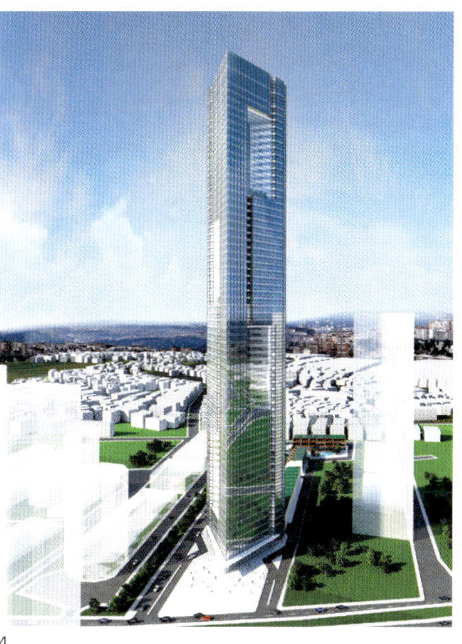

4

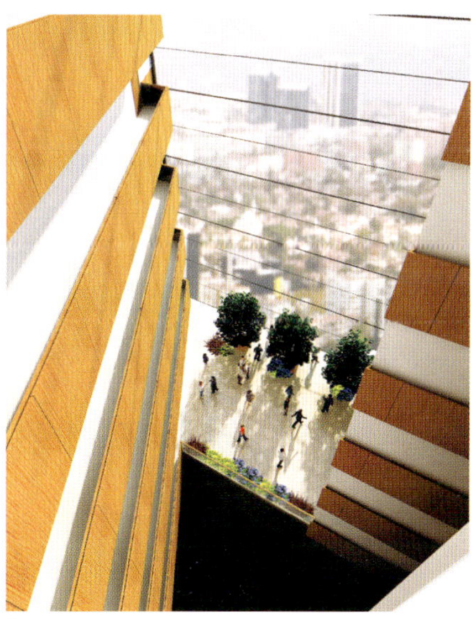

5

Şahinler

Client Şahinler Holding
Project Date 2007
Area 320,000 m²
Location İstanbul

The project site is on the E5 Highway, one of İstanbul's most important transportation axes. The building is situated on two plots of different sizes. The main functions include a shopping mall, an office-residence block, and social spaces.

The design is a result of several contributions relating to topography, urban panorama, environmental impacts, and social requirements. The project is about to create an urban focal point for its surroundings. With its plaza, the shopping mall is designed as a dynamic shell, which also includes the lively and active use of the commercial spaces.

The residential and office tower includes housing units and open office layouts. There are several apartment sizes and layouts and the social spaces underneath afford residents and visitors visual and recreational opportunities.

The forms of the residential blocks, shopping mall, and the office tower create a distinct element in the urban skyline.

1 General layout
2 Residential blocks
3,4 General view
5 Sketch exploring pedestrian flow by Ali Osman Öztürk
6 Sketch of the entrances and spatial organization by Ali Osman Öztürk

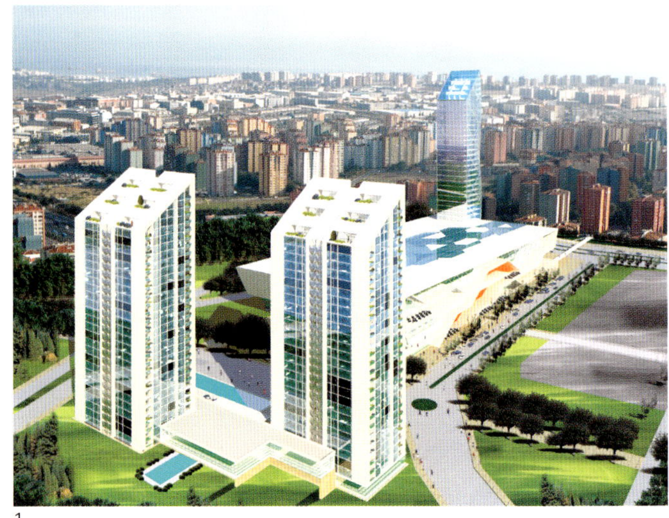
1

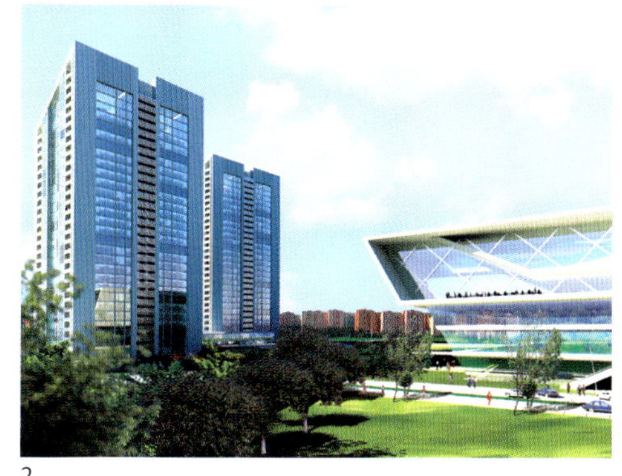
2

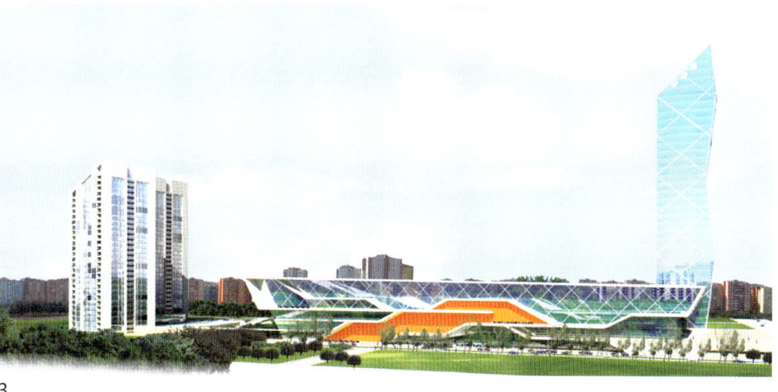
3

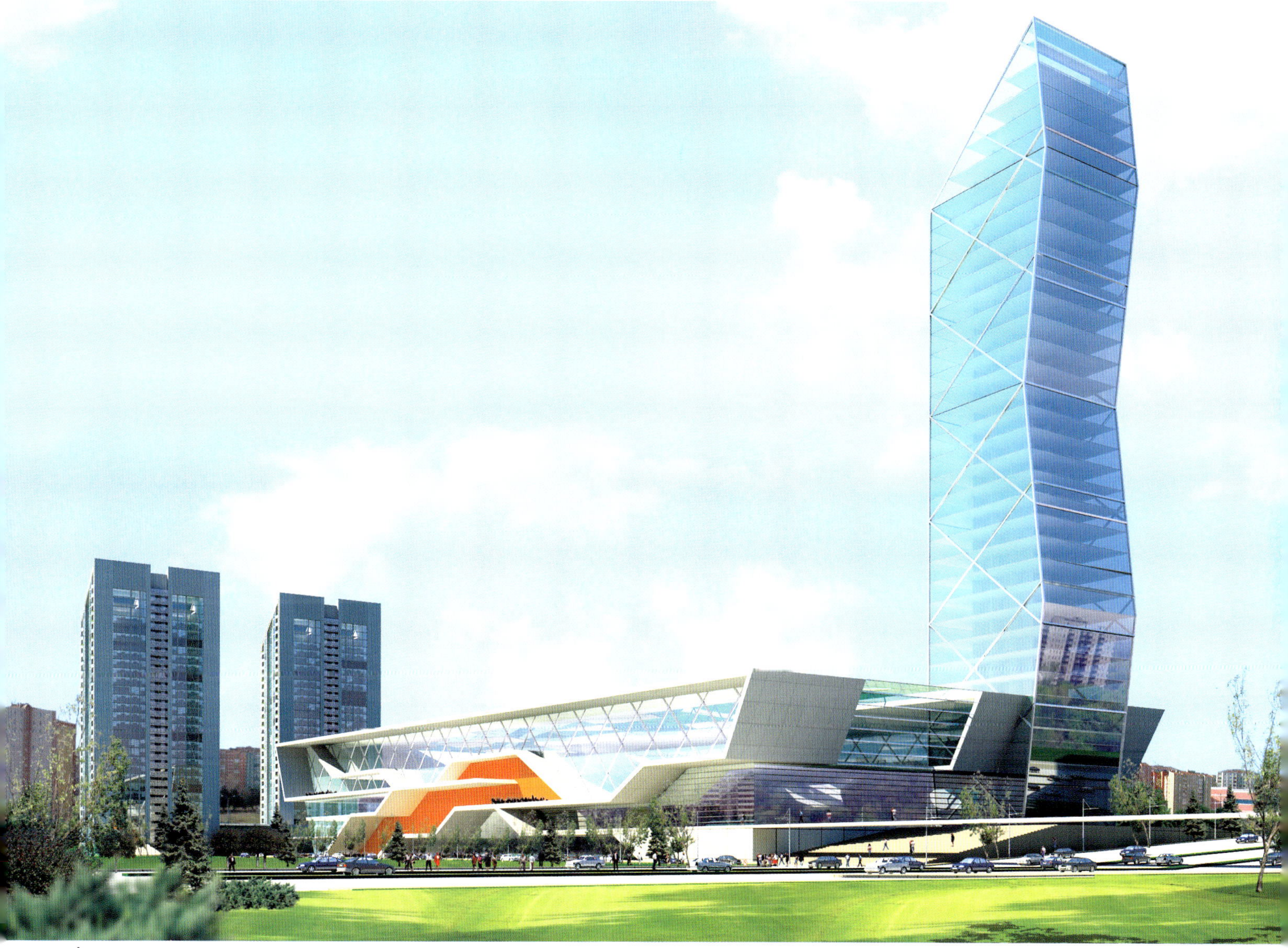

4

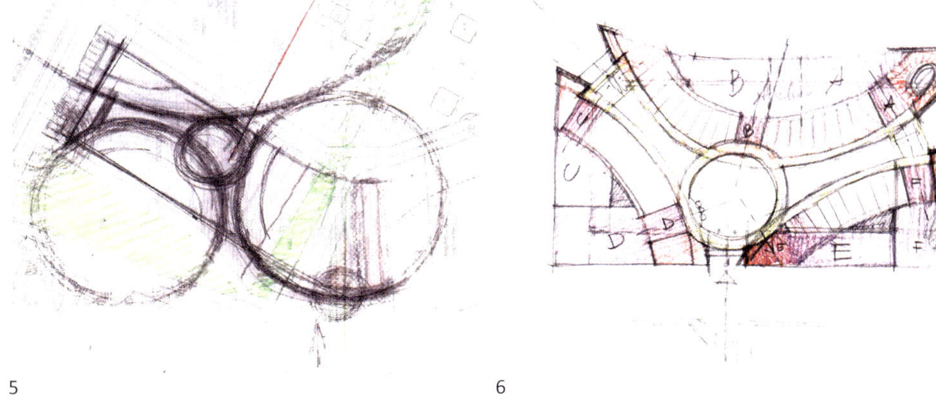
5

6

Kızılırmak Mixed-Use Center

Client Usta Construction
Project Date 2008
Area 97,695 m^2
Location Ankara

The project site is very close to the housing and commercial district that is being built in Söğütözü area. A variety of spaces that contain different building programs have been proposed for the building block, which is surrounded on all sides by roadways. The urban spaces created between the buildings with convex and concave lines can be accessed from various levels. These high-rise buildings can be used as apartments or offices. Many connection points are provided for the independent commercial units designed within the lower mass. The fragmental order of the masses creates alternative spaces for functional diversity.

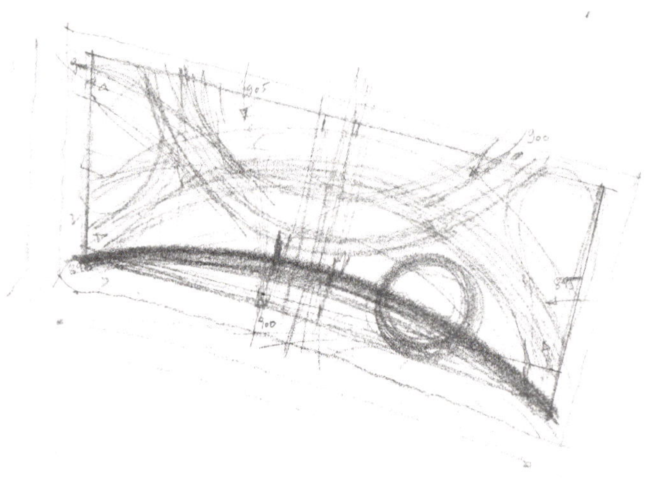

1

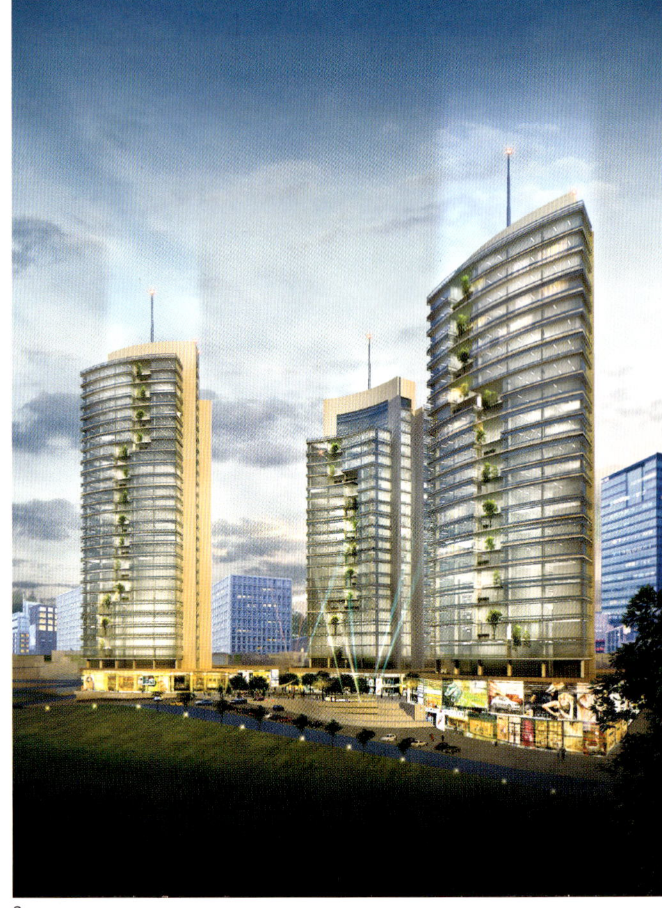

2

1 Sketch by Ali Osman Öztürk
2 Rendering of the buildings
3 Aerial view of the plaza

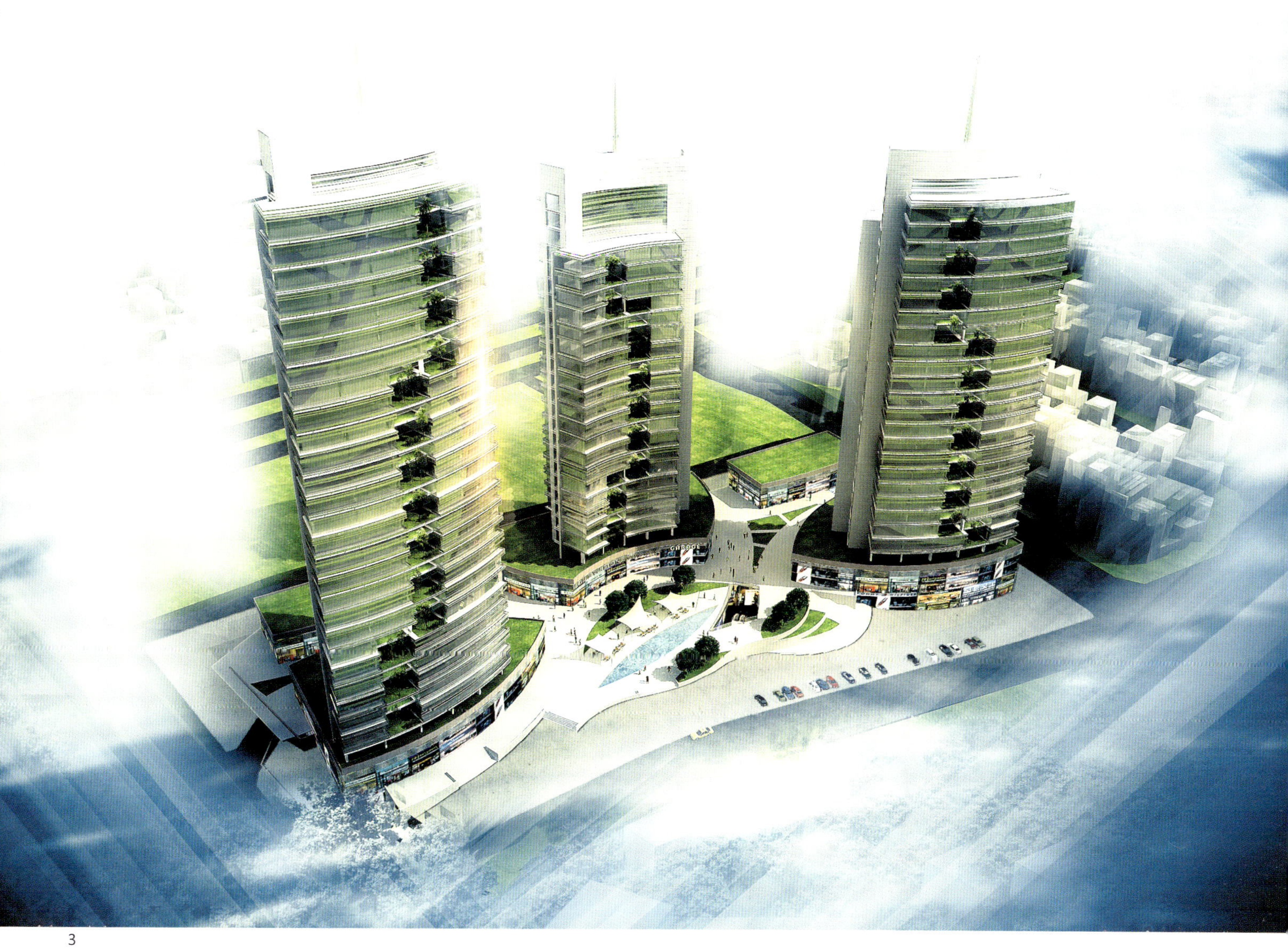

3

Farilya

Client Ufuk Mesken Construction
Project Date 2008
Area 25,415 m^2
Location Ankara
Structural Engineer Yüksek Project
Mechanical Engineer BTC Engineering
Electrical Engineer BTC Engineering
Contractor Ufuk Mesken Construction

As the functions of the increasingly central Söğütözü area expand, there is demand for new business spaces. This building has a design approach that integrates the base mass with the upper structure. There are four units, which are offices of various sizes and types, on each floor of the building. The ground floor contains rows of units with mezzanines.

1 Night view of Farilya in the front with Congresium at the back
2 General view

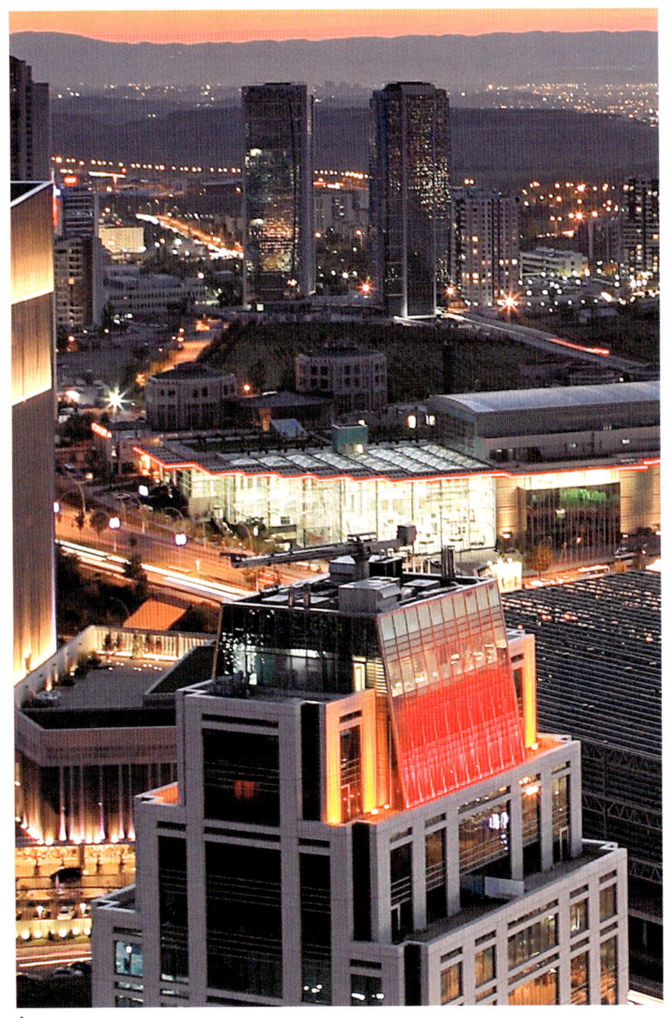

1

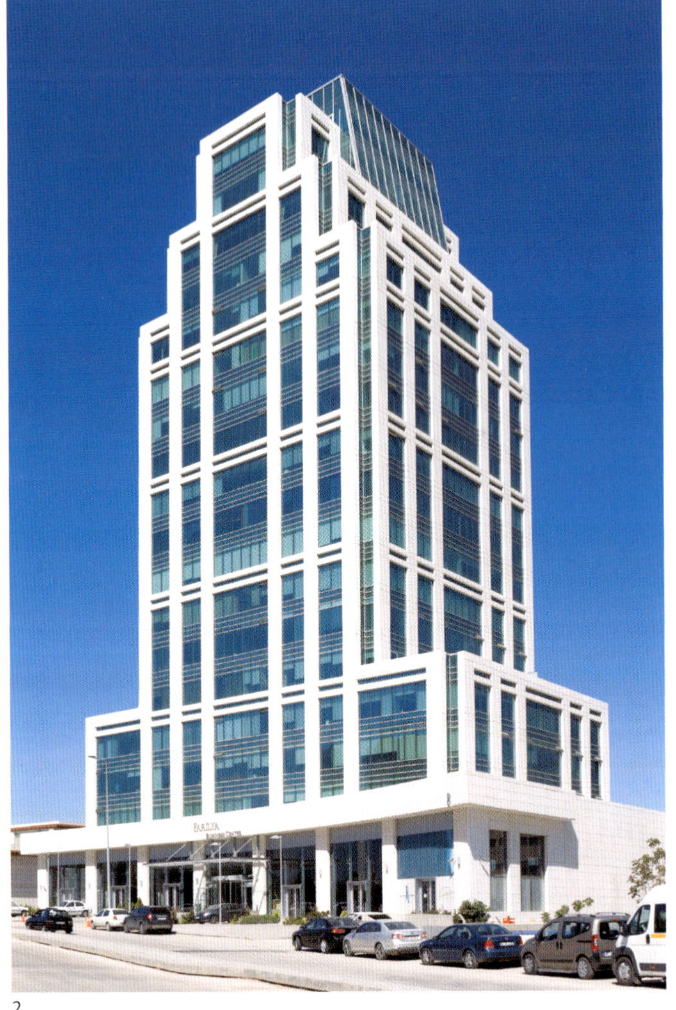

2

Via/Life

Client Bayraktar Construction
Project Date 2003
Area 42,000 m^2
Location Ankara
Structural Engineer Yüksek Project
Mechanical Engineer BTC Engineering
Electrical Engineer BTC Engineering
Contractor Bayraktar Construction

Via/Life is a multi-use building composed of a horizontal outlet shopping mall and a vertical office block. The office block comprises 59 offices, including a variety of spatial configurations to enable different office uses. The shopping mall block includes 55 shops, restaurants, and administrative offices.

1 Sketch of the ground floor by Ali Osman Öztürk
2 General view

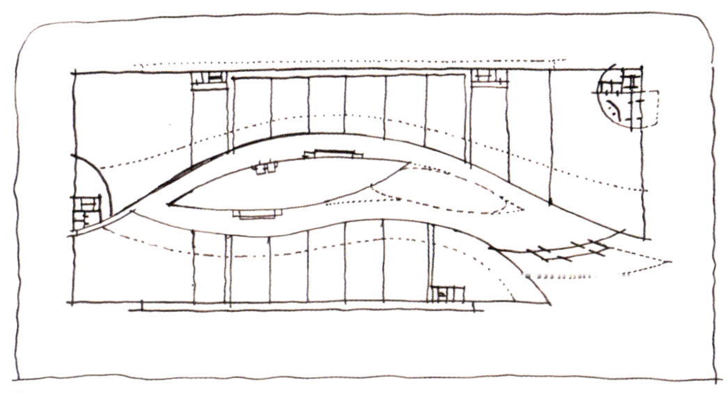

1

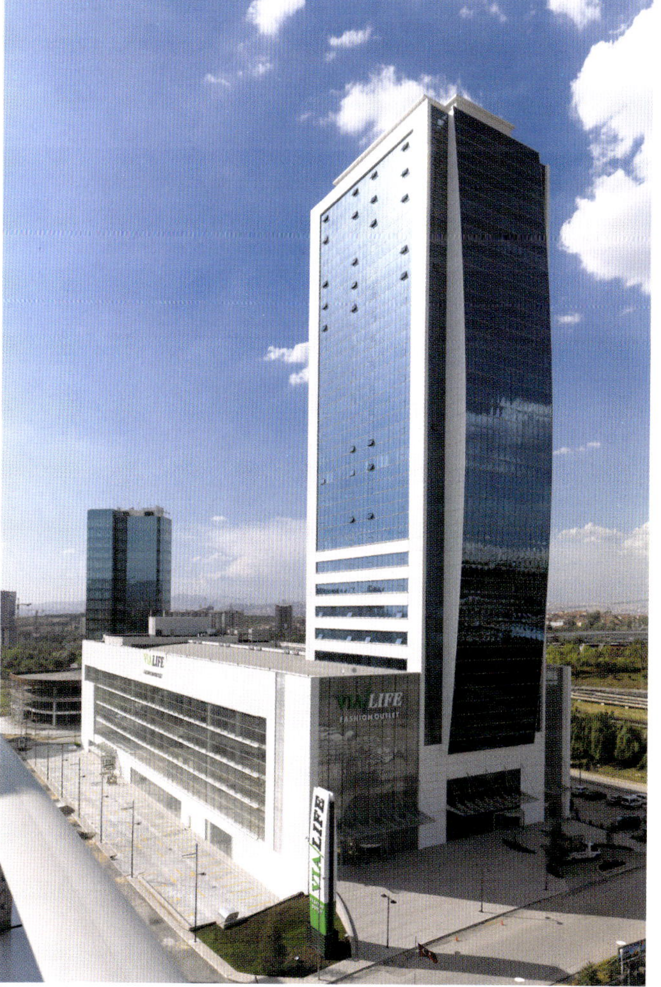

2

METU Technopolis Projects

METU Slicon Block
Client METU
Project Date 2003
Area 8,440 m^2
Location Ankara
Structural Engineer Yüksek Project
Mechanical Engineer Okutan Engineering
Electrical Engineer Akay Engineering

METU Gallium Block
Client METU
Project Date 2005
Area 8,410 m^2
Location Ankara
Structural Engineer Yüksek Project
Mechanical Engineer Okutan Engineering
Electrical Engineer Akay Engineering

METU Titanium Block
Client METU
Date 2005
Area 3,780 m^2
Location Ankara

These proposals have been submitted to various invitation-only competitions for the METU Technopolis campus. **The Silicon Block** proposal has been designed for the northern entry point to the technopolis, with an ecological park in the western section of the building. The park is visually connected to the dormitories and sports facilities, with the assumption that it will constitute a buffer between the future technopolis campuses. Observation terraces are located around the ecological park and the flow of pedestrian, bicycle, and car traffic is taken into account.

The Titanium Block proposal has been designed for an important developmental axis in METU. Designed with an ecological and sustainable approach, the project proposes functional solutions for modern office needs.

The Gallium Block's main façade has been designed to face the traffic and pedestrian alley from the METU campus, while the back façade looks out over the recreational area. This ensures that the building is a permeable site within the campus's green fabric. The form of the mass is intended to sit harmoniously with neighboring buildings as well as the topography. The building's offices are placed around an indoor corridor and there is a cafeteria on the ground floor—a gathering point for both employees and visitors.

The Modsim Block, an office block proposal, defines itself as a separate block while being in harmony with the architecture surrounding it. In the two-story linear structure, offices are located on the ground floor while the meeting room and a large observation patio that can host cocktail parties is located on the upper floor.

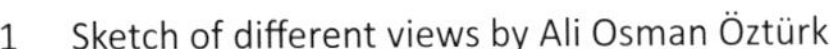

1 Sketch of different views by Ali Osman Öztürk
2 Sketch of the geometrical analysis and pedestrian movement near the building by Ali Osman Öztürk
3 Rendering of the building
4 Aerial view
5 View of the canopy
6 Sketch of the general layout by Ali Osman Öztürk

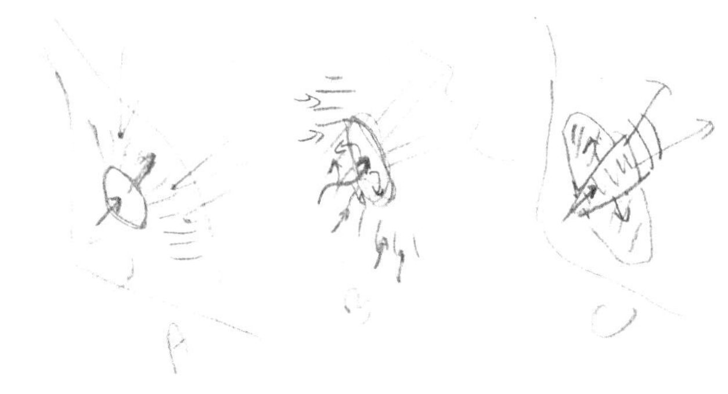

1

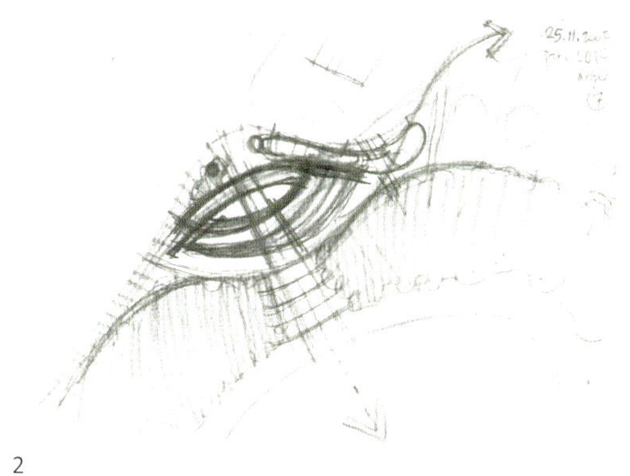
2

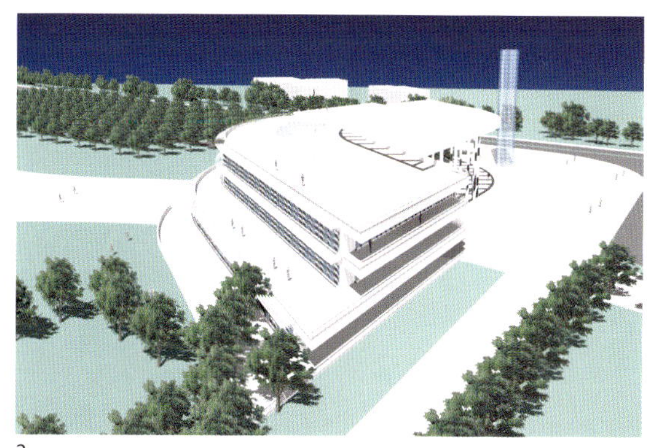
3

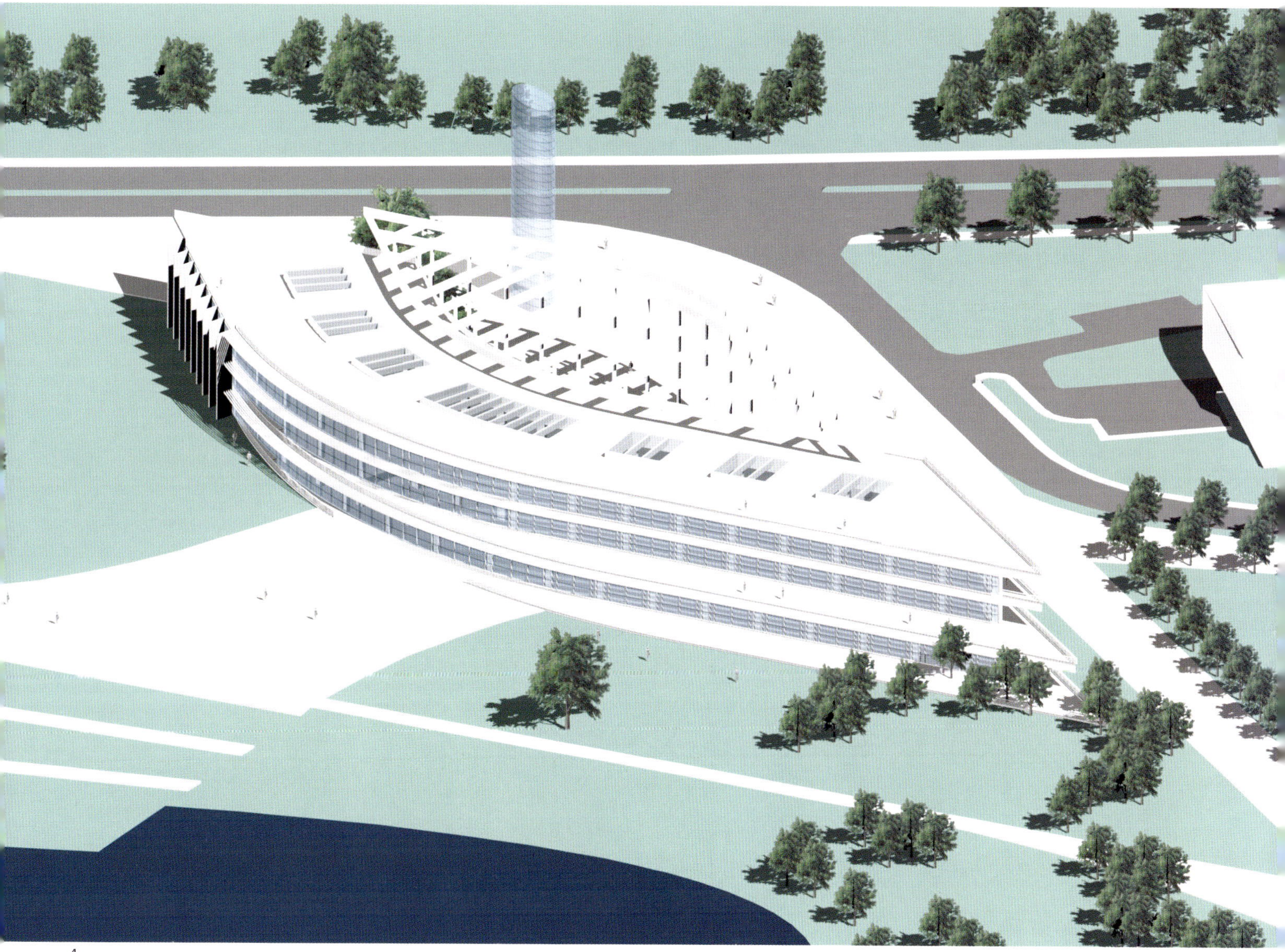

4

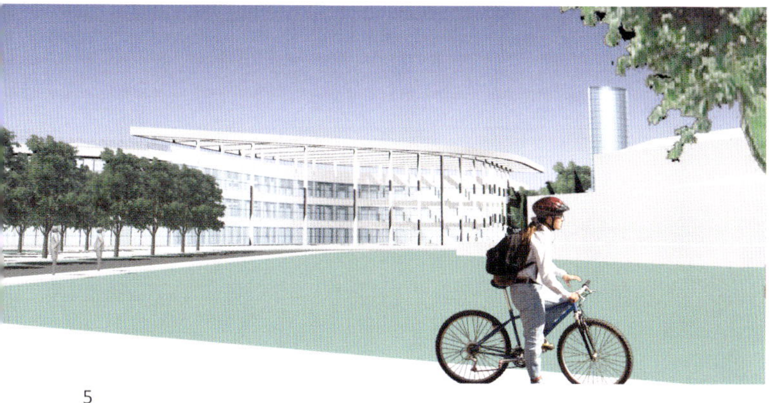
5

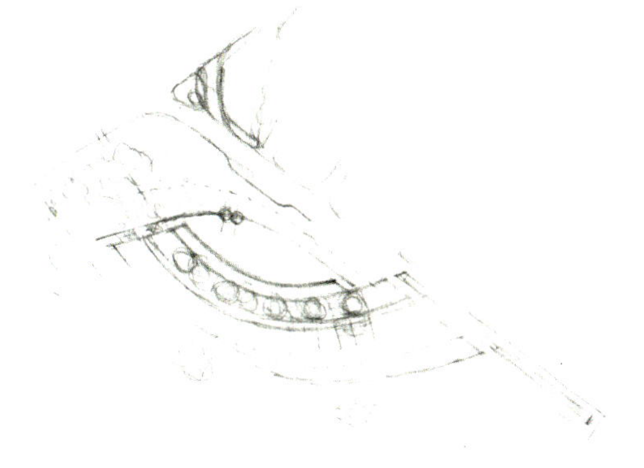
6

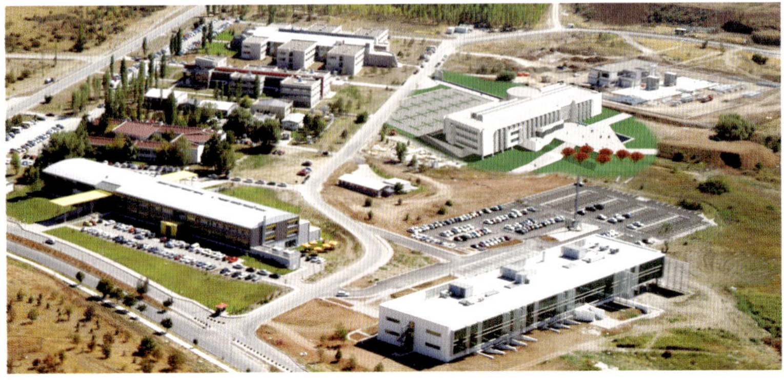

7

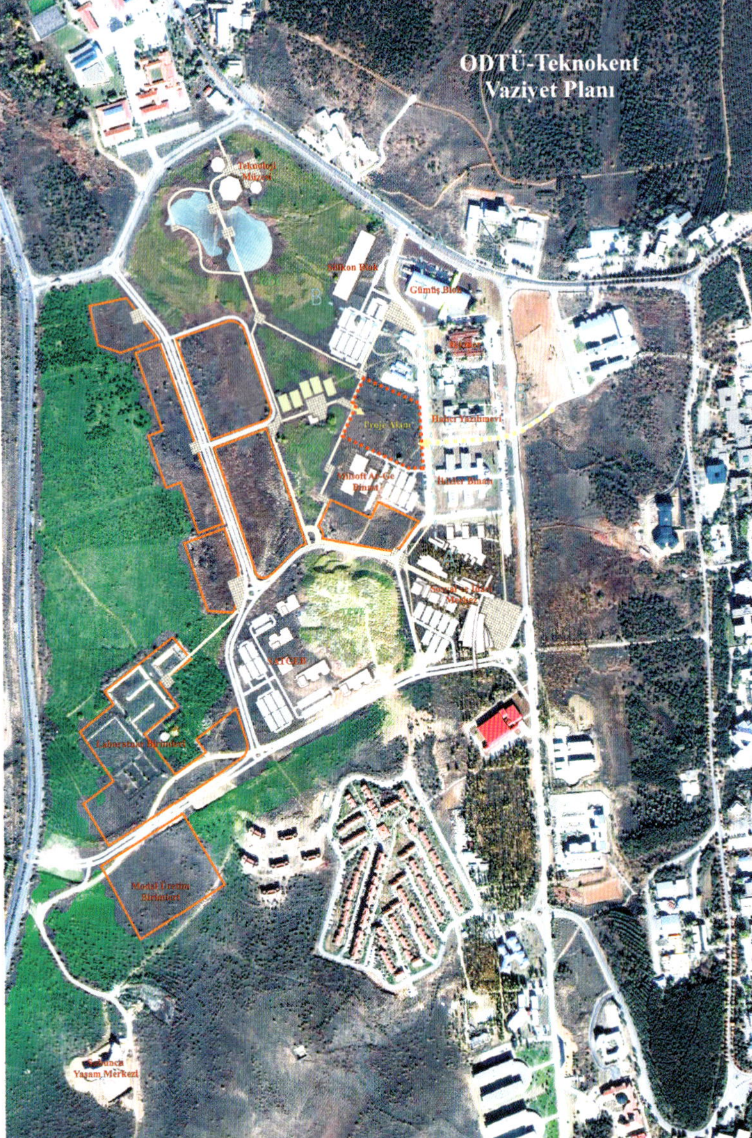

8

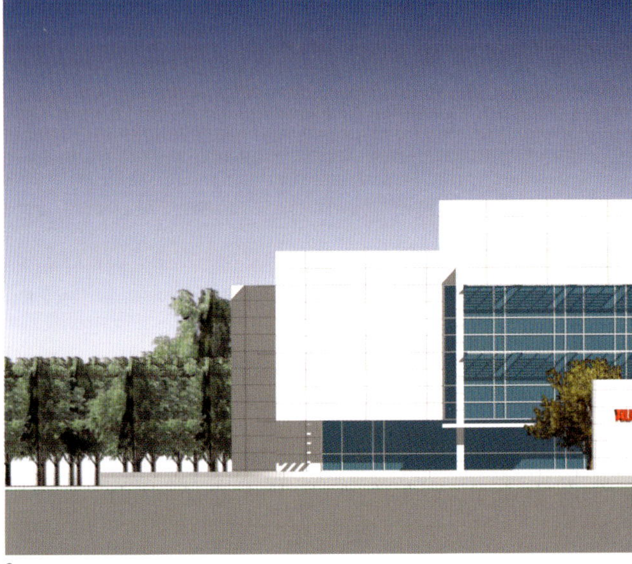

9

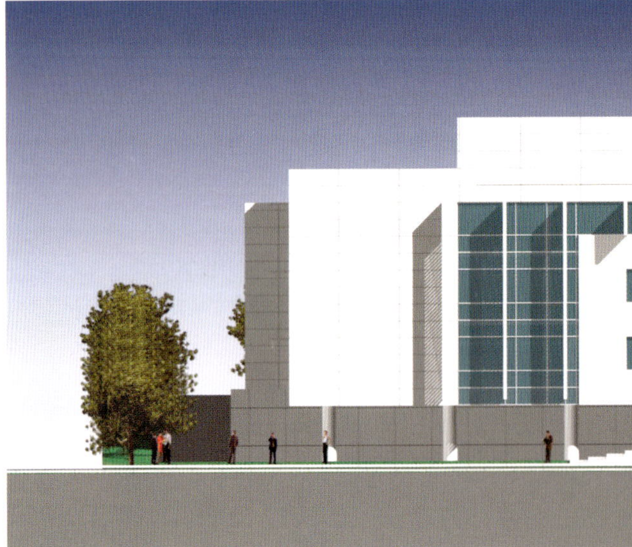

10

7 Aerial view of the Gallium Block showing the existing buildings located in the METU Technopolis area
8 Map of METU Technopolis
9 Model view of the Titanium Block
10 Northeast façade of the Gallium Block
11 Southwest façade of the Gallium Block
12,13 Side elevations of the Gallium Block

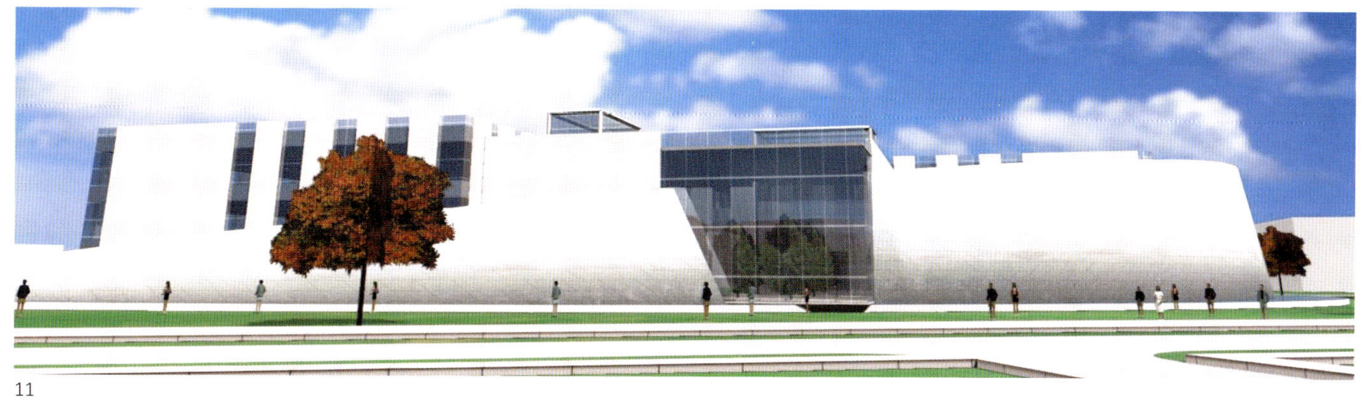
11

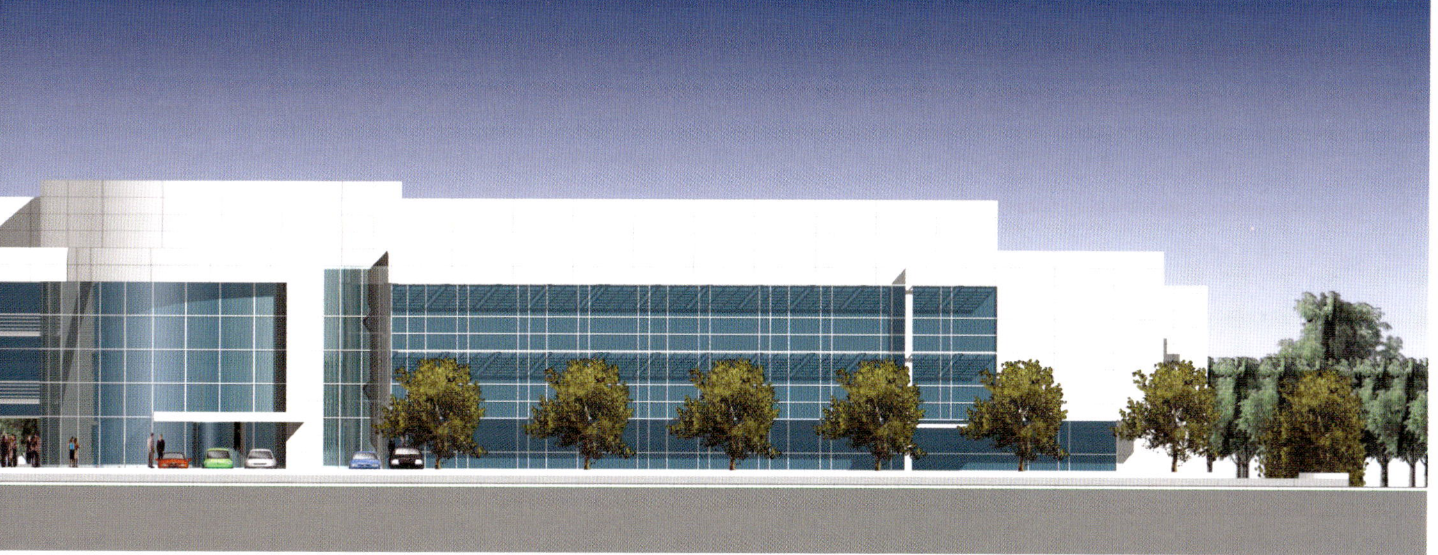

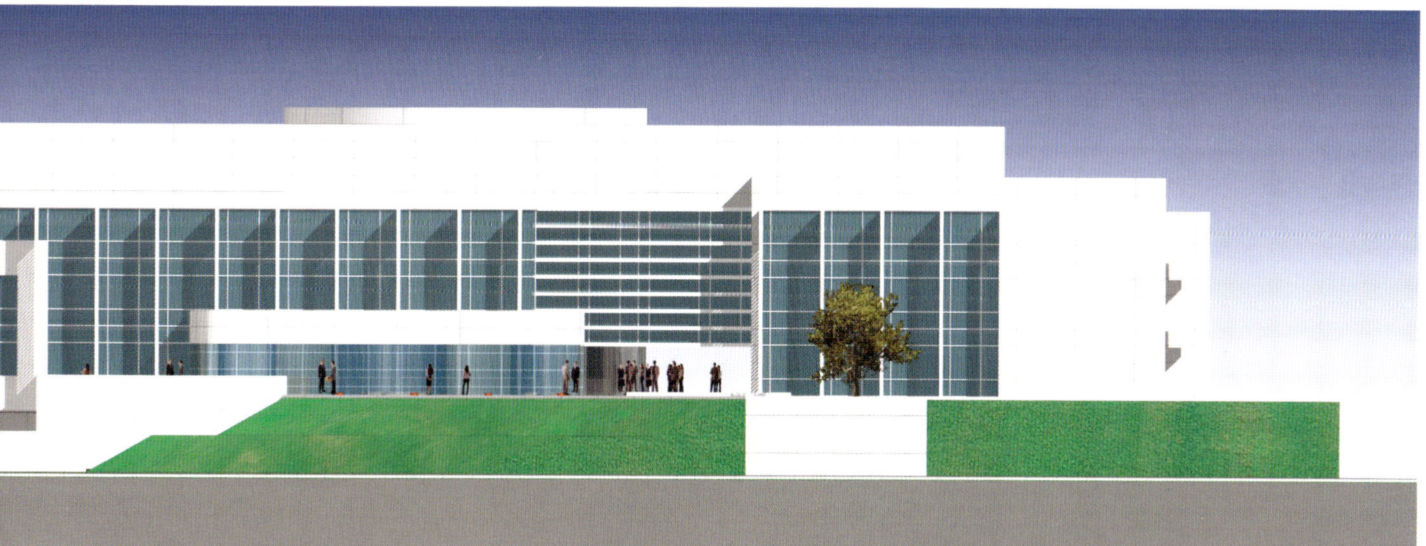

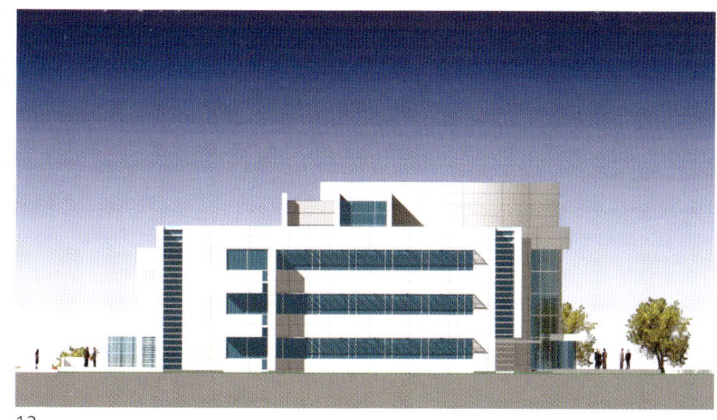
12

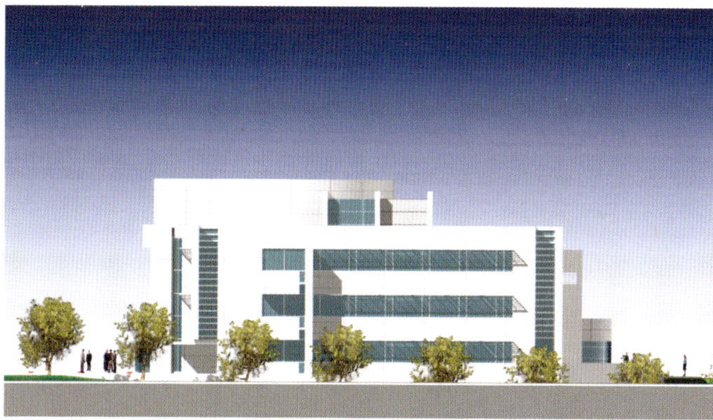
13

TOBB University of Economics and Technology Master Plan

Client TOBB University of Economics and Technology
Project Date 2004
Planned Area 300,000 m^2
Location Ankara

Founded by The Union of Chambers and Commodity Exchanges of Turkey, the University of Economics and Technology (TOBB UET) has an inner city campus situated in Söğütözü, Ankara. A group of existing school buildings owned by the University was renovated to form the new campus. The implementation of the design was completed in several stages, and educational and administrative buildings, a sports center, and an institutional building were all grouped around a communal courtyard. This courtyard was conceived as a public area that could host a variety of activities.

In the course of designing the master plan, adjacent sites were added to the campus area, thus forming new areas for future development. This process emphasized the concept of urban renewal where the principal aim was to transform the campus and its surrounds into an area filled with abundant educational and student-oriented functions.

The campus development scheme was determined according to the university's academic programs. Hence, the Faculty of Engineering, the Cultural Center and the Faculty of Fine Arts, the University Library, and the Library for the Faculty of Law are located at the center of the academic scheme.

The master plan was designed to include several different alternatives, and urban arrangements were proposed to structure and strengthen the relationship between the existing urban context and building stock with the campus layout. Overall, the study presents a unique process of planning an existing fragmented urban context from a single architectural unit.

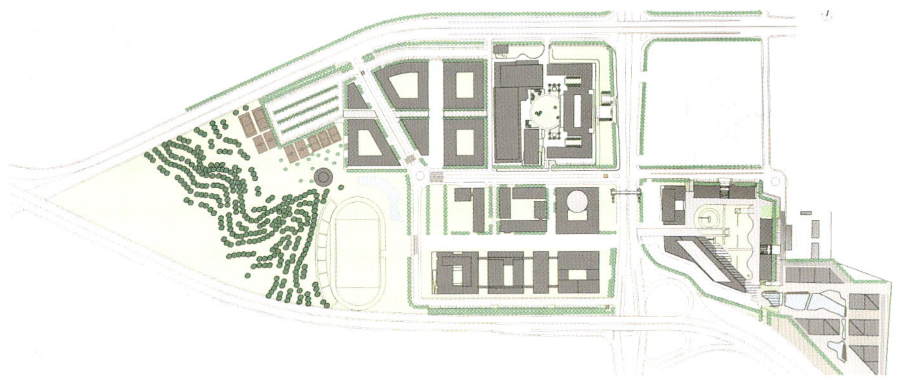

1

1 TOBB University of Economics and Technology Master Plan
2 Rendering of the buildings located in the Master Plan
3 View of TOBB UET Student Guesthouses
4 Pedestrian axes between faculty buildings

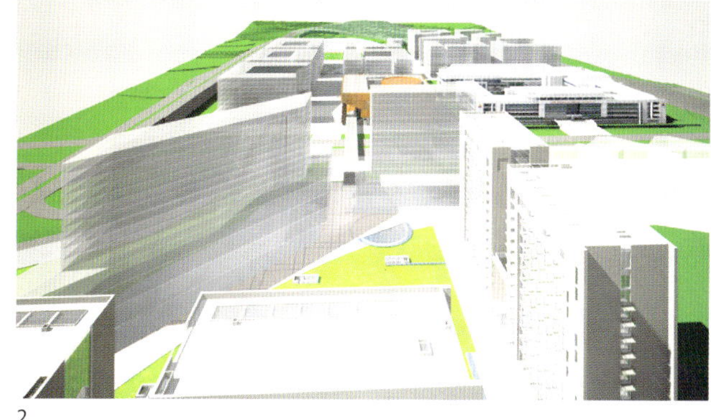

2

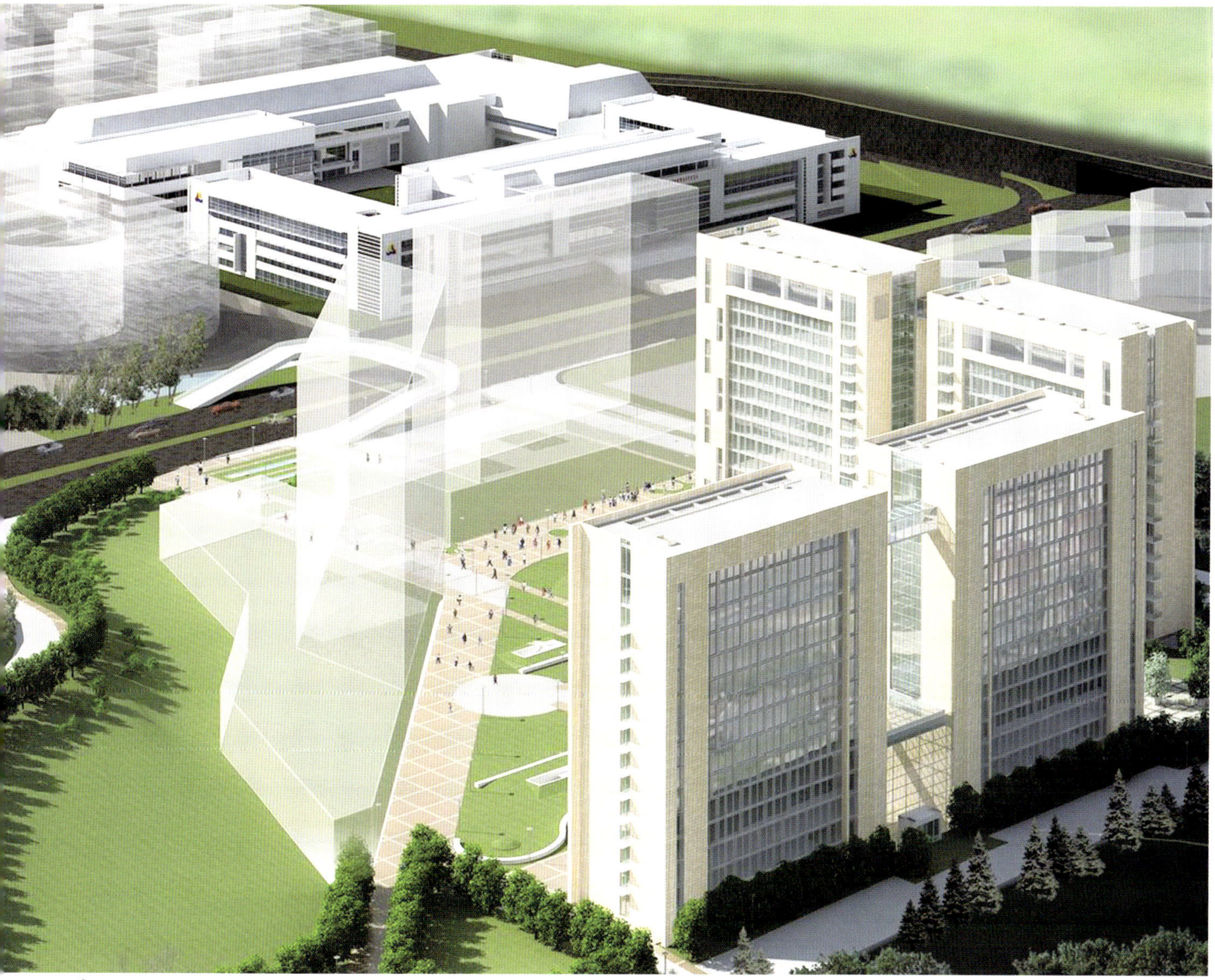

3

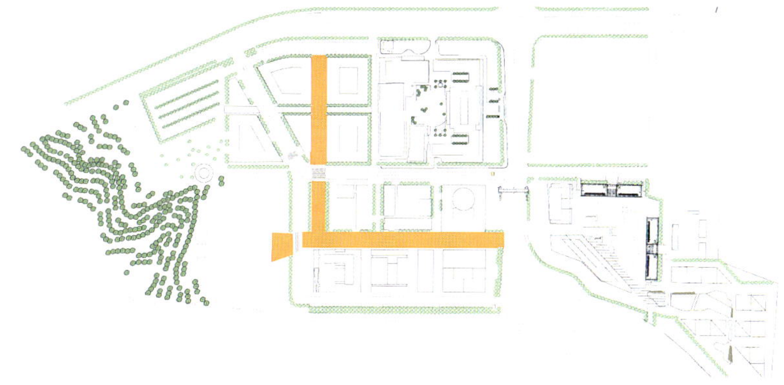

4

TOBB University of Economics and Technology Campus

Client TOBB University of Economics and Technology
Project Date 2003
Area 31,000 m^2
Location Ankara
Structural Engineer Yüksek Project
Mechanical Engineer Okutan Engineering
Electrical Engineer Akay Engineering
Landscape Design On Design
Consulting Firm Tür-Sum Construction, Yüksel Project International Inc.
Construction Manager Seviye Akı
Contractor Yavuzlar Construction Inc.

The first buildings completed for the TOBB University of Economics and Technology campus were the educational, administrative, and sports facilities, which were all refurbished and renovated from an existing group of elementary school buildings. The tension between the existing buildings' decisive style and the architectural image sought for the new university was resolved through the addition of rich interior spaces and the renewal of existing building façades, thereby providing an architectural setting for contemporary university education.

The campus buildings were completed in several successive stages. The educational and administrative buildings were completed in the first stage while the second stage comprised an Olympic swimming pool, a multi-functional indoor sports hall, and an office building. The dormitory buildings and a guest house were completed in the third stage of the design and the building of research laboratories, lecture halls, a media-tech block, conference center, dining hall, sports stadium, and eight new faculty buildings are planned for completion in the fourth stage.

The existing buildings were refurbished to house the educational, administrative buildings, and the sports center and were initially architecturally and structurally unsound. The façades of these reinforced concrete structures were stripped off and reinforced with the addition of a modular system, which transformed the close-knit pattern of load-bearing columns into a spatial advantage inside. By doing so, the congestion of columns and the rigid symmetry of the existing structural system were both utilized as an architectural language in designing the building interiors.

While the campus buildings are interconnected by way of inner gardens, new spaces have been introduced to define the additional areas, the most significant being the atrium. An outdoor area located between the rear building block, which houses lecture halls, the library, and cafeterias, and the front building block, which houses classrooms and administrative offices, was covered with a steel glass roof light to create an atrium, which would function as a social area. This atrium functions as a lively public space and includes facilities such as conference halls, exhibition areas, cafeterias, a health-care center, Xerox center, bookstore, bank, and souvenir shops. This space offers a rich spatial experience with magnolia trees set among glass stairs that connect the garden level with the main entrance, and a glass bridge leading to the library.

Opposite:
A lively public space is formed by the new design of additional spaces to the existing old college buildings

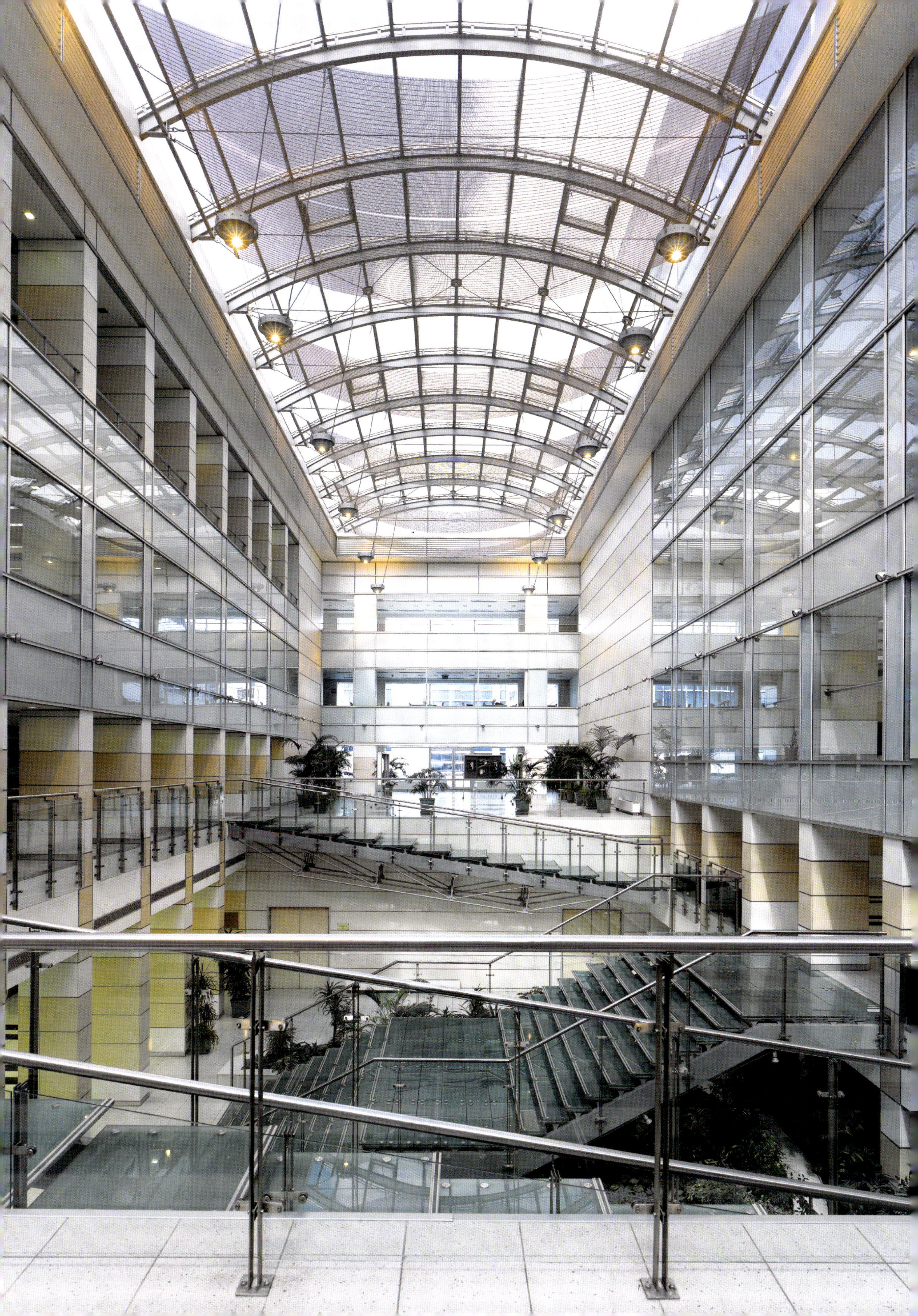

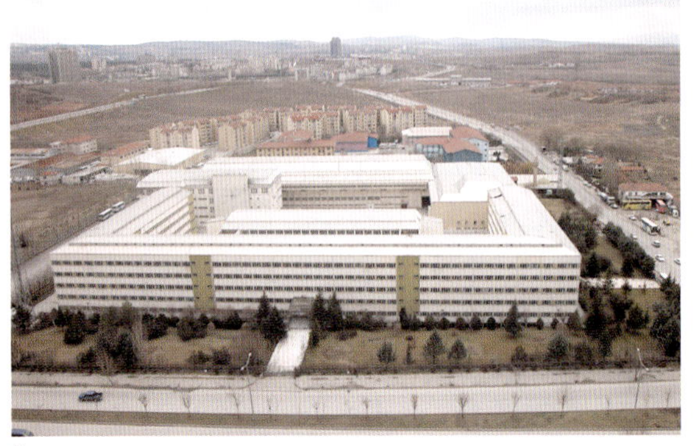
2

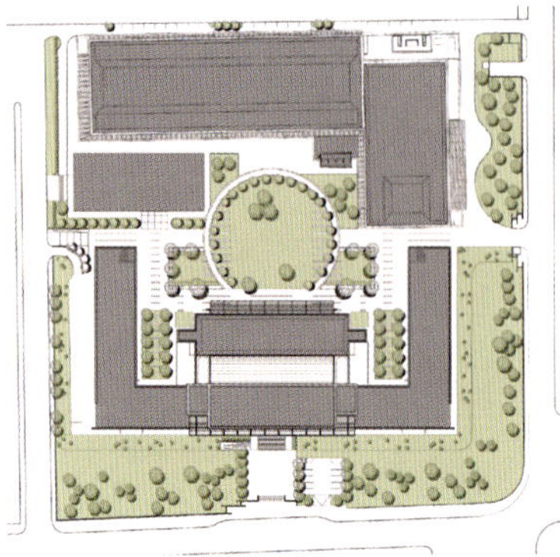
3

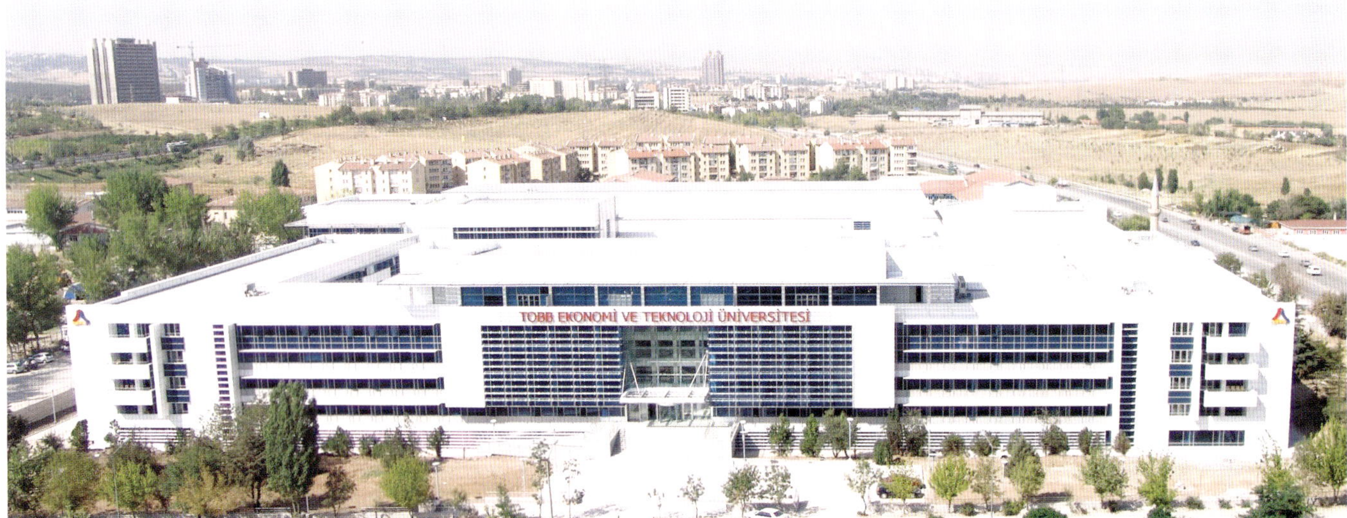

4

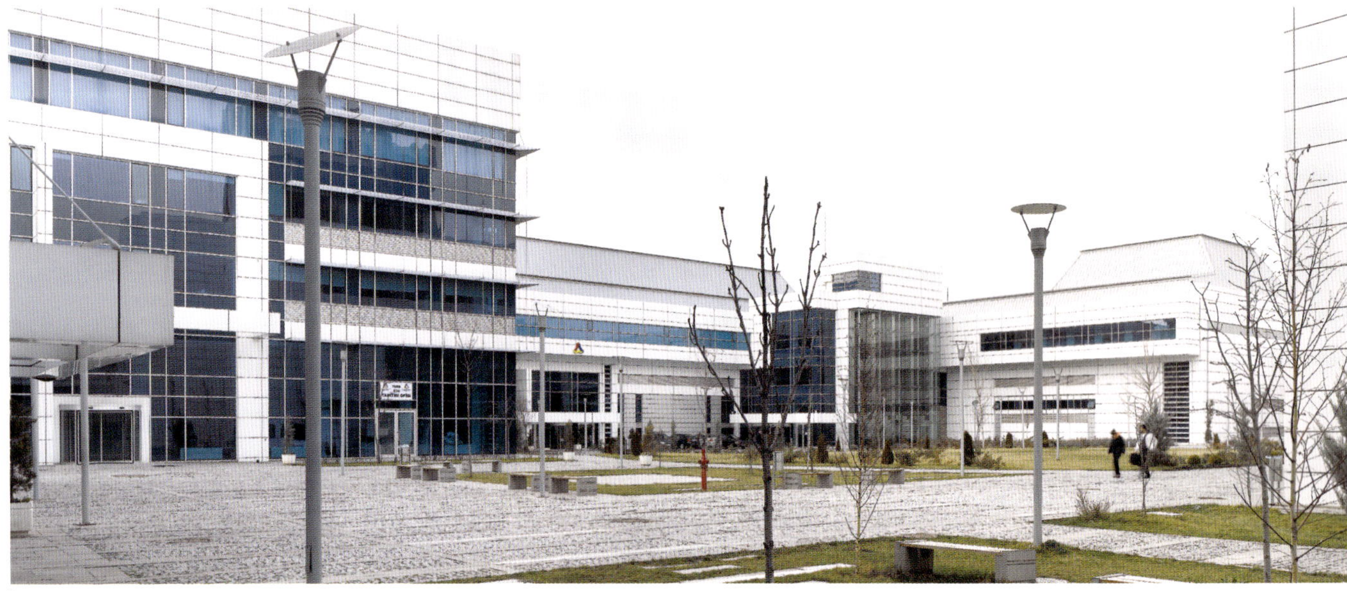
5

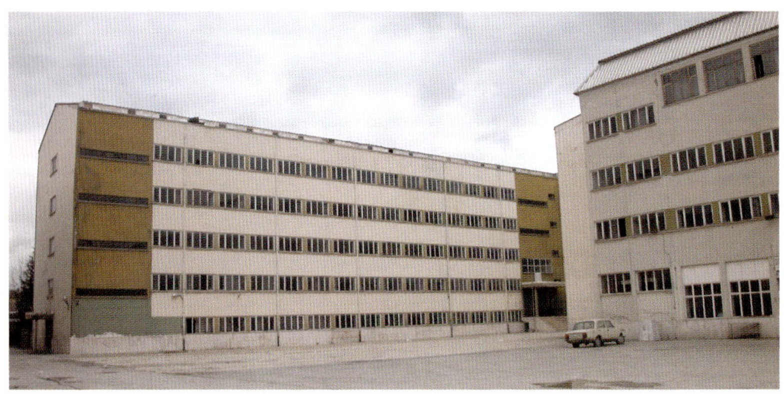
6

2 General view of the former buildings before renovation
3 Site plan of the buildings after renovation
4 General view of the buildings after renovation
5 View of the renovation from the courtyard
6 Before renovation
7 Façade detail
8 Longitudinal section from the first phase of the buildings

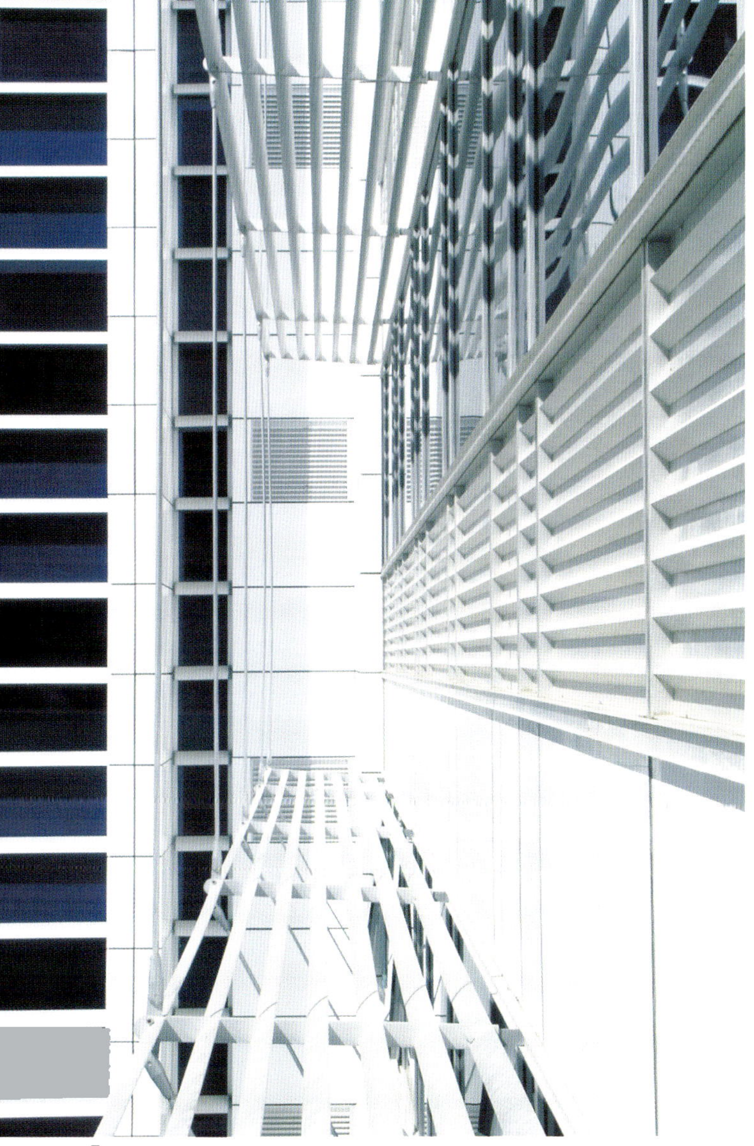
7

Classrooms are located on the wings located on both sides of the educational and administrative block. The corner of the building is reserved for balconied foyers, which act as communal spaces for faculty members and students, while academic staff rooms are located between these corner spaces and the upper administrative block.

All floors of the building were designed as open, undivided spaces, allowing maximum flexibility. Dividing plasterboard panel walls are fixed to the finished floors with aluminum profiles and may be demounted and re-arranged for different uses. All ceilings, floors, and walls were designed to complement each other. Metal and plasterboard were used for the suspended ceilings to match the walls and floors. Wall surfaces in the corridors were covered with frosted cam panels, allowing daylight into all the interior spaces. Laminated maple cladding was used in the interiors and the freestanding furniture is white and maple to complement the interior color scheme.

The vertical and horizontal planes on the building façades, the transparent surfaces, the overhangs, and the general dynamics of the building were all designed in accordance to the functional variety of the building. The architectural language of the building façades, formed through the use of material and details, was revised according to differing building functions and repeated throughout the campus.

Beyond its own program, this building represents an original design process consisting of the re-evaluation and refurbishment of existing buildings.

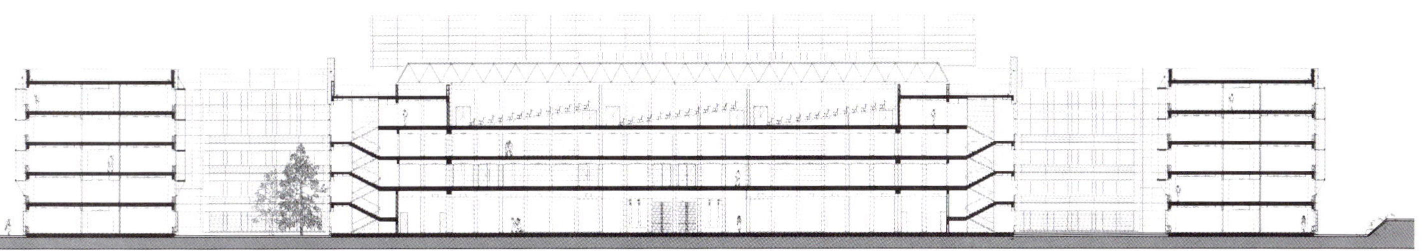
8

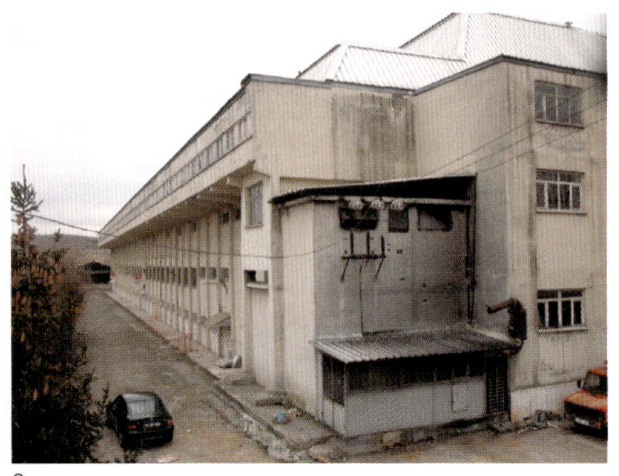
9

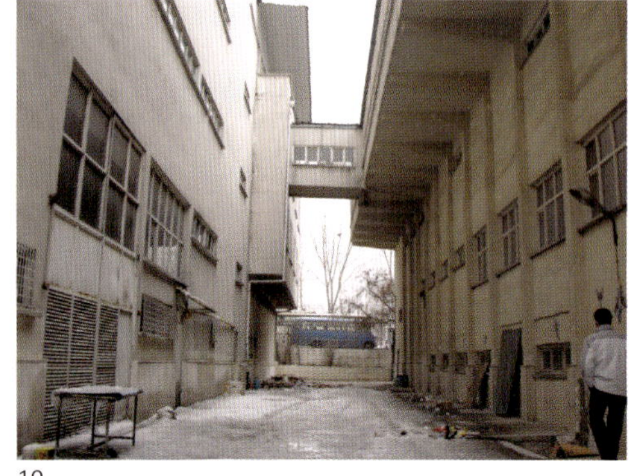
10

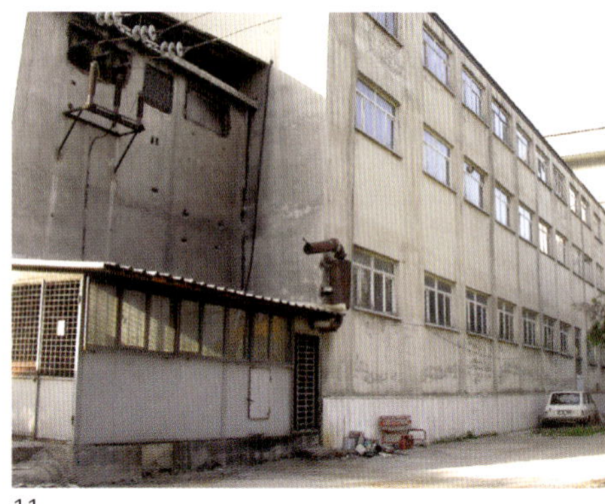
11

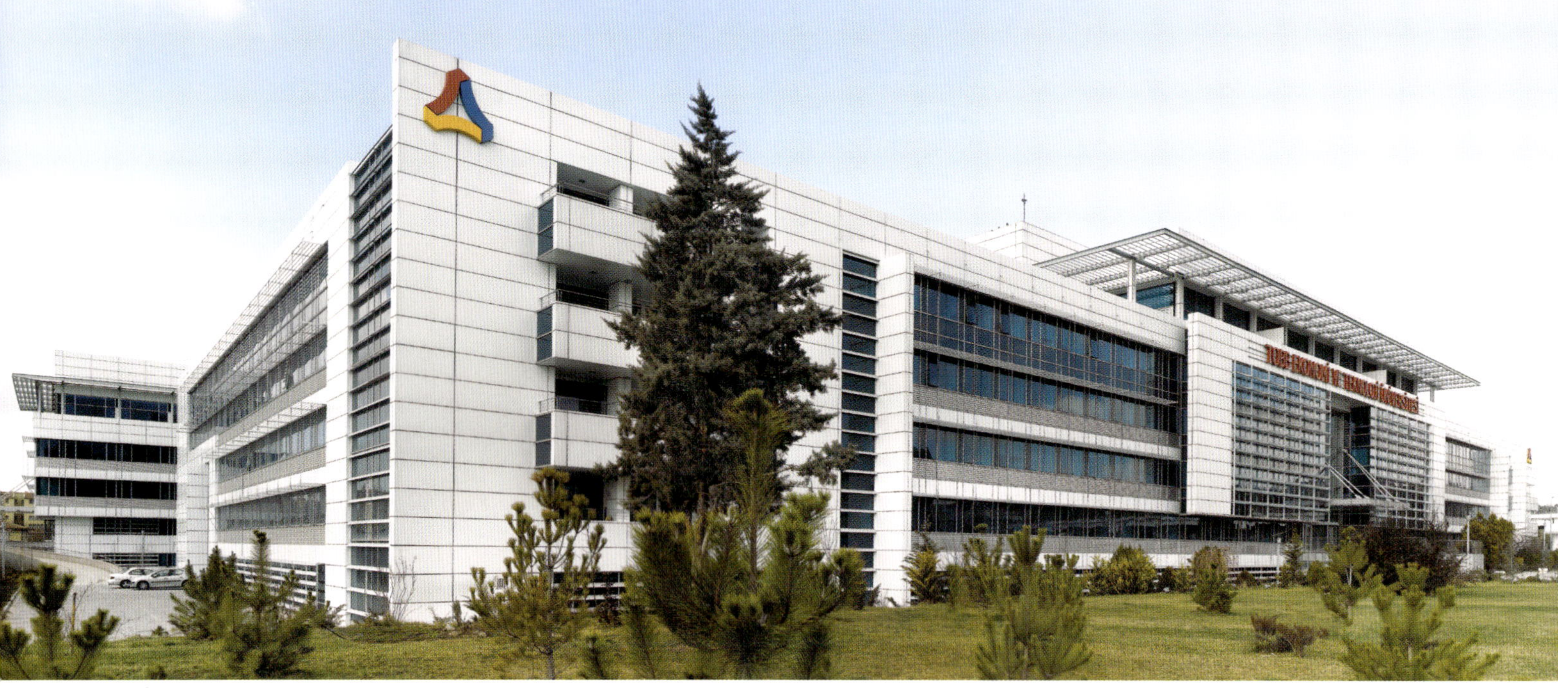
12

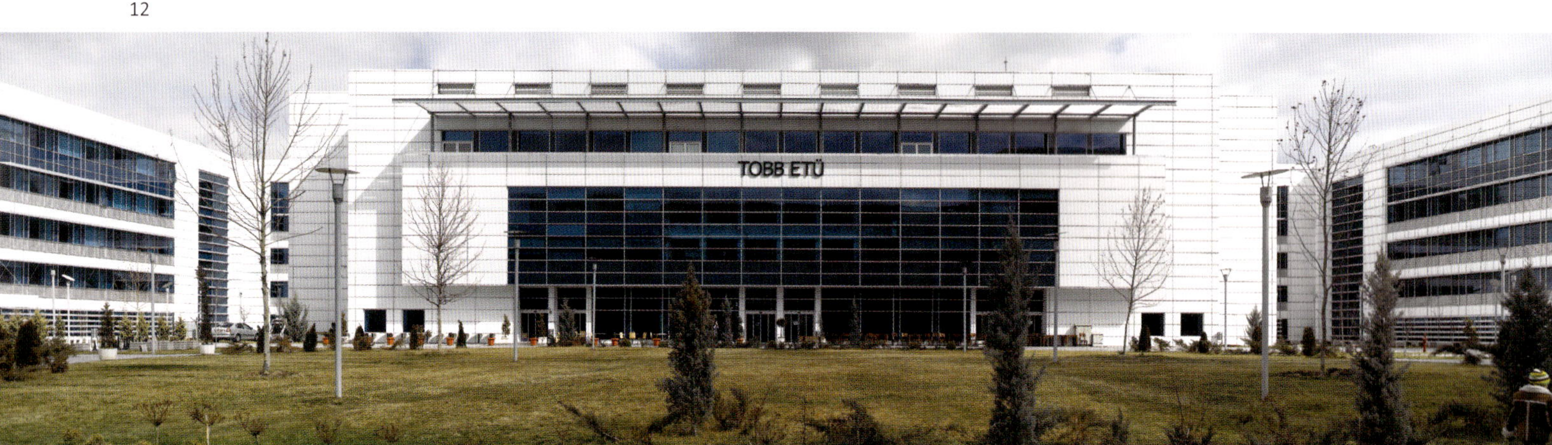

13

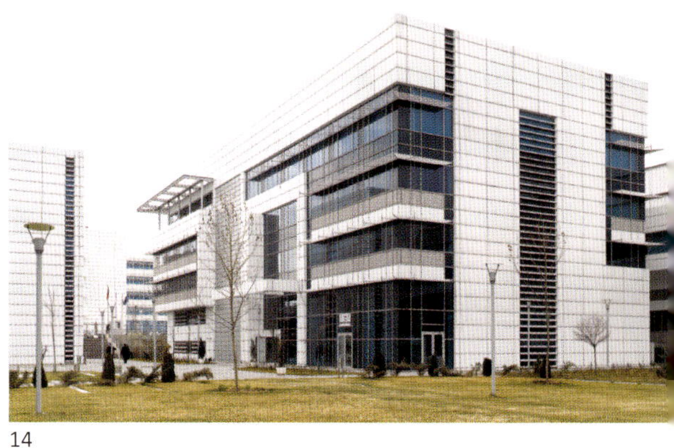
14

9–11 General view prior to renovation
12 Front façade after renovation
13 View of the buildings from the courtyard after renovation
14 TEPAV building after renovation
15 Façade view after renovation
16 Façade view before renovation
17 Main entrance after renovation

Following pages:
Transitory space showing the glass stairs connecting the garden level with the main entrance

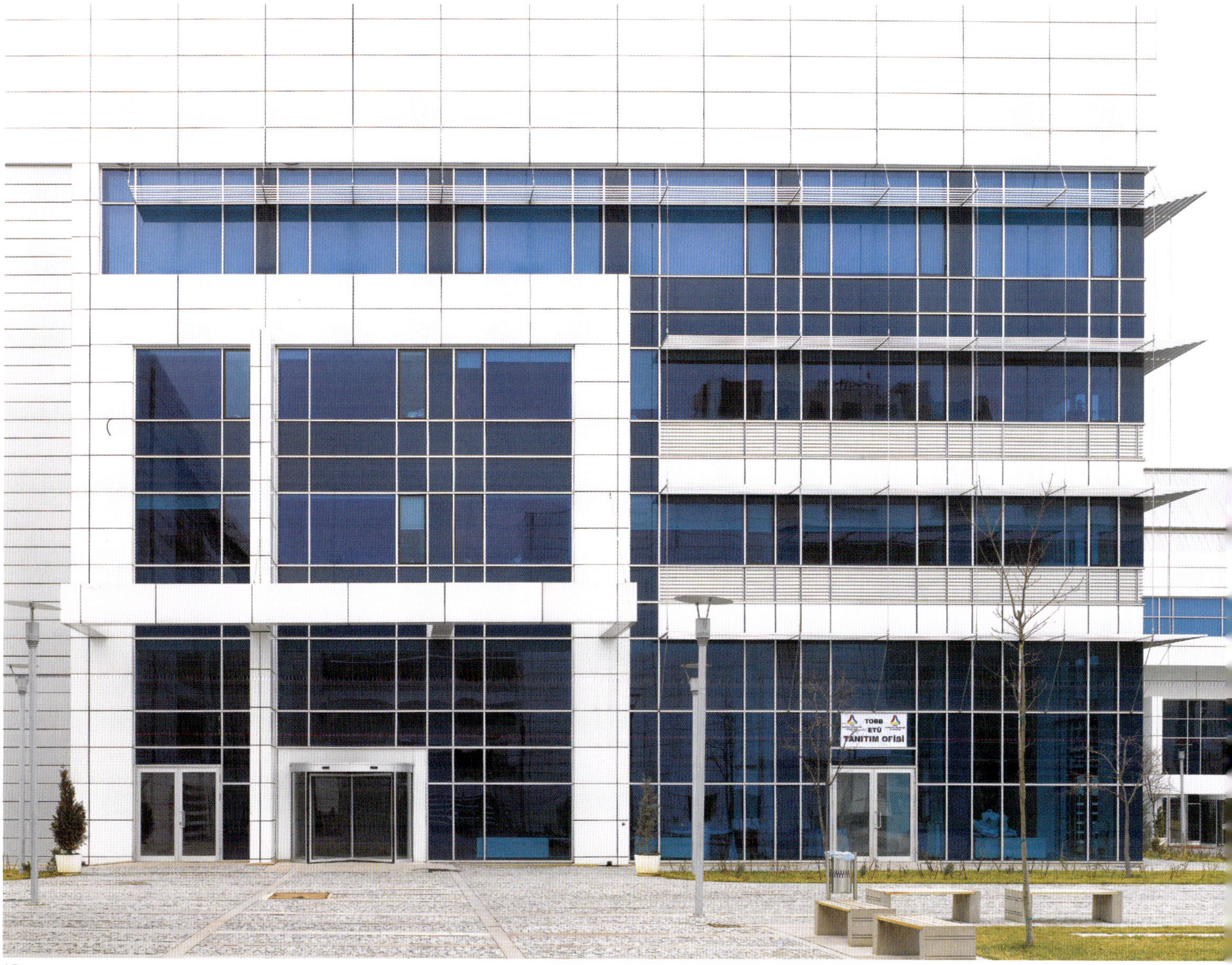

15

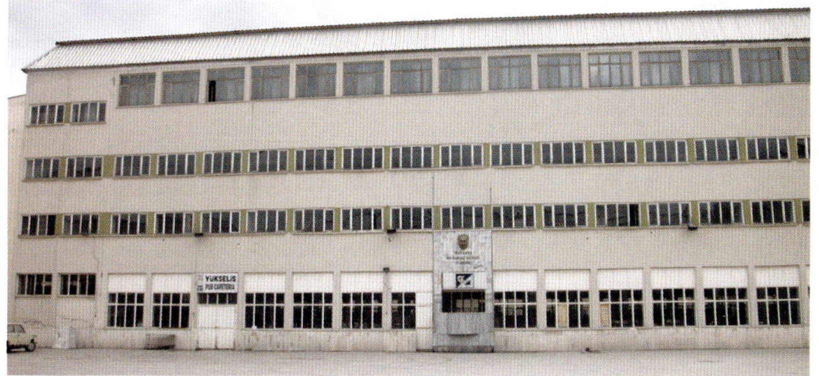

16

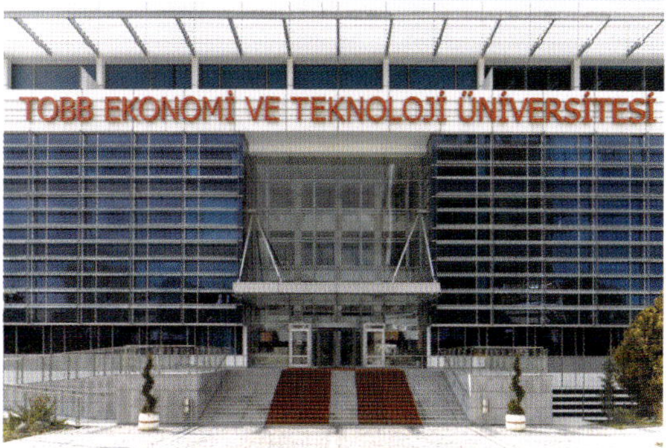

17

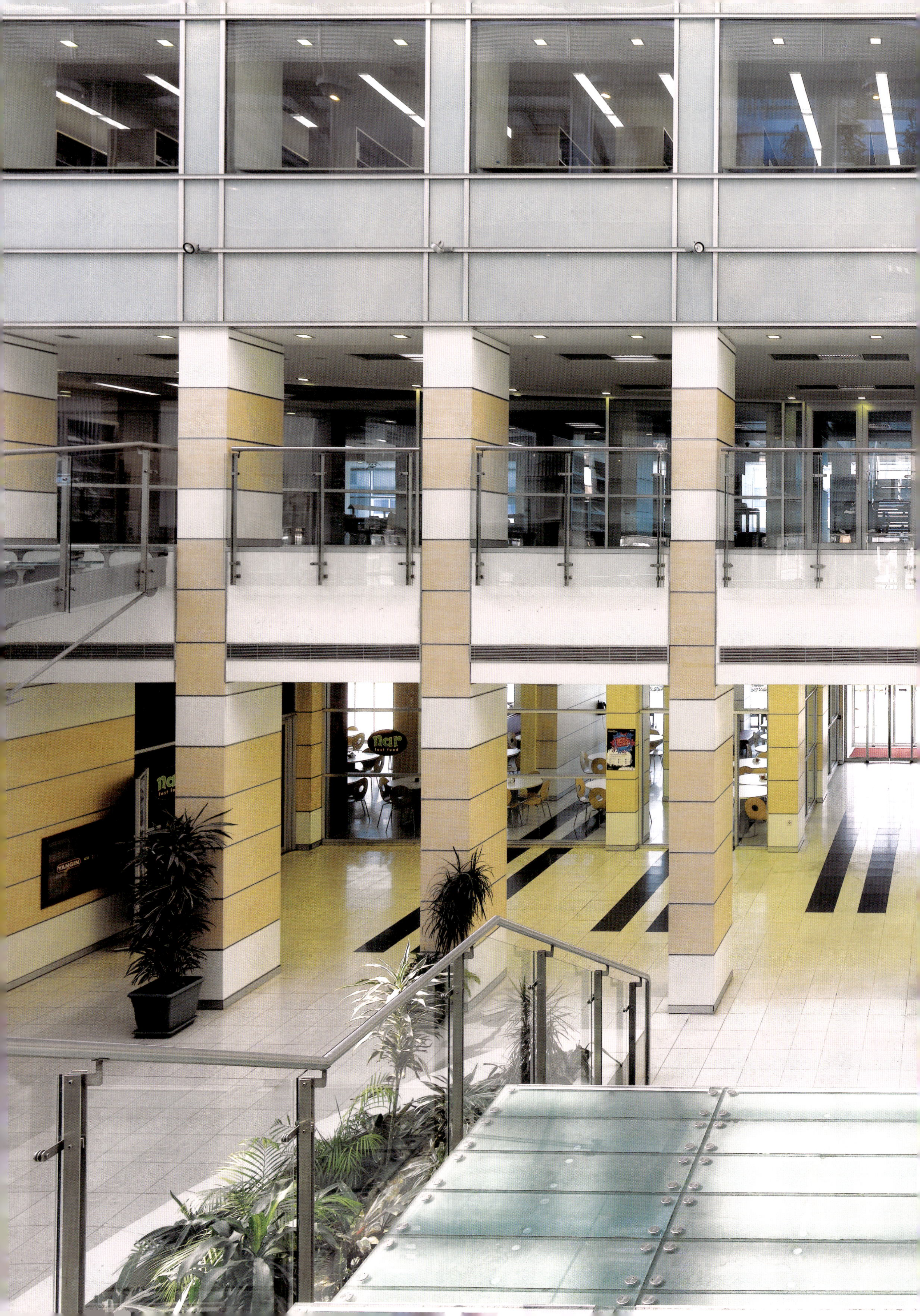
YANGIN
nar
fast food

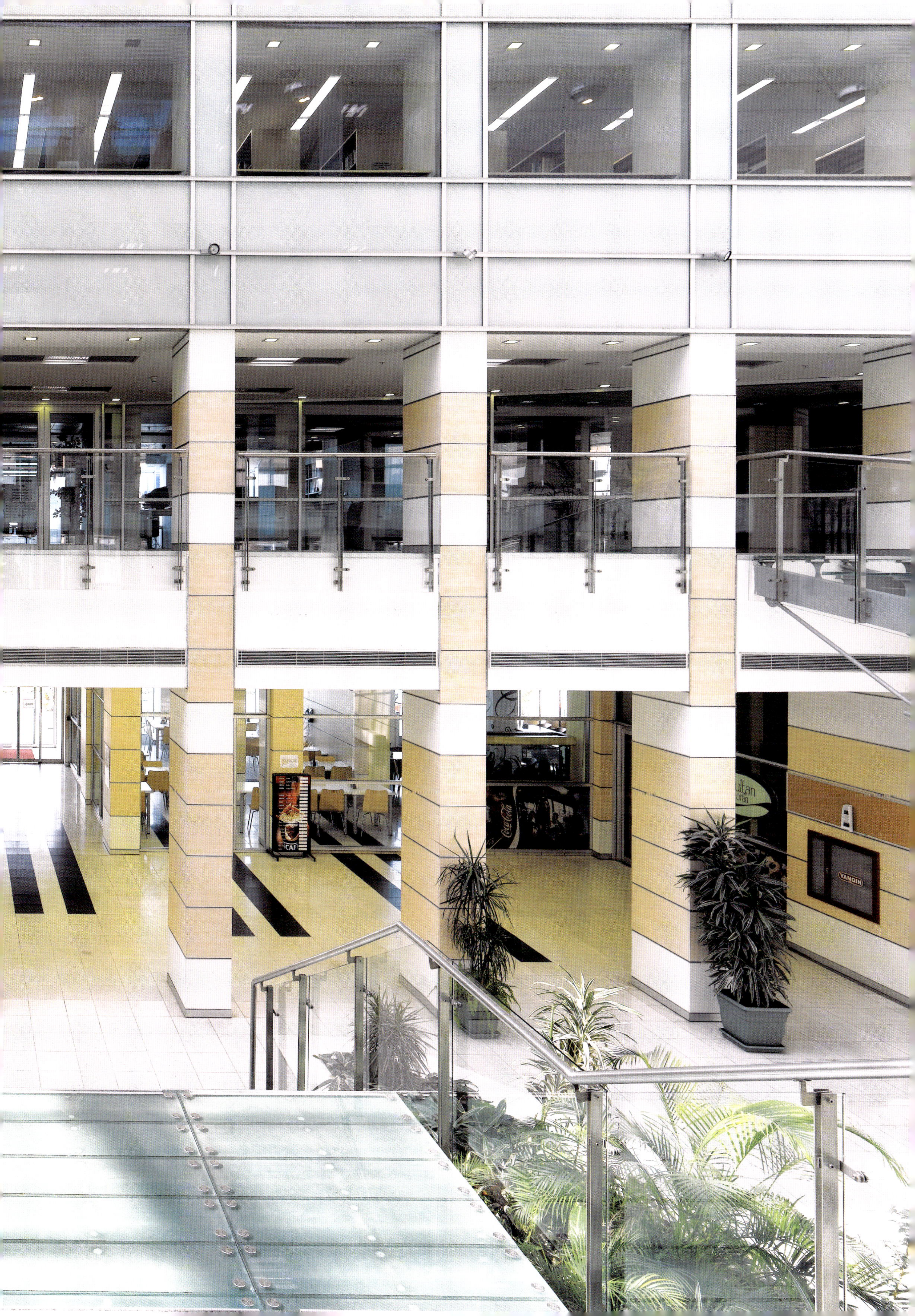
YANGIN
Coca-Cola

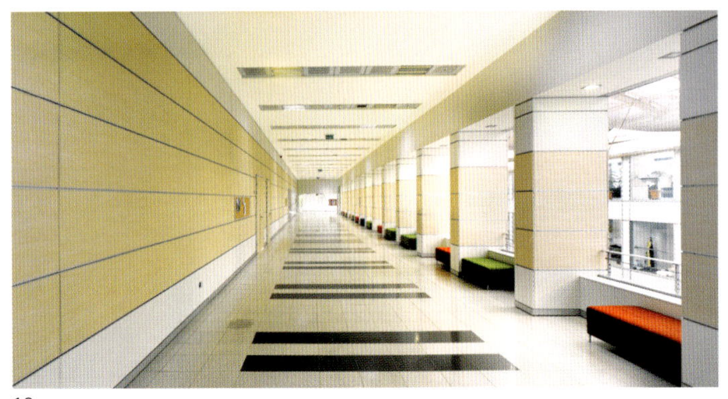
19

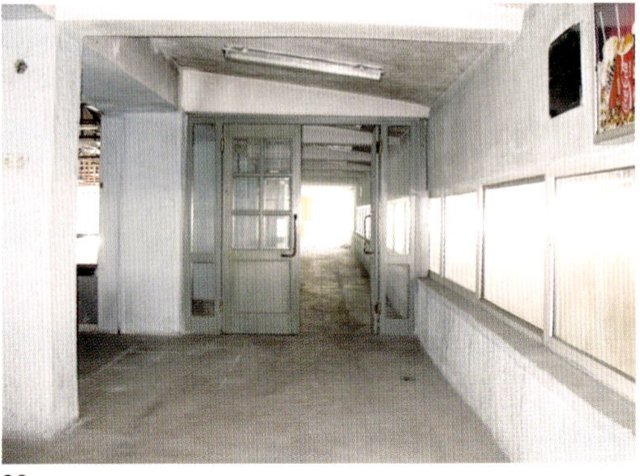
20

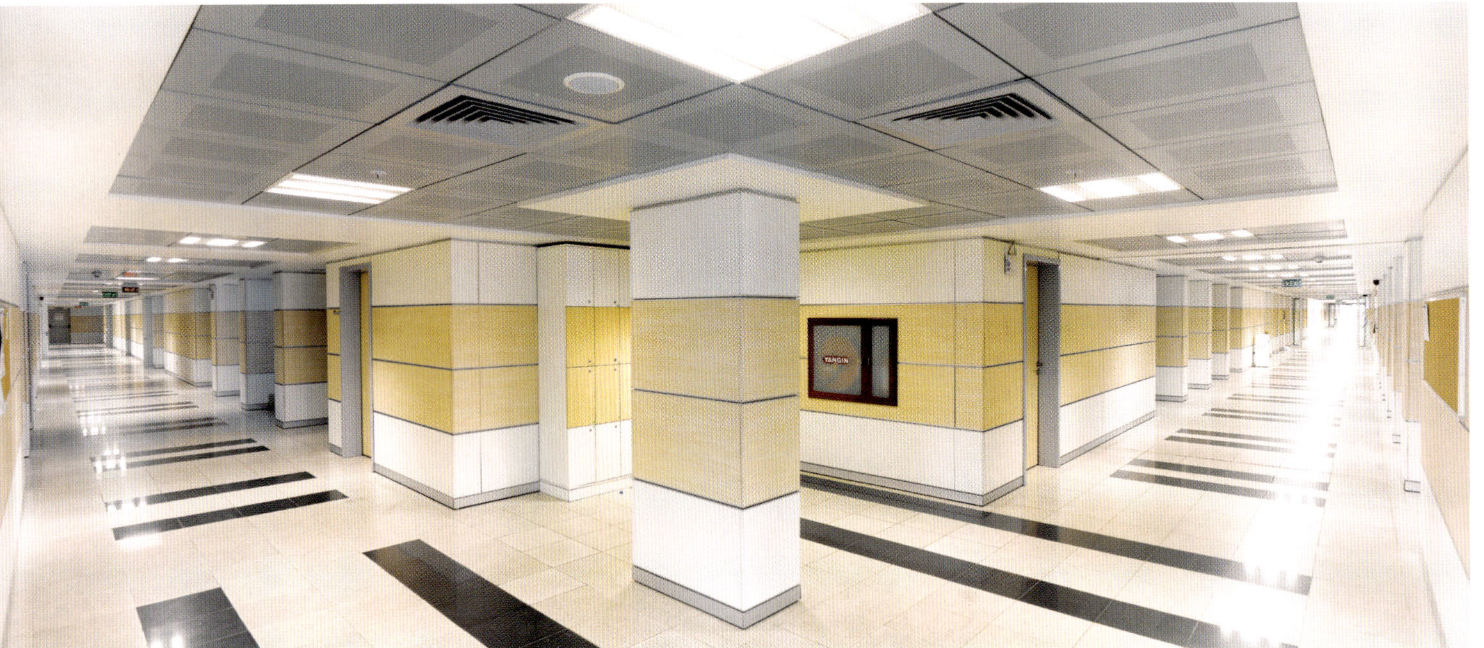

21

22

19 View of the renovated circulation area
20 View of the circulation area before renovation
21 View of the circulation area showing modular design floor and ceiling
22 Cross-section showing the different levels and foyer
23 Interior view of the circulation hall
24,25 Detail view of the glass stairs
26 General view of the renovated foyer
27 Fourth floor plan
28 Ground floor plan
29 Courtyard level plan
30 General view of the foyer before renovation

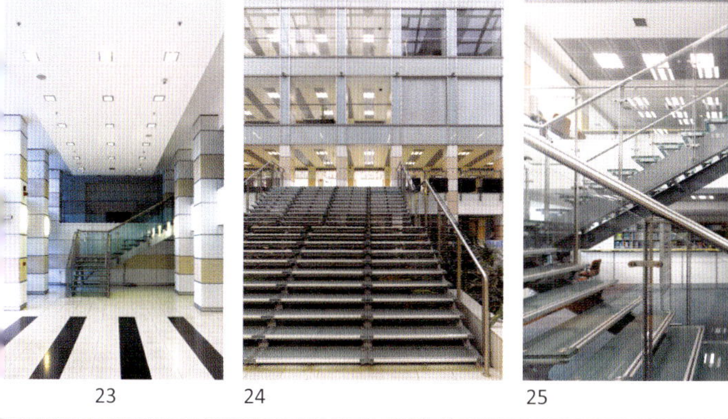

23 24 25

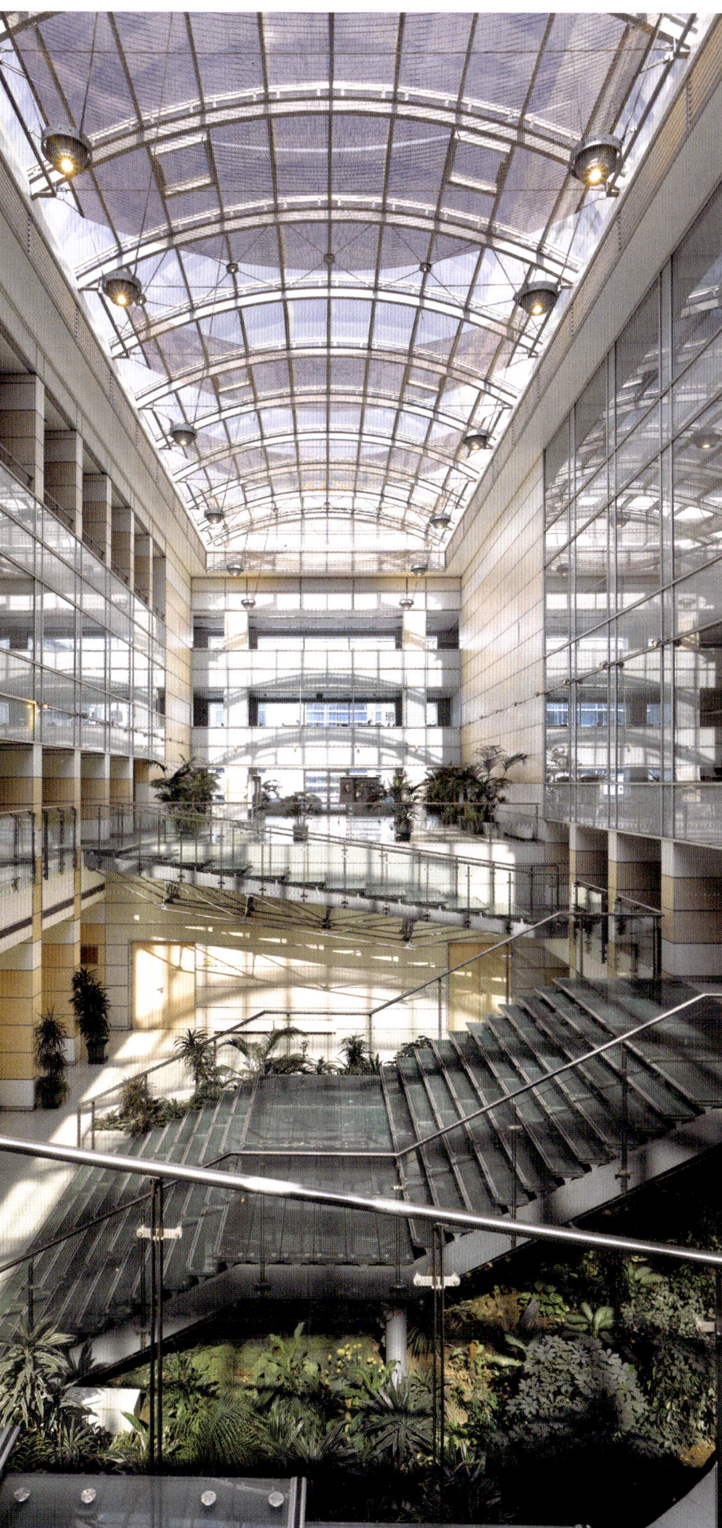

26

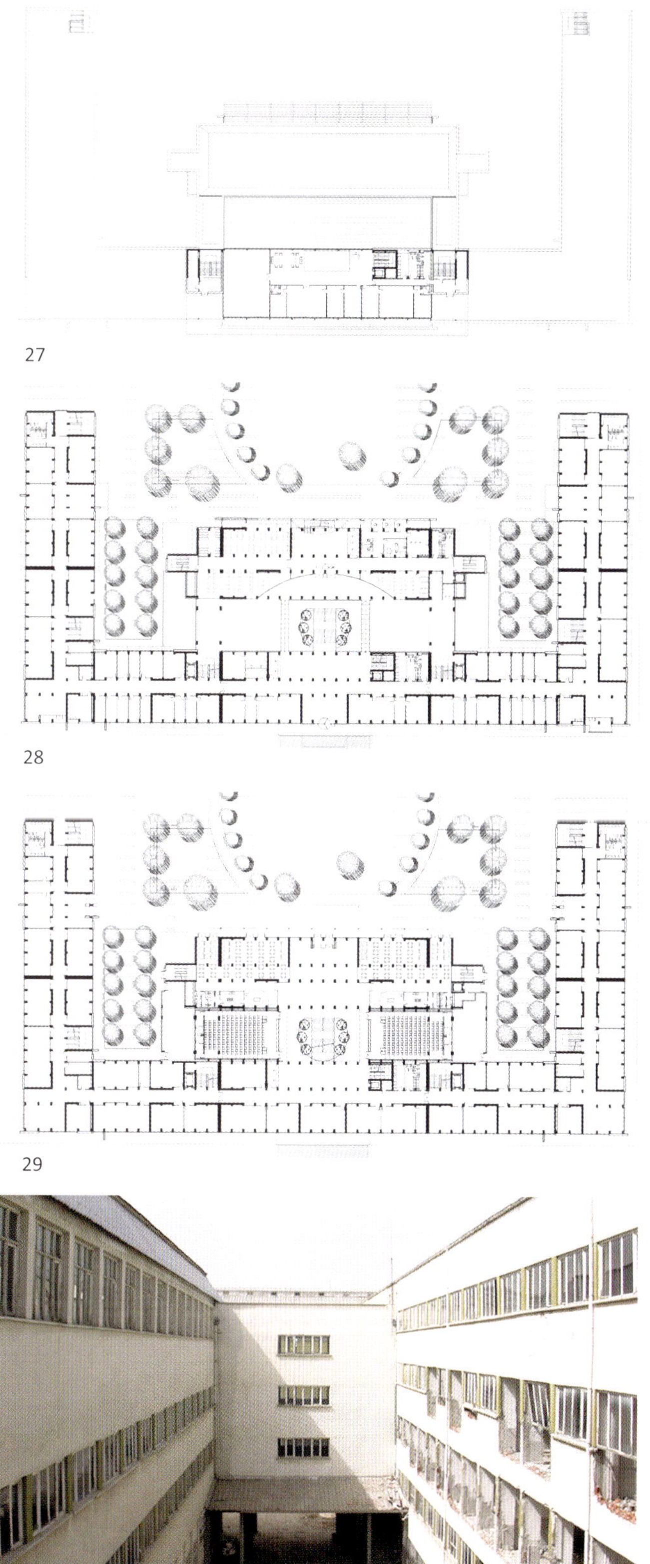

27

28

29

30

TOBB University of Economics and Technology Sports Complex

Client TOBB University of Economics and Technology
Project Date 2004
Area 31,000 m^2
Location Ankara
Structural Engineer Yüksek Project
Electrical Engineer Akay Engineering
Consulting Firm Yüksel Project International Inc.
Contractor Koçoğlu Inc.

The sports complex is a part of the second stage of buildings in the TOBB UET Söğütözü campus and it had previously been used as the sports facilities of a secondary educational institution. The buildings have not been demolished but reused and a new sports center has been created for the university according to international standards. The existing space frame system has been preserved while all of the materials are new. This renovation allows the multi-purpose sports center to be used by the public as well as the university. The sports complex contains an Olympic-size swimming pool, basketball and volleyball courts, a sauna, spa, and gymnastics and aerobics rooms.

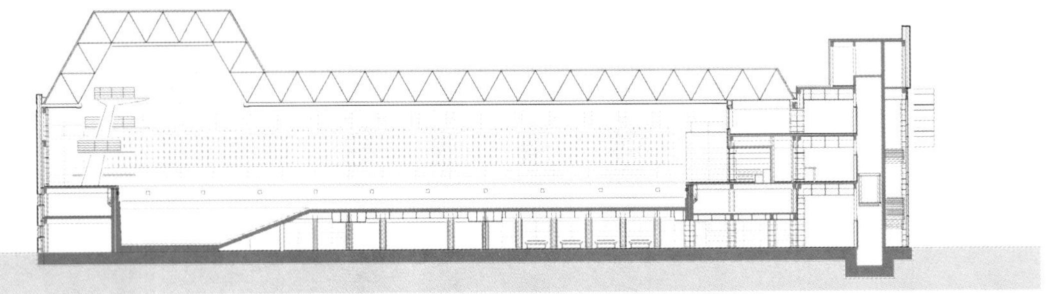

1

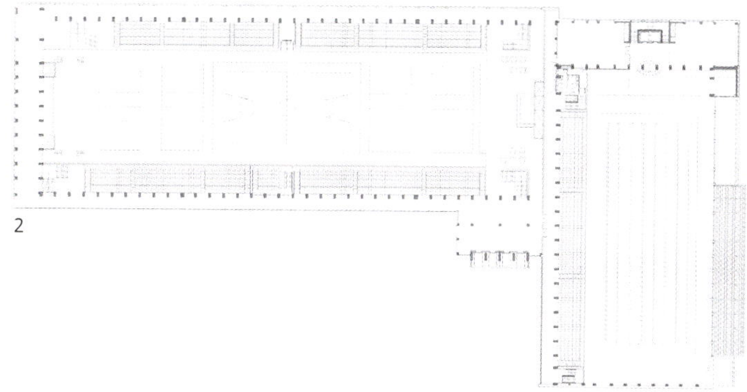
2

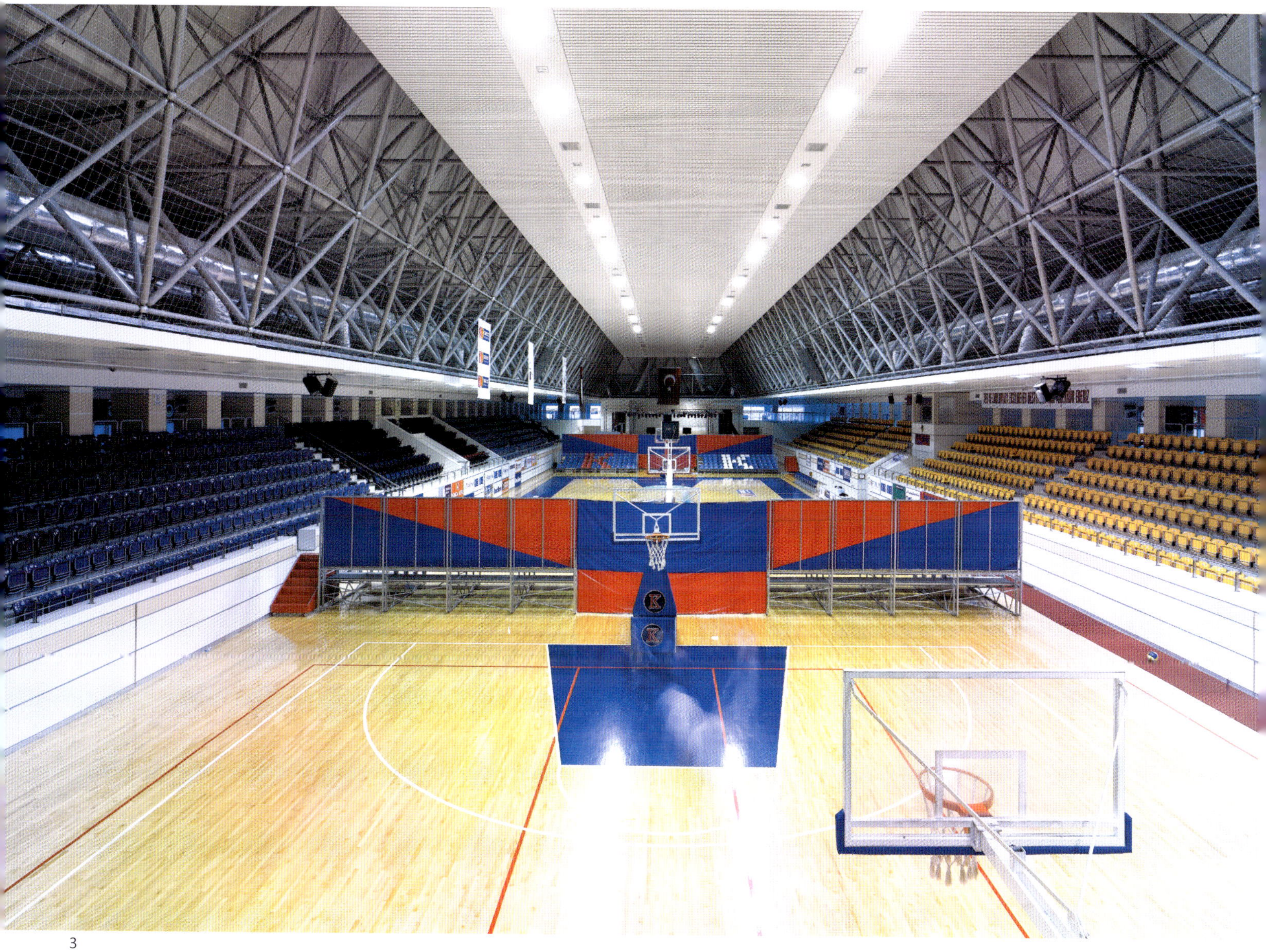

3

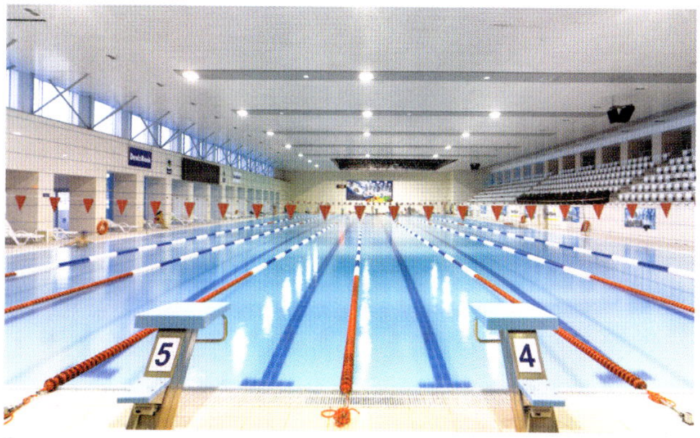

4

1 Cross-section through the swimming pool
2 Floor plan of sports hall and swimming pool
3 Renovated sports hall
4 Renovated swimming pool

TOBB University of Economics and Technology School of Foreign Languages

Client TOBB University of Economics and Technology
Project Date 2008
Area 10,500 m^2
Location Ankara
Structural Engineer Yüksek Project
Mechanical Engineer Okutan Engineering
Electrical Engineer Akay Engineering
Landscape Design On Design
Consulting Firm Tür-Sum Construction
Construction Manager Mustafa Tekinel
Contractor Tür-Sum Construction

The School of Foreign Languages was constructed in the development area of TOBB University of Economics and Technology (UET) Söğütözü Campus. Located on the planned pedestrian alley, the building has been designed to leave space for future buildings. The planned expansion of the building will create a courtyard in its center.

A modular system was developed for a rapid construction process. Classrooms and lecturer offices are located in separate annexes and common social spaces can be found in the inner sections. Connecting patios face the expansion area. The colors and materials used in the campus's first buildings were repeated for this building, ensuring the new structure matches the existing buildings.

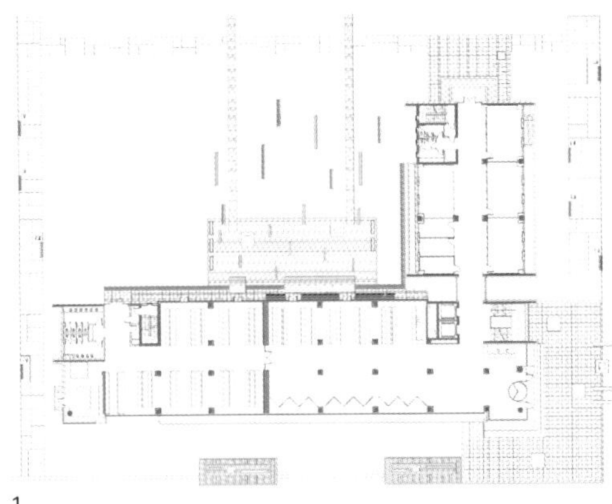
1

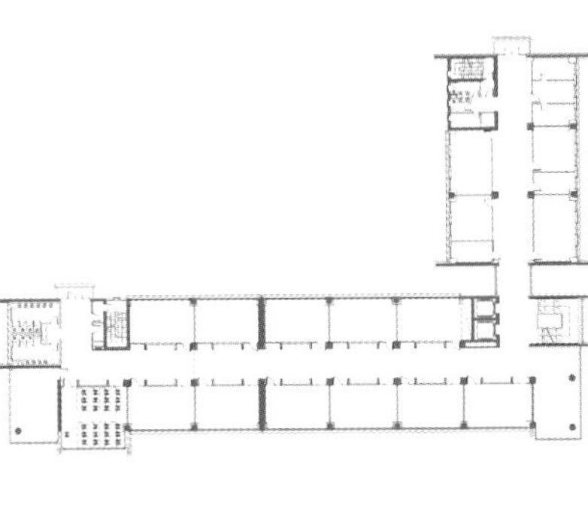
2

1 Ground floor plan
2 Typical floor plan
3 Cross-section and elevation
4 South view of the building
5 View of the building with the outdoor greenery
6 Main entrance through the parking lot

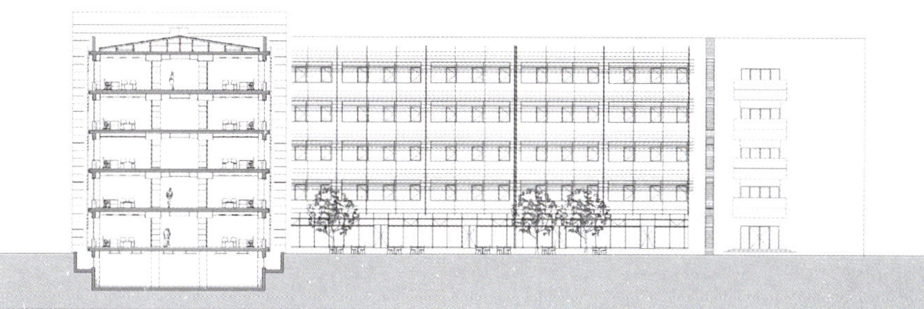

3

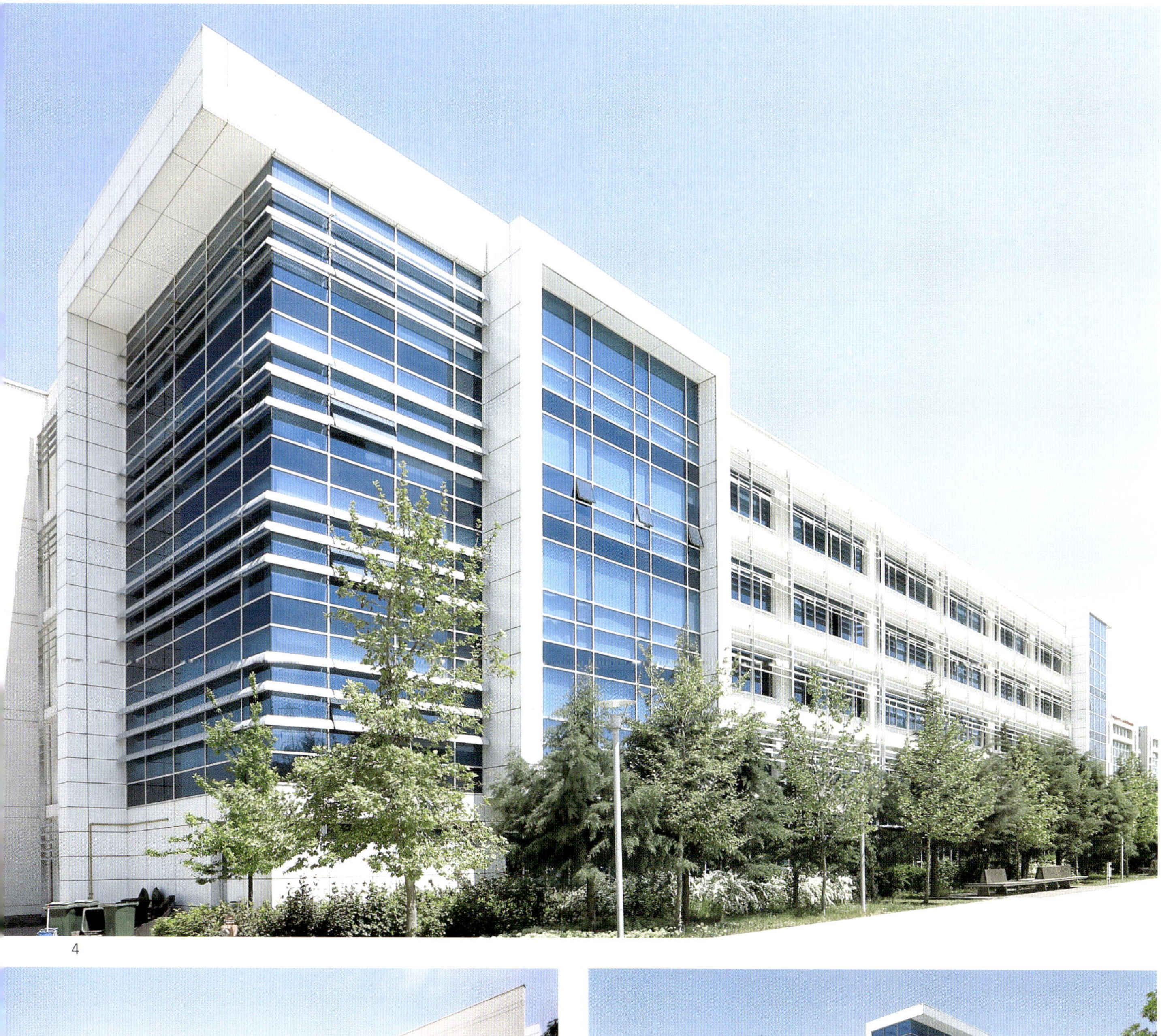

4

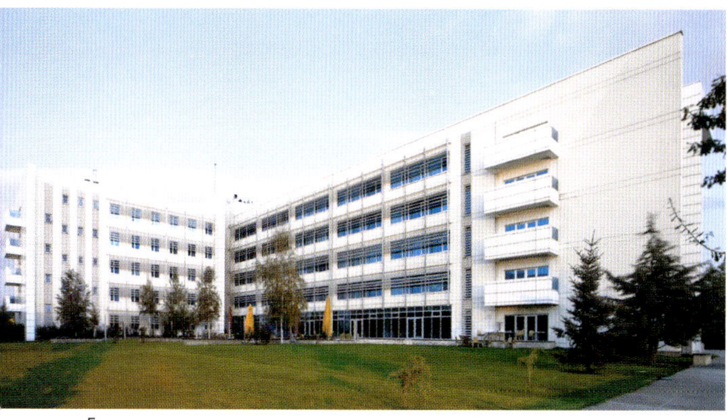

5

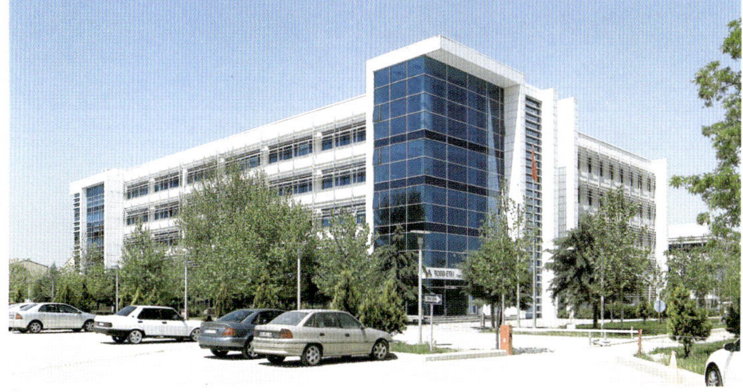

6

TOBB University of Economics and Technology Student Guesthouses

Client TOBB University of Economics and Technology
Project Date 2004
Area 70,000 m^2
Location Ankara
Structural Engineer Yüksek Project
Mechanical Engineer Okutan Engineering
Electrical Engineer Akay Engineering
Landscape Design On Design
Consulting Firm Tür-Sum Construction
Construction Manager Mustafa Tekinel
Contractor Ender Construction

Opposite:
Night view of the front façade and the main entrance
Following pages:
Night view of the building showing the courtyard

Following the completion of the faculty buildings for the TOBB University of Economics and Technology at the Söğütözü Campus, the esteem earned by the institution led to the need for new developments in the campus. At this time, the university acquired several adjacent building sites and a new master plan was designed for the enlarged campus.

In the campus development plan, the student guesthouses buildings are located along Söğütözü Avenue, facing the faculty buildings. The student dormitory blocks, academic guesthouse, life center, and studio flats are also designed at this location, thus aiming to create a lively social area for the campus. Students can access the guesthouses by the pedestrian route passing through the trainee hotel and student union buildings, which will be built in the later phases of the campus development. There are two individual blocks for men and women, which are connected by atriums that include the entrance halls. The transparent entrance halls rise above the standard story height of the blocks, thus creating spacious social areas for the buildings.

To meet the minimal construction time requirement, the structural system of the buildings was prepared via tunnel formwork. A spatial design that offers flexibility of use was designed with this system. Within the limits of the tunnel formwork system, the ground level consisting of the restaurants, the basement floor consisting of the social activity spaces, and the terrace floor consisting of the sports area and café were designed to have higher ceilings than the typical floors. The lower levels house a series of cafeterias, which have access to the inner courtyard, and the lobby, a library, study halls, and offices. Student rooms, communal kitchens, and resting areas can be found on the upper levels.

The design of the double rooms offers each student an equal amount of space. Single rooms may be turned into double rooms on demand. Bathrooms have a separate door for the toilet area, thus allowing simultaneous use of the lavatory and shower by roommates. Study and bedroom areas are clad in wood for a simple interior effect. Doors to the rooms are timber, and have been designed to match the lighting fixtures.

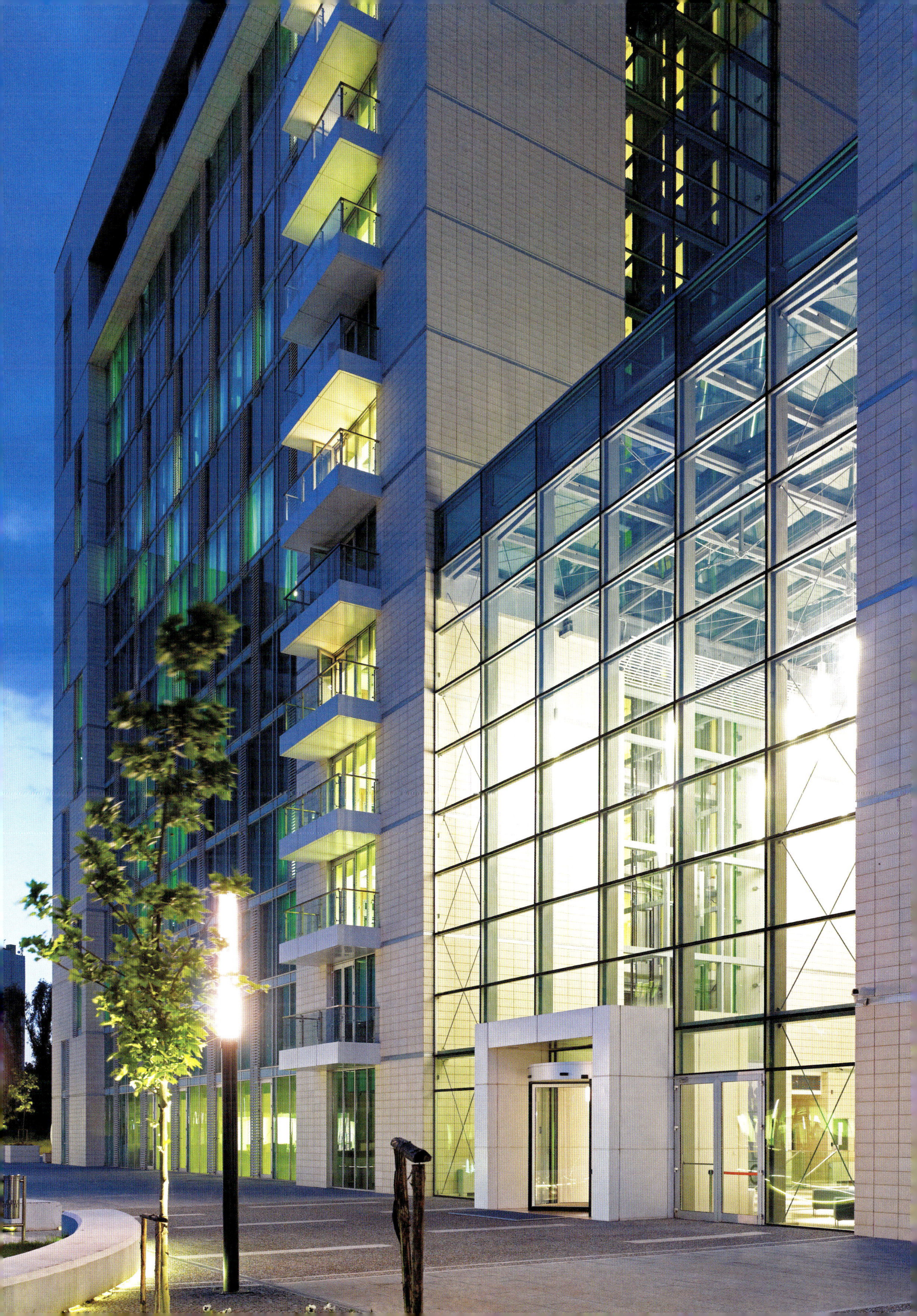

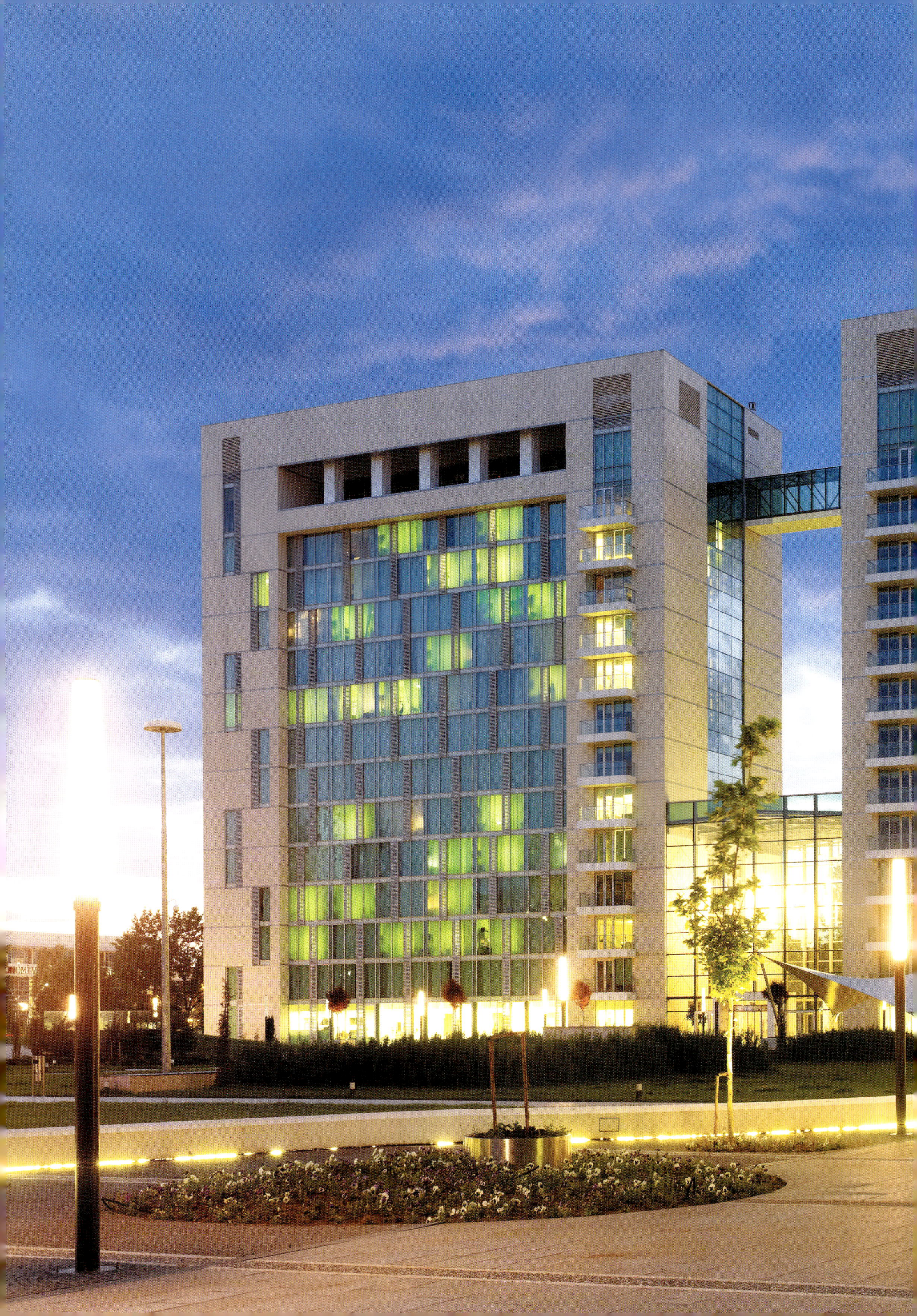

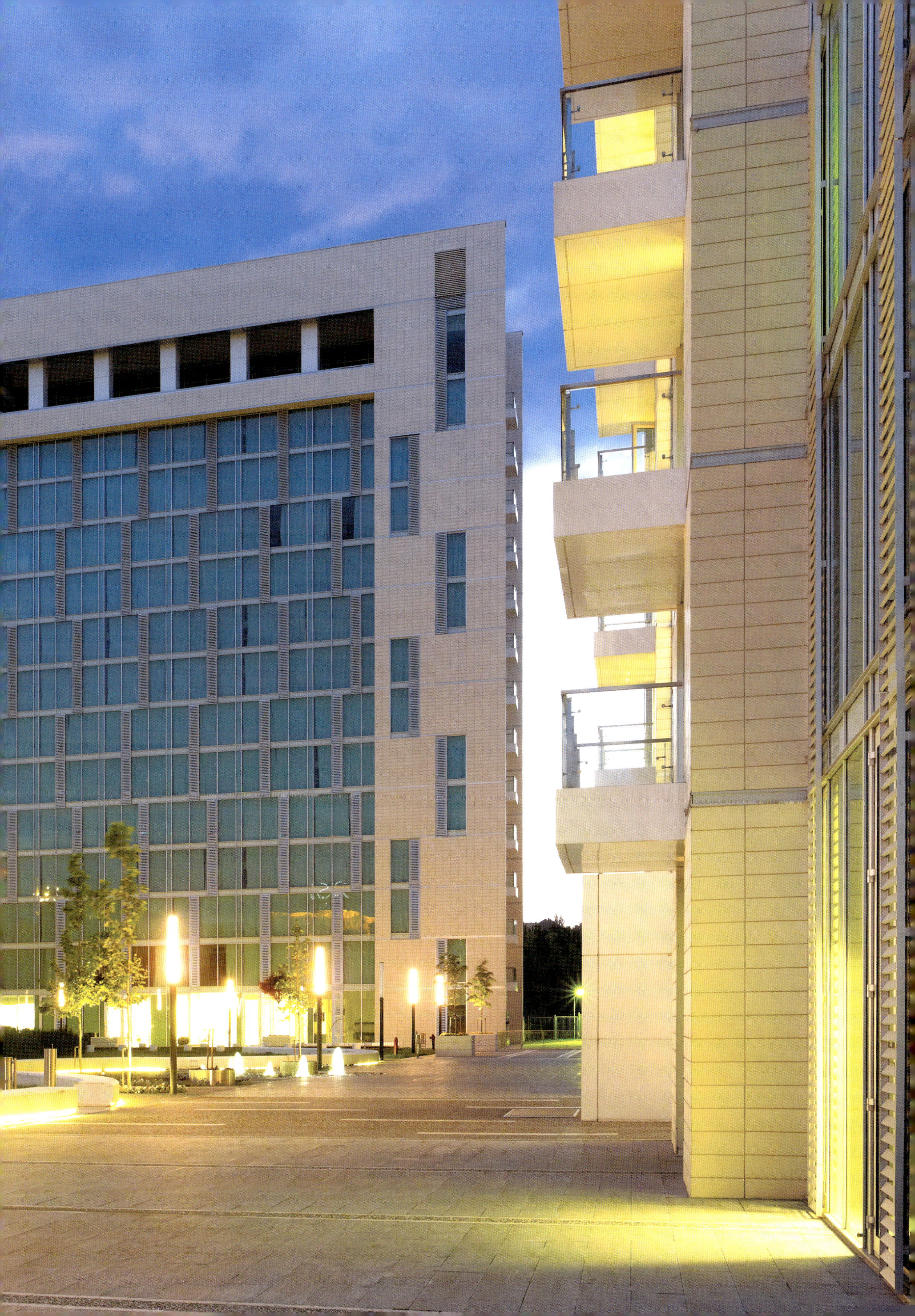

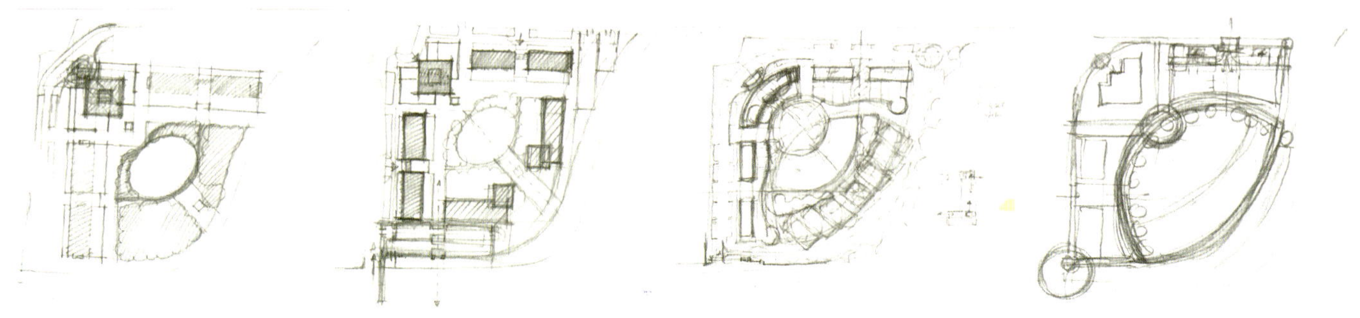

3

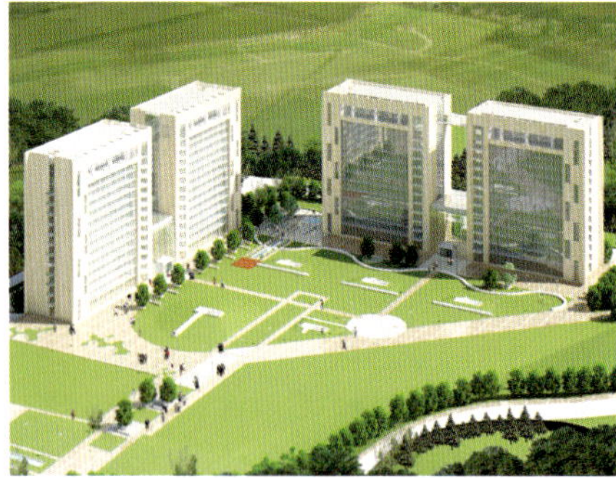

4

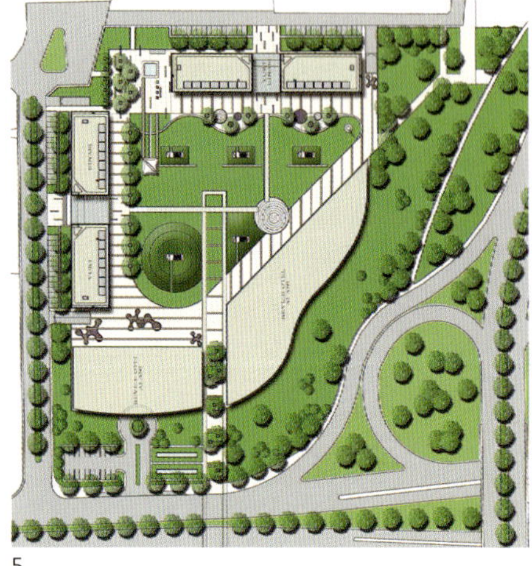

5

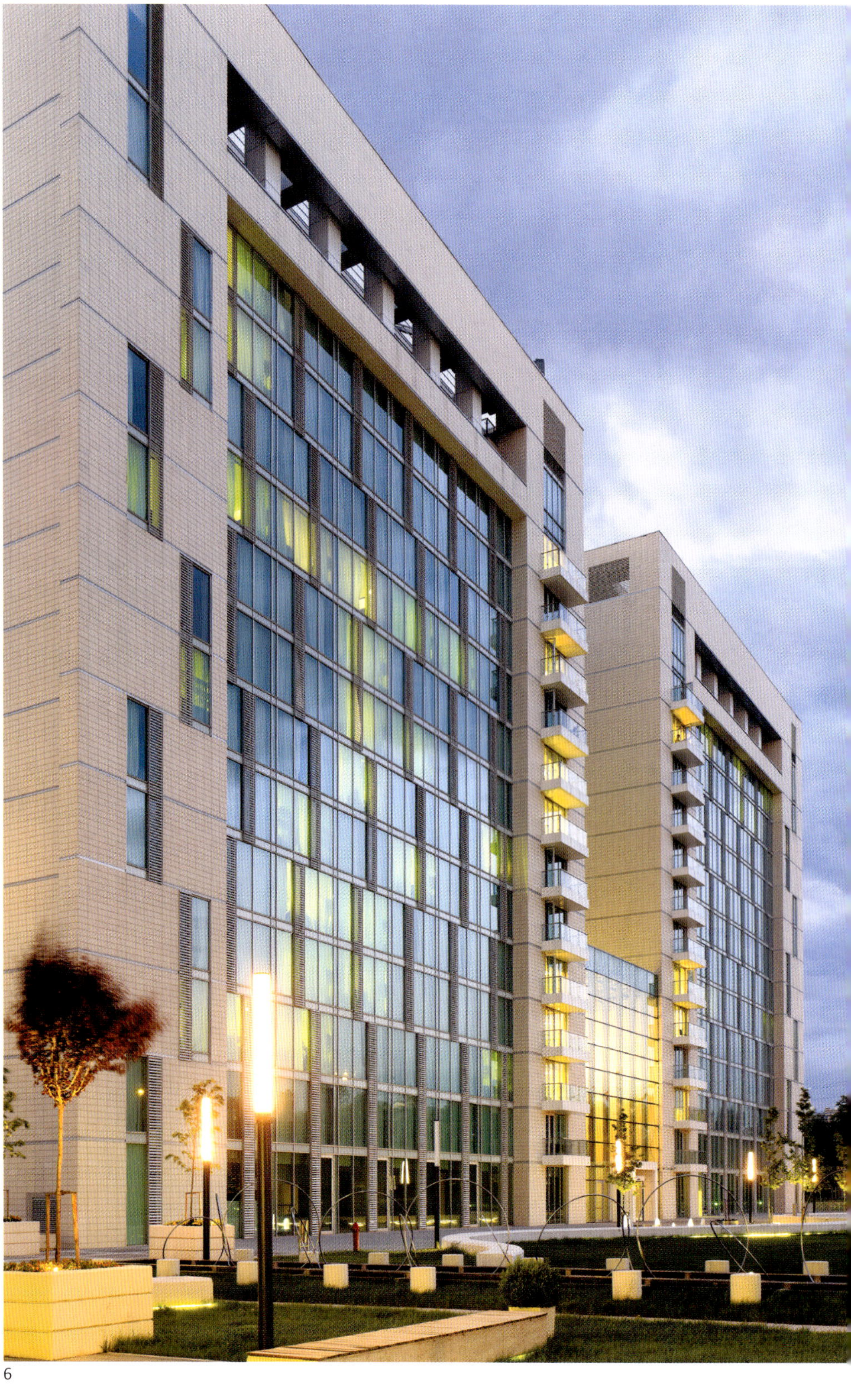

6

3 Early sketches by Ali Osman Öztürk exploring the relations between buildings and the courtyard
4 Aerial view of the building
5 Site plan
6 Façade of the building at night
7 Ground floor plan and typical floor plan
8 Plan of the double rooms and single rooms
9 Interior view of the double rooms
10 Interior view of the single rooms
11 View of the entrance hall
12 Cross-section and elevation

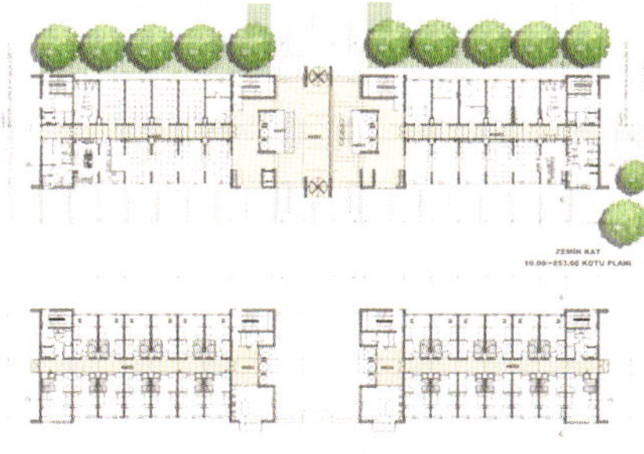

7

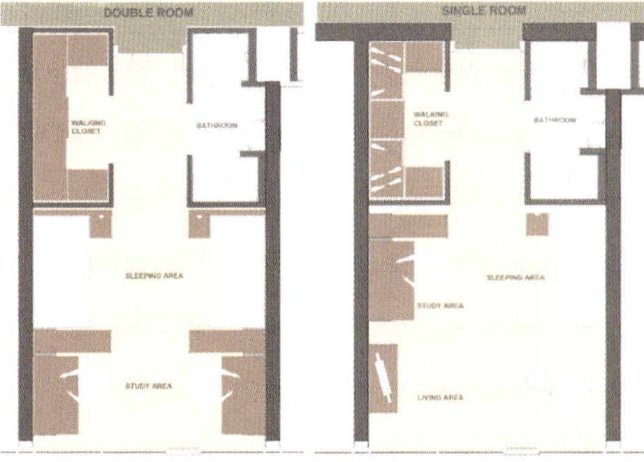

8

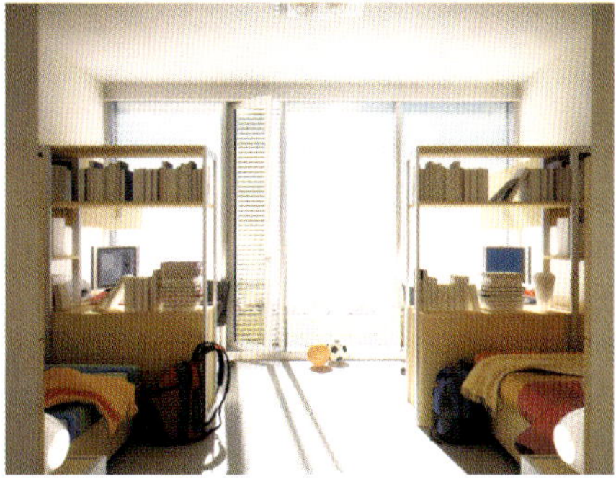

9

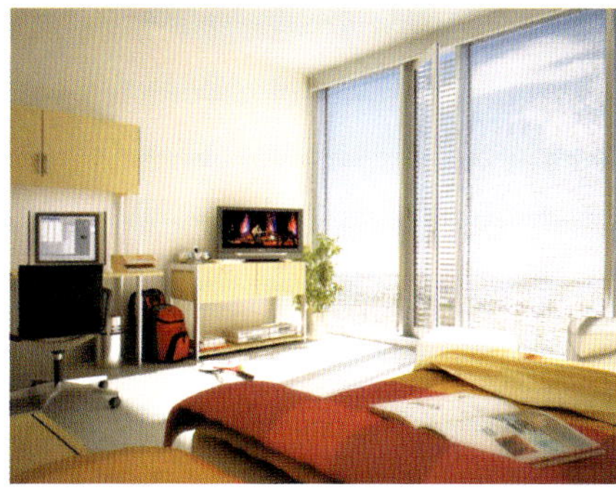

10

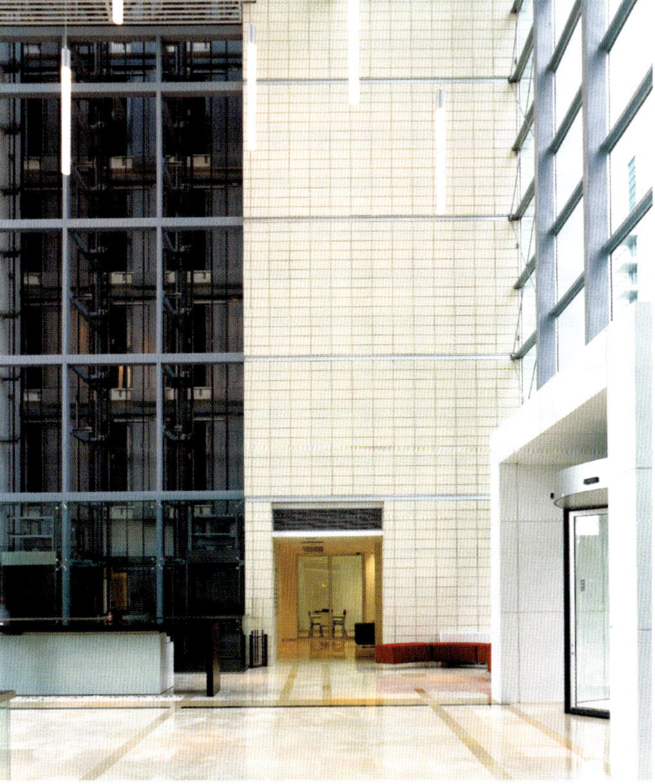

11

Storage areas include wardrobes as well as areas for built-in refrigerators and kettles. All rooms have curtain walls from floor to ceiling, which are also decked with ventilation panels. Panels on the higher levels are embedded in the façade system for security. The bricks that were mechanically mounted to the curtain walls on the outer façade allude to the conventional use of brickwork on dormitory buildings. These bricks were chosen in different color tones and shades to accentuate the natural quality of the material.

The dormitories have been designed to provide students with a liberating urban and social setting as well as a relaxing environment where they can feel at home and have privacy.

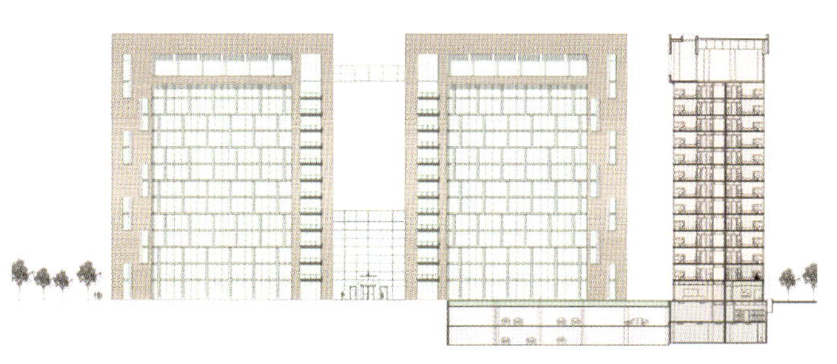

12

TOBB University of Economics and Technology Technology Center

Project Date 2010
Area 23,000 m^2
Location Ankara
Structural Engineer Yüksek Project
Mechanical Engineer Okutan Engineering
Electrical Engineer Akay Engineering
Landscape Design On Design
Consulting Firm Tür-Sum Construction
Construction Manager Mustafa Tekinel
Contractor Tür-Sum Construction

Within the TOBB UET Söğütözü Campus development plan, the designated area for the Engineering and Fine Arts Departments is to the left of the School of Foreign Languages. The engineering buildings to be designed in this area will connect to the Fine Arts building and the library. A new building with similar size and organization is designed in a way that allows for future development, with reserve sections left at the end of the connecting corridors.

The transparent façades of the shared spaces, the laboratories, and the water turbine test center planned for the basement floor, as well as the indoor garden surrounded by patios, can be seen from almost every point in the building. The completely transparent indoor garden façade visually connects all the spaces. The lecture hall is designed in proximity to the corridor, and the entrance on the basement floor provides access to the indoor garden from the cafeteria. The intention is to make it easy for students to actively use the indoor garden that constitutes the heart of the building.

The building program includes a total of 82 laboratories that vary between 64 and 200 square meters for the mechanical engineering, industrial engineering, computer engineering, electrical engineering, biomedical engineering, materials science, and nanotechnology engineering departments. Twelve studios and design and modeling workshops were also designed for the Fine Arts department.

1 View of the building at night
2 View of the courtyard

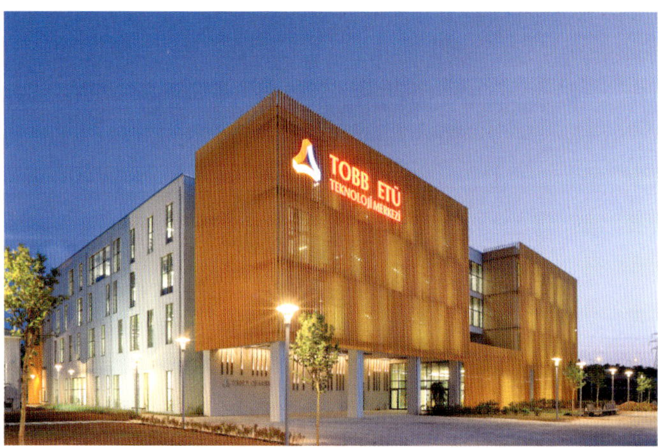

1

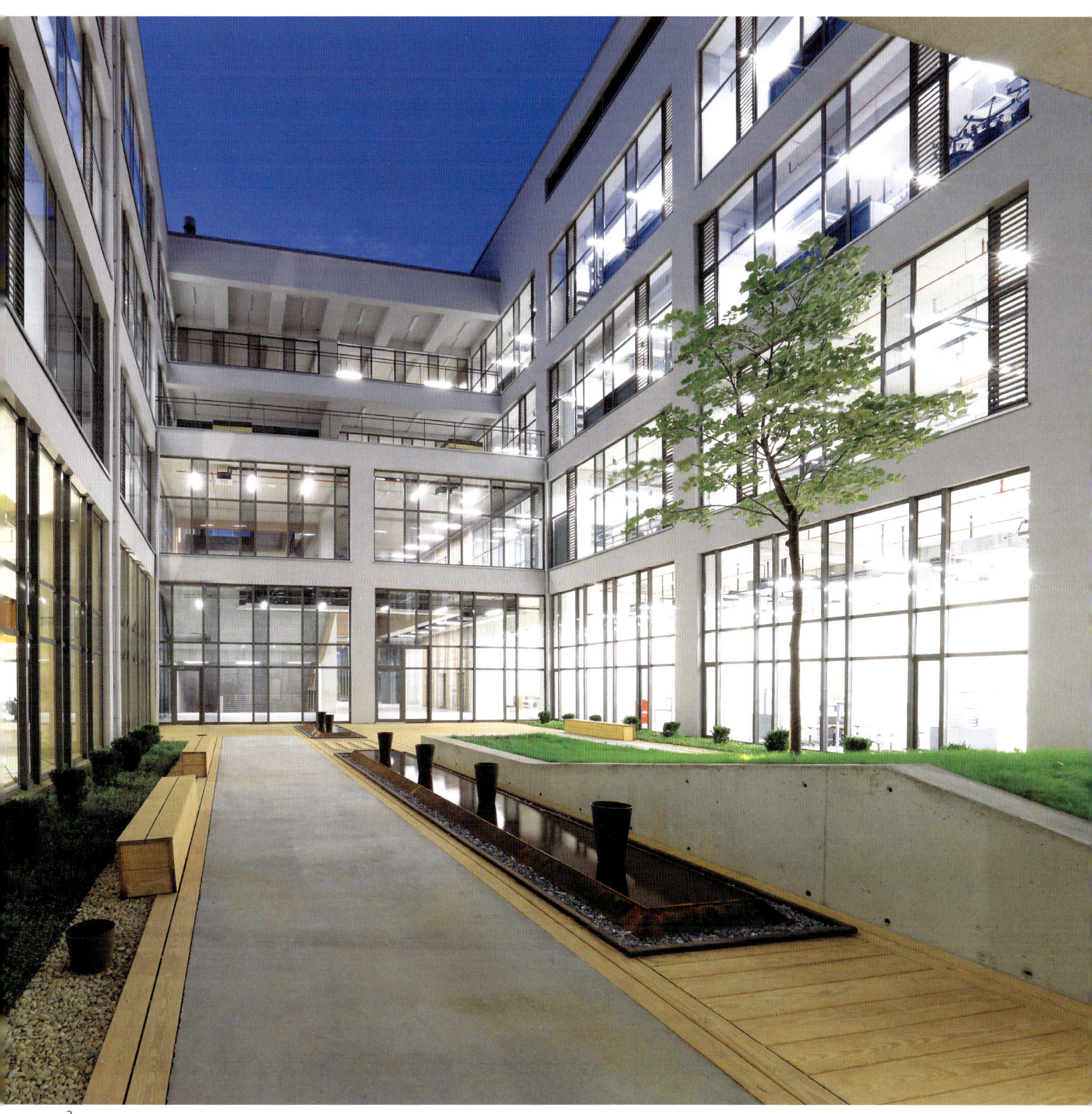

2

3 View of courtyard
4 Courtyard view showing the seating and pool
5 Cross-section through the water turbine test center illuminated by sunlight from the inner garden and façade
6 Façade detail
7 Aerial view of the courtyard showing the landscape
8 Interior view of the laboratory towards the courtyard
9 Typical floor plan
10 Ground floor plan
11 First basement floor plan

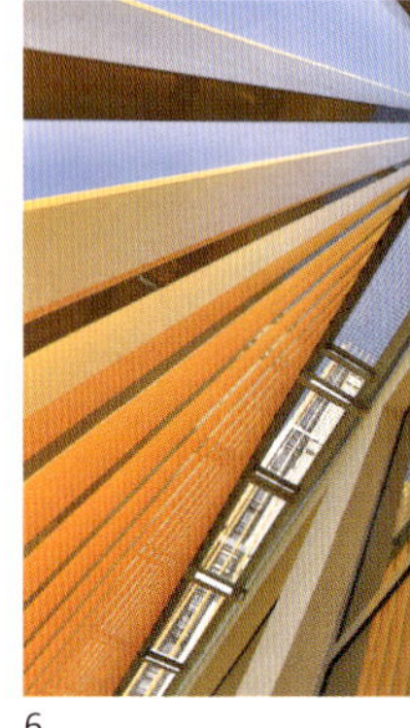
6

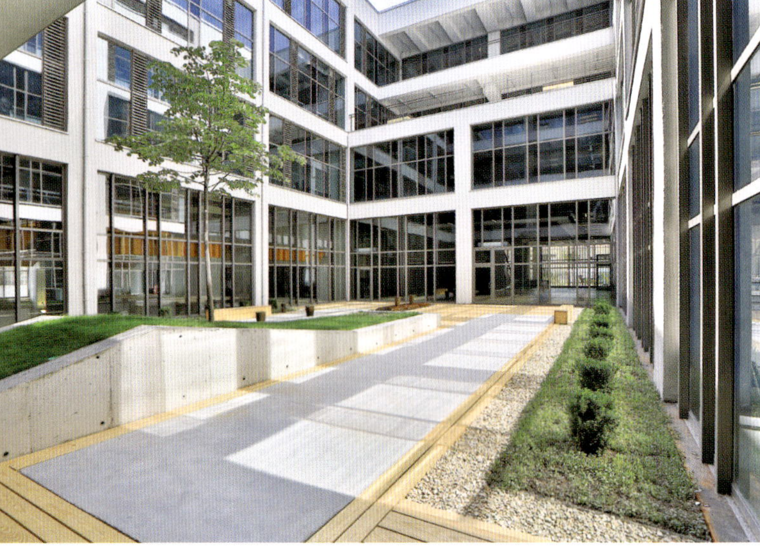
3

The largest water turbine test center in the world, TOBB UET HYDRO, is planned for a 600-square-meter area on the basement floor. The space is 12 meters high and receives daylight from the indoor garden as well as the façade, even though it is located in the basement. The reinforced concrete box has a depth of 7 meters and is separated from the building and covered with prefabricated planks containing the underfloor section of the mechanism and the water tank for the test center.

Many ducts have been planned for, allowing unlimited development of the functions and the technical character of the building program. Provisions have been made for the eventual expansion and modification of the technical fittings, as this is essential in order to continually satisfy such needs.

The basement has wide corridors that allow for vehicle entry and the laboratories are accessible via forklift corridors and cargo lifts that connect to each floor and receive service from outside. The floor is made of hardened concrete and the technical fittings are exposed—avoiding the use of suspended roof systems—which complements the architectural language.

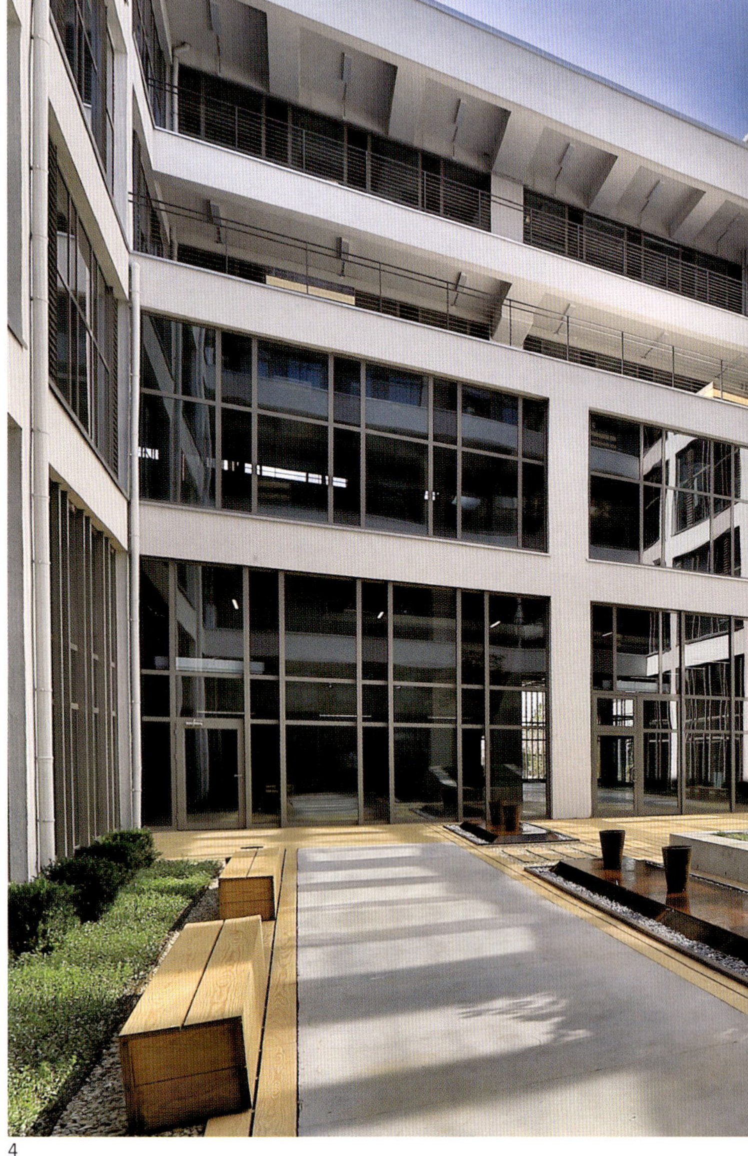
4

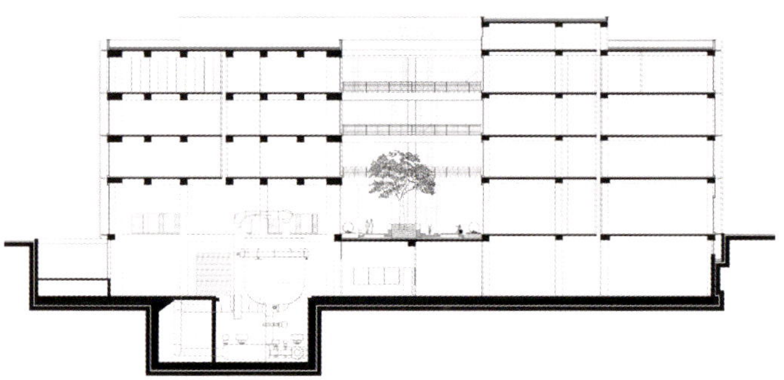
5

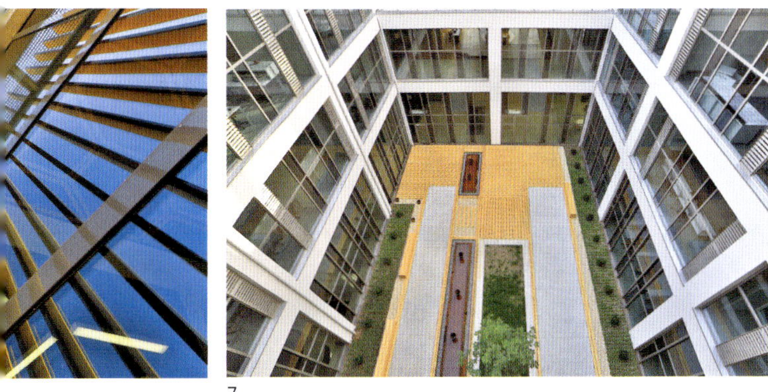

7

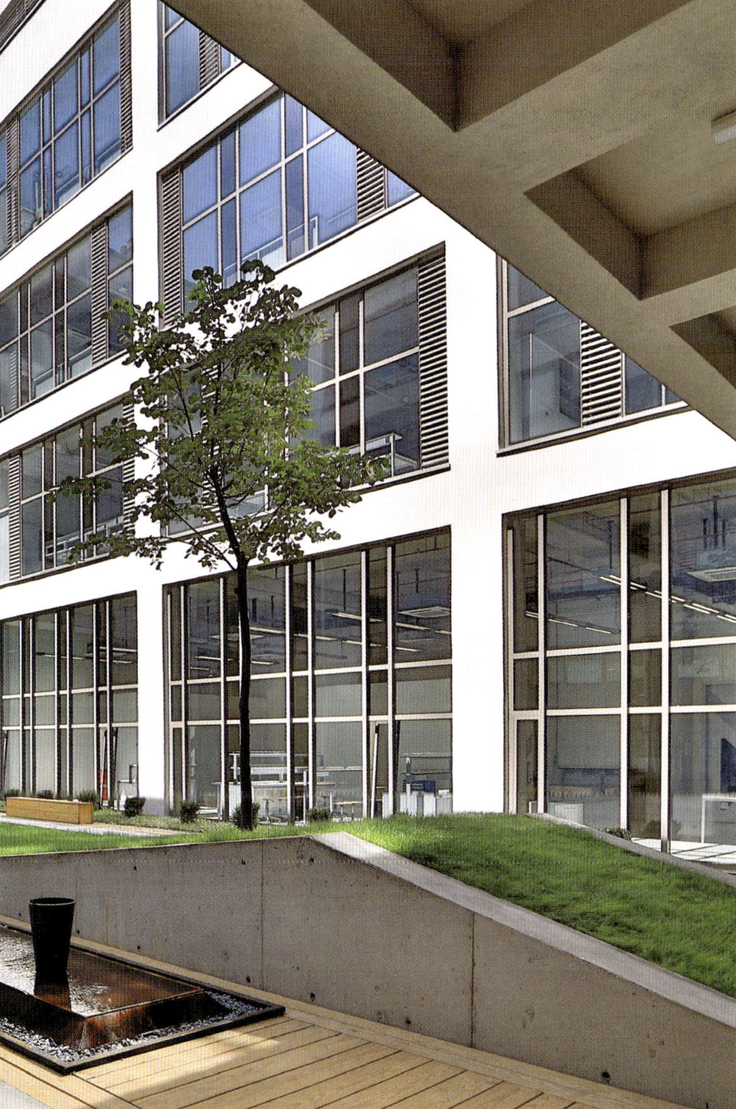

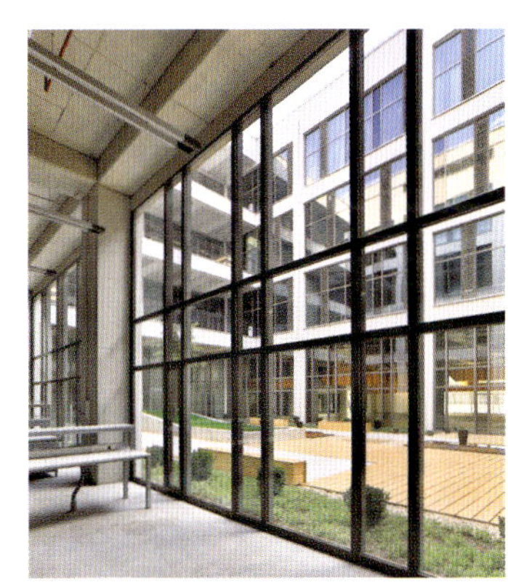

8

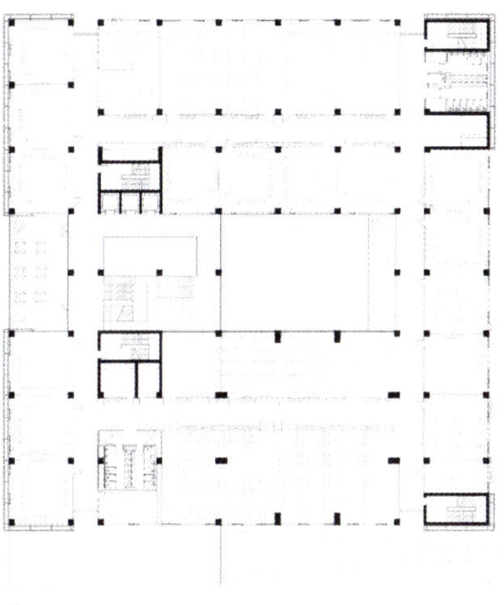

9

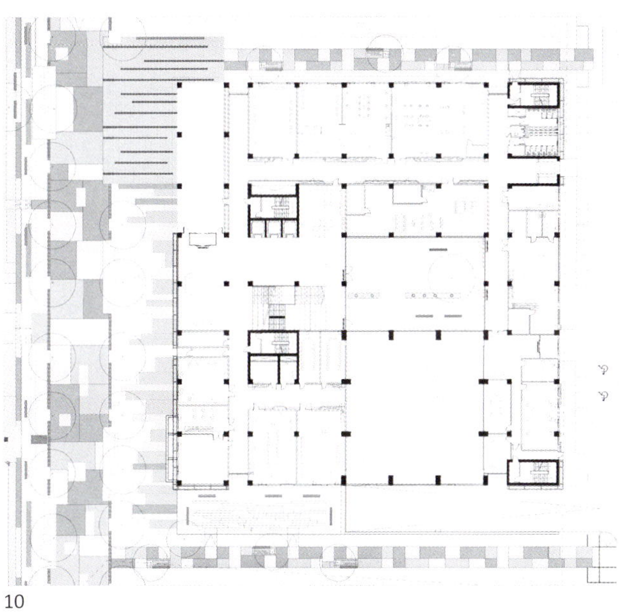

10

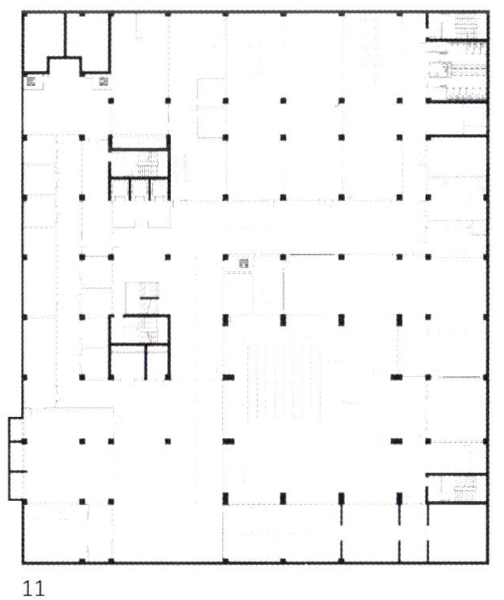

11

12 Laboratory view
13 Interior view
14 Laboratory interior
15 Stair detail
16 View of the entrance hall with the information desk
17 Cross-section through the courtyard showing the vertical circulation
18–20 TOBB UET color codes used in circulation spaces

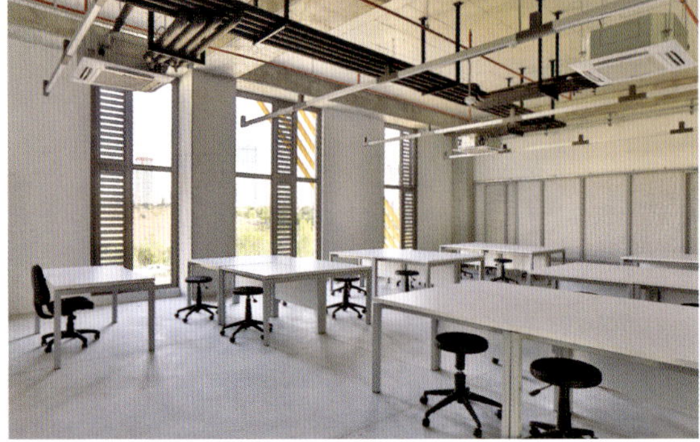
12

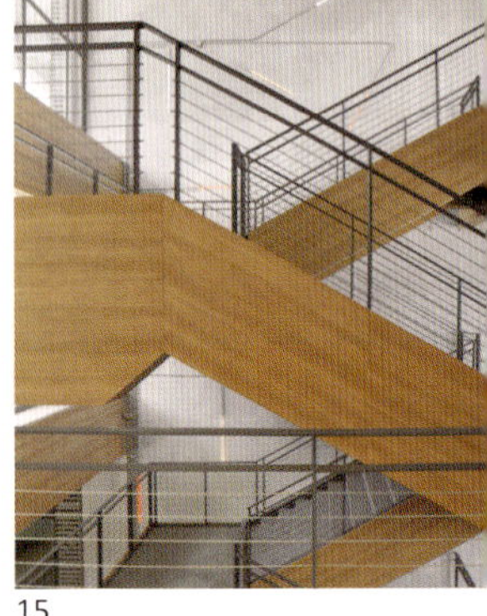
15

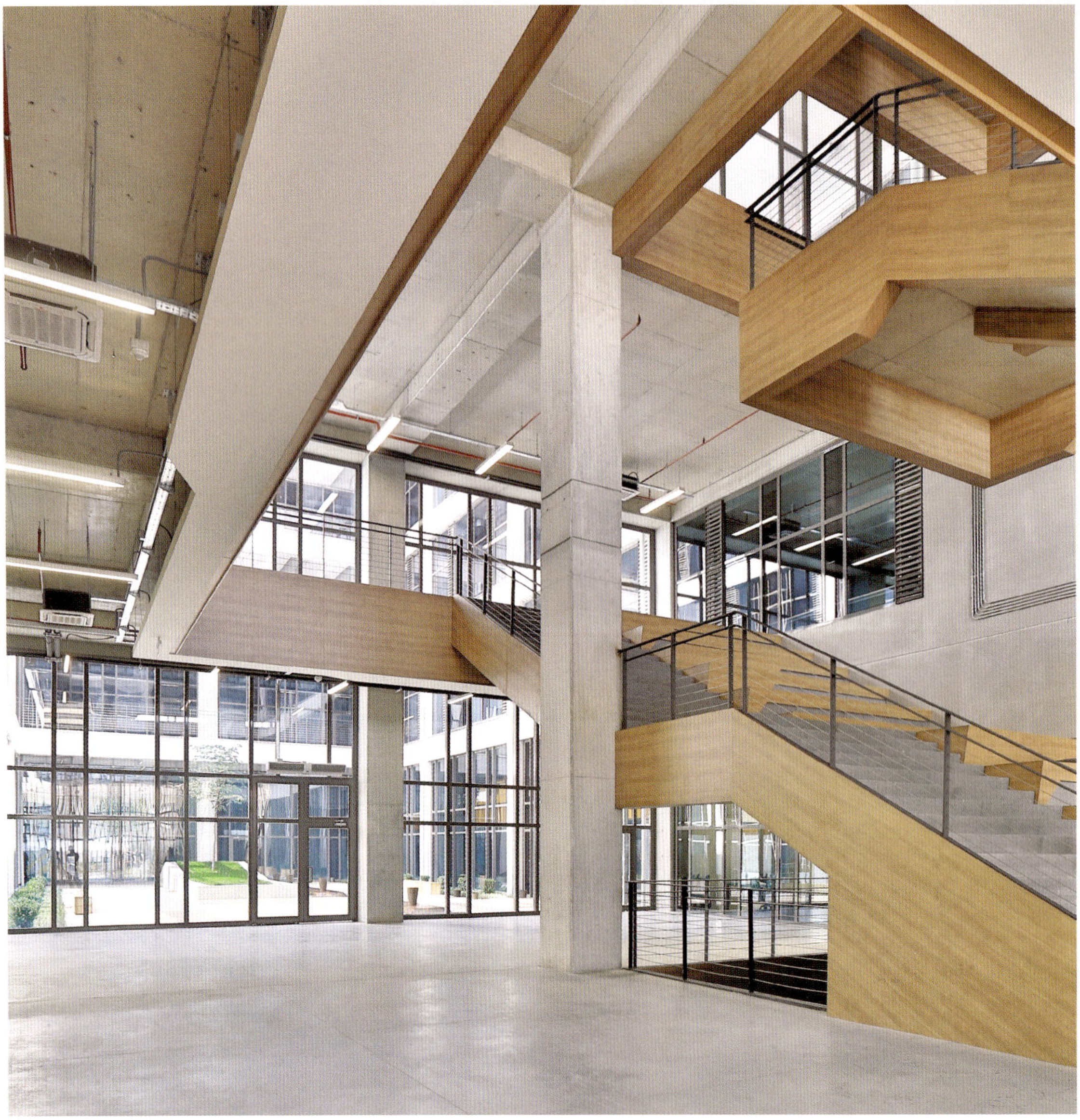

13

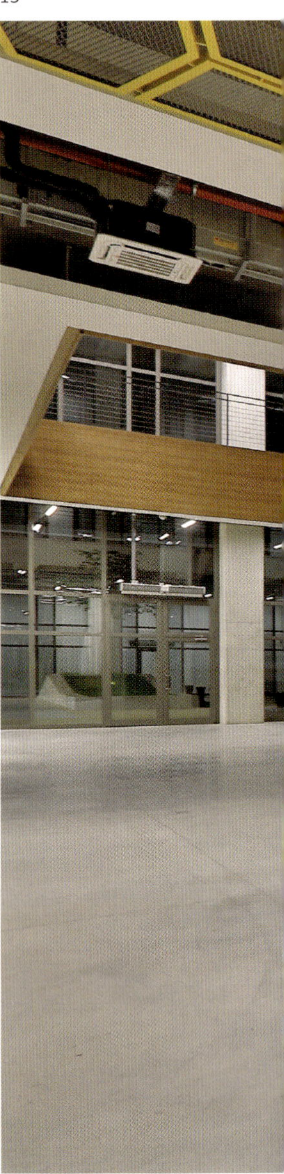
16

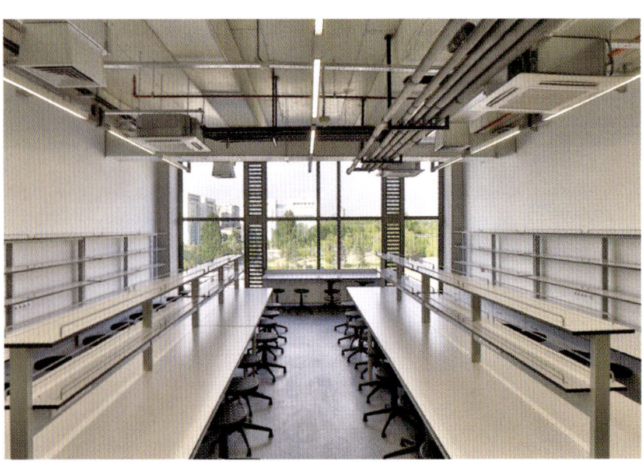
14

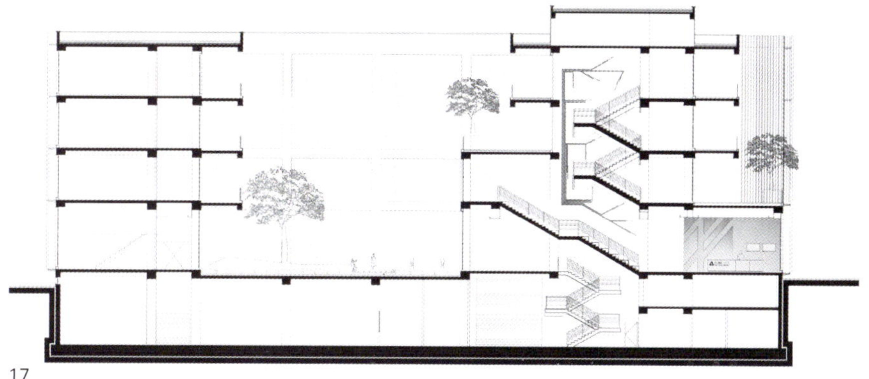

17

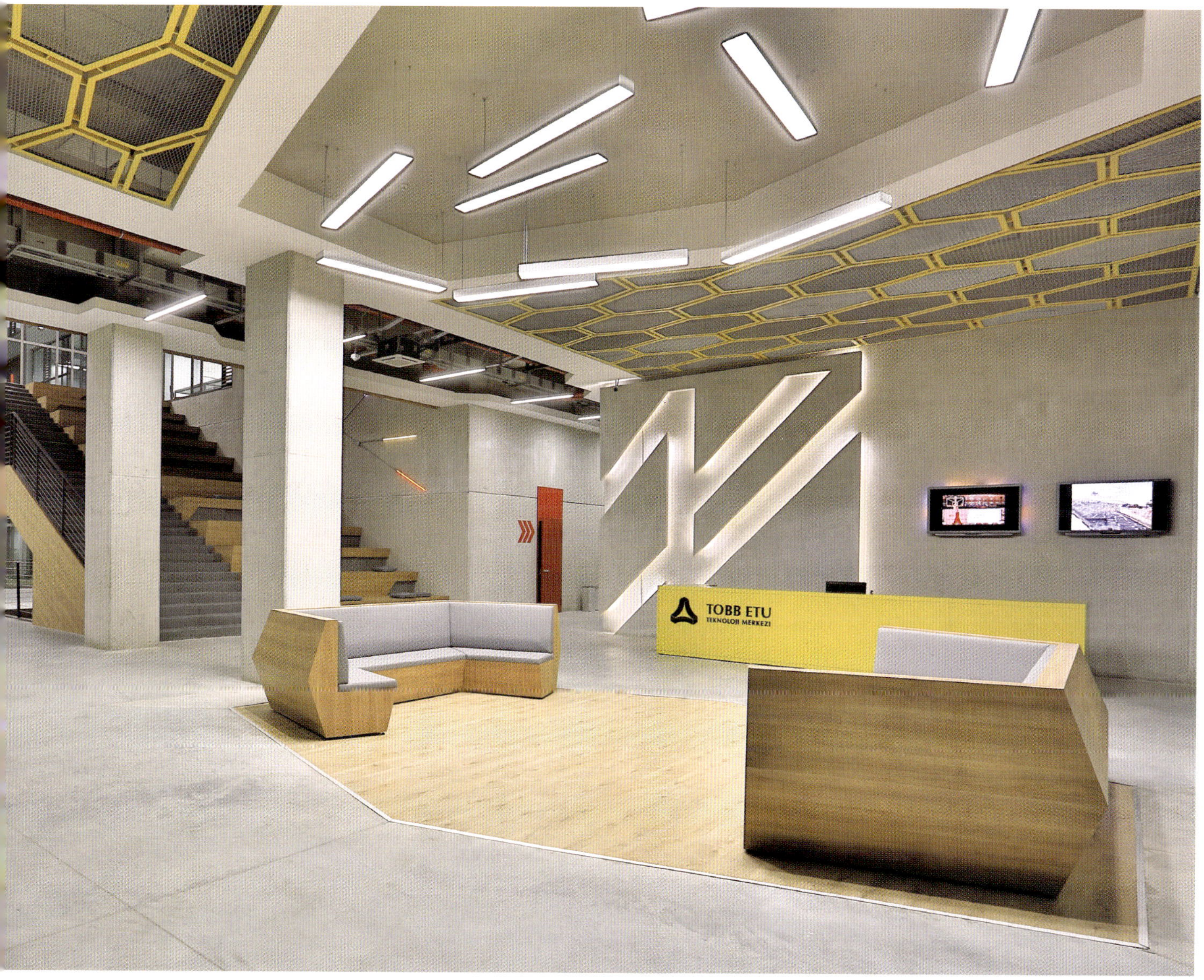

18

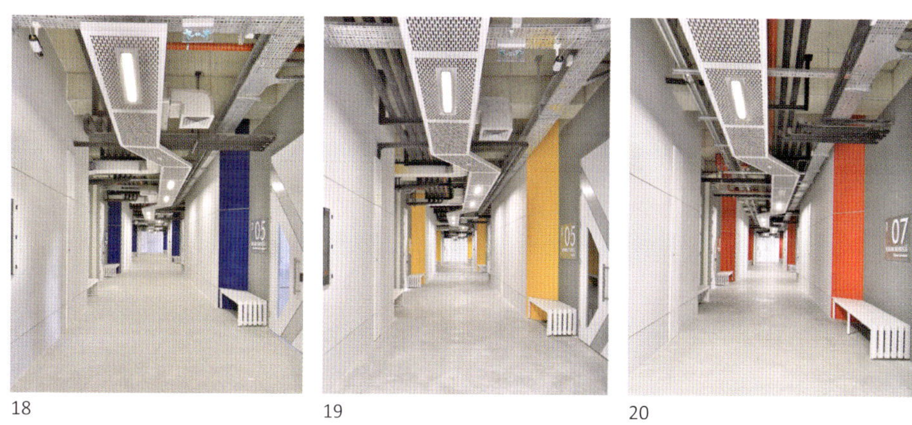

19

20

Kipaş High School Campus

Client Kipaş Holding Inc.
Project Date 2004
Area 23,200 m²
Location Kahramanmaraş
Structural Engineer Yüksek Project
Mechanical Engineer Okutan Engineering
Electrical Engineer Akay Engineering

This project consists of an education block, management building, pre-school, conference room, and an indoor sports hall located on a sloping site.

The management offices, conference room, and indoor sports hall surround a formal area at the campus entrance. The management block is connected to the classroom by bridges while there is a separate entrance for the pre-school.

The courtyard created by the school block functions as an outdoor playground for the students. The outdoor sports facilities are designed for various activities including basketball, volleyball, soccer, and tennis.

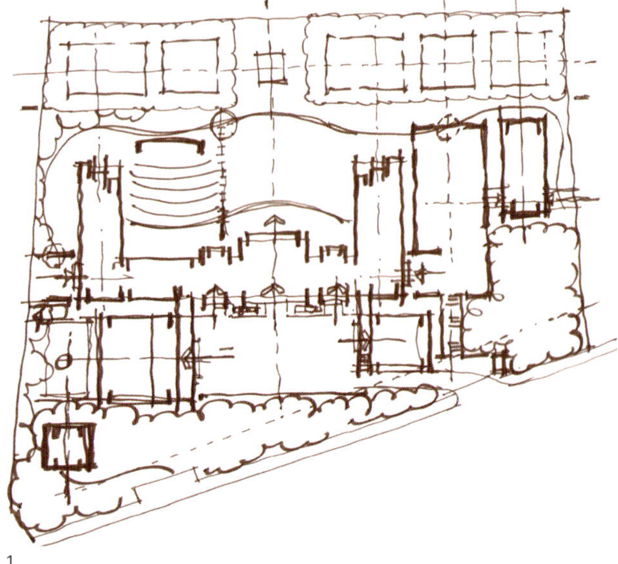
1

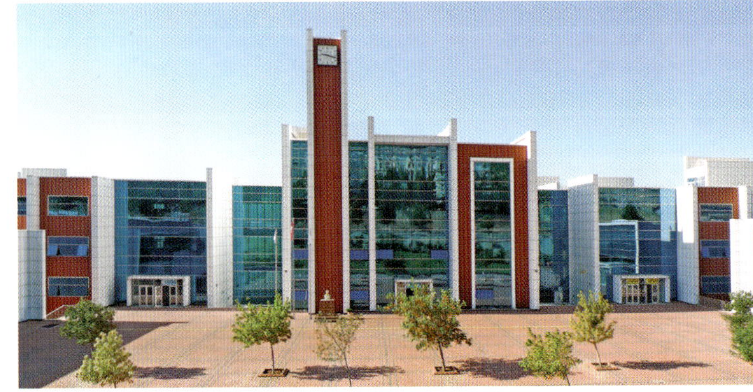
2

1 Sketch by Ali Osman Öztürk
2 Front view of the building
3 Model of the building
4 View of the entrance showing the ceremonial space in front of the building
5 Side view
6 View of the courtyard

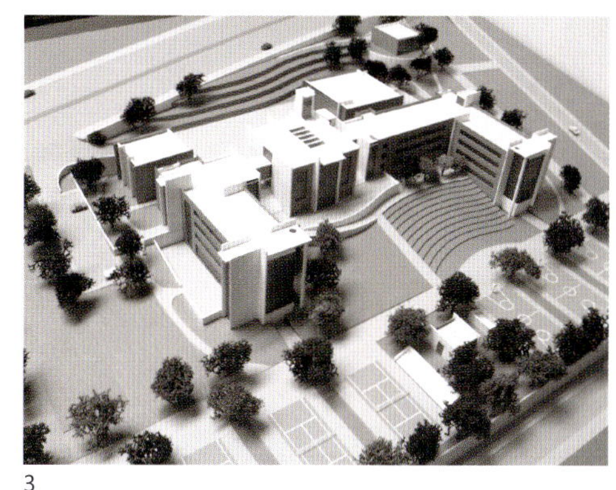

3

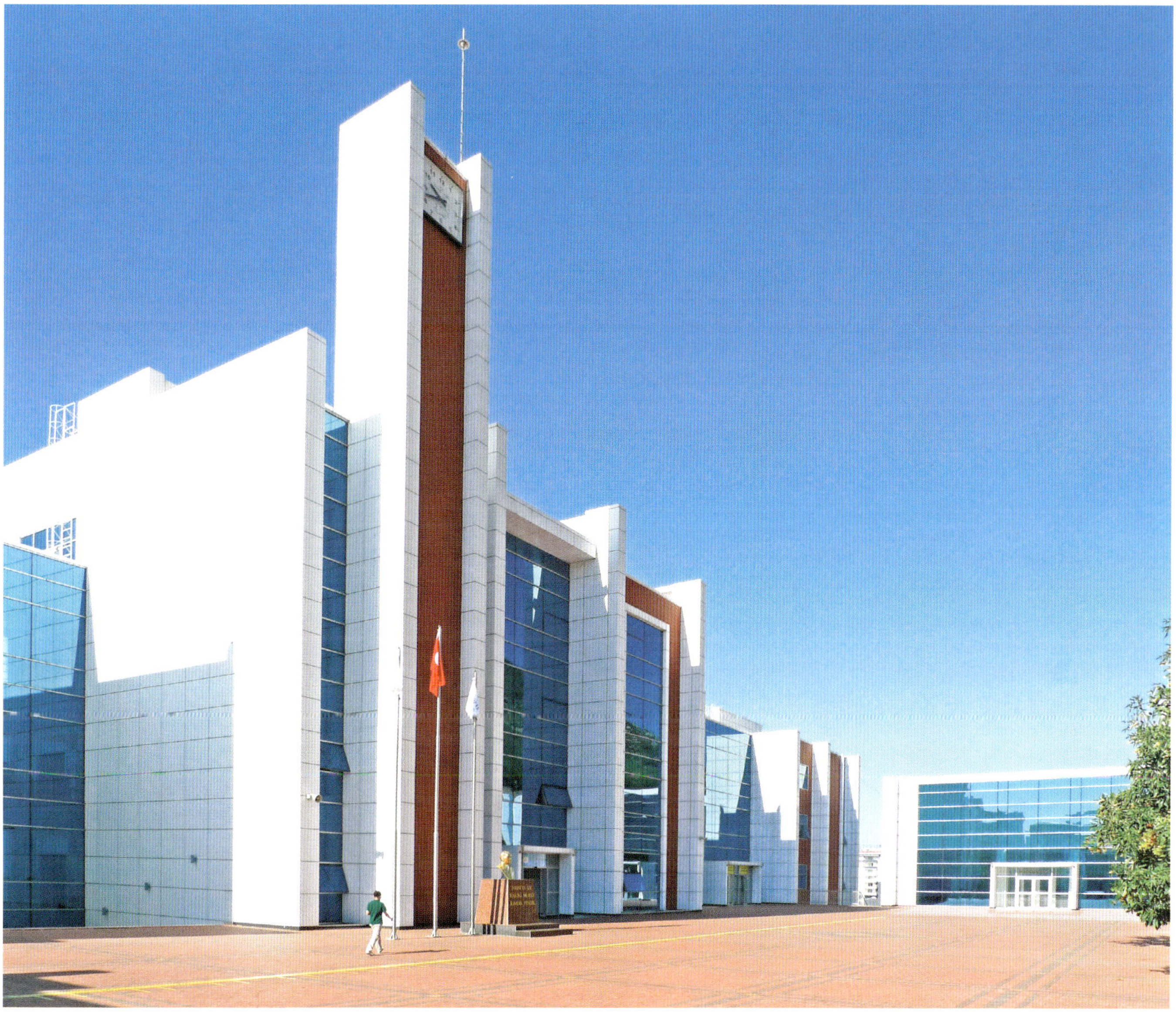

4

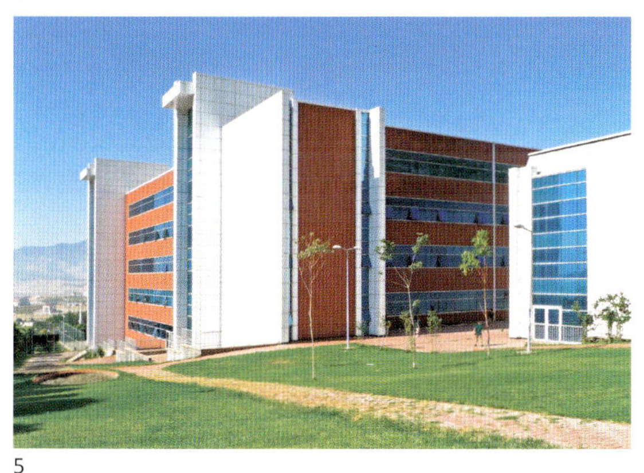

5

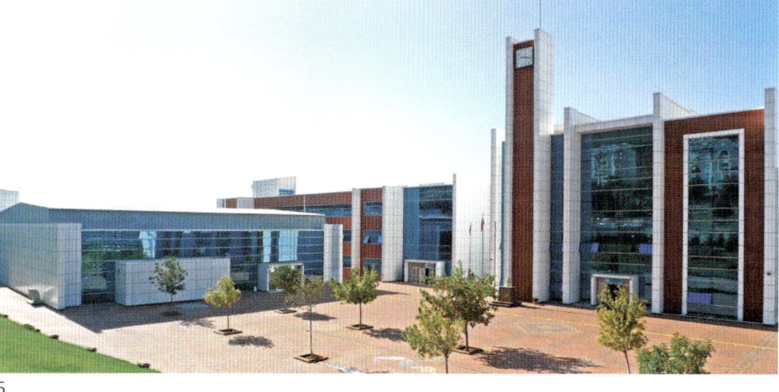

6

Courthouses

İstanbul Courthouse-Anatolian Side
Client The Foundation of Justice Organization
Project Date 2004
Area 210,000 m^2
Location İstanbul
Structural Engineer Yüksek Project
Mechanical Engineer Okutan Engineering
Electrical Engineer Akay Engineering

These projects are submissions for limited competitions for various locations in Turkey. The designs were created by reinterpreting the given building programs with an approach that re-examines the modern image of the office/courthouse.

The **İstanbul Courthouse-Anatolian Side**, a symbolic public building, involved a different approach in order to generate a diversity of spaces in a plain, transparent cubic form. The courtrooms, clerk offices, and judicial chambers that constitute the basis of the program wrap around the structure, defining the glass façade on the outside and the atrium on the inside. The atrium is a glass-covered transparent steel structure that serves as the main entrance of the building, the circulation area, and the primary social space for visitors. In this space, office functions, apart from the courtrooms, are designed as "buildings within the building," or independent prisms. Communal staff spaces, such as the cafeteria and kindergarten, are located on the upper floors. The conference room and the library are also designed as separate atrium spaces in the form of a wood and glass cylinder. The nodes that are located on the edge of the main atrium allow visitors to circulate vertically and easily find their way. The parking area and other services are located in the basement. This proposal for the limited project competition was not implemented.

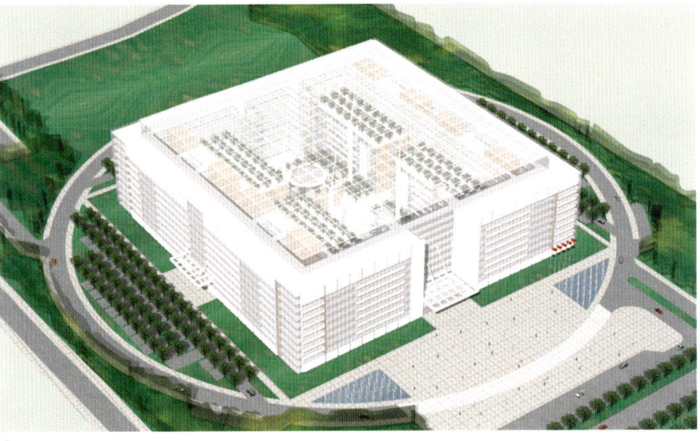

1

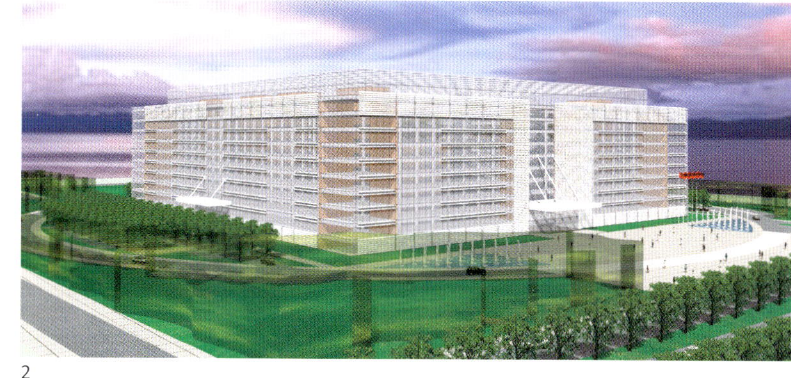
2

3

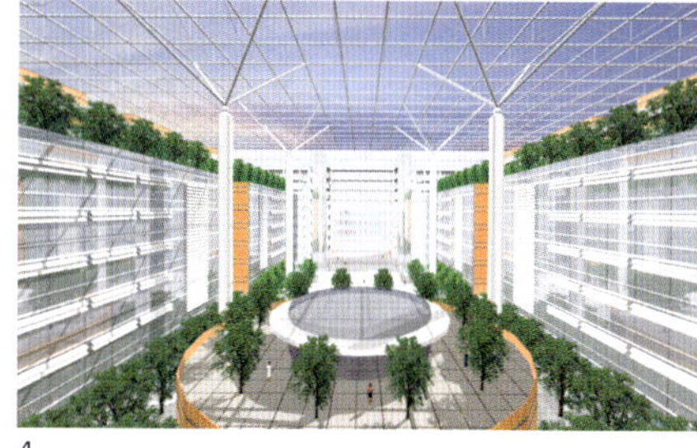
4

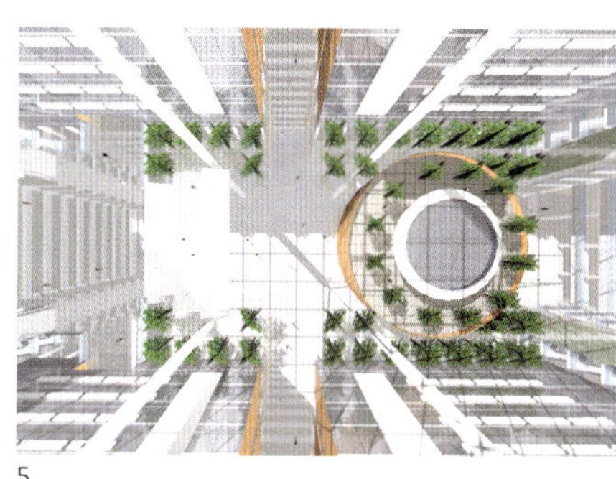
5

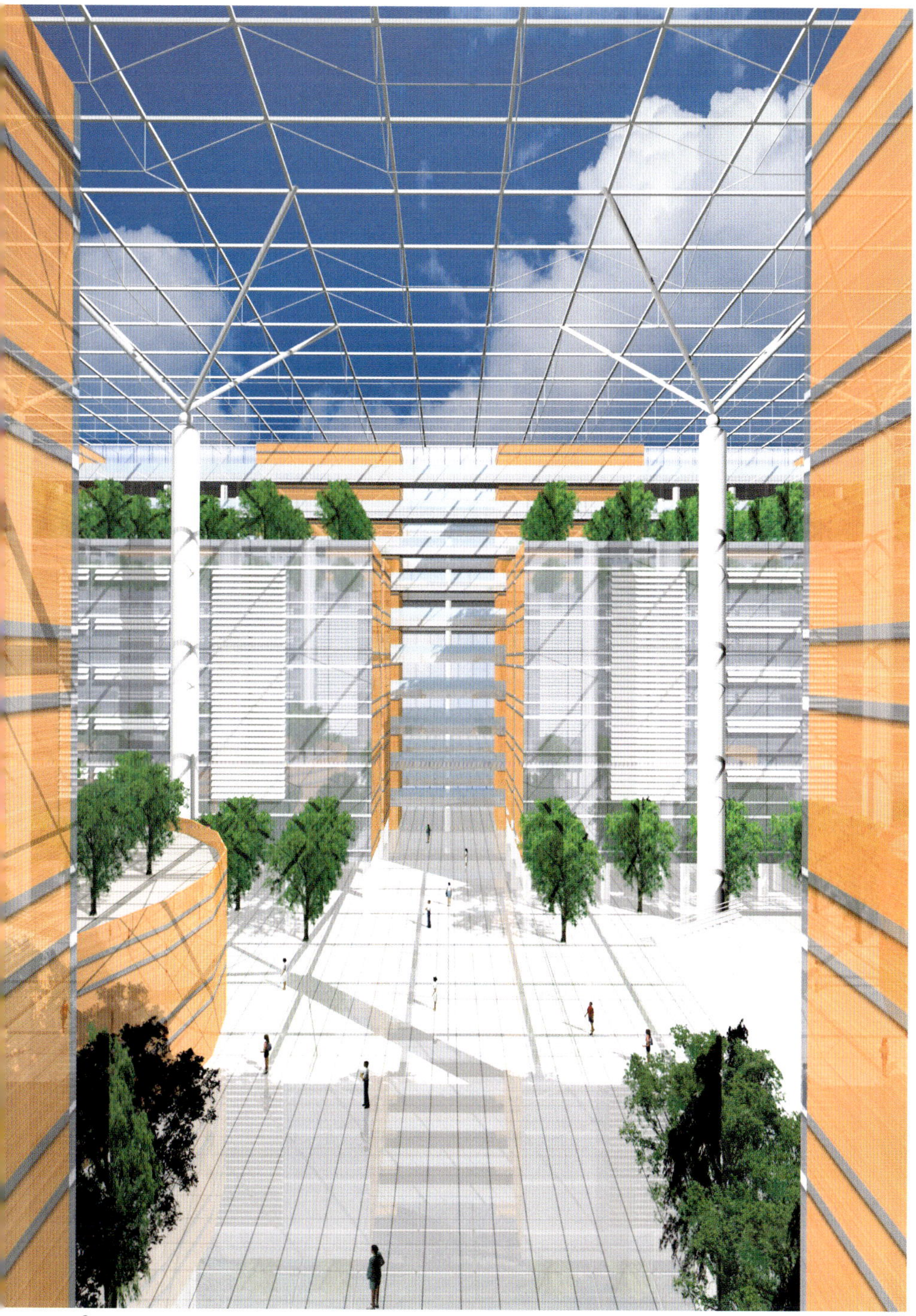

1 Aerial view
2 General view
3–5 View into the separate atrium spaces

İstanbul Courthouse-European Side

Client The Foundation of Justice Organization

Project Date 2006

Area 210,000 m^2

Location İstanbul

Structural Engineer Yüksek Project

Mechanical Engineer Okutan Engineering

Electrical Engineer Akay Engineering

Zonguldak Courthouse

Client Republic of Turkey Ministry of Justice

Project Date 2009

Area 7,560 m^2

Location Zonguldak

Structural Engineer Yüksek Project

Mechanical Engineer Setes Engineering

Electrical Engineer Akay Engineering

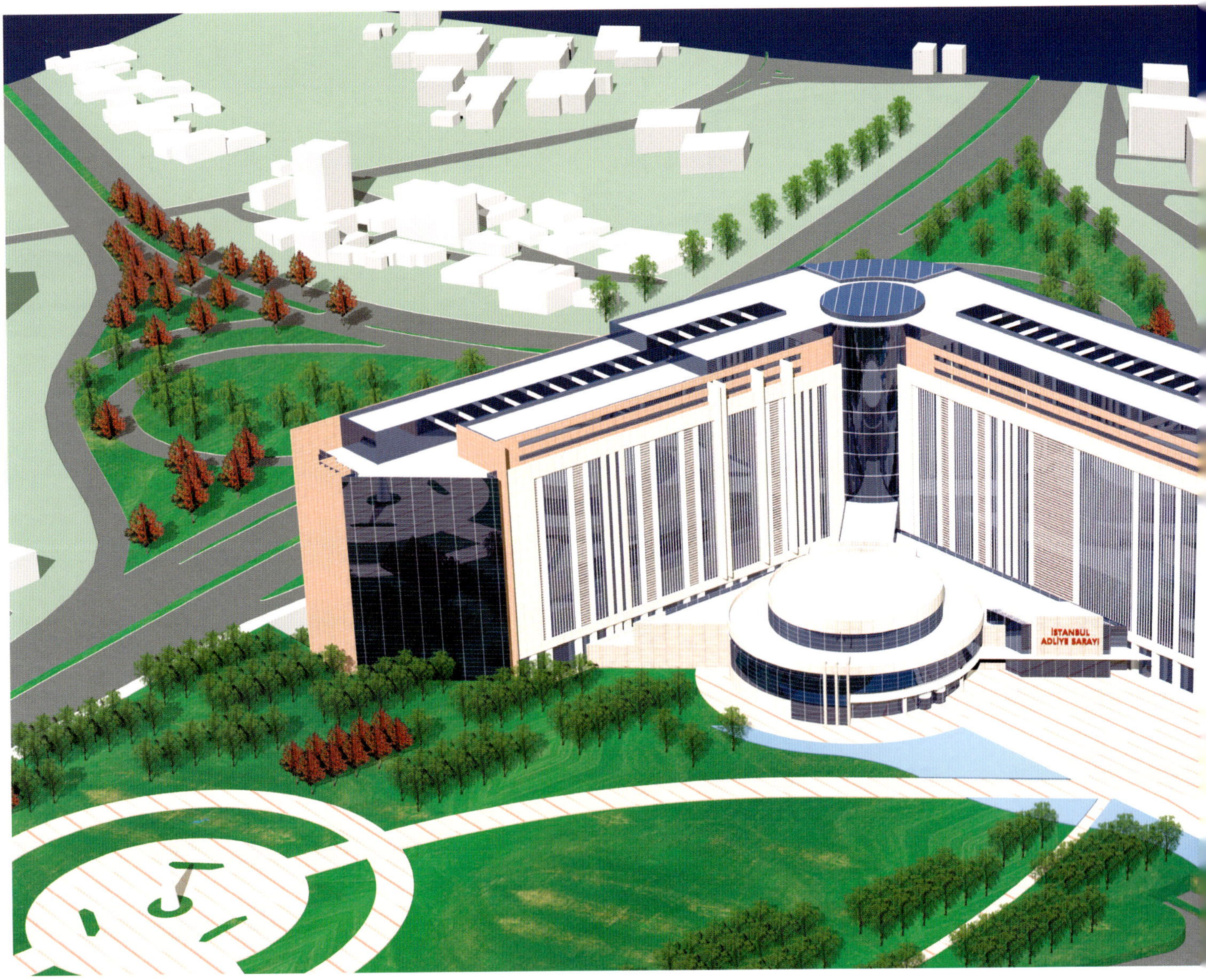

1

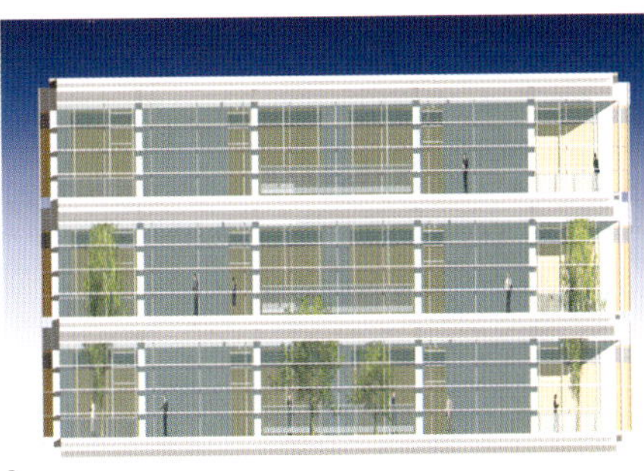

2

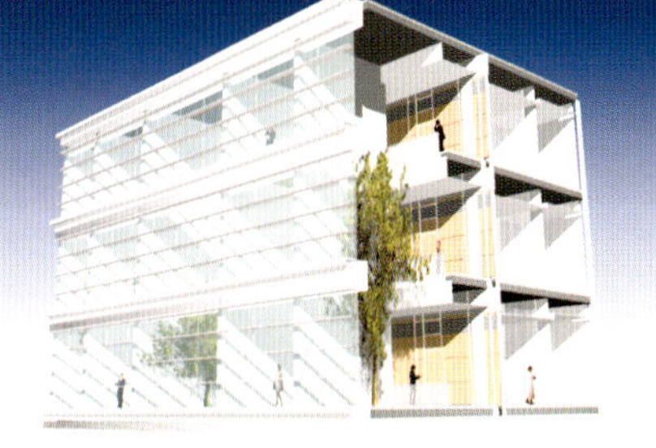

3

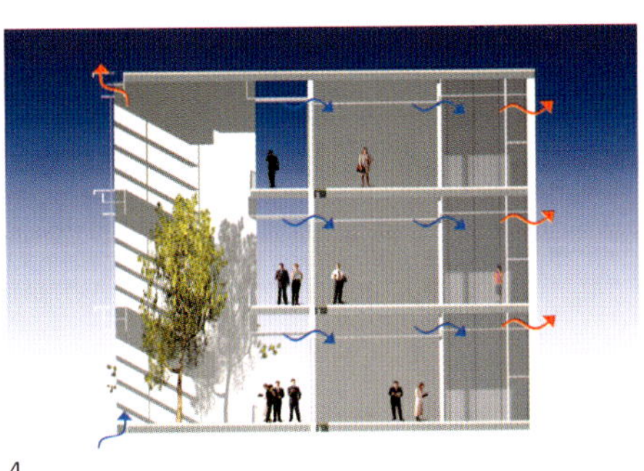

4

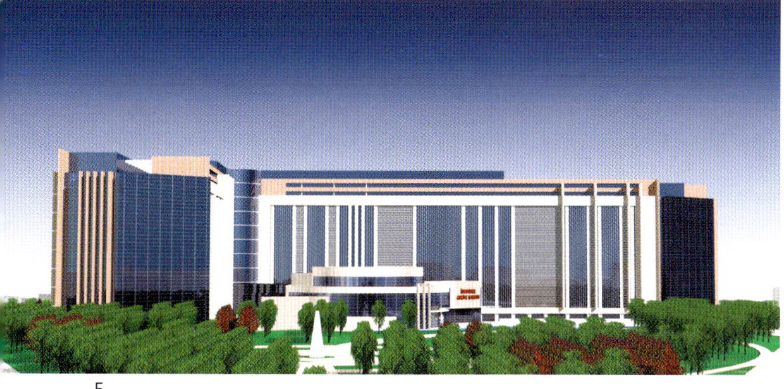

5

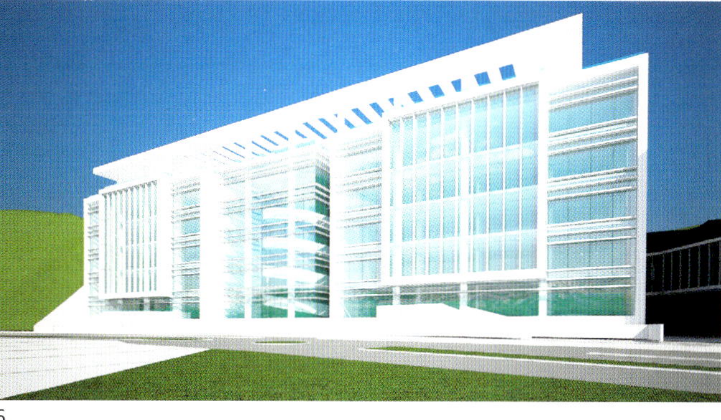

6

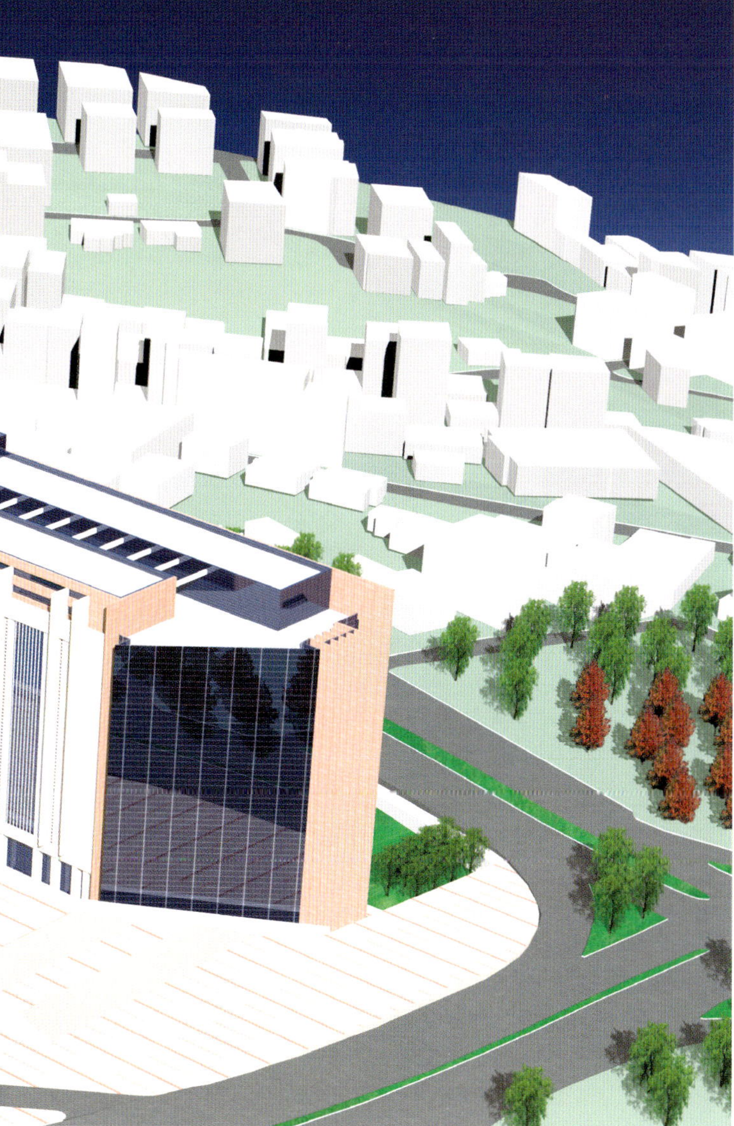

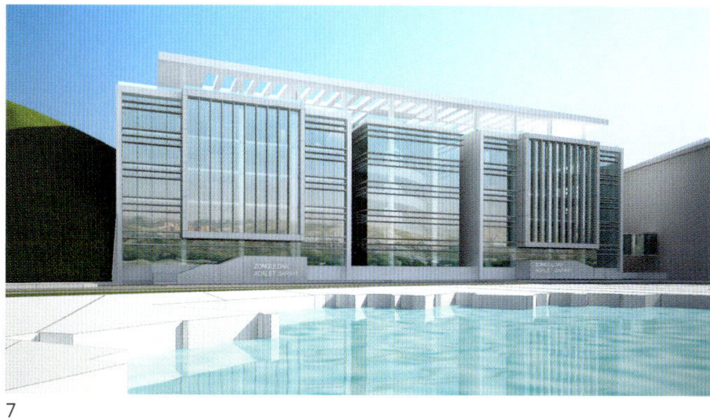

7

1 Model view of İstanbul Courthouse-European Side
2 Model of the partial section of İstanbul Courthouse-European Side
3 Perspective section of İstanbul Courthouse-European Side
4 Model showing the air flow through the inner gardens in İstanbul Courthouse-European Side
5 Façade of İstanbul Courthouse-European Side
6,7 Zonguldak Courthouse

The **İstanbul Courthouse-European Side** is located at an intersection of the city's main transportation arteries. Located next to the Abide-i Hurriyet Park, the building was designed to integrate its southern and eastern façades with the city and its northern and western façades with the park and the public.

With a techno-ecological building approach and an urban environmental consciousness, the perception of urban space increases on the upper floors, with a view of the Bosphorus and the Golden Horn. The double façade indoor gardens are designed to create a spacious work environment that allows for natural light and airflow. This proposal for the limited project competition was not implemented.

The parcel designated for an **additional service building** for **Zonguldak Courthouse** is located next to the existing building and it has a steep slope. According to the building program, the courtrooms and offices face the sea, and the circulation spaces are on the other side. The building, located on rocky ground, is designed to include four stories.

The symmetrical mass has an official entrance for prosecutors on one side and a public entrance on the other. Vertical and horizontal circulation within the building has been simplified with the easily accessible staircase and elevators located in the middle axis. Various connections between the new building and the existing building have been proposed. The use of natural stone and glass is intended to create a minimalist effect.

Samsun Courthouse

Client The Foundation of Justice Organization

Project Date 2009

Area 71,800 m^2

Location Samsun

Structural Engineer Yüksek Project

Mechanical Engineer Setes Engineering

Electrical Engineer Akay Engineering

Landscape Design DDS Dalokay Design Studio

Adana Courthouse

Client The Foundation of Justice Organisation

Project Date 2010

Area 166,800 m^2

Location Adana

Structural Engineer Yüksek Project

Mechanical Engineer Metta Engineering

Electrical Engineer Akay Engineering

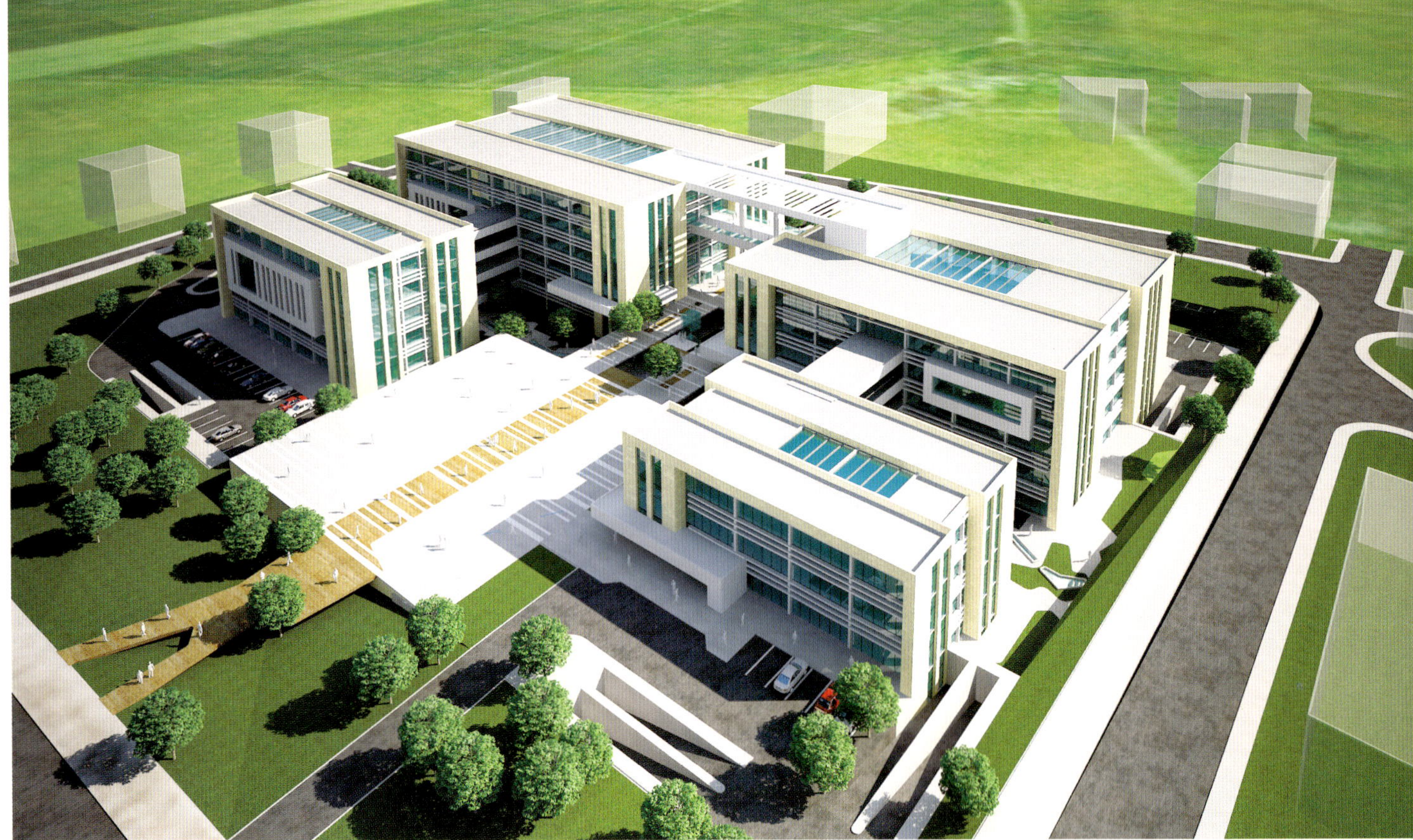

1

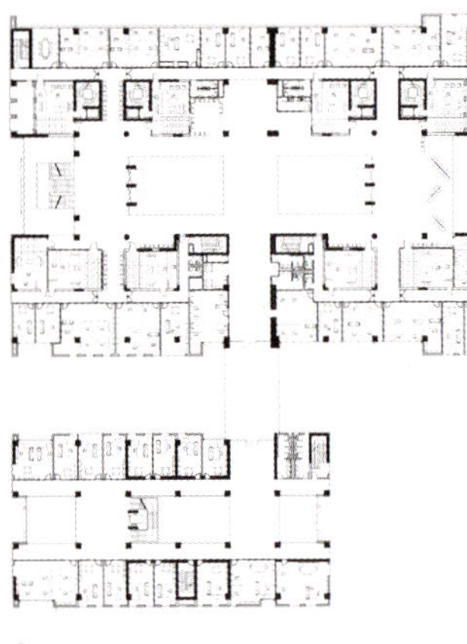

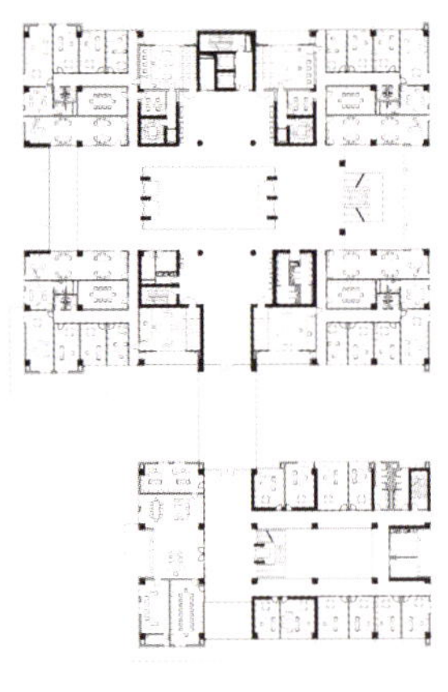

2

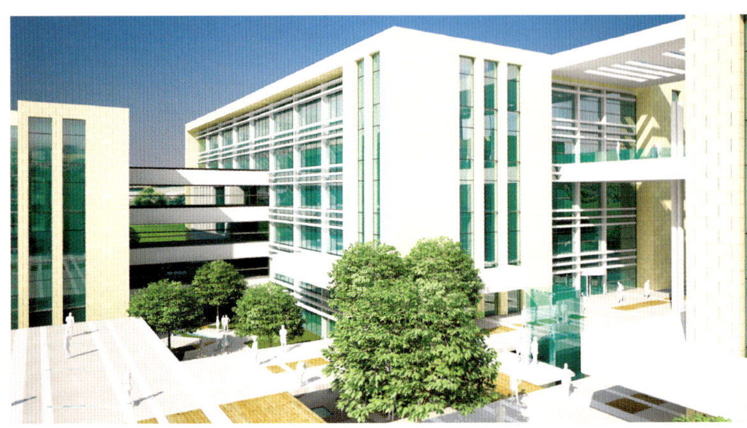

3

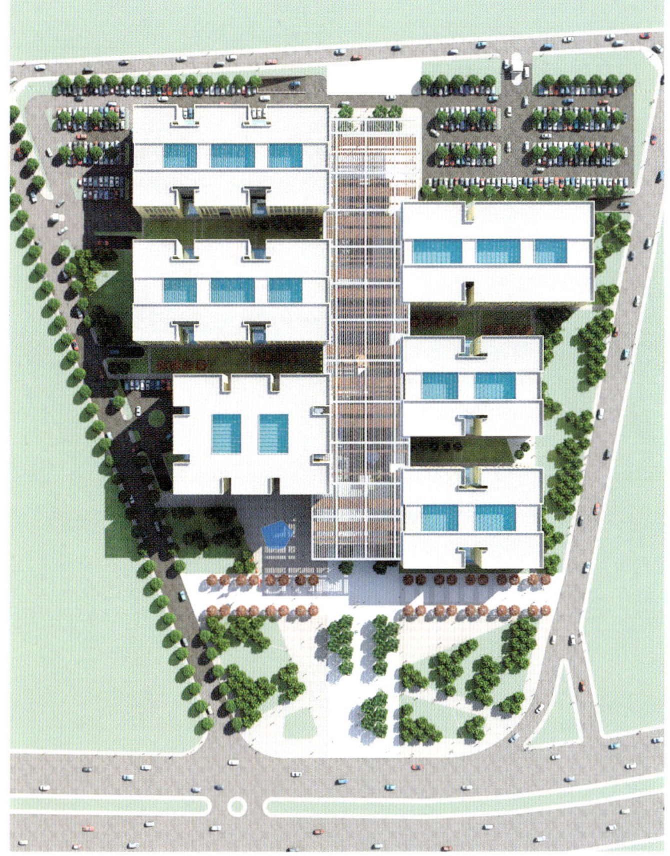

4

The **Samsun Courthouse** is located on one of the most important avenues in the city, Cumhuriyet Avenue, which runs behind Ataturk Boulevard parallel to the coastline. The Palace of Justice and the Regional Courthouse service building design intends these two separate buildings to be located on a single plot with similar masses and functional schemes. The public space created at the entrance forms a continuum with the circulation spaces within the buildings. The courtrooms in both buildings are placed to the left and the right sides of this space.

The existing greenery on the plot has been preserved and extended with new indoor and outdoor green spaces. A positive atmosphere is to be maintained both inside and outside the building with brightness and spacious effects.

Open, semi-open, and closed axial connections between the buildings provide continuity of space. Functional organization has been achieved with modular repetition and simple vertical and horizontal circulation. The atriums are repeated in all four structures, which increase the effect of daylight receiving spaces. The blocks are oriented to allow the sea breeze to enter, bringing fresh air to both the pedestrian path between the buildings and to the atriums inside.

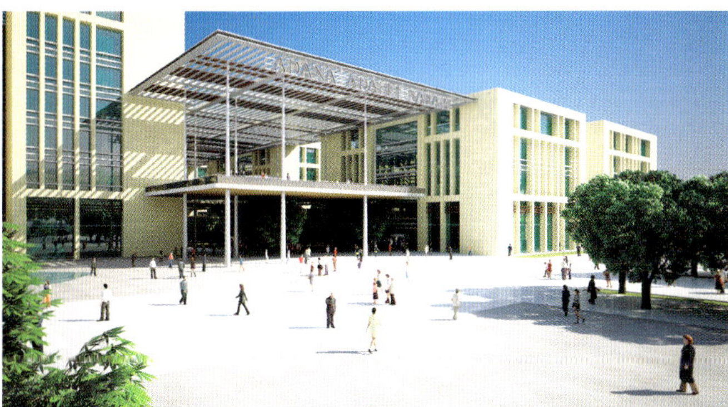

5

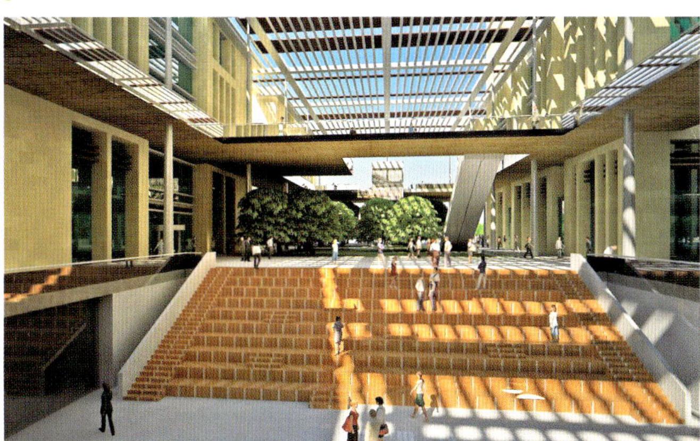

6

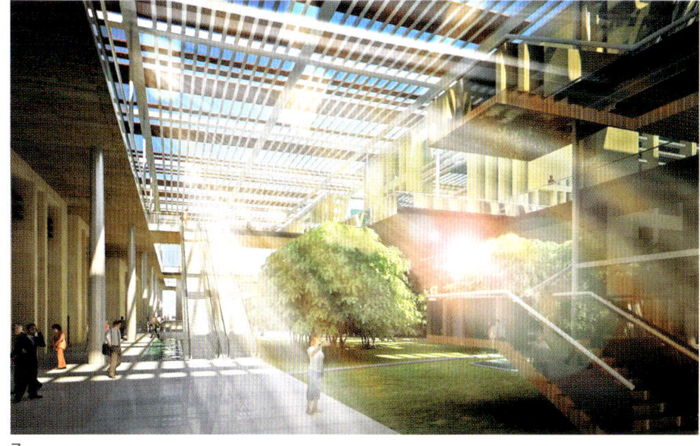

7

1 Model view of Samsun Courthouse
2 Typical floor plan of Samsun Courthouse
3 The exterior of Samsun Courthouse showing the connections
4 Aerial view of Adana Courthouse
5 Adana Courthouse view showing the plaza
6,7 Adana Courthouse canopy details and the sunlight over the transitional space

1 Model of Ankara Courthouse Extension Building
2 Model of Kayseri Regional Court and Regional Administrative Courthouse.
3 Kayseri Regional Court and and Regional Administrative Courthouse
4 Site plan of Erdemli Courthouse
5 View of Erdemli Courthouse
6 Aerial view of Kayseri Regional Court and Regional Administrative Courthouse
7 Ground floor plan of Kayseri Regional Court and Regional Administrative Courthouse
8 Typical floor plan of Kayseri Regional Court and Regional Administrative Courthouse

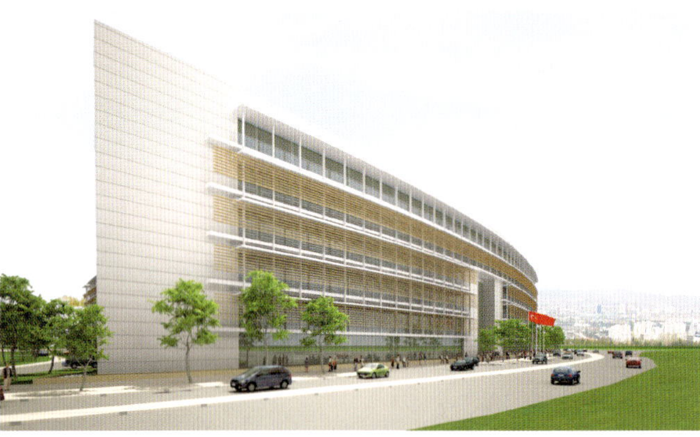

1

Ankara Courthouse

Client Republic of Turkey Ministry of Justice

Project Date 2008

Area 166,105 m^2

Location Ankara

Kayseri Regional Court and Regional Administrative Court of Justice

Client The Foundation of Justice Organization

Project Date 2012

Area 48,075 m^2

Location Kayseri

Structural Engineer Yüksek Project

Mechanical Engineer Metta Engineering

Electrical Engineer Akay Engineering

Landscape Design Dalokay Design Studio

Fire Consultant Alara Design and Engineering

Erdemli Courthouse

Client Republic of Turkey Ministry of Justice

Project Date 2011

Area 12,540 m^2

Location Mersin

Structural Engineer Yüksek Project

Mechanical Engineer Metta Engineering

Electrical Engineer Akay Engineering

Fire Consultant Alara Design and Engineering

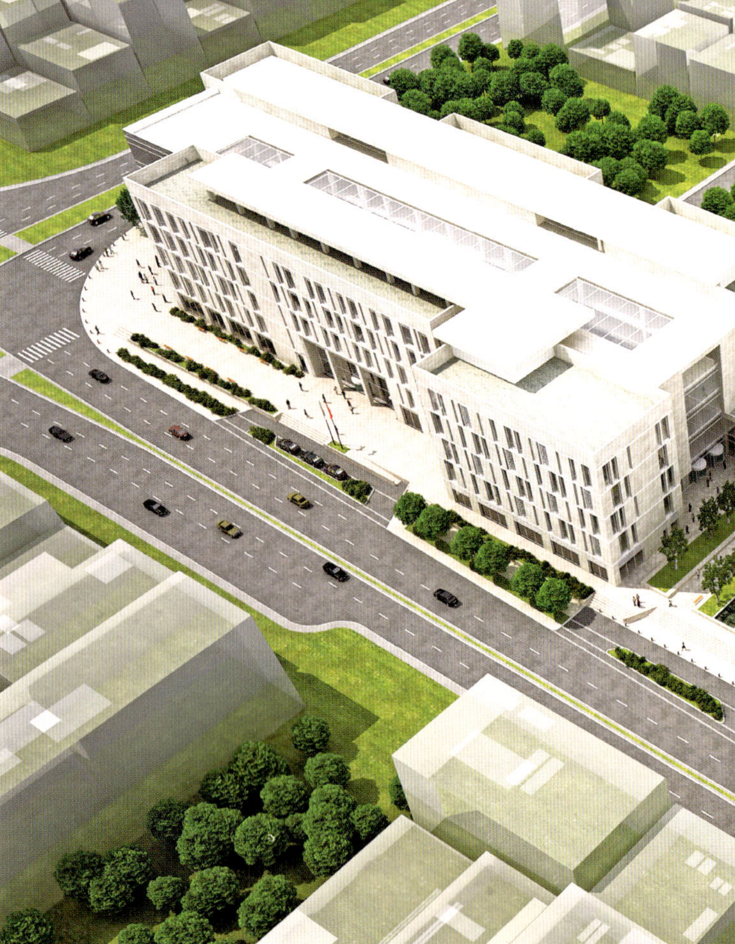

2

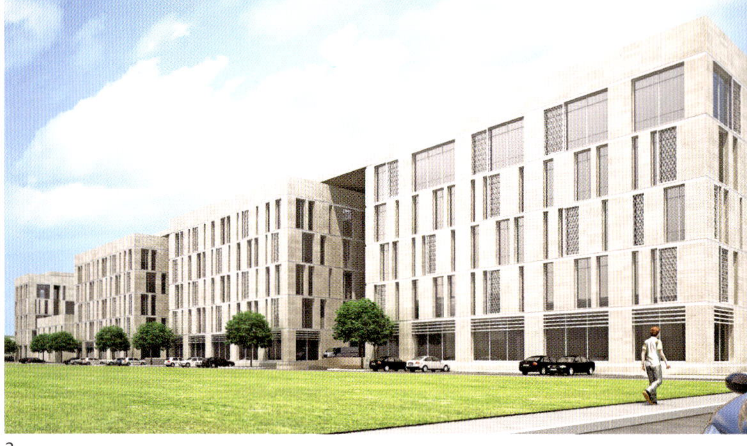

3

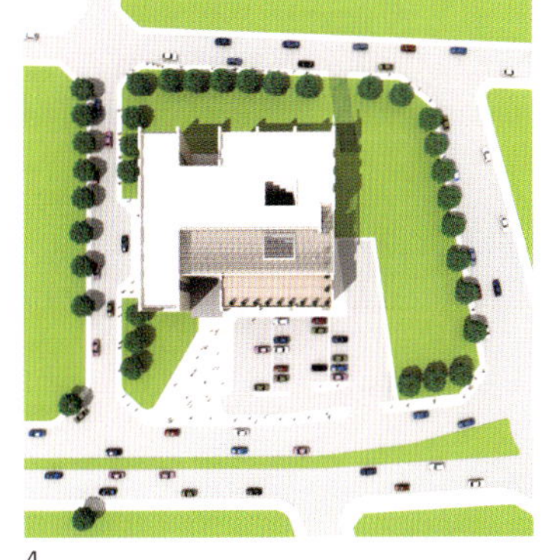
4

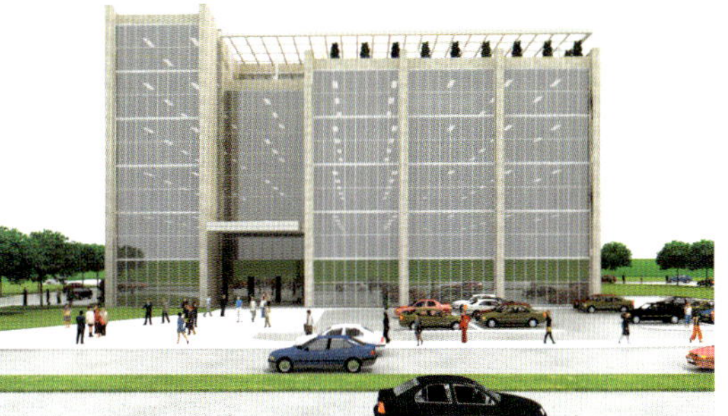
5

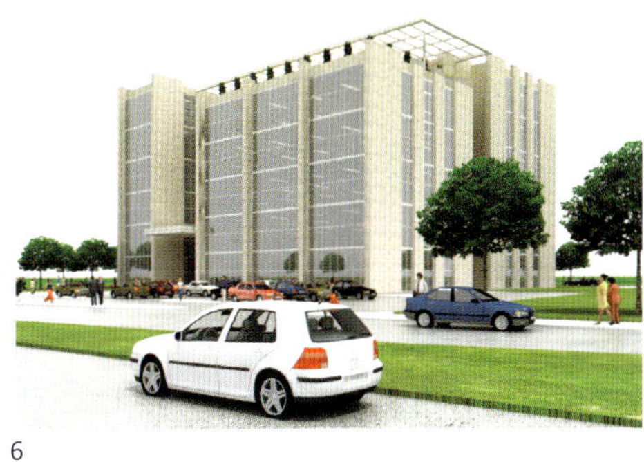
6

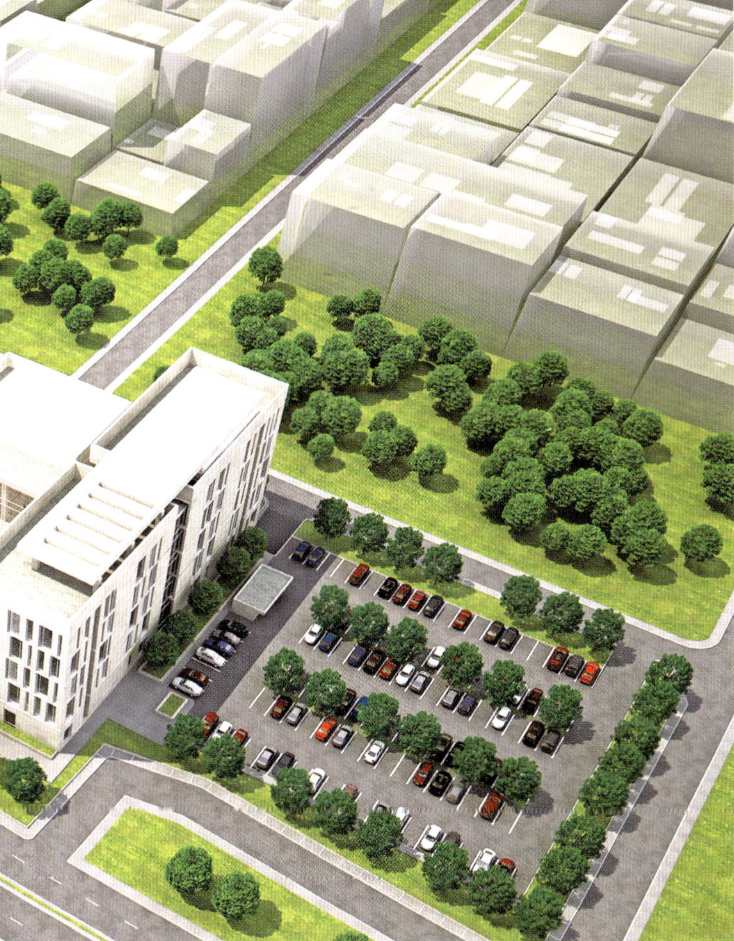

The proposal for **Ankara Courthouse** concerns a location designated for an additional service building near the existing structure on the main connection between Ataturk Boulevard and Talatpaşa Boulevard. Spatial arrangements have been proposed to create a unified perception for the proposed building, which is located on the important urban artery connecting the Opera Bridge to Sıhhiye Square. The location of the Attorney General's Office block can be seen from Atatürk Boulevard. The circulation hallways in front of the court waiting rooms connect to the main atrium. The cylindrical forms on the circulation hallways house service spaces for public use. Controlled circulation hallways are designed for the use of the prosecution and staff.

The functions of **Kayseri Regional Courthouse and Regional Administrative Tribunal** have been organized in three main blocks—the courtrooms, the prosecution, and the administrative tribunal. Located across the Kayseri Courthouse building that is currently under construction, the new building will connect to the Courthouse. Its main entrance opens to a plaza that supports this connection. The building blocks are placed around a main circulation axis and two plazas define the entrances, which also shape communal life in the building. The building is integrated with the city by means of these plazas.

The main circulation axis in the project is supported by the layout and elevation as well as a skylight that follows this axis. The circulation axis also allows natural light to enter the building. This, in turn, increases the structures' efficiency and creates continuity between the interior spaces.

The natural stone elements used in the building give the impression of a public building, while the apertures that let light in give it a dynamic look. The aim of this design is to create a building for the city that transforms and improves the district, with a design approach that reveal the modern face of the city and its judicial buildings, as well as symbolizing the city itself.

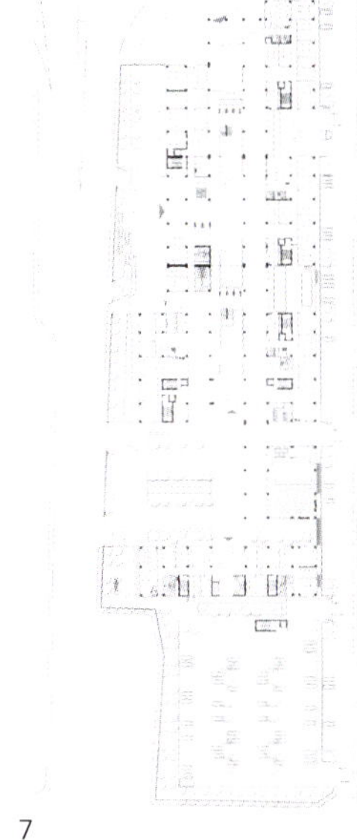
7

8

NATA İncek Housing

Client NATA Group and MNM Eurasia Forest Foundation
Project Date 2011
Area 55,000 m²
Location Ankara
Structural Engineer Yüksek Project
Mechanical Engineer Metta Engineering
Electrical Engineer Akay Engineering
Landscape Design Dalokay Design Studio
Fire Consultant Alara Design and Engineering
Contractor NATA Group and MNM Eurasia Forest Foundation

The NATA İncek Housing project consists of four separate 18–20-story blocks. The main façade faces the southeast with a view of Lake Mogan. The campus contains 2+1, 3+1, 4+1, and duplex apartments. The kitchens, living rooms, and guest rooms of the apartments are closely connected, and the balconies are oriented towards the view. The common social facility for the houses contains a fitness center, swimming pool, Turkish bath, sauna, and playgrounds. There are green areas, pools, playgrounds, and hiking and running trails between the building blocks.

Commercial spaces that provide essentials and can be accessed from the outside have been proposed for this campus, which is located outside the city center.

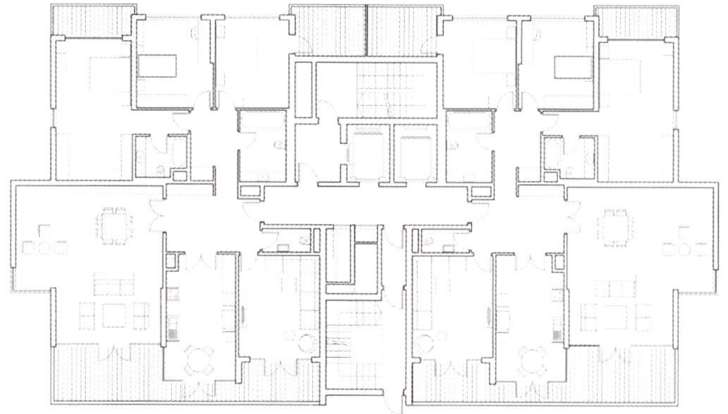

1

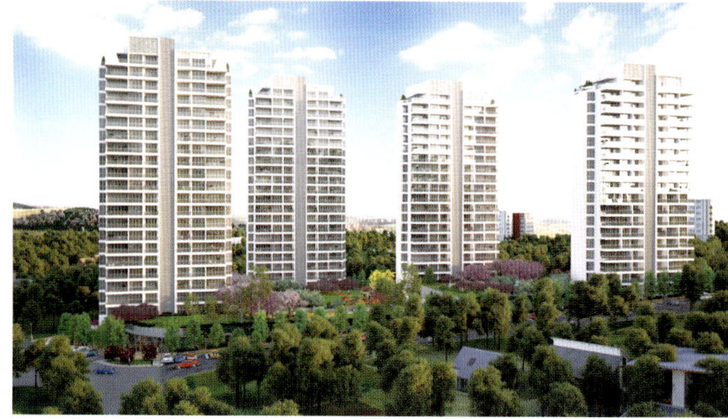

2

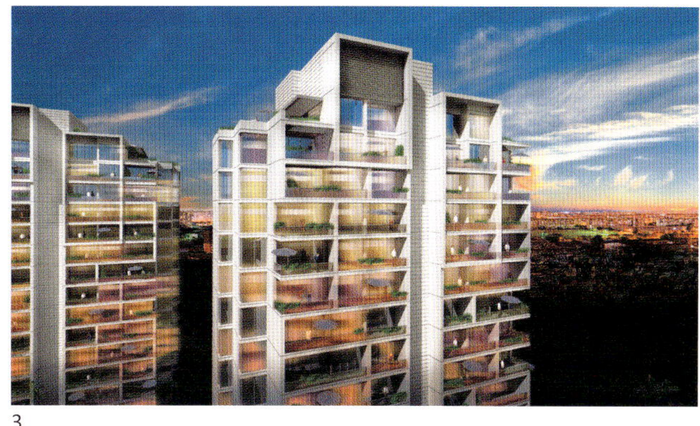

3

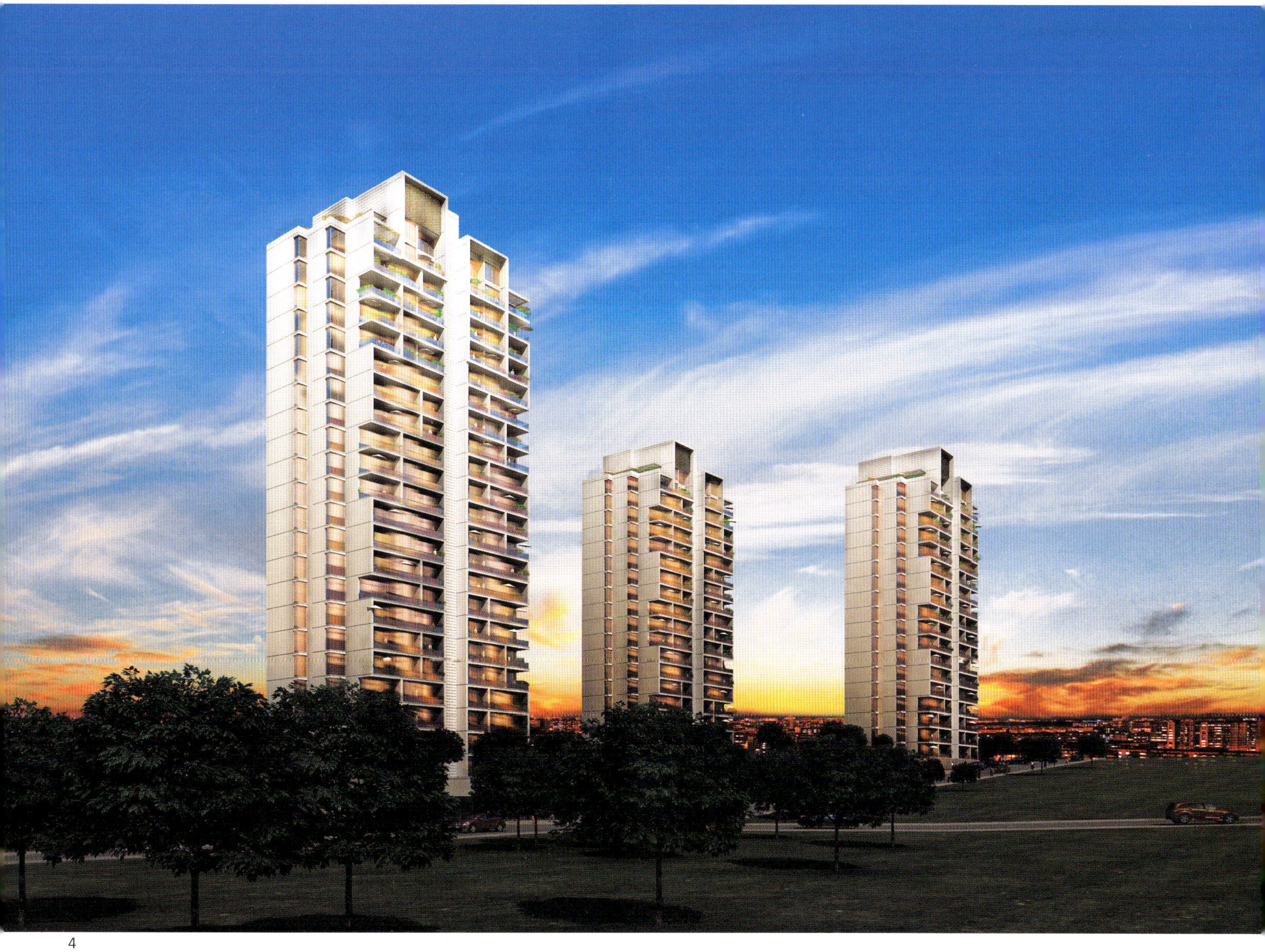

4

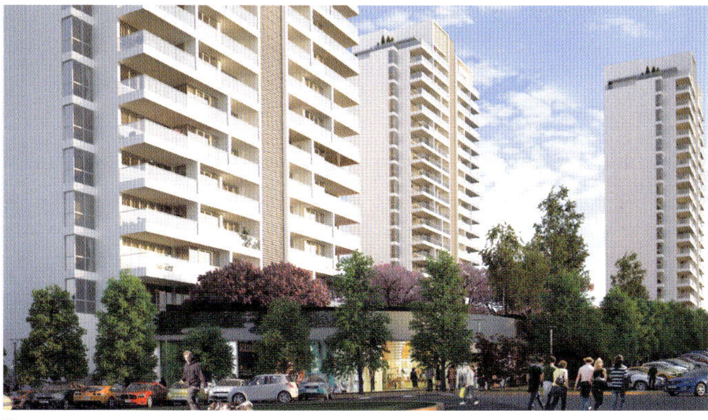

5

1 Typical floor plan
2 General view
3 Partial view of the buildings
4 Night view
5 View of the buildings from street level

NATA Vega Housing

Client NATA Group and MNM Eurasia Forest Foundation
Project Date 2010
Area 80,000 m²
Location Ankara
Structural Engineer Yüksek Project
Mechanical Engineer Metta Engineering
Electrical Engineer Akay Engineering
Landscape Design Dalokay Design Studio
Fire Consultant Alara Design and Engineering
Contractor NATA Group and MNM Eurasia Forest Foundation

The 46-story towers in this project are among the tallest housing structures in Ankara. The buildings will be seen from many points in the city, and they are designed to connect to the shopping mall. Constructed with a tunnel framework system, the buildings contain 400 apartments of various types, including 1+1, 2+1, 3+1, 4+1, and duplex apartments. The common areas that will serve the residential block include a recreational facility, children's club, and fitness center, aiming to offer a self-sufficient living environment.

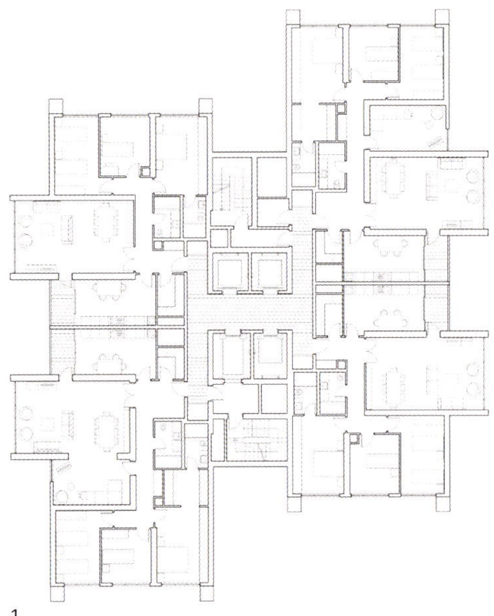

1

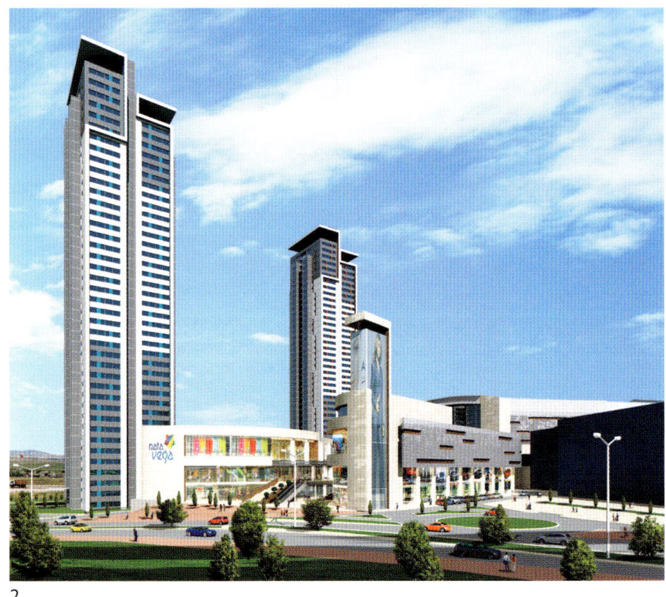

2

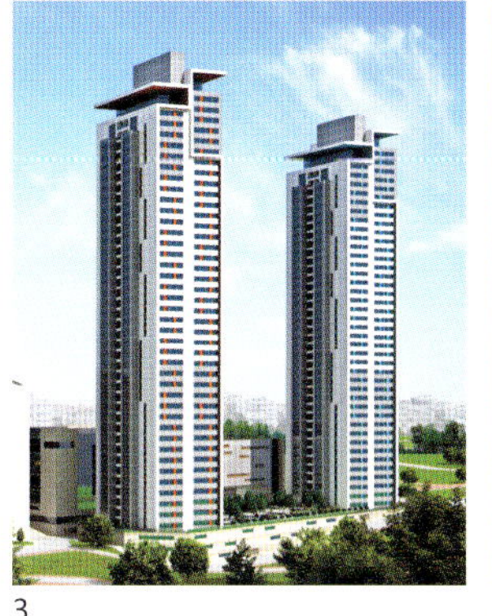

3

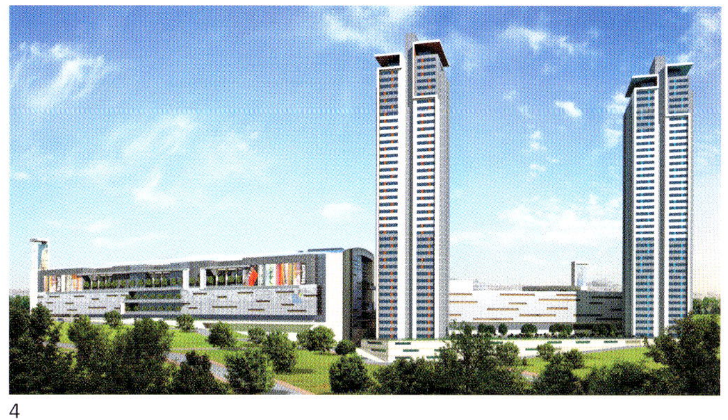

4

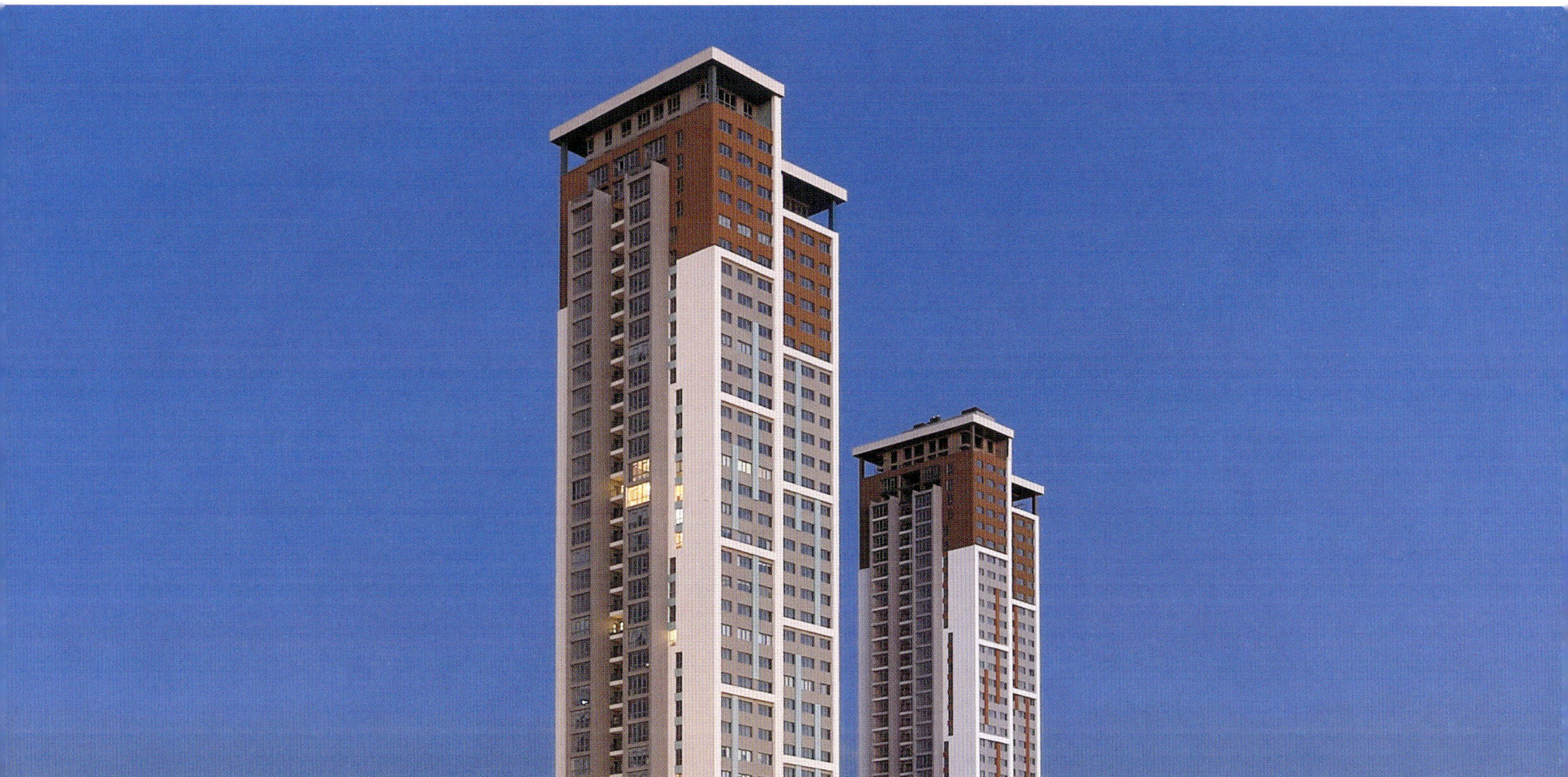

5

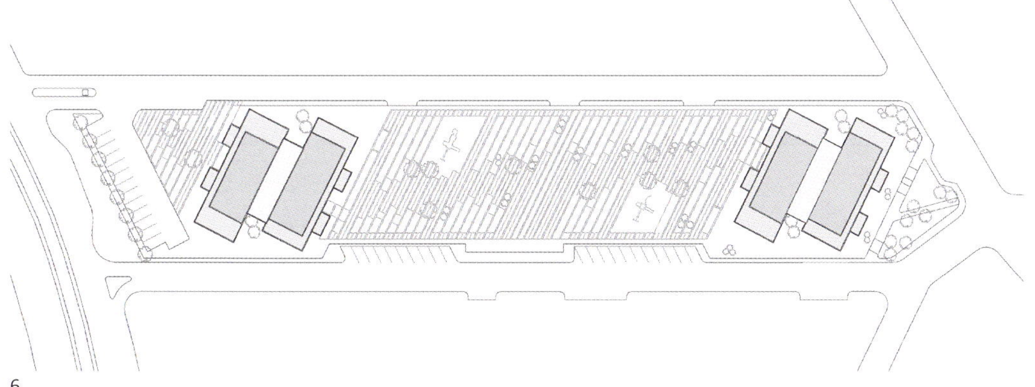

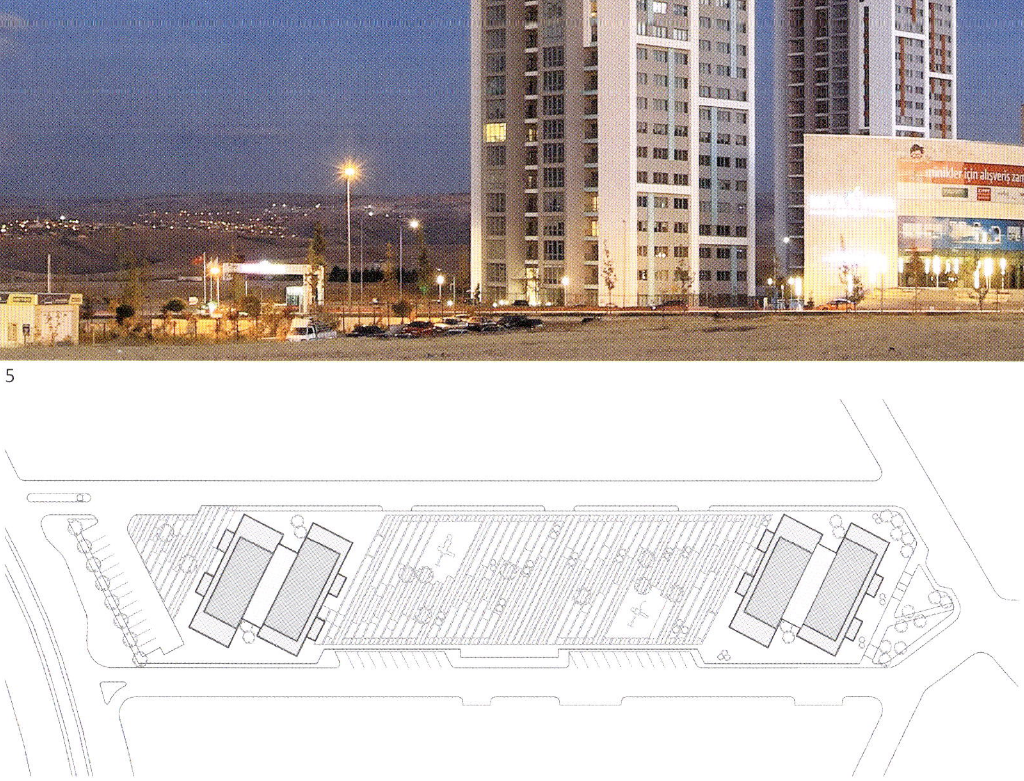

6

1 Typical floor plan
2 Model view
3,4 Model view showing the residential blocks from the valley
5 General view
6 Site plan

Antares Housing

Client Dolunay Forest Trade Ltd.
Project Date 2005
Area 206,360 m^2
Location Ankara
Structural Engineer Dumanoğlu Engineering
Mechanical Engineer Aydın Bingöl
Electrical Engineer Promete Engineering
Landscape Design Dalokay Design Studio
Fire Consultant Alara Design and Engineering
Contractor Dolunay Forest Trade Ltd.

The houses, designed at the same time as the Antares campus, are located towards the back of the complex. In order to maximize green spaces, a small number of houses with good vistas have been organized vertically.

The relationships among the six residential blocks, as well as their relationship with the plot and city, are arranged in terms of architectural composition and coherence. Landscaping connects the blocks to the shopping center and the northern side of the road passing through the area is designed for parking, while the southern side is designated for parklands.

There are approximately 800 dwelling units located in 27-story blocks, offering 4+1, 3+1, and 2+1 homes. The top floors contain duplex apartments while the lower floors comprise sports and hobby facilities for the residents. The open parklands, which surround the residential blocks and connect to the upper entrance of the mall, are lush and come complete with running, hiking, and cycling trails, playgrounds, and outdoor sports fields.

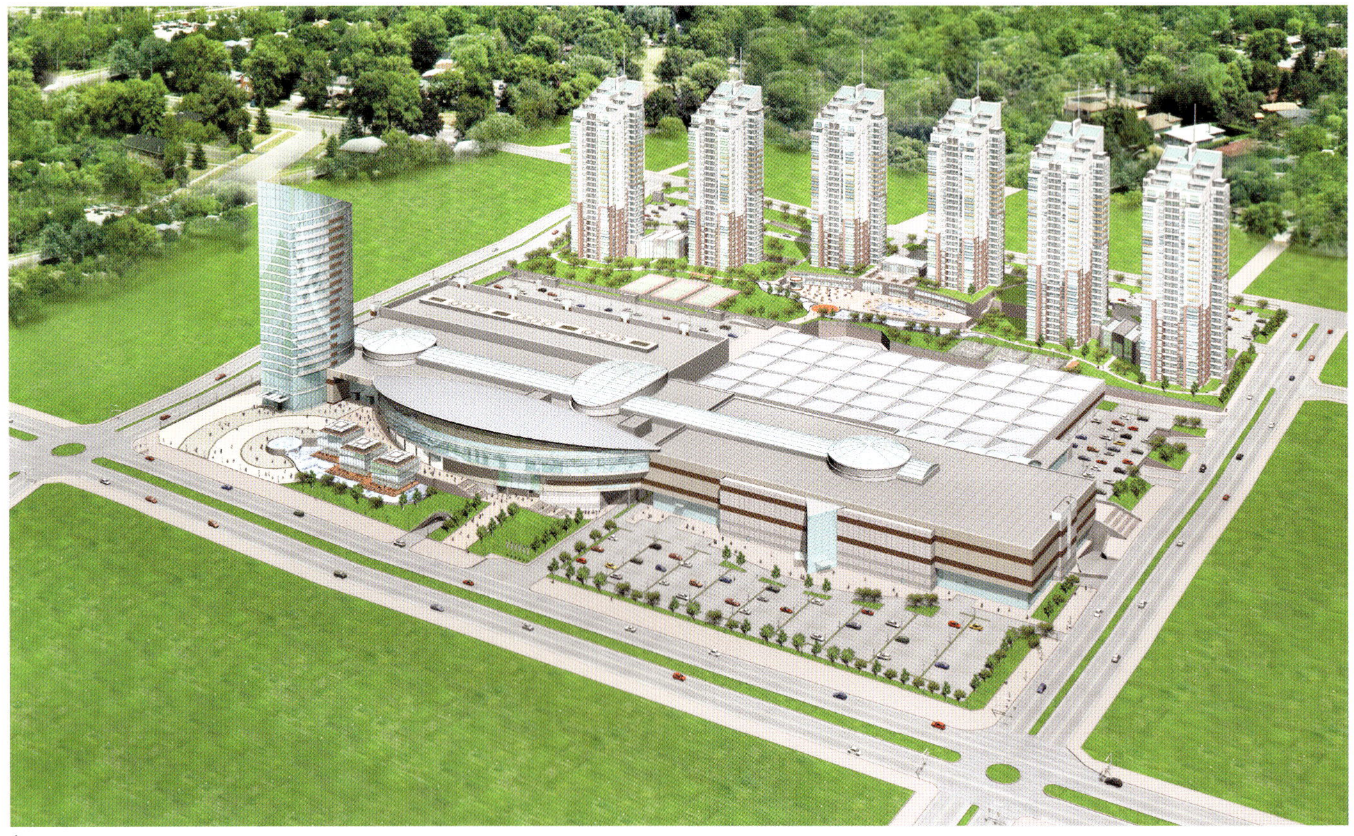

1

1 Rendering of the general layout showing the complex with apartments
2 General view of shopping mall and the residential blocks
3,4 South view of the residential block
5 Site plan
6 Typical floor plan

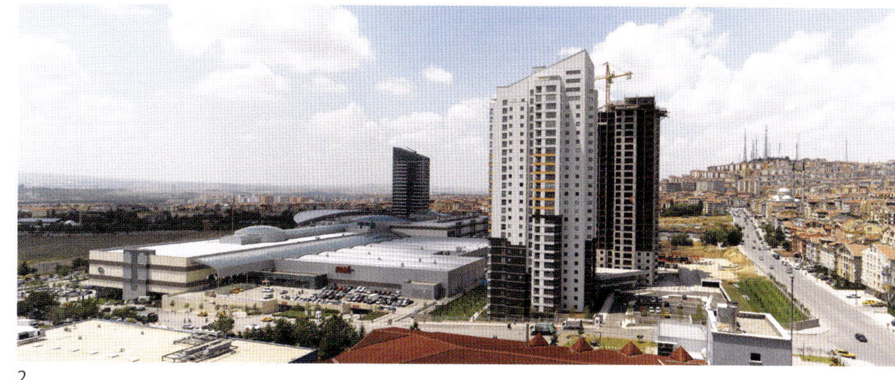

2

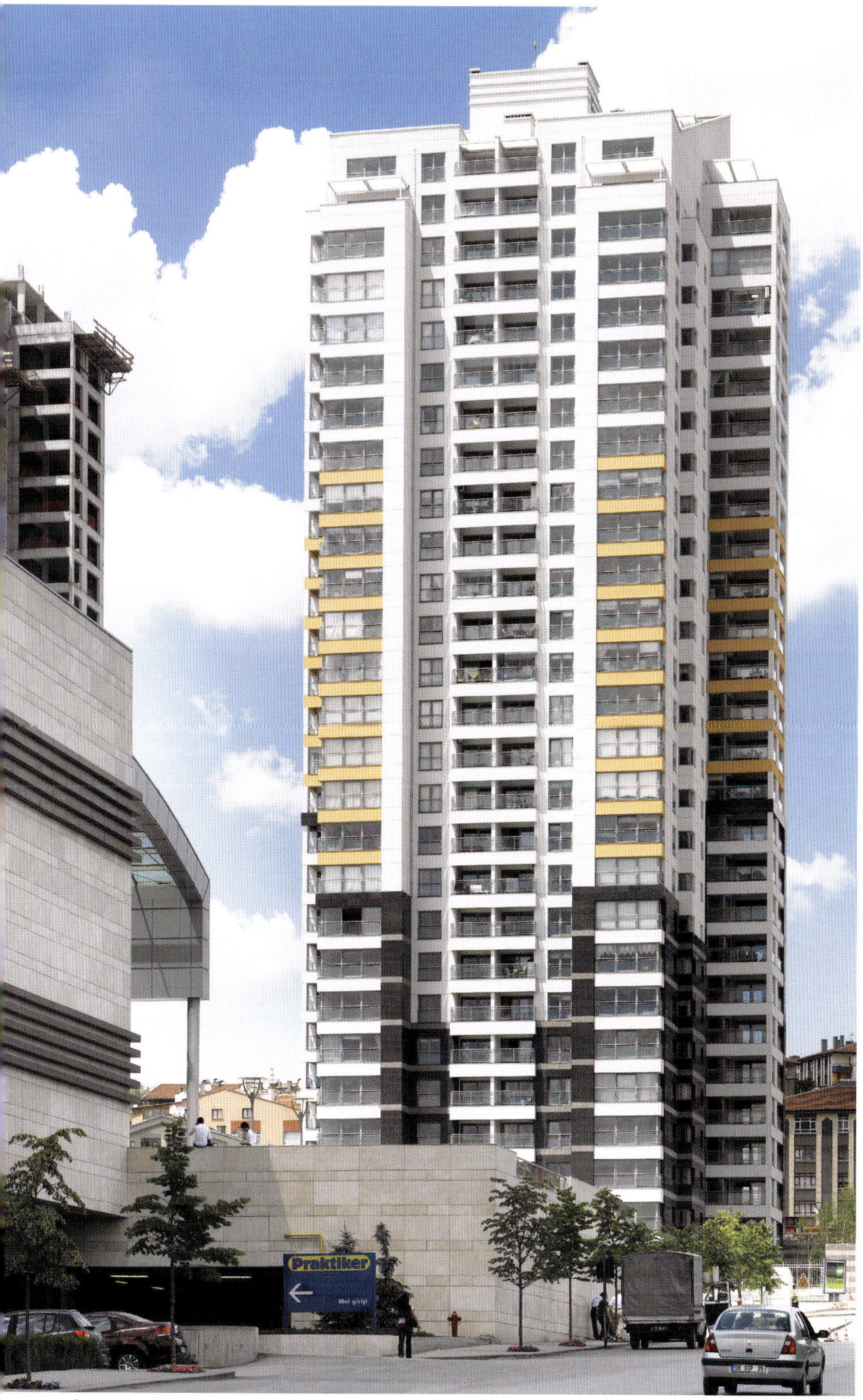

3

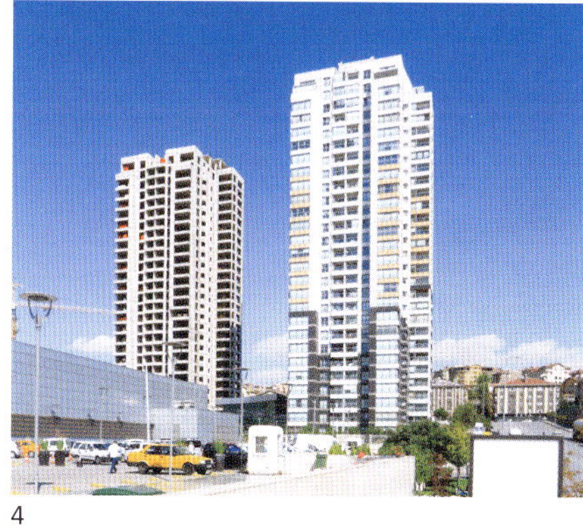

4

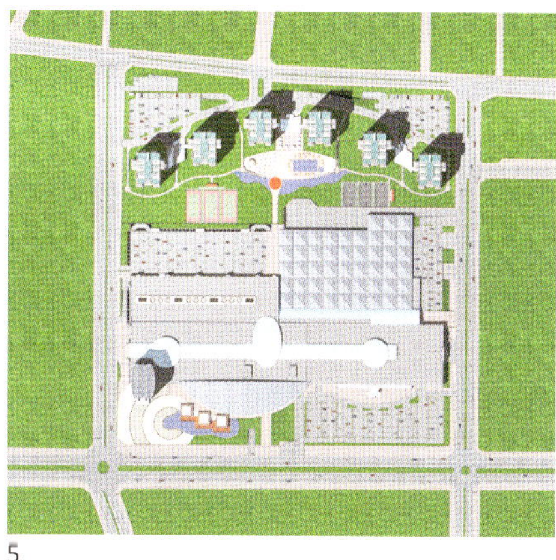

5

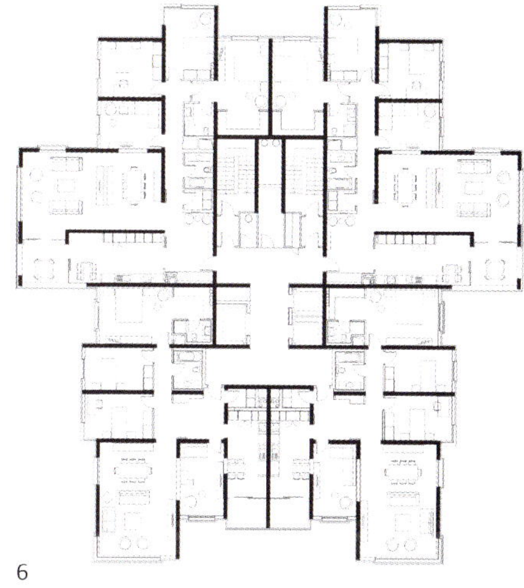

6

Nexus

Client Tepe Construction Inc.
Project Date 2011
Area 123,000 m²
Location İstanbul
Structural Engineer Yüksek Project
Mechanical Engineer GMD Engineering
Electrical Engineer Akay Engineering
Landscape Design Dalokay Design Studio

The Nexus project site is located next to Maltepe Narcity, above a valley with a view of the Prince Islands. The most important design criterion for the high-density parcel is the southwest and southeast orientation of the apartments. Apartments of various sizes have been placed in such a way to create a shared courtyard, which complements the valley. Social facilities are designed on different levels and the low-rise blocks include garden duplexes, which are oriented towards the view of the Prince Islands. Each of the blocks' curved façades vary, creating a sense of movement.

The entrance to the site is at the lowest level of the approaching road. Outdoor playgrounds are located next to the park and the slope of plot has been exploited to provide entrances to the apartments and indoor parking lots at different levels.

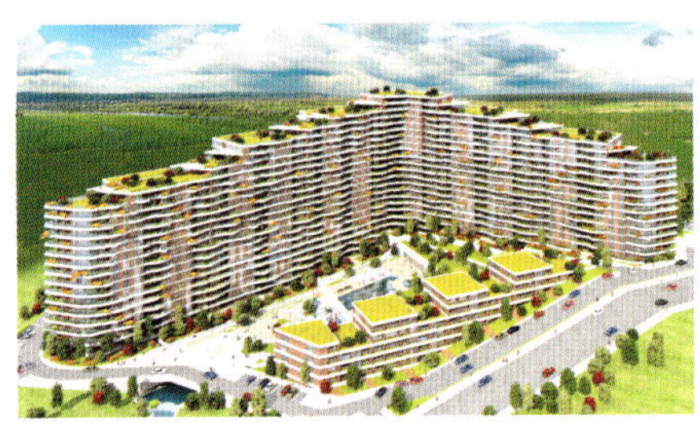
1

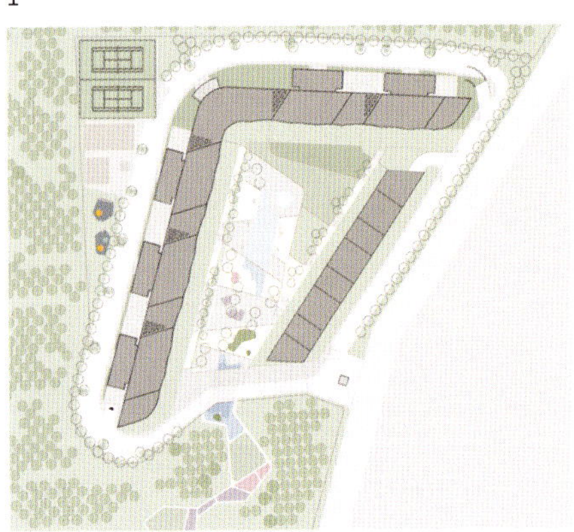
2

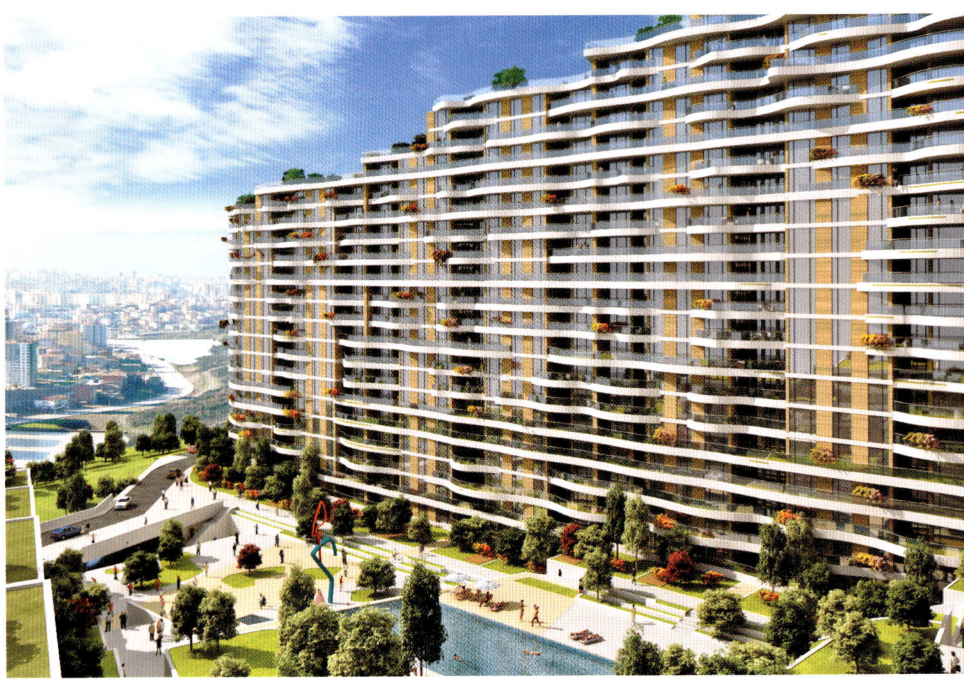
3

1 Model showing the apartments
2 Site plan
3 Model showing the courtyard

Turan Güneş Boulevard Housing

Client Tepe Construction Inc.
Project Date 2011
Area 100,000 m^2
Location Ankara

A variety of uses were proposed for a parcel of land designated to be a shopping mall. The site is located in a mixed residential and commercial district. A landmark housing–office–commerce tower is proposed for the most elevated part of the terrain. Entrances are located on various levels for this section. A public area was designed around the tower. Low-rise row houses were designed for the rest of the parcel.

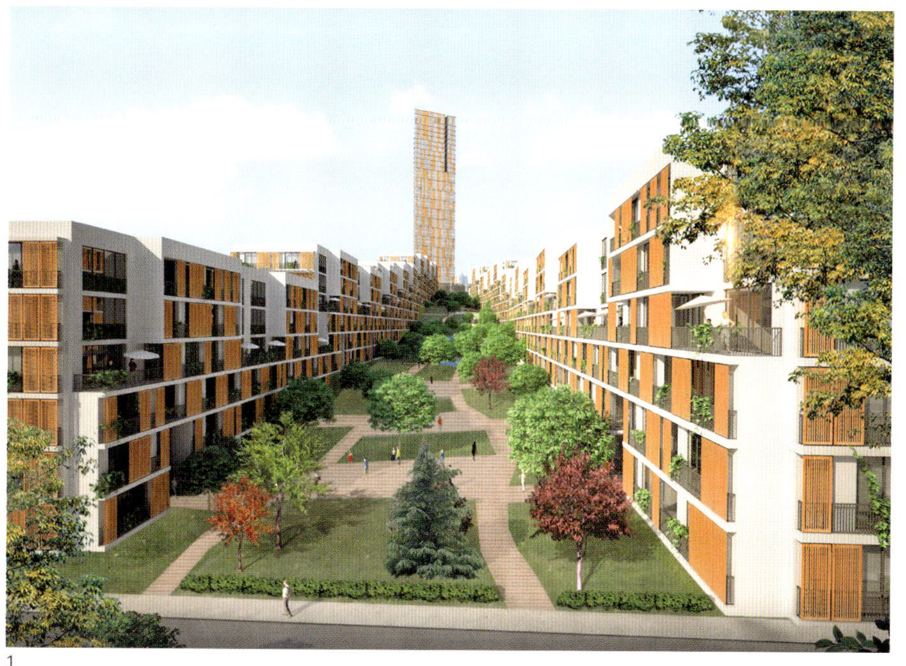
1

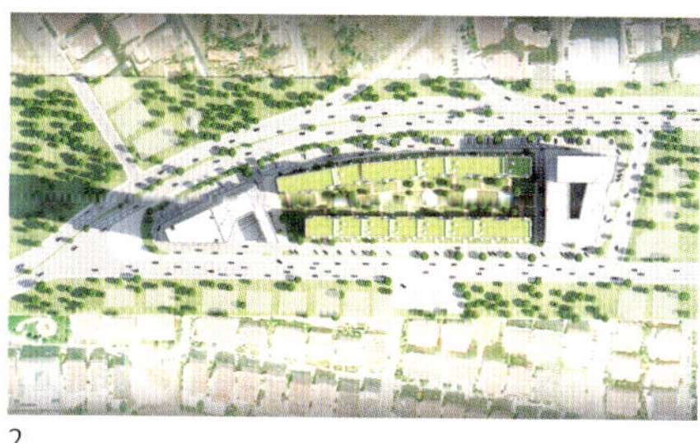
2

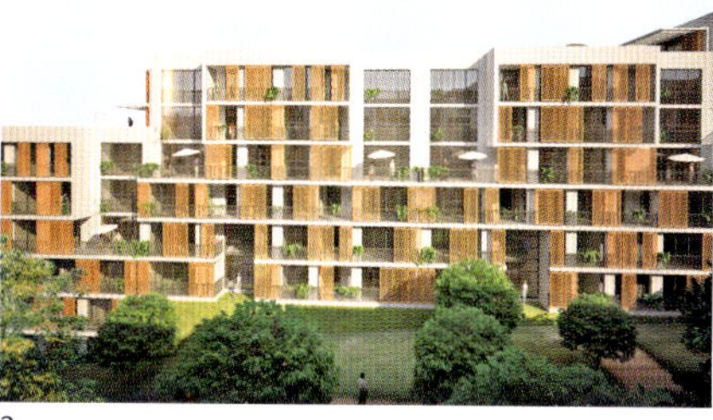
3

1 Model view showing the housing units
2 Site plan
3 View of the row houses from the courtyard

Koza Residence

Client Koza İpek Holding
Project Date 2012
Area 145,415 m^2
Location Ankara

This is a residential project prepared for a parcel with high building density. The restrictions on the distance between building heights influenced the layout and two residential towers of different heights were placed on a seven-story base. There are 335 houses of various types in the complex. The living spaces in the apartments are oriented towards a nearby park.

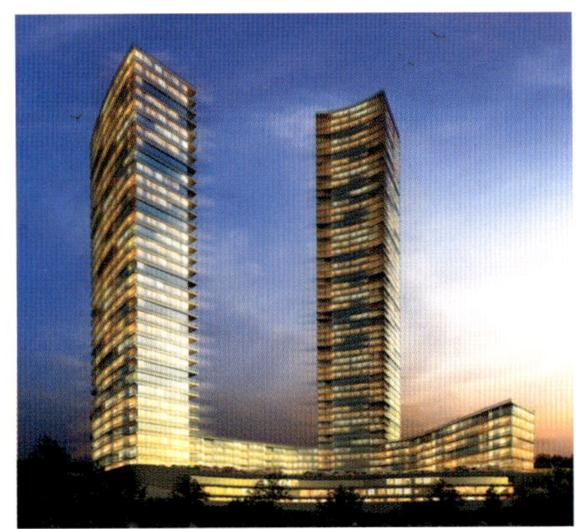
1

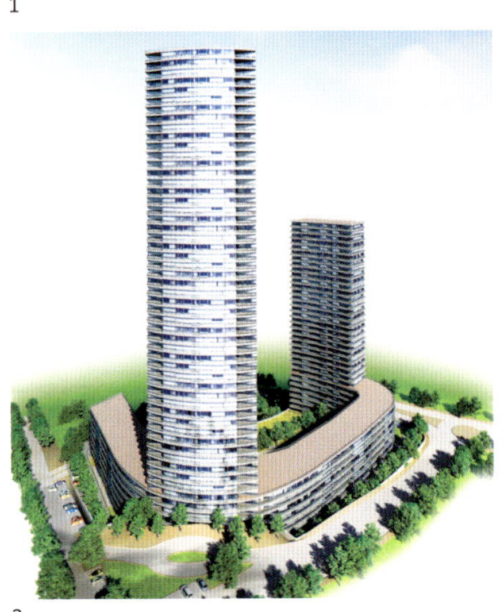
2

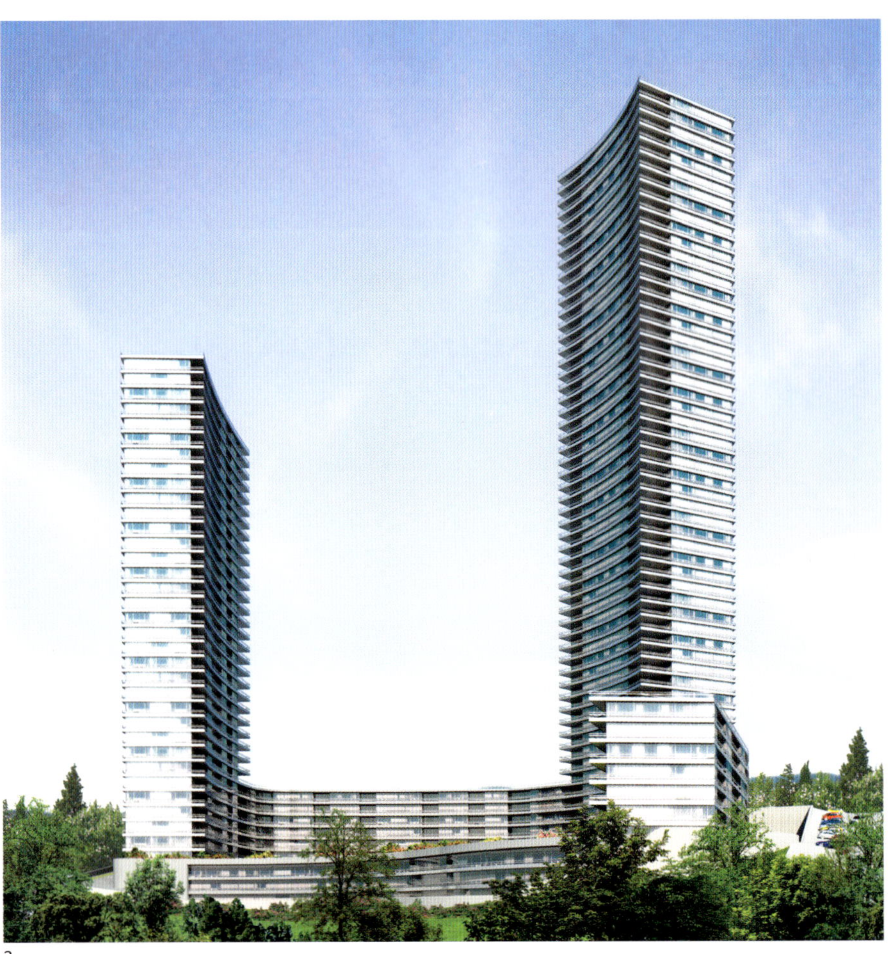
3

1 Night view
2,3 Model view showing the different heights of the unit

Sinpaş Bursa Housing

Client Sinpaş REIT
Project Date 2011
Area 173,000 m^2
Location Bursa
Landscape Design Dalokay Design Studio

This is a residential project prepared for a parcel with high building density. The restrictions on the distance between building heights influenced the layout and two residential towers of different heights were placed on a seven-story base. There are 335 houses of various types in the complex. The living spaces in the apartments are oriented towards a nearby park.

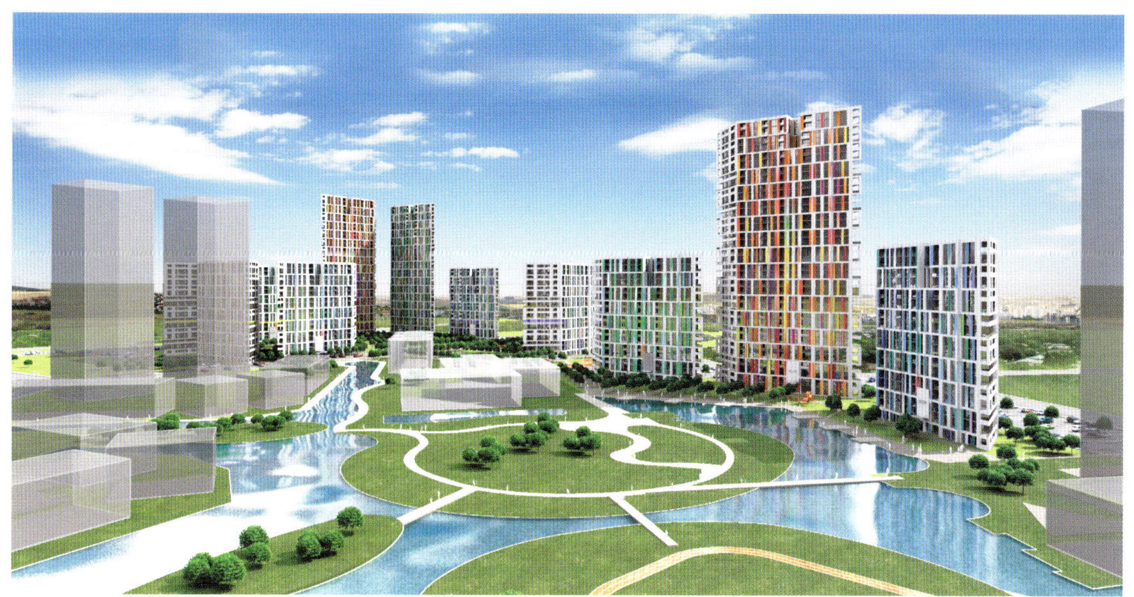

1

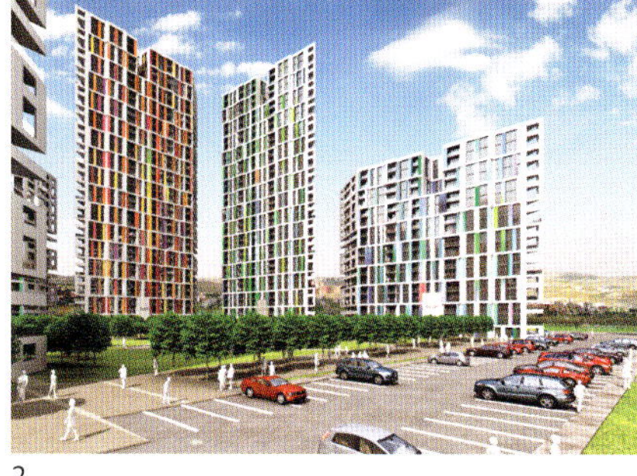

2

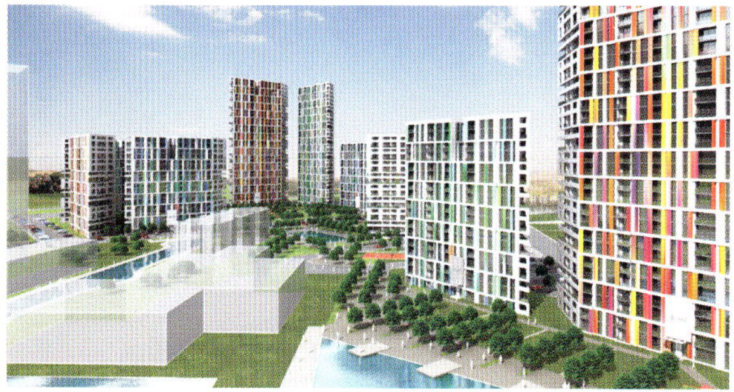

3

1 General view
2 View from the parking lot
3 Façade detail

Güneşli Park

Client Gül Construction
Project Date 2008
Area 103,000 m^2
Location İstanbul
Structural Engineer AS Engineering
Mechanical Engineer AMK Engineering
Electrical Engineer AKC Group
Landscape Design Spiga Landscape
Contractor Gül Construction

Designed as a recreational center within the existing residential area, this structure contains a number of shops, banks, agencies, offices, cafés, and restaurants. Residential blocks are located on the periphery of the campus in order to create a central social area in the courtyard. The design opens toward the exterior and brings an independent organization to the adjacent commercial units. This section, which can be accessed from the street, contains 122 shops, a supermarket, techno-market, and eight restaurants. The patio gardens created at different levels allow the open spaces to be used and enjoyed. The restaurant and café block and the low-rise commercial spaces are intended to serve the surrounding area as well as Güneşli Park's own residential units.

The high-rise residential blocks contain a variety of apartment types ranging from 1+1, 2+1, 3+1, 4+1, and 5+1. There are a total of 264 apartments in this section as well as recreational facilities to be used by the residents. With indoor and outdoor swimming pools, a sports center, and social and cultural facilities, Güneşli Park aims to become a local attraction, not only serving its own residents, but also the surrounding neighborhoods.

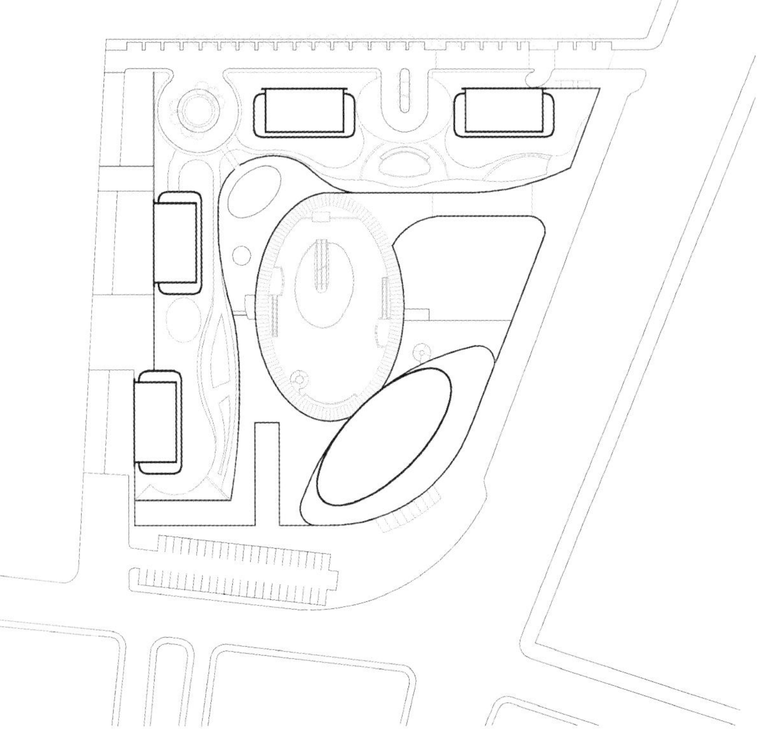

1

1 Site plan
2 Street view of the project showing the commercial space including a number of shops, banks, agencies, offices, cafés, and restaurants
3 General view of the residential and recreational space

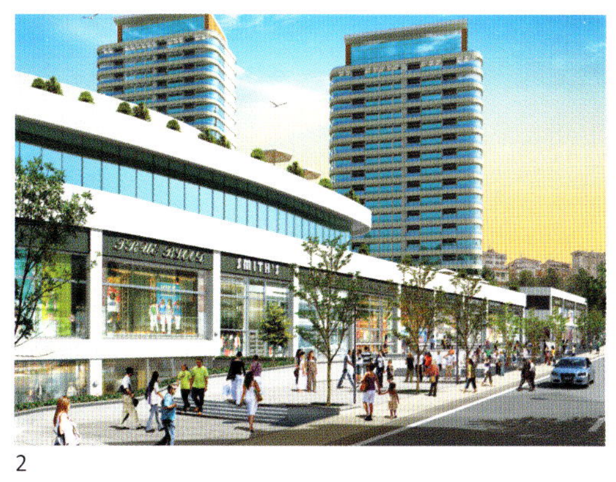

2

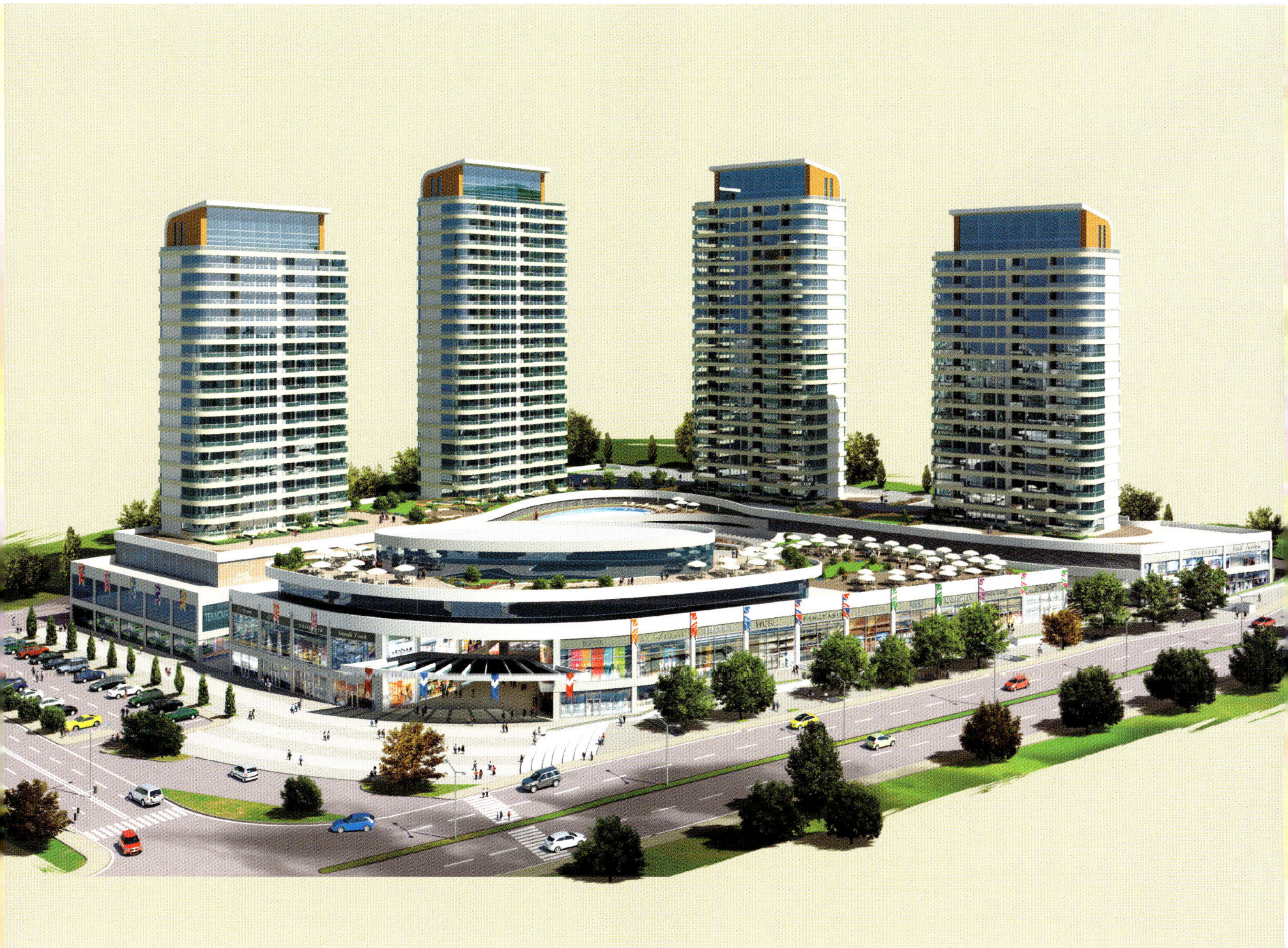

3

Gardenya

Gardenya is located in Bağcılar İstanbul, a rapidly developing and transforming district. The project, which aims to create an alternative living space, contains 306 apartments of varying types from 1+1 to 4+1. The campus also includes six shops and a supermarket.

Client Gül Construction and Mutlu Construction
Project Date 2009
Area 69,355 m^2
Location İstanbul
Structural Engineer Yüksek Project
Mechanical Engineer Setes Engineering
Electrical Engineer Akay Engineering
Landscape Design Defne Akşin Akyol
Contractor Gül Construction and Mutlu Construction

1 Rendering of the project at dusk
2 Typical floor plan
3,4 Rendering of the project at night

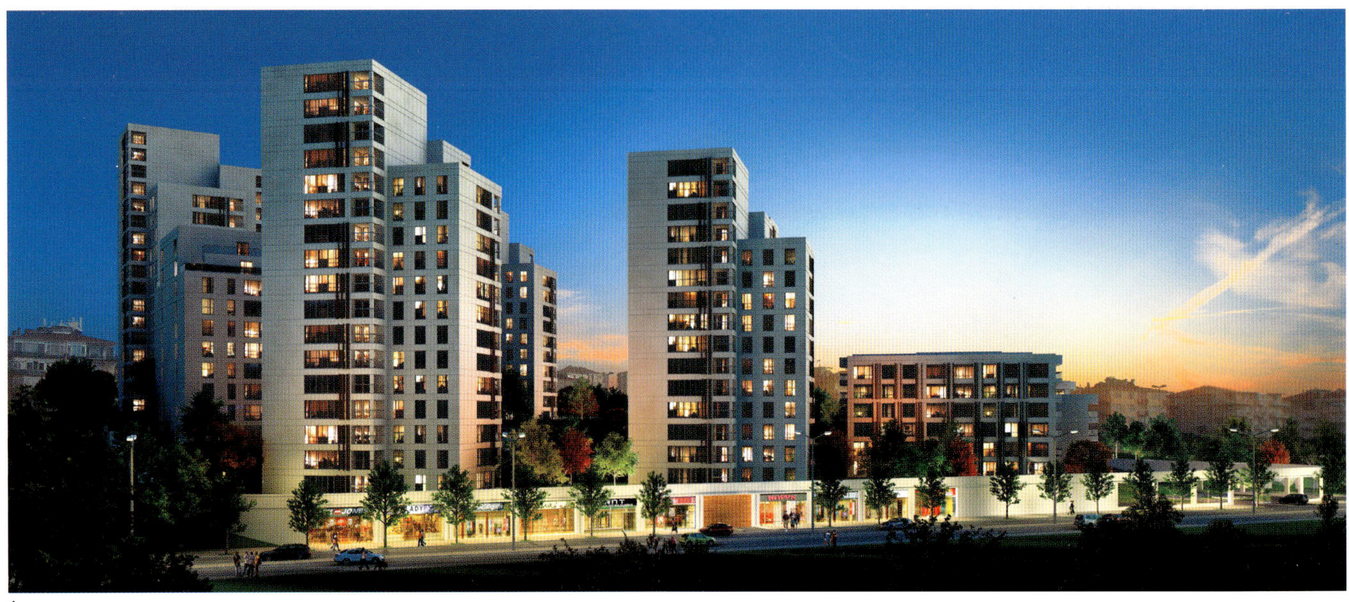

1

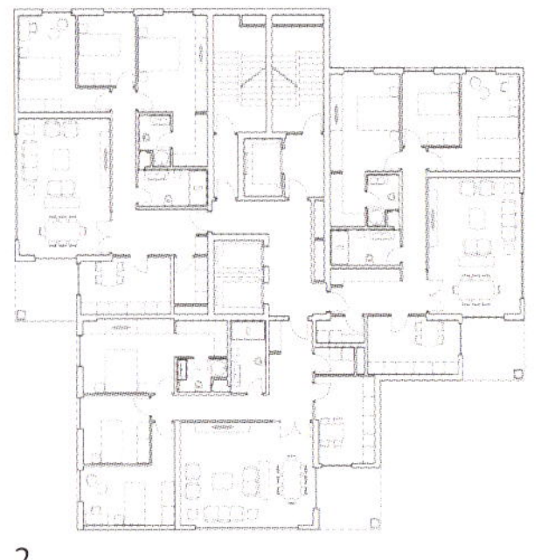

2

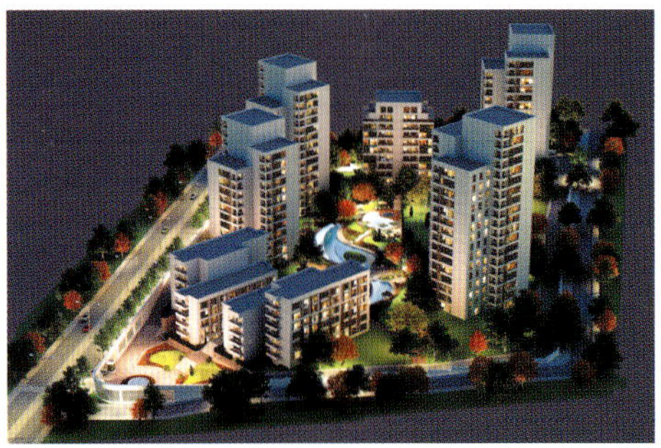

3

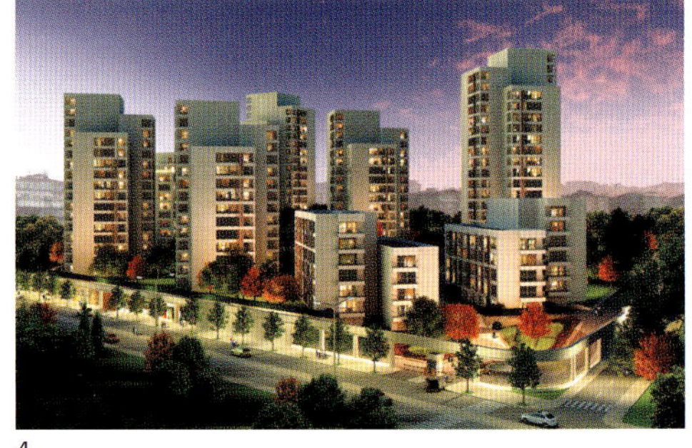

4

Avcılar Park

Client Gül Construction
Project Date 2010
Area 40,000 m^2
Location İstanbul
Structural Engineer Birim Engineering
Mechanical Engineer AMK Engineering
Electrical Engineer Çiçek Electrics
Contractor Gül Construction

These low-rise housing blocks are designed in a park arrangement. The campus includes commercial activities such as a supermarket, pharmacy, and shops along with the residences. In the layout plans for the houses, main living spaces are oriented towards the park. There are 275 apartments in the campus that vary in type. The park contains indoor and outdoor swimming pools, playgrounds, hiking trails and observation terraces.

1 Street view showing the commercial activities
2 Model
3 View of the pool area from the terrace
4,5 View of the housing blocks

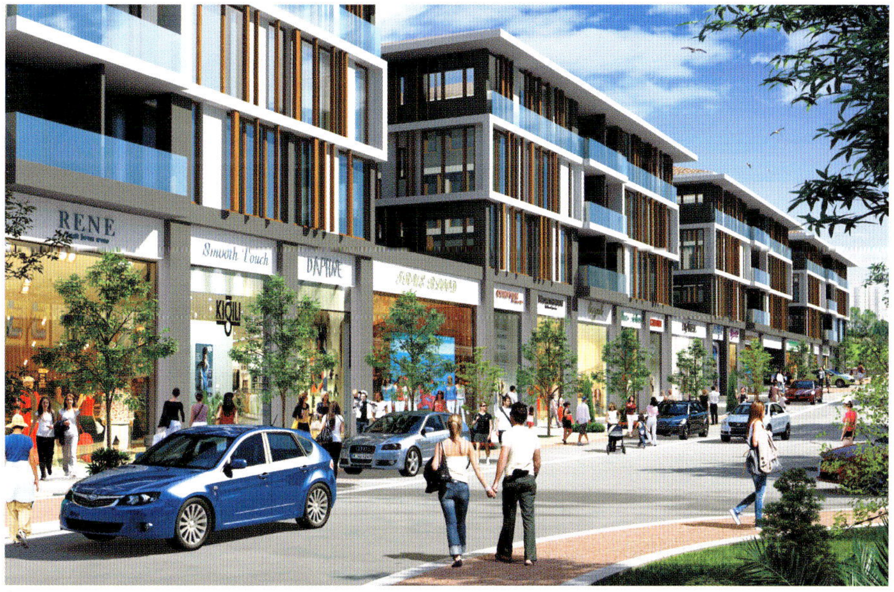

1

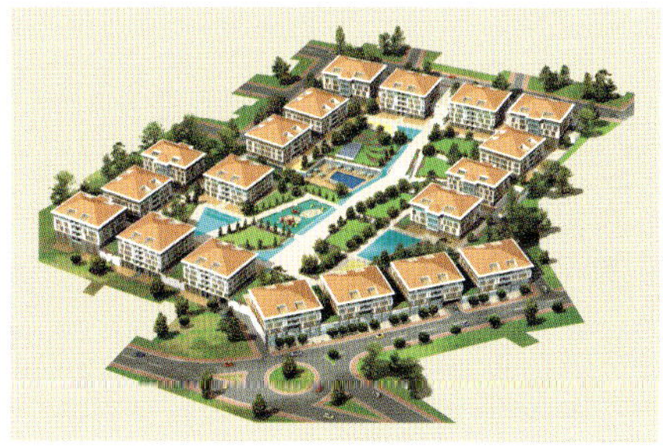
2

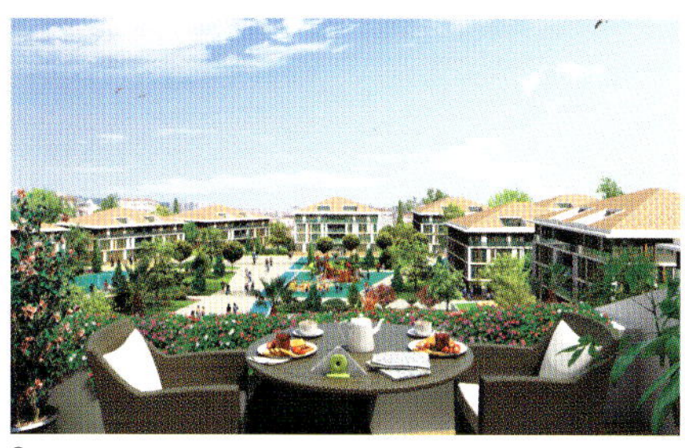
3

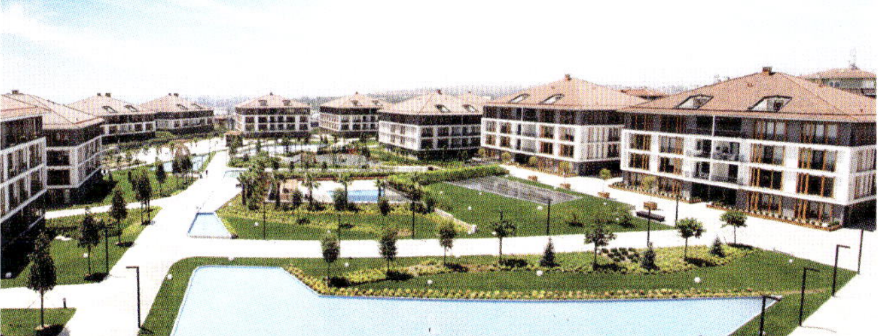
4

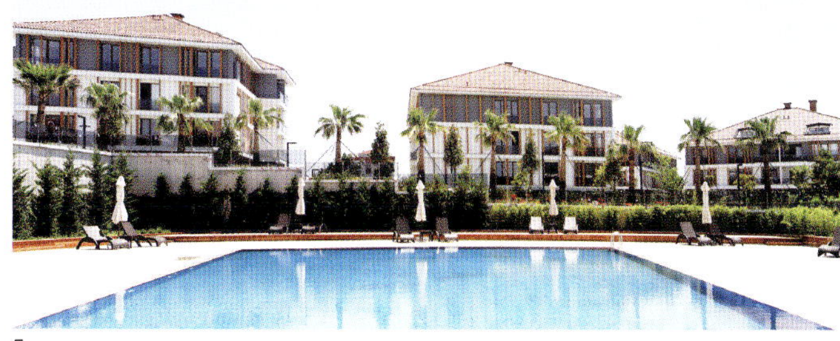
5

Eyüp Park

Client Gül Construction
Project Date 2011
Area 92,300 m^2
Location İstanbul
Structural Engineer AS Engineering
Mechanical Engineer Sadıkoğlu Engineering
Electrical Engineer Tepas Engineering
Contractor Gül Construction

With social and cultural facilities, Eyüppark aims to offer a regional meeting and living space not only to its own residents, but also for the surrounding neighborhoods. Designed as a recreation center for the surrounding population, the complex contains residential units, shops, cafés, and restaurants. The residential blocks rise on the periphery, leaving an open space in the middle. The commercial units are designed to be accessible from the exterior and are located side-by-side in an independent structure. The commercial center consists of 133 shops, a supermarket, an entertainment center, a movie theater, and restaurants. The building is accessible on different levels from the surrounding roads, and the rooftop patio gardens contribute to the sense of open space.

Three 14-story housing blocks offer good vistas due to their elevation and architectural layout. The apartments are oriented towards the green patios and the indoor atrium on lower floors, while the upper floors are oriented towards the view of the surrounding area. There are a total of 343 housing units in these blocks together with shared recreational facilities designed especially for the residents. The indoor swimming pool and the sports center are both available for residents and the project offers the region and residents an alternative living space.

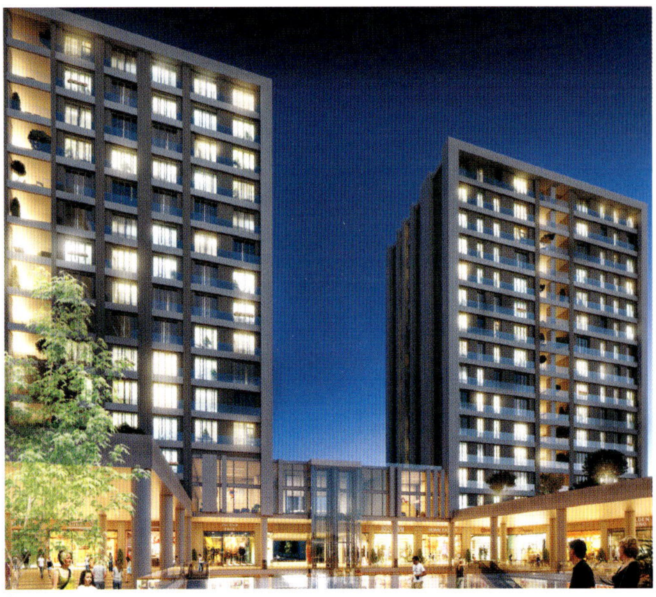
1

1 Rendering of the buildings at night
2 Model emphasizing the metro connection with the complex
3 View of the rooftop patio gardens and the inner space

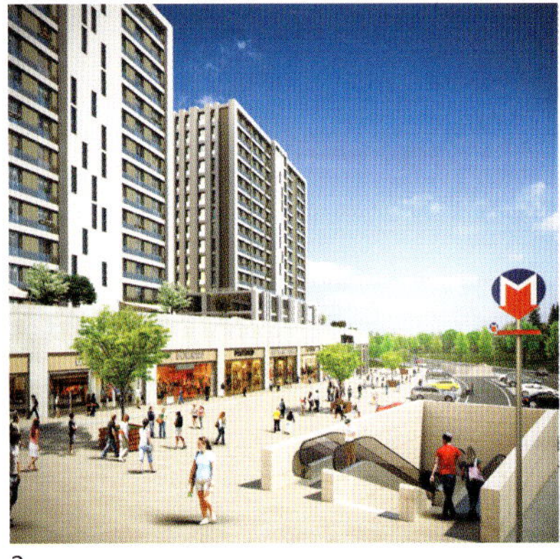
2

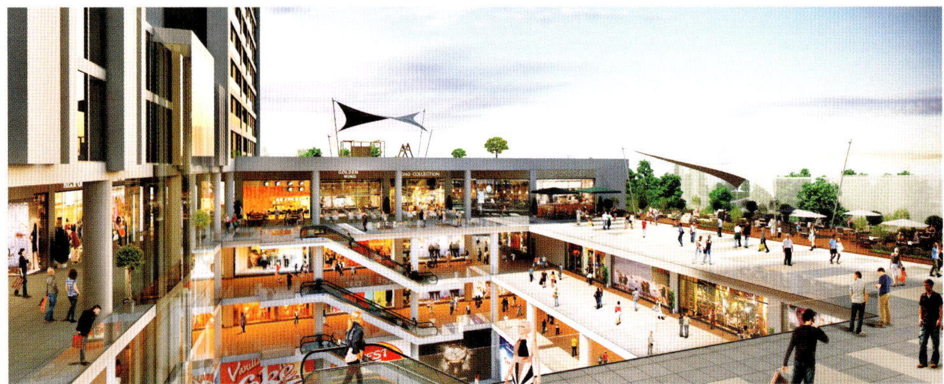
3

Yakuplu Park

Client Saray Aluminium
Project Date 2010
Area 120,000 m^2
Location İstanbul
Structural Engineer Yüksek Project
Mechanical Engineer Sadıkoğlu Engineering
Electrical Engineer Akay Engineering
Landscape Design Defne Akşin Akyol

The site for Yakuplu Park is located next to the city's commercial axis. Commercial spaces, apartments, and offices are proposed for the front parcel. The apartments designed for the second parcel are situated in a linear arrangement, and they form a courtyard. Shared social spaces are located in the green area.

1 Model of the buildings from the road
2,3 Rendering of the apartments

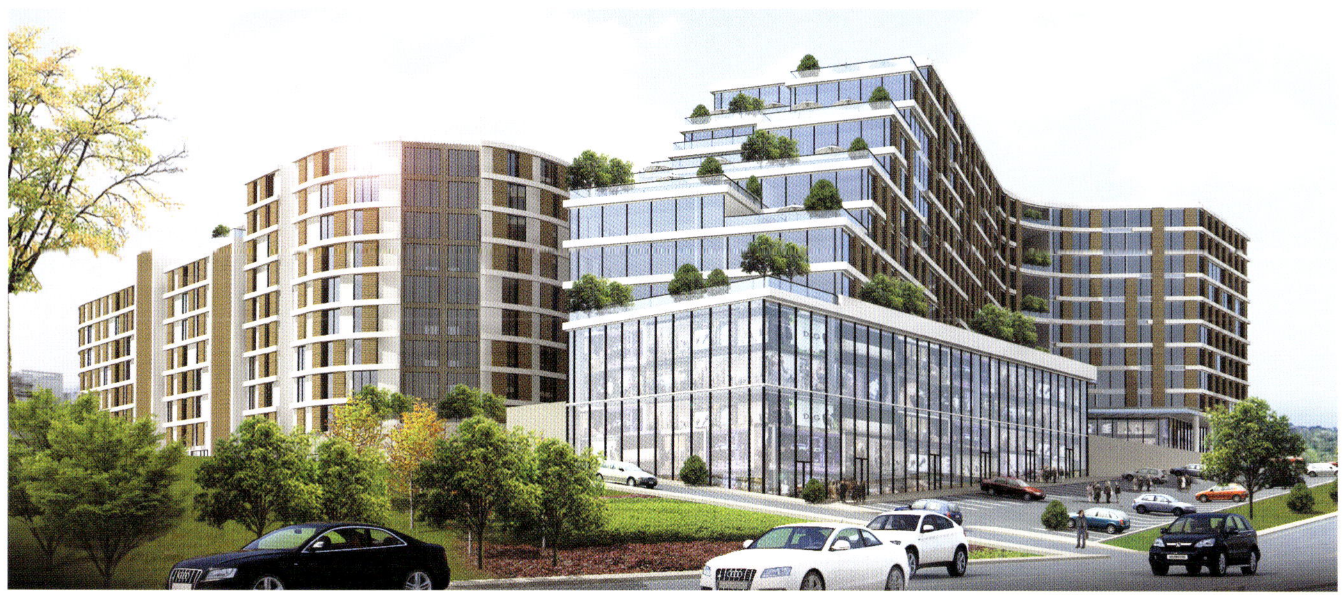

1

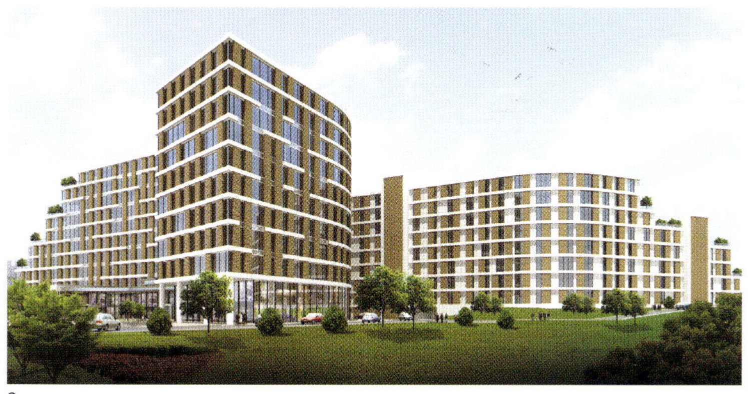

2

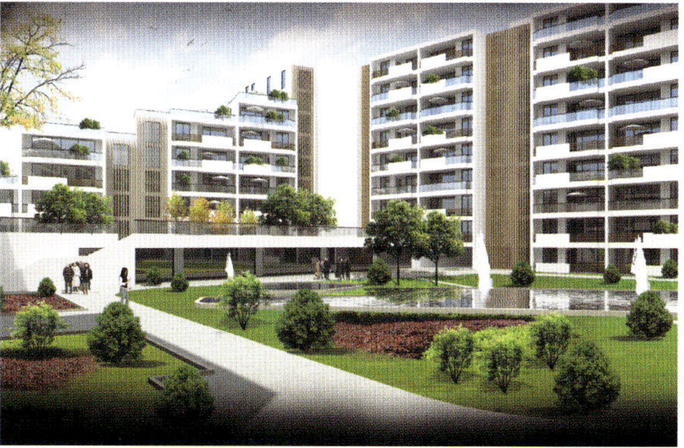

3

Ginza Lavinya

Client Keleşoğlu Group, Kullar Construction
Project Date 2007
Area 95,000 m^2
Location İstanbul
Structural Engineer Gündüz Çetemen
Mechanical Engineer Cengiz Erturhan
Electrical Engineer Hakan Yüksel, Enver Şengüler
Landscape Design Dalokay Design Studio
Contractor Keleşoğlu Group, Kullar Construction

Ginza Lavinya is centrally located in the district of Beylikdüzü on the E5 motorway. The mixed-use building program includes offices, housing, and shops looking out on to the street.

The offices vary between 60 and 70 square meters in size and are arranged in a linear fashion. The atriums shaped by the hollow spaces created in the façade become indoor gardens on the upper floors, allowing for maximum use of daylight. Dominated by horizontal lines, the upper floor gardens give the space pockets of deep shade.

The entrances to the residential blocks can be accessed through the courtyard via security gates in the main lobby. There are five apartments on each floor opening up to the inner atrium and four apartments on the upper floors.

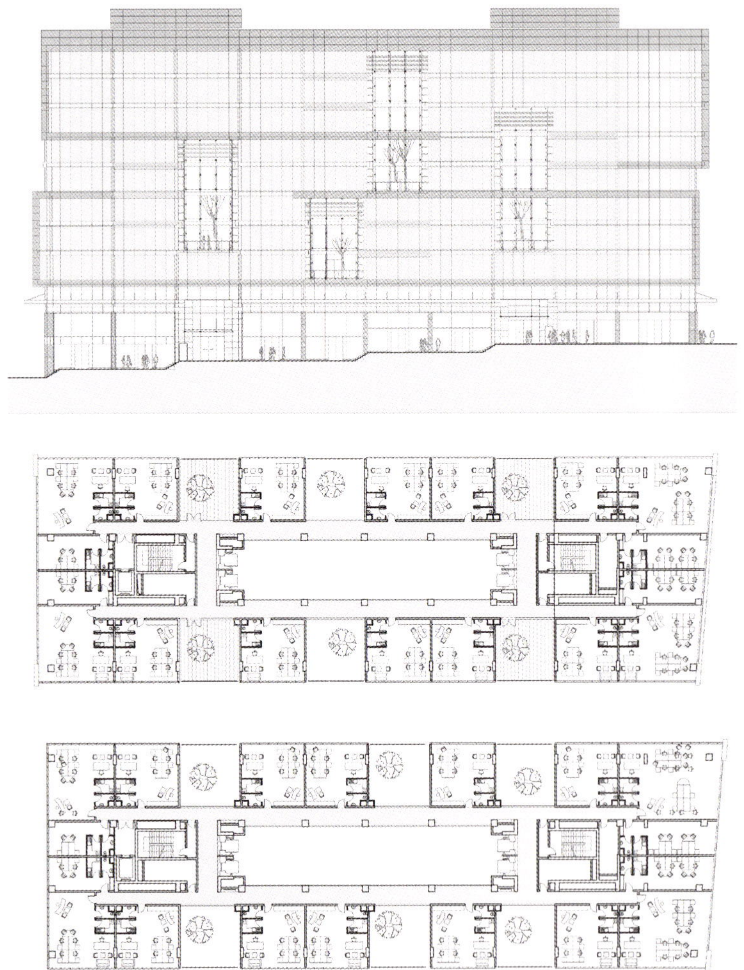
1

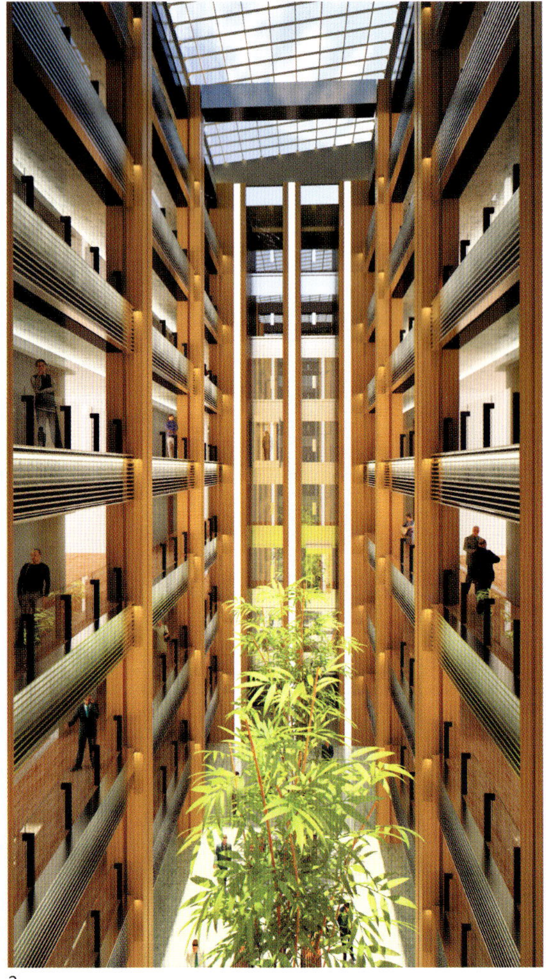
2

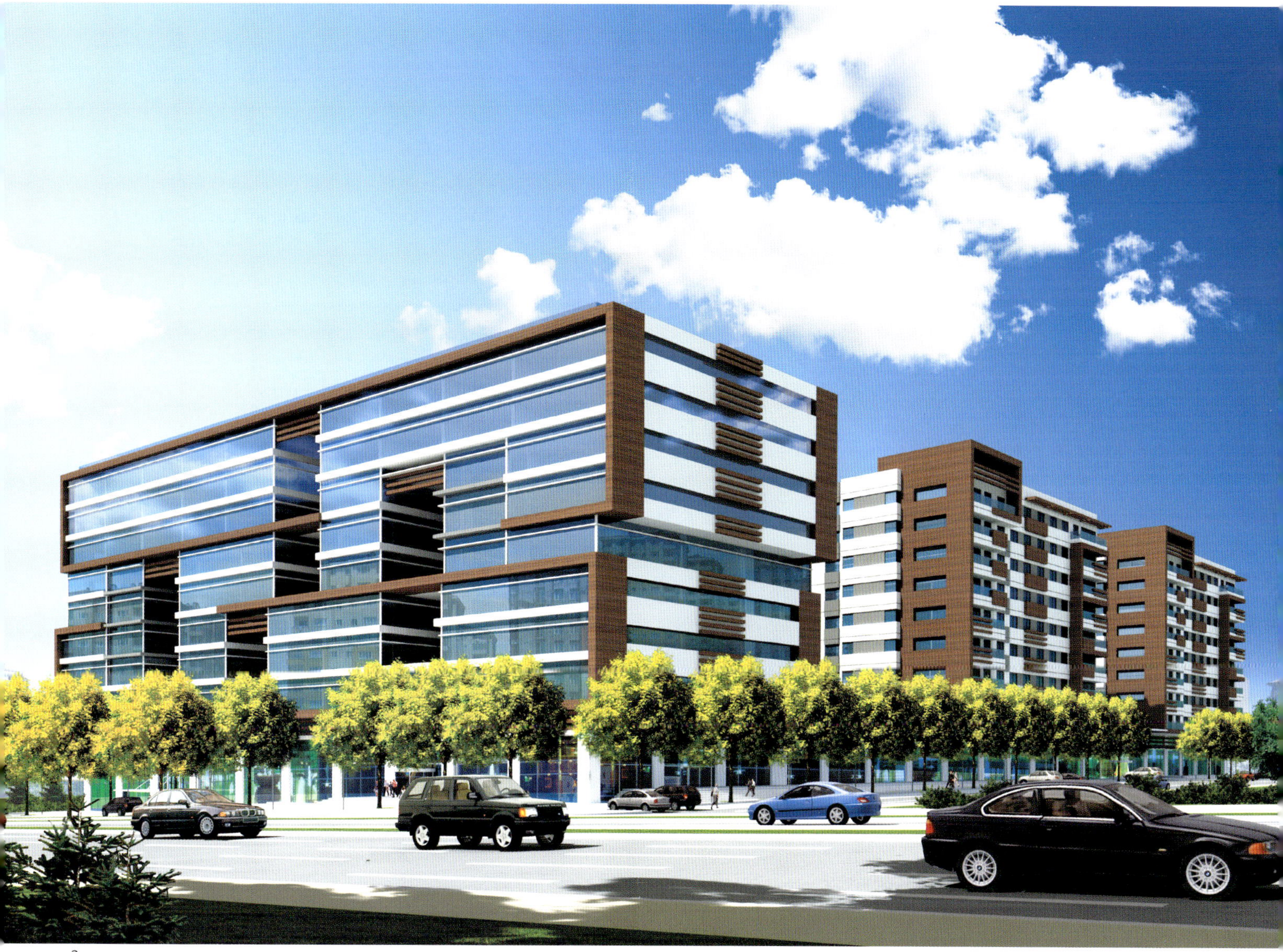

3

1 Drawing of 10.60 level plan, 21.40 level plan, and the façade
2 Looking along the atrium
3 Model of the office and the residential blocks
4 Night view
5 Façade detail

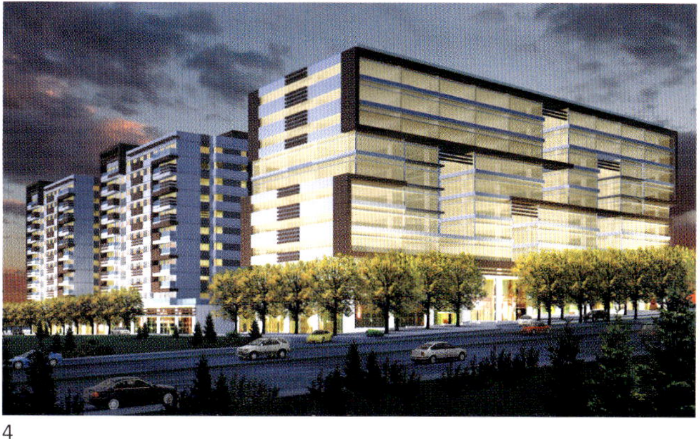

4

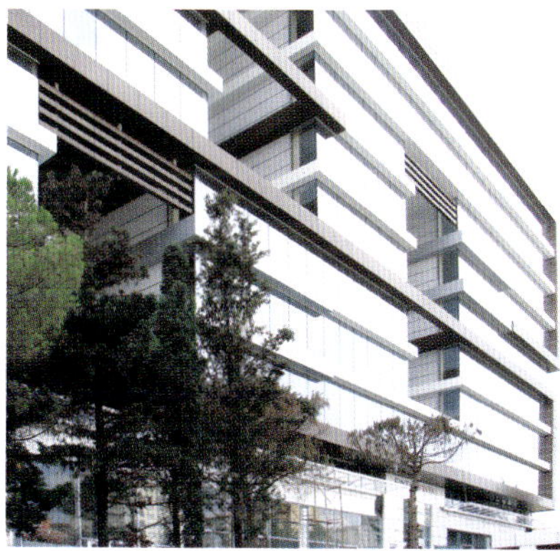

5

Gökyüzü Residence

Client Keleşoğlu Construction Tourism
Project Date 2006
Area 23,000 m^2
Location İstanbul
Structural Engineer Osman Tatlısu
Mechanical Engineer Mehmet Demiroğlu
Electrical Engineer Recai Bulan

The Gökyüzü Residence is located in Kemerburgaz, one of the most popular neighborhoods in İstanbul. It has been developed intensely since the 1980s. This attached housing scheme's milieu is defined by the courtyard and outdoor arrangement. The housing blocks define the courtyard along with the elliptical condominium block. The main living spaces of the dwelling units have a view of the inner courtyard.

The seven blocks contain 88 dwelling units, with the apartments on the ground floor boasting private patios, as a result of the differences in elevation. The wellness center located at the entrance of the site contains recreational and other amenities, including a multi-purpose hall, a fitness room, indoor and outdoor swimming pools, a Turkish bath, and a sauna. There is also an observatory on the roof of the elliptical block.

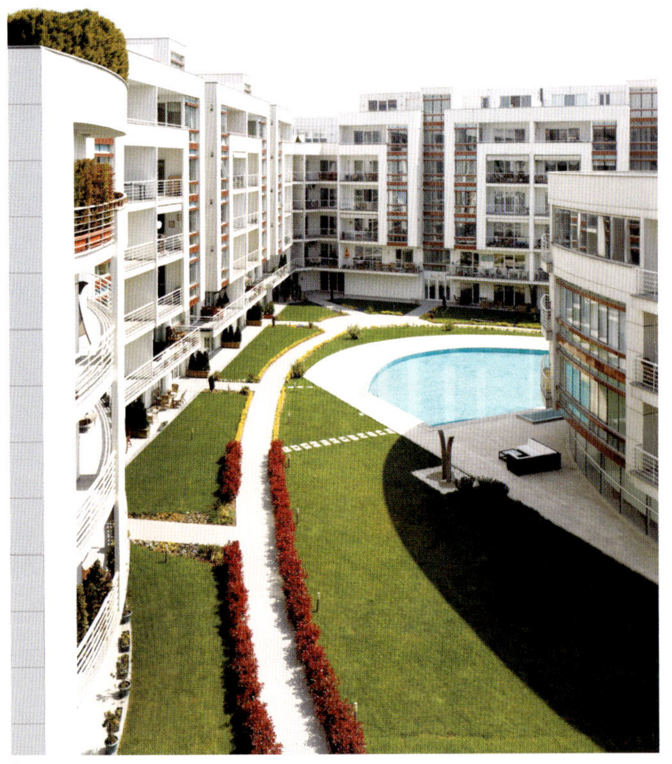

1

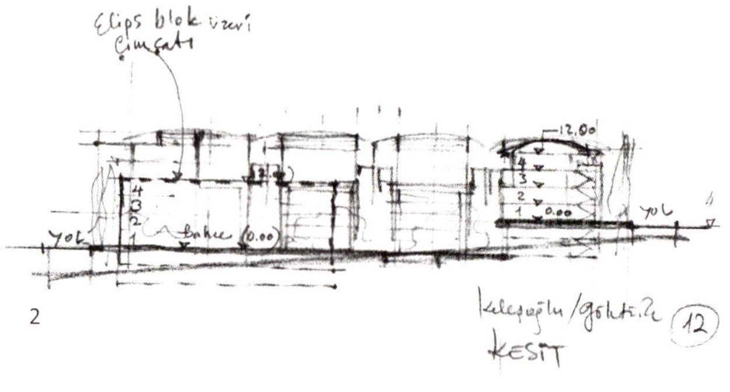

2

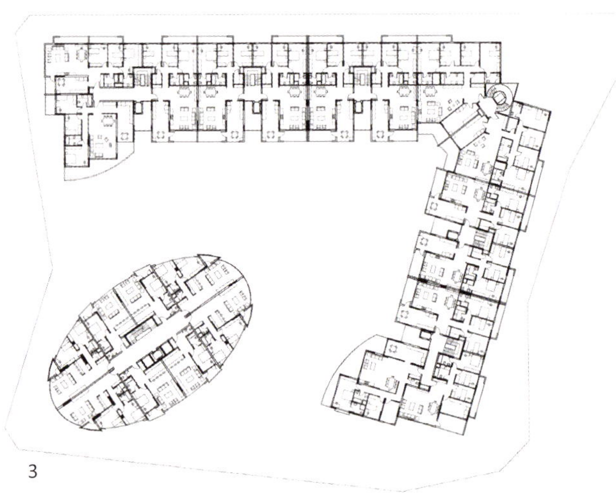

3

1 View of the courtyard
2 Sketch by Ali Osman Öztürk, explaining the level studies
3 Typical floor plan
Opposite:
Residential units

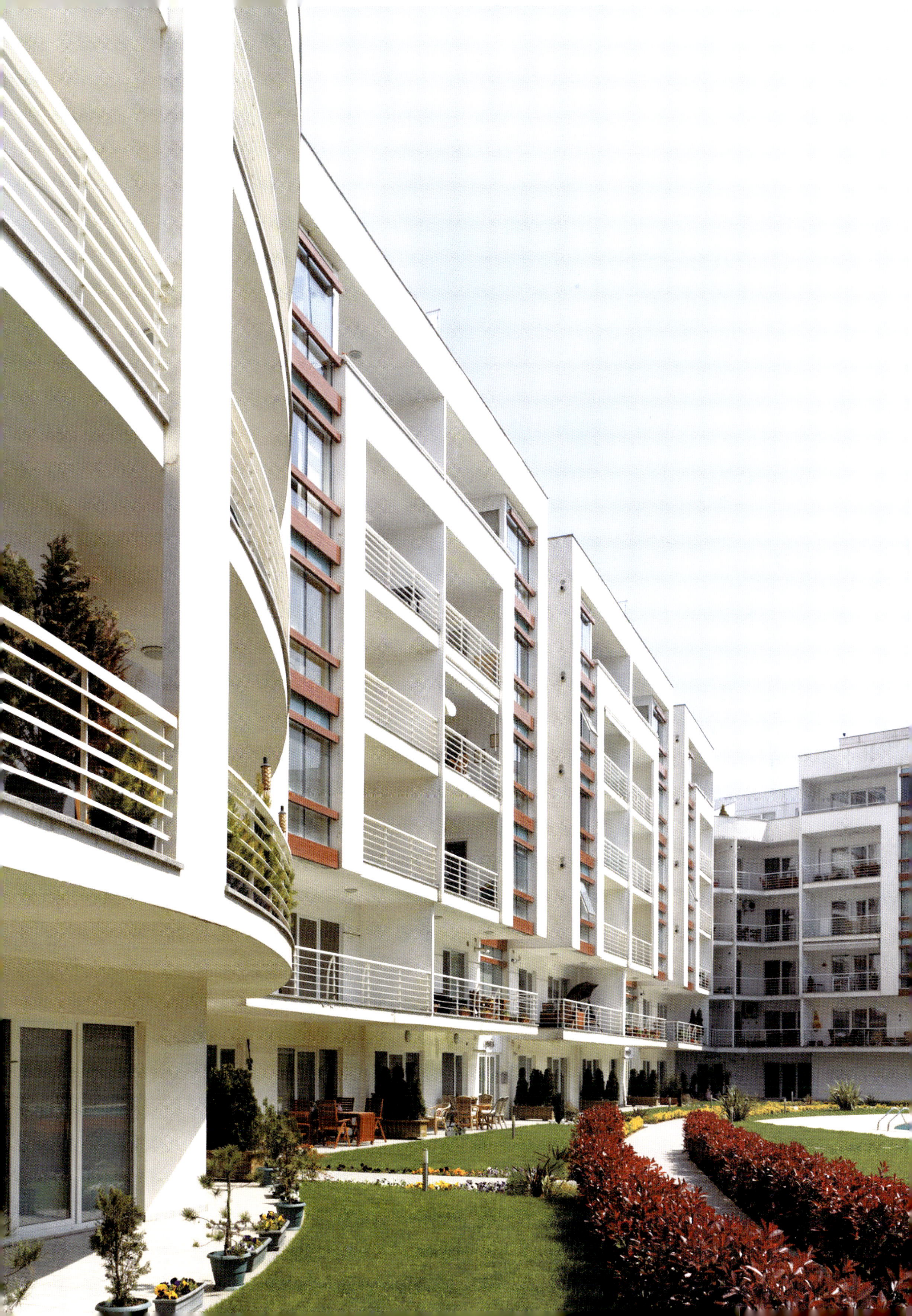

Limak Euroasia Hotel

Client Limak Holding
Project Date 2007
Area 20,000 m^2
Location Ankara
Structural Engineer Yüksek Project
Mechanical Engineer Wemeks Engineering
Electrical Engineer Melyap Engineering

The rooms and general-purpose spaces of this 33-bed capacity five-star hotel are all oriented towards the Kavacık recreation area. A circular layout was chosen to capitalize on the views and the rooms have been laid out in a radial plan. The left and right wings are both designed to have maximum exposure to the views.

The service corridor and customer circulation hallway are both located at the back of the building. The elevation differences in the parcel are exploited in order to create two entrance options. The lower entrance on the park side is accessed via a 15-meter-wide road. The upper entrance is accessed via a 10-meter-wide path to the hotel's west. The guest elevators and stairs are easily accessible from both entrances.

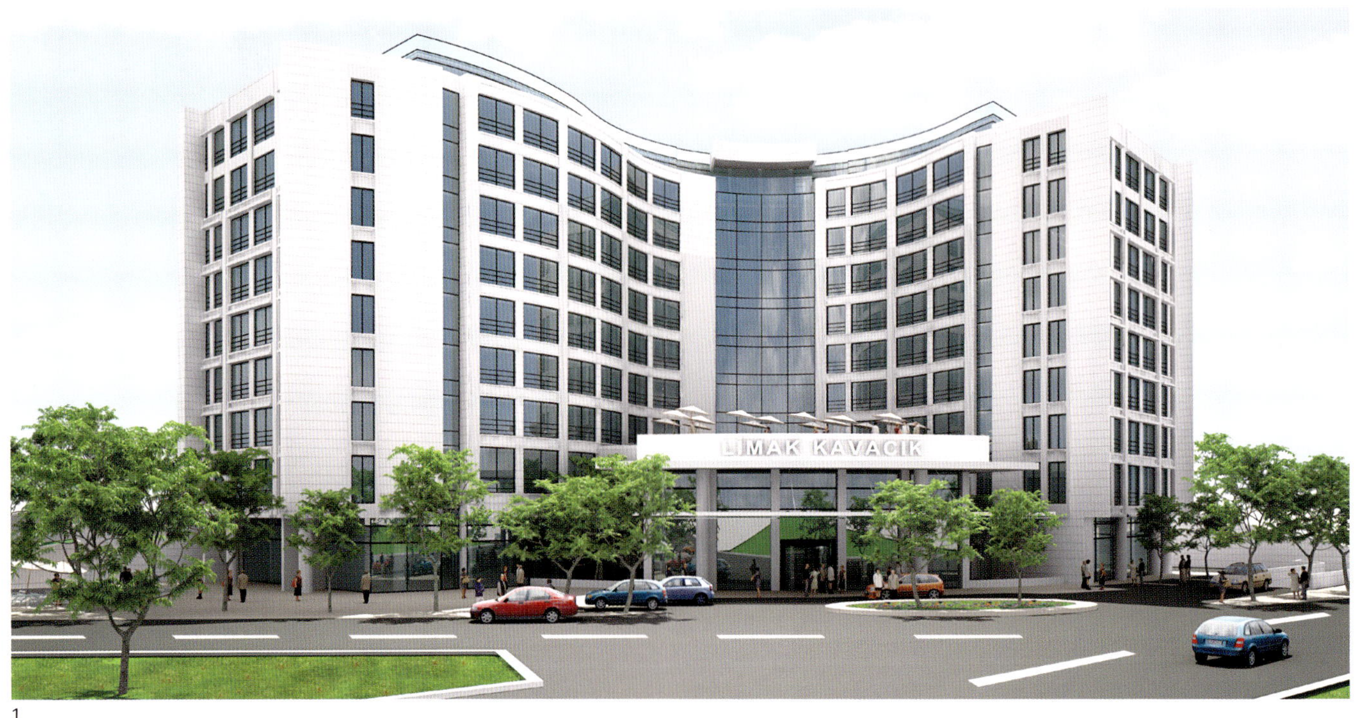

1

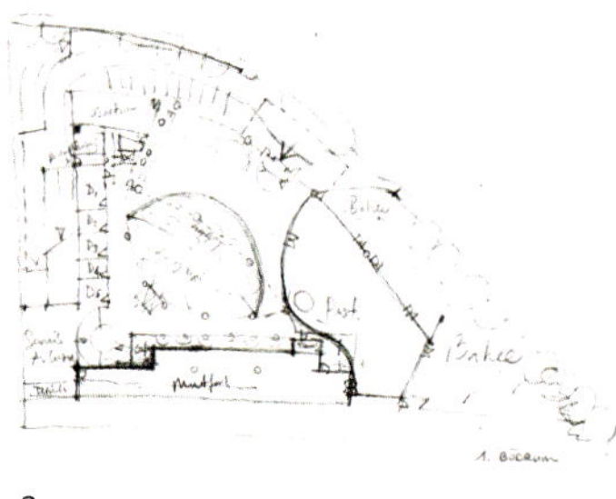

2

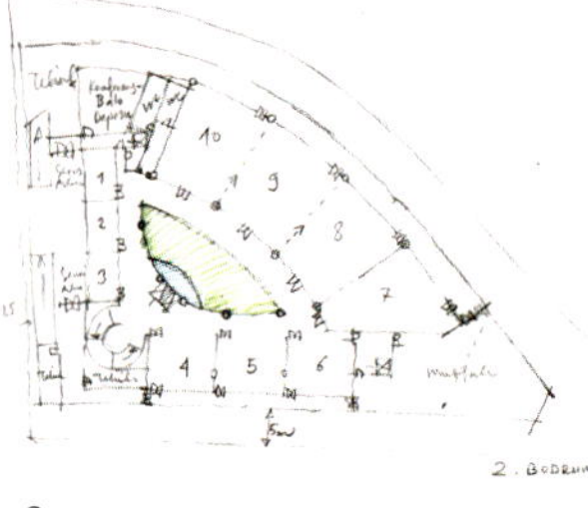

3

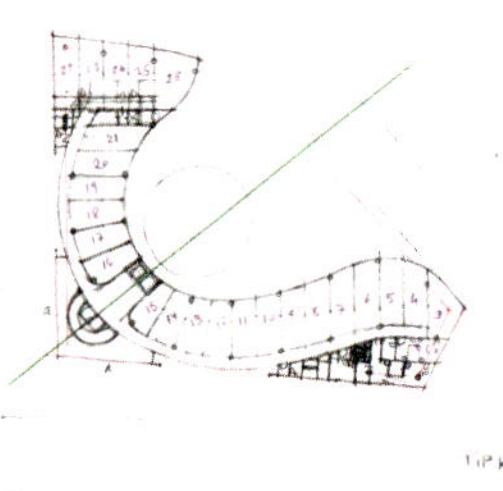

4

1 General rendering
2–4 Sketch by Ali Osman Öztürk, showing the different levels of the hotel

Via/Port Hotel

Client Bayraktar Construction
Project Date 2007
Area $42,000m^2$
Location İstanbul
Structural Engineer Yüksek Project
Mechanical Engineer BTC Engineering
Electrical Engineer BTC Engineering
Contractor Bayraktar Construction

Located in the Via/Port area, Via/Port Hotel has been designed to serve business and conference functions as part of a shopping center, exhibition, recreation, and entertainment park complex. The 33-room hotel has a ballroom with the capacity to seat 1,200 people, a conference room, meeting rooms, a spa, and a fitness center. The front façade of the building has separate entrances for the hotel and the conference center. The conference and meeting rooms are directly connected to the lobby, and the main foyers are oriented towards the recreation area.

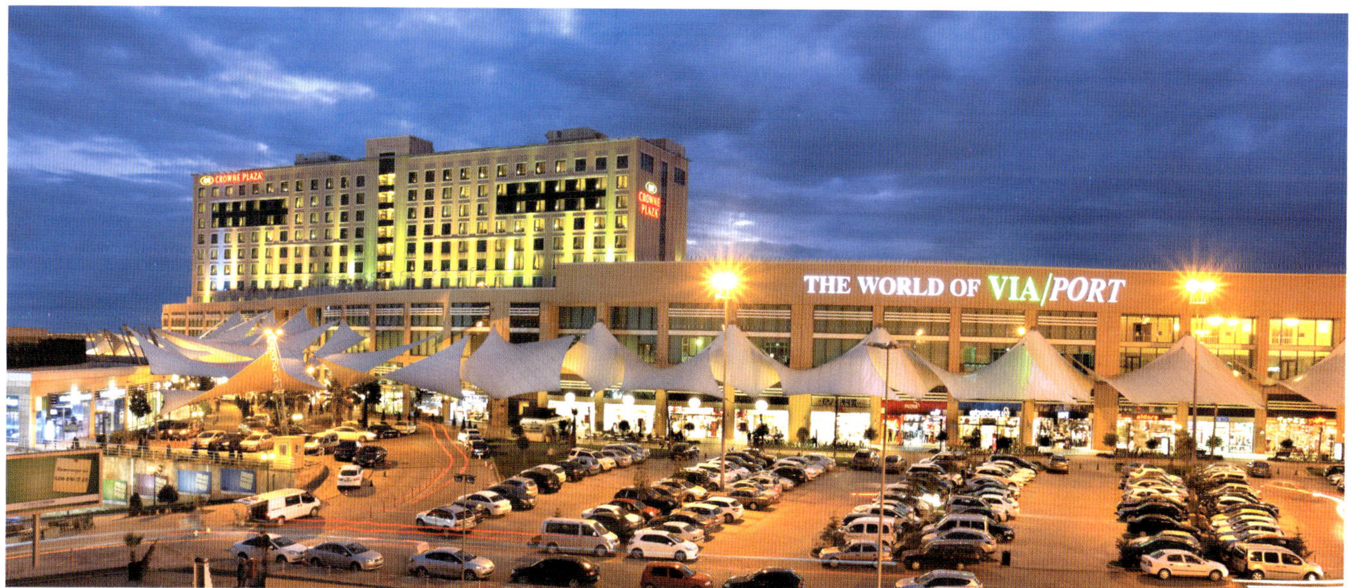

1

2

1 The hotel at night
2 Front façade

İstoç

Client İstanbul Wholesale Trade and Small Industries Cooperative

Project Date 1998–2012

Area 145,250 m²

Location İstanbul

Structural Engineer Yüksek Project

Mechanical Engineer Akdeniz Engineering

Electrical Engineer Akay Engineering

Contractor İstanbul Wholesale Trade and Small Industries Cooperative

İstoç Center has been designed as a multi-functional building complex on TEM Highway and the design phase took place over the course of a decade. The building complex is composed of a hotel and a shopping mall. The 400-bed five-star capacity hotel includes an outdoor swimming pool, meeting rooms, a ballroom, and restaurants. The shopping mall, which has a direct link to the metro station, includes a supermarket, a construction materials market, shops, movie theaters, cafés, food-court, playground, and recreational activity areas.

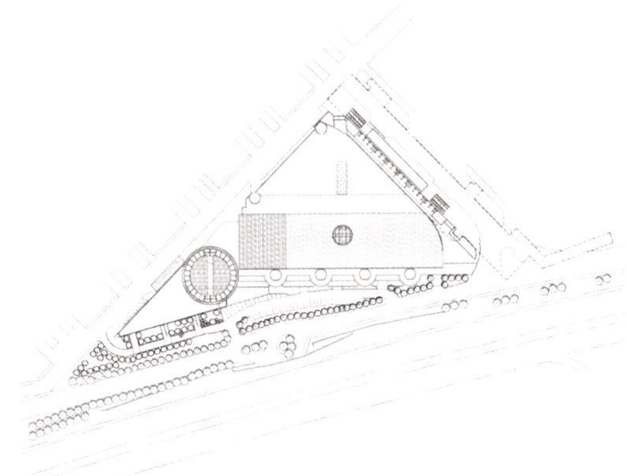

1

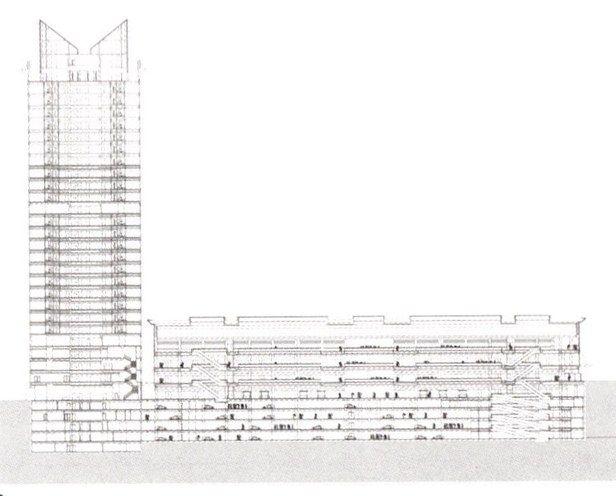

2

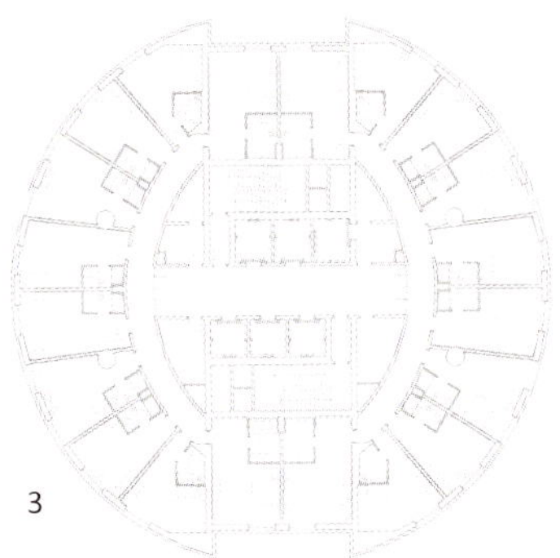

3

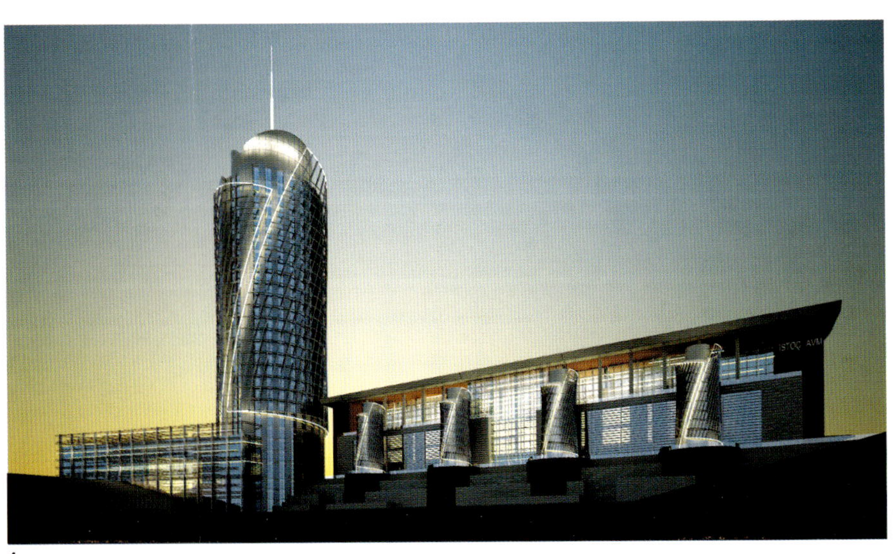

4

1 Site plan
2 Cross-section through the high-rise building and the podium
3 Typical floor plan
4 Model showing the complex illuminated at night

Arma Hotel

Client Besa Construction
Project Date 2002
Area 12,000 m^2
Location Antalya
Structural Engineer Yüksek Project
Design Consultants Salih Bezci, Vecihi Yıldız
Mechanical Engineer Setes Engineering
Electrical Engineer Akay Engineering
Contractor Besa Construction

The Arma Hotel has been designed as a linear block parallel to a private 220-meter-long coastline. As a result, each room has a view to the sea or the mountains. There is a private outdoor pool and a landscaped area on the coastline. The unique roof form proposed for the hotel distinguishes itself from the rest of the fabric of the district and allows for penthouse rooms to be built. The restaurant on the lower ground floor is connected to the open landscaped space in front of the building. The indoor pool, spa, and sports center are located in this section.

Apartment villas run by the hotel are located next to the linear hotel block. The design of these blocks is similar to the hotel block. The construction materials are mainly natural stone and white plaster, while a green copper color was chosen for the roof.

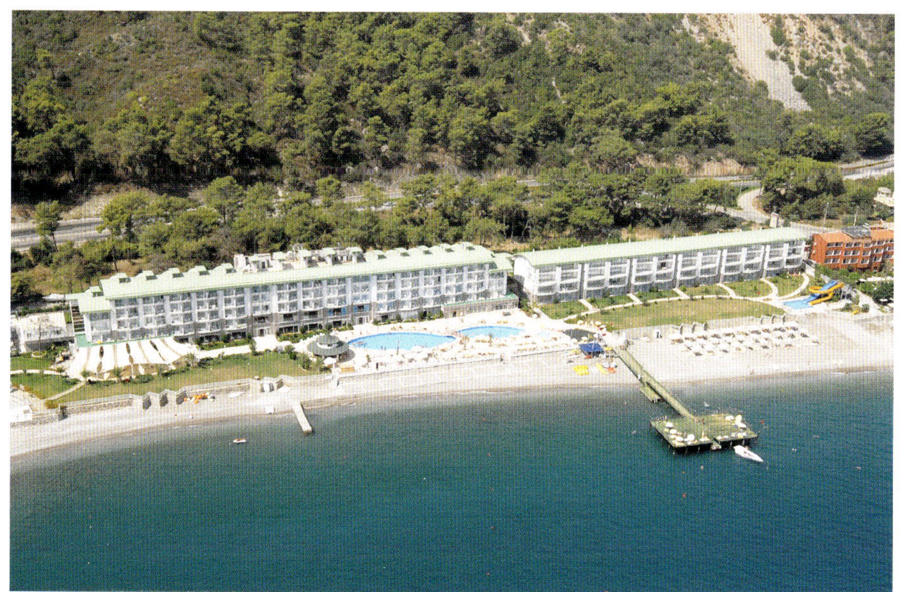
1

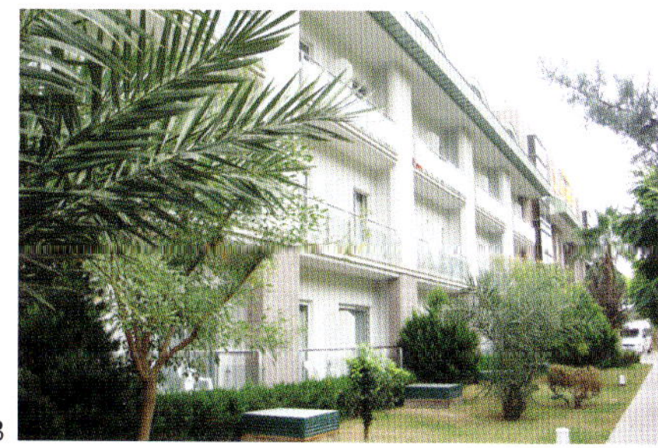
3

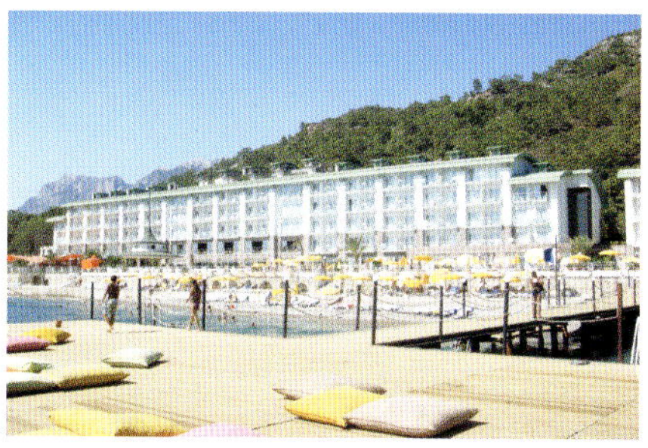
4

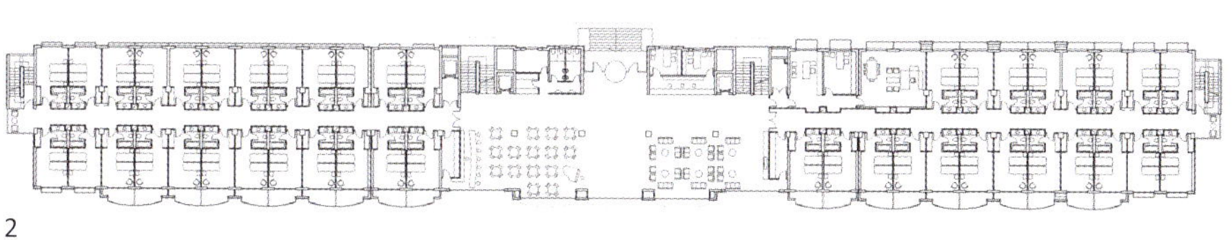
2

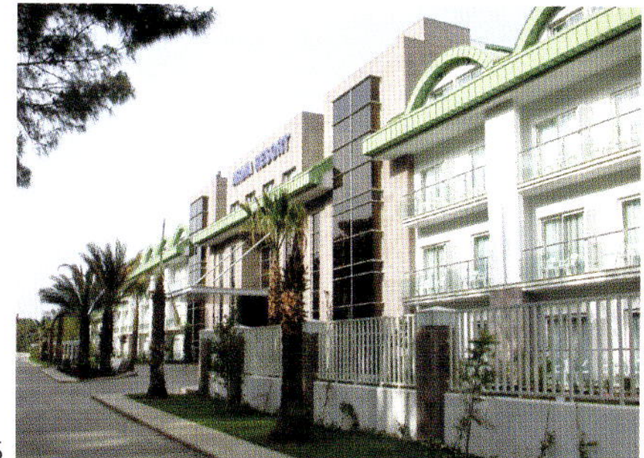
5

1 Aerial perspective of the hotel
2 Ground floor plan
3–5 Visuals of the hotel from different perspectives

Tripoli Ministry Buildings and Conference Center Mosque

Client Gür-iş Construction and Engineering Inc.
Project Date 2008
Area 499,145 m^2
Location Tripoli, Libya
Structural Engineering Yüksek Project
Mechanical Engineering Okutan Engineering
Electrical Engineering Akay Engineering
Landscape Design Dalokay Design Studio
Infrastructure Sigal Engineering

The former Great Socialist People's Libyan Arab Jamahiriya, represented by the Organization for Development of Administrative Centers (ODAC), held an urban design and architecture competition in early 2007 for "The Administration Complex in Tripoli", the development of a complex for governmental and administration building at an recently established government site. The area is located approximately 7 kilometers south of Tripoli city center and is situated directly on both sides of the highway that connects the old city center with the international airport.

The design competition was won by a German firm, Léon Wohlhage Wernik Architekten (LWW), and their proposal centered on a quad around which the buildings would be grouped. The buildings, which include a conference center, VIP hotel, mosque, and General People Committee buildings, along with underground car parking. The project also includes highways, interchanges, a rail tunnel, service tunnels, and an energy center to serve the significant needs of such a complex. LWW has also taken note of an adjacent forest and included these areas as a public park within the competition boundary.

Gür-iş has been commissioned as contractor for The Administration Complex projects in Tripoli. The design package comprises the concept and final design phases of the General People's Committee buildings (small, medium, and large), underground car parking, a mosque, and service buildings, as well as the application design phase of underground car parking and service buildings.

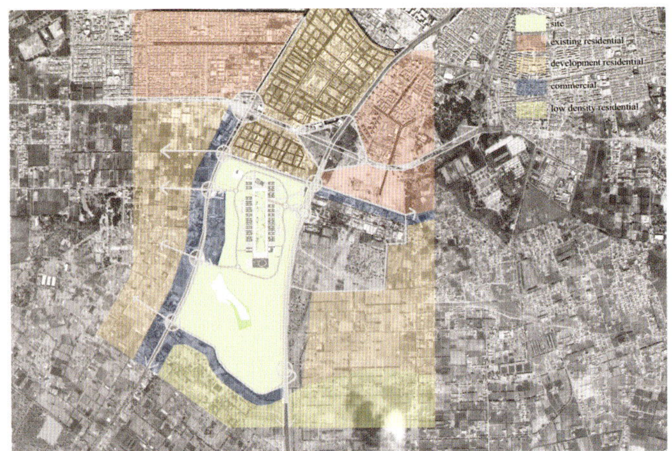

1

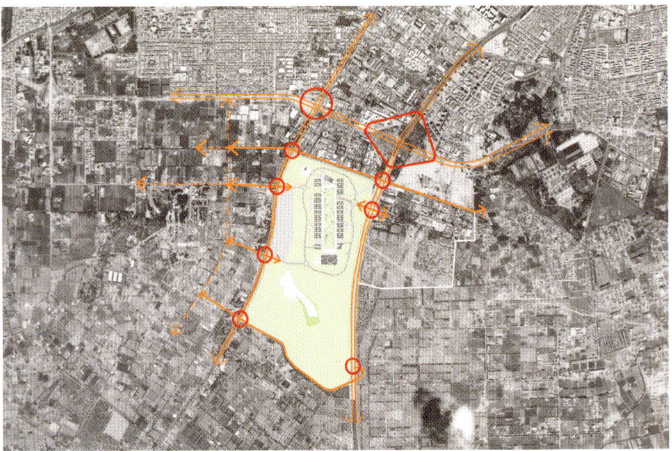
2

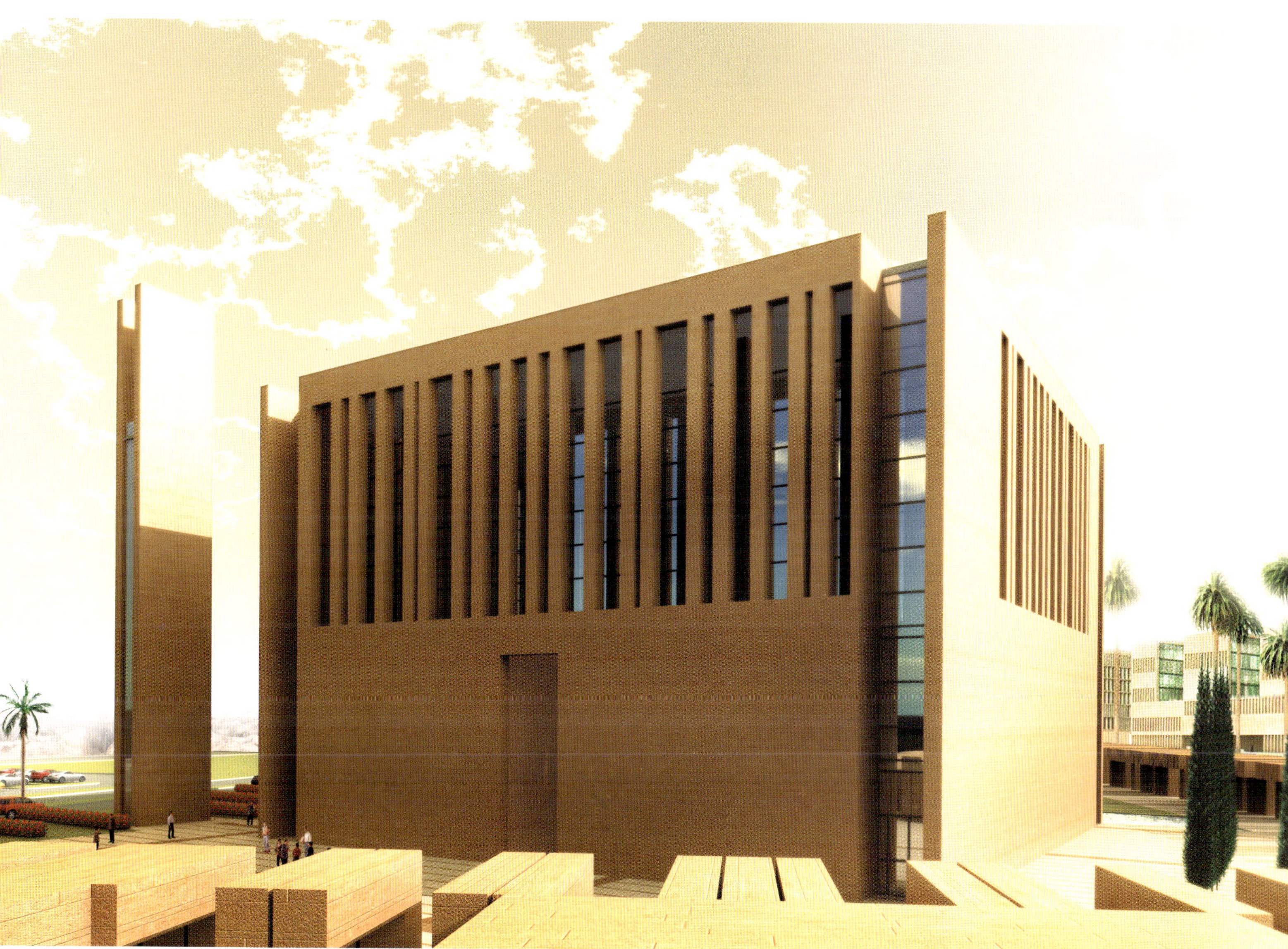

3

1 Map showing the commercial and residential area in the district
2 Map showing the main junctions and entrances
3 Mosque exterior

Bakü Marina and Public Park

Client Asnaf-Alkon
Project Date 2007
Area 179,500 m^2
Location Bakü, Azerbaijan

Baku Marina and City Park is located in the harbor area at the end of the coastal strip of the city of Baku. The project is intended to be a mixed-use project that will give a new identity to the district by including a variety of functions such as a marina, commerce, accommodation, entertainment, and culture. One of the main objectives of the project is to create a new living space by opening the formerly inaccessible harbor area to the public.

The project is located on approximately 13 hectares of land. By providing wide green areas, it will create a continuum for the existing pedestrian axes on the coastal strip. The area can easily be accessed by motorway connections and public transport via a service lane on the eastern border of the project area.

The project offers a new urban planning proposal for the district, and contains forms that utilize reflections of the water on a waterfront property. A shopping mall has been integrated with the existing parklands and coastal strip and is situated at the center of the complex. The park surrounding the mall integrates the elements of air, earth, and water. All of the buildings are constructed on a single base, which contains the indoor parking area that serves the shopping mall and the hotel.

The three-story shopping mall combines commercial and cultural activities. The cultural center, movie theater, and playgrounds comprise the complex's cultural functions and the surrounding landscape complements the entertainment and commercial center. Commercial spaces can be accessed from both inside the mall as well as from outside, which is a new concept in mall design, and these units help to connect the mall with the landscape. Restaurants with a view of the coastal strip are located on the ground floor of the mall. The commercial scheme's building has a clear and striking layout, consisting of three large atriums. These have been designed as the entrance of the mall and the center of the axes that lead to the park. The shops located around the indoor street and the atriums can be easily seen from different floors. The top floor is designated for food and entertainment functions and contains patios offering excellent vistas over the park and coastline.

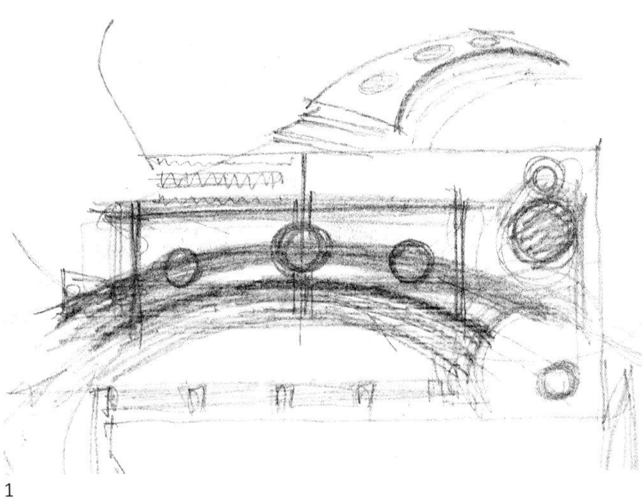

1

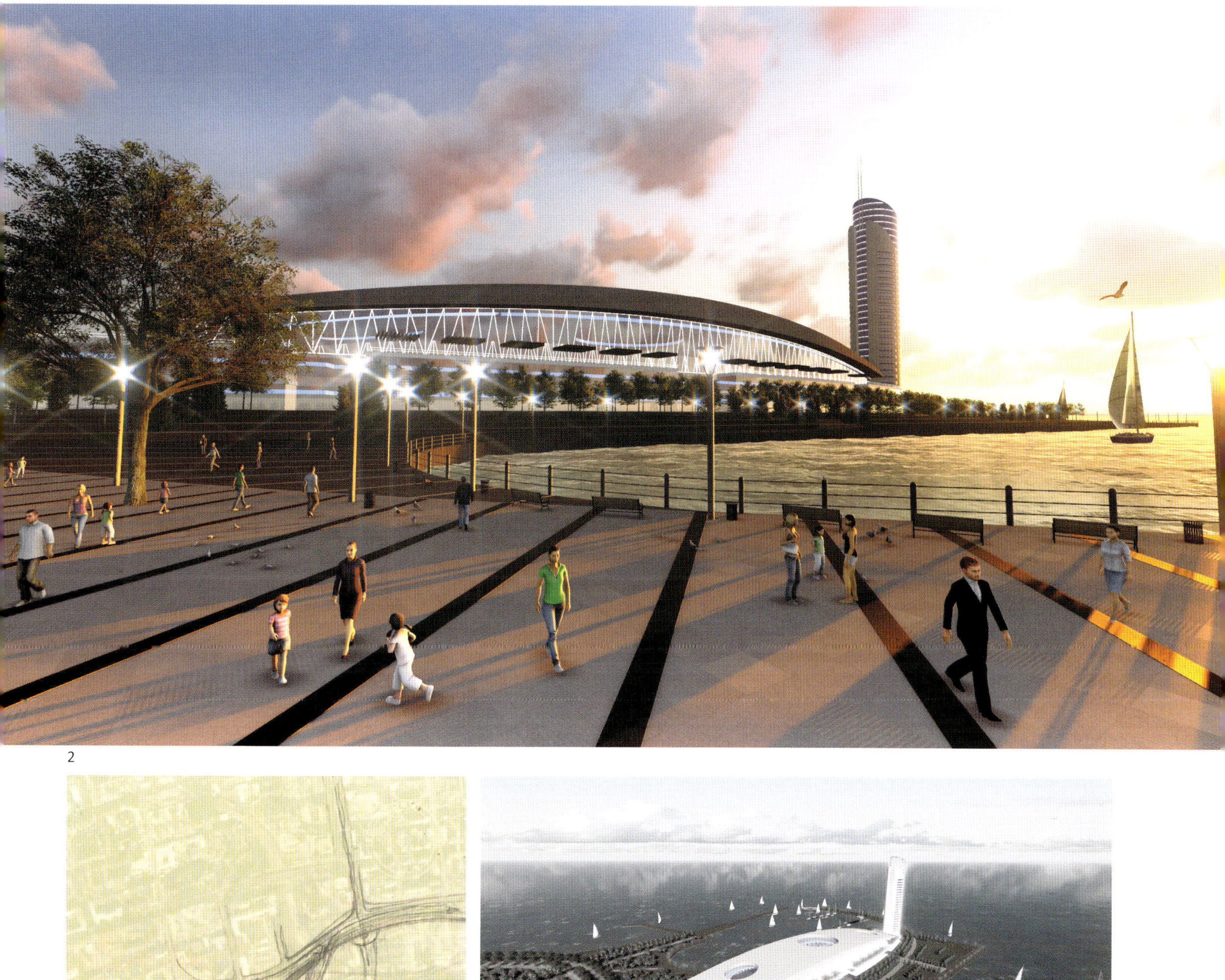

2

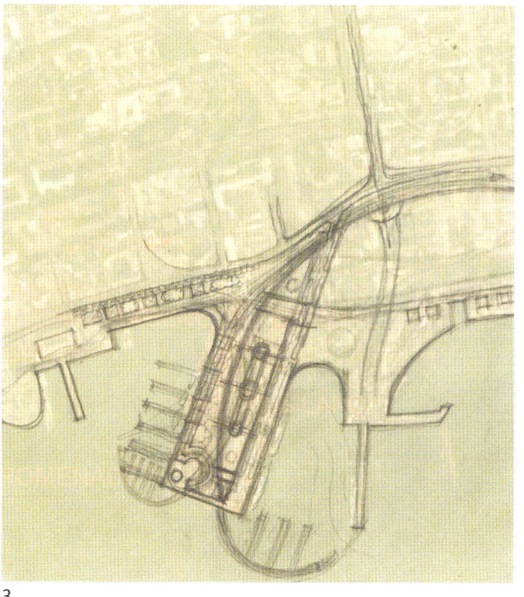

3

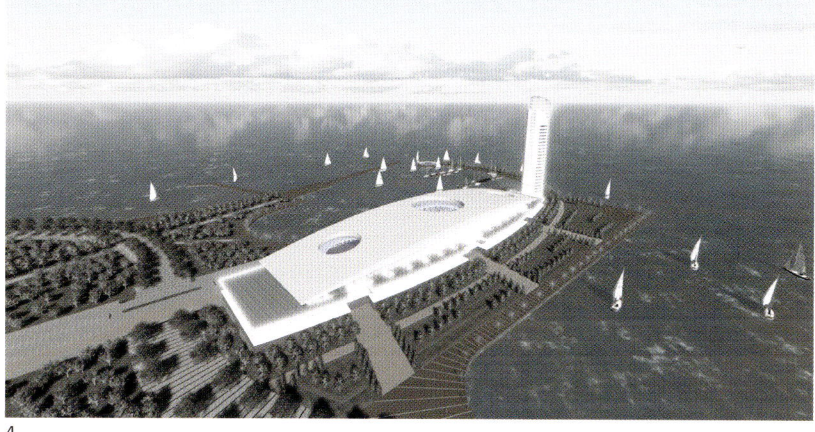

4

1 Sketch by Ali Osman Öztürk
2 Model view, showing the marina at twilight
3 Sketch by Ali Osman Öztürk
4 Aerial rendering

Bucharest International Exhibition and Convention Center

Client TOBB

Project Date 2010

Location Bucharest, Romania

This project consists of proposals for renovating the existing exhibition center located in a valuable area of downtown Bucharest. The project preserves the site's current functions while the new building program will add new functions. The proposal aims to create an urban space that will allow for exhibitions, gathering, commerce, accommodation, and mixed-use facilities and give the district a new identity. These changes also aim to renovate the Convention Center to international standards. A mixed-use building and a symbolic structure have been proposed for the section facing the road on the site's south side. The hotel tower has a view of the city and the artificial lake.

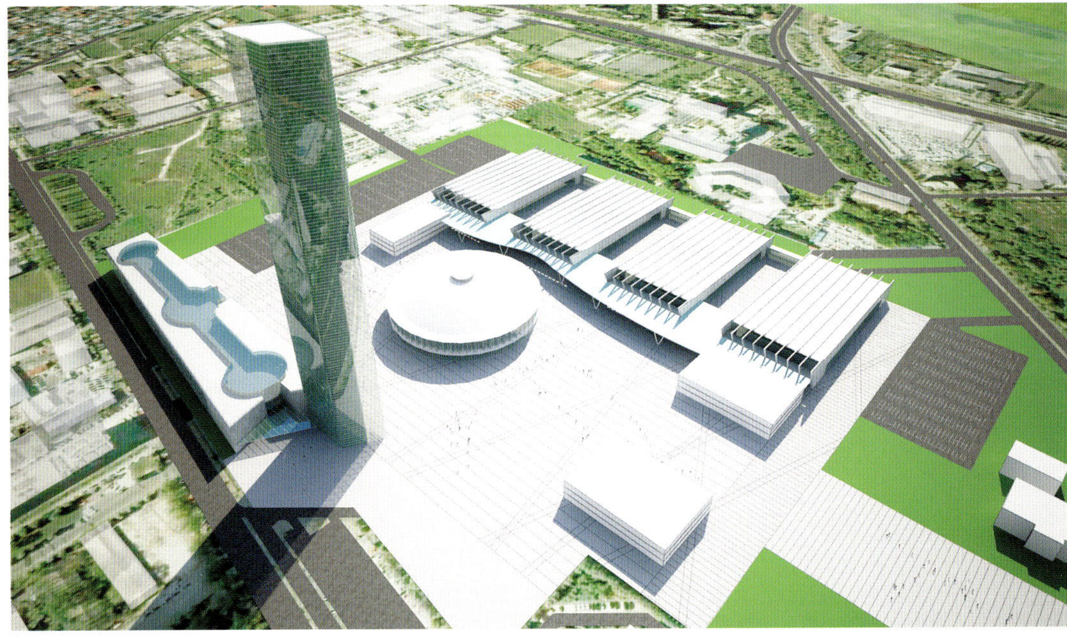

1

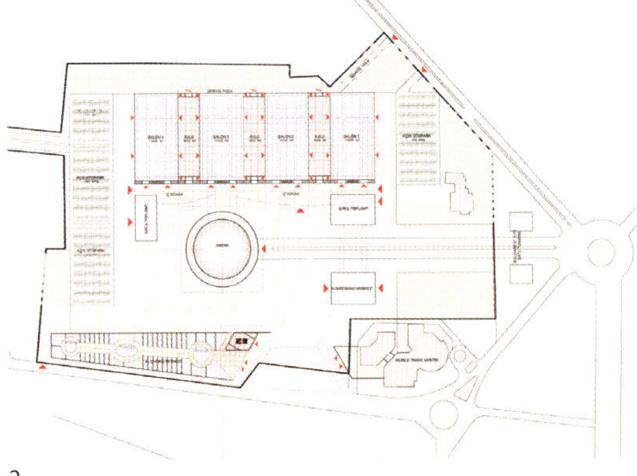

2

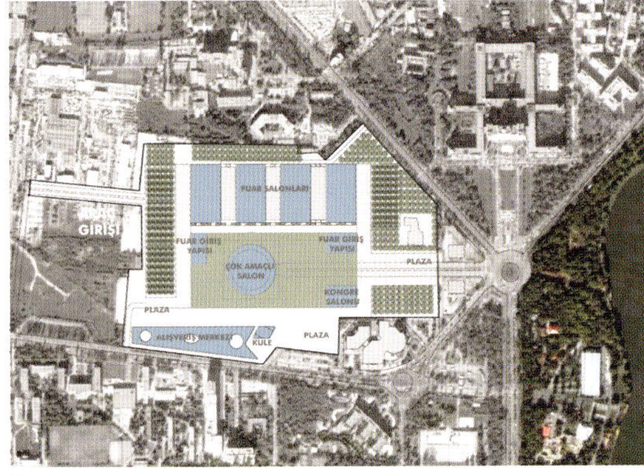

3

1 Aerial view of the project

2,3 Plans showing the functions of the center

Tiraspol Life Center

Client Summa Inc.
Project Date 2011
Area 44,925 m^2
Location Tiraspol, Moldova

This building was designed for a location in downtown Tiraspol. It combines a variety of functions, including a bookstore, children's entertainment center, showroom, and a bank, as well as commercial facilities, food and beverage units, cafés, and accommodation units.

The shops on the main street can be accessed from the outside of the complex. The 3,500-square-meter supermarket is to be used by the surrounding residential areas. The second floor contains food and entertainment facilities, and there are patios with a view of the river.

The ground floor of the bank building located on the eastern corner of the site is designated for customer service, while the upper floors house offices. The bank floors and the commercial floors are connected.

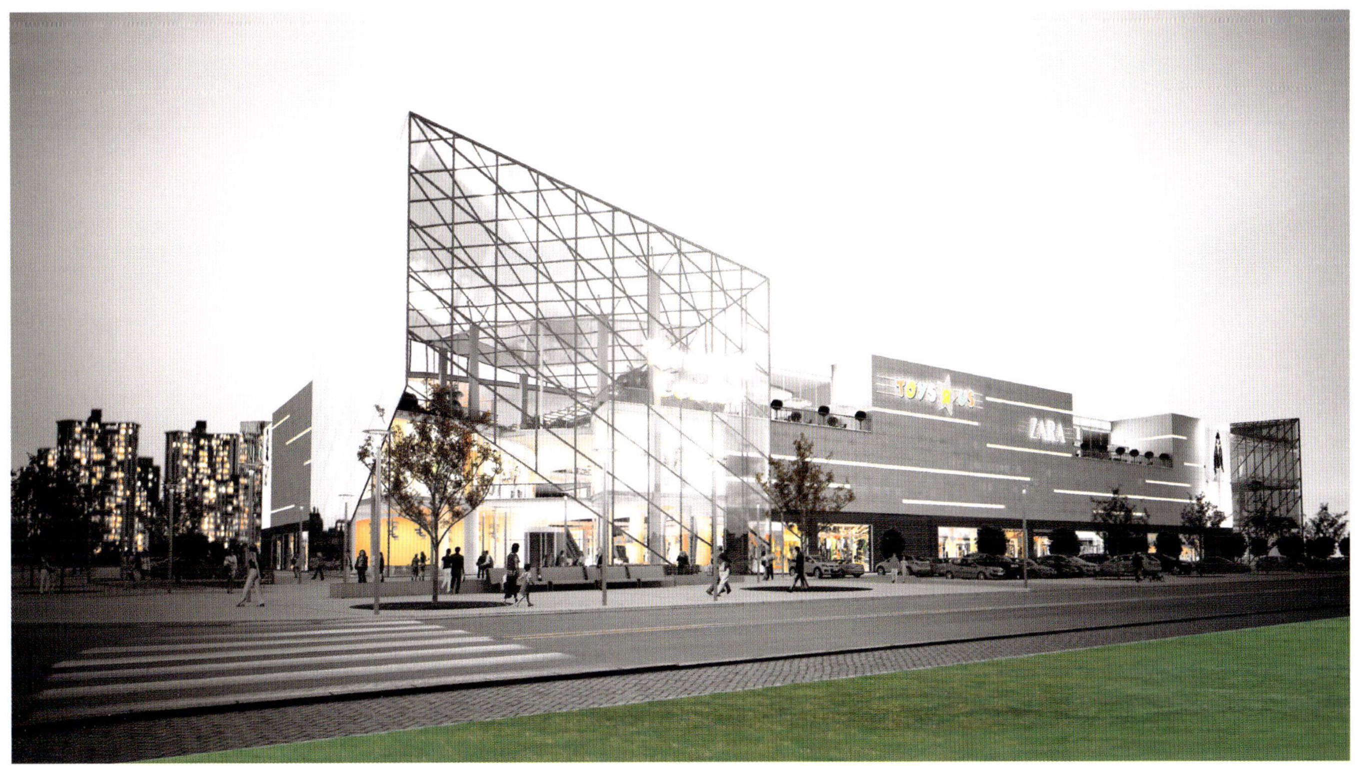

Exterior view

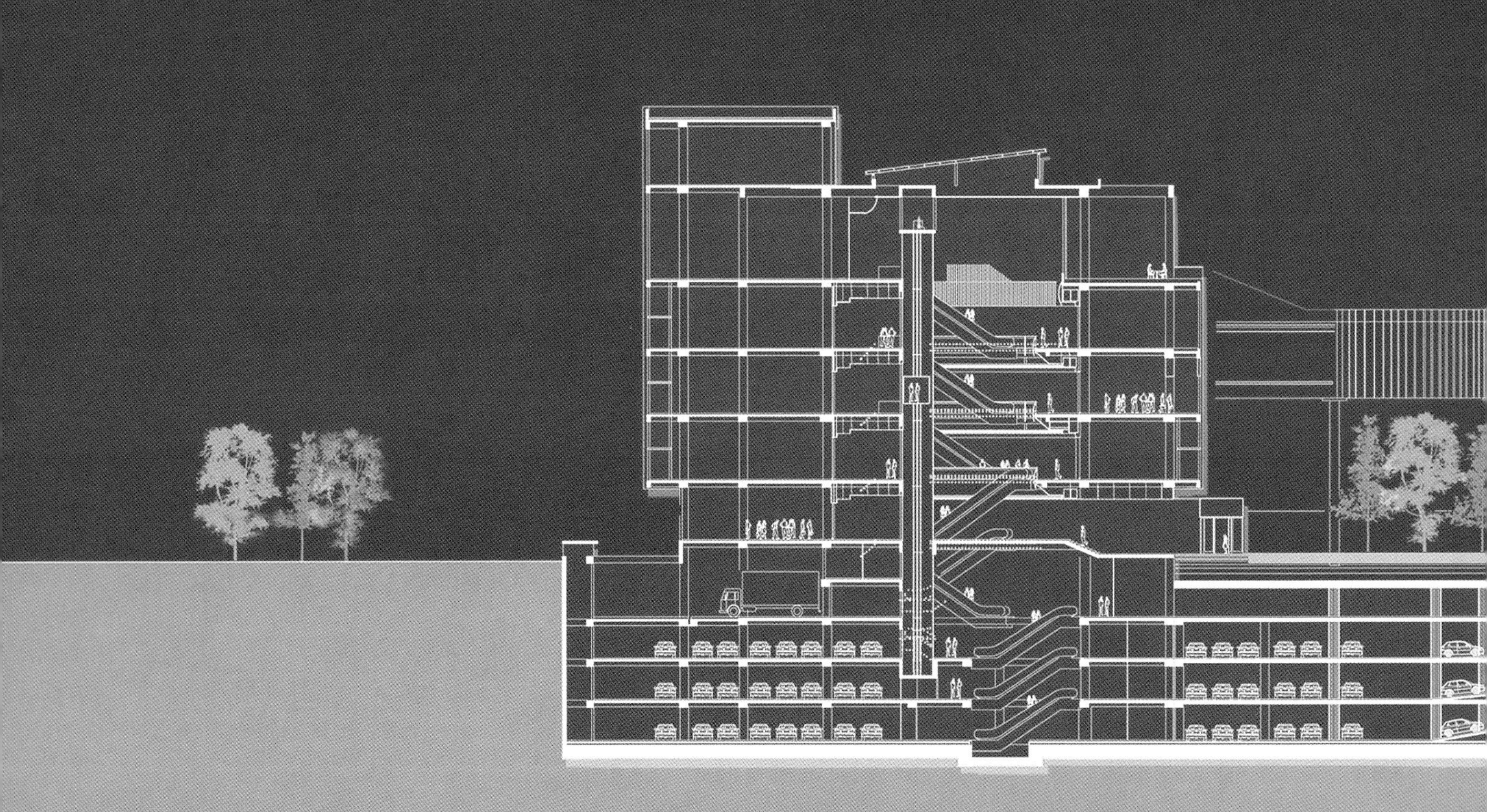

Profiles

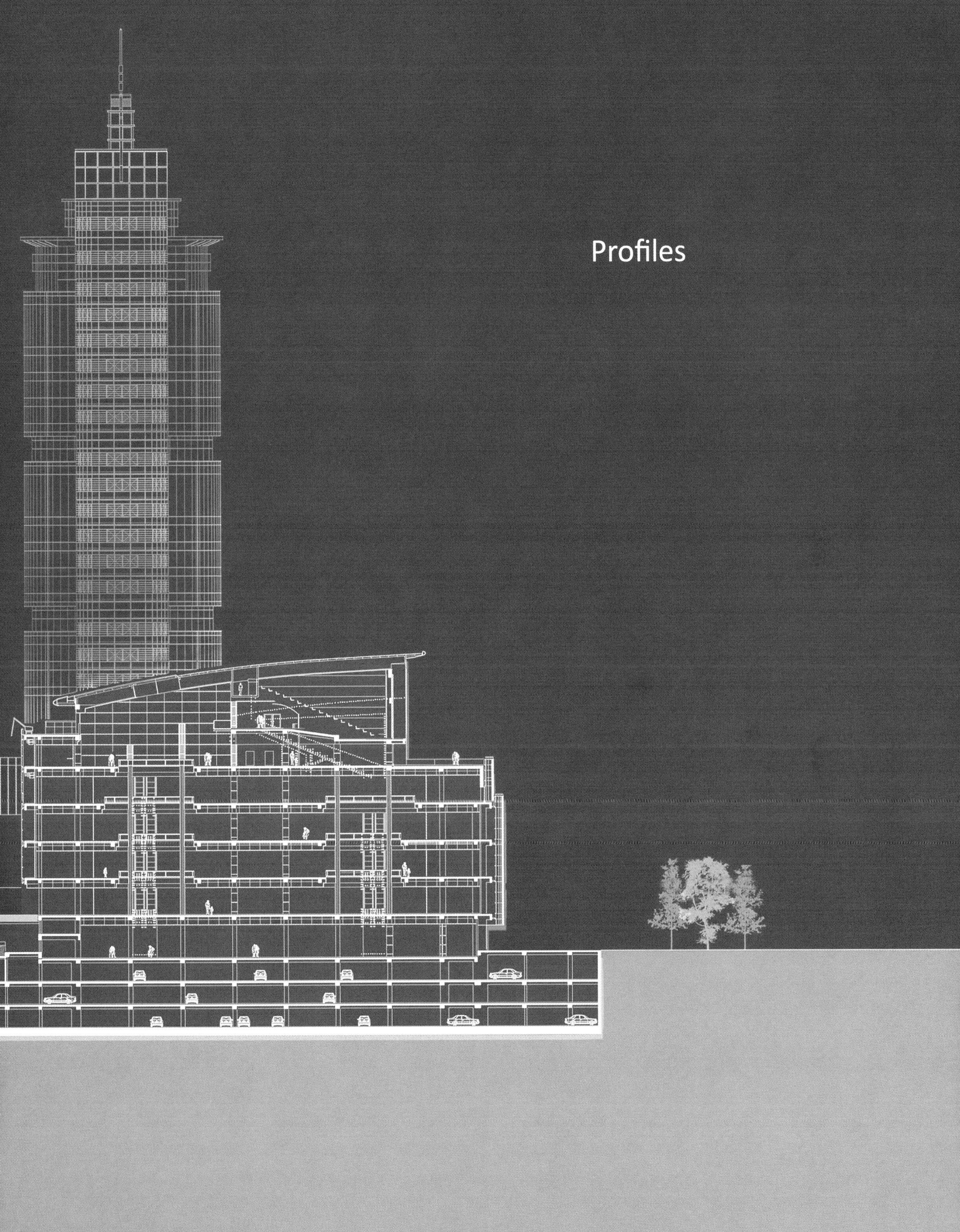

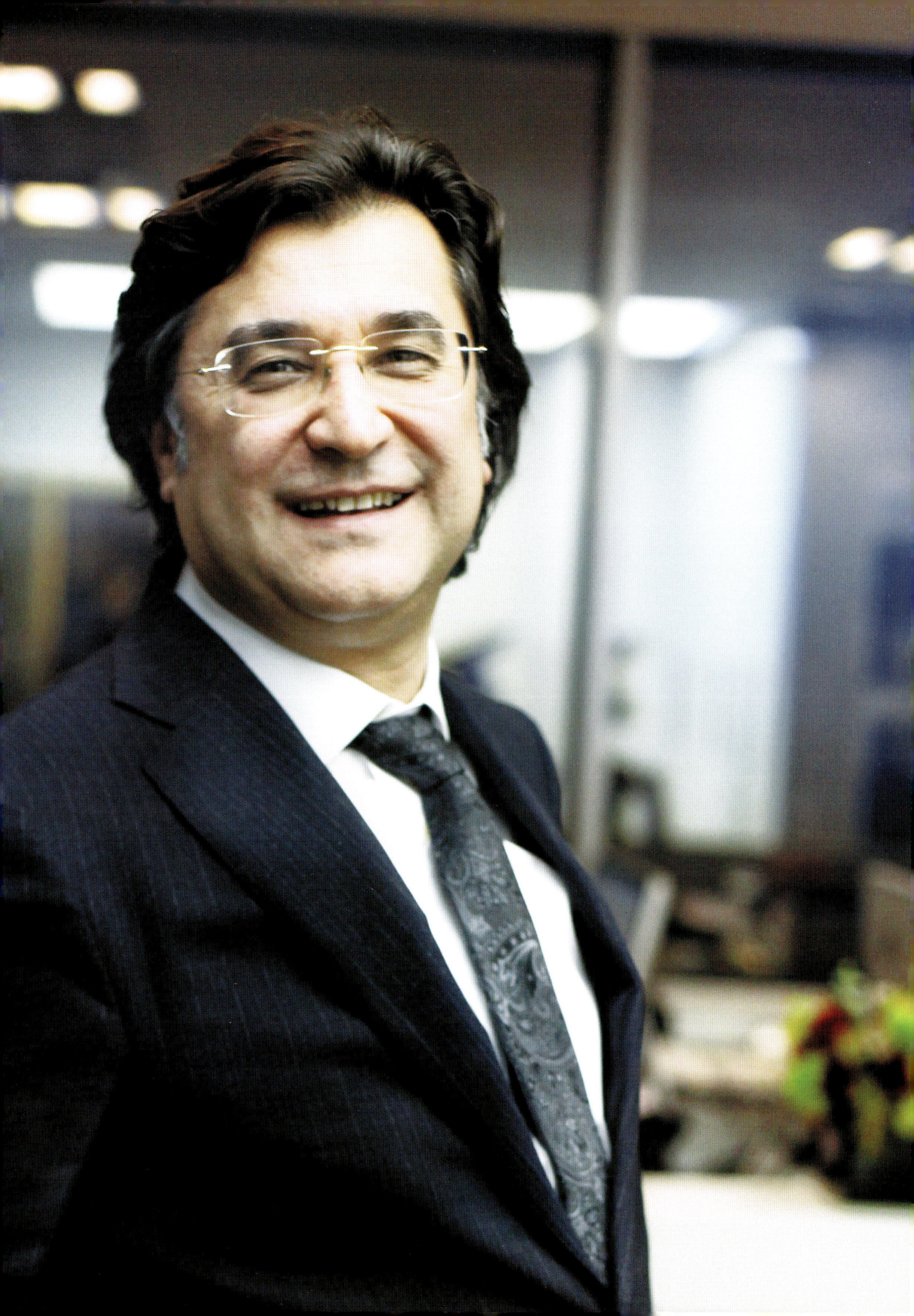

Ali Osman Öztürk

Born in 1965, Ali Osman Öztürk graduated from the Middle East Technical University Department of Architecture, pursuing his master's degree in the same department with a thesis called "The City as a Meeting Place."

Employed as research assistant at METU design studios between 1987 and 1993, he then worked as a part-time instructor until 1997 at METU and, the following year, he instructed at Gazi University. During this period, Öztürk took an active role on revolving funds projects in Middle East Technical University.

In 1997, Ali Osman Öztürk founded his own firm, A Tasarım Mimarlık, and completed many significant and prestigious projects. Throughout his career, he has had the opportunity to gain valuable work experience in the Chamber of Architects Turkey, Turkish Association of Architects in Private Practice, METU Faculty of Architecture, and *Arkitekt* magazine.

Among his most well-known projects are Türk Telekom, Armada, Yaşamkent Mosque, Tepe Prime, Panora, Via/Port, Antares, TOBB University of Economics and Technology, Congresium, and Metroport. With his firm, he has been awarded the ICSC International Design and Development Awards Certificate of Merit for Armada in 2005, ICSC European Shopping Centre Awards First Prize for Armada in 2004, and the ICSC European Shopping Centre Awards Certificate of Merit for Panora in 2009.

Ali Osman Öztürk has played an active role in projects and developments in Ankara. For many years, he has also been developing relationships with international architectural firms and carrying out significant projects. A member of Association of Architects 1927, Turkish Association of Architects in Private Practice, and Ankara Chamber of Commerce, he is currently the president of A Tasarım Mimarlık, where he continues his architectural projects.

The Practice

Ali Osman Öztürk

I am the first in my family to receive an education in architecture. In the beginning, I naturally did not have many ideas about it. But I always had this penchant, this interest in the art of painting. While I was at school, I collected a number of awards in a variety of painting competitions; and my dear high school painting teacher, Gönül Akbay, had always spoken about architecture. Vecihi Yıldız, with whom I later had a chance to work, is also one of those who steered me in this direction.

After Ankara Cumhuriyet High School, I began studying at the Faculty of Architecture of the Middle East Technical University, which was my first choice in the university entrance exams in 1982. First as a student and then as an assistant, I spent some 11 years on this campus and in the faculty, both of which influenced me greatly. Altuğ and Behruz Çinici are the architects of both the campus and the faculty and our faculty building is one of the most beautiful examples of the era in which it was built and is also among the pioneers of the exposed concrete movement. I still recall those days, so fresh in my memory as I walk through that building where we used to sit in the garden, watch the fish in the pool, and spend the nights in the studios.

I want to commemorate once again our dear professors who have invested so much in us: İnci Aslanoğlu, Kemal Aran, Raci Bademli, Ali Cengizkan, Alaaddin Egemen, Feyyaz Erpi, Jale Erzen, Gönül Evyapan, Baykan Günay, Suna Güven, Celal Abdi Güzer, Vacit İmamoğlu, İlhan Kural, Haluk Pamir, Önder Seren, Eşber Yolal, our Dean, Rüştü Yüce, and others.

My education was great fun in a hard-working and resolute class. It was a crowded class and the faces that come to mind immediately are Ahmet Ardıçoğlu, Turgut Aygördü, Süreyya Atalay, Cânâ Bilsel, Hüseyin Bütüner, Şuayip Çavuşlar, Aysun Coşar, Esfendiyar Dilmeghani, Gülay Dülger, Yunus Eşkinat, Elif Elmas, Boran Ekinci, Hilmi Güner, Serdar Kaftancıoğlu, Lale Kaya, Zeynep Kezer, Bilge Oğan, Korkut Onaran, Filiz Öngüç, Ümit Ünal, and Teoman Üstoğlu. Many brilliant architects have walked out of this class and the friendships that were established there still continue to a great extent.

Zafer Akay, Cüneyt Budak, Cumhur Keskinok, Ayşen Savaş, and Güven Sargın are also important names to remember from those days.

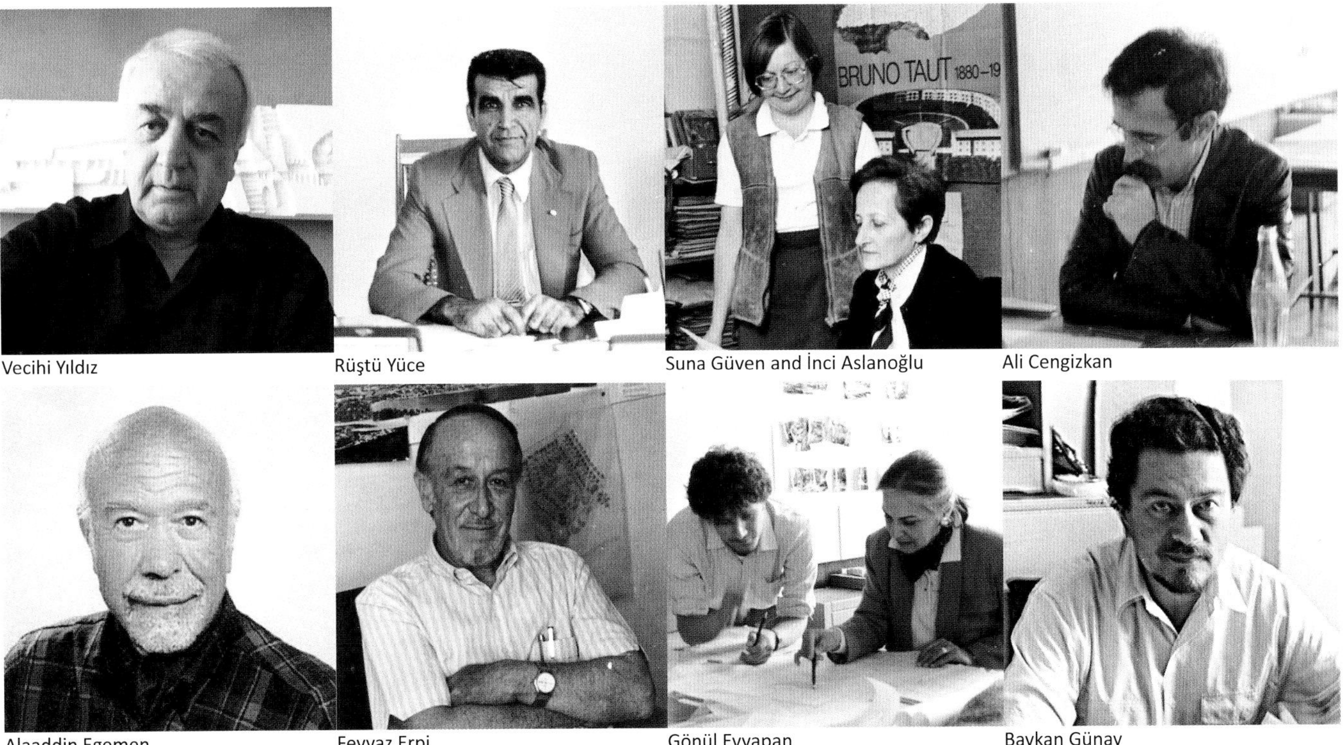

Vecihi Yıldız | Rüştü Yüce | Suna Güven and İnci Aslanoğlu | Ali Cengizkan

Alaaddin Egemen | Feyyaz Erpi | Gönül Evyapan | Baykan Günay

I graduated in 1987 and started at the third-grade studio as an assistant to Professor Enis Kortan. Throughout my six years as an assistant in that studio, I worked with valuable people who later became friends and colleagues: Cem Altınöz, Çağla Aysal, Erkin Aytaç, Tamer Bozoklar, Sibel Dalokay, Gamze Demiröz, Elvan Altan Ergut, Namık Erkal, Özlem Gürses, Mehmet Kütükçüoğlu, Enis Öncüoğlu, Şebnem Yalınay, and Kerem Yazgan.

During the winter holidays when I was at the second grade, I visited Erdoğan Elmas' office—the father of Elif Elmas, a classmate—and that was the first professional architectural environment I had seen. I visited that office at every opportunity until graduation, and worked there. That office has an important place in the cultivation of my professional discipline.

One summer, I had a opportunity to work with Behruz Çinici and Can Çinici on the mosque project for the Grand National Assembly of Turkey (TBMM). It was, for me, a very important experience that showed me the architect's "stance"—the relationship the architect establishes with employers—and the architect's place in society.

Another uplifting place was Erkut Şahinbaş' office, just like the offices of Hasan Özbay, and Davran Eşkinat, the father of dear Yunus Eşkinat, where we used to visit frequently. In those years, with Zafer and Boran, we had some high-spirited talks on architecture and we were also trying to revive *Arkitekt* magazine.

While I was an assistant, I was drawing projects for the revolving fund, participating in some competitions, and completing my Master of Arts. As a student, I had always been a part of many social activities including, upon an invitation, study visits to the University of Dortmund. With Korkut, Ahmet and Namık we have organized a total of ten coach tours abroad from the Swedish fjords to Petra, from Andalucia to Cairo, from London to Moscow. During one of those trips, we even stopped in Geneva to visit Suha Özkan. Years have passed, but our friends at the faculty and us as A Tasarım Mimarlık still continue this tradition. The A Tasarım Mimarlık team completed its tenth round of these trips in 2013.

My first step into professional life came upon winning the award at the Saraçlar Çarşısı (Saddlers' Bazaar) with Hilmi Güner and Hüseyin Bütüner. We established Artı Tasarım in

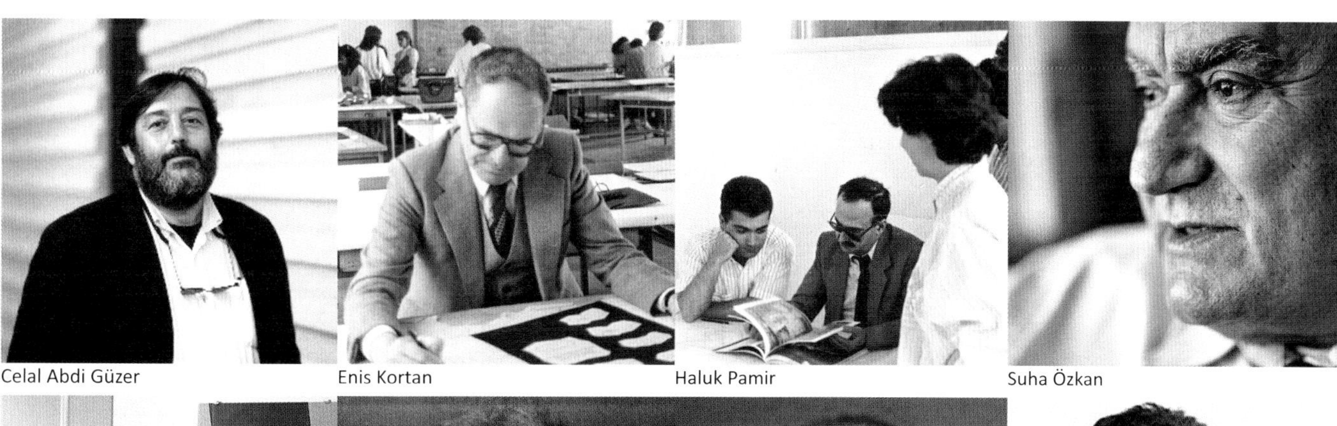
Celal Abdi Güzer Enis Kortan Haluk Pamir Suha Özkan

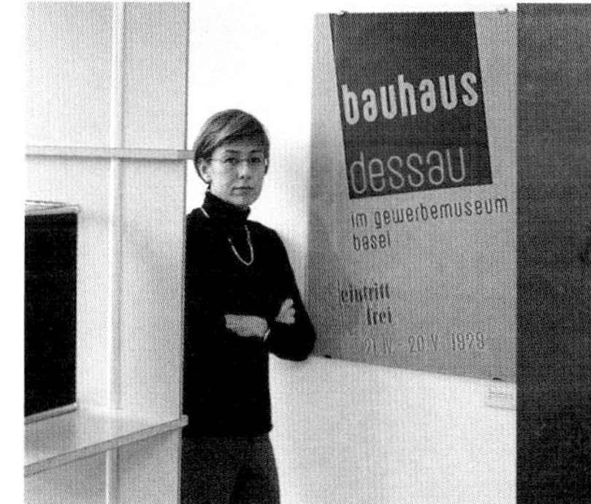

Ayşen Savaş

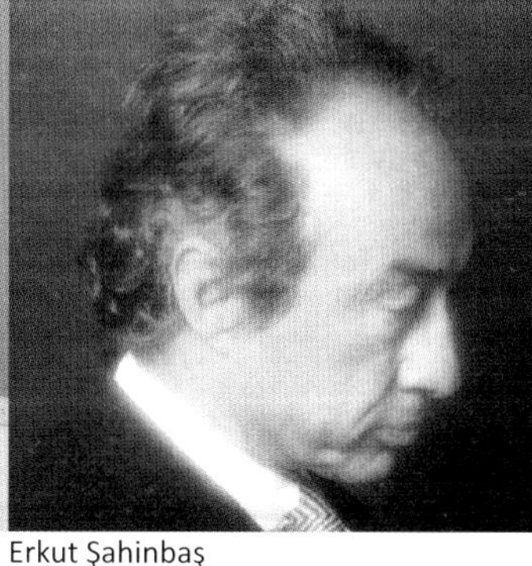
Erkut Şahinbaş

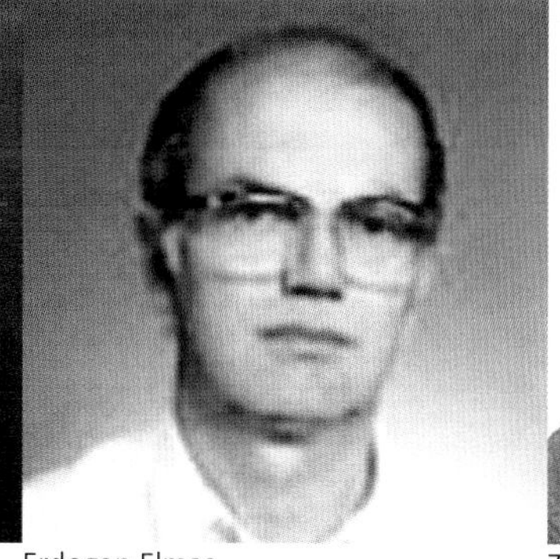
Erdogan Elmas

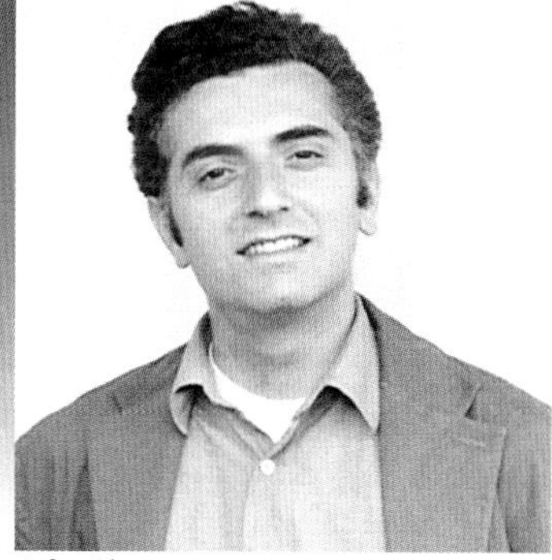
Zafer Akay

1992 and worked and experienced together, entered many competitions, went through many hardships, and dissolved the company in 1996.

In 1997, with my wife İlgiz, I established **A Tasarım Mimarlık**. Our first office was in an apartment on Çevre Street and we shared our office with Yüksek Project Engineering, run by İbrahim Öztürk, a relative and one of my childhood friends. After many successful projects we have completed, İbrahim is a dear friend and even a partner to me. A Tasarım Mimarlık and Yüksek Engineering are two sibling companies that work closely together.

My dear team from those days, with whom we have been working together since—Niyazi Ayvaz, Ebru Laçin Bilir, Eser Çengel, and my dear uncle Yakup Öztürk—we cannot forget that office; our days and our life there. And our neighbor, the architect Adnan Aksu with his door that was always open to us.

In the very first years after we established our office, I received an invitation from the faculty of architecture at Gazi University for a part-time teaching job, which lasted two years. It was a very enjoyable experience for me as a scholar. During the same period, we also worked on joint projects with Professor Enis Kortan, and Numan Cebeci, a colleague of ours.

In 2005, we moved to our present office in Armada, which marked the beginning of a new era for **A Tasarım Mimarlık**. It gave our team a new perspective and a new impetus. We also reorganized our office into groups at this time.

The Armada project marked a turning point in our professional lives and was conceived in our office on Çevre Street. It is the same project that introduced us to Salih Bezci, who trusted us and awarded us this crucial project. The Armada Project was a great success and won many international awards. As we continued working with Salih Bezci on new projects, he also recommended and introduced us to other employers. He was an architect and, as a result, we shared the same language. This brought a whole new perspective in our work and his comments during the development phases of our projects, our study visits, and the work we attended to on sites have gained both parties considerable experiences.

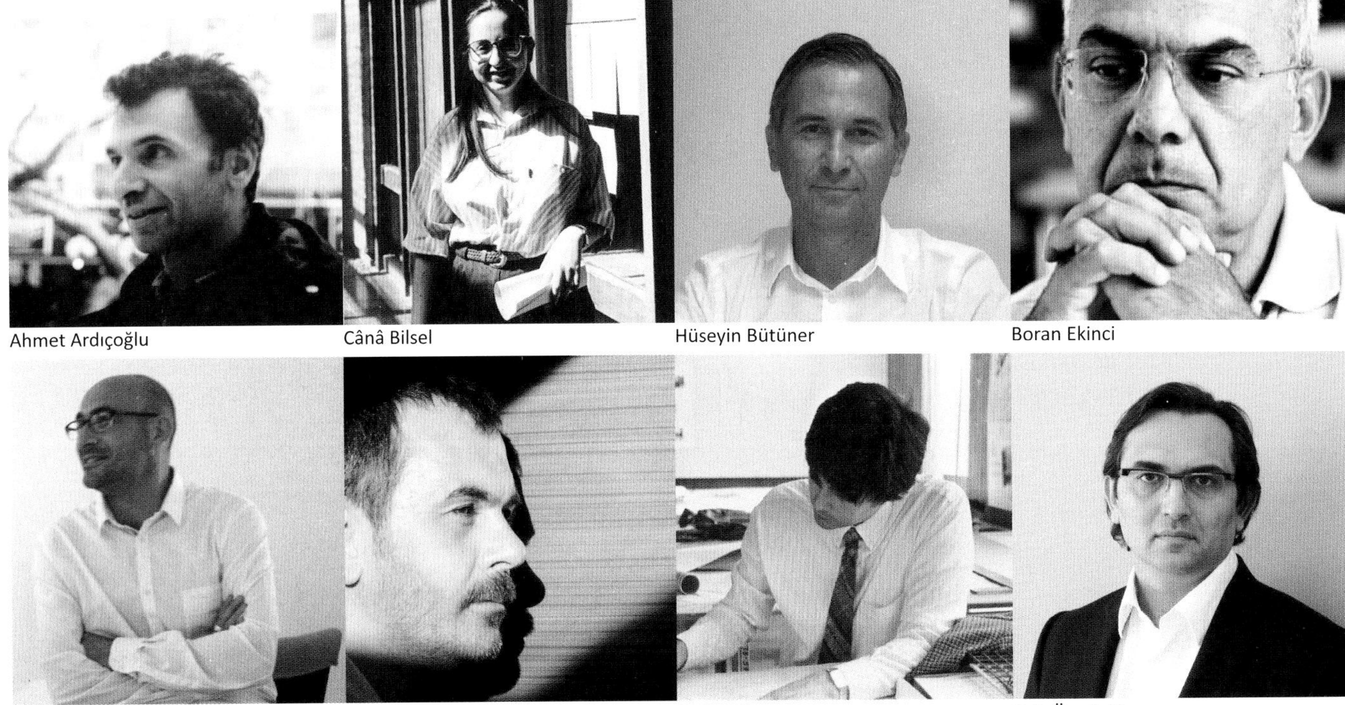

Ahmet Ardıçoğlu | Cânâ Bilsel | Hüseyin Bütüner | Boran Ekinci

Namık Erkal | Hilmi Güner | Korkut Onaran | Enis Öncüoğlu

We have also worked with Rıfat Hisarcıklıoğlu, whom we met as the former Chair of the Board of Armada, now the President of the Union of Chambers and Commodity Exchanges of Turkey (TOBB) on many projects. In the 10 years since the foundation of the TOBB University of Economics and Technology (UET), we have worked to shape the campus with Professor. Dr. Adem Şahin, the vice-president of TOBB UET and the General Secretary of the University, and Ahmet Akpınar's team (TÜRSUM). Today, TOBB UET is one of the most successful universities in Turkey, honoring us through its continuous improvement on the basis of the master plan that we had prepared.

On the other hand, another important figure, a valuable employer with whom we have carried out some large-scale projects is Namık Tanık, including projects such as the Ziraat Bank, the Ministry of Justice, Türk Telekom, and Türksat in the public sector and our work for MESA Construction, TEPE Construction, Limak, and Summa Construction in the private sector.

In 1987, the year I graduated, we received an invitation to a workshop from the University of Dortmund and our dear dean, Rüştü Yüce, brought together a team of successful graduates from that year from a variety of departments, including architecture, city planning, and industrial product design. However, as we arrived at the University of Dortmund, we discovered that the workshop was about cities and city planning. Since we were there, we were more than happy to attend the program that revolved around classes at the faculty, meetings with municipalities and NGOs, and on-the-job sessions followed by a trip to Berlin. At the time, the International Building Exhibition Berlin (IBA) was there and it was such a great experience for me that it made me think about "the city." Later I visited Paris, London, Rome, Florence, İstanbul, Bursa, and other cities, and seeing those cities, urban spaces, and even the design of empty areas was simply enchanting for me.

For me, the city is our *magnum opus*. It is why we need to start from the whole, from this complex structure, and descend towards parts, pieces, and finally, to the building. We always try to design our buildings with the environment that surrounds them. In this way, we believe that each building we design will be genuine and belong in its environment.

We also think that a building is shaped by the limitations and the capabilities of the era, as well as the builder and the patron. This requires a sustained balance of both the local and universal contexts.

We cherish the idea that buildings are built for human beings. We want the users to enjoy their spaces, embrace them, and make them their own.

With these thoughts in mind, let's continue towards an even better architecture.

***Ali Osman Öztürk** is the founder of A Tasarım Mimarlık*

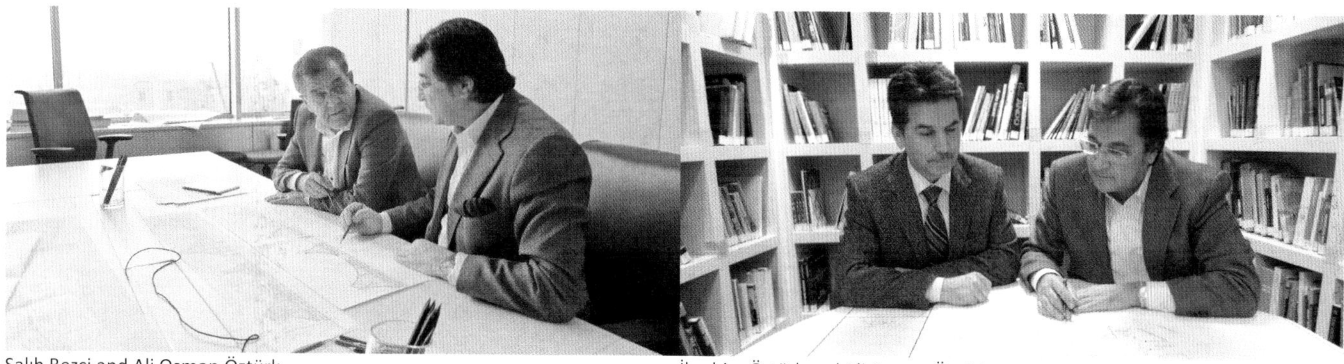

Salıh Bezci and Ali Osman Öztürk

İbrahim Öztürk and Ali Osman Öztürk

Group 1 Ankara

Group 1 is led by Eser Çengel with the assistance of Canan Karakaya. The group's projects vary from mixed-use to urban design and their responsibilities begin with the concept project phase and continue with preliminary and final project design, including construction documents and workplace consultancy. The IIFC Ziraat Bank, which has been designed in collaboration with international architectural practice Kohn Pedersen Fox Associates (KPF), is one of Group 1's major projects, and other projects include Yaşamkent Housing, Atakule, Tepe Prime, Antares, Nata Vega, and Congresium.

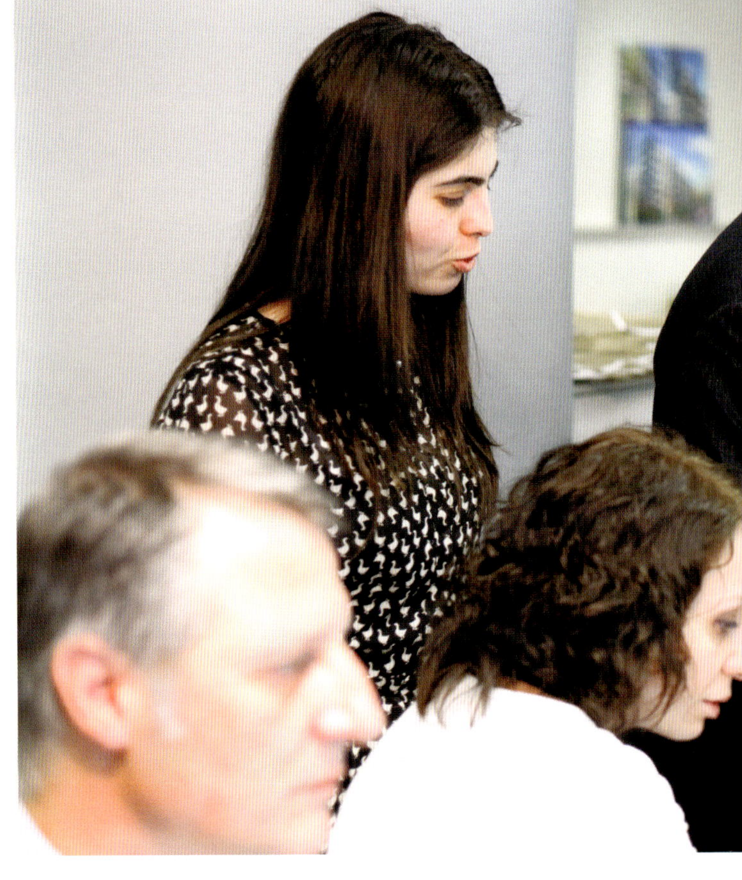

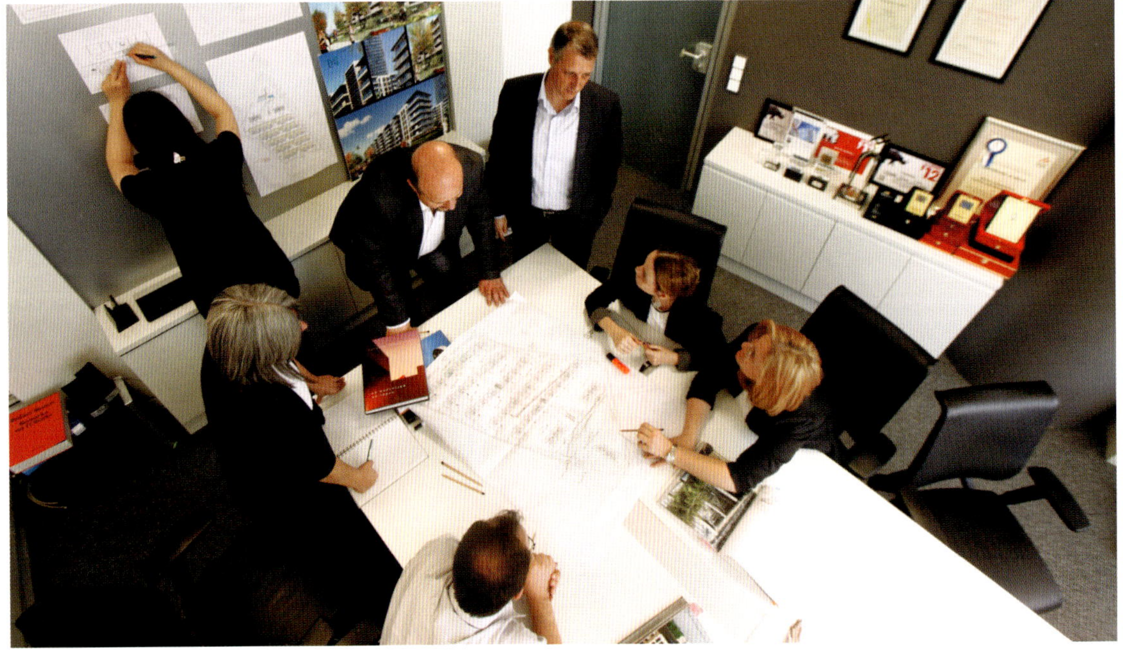

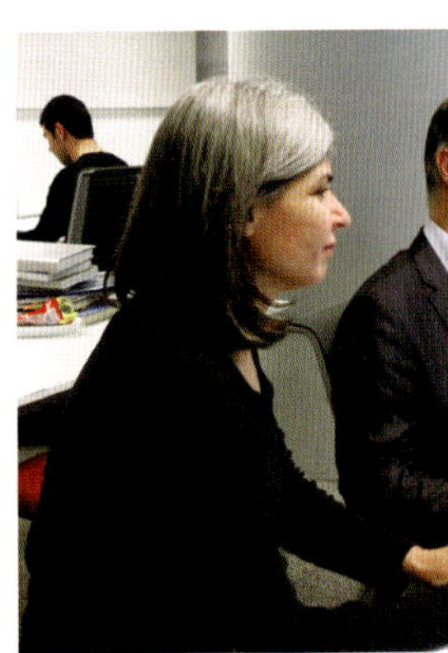

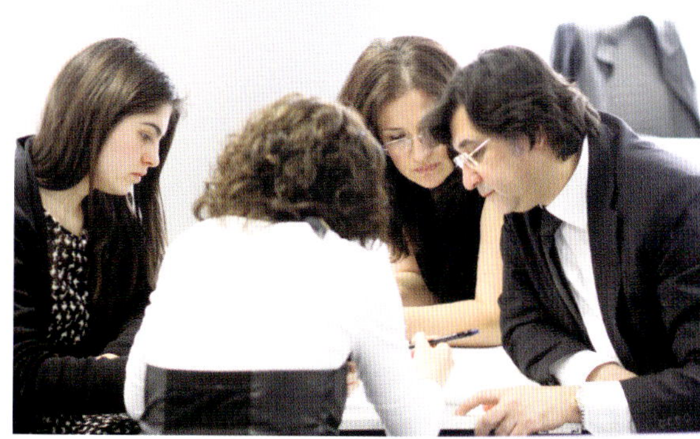

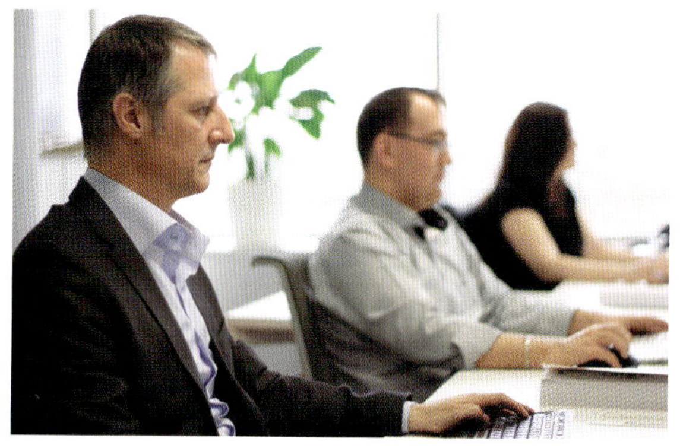

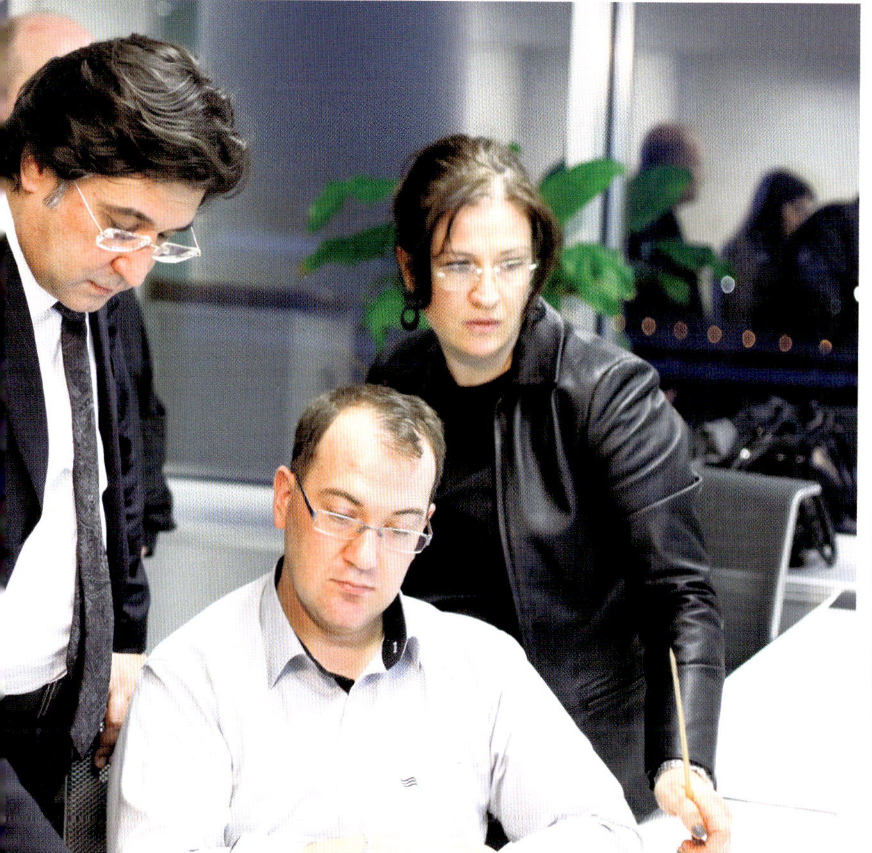

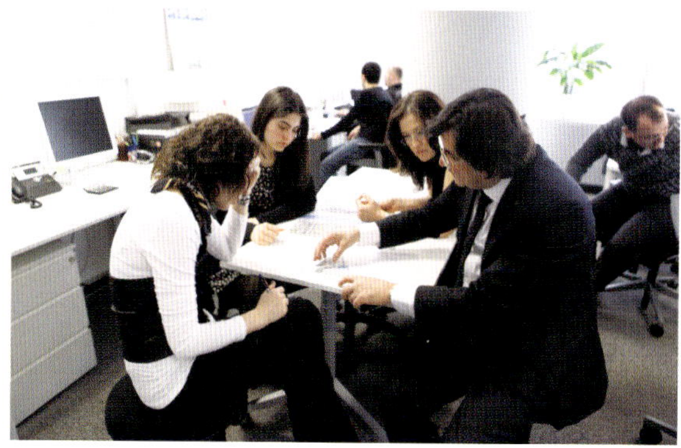

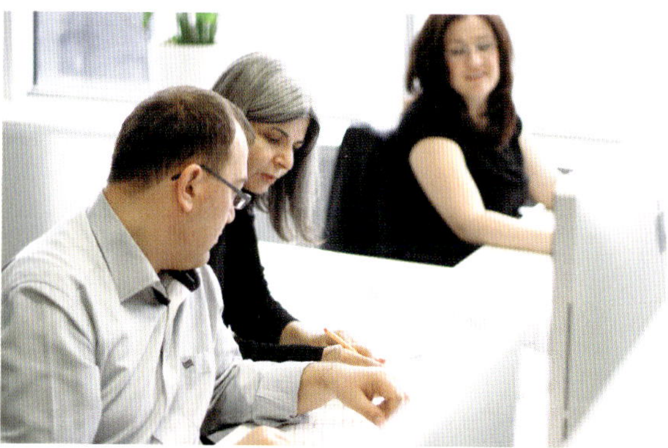

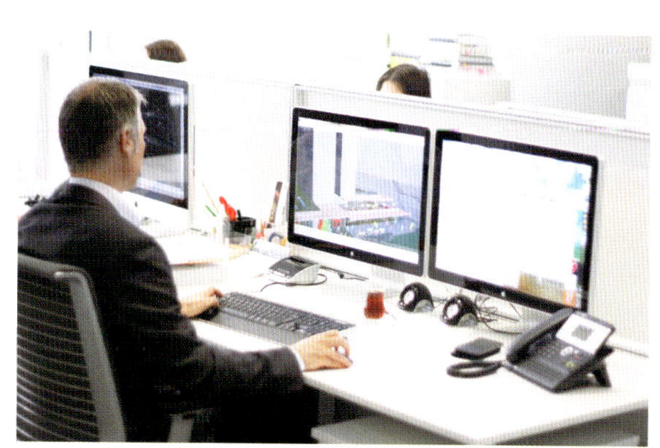

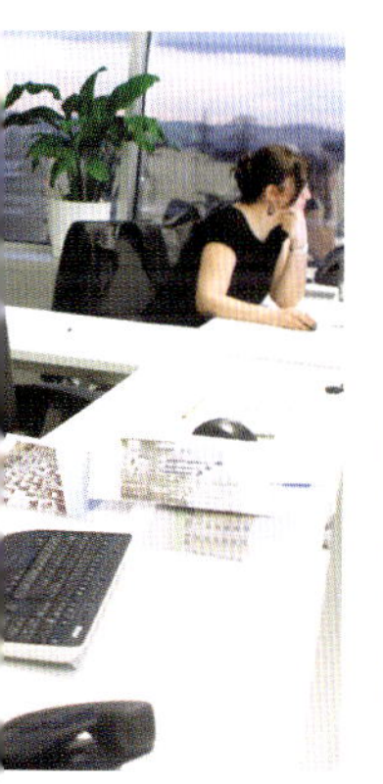

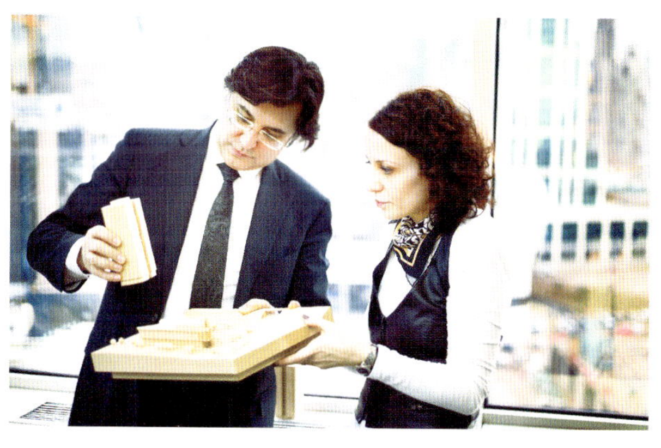

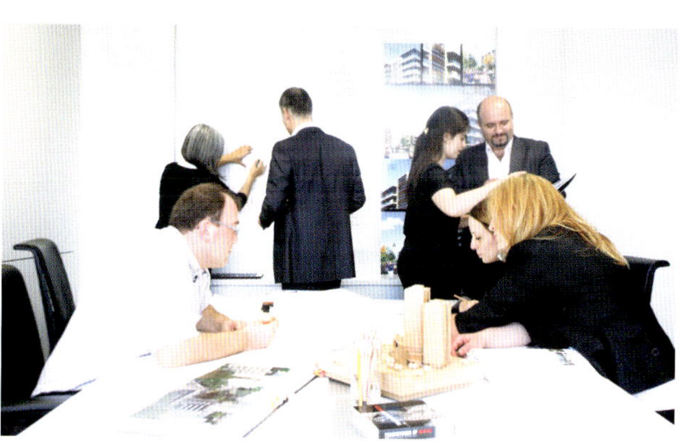

Group 2 Ankara

Group 2 is led by İrem Aker Büyükkalay with the assistance of Niyazi Ayvaz and Levent Balcı. The group's projects include public and commercial spaces and mixed-use projects. The group's responsibilities begin with the concept project phase and continue with preliminary and final project design, including construction documents and workplace consultancy. Projects include Ankara High Speed Train Station, Skopje Mixed-Use Center, Türk Telekom, Armada Development Project, Malabo Shopping Center, Samsun and Kayseri Courthouses, and Panora.

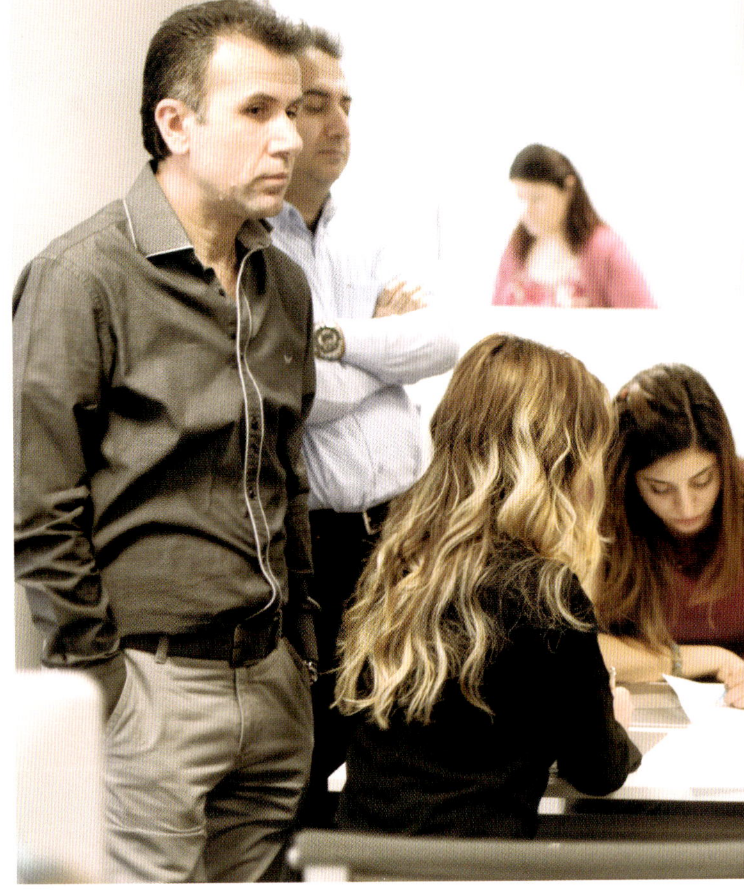

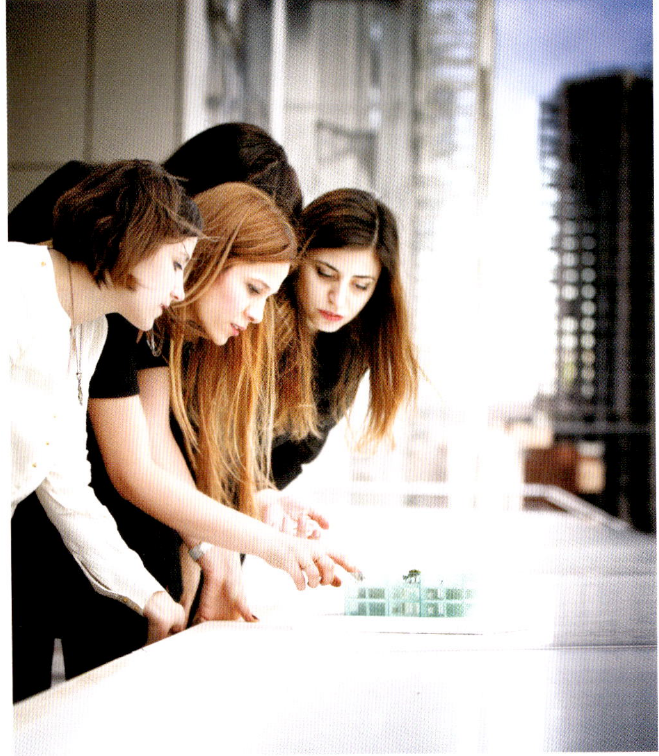

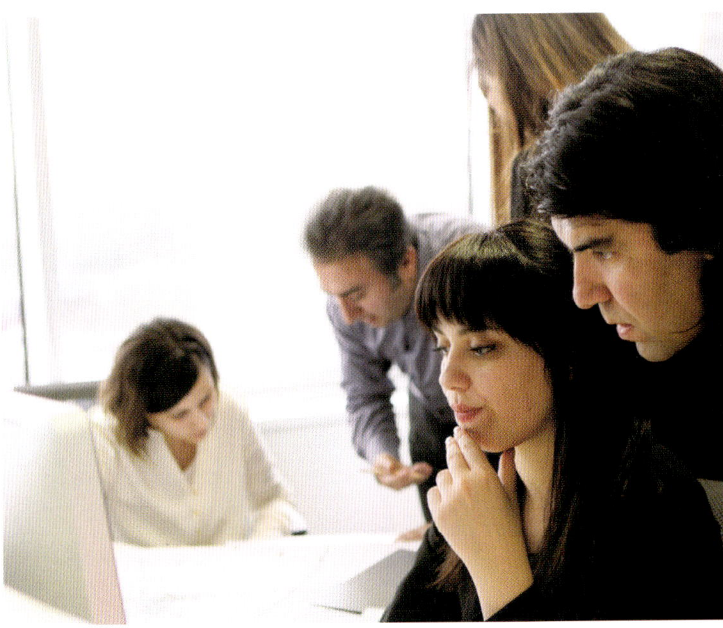

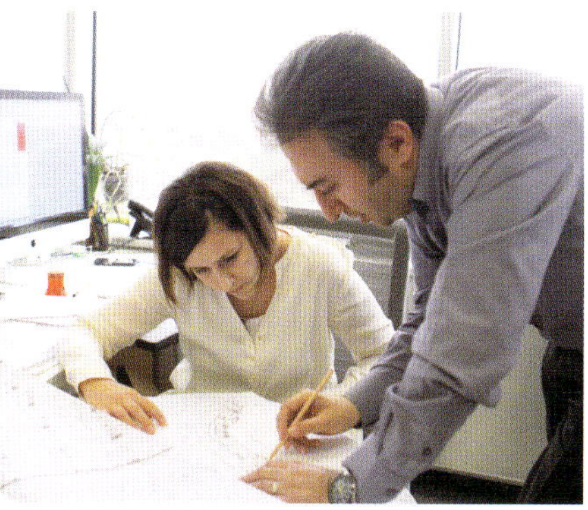
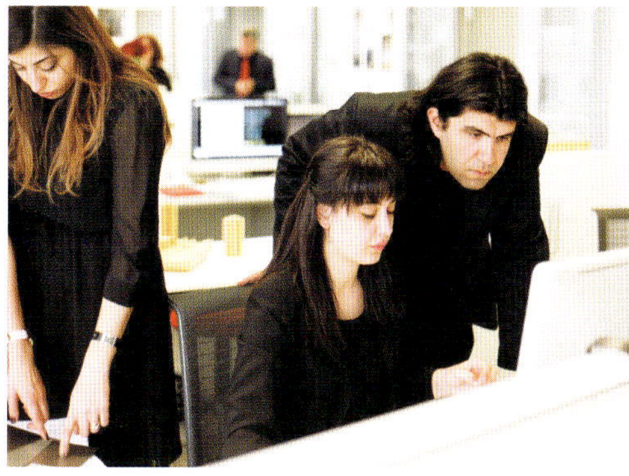
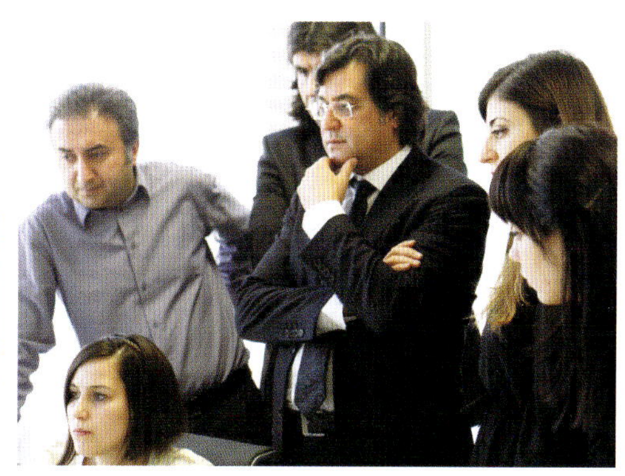
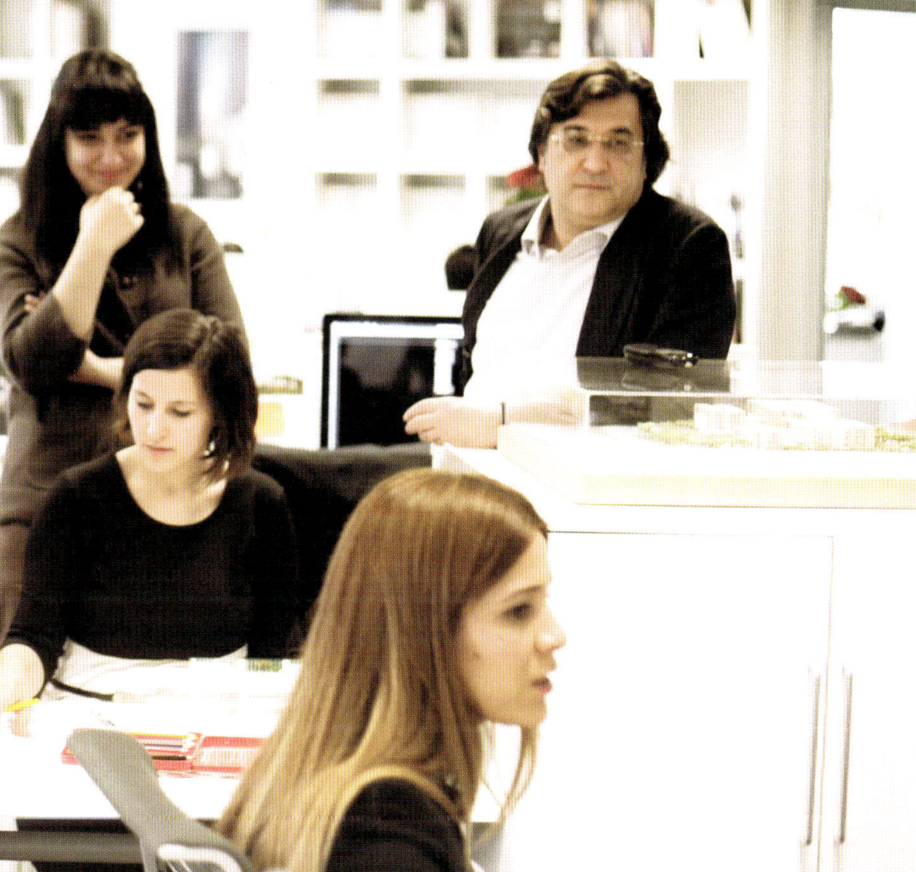
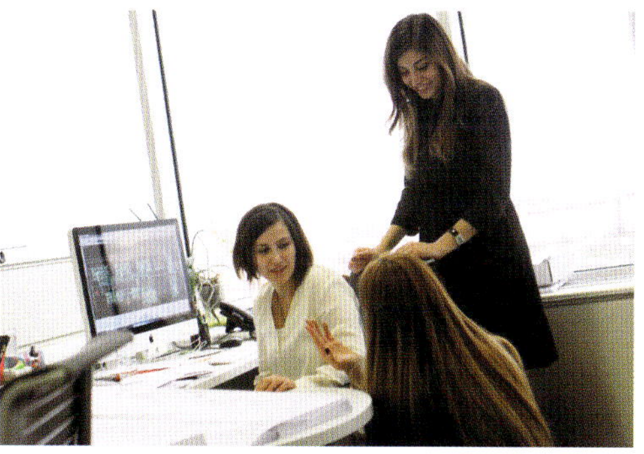
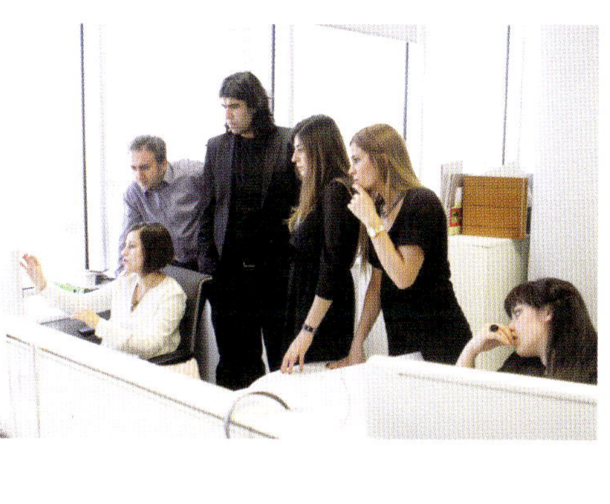
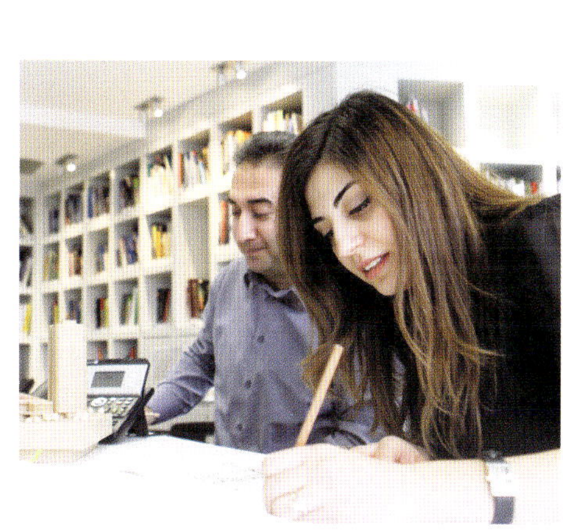
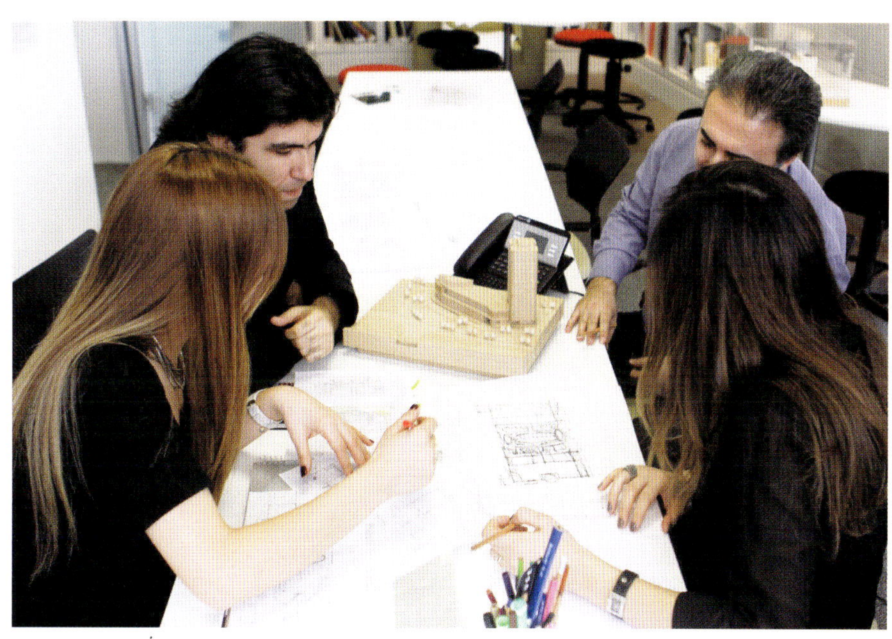

Group 3 Ankara

Group 3 is led by Harun Karabulut with the assistance of Nil Ece İnce. The group's responsibilities begin with the concept project phase and continue with preliminary and final project design, including construction documents and workplace consultancy. Ankara International Exhibition and Congress Center, which has been designed in collaboration with international architectural practice Gmp, is one of Group 3's major projects and other projects include Taurus, Yaşamkent Mosque, TOBB ETU Development Projects, and Kipaş Headquarters.

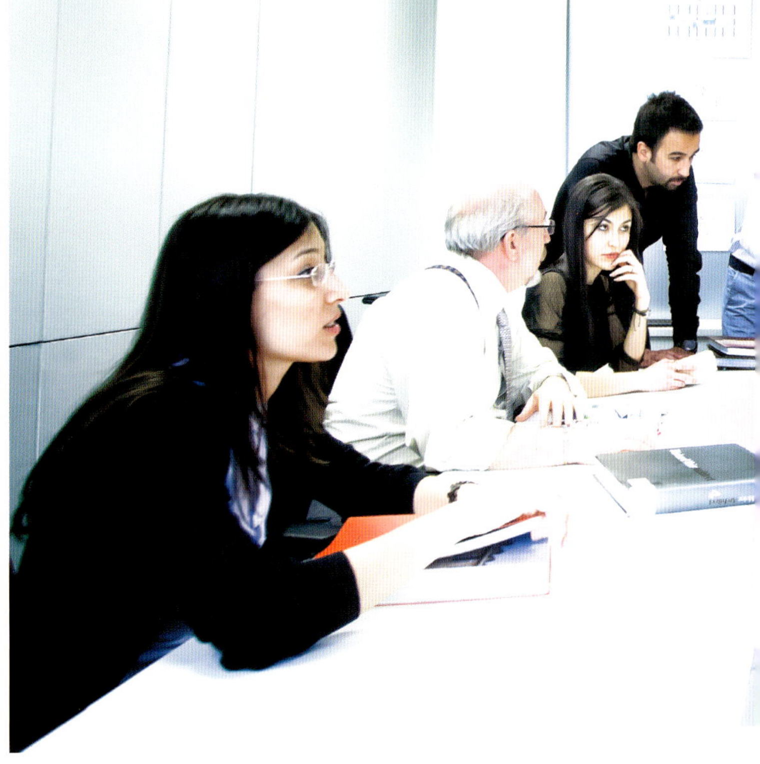

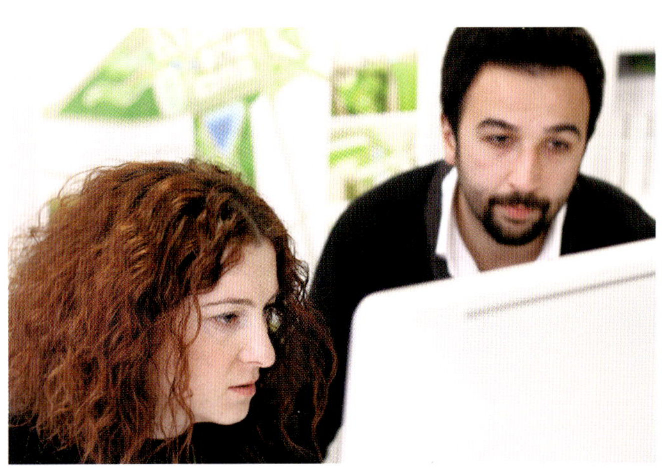

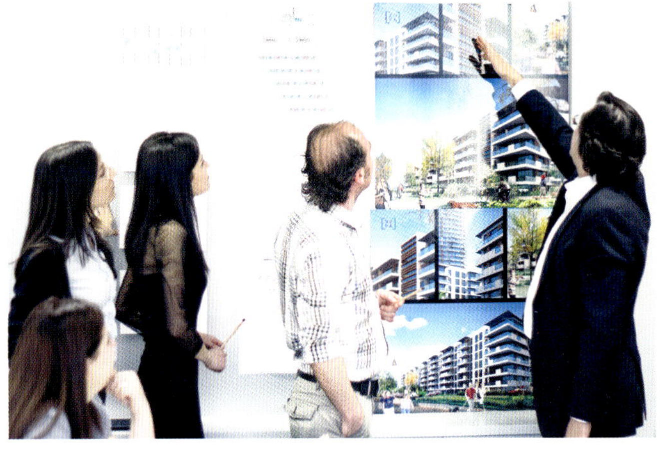

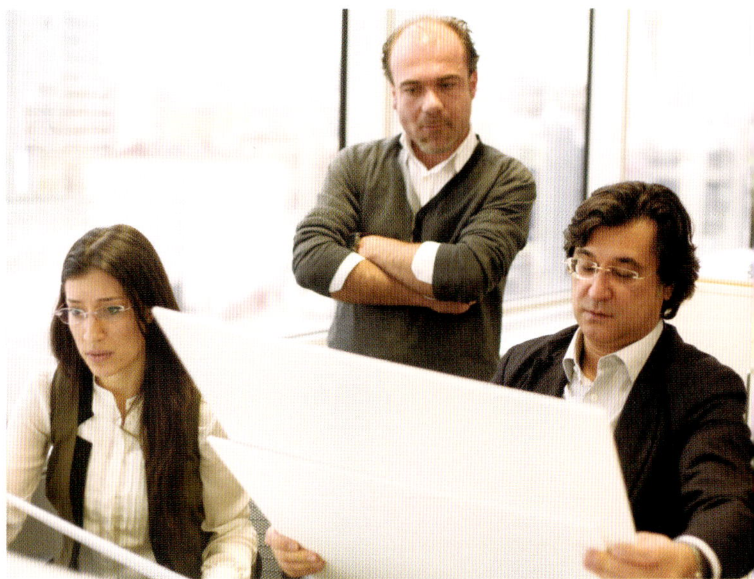

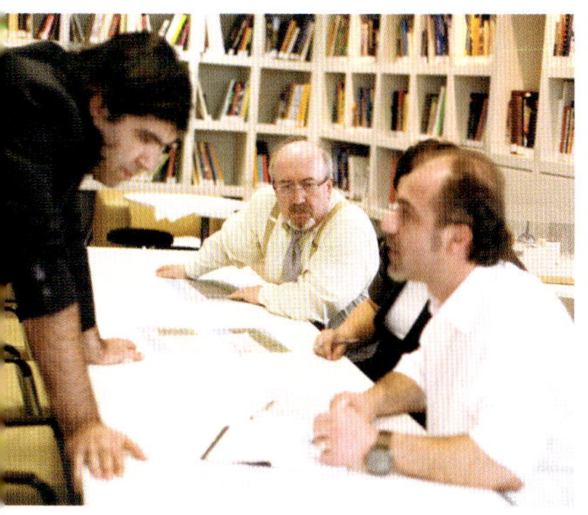
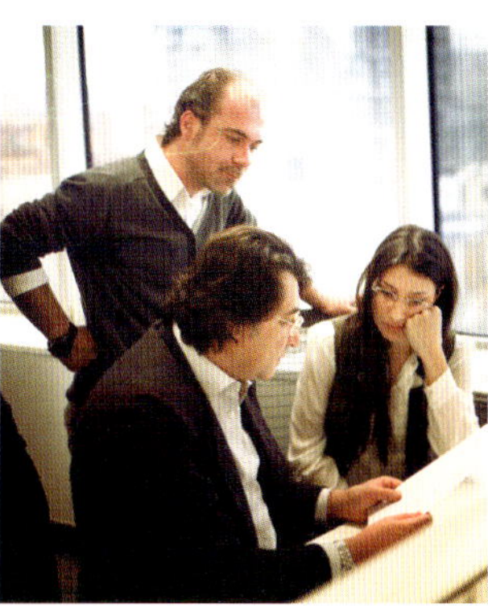
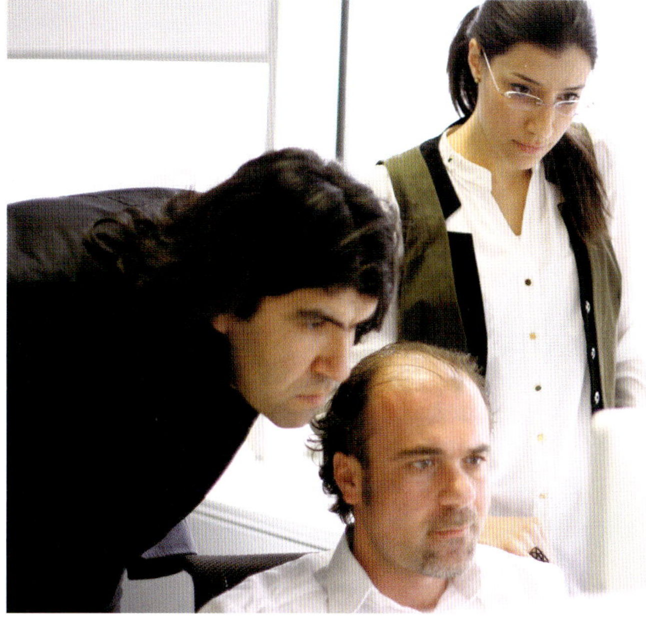
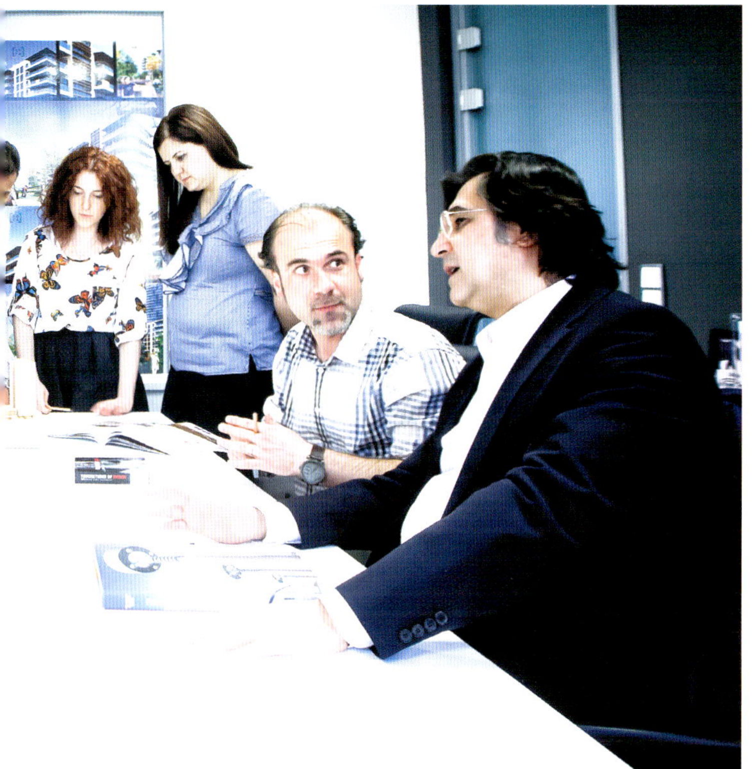
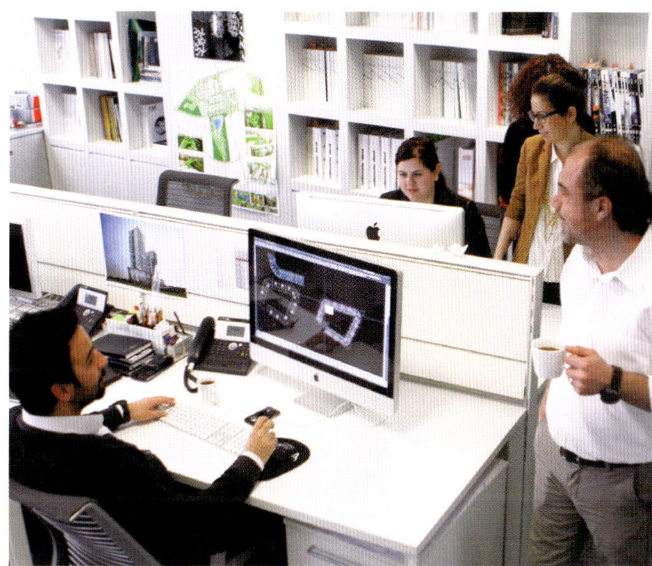
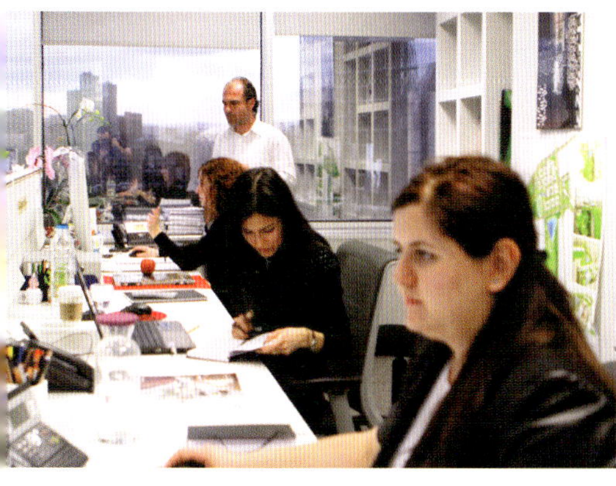
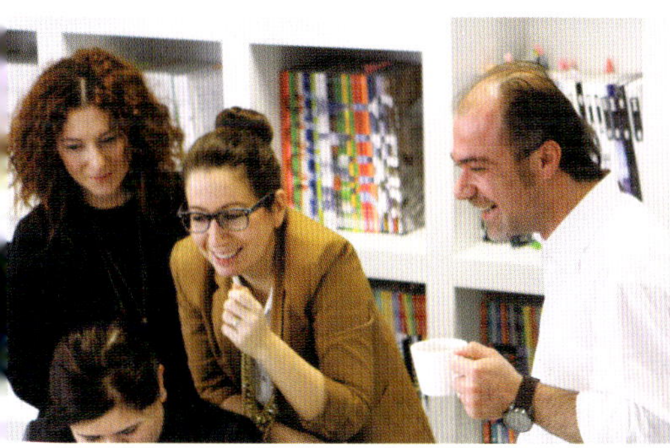
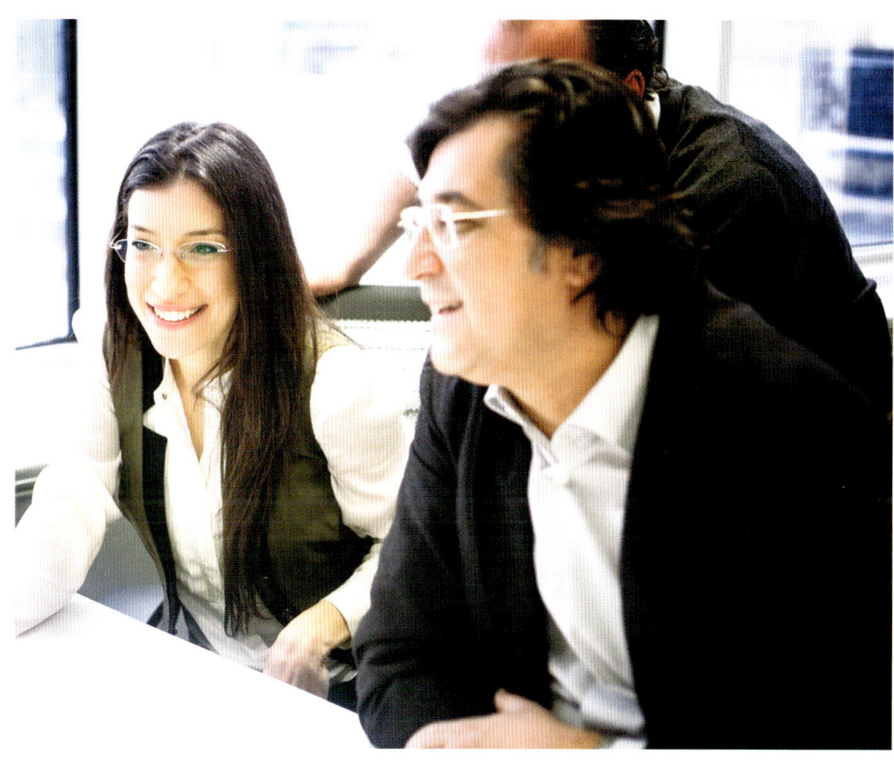

Group 4 İstanbul

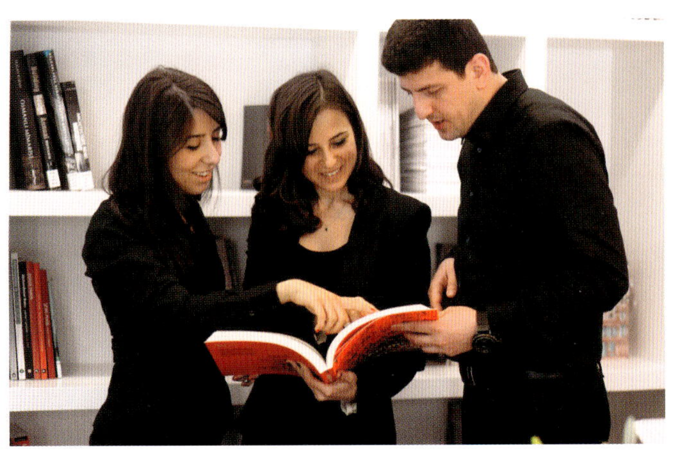

Group 4 is led by İhan Şimşek. The projects of Group 4 are mainly located in İstanbul and include office, residential, and mixed-use projects. The group's responsibilities begin with the concept project phase and continue with preliminary and final project design, including construction documents and workplace consultancy. Group 4's projects include Küçükyalı Business Center, Avcılar Park, Eyüp Park, Yakuplu Park, Güneşli Park, and Gardenya.

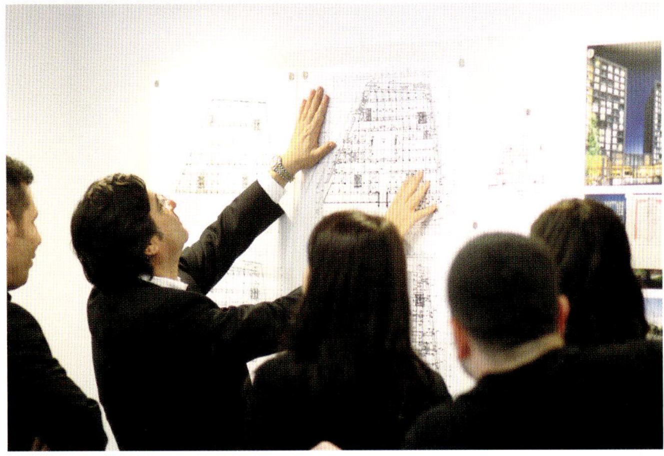

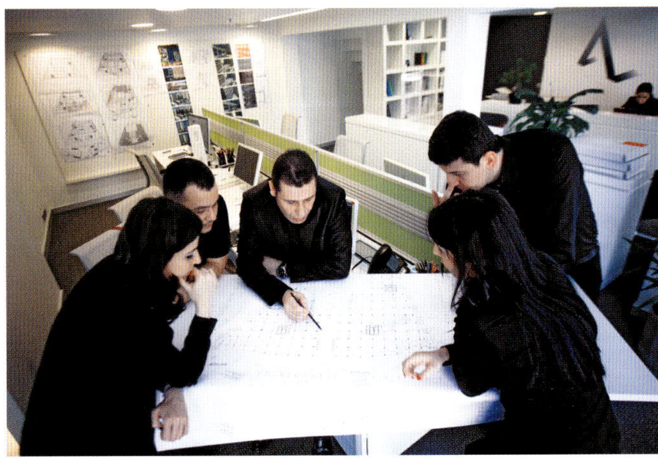

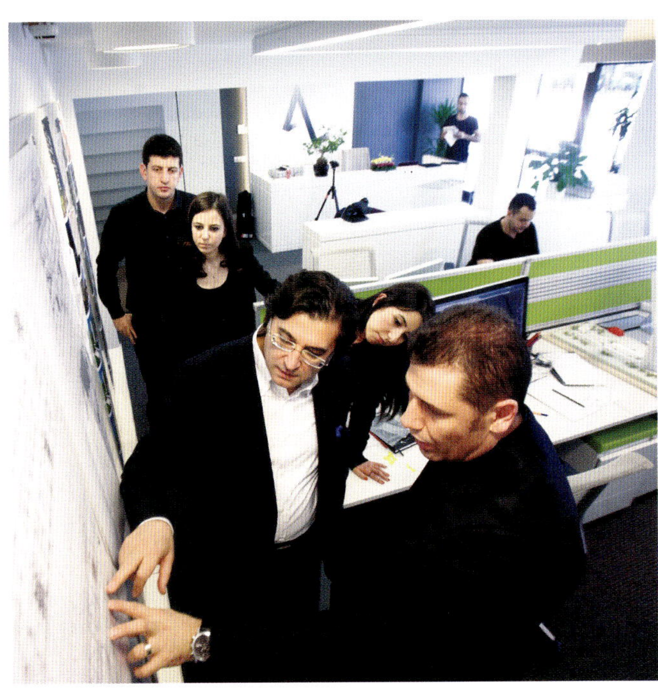

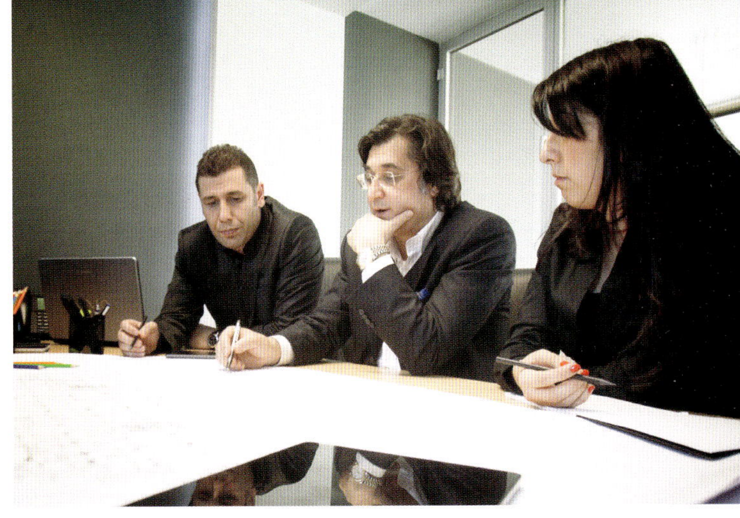

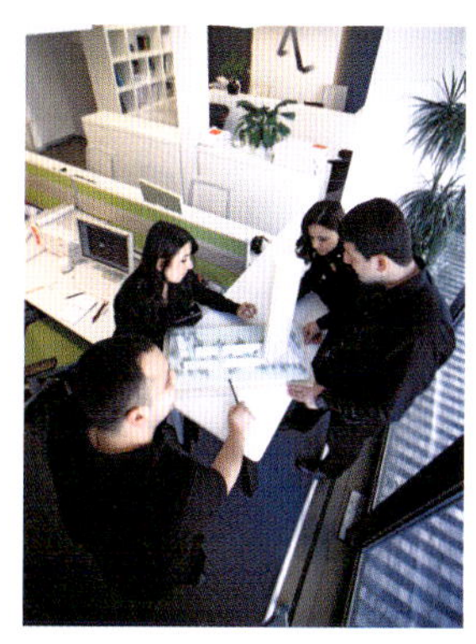
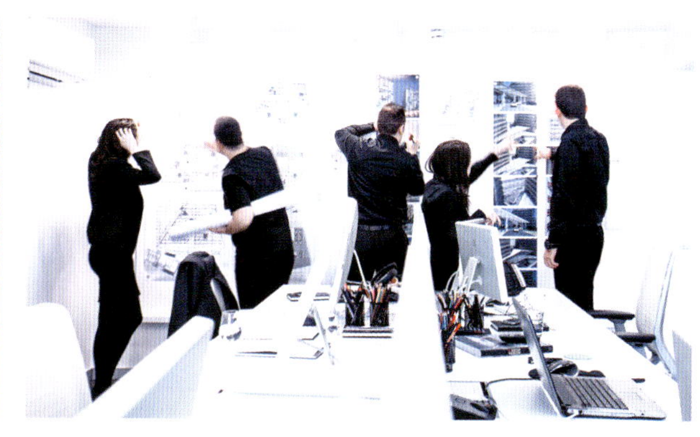
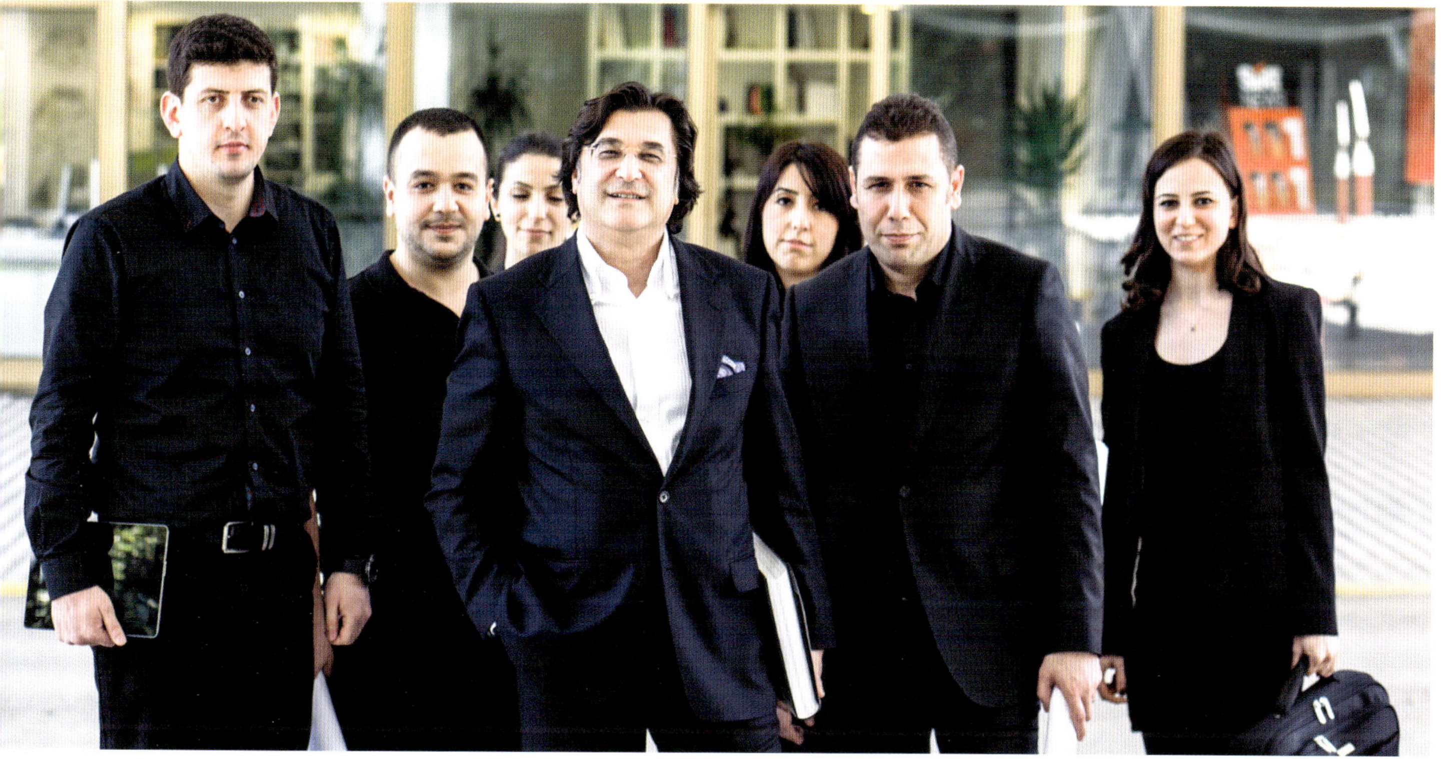
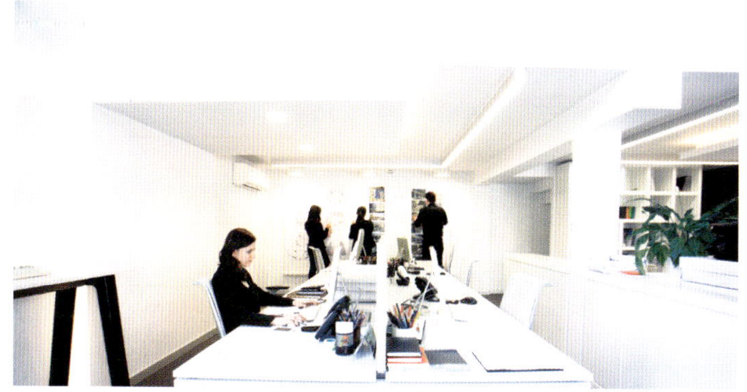
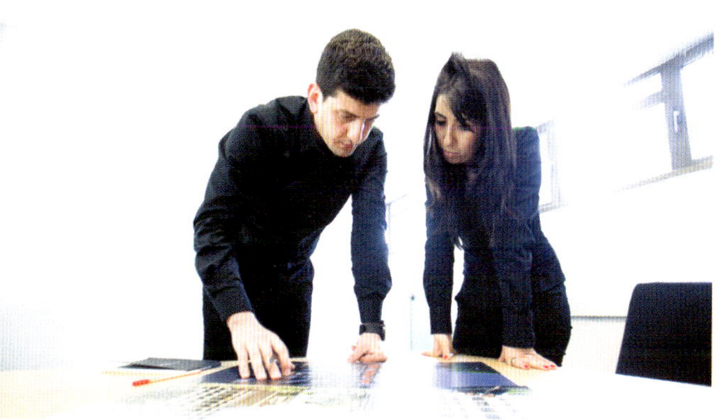
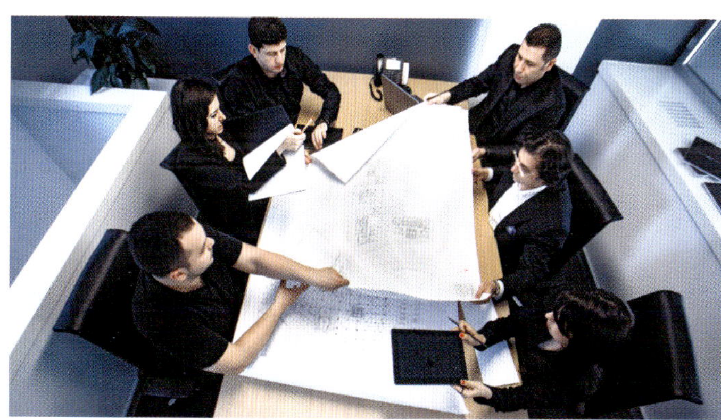
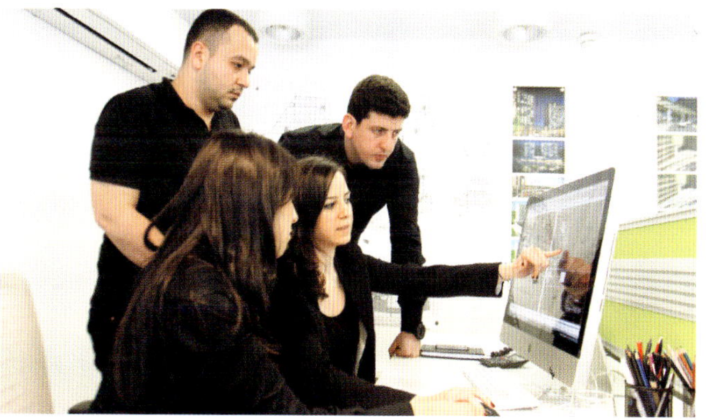

International Trips and Workshops

International trips are one of the major social activities for A Tasarım Mimarlık. These trips are not only important as a chance for the team to bond, work together, and share the same social environment outside of the office; but they are also valuable as an architectural and technical educational workshop. Organized by the office travel committee, the trips are attended by the entire team as well as occasional special guests. It is a chance for the team to see the evolution of the urban areas, different building methods, material technologies, and detail solutions on-site with the appropriate technical information. Through these workshops, the team has had the opportunity to visit a variety of architectural offices around the world, as well as to visit the constructions along with their architects.

Starting with Paris in 2004 and continuing with Berlin in 2005, Frankfurt-Düsseldorf-Cologne in 2006, London in 2007, Roma-Florence-Siena-Venice in 2008, Milan in 2009, Berlin in 2009, Paris in 2010, Barcelona in 2011, Munich in 2012, and Hamburg-Lübeck in 2013—these international workshops have become a tradition.

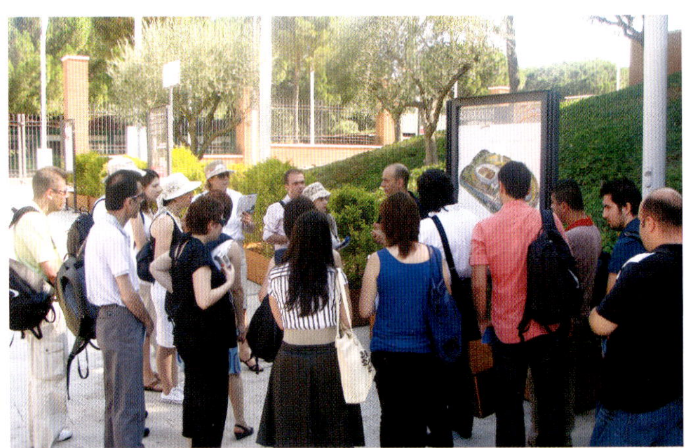

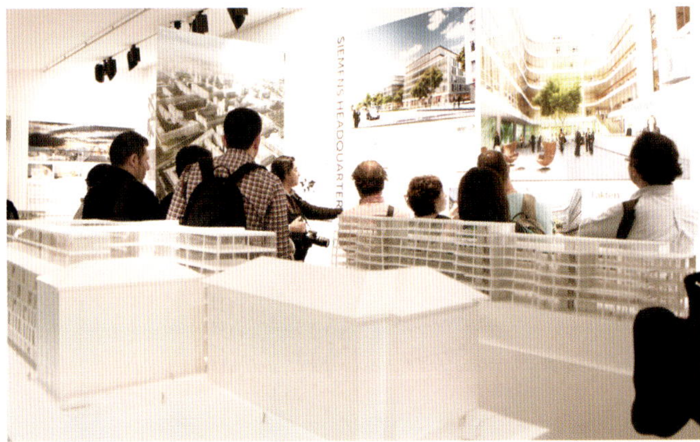

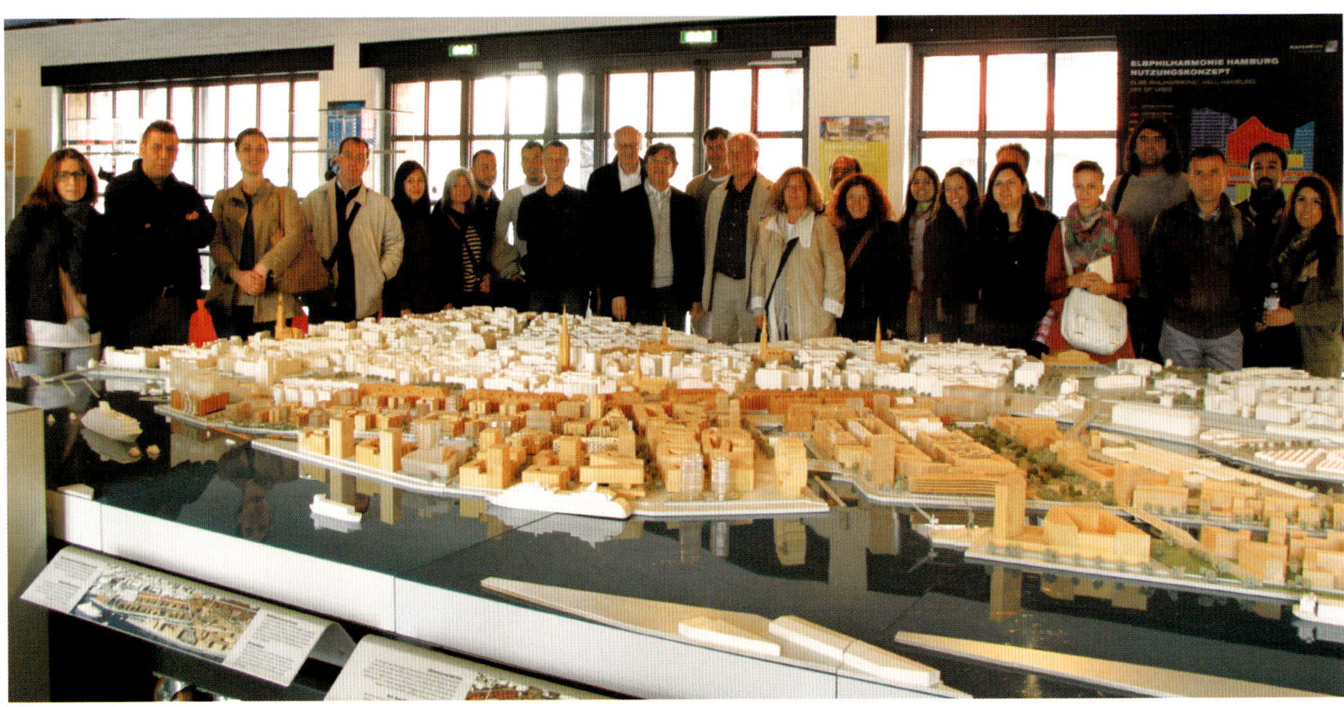

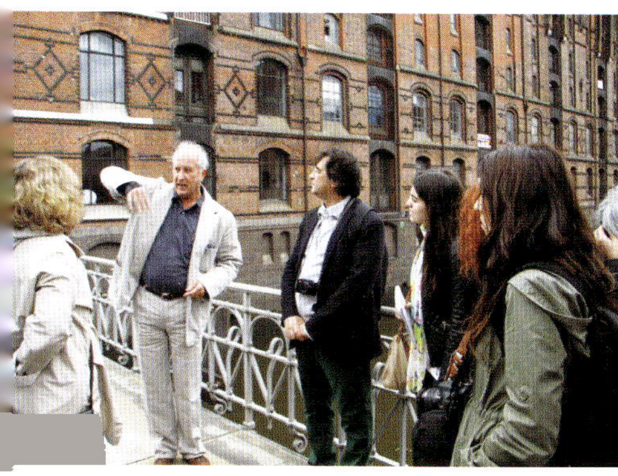

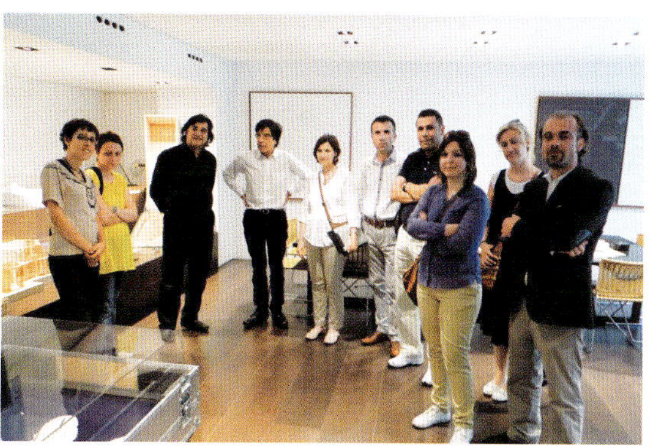

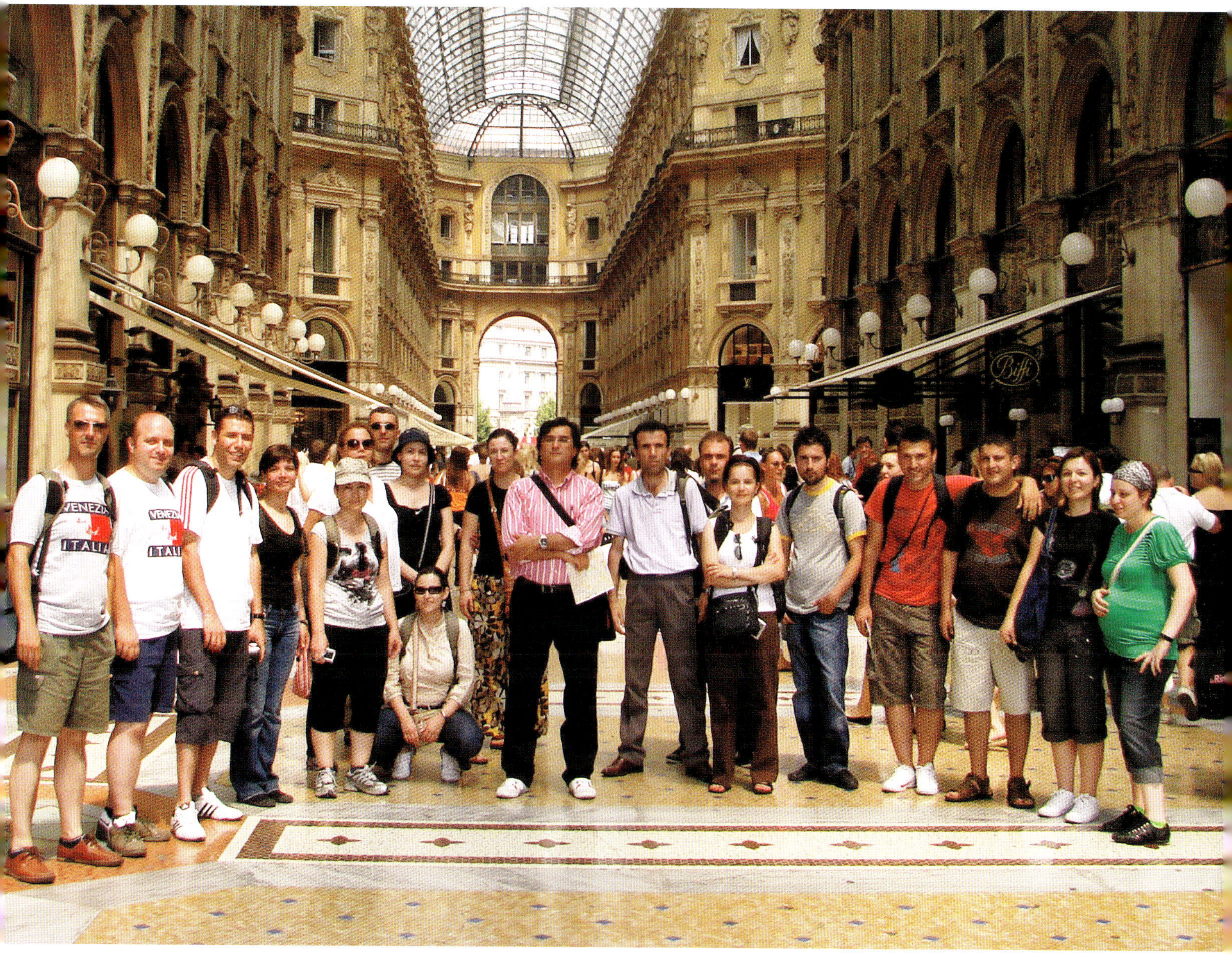

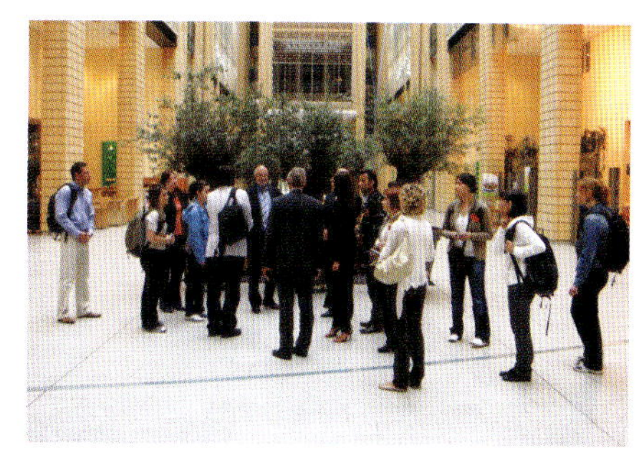

The Team

Founder and President

Ali Osman Öztürk

Board of Directors

Ali Osman Öztürk
İlgiz Öztürk
Yakup Öztürk
Eser Çengel
İrem Aker Büyükkalay
Harun Karabulut
İlhan Şimşek
Ebru Laçin Bilir

Administration

İlgiz Öztürk
Yakup Öztürk
Ebru Laçin Bilir
Aylin Temel Ak
Satı Demirhan
Mehmet Ali Öztürk

Group Coordinators

Eser Çengel
İrem Aker Büyükkalay
Harun Karabulut
İlhan Şimşek

Group 1

Eser Çengel
Canan Karakaya
Mehmet Güner
Süreyya Atalay
Burcu Şenal
Güray Tekin
Bülent Karakaya
Cenk Erkoçoğlu
Öznur Yıldız

Group 2

İrem Aker Büyükkalay
Niyazi Ayvaz
Levent Balcı
Hasret Devran İnce
Nihan Ürek
Canan Arslan
Sinan Özkan
Aslı Altıntaş

Group 3

Harun Karabulut
Nil Ece İnce
Hatice Baştabak
Ceyda Er Çelik
Ersin Candan
Yasemin Rençber Ünal
Cüneyt Öztürk
Durmuş Ursun

Group 4

İlhan Şimşek
Ayça Yontarım
Mehmet Aydın
Serra Aslı Say
Eyüp Hayri Yıldırım
Henife Tan

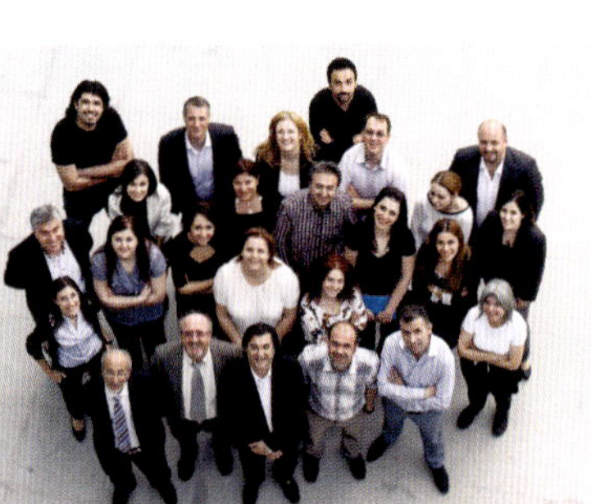

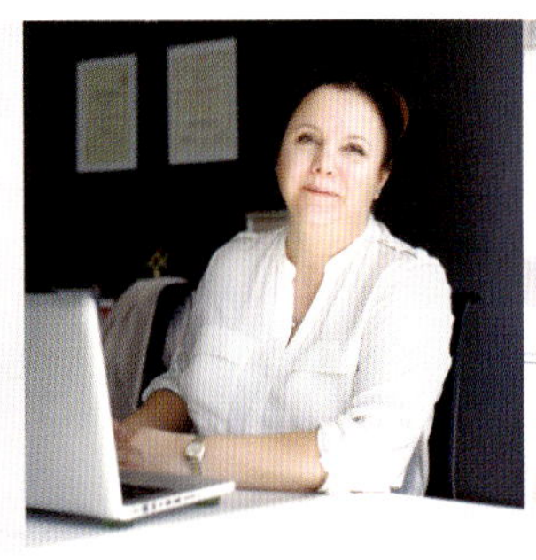

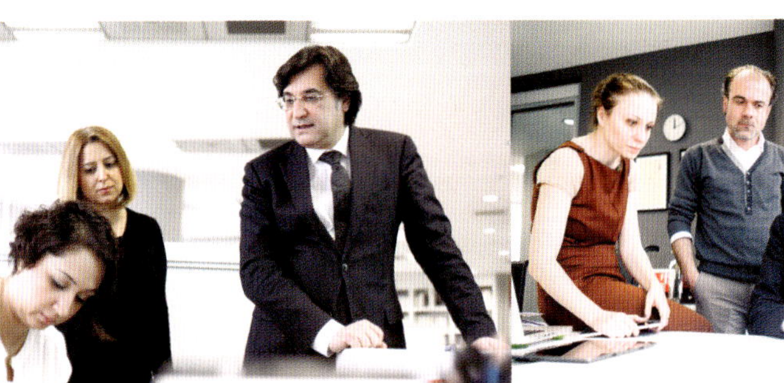

The Team 1997–2014

Aylin Temel Ak
Çağrı Akay
Mehmet Albayrak
Aslı Altıntaş
Canan Arslan
Ebru Güzelöz Aşan
Nurten Asil
Atilla Murat Aslangöz
Süreyya Atalay
Mehmet Aydın
Murat K. Aydoğmuş
Aydın Ayvaz
Niyazi Ayvaz
Levent Balcı
Yavuz Selim Barbaros
Oğuz Baykal
Ebru Laçin Bilir
Ferdi Bozkurt
İrem Aker Büyükkalay
Ersin Candan
Eren Ceylan
Filiz Cingi
Fatih Çaylan
Ceyda Er Çelik
Eser Çengel
Asu Çetinkaya
Devrim Çimen
Satı Demirhan
Ertan Demirkan
Erol Engin
Cenk Erkoçoğlu
Mehmet Güner
Solmaz Hisarcıklıoğlu
Hasret Devran İnce
Nil Ece İnce
J. Filiz Kadiroğlu
Hatice Baştabak Kantar
Harun Karabulut
Erhan Karahaliloğulları
Bülent Karakaya
Canan Karakaya
Özlem Yıldız Kaya
Tuncay Kaya
Türker Kesiktaş
Evren Kocabıçak
Burçin Öğreten
Sinan Özkan
Yakup Öztürk
Meltem Öztürk
Cüneyt Öztürk
Mehmet Ali Öztürk
Rasim Özveren
Serra Aslı Say
Mustafa Selçuk
Murat Şalcıgil
Burcu Şenal
İlhan Şimşek
Henife Tan
Güray Tekin
Durmuş Ursun
Banu Refia Uslu
Yasemin Rençber Ünal
Nihan Kocaoğlu Ürek
Eyüp Hayri Yıldırım
Öznur Yıldız
Ayça Yontarım

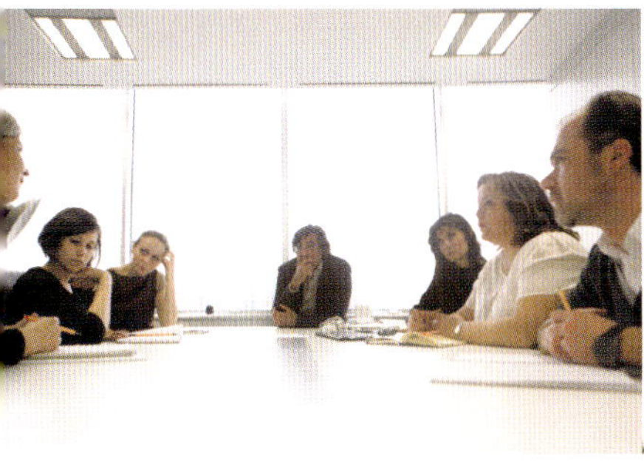
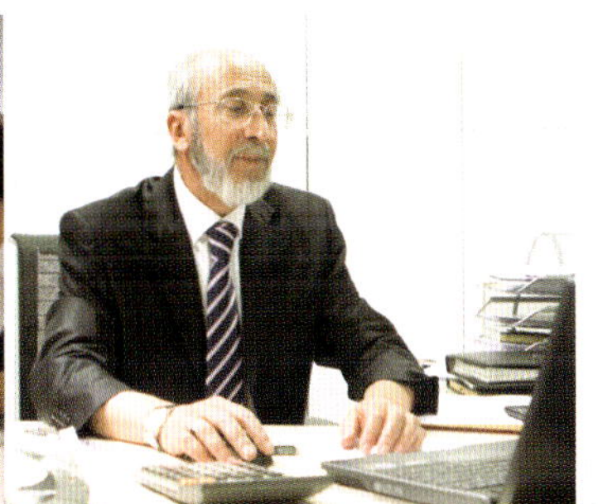
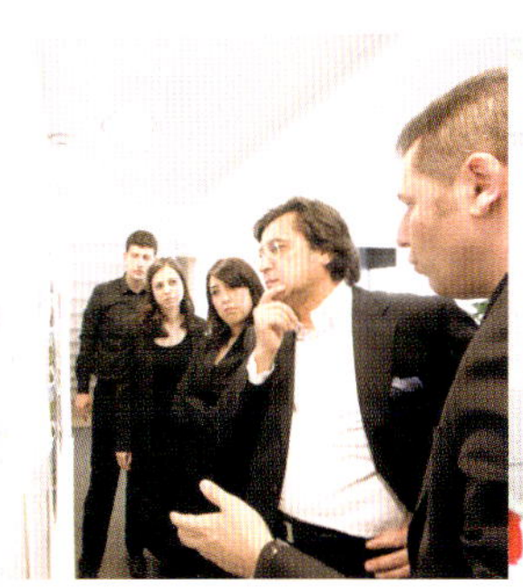
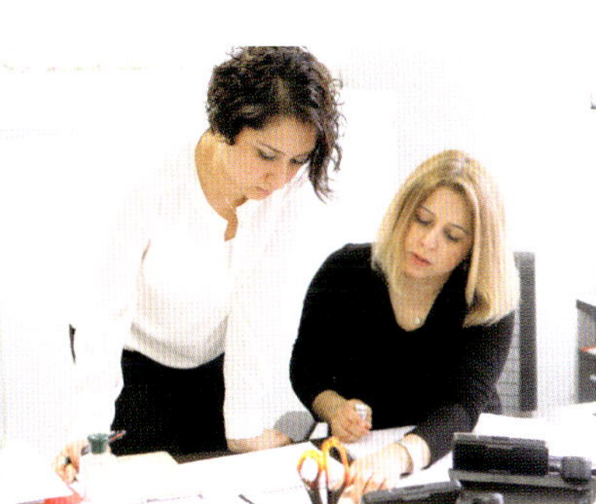

Engineers, Consultants, and Collaborators

Structural Engineering İbrahim Öztürk/Yüksek Project, Dumanoğlu Engineering, Prota Engineering, Arup

Mechanical Engineering Celal Okutan, Mehmet Okutan/Okutan Engineering, Meriç Sapçı/Metta Engineering, Nevzat Öztürk/Setes Engineering

Electrical Engineering Mustafa Ülkü, Cengiz Özkan/Akay Engineering, Mehmet Yurdakul, Özgür Ulupınar/Yurdakul Engineering

Landscape Design Belemir Dalokay/Dalokay Design Studio, Oktan Nalbantoğlu/On Tasarım, Promim Urban and Environmental Design, Çevre Landscaping

Architectural Design Consultants Salih Bezci, Vecihi Yıldız

Financial Consultants İsmail Koş/Referans, Abdülkadir Öztürk

Fire Consultants Alara Design and Engineering, Karina Design

Leasing Consultants Avi Alkaş, Nilgün Dil Erman/Jones Lang Lasalle Turkey, Metro Assetment Management, Reval, AVM MFI Partners

Acoustics Consultant Prof. Dr. Mehmet Çalışkan, Mezzo Studio Acoustical Design and Consultancy

Lighting Consultant Attila Uysal

Façade Consultant Kaan Kuran/Priedemann Building Envelope Consultants

Visualization AD Design, Min Tasarım, Archfon Concept, Simple Tree, Frontop, A-promise

Post Processing Burçin Öğreten

Physical Models Selahattin Yazıcı Modelling Atelier, Mehmet Savaş, Serdar Gürol, Model Maket

Photographers Cemal Emden, Kadir Kır, Umut Akgün, Gürkan Akay, Fethi Mağara, Melih Uçar, Kerem Şeker, Salih Kılıç

Corporate Identity Design Murat Dorkip

Graphics and Printing Rekmay

Web Design iconpm

Communication and Design Consultant Funda Mehter

English translation for the book Emre Akçaoğlu, Alev Erkmen, İlknur Urkun Kelso

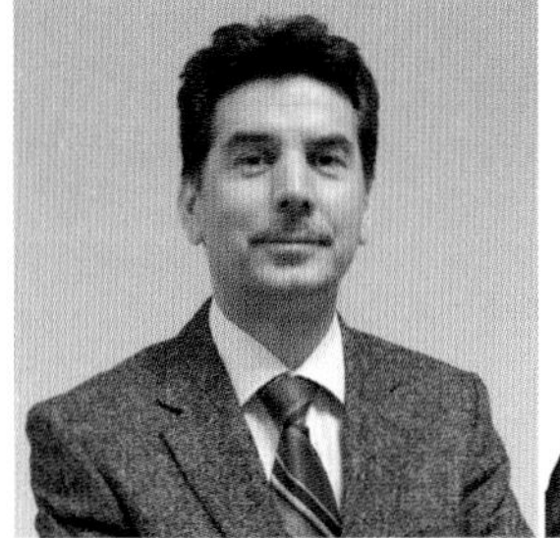
İbrahim Öztürk

Celal Okutan

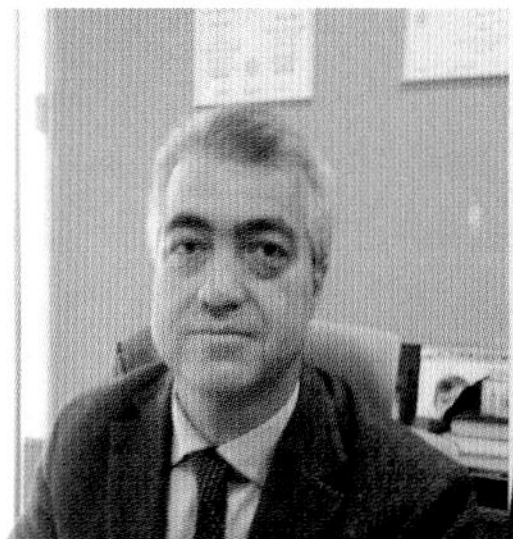
Meriç Sapçı

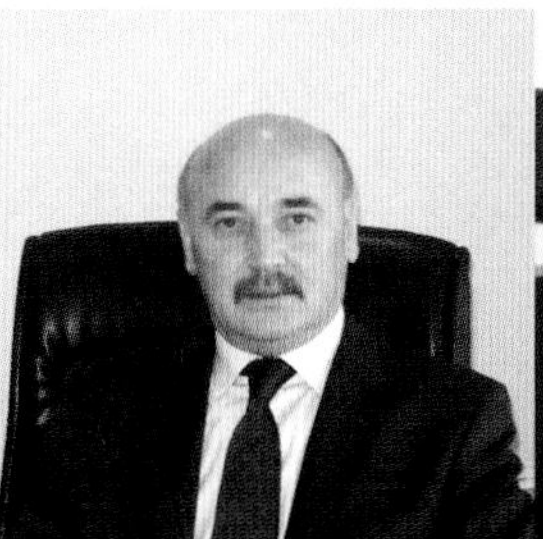
Nevzat Öztürk

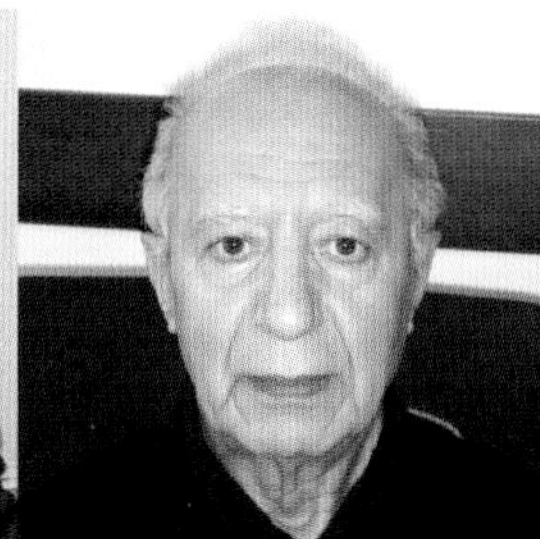
Mustafa Ülkü

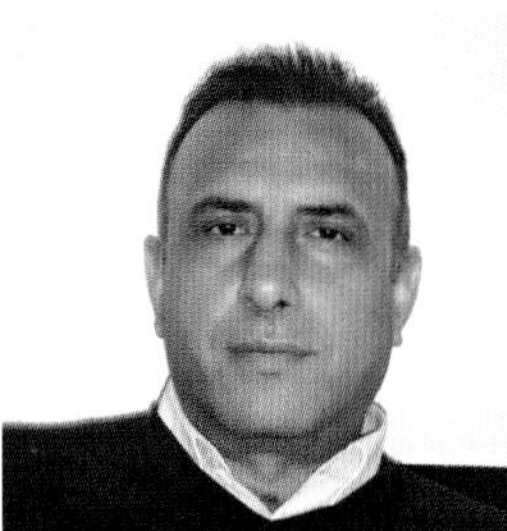
Cengiz Özkan

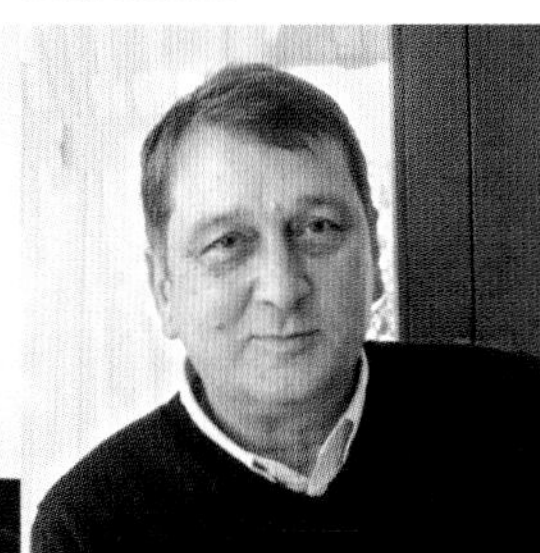
Mehmet Yurdakul

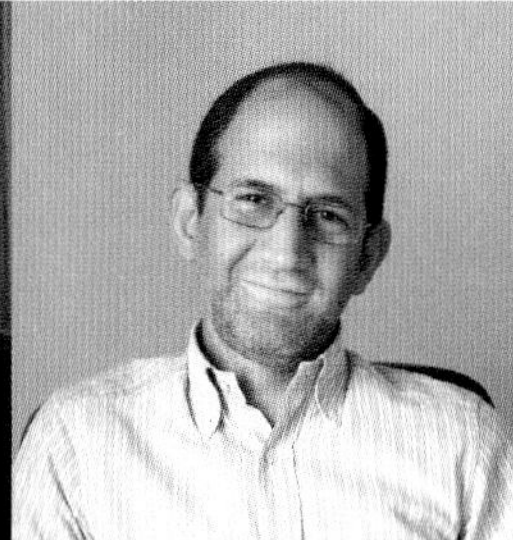
Özgür Ulupınar

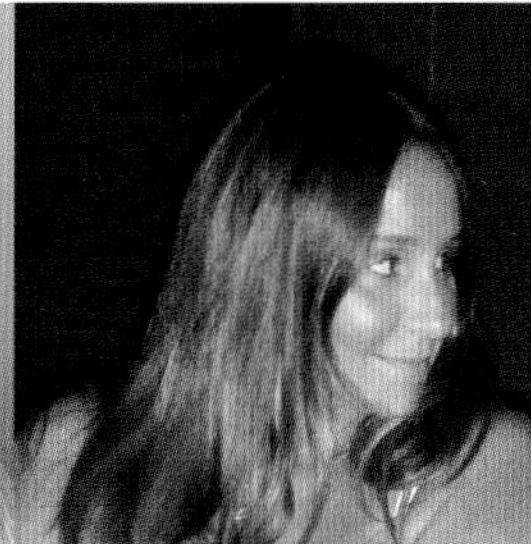
Belemir Dalokay

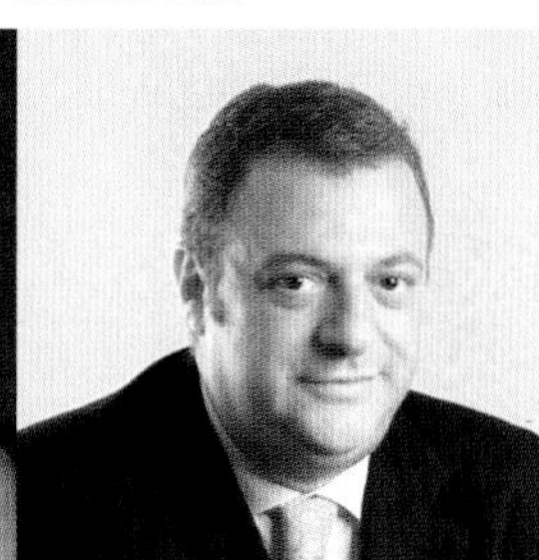
Avi Alkaş

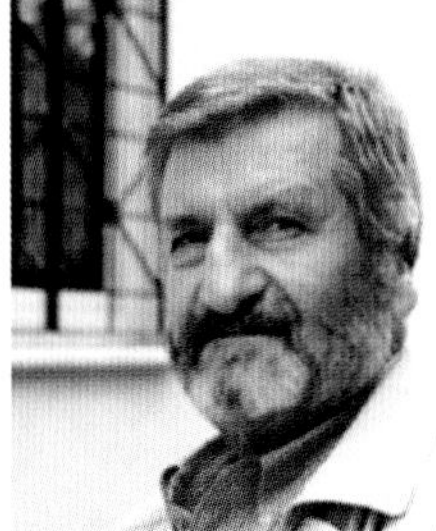
Selahattin Yazıcı

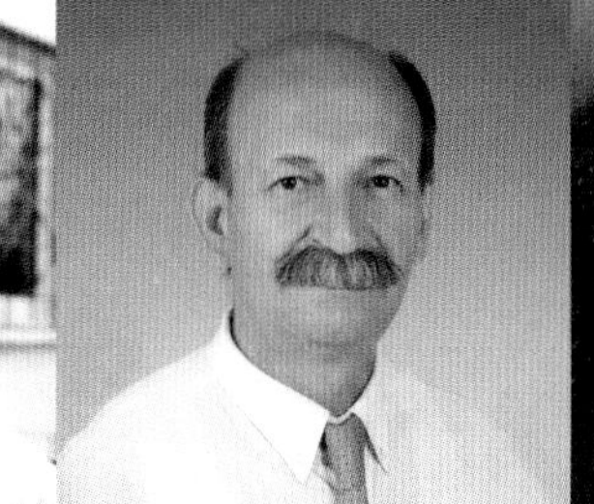
Mehmet Savaş

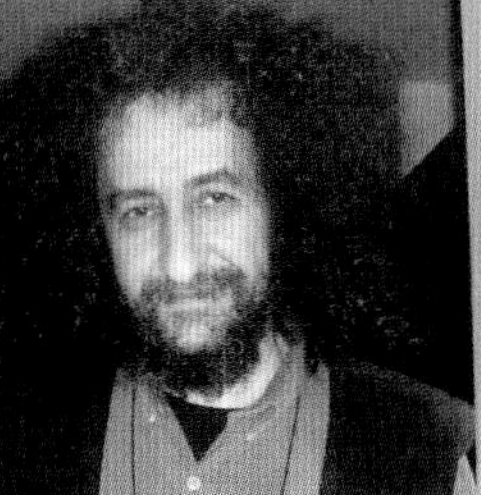
Serdar Gürol

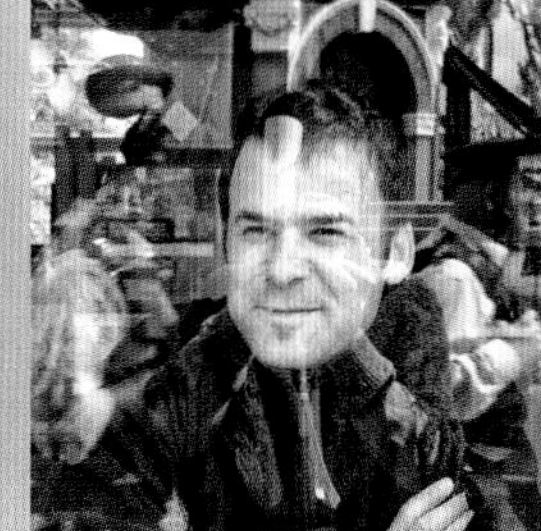
Cemal Emden

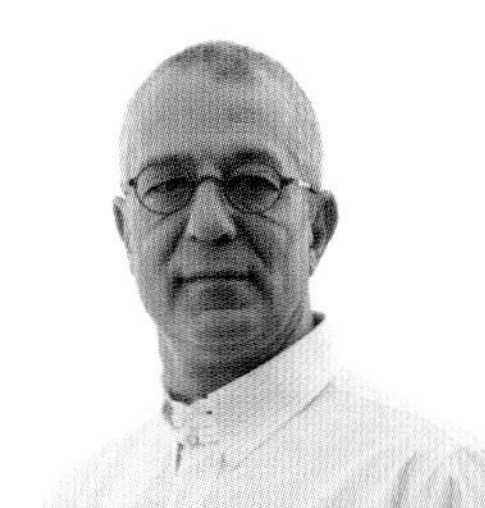
Murat Dorkip

Awards and Competitions

2013 Tepe Prime-Retail and Leisure International Awards // Finalist
2012 Tepe-Mesa Yaşamkent Housing // 1st Prize
2012 Yaşamkent Mosque, Cityscape Dubai // Finalist
2012 Yaşamkent Mosque, WAF // Finalist
2012 Tepe Prime, Arkiparc'12 Awards // Finalist
2010 Türk Telekom // 1st Prize
2010 Via/Port Outlet, Cityscape Abu Dhabi // Finalist
2010 Via/Port, ICSC European Shopping Center Awards // Finalist
2010 Adana Courthouse // 2nd Prize
2009 Panora, ICSC European Shopping Center Awards // Merit
2009 Via/Port, AMPD Awards // Award
2009 Samsun Courthouse // 1st Prize
2009 Kazıkiçi Bostanları Central Business District, UIA Celebration of the Cities // Participation
2009 Congresium, Union of Steel Awards // Participation
2008 Via/Port, Arkiparc Best Shopping Center // Finalist
2008 Ankara Courthouse Extention Building // 2nd Prize
2006 İstanbul European Side Courthouse // 2nd Prize
2005 İstanbul Anatolian Side Courthouse // 2nd Prize
2005 METU Technopolis Gallium Block // 2nd Prize
2005 Armada, ICSC International Design and Development Awards // Merit
2004 Armada, ICSC European Shopping Centre Awards // 1st Prize
2002 METU Technopolis Research and Development Building // 2nd Prize
2001 Kadıköy Square Haydarpaşa, Harem Urban Design Competition (with Hüseyin Bütüner) // Mention
2001 International Urban Design Idea Competition for the Port District of İzmir // Participation
2000 The Greater Metropolitan Municipal Building & City Hall for Ankara with Social–Commercial Facilities (with Boran Ekinci) // Participation
1997 The Grand National Assembly of Turkey Office Building // Participation
1997 Turkish Pharmacists' Association Social Facilities Architectural Competition (with Hüseyin Bütüner and Hilmi Güner) // Mention
1995 Harran University Campus Architectural Competition (with Hüseyin Bütüner and Hilmi Güner) // 3rd Prize
1994 Tariş Headquarters Architectural Competition (with Hüseyin Bütüner) // Mention
1992 Ulus Historical City Center Saraçlar Bazaar Architectural Competition (with Hüseyin Bütüner and Hilmi Güner) // 1st Prize
1991 Ulus Tunnel and Hergelen Square Urban Design Competition (with Prof. Dr. Enis Kortan on behalf of Tepe Construction and Hüseyin Bütüner) // 2nd Prize
1989 METU Housing Research Symposium, Technology and Housing Architectural Competition // 1st Prize
1998 TED Campus Student Union Building, The National Architecture Exhibition and Awards // Participation
1988 Ankara Castle Development Plan Architectural Competition (with Ahmet Ardıçoğlu, Korkut Onaran, and Hüseyin Bütüner) // Mention
1988 Bursa Zafer and Şehreküstü Squares Urban Design(with Dr. Turgay Ateş and Hüseyin Bütüner) // 3rd Prize
1987 Ulus Historical City Center Development Plan (with Boran Ekinci, Zafer Akay, Ayşen Savaş, and Ahmet Ardıçoğlu) // Mention
1987 21. Century Housing and Environment Architectural Competition // 1st Prize
1987 Economical Housing Design Architectural Competition (with Hüseyin Bütüner and Kevser Kantar) // 3rd Prize
1987 208 Housing Architectural Competition for Students // Mention
1987 RIBA, 'New in the Old' Architectural Competition for Students // Participation
1986 Afyonkarahisar Square Urban Design Project Architectural Competition // 1st Prize
1986 Kelebek Furniture 'Modular Furniture for Youth' Competition // Participation
1986 Kent-Koop 'Batıkent Administration Center' Architectural Competition for Students // Mention
1985 RIBA, 'Hockney and Caro Museums' Architectural Competition for Students // Participation
1985 Kent-Koop, 'Batıkent District Center' Architectural Competition for Students // 2nd Prize

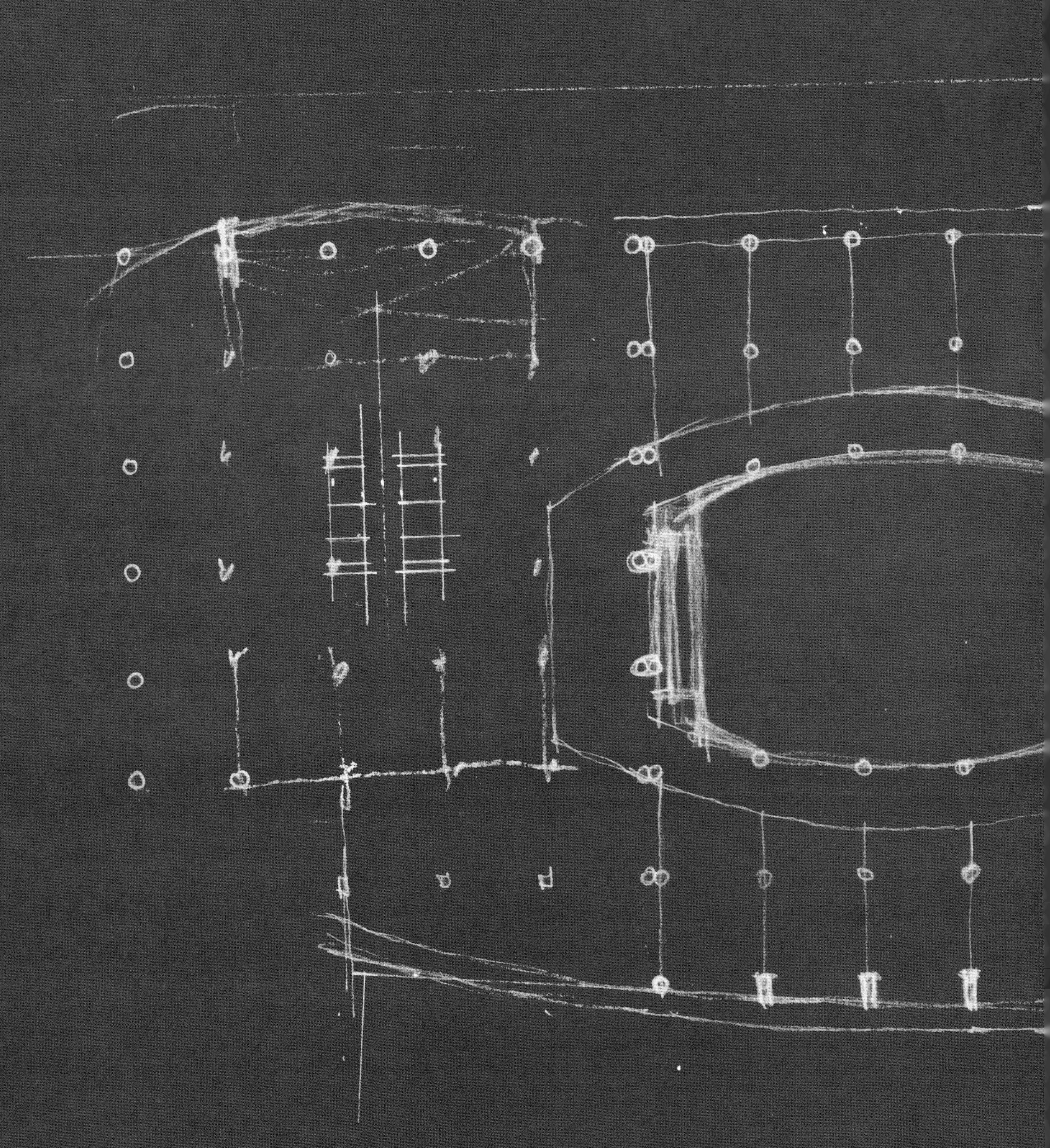

Project Chronology

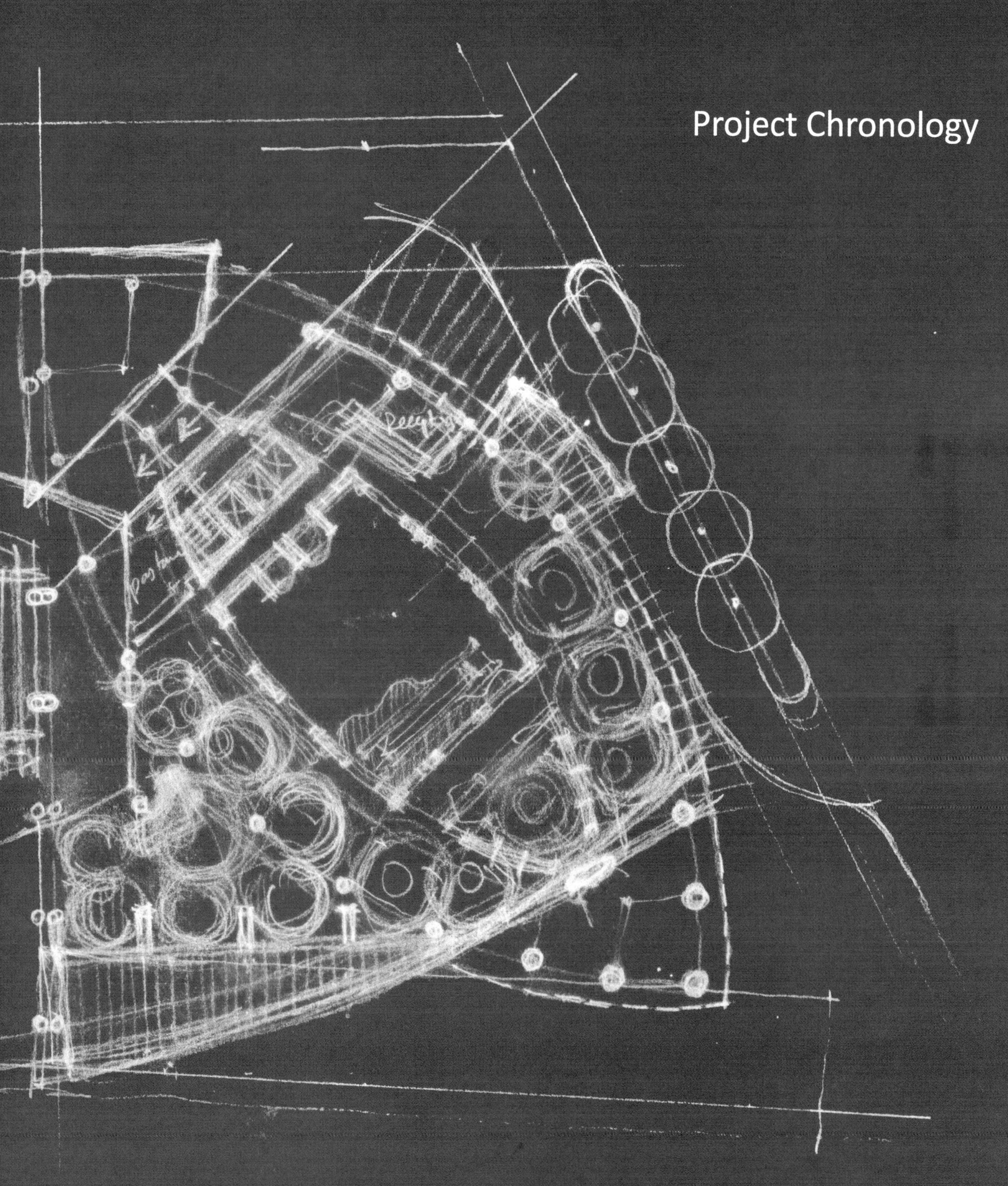

Chronological Projects

Armada

Client Söğütözü Construction and Management
Project Date 1998–2002
Area 125,000 m^2
Location Ankara
Design Consultant Salih Bezci, Vecihi Yıldız and GMW Architectural Ltd.
Structural Engineer Yüksek Project
Mechanical Engineer Ünlü Engineering
Electrical Engineer Emak Engineering
Leasing Consultant Alkaş Consultancy, Avi Alkaş
Mechanical Consultant İhsan Önen
Construction Supervisor Ömer Genç, Sonay Ozar
Contractor Söğütözü Construction and Management
Status Built
2005 ICSC International Design and Development, Merit
2004 ICSC European Shopping Center Awards First Prize

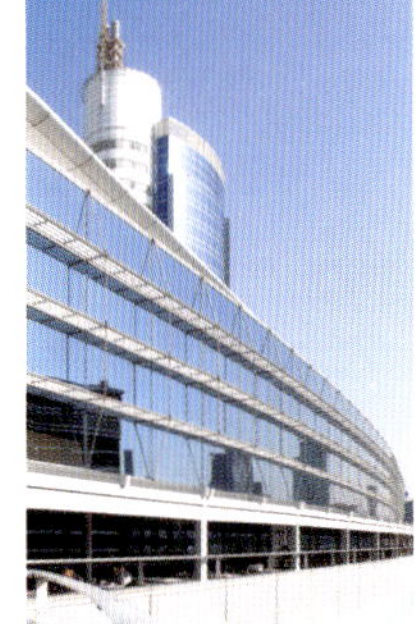

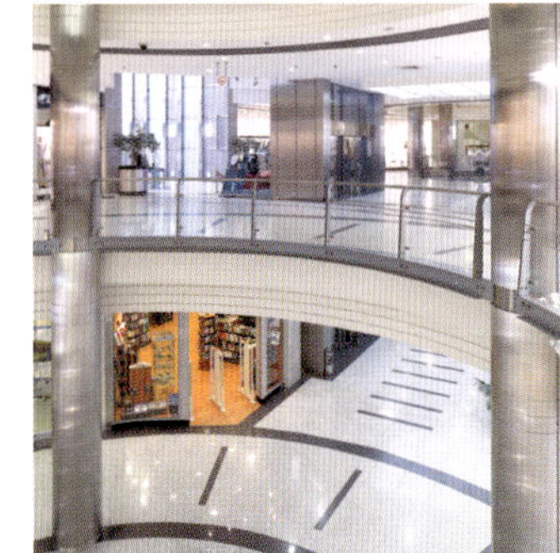

İstoç

Client İstanbul Wholesale Trade and Small Industries Cooperative
Project Date 1998–2012
Area 145,240 m^2
Location İstanbul
Structural Engineer Yüksek Project
Mechanical Engineer Akdeniz Engineering
Electrical Engineer Akay Engineering
Contractor İSTOÇ
Status Under construction

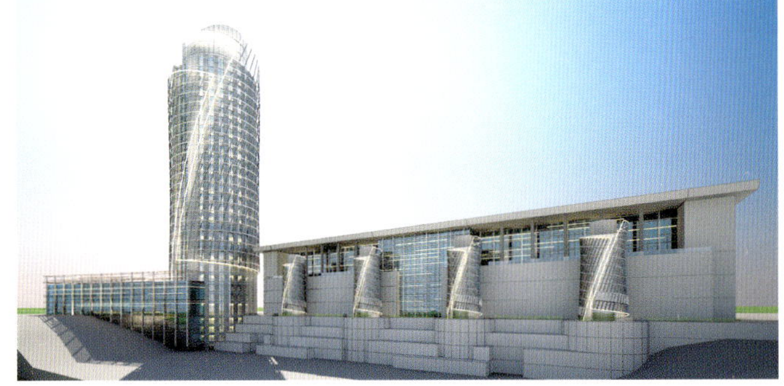

ODC

Client ODC
Project Date 1998
Area 2,500 m^2
Location Ankara
Design with Prof. Dr. Enis Kortan
Status Built

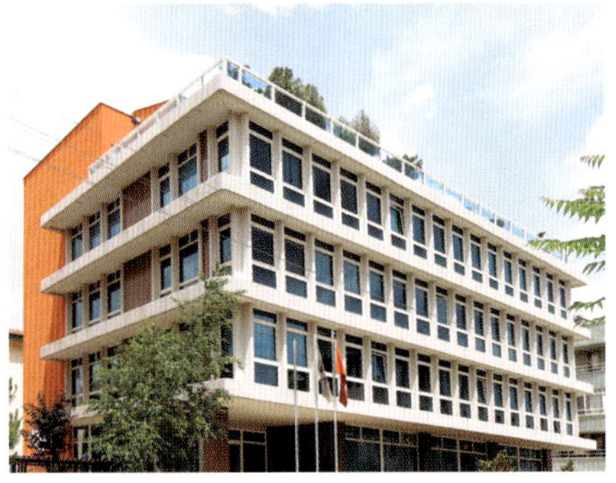

Ali Babacan Trade and Social Center

Client Ali Babacan Inc.
Project Date 1999
Area 10,500 m^2
Location Ankara
Structural Engineer Yüksek Project
Mechanical Engineer Akay Engineering
Electrical Engineer Setes Engineering
Status Built

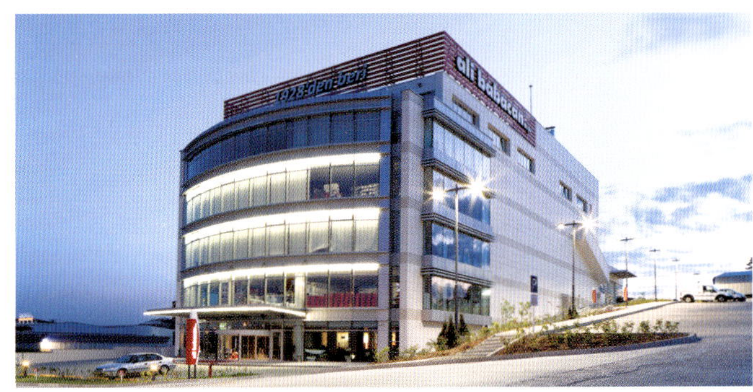

Akbak Plaza 1

Client Tevfik Akbak
Project Date 1999
Area 3,800 m^2
Location Ankara
Status Built

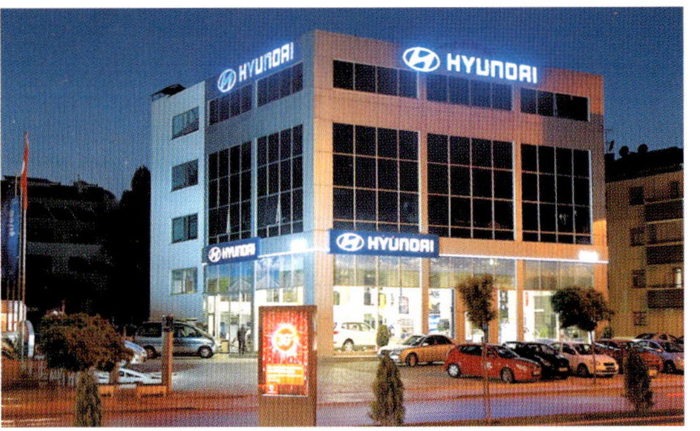

Lokman Hekim Hospital

Client Lokman Hekim Hospital
Project Date 2000
Area 3,000 m²
Location Ankara
Structural Engineer Yüksek Project
Status Built

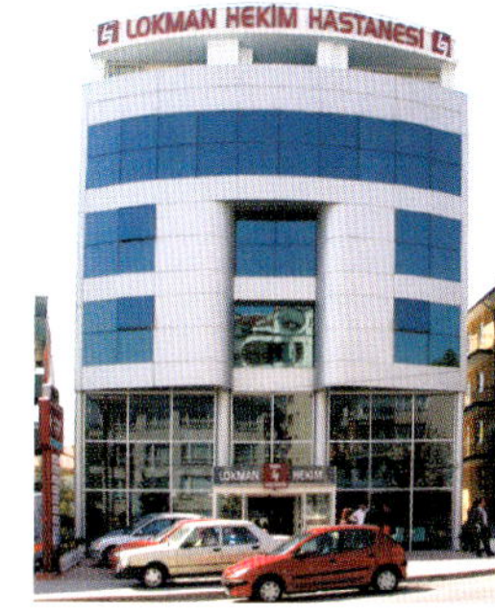

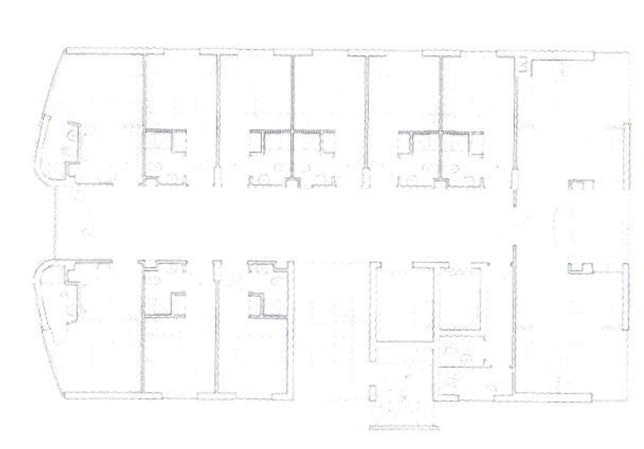

İzmir Port District Urban Design Competition

Client İzmir Municipality
Project Date 2001
Location İzmir
Status Unbuilt

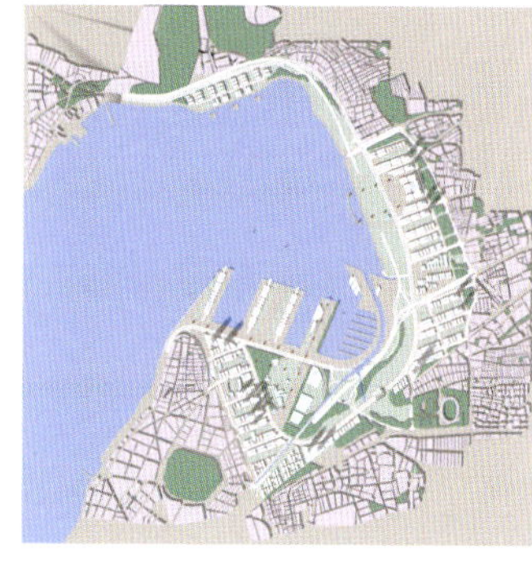

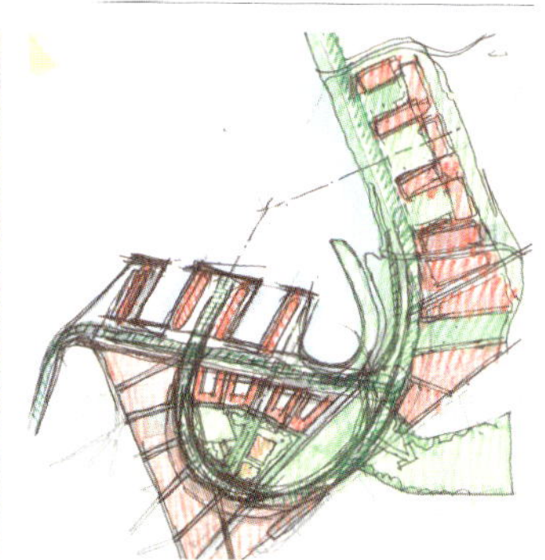

Congresium

Client Ankara Chamber of Commerce
Project Date 2001–2007
Area 80,490 m²
Location Ankara
Design Consultant Salih Bezci
Structural Engineer Yüksek Project
Mechanical Engineer Celal Okutan Engineering
Electrical Engineer Akay Engineering
Landscape Design Dalokay Design Studio
Project Manager Rüstem Gezen
Fire Consultant Alara Design and Engineering
Acoustic Consultant Prof. Dr. Mehmet Çalışkan
Sound/Light/Video System Consultant Yesa Electronics Systems
Contractor Ankara Chamber of Commerce
Status Built

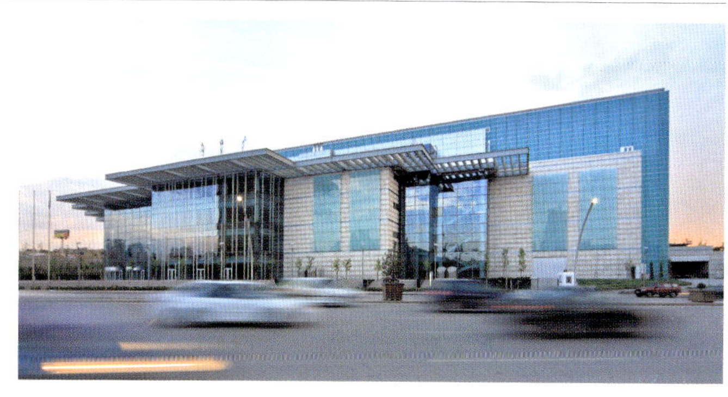

Metroport

Client Mutlu Evren Construction
Project Date 2001–2008
Area 100,000 m²
Location İstanbul
Structural Engineer Yüksek Project
Mechanical Engineer Çilingiroğlu Engineering
Electrical Engineer Elsan Electricity
Interior Design Dara Kızıltoprak
Contractor Mutlu Evren Construction
Status Built

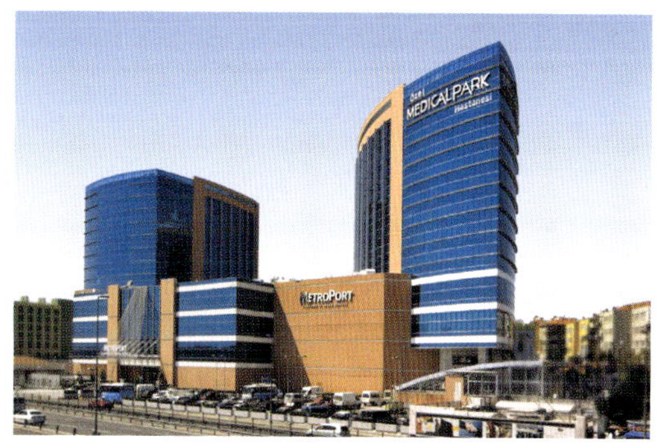

Tunalı Apartment

Client GESTAŞ
Project Date 2002–2004
Area 3,000 m²
Location Ankara
Structural Engineer Yüksek Project
Status Built

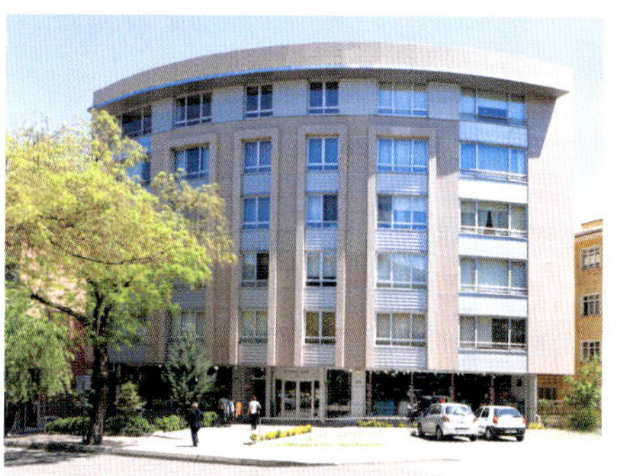

Arma Hotel

Client Besa Construction
Project Date 2002
Area 12,000 m²
Location Antalya
Design Consultant Salih Bezci, Vecihi Yıldız
Structural Engineer Yüksek Project
Mechanical Engineer Setes Engineering
Electrical Engineer Akay Engineering
Status Built

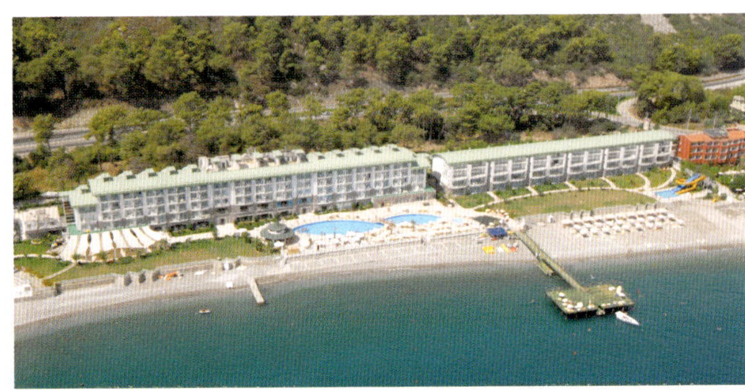

Ataport

Client Rönesans & Koçhan Consortium
Project Date 2002
Area 2,500,000 m²
Location İstanbul
Status Unbuilt

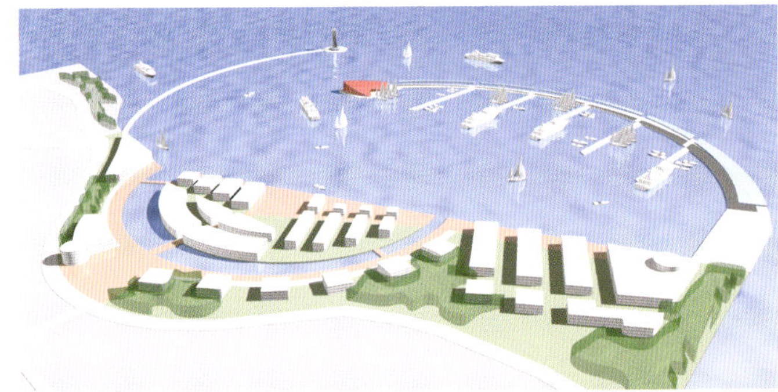

Ata Plaza

Client Platin Construction
Project Date 2002
Area 40,000 m²
Location Ankara
Structural Engineer Yüksek Project
Mechanical Engineer Akay Engineering
Electrical Engineer Okutan Engineering
Status Built

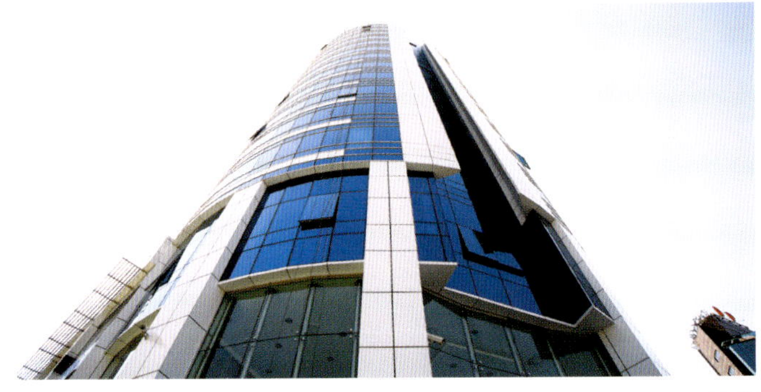

Bayraktar Business Center

Client Bayraktar Construction
Project Date 2003
Area 50,000 m²
Location Ankara
Structural Engineer Yüksek Project
Mechanical Engineer Okutan Engineering
Electrical Engineer Akay Engineering
Contractor Bayraktar Construction
Status Built

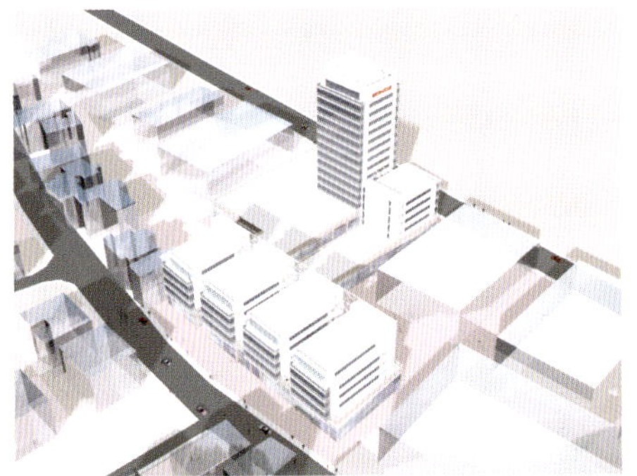

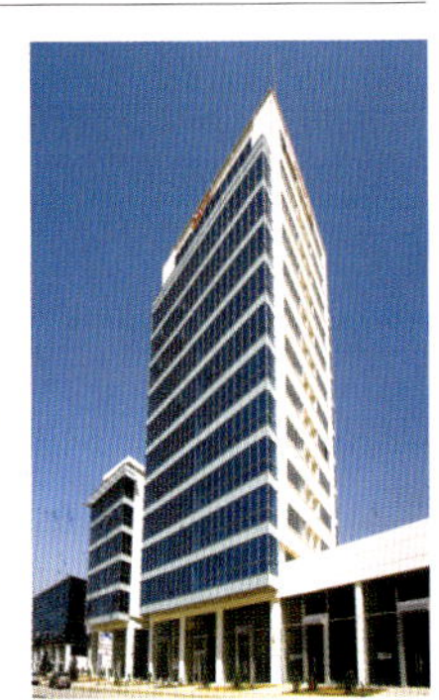

Via/Life

Client Bayraktar Construction
Project Date 2003
Area 42,000 m²
Location Ankara
Structural Engineer Yüksek Project
Mechanical Engineer BTC Engineering
Electrical Engineer BTC Engineering
Contractor Bayraktar Construction
Status Built

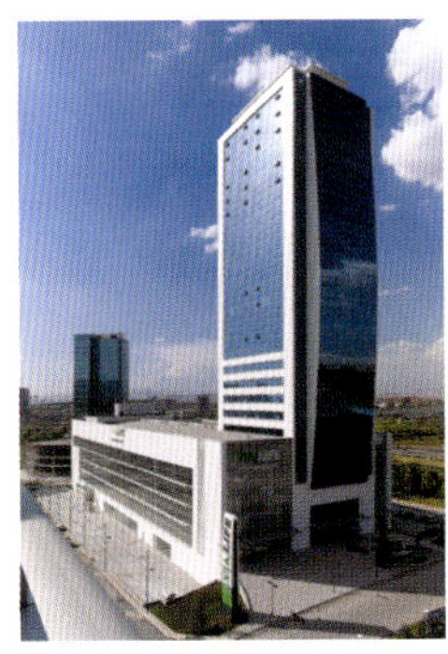

TOBB University of Economics and Technology Campus

Client TOBB University of Economics and Technology
Project Date 2003
Area 31,000 m^2
Location Ankara
Structural Engineer Yüksek Project
Mechanical Engineer Okutan Engineering
Electrical Engineer Akay Engineering
Landscape Design On Design
Consulting Firm Tür-Sum Construction, Yüksel Project International Inc.
Construction Manager Seviye Akı
Contractor Yavuzlar Construction Inc.
Status Built

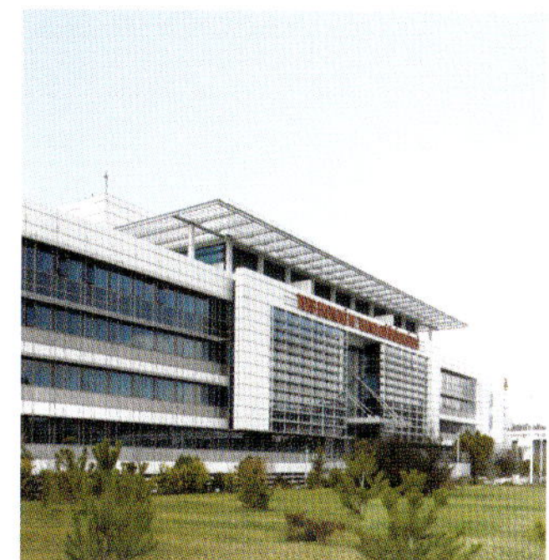

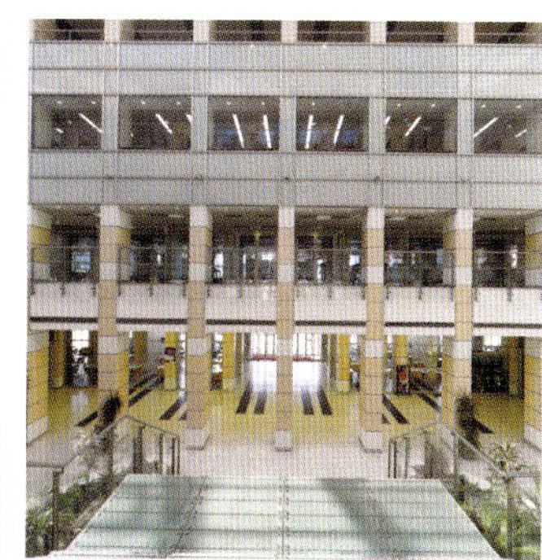

METU Silicon Block

Client METU
Project Date 2003
Area 8,440 m^2
Location Ankara
Structural Engineer Yüksek Project
Mechanical Engineer Okutan Engineering
Electrical Engineer Akay Engineering
Status Unbuilt

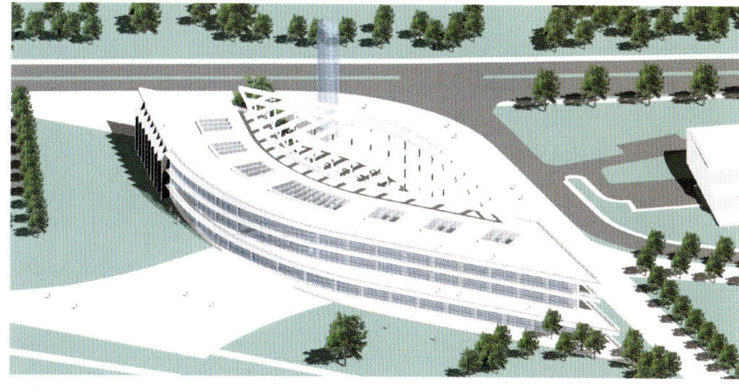

TOBB University of Economics and Technology Sports Complex

Client TOBB University of Economics and Technology
Project Date 2004
Area 31,000 m^2
Location Ankara
Structural Engineer Yüksek Project
Electrical Engineer Akay Engineering
Consulting Firm Yüksel Project International Inc.
Contractor Koçoğlu Inc.
Status Built

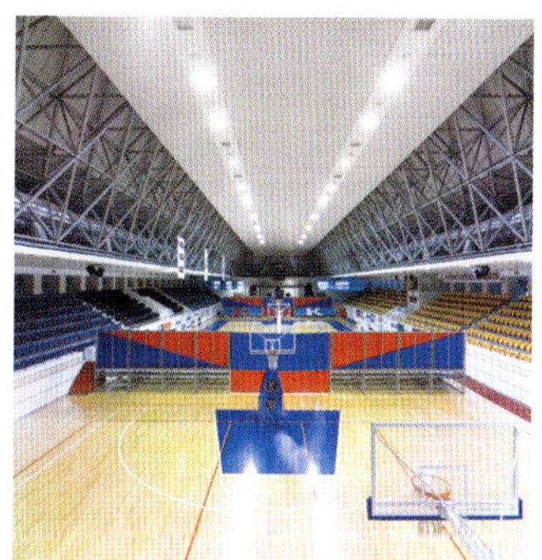

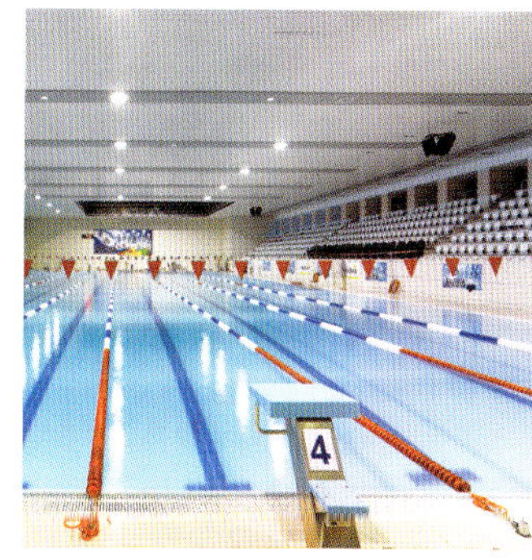

Mesa Plaza

Client MESA Housing Industries Inc.
Project Date 2004
Area 19,800 m^2
Location Ankara
Architectural Design A Architectural Design, Mesa Design Group
Structural Engineer Mesa Housing Industries, Yüksek Project
Mechanical Engineer Mesa Mechanical Group, Beşeli Engineering
Electrical Engineer Mesa Electrical Group
Contractor Mesa Housing Industries Inc.
Status Built

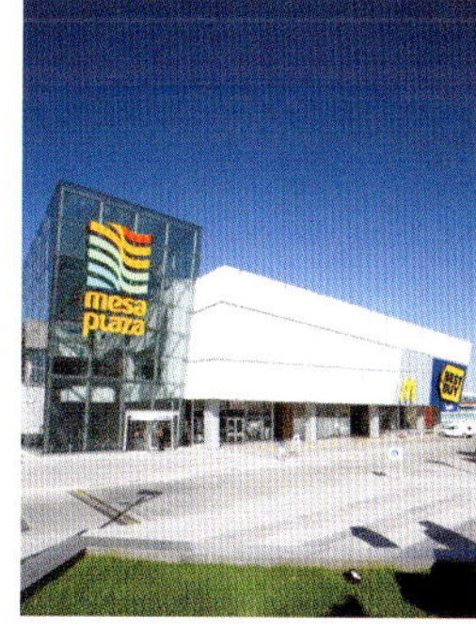

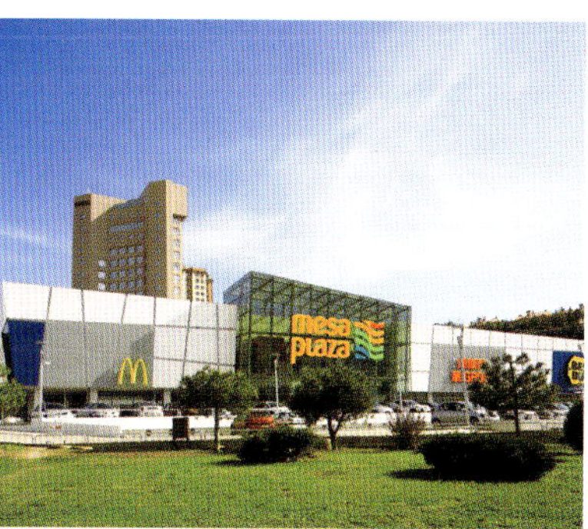

Kayseri Park

Client Doruk Furniture
Project Date 2004–2005
Area 40,000 m^2
Location Kayseri
Structural Engineer Yüksek Project
Mechanical Engineer BTC Engineering
Electrical Engineer Seferoglu Engineering
Status Built

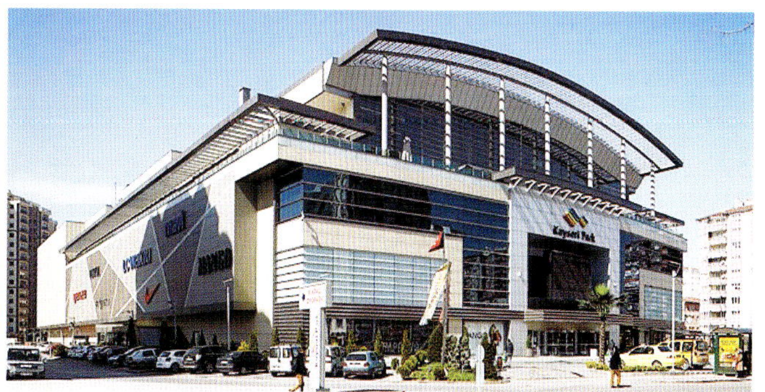

Kipaş High School Campus

Client Kipaş Holding
Project Date 2004
Area 23,200 m^2
Location Kahramanmaraş
Structural Engineer Yüksek Project
Mechanical Engineer Okutan Engineering
Electrical Engineer Akay Engineering
Status Built

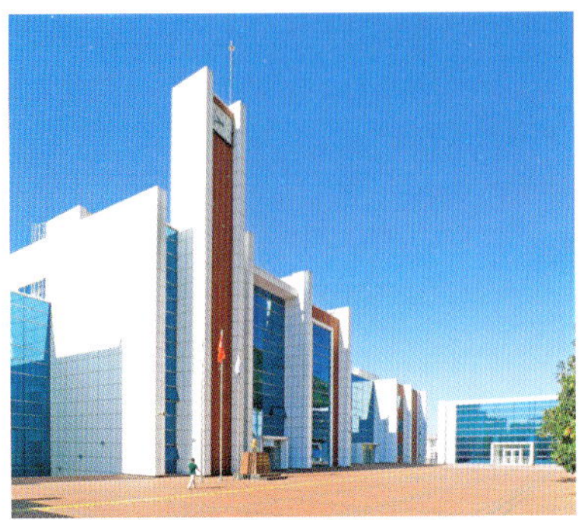

İpek Furniture Showroom

Client Adanır Logistics
Project Date 2004
Area 12,000 m^2
Location Ankara
Structural Engineer Yüksek Project
Mechanical Engineer Okutan Engineering
Electrical Engineer Akay Engineering
Status Built

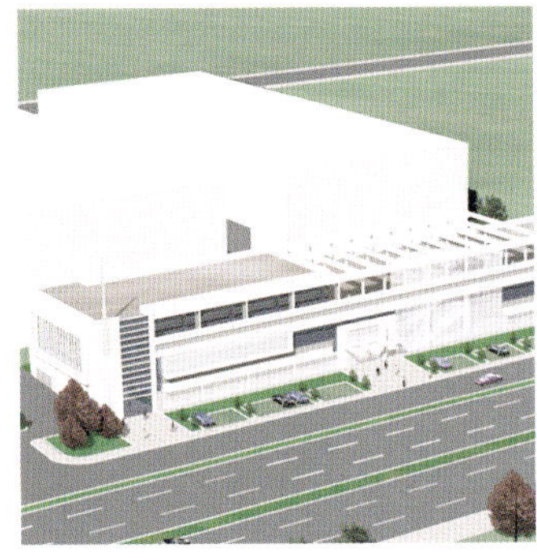

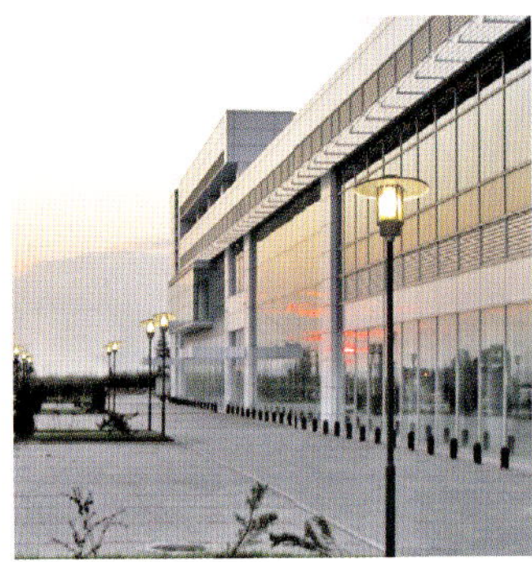

TEPAV

Client TOBB University of Economics and Technology
Project Date 2004
Area 6,000 m^2
Location Ankara
Structural Engineer Yüksek Project
Mechanical Engineer Okutan Engineering
Electrical Engineer Akay Engineering
Consulting Firm Yüksel Project International Inc.
Contractor Koçoğlu Inc.
Status Built

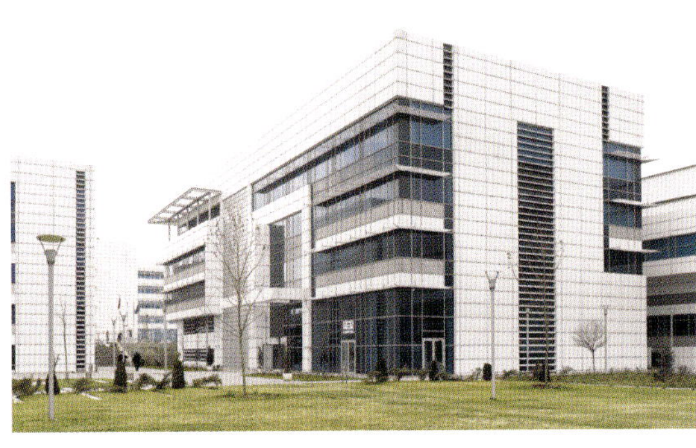

Tüzün

Client Tüzün
Project Date 2004
Area 6,330 m^2
Location Ankara
Renovation Project A Architectural Project
Structural Engineer Yüksek Project
Mechanical Engineer Melis Engineering
Status Built

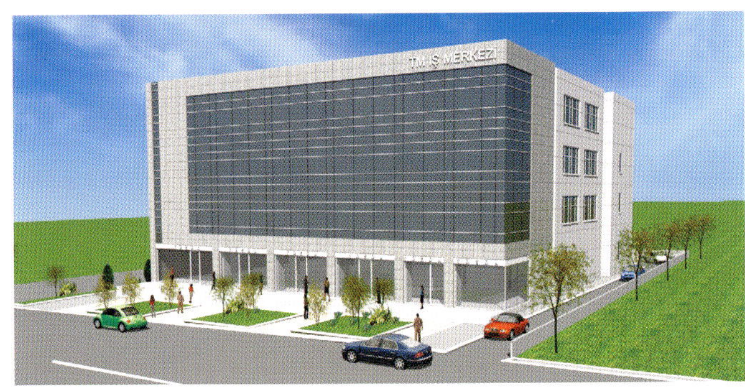

Via/Port

Client Bayraktar Construction
Project Date 2004–2007
Area Outlet 90,000 m^2, Convention and Exhibition Center 120,000 m^2, Hotel 42,000 m^2
Location İstanbul
Structural Engineer Yüksek Project
Mechanical Engineer BTC Engineering
Electrical Engineer BTC Engineering
Contractor Bayraktar Construction
2009 AMPD Foundation for Shopping Malls and Retailers Mall of the Year
2010 ICSC Finalist
2010 Cityscape Abu Dhabi Best Commercial/Retail Project Category Finalist
Status Built

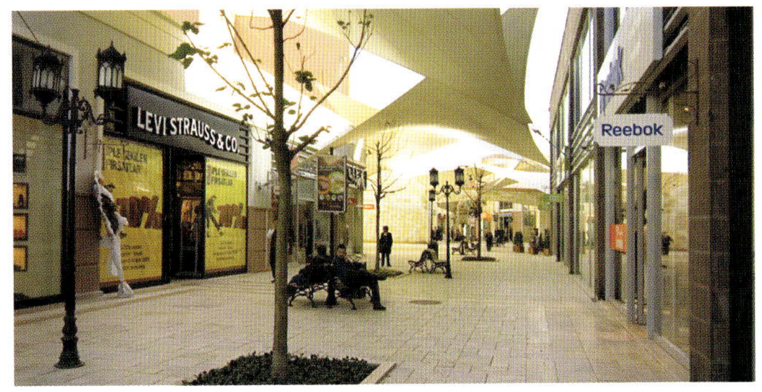

Ziraat Bank Kadıköy Branch

Client Ziraat Bank General Directorate
Project Date 2004
Area 4,000 m^2
Location İstanbul
Structural Engineer Yüksek Project
Mechanical Engineer Okutan Engineering
Electrical Engineer Akay Engineering
Status Built

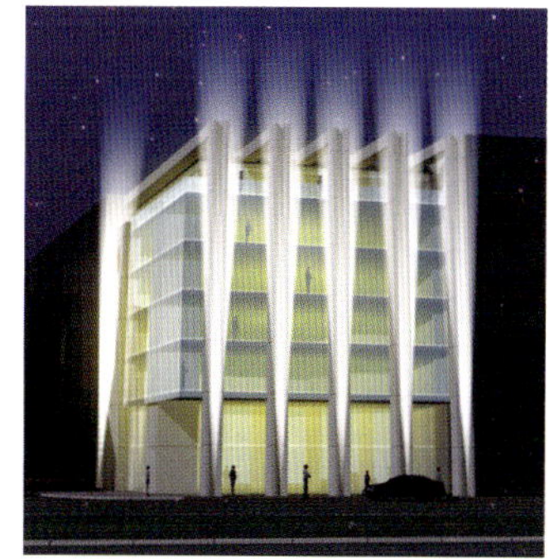

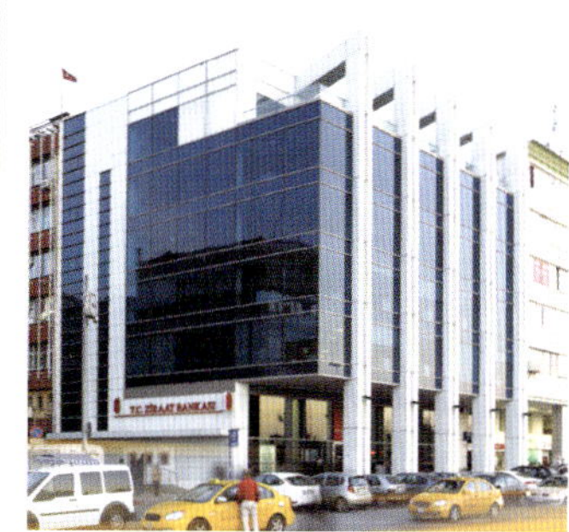

Panora

Client Merkez Construction, Tourism and Management Inc.
Project Date 2004–2007
Area 180,000 m^2
Location Ankara
Design Consultant Salih Bezci, Vecihi Yıldız
Construction Supervisor Sonay Ozar
Structural Engineer Yüksek Project
Mechanical Engineer GMD Engineering
Electrical Engineer Yurdakul Engineering
Landscape Design Dalokay Design Studio
Leasing Consultant Jones Lang LaSalle Turkey
Contractor Merkez Construction, Tourism and Management Inc.
Status Built
2004 ICSC (International Council of Shopping Centres)
European Shopping Center Awards Certificate of Merit

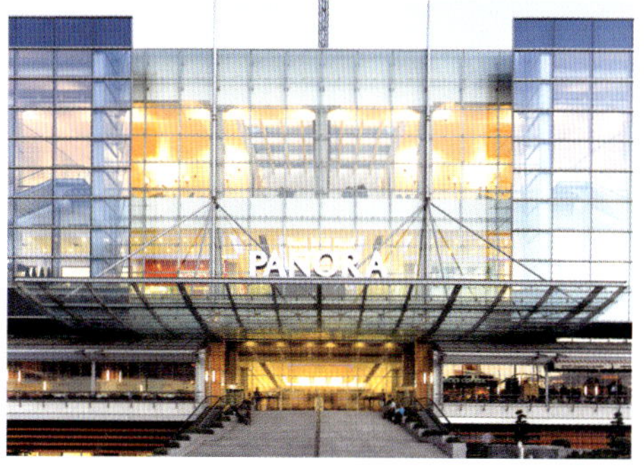

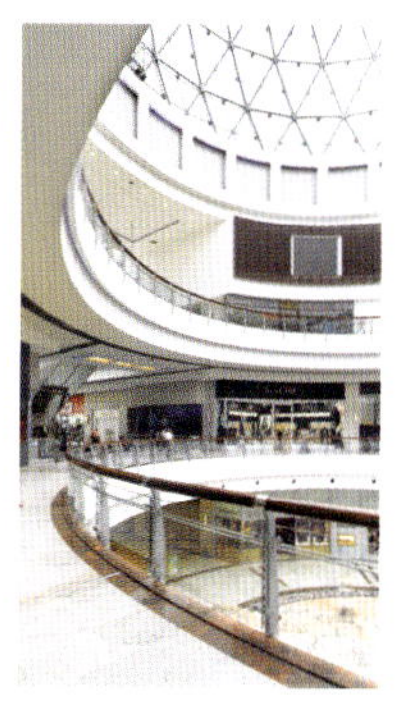

Armada Development Project

Client Söğütözü Construction Management Inc.
Project Date 2004–2010
Area 80,000 m^2
Location Ankara
Design Consultant Salih Bezci
Structural Engineer Yüksek Project
Mechanical Engineer Metta Engineering
Electrical Engineer Akay Engineering
Landscape Design Promim Urban and Environmental Design
Construction Supervisor Sonay Ozar
Fire Consultant Karina
Leasing Consultant Jones Lang LaSalle Turkey
Contractor Söğütözü Construction Management Inc.
Status Built

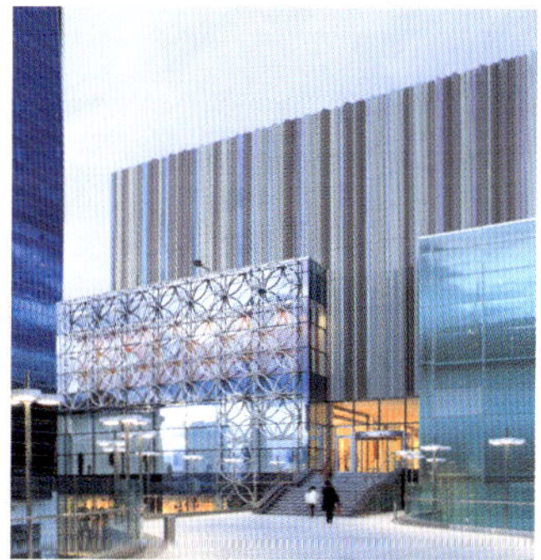

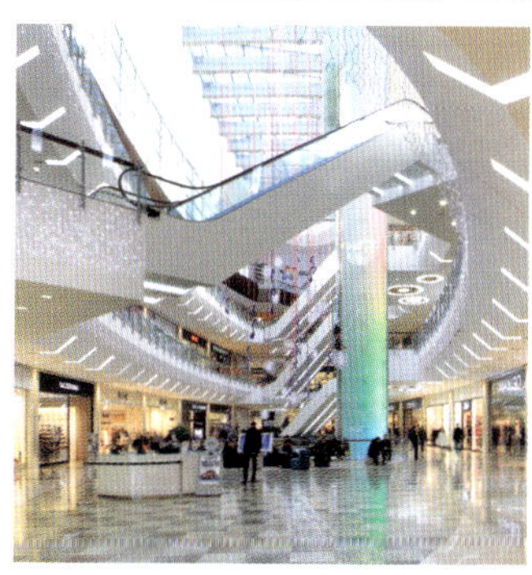

TOBB University of Economics and Technology Student Guesthouses

Client TOBB University of Economics and Technology
Project Date 2004
Area 70,000 m^2
Location Ankara
Structural Engineer Yüksek Project
Mechanical Engineer Okutan Engineering
Electrical Engineer Akay Engineering
Landscape Design On Design
Consulting Firm Tür-Sum Construction
Construction Manager Mustafa Tekinel
Contractor Ender Construction
Status Built

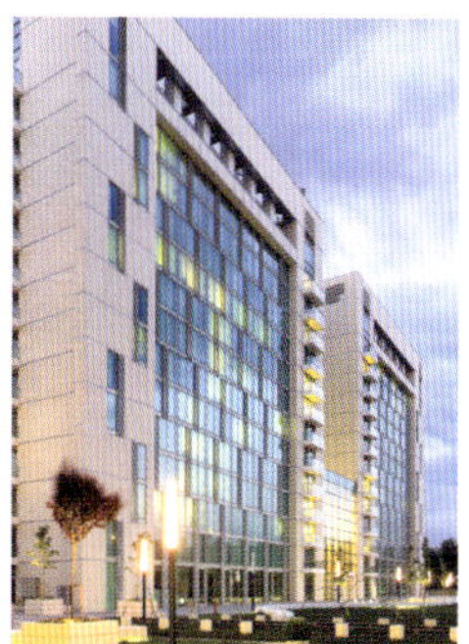

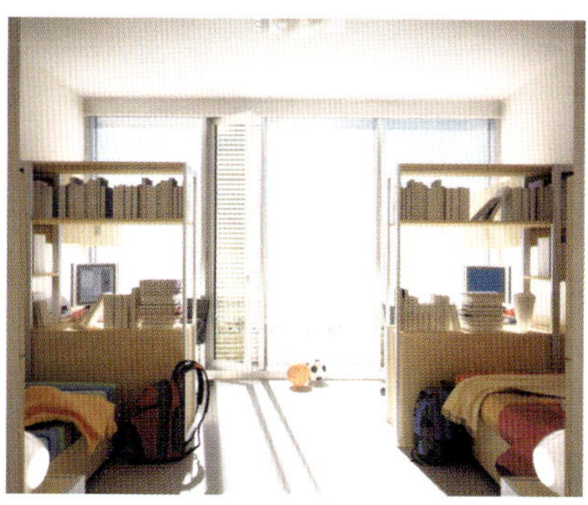

İstanbul Courthouse-Anatolian Side

Client The Foundation of Justice Organization
Project Date 2004
Area 210,000 m^2
Location İstanbul
Structural Engineer Yüksek Project
Mechanical Engineer Okutan Engineering
Electrical Engineer Akay Engineering
Status Unbuilt

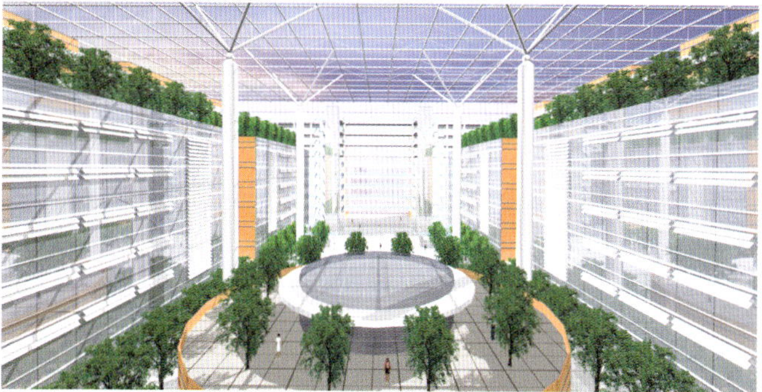

TOBB Twin Towers Repurposing

Client TOBB
Project Date 2004
Area 95,000 m²
Location Ankara
Architectural Design Umut İnan
Repurposing Project A Tasarım Mimarlık
Structural Engineer Yüksek Project
Mechanical Engineer Akdeniz Engineering
Electrical Engineer Akay Engineering
Consultancy Firm Türsum Construction
Status Built

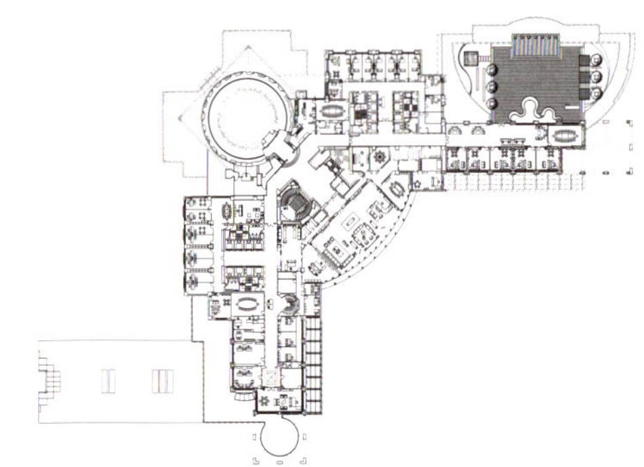

TOBB University of Economics and Technology Masterplan

Client TOBB University of Economics and Technology
Project Date 2004
Planned Area 300,000 m²
Location Ankara
Status Ongoing

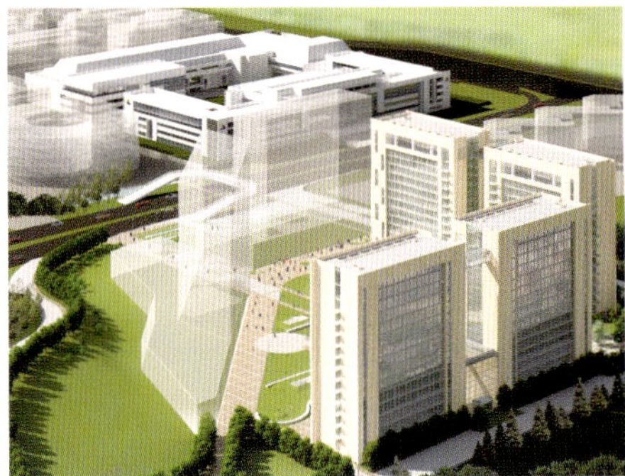

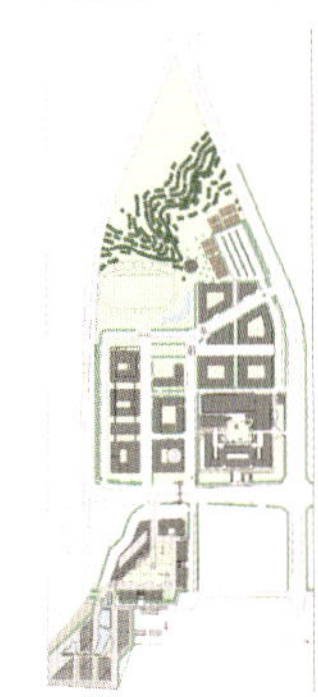

Barutçuoğlu Shopping Center and Municipality Building

Client Barutçuoğlu Construction
Project Date 2005
Area 20,000 m²
Location Kastamonu
Structural Engineer Yüksek Project
Mechanical Engineer Okutan Engineering
Electrical Engineer Akay Engineering
Status Built

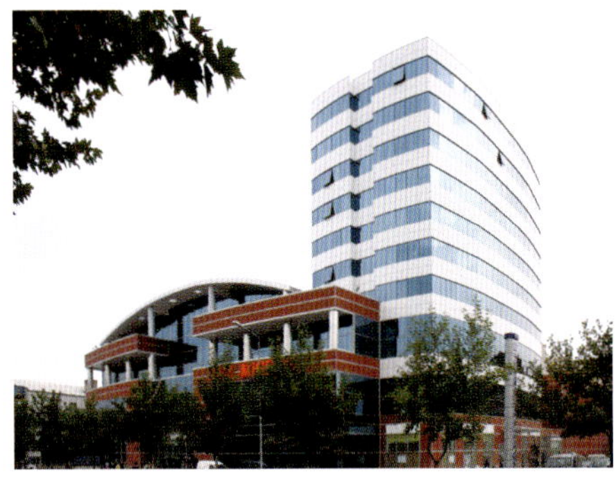

İstoç C Block

Client İSTOÇ Building Society
Project Date 2005
Area 25,000 m²
Location İstanbul
Structural Engineer Yüksek Project
Mechanical and Electrical Engineer Aslı Engineering
Status Unbuilt

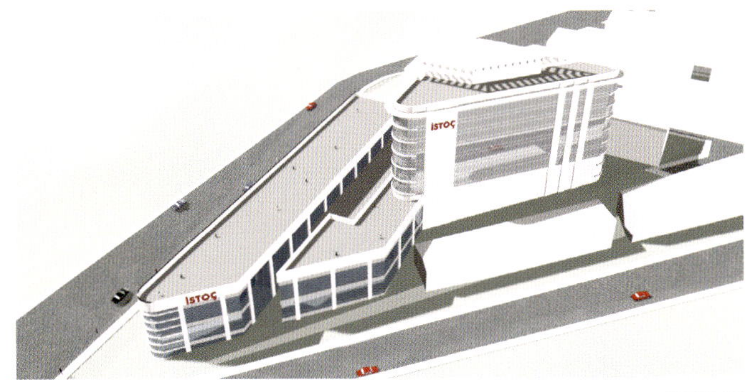

Antares

Client Dolunay Forest Trade Ltd.
Project Date 2005
Area 222,205 m²
Location Ankara
Structural Engineer Yüksek Project
Mechanical Engineer GMD Engineering
Electrical Engineer Yurdakul Engineering
Landscape Design Dalokay Design Studio
Fire Consultant Alara Design and Engineering
Leasing Consultant Metro, Jones Lang LaSalle Turkey
Contractor Dolunay Forest Trade Ltd.
Status Built

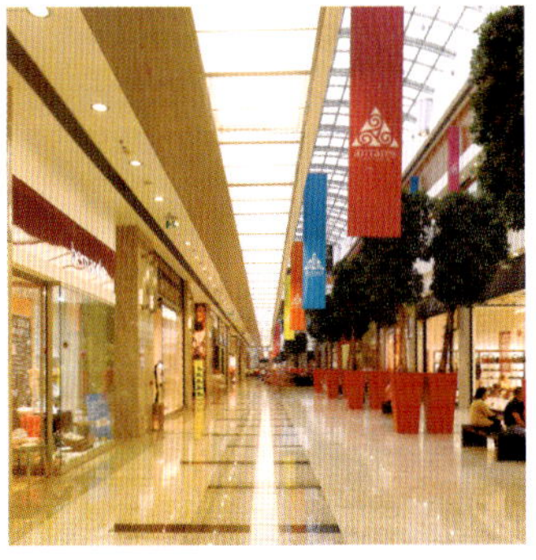

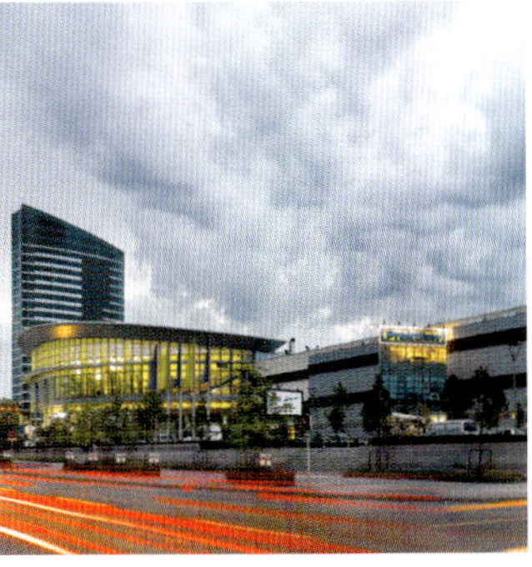

METU Titanium Block

Client METU
Project Date 2005
Area 3,780 m²
Location Ankara
Status Unbuilt

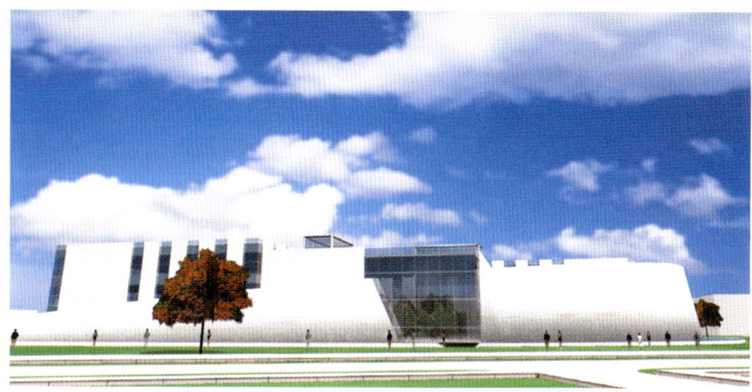

METU Gallium Block

Client METU
Project Date 2005
Area 8,410 m²
Location Ankara
Structural Engineer Yüksek Project
Mechanical Engineer Okutan Engineering
Electrical Engineer Akay Engineering
Status Unbuilt

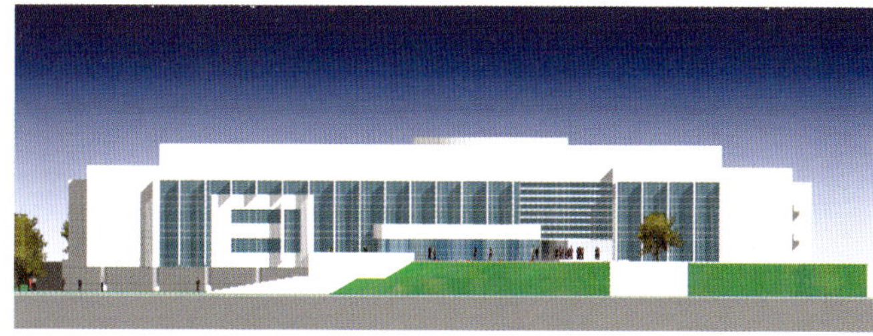

Antares Housing

Client Dolunay Forest Trade Ltd.
Project Date 2005–2007
Area 206,359 m²
Location Ankara
Structural Engineer Dumanoğlu Engineering
Mechanical Engineer Aydın Bingöl
Electrical Engineer Promete Engineering
Landscape Design Dalokay Design Studio
Fire Consultant Alara Project
Contractor Dolunay Forest Trade Ltd.
Status Ongoing

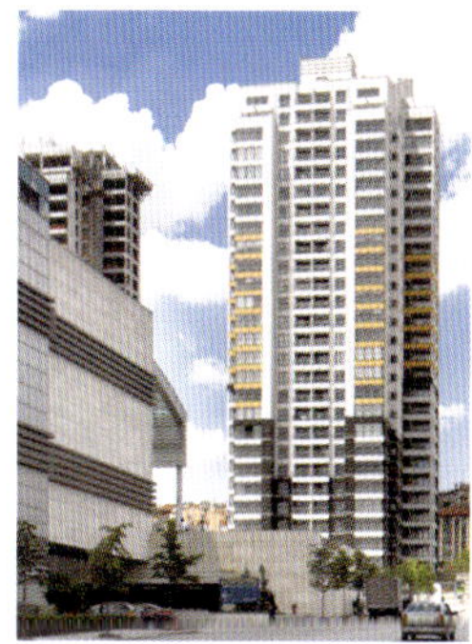

Medicana

Client Gözüm Construction
Project Date 2006
Area 15,000 m²
Structural Engineer Güncel Engineering
Mechanical–Electrical Engineer BTC Engineering
Status Built

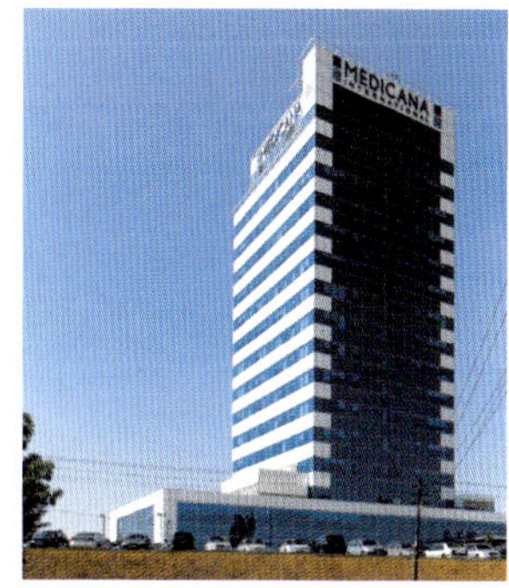

Gökyüzü Residence

Client Keleşoğlu Construction Tourism
Project Date 2006
Area 23,000 m²
Location İstanbul
Structural Engineer Osman Tatlısu
Mechanical Engineer Mehmet Demiroğlu
Electrical Engineer Recai Bulan
Contractor Keleşoğlu Construction Tourism
Status Built

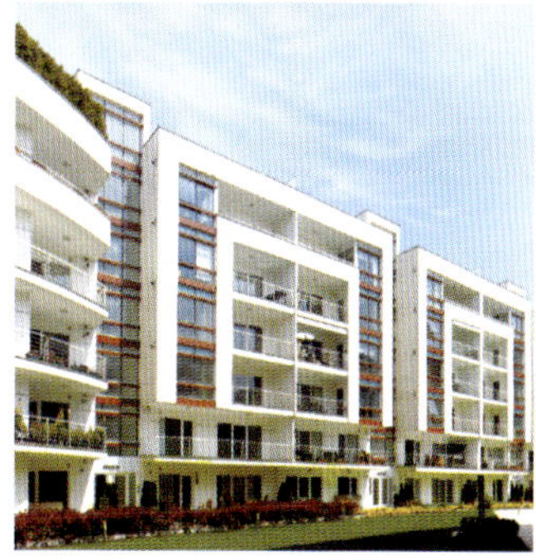

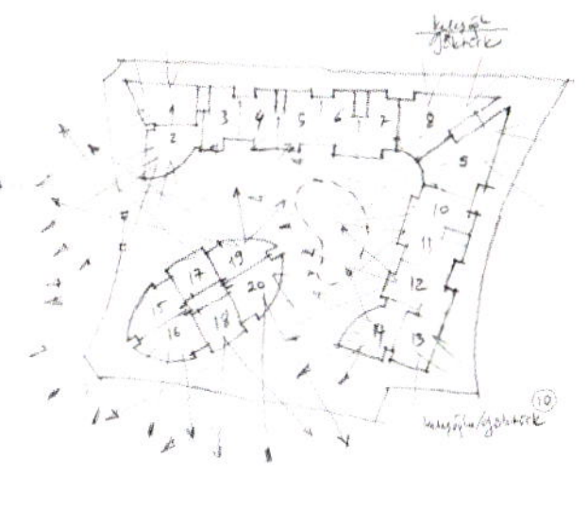

İstanbul Courthouse-European Side

Client The Foundation of Justice Organization
Project Date 2006
Area 210,000 m^2
Location Istanbul
Structural Engineer Yüksek Project
Mechanical Engineer Okutan Engineering
Electrical Engineer Akay Engineering
Status Unbuilt

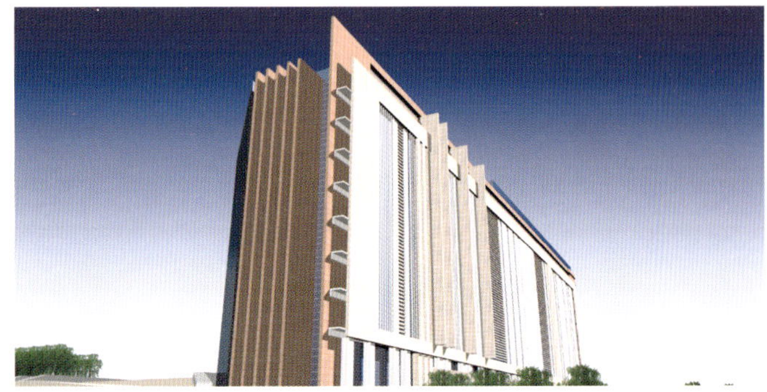

Ömer Çobanoğlu House

Client Dr. Ömer Çobanoğlu
Project Date 2006
Area 1,850 m^2
Location Ankara
Structural Engineer Yüksek Project
Mechanical Engineer Okutan Engineering
Electrical Engineer Yurdakul Engineering
Status Unbuilt

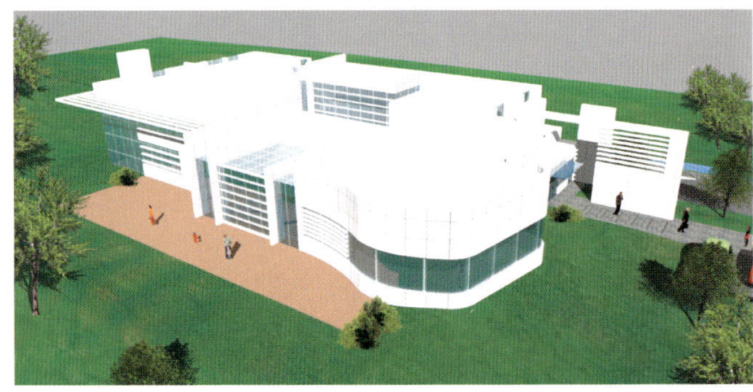

Zeugma Center

Client Akfen Holding
Project Date 2006
Area 86,000 m^2
Status Unbuilt

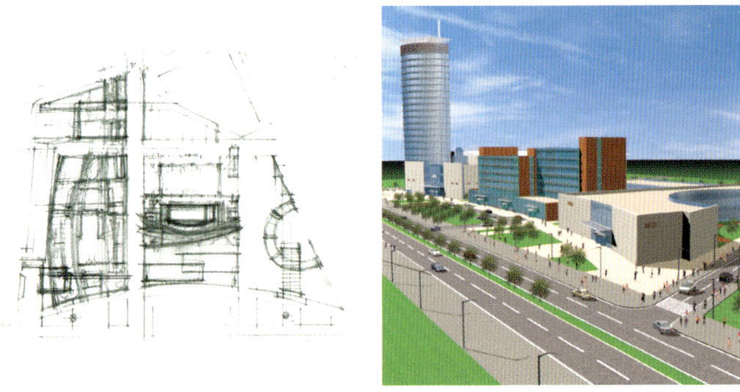

Tepe Prime

Client Tepe Construction Inc.
Project Date 2007
Area 92,750 m^2
Location Ankara
Project Director Fehmi Çataltepe
Structural Engineer Yüksek Project
Mechanical Engineer GMD Engineering
Electrical Engineer Yurdakul Engineering
Landscape Design Dalokay Design Studio
Fire Consultant Alara Design and Engineering
Contractor Tepe Construction Inc.
Construction Supervisor Tepe Construction Team
Status Built
2012 Arkiparc Mixed-Use Category Finalist, 2013 Global RLI Awards International Retail and Leisure Destination Category Finalist

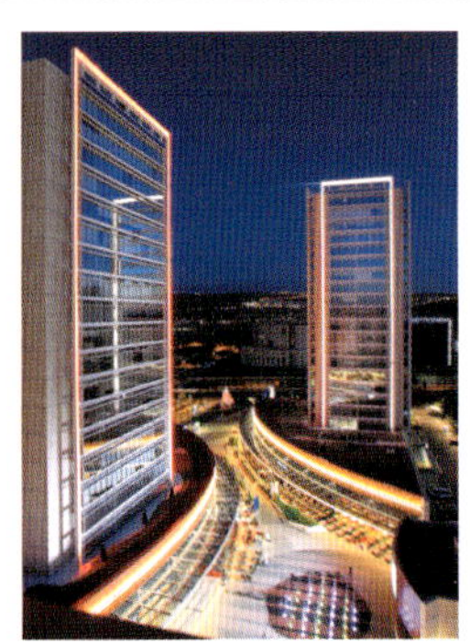

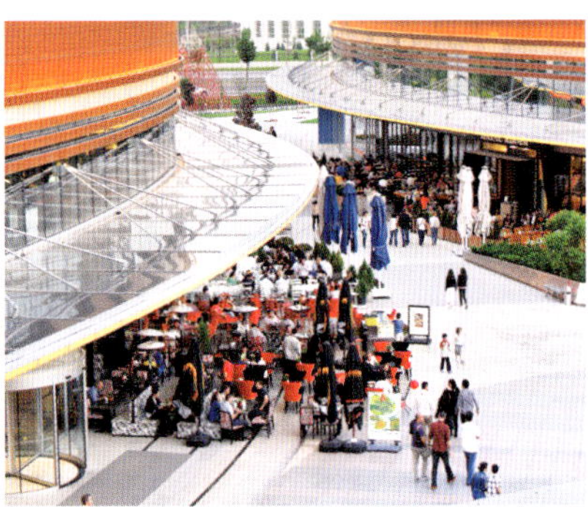

Baku Marina and Public Park

Client Asnaf-Alkon
Project Date 2007
Area 179,500 m^2
Location Baku, Azerbaijan
Status Unbuilt

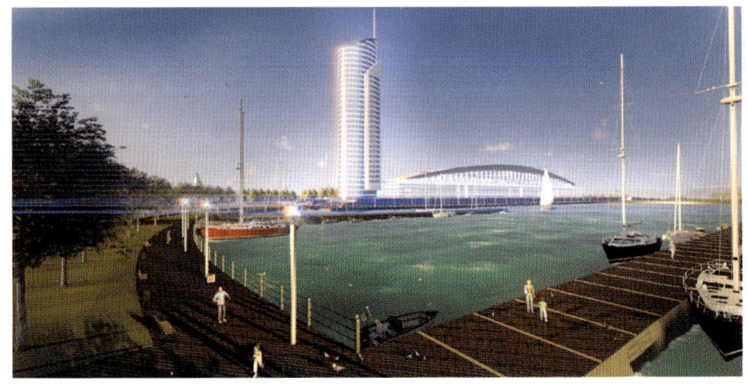

Akgül Office

Client Akgül Construction
Project Date 2007
Area 18,715 m²
Location Ankara
Structural Engineer Güncel Engineering
Mechanical Engineer BTC Engineering
Electrical Engineer Özer Engineering
Contractor Akgül Construction
Status Built

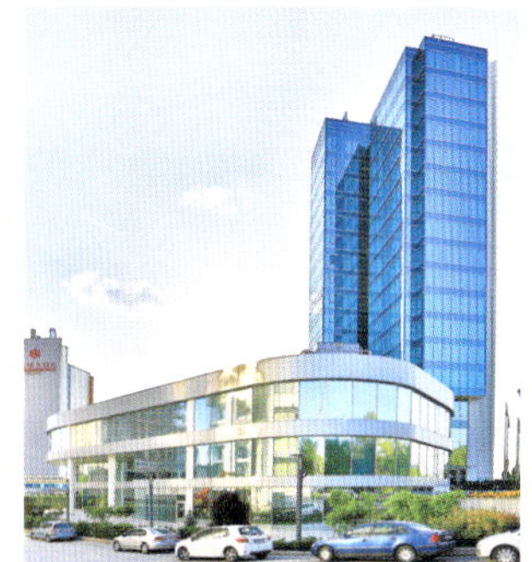

Zeki Demirci Business Center

Client Ekol
Project Date 2007
Area 24,250 m²
Location Ankara
Structural Engineer Yüksek Project
Mechanical Engineer Akay Engineering
Electrical Engineer Setes Engineering
Contractor Platin Construction
Status Built

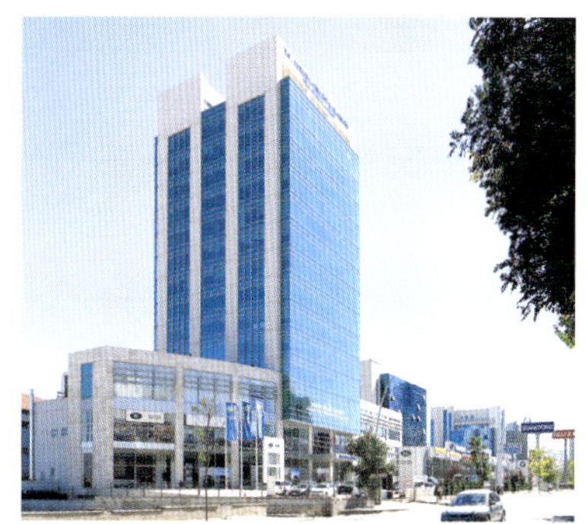

Şahinler

Client Şahinler Holding
Project Date 2007
Area 320,000 m²
Location İstanbul
Status Unbuilt

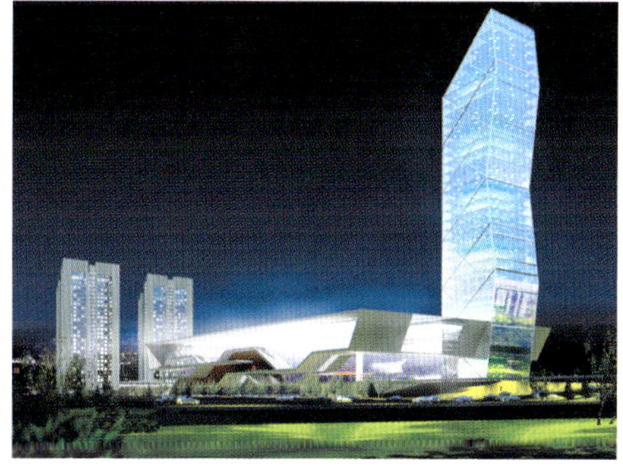

Nata Delta

Client Nata Group
Project Date 2007
Area 167,000 m²
Location Ankara
Status Unbuilt

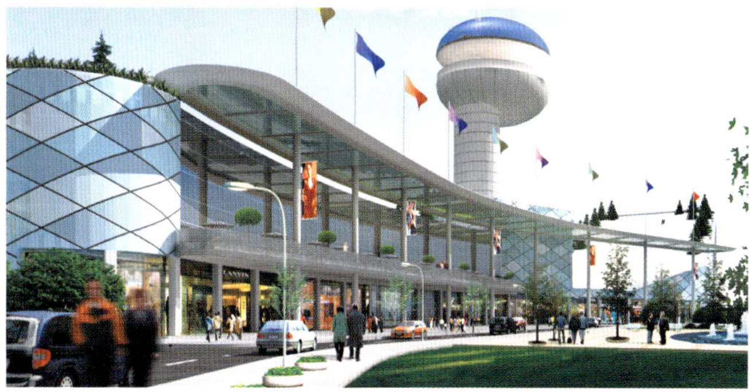

Ginza Lavinya

Client Keleşoğlu Grup, Kullar Construction
Project Date 2007
Area 95,000 m²
Location İstanbul
Structural Engineer Gündüz Çetemen
Mechanical Engineer Cengiz Erturhan
Electrical Engineer Hakan Yüksel, Enver Şengüler
Landscape Design Dalokay Design Studio
Contractor Keleşoğlu Grup, Kullar Construction
Status Built

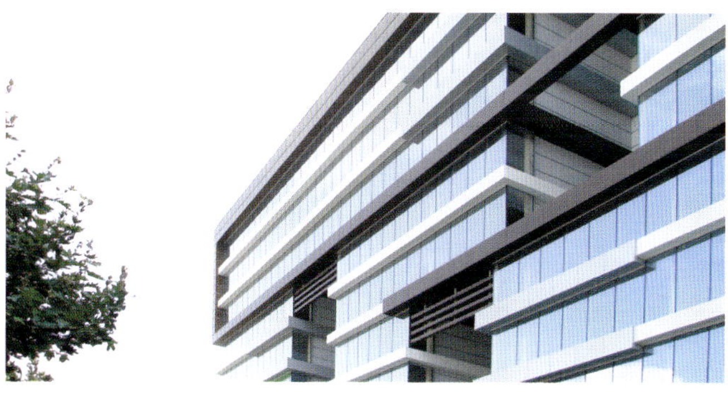

Limak Euroasia Hotel
Client Limak Holding
Project Date 2007
Area 20,000 m²
Location Ankara
Structural Engineer Yüksek Project
Mechanical Engineer Wemeks Engineering
Electrical Engineer Melyap Engineering
Contractor Limak Holding
Status Built

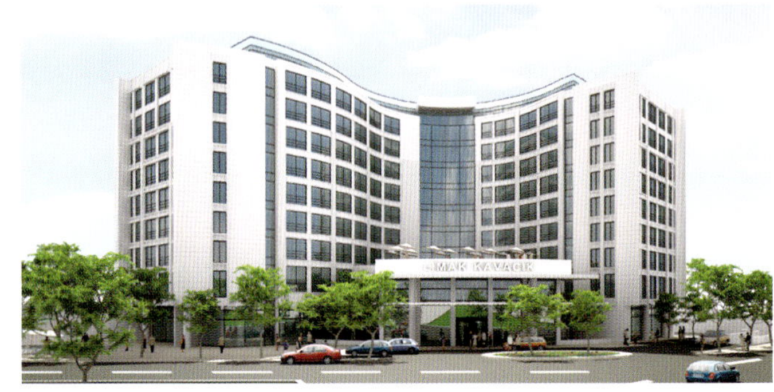

İncekara Headquarters
Client Incekara Holding
Project Date 2007
Area 5,300 m²
Location Ankara
Structural Engineer Yüksek Project
Mechanical Engineer Setes Engineering
Electrical Engineer Akay Engineering
Status Unbuilt

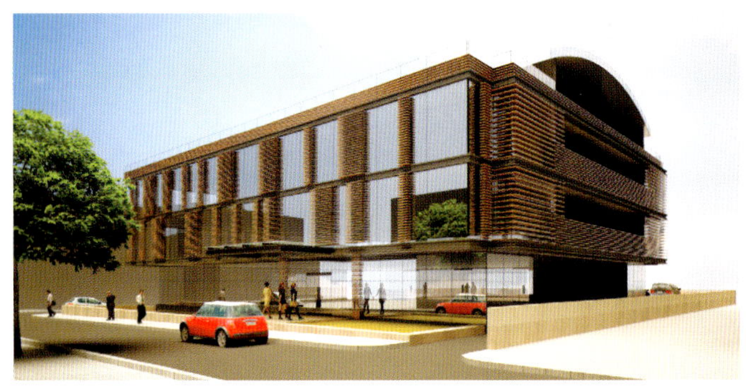

Edirne Courthouse
Client Republic of Turkey Ministry of Justice
Project Date 2007
Area 39,500 m²
Location Edirne
Status Unbuilt

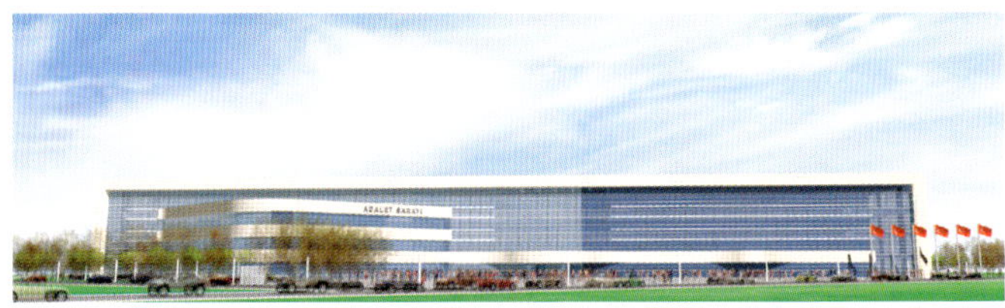

Via/Port Hotel
Client Bayraktar Construction
Project Date 2007
Area 42,000 m²
Location İstanbul
Structural Engineer Yüksek Project
Mechanical Engineer BTC Engineering
Electrical Engineer BTC Engineering
Construction Bayraktar Construction
Status Built

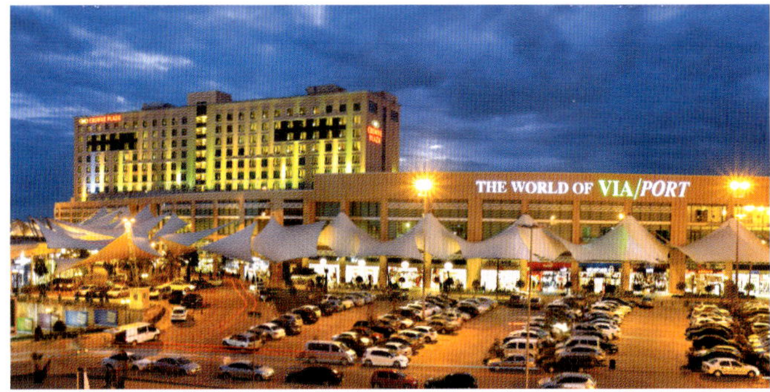

Ankara Courthouse Extension Building
Client Republic of Turkey Ministry of Justice
Project Date 2008
Area 166,105 m²
Location Ankara
Status Unbuilt

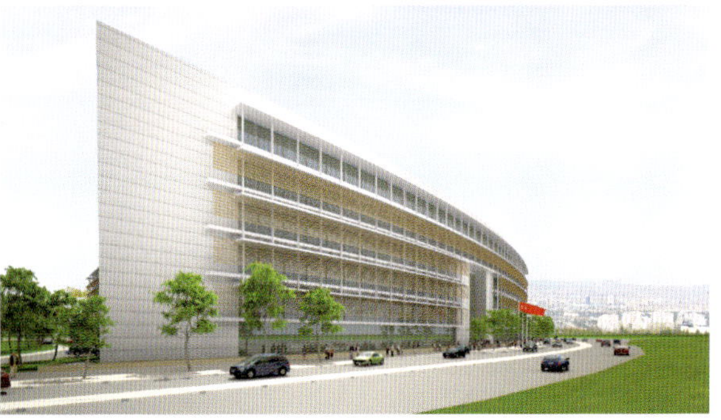

Kazıkiçi Bostanları Central Business District Master Plan

Client İskitler Union of Building Cooperatives
Project Date 2008
Lot Area 640,000 m²
Location Ankara
Status Ongoing

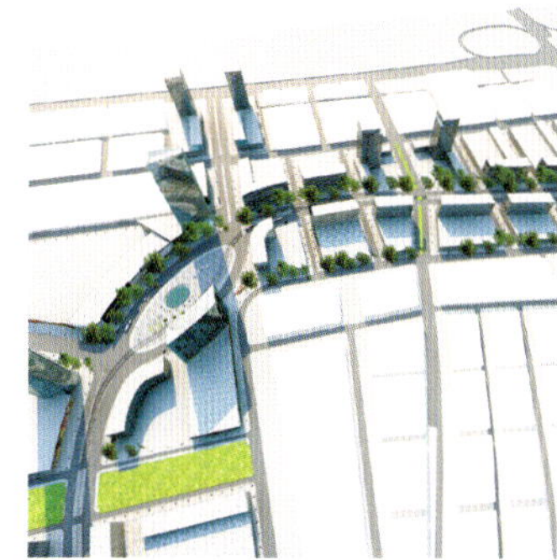

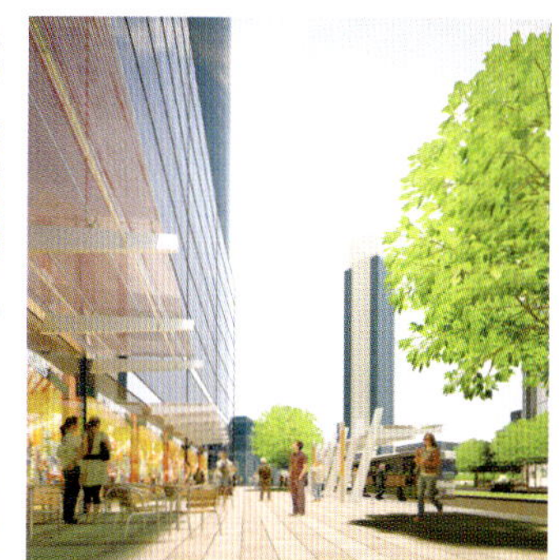

TOBB University of Economics and Technology School of Foreign Languages

Client TOBB University of Economics and Technology
Project Date 2008
Area 10,500 m²
Location Ankara
Structural Engineer Yüksek Project
Mechanical Engineer Okutan Engineering
Electrical Engineer Akay Engineering
Landscape Design On Design
Consulting Firm Tür-Sum Construction
Construction Manager Mustafa Tekinel
Contractor Tür-Sum Construction
Status Built

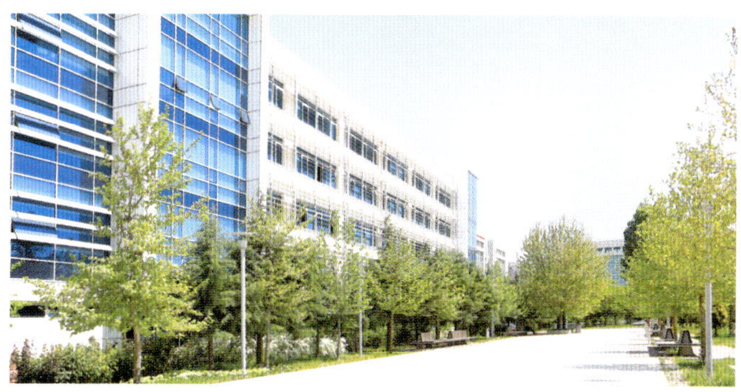

Çankırı Shopping Center

Client Yunus Inc.
Project Date 2008
Area 32,000 m²
Location Çankırı
Structural Engineer Yüksek Project
Mechanical Engineer Setes Engineering
Electrical Engineer Akay Engineering
Status Built

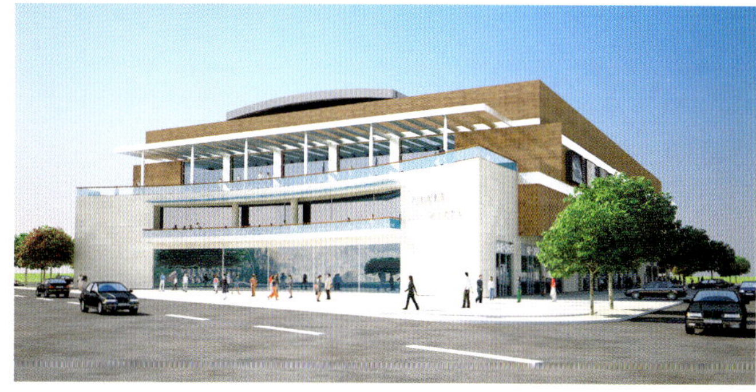

Güneşlipark

Client Gül Construction
Project Date 2008
Area 103,000 m²
Location Istanbul
Structural Engineer AS Engineering
Mechanical Engineer AMK Engineering
Electrical Engineer AKC Group
Landscape Design Spiga Landscape
Contractor Gül Constraction
Status Built

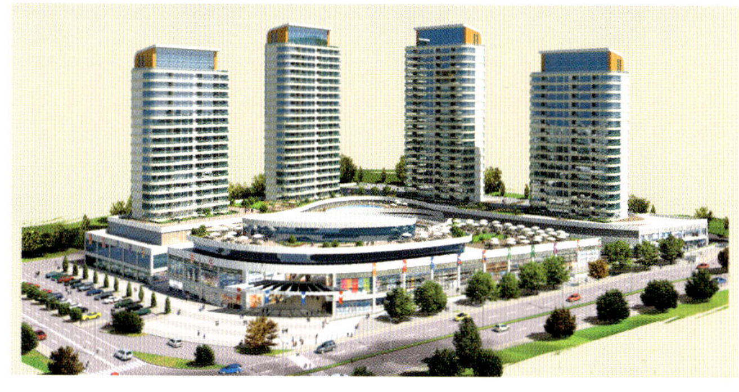

Farilya

Client Ufuk Mesken Construction
Project Date 2008
Area 25,415 m²
Location Ankara
Structural Engineer Yüksek Project
Mechanical Engineer BTC Engineering
Electrical Engineer BTC Engineering
Status Built

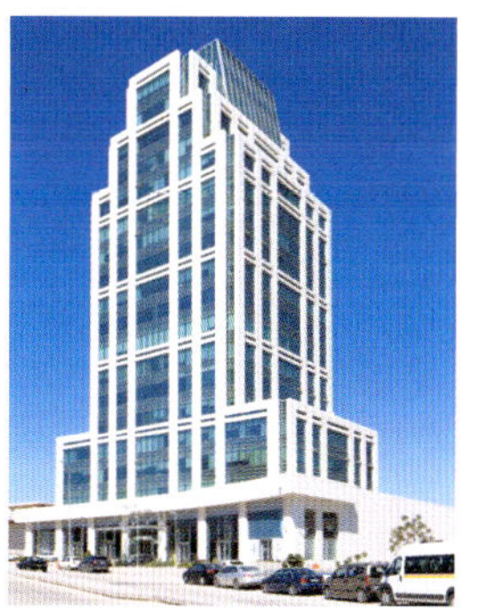

Ceylan Karavil Park

Client Ceylan Construction and Trade Co. Inc., Karavil Group
Project Date 2008
Area 210,000 m²
Location Diyarbakır
Structural Engineer Yüksek Project
Mechanical Engineer Setes Engineering
Electrical Engineer Akay Engineering
Landscape Design Dalokay Design Studio
Fire Consultant Alara Design and Engineering
Status Under construction

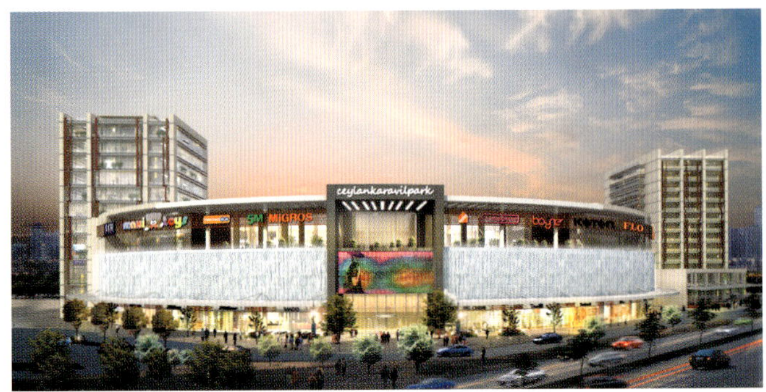

Osmaniye Shopping Center

Client Osmaniye Provincial Administration, Pekintaş Building
Project Date 2008
Area 42,840 m²
Location Osmaniye
Structural Engineer Yüksek Project
Mechanical Engineer Setes Engineering
Electrical Engineer Akay Engineering
Status Built

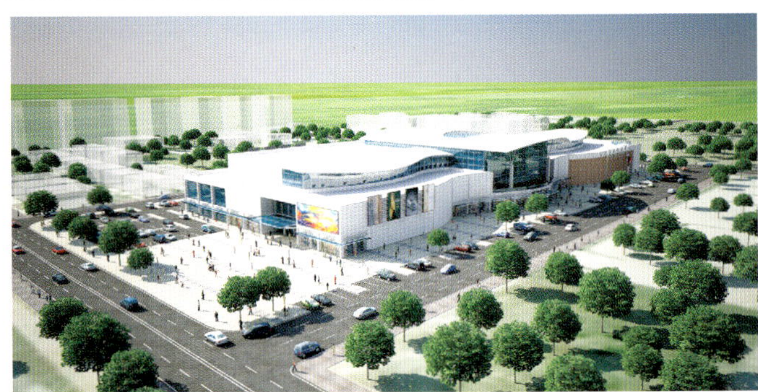

Kızılırmak Mixed-Use Center

Client Usta Construction
Project Date 2008
Area 97,695 m²
Location Ankara
Status Ongoing

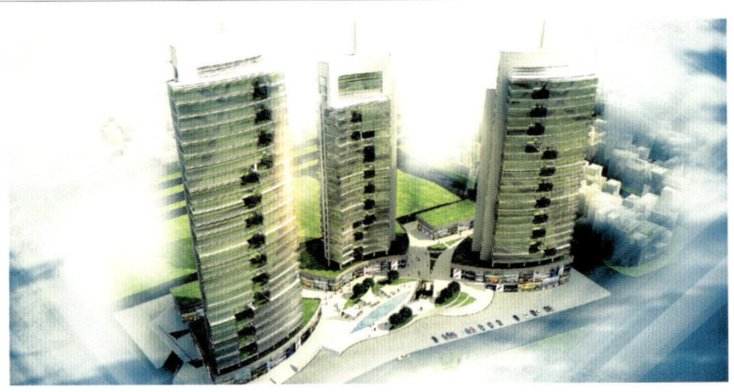

Tripoli Ministry Buildings

Client Gür-iş Construction and Engineering Inc.
Project Date 2008
Area 447,145 m²
Location Tripoli, Libya
Structural Engineering Yüksek Project
Mechanical Engineering Okutan Engineering
Electrical Engineering Akay Engineering
Landscape Design Dalokay Design Studio
Infrastructure Sigal Engineering
Status Unbuilt

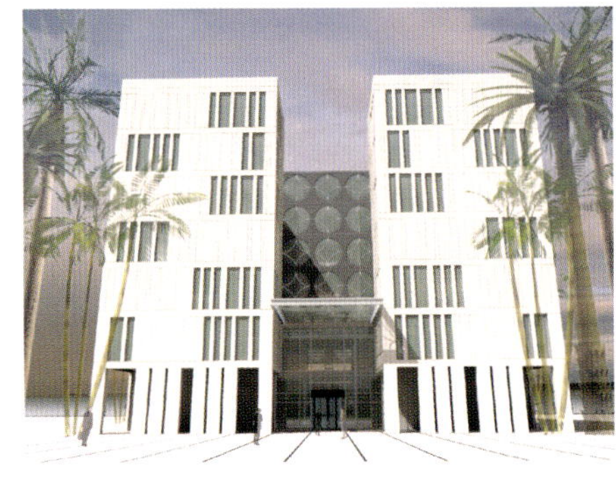

Tripoli Conference Center Mosque

Client Gür-iş Construction and Engineering Inc.
Project Date 2008
Area 2,000 m²
Location Tripoli, Libya
Status Unbuilt

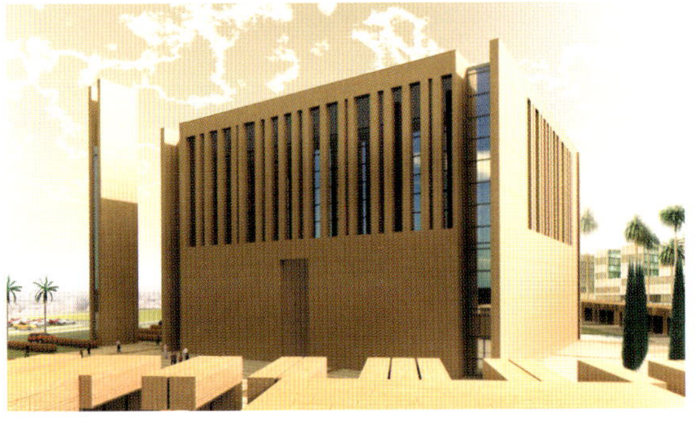

Çorlupark
Client Prokon
Project Date 2008
Area 120,000 m^2
Location Çorlu
Status Unbuilt

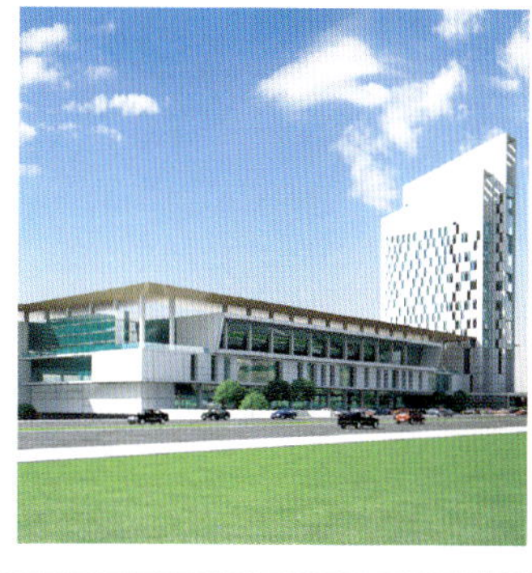
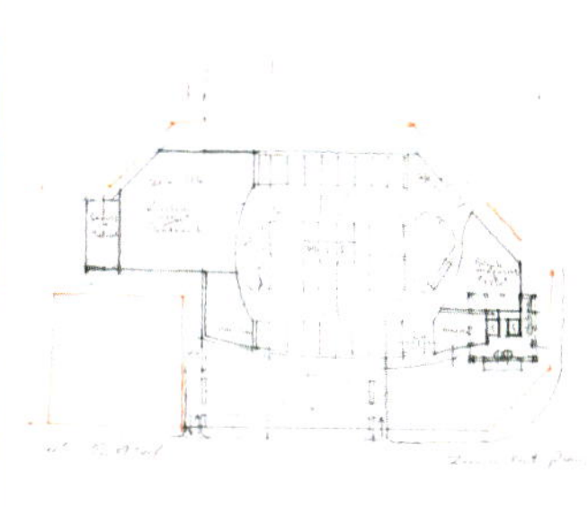

Turgut Plaza
Client Tepe Construction Inc.
Project Date 2008
Area 123,500 m^2
Location İstanbul
Status Unbuilt

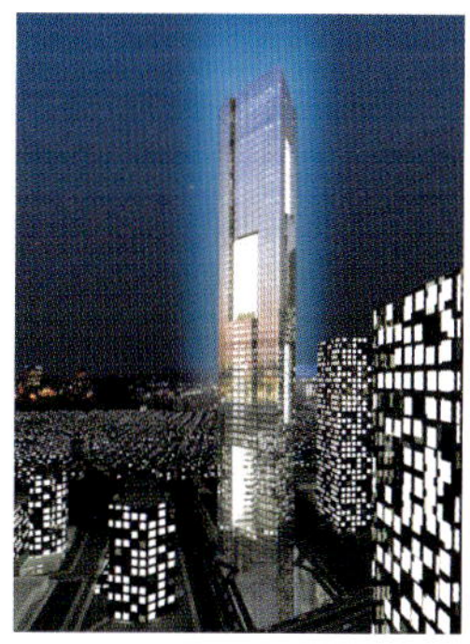

Nata Vega Housing
Client NATA Group and MNM Eurasia Forest Foundation
Project Date 2008–2010
Area 184,510 m^2
Location Ankara
Structural Engineer Yüksek Project
Mechanical Engineer Metta Engineering
Electrical Engineer Akay Engineering
Landscape Design Dalokay Design Studio
Leasing Consultant Jones Lang LaSalle Turkey
Fire Consultant Alara Design and Engineering
Contractor NATA Group and MNM Eurasia Forest Foundation
Status Built

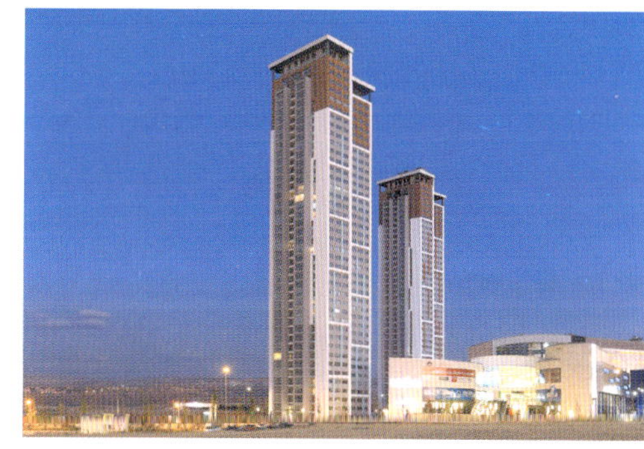

Gardenya
Client Gül Construction and Mutlu Construction
Project Date 2009
Area 69,355 m^2
Location İstanbul
Structural Engineer Yüksek Project
Mechanical Engineer Setes Engineering
Electrical Engineer Akay Engineering
Landscape Design Defne Akşin Akyol
Contractor Gül Construction and Mutlu Construction
Status Under construction

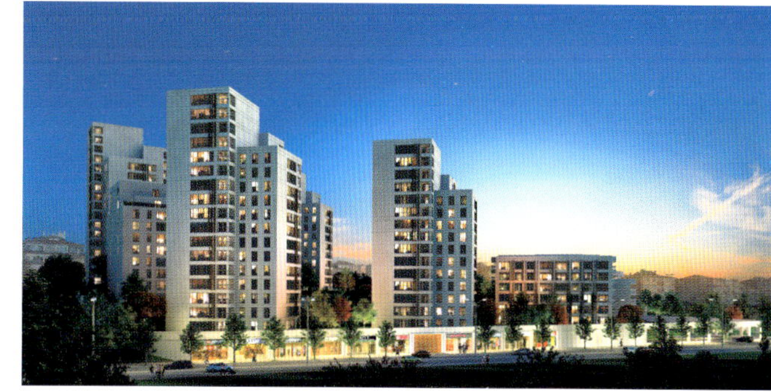

Zonguldak Courthouse
Client Republic of Turkey Ministry of Justice
Project Date 2009
Area 7,560 m^2
Location Zonguldak
Structural Engineer Yüksek Project
Mechanical Engineer Setes Engineering
Electrical Engineer Akay Engineering
Status Under construction

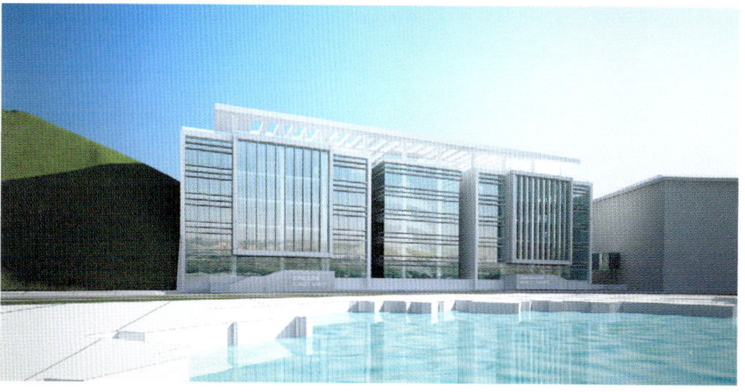

Samsun Courthouse

Client The Foundation of Justice Organization
Project Date 2009
Area 71,800 m²
Location Samsun
Structural Engineer Yüksek Project
Mechanical Engineer Setes Engineering
Electrical Engineer Akay Engineering
Landscape Design Dalokay Design Studio
Contractor Vera Construction
Status Under construction

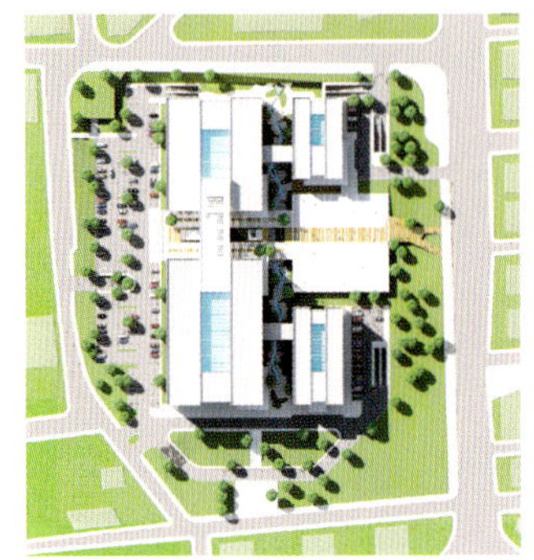

Besa Tower

Client BESA Construction Inc.
Project Date 2010
Area 19,400 m²
Location Ankara
Design Consultant Salih Bezci
Structural Engineer Yüksek Project
Mechanical Engineer Metta Engineering
Electrical Engineer Akay Engineering
Fire Consultant Karina Design
Contractor BESA Construction Inc.
Status Under construction

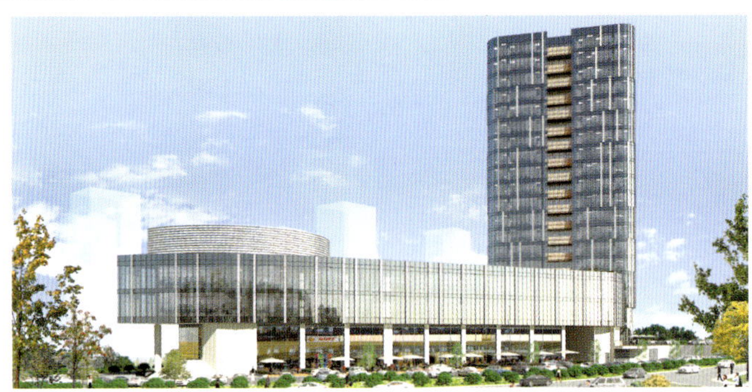

Yaşamkent Mosque

Client Association of Ankara Ataşehir Mosque
Project Date 2009
Area 2,685 m²
Location Ankara
Design Consultant Salih Bezci, Vecihi Yıldız
Project Manager Ömer Tunavelioğlu
Structural Engineer Yüksek Project
Mechanical Engineer Metta Engineering
Electrical Engineer Akay Engineering
Contractor BESA Construction Inc.
Status Under construction
2012 Cityscape Dubai Finalist
2012 WAF Finalist

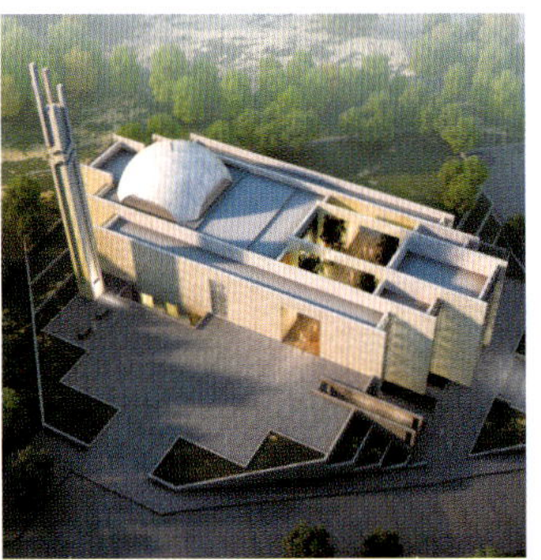

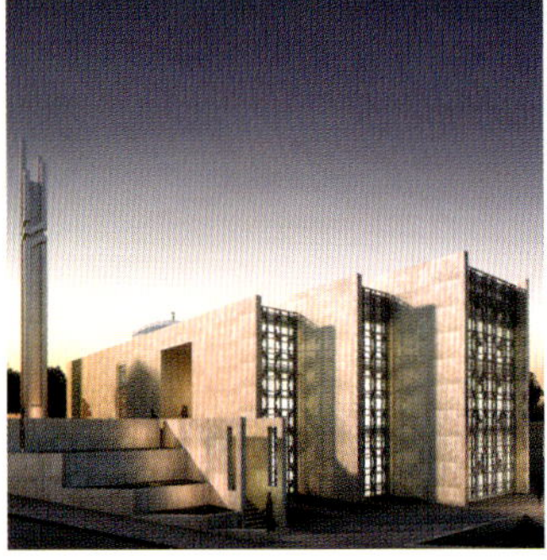

İzmit Park

Client Nur Construction
Project Date 2009
Area 99,300 m²
Location İzmit
Status Unbuilt

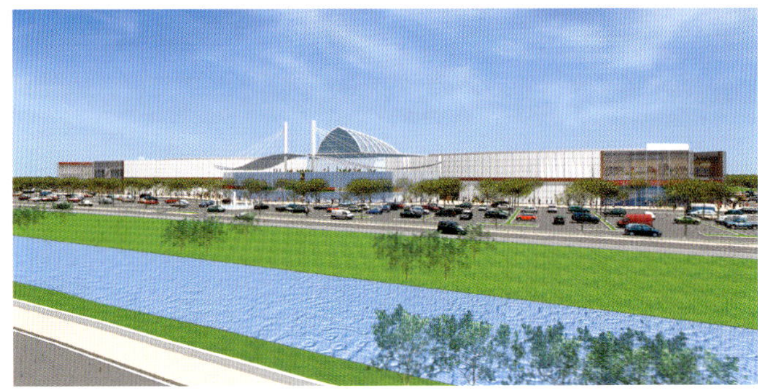

Ankara Anatolium

Client ADMA Construction Inc.
Project Date 2010
Area 160,000 m²
Location Ankara
Concept Design CPU
Structural Engineer Barka Engineering, Prota
Mechanical Engineer Özmak Machine Construction
Electrical Engineer Erk Project
Landscape Design Dalokay Design Studio
Contractor Mayser Construction Inc.
Status Built

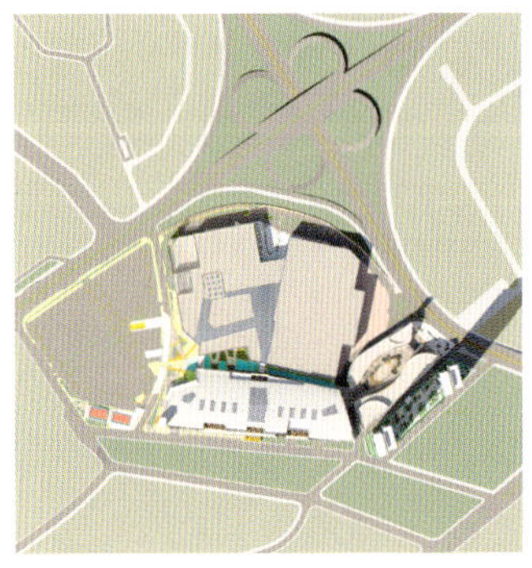

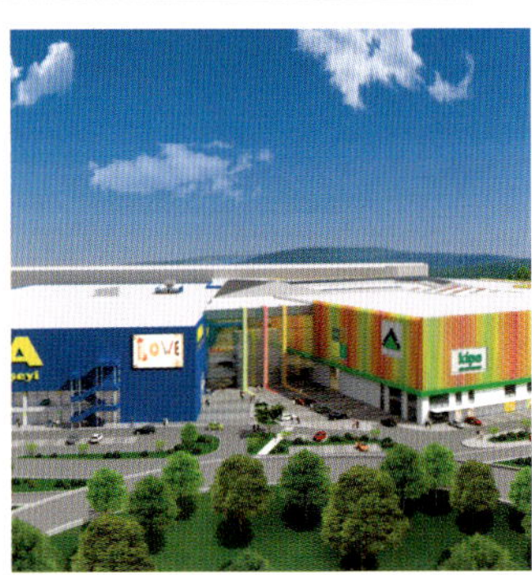

Taurus

Client Taurus Balgat Shopping Center Investment Inc.
Project Date 2010
Area 153,000 m²
Location Ankara
Structural Engineer Yüksek Project
Mechanical Engineer Metta Engineering
Electrical Engineer Yurdakul Engineering
Landscape Design Çevre Landscaping
Fire Consultant Alara Design and Engineering
Acoustics Mezzo Studio
Contractor Tepe Construction Industry Inc.
Status Built

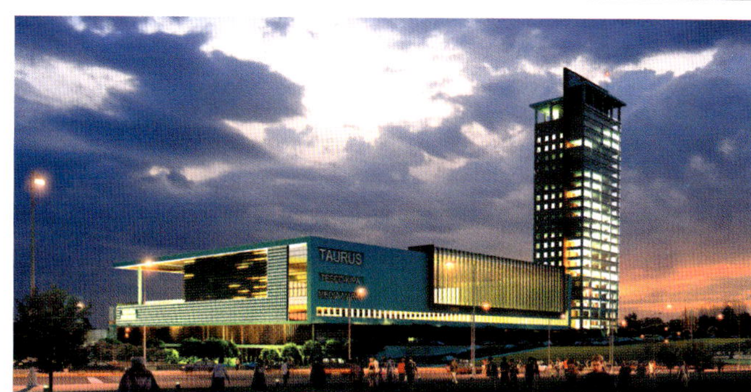

Nata Vega

Client NATA Group and MNM Eurasia Forest Foundation
Project Date 2010
Area 80,000 m²
Location Ankara
Structural Engineer Yüksek Project
Mechanical Engineer Metta Engineering
Electrical Engineer Akay Engineering
Landscape Design Dalokay Design Studio
Fire Consultant Alara Design and Engineering
Contractor NATA Group and MNM Eurasia Forest Foundation
Status Built

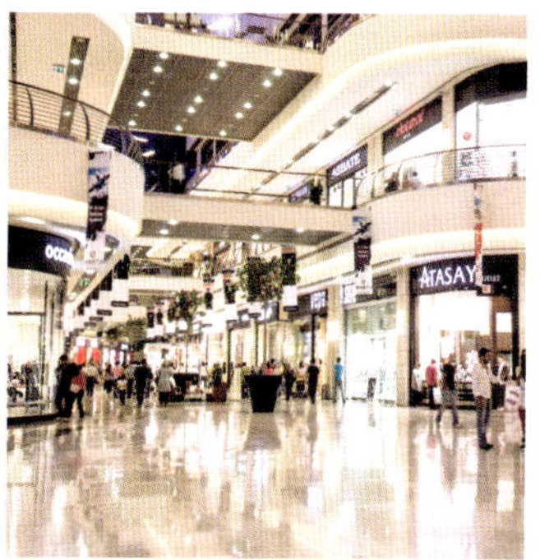

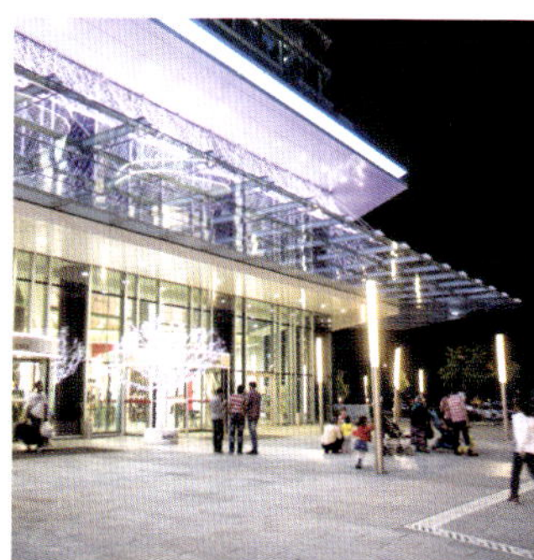

Batıpark

Client Ons Inc.
Project Date 2010
Area 60,000 m²
Location Ankara
Structural Engineer Yüksek Project
Mechanical Engineer Setes Engineering
Electrical Engineer Akay Engineering
Landscape Design Çevre Landscaping
Contractor Ons Inc.
Status Built

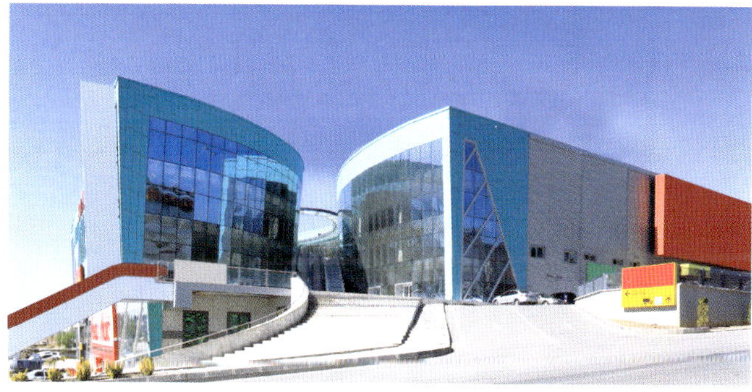

Atakent

Client Artaş Construction
Project Date 2010
Area 60,000 m²
Location İstanbul
Status Unbuilt

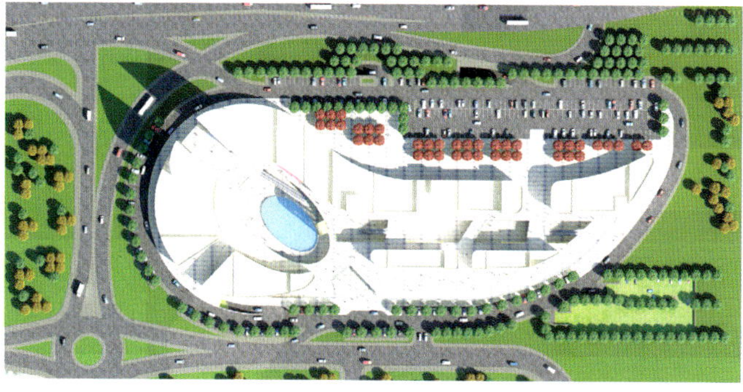

KOSGEB

Client KOSGEB (Republic of Turkey, Small and Medium Enterprises Development Organization)
Project Date 2010
Area 36,885 m²
Location Ankara
Engineering Projects Aliş Project
Contractor Özoğuz Construction
Status Under construction

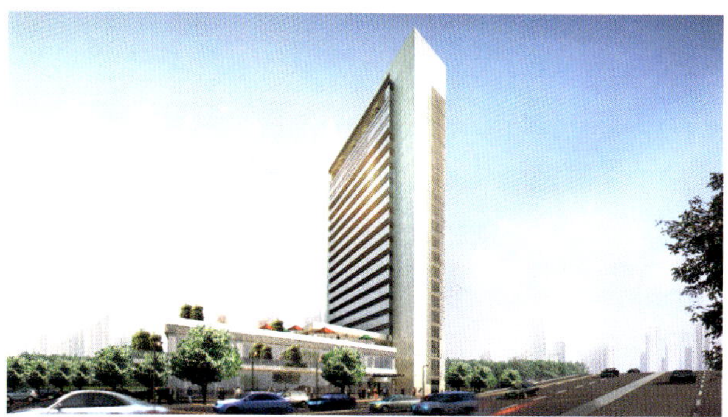

Akyurt Auto City
Client Ankara Metropolitan Municipality
Project Date 2010
Area 467,000 m²
Location Ankara
Status Unbuilt

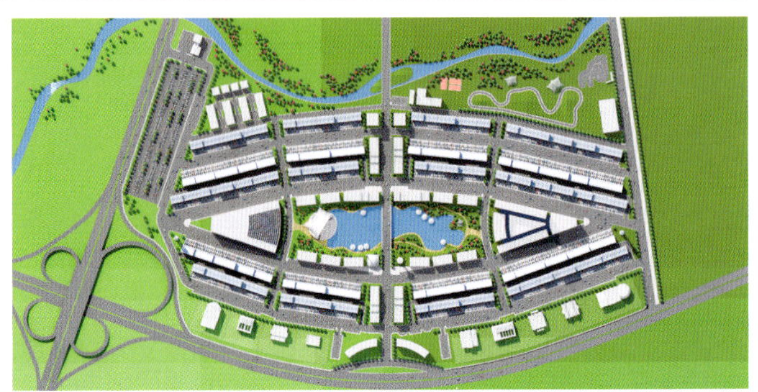

Bucharest Exhibition and Convention Center
Client TOBB
Project Date 2010
Location Bucharest, Romania
Status Unbuilt

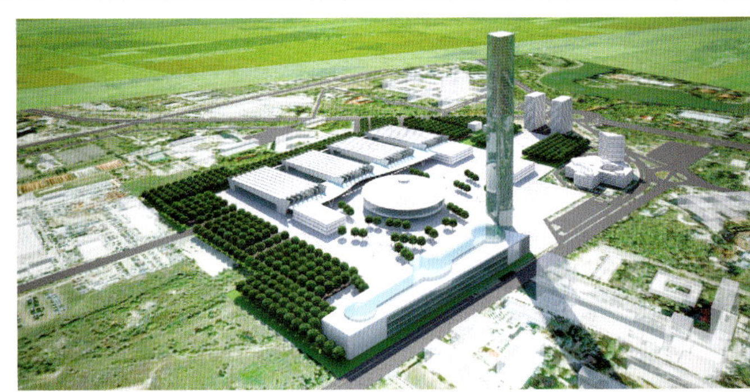

TOBB Brussels
Client TOBB
Project Date 2010
Area 2,700 m²
Location Brussels, Belgium
Architectural Design Willen Associates Architekten
Local Architect Pierre Accarain Architectes, Marc Bouillot Associés SA
Renovation Design A Tasarım Mimarlık
Structural Engineer Be Franz Dupont
Mechanical Engineer Crea-Tec S.P.R.L
Electrical Engineer Crea-Tec S.P.R.L
Consultants A.A.U. SA
Status Under construction

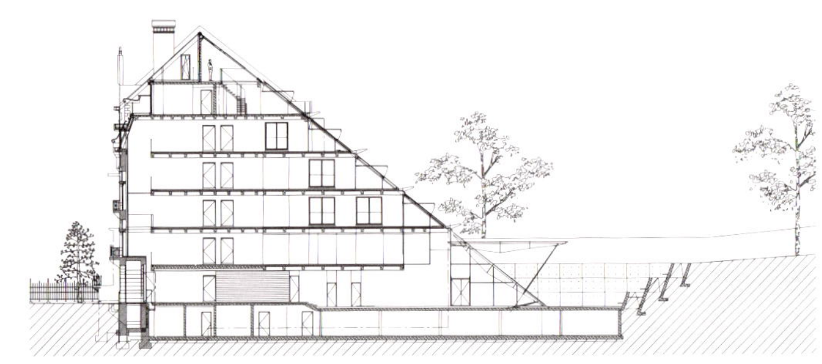

Türk Telekom
Client Türk Telekom
Project Date 2010
Area 54,000 m²
Location Ankara
Structural Engineer Yüksek Project
Mechanical Engineer Metta Engineering
Electrical Engineer Yurdakul Engineering
Landscape Design Dalokay Design Studio
Fire Consultant Alara Design and Engineering
Façade Consultant Pridemann
Building Envelope Consultants Kaan Kuran
Lighting Consultant Atilla Uysal
Acoustic Consultant Mezzo Studio—Prof. Dr. Mehmet Çalışkan
Contractor Burkay Construction
Status Under construction

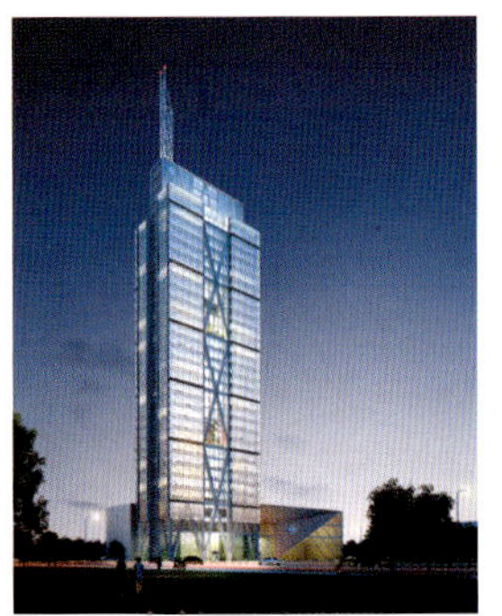

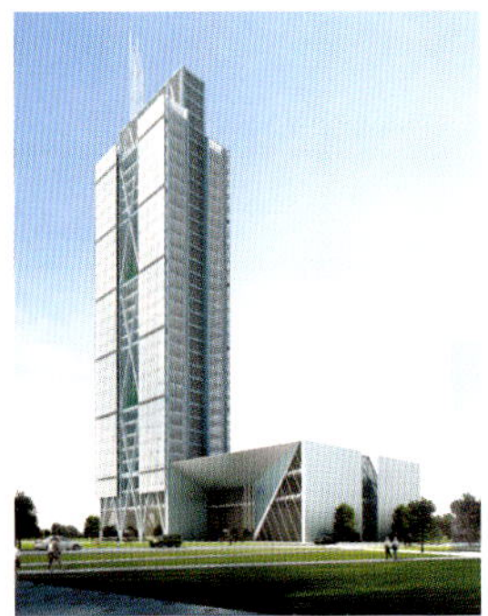

TOBB World Trade-Business Center and Technopolis Master Plan
Client The Union of Chambers and Commodity Exchanges of Turkey (TOBB)
Project Date 2010
Area 133,340 m²
Location Ankara
Status Ongoing

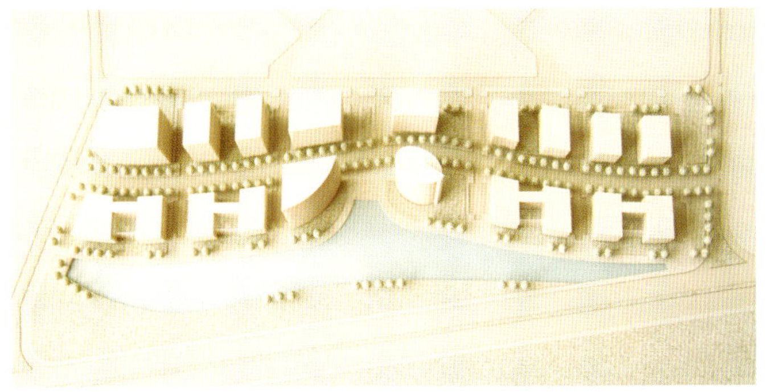

TOBB University of Economics and Technology Technology Center

Client TOBB University of Economics and Technology
Project Date 2010
Area 23,000 m^2
Location Ankara
Structural Engineer Yüksek Project
Mechanical Engineer Okutan Engineering
Electrical Engineer Akay Engineering
Landscape Design On Design
Consulting Firm Tür-Sum Construction
Construction Manager Mustafa Tekinel
Contractor Tür-Sum Construction
Status Built

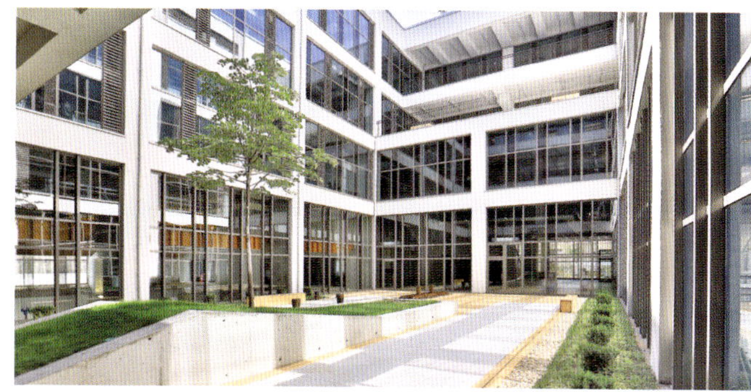

Atakule

Client Atakule Real Estate Investment Trust
Project Date 2010
Area 50,000 m^2
Location Ankara
Existing Tower Design Ragıp Buluç
Structural Engineer Yüksek Project
Mechanical Engineer Metta Engineering
Electrical Engineer Akay Engineering
Leasing Consultant Jones Lang LaSalle Turkey
Fire Consultant Alara Design and Engineering
Status Ongoing

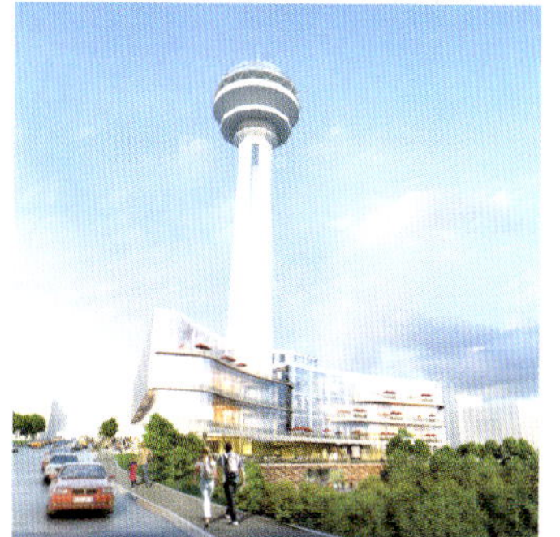

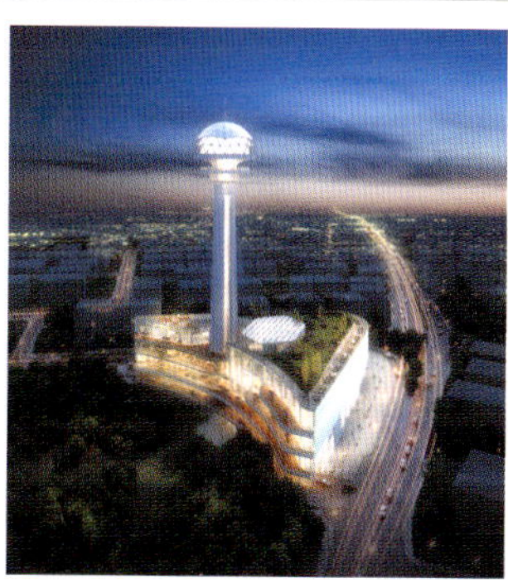

Yakuplu Park Data Center

Project Date 2010
Area 120,000 m^2
Location İstanbul
Structural Engineer Yüksek Project
Mechanical Engineer Sadıkoğlu Engineering
Electrical Engineer Akay Engineering
Landscape Design Defne Akşin Akyol
Status Ongoing

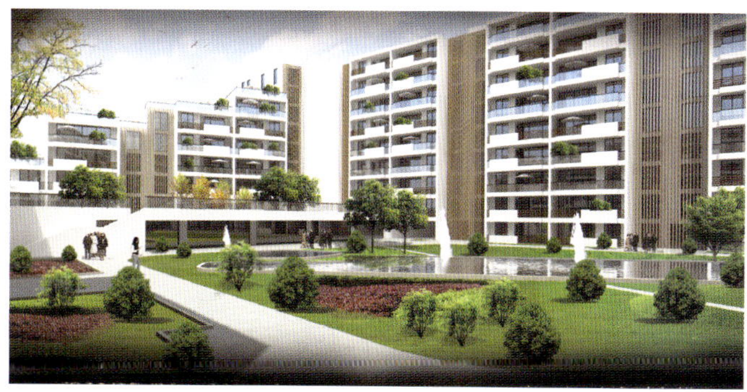

Avcılar Park

Client Gül Construction
Project Date 2010
Area 40,000 m^2
Location İstanbul
Structural Engineer Birim Engineering
Mechanical Engineer AMK Engineering
Electrical Engineer Çiçek Electrics
Contractor Gül Construction
Status Built

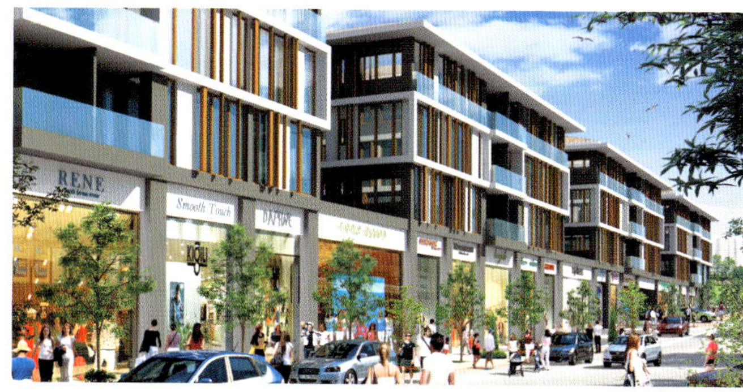

Türksat Konya Data Center

Client Türksat Inc.
Project Date 2010
Area 23,080 m^2
Location Konya
Structural Engineer Yüksek Project
Mechanical Engineer Setes Engineering
Electrical Engineer Akay Engineering
Consultants Uptime Institute
Status Ongoing

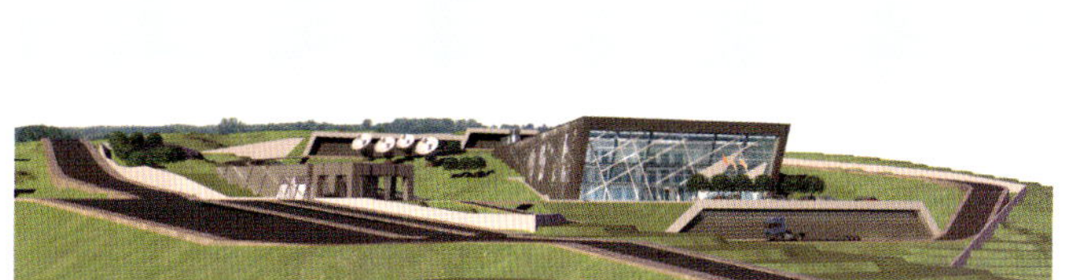

Adana Courthouse

Client The Foundation of Justice Organisation
Project Date 2010
Area 166,800 m²
Location Adana
Structural Engineer Yüksek Project
Mechanical Engineer Metta Engineering
Electrical Engineer Akay Engineering
Status Unbuilt

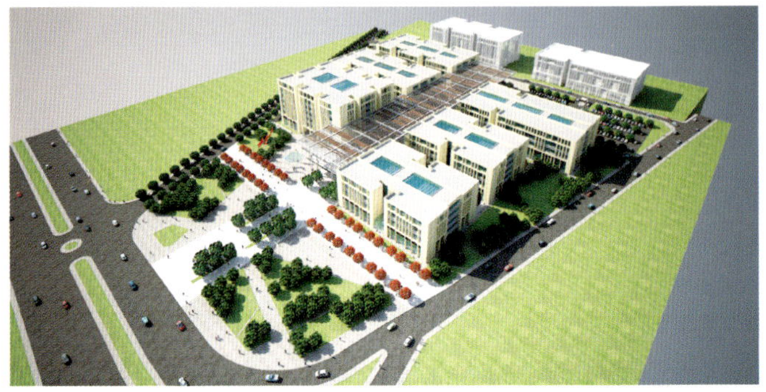

NATA Beta

Client NATA Group
Project Date 2010
Area 100,000 m²
Location Ankara
Status Unbuilt

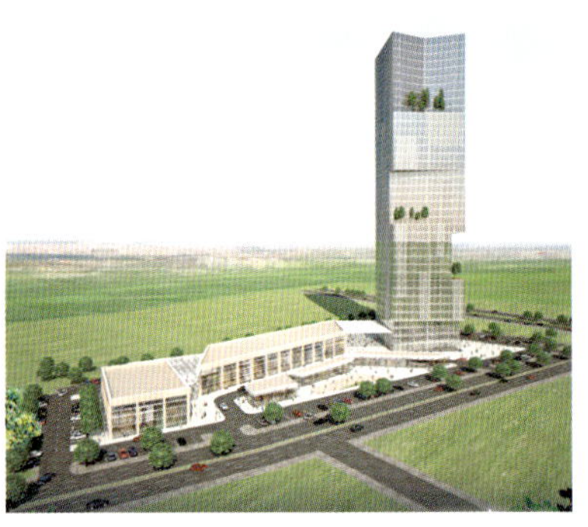

Afyon Thermal Center

Client Özer Tourism Inc.
Project Date 2010
Area 300,000 m²
Location Afyon
Status Unbuilt

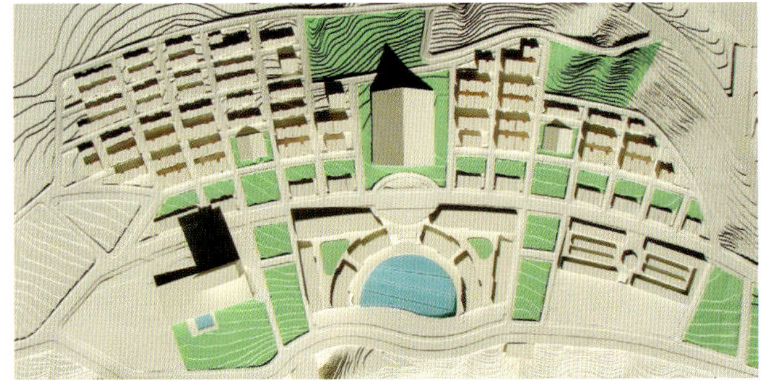

TOBB University of Economics and Technology Center Pedestrian Bridge

Client TOBB University of Economics and Technology Center Pedestrian Bridge
Project Date 2010
Location Ankara
Structural Engineer Amiral Engineering
Contractor Türsum Construction
Status Built

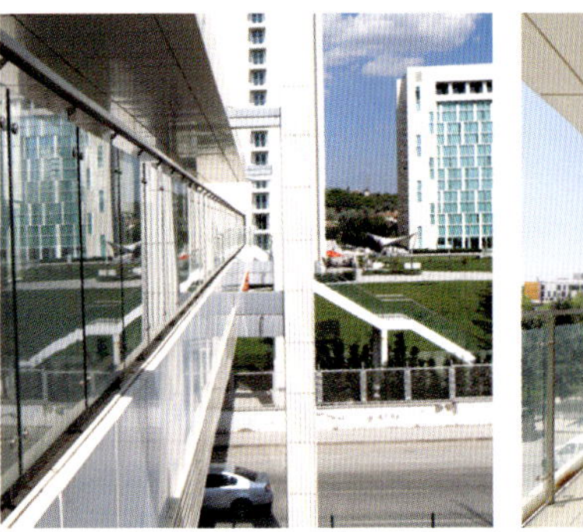

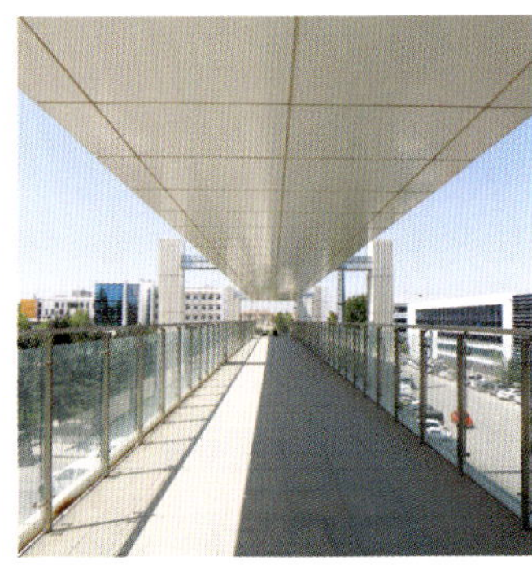

Eyüp Park

Client Gül Construction
Project Date 2011
Area 92,300 m²
Location İstanbul
Structural Engineer AS Engineering
Mechanical Engineer Sadıkoğlu Engineering
Electrical Engineer Tepas Engineering
Contractor Gül Construction
Status Under construction

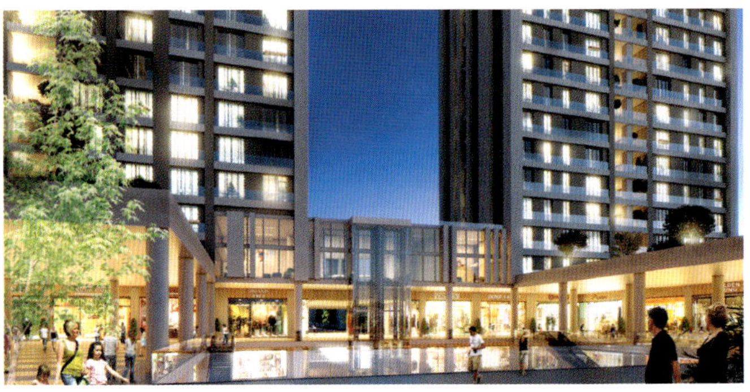

Nexus

Client Tepe Construction Inc.
Project Date 2011
Area 123,000 m²
Location İstanbul
Structural Engineer Yüksek Project
Mechanical Engineer GMD Engineering
Electrical Engineer Akay Engineering
Landscape Design Dalokay Design Studio
Status Unbuilt

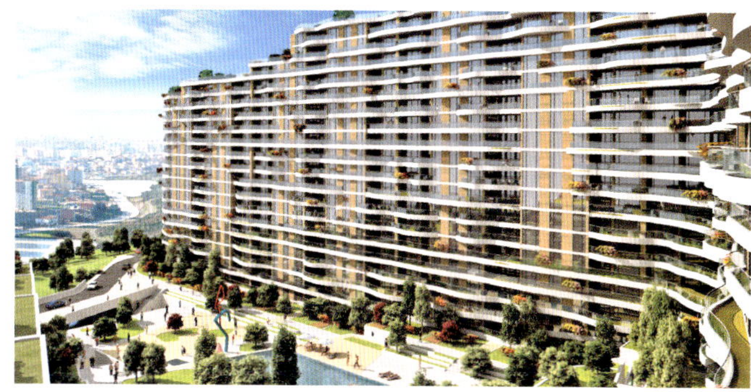

Gölbaşı University

Client Tek-Dav Foundation University
Project Date 2011
Site Area 900,000 m²
Location Ankara
Status Unbuilt

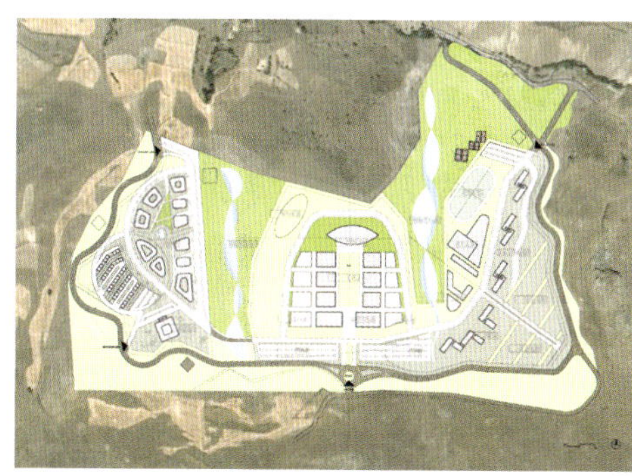

KİPAŞ Headquarters

Client Kipaş Holding
Project Date 2011
Area 12,840 m²
Location Kahramanmaraş
Structural Engineer Yüksek Project
Mechanical Engineer Setes Engineering
Electrical Engineer Akay Engineering
Landscape Design Dalokay Design Studio
Status Built

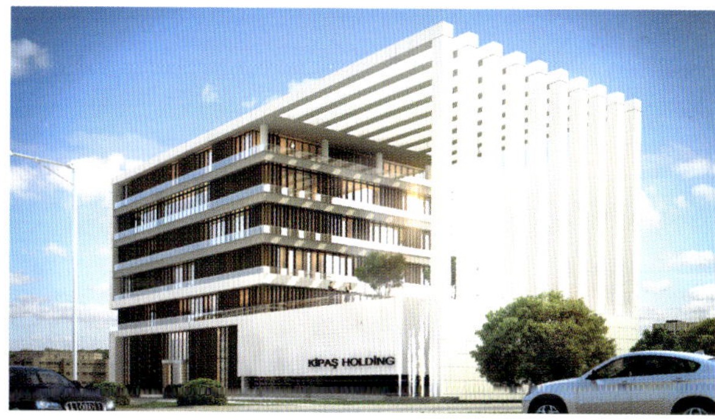

MFS Business Center

Client Alternatif Construction
Project Date 2011
Area 60,000 m²
Location Ankara
Structural Engineer Yüksek Project
Mechanical Engineer Setes Engineering
Electrical Engineer Akay Engineering
Status Under construction

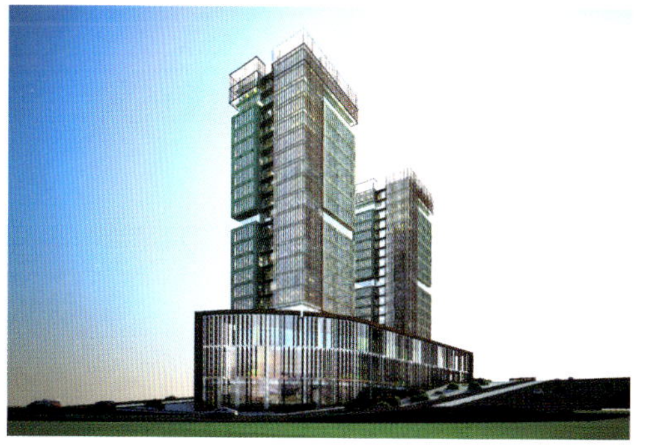

Sinpaş Bursa Housing

Client Sinpaş REIT
Project Date 2011
Area 173,000 m²
Location Bursa
Landscape Design Dalokay Design Studio
Status Unbuilt

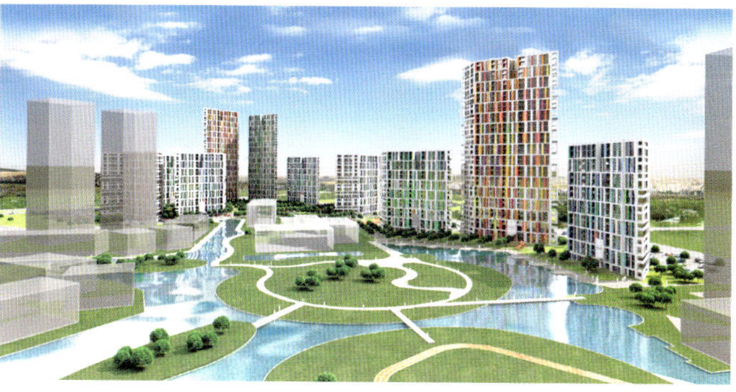

Akbak Plaza 2

Client Tevfik Akbak
Project Date 2011
Area 9,500 m²
Location Ankara
Status Unbuilt

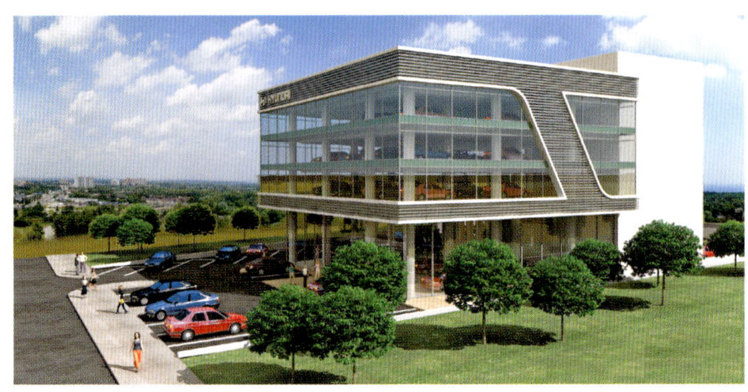

Balıkuyumcu

Client BESA Construction Inc.
Project Date 2011
Area 413,000 m²
Location Ankara
Status Ongoing

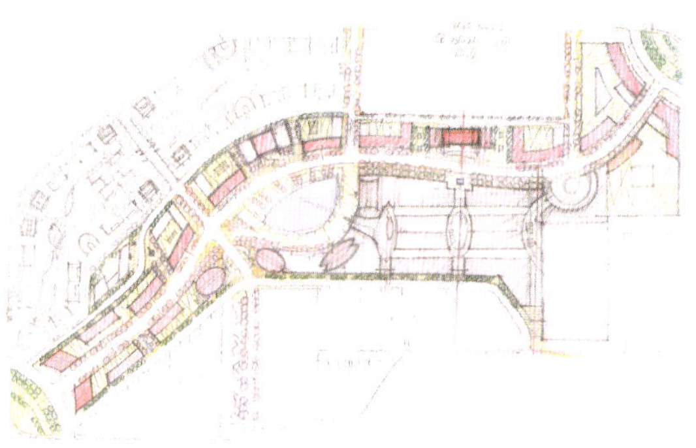

Ankara International Exhibition and Convention Center

Client Ankara International Exhibition and Convention Organization Inc.
Project Date 2011
Area 168,000 m²
Location Ankara
Architectural Design gmp Architekten von Gerkan, Marg und Partner, A Architectural Design
Structural Engineer Binnewies, Yüksek Project
Mechanical Engineer Protec, Metta Engineering
Electrical Engineer Protec, Yurdakul Engineering
Landscape Design Breimann&Bruun, Dalokay Design Studio
Signage Form Kombinat/Katharina Marg
Status Ongoing

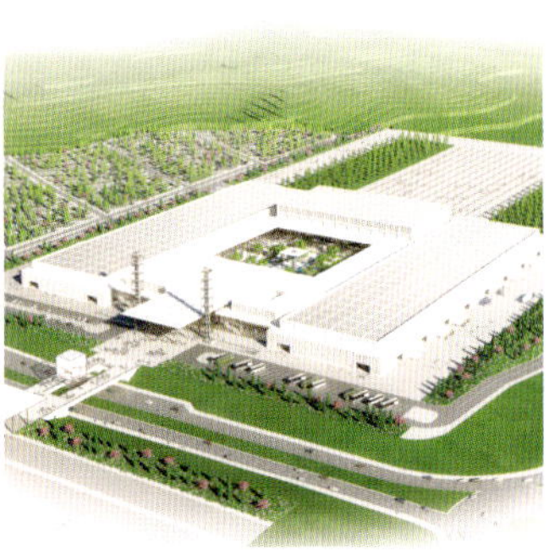

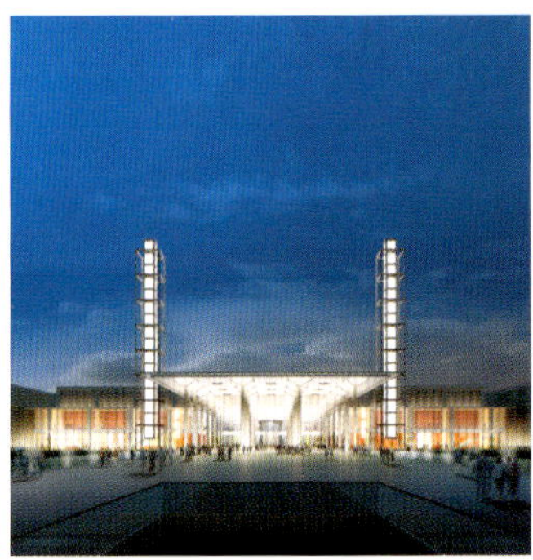

Tiraspol Life Center

Client Summa Inc.
Project Date 2011
Area 44,925 m²
Location Tiraspol, Moldova
Status Unbuilt

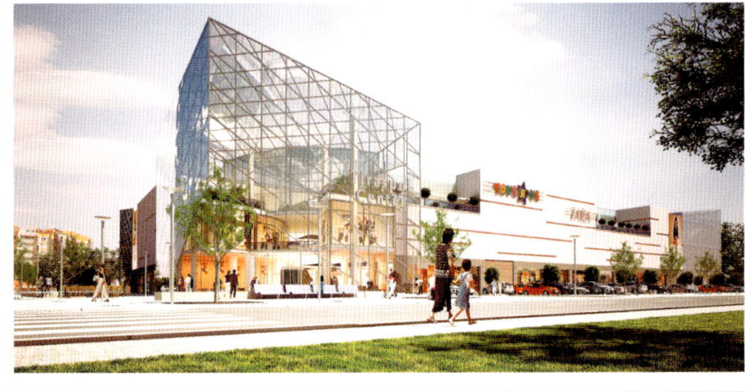

Kayseri Outlet

Client Küçükçalık Group
Project Date 2011
Area 82,000 m²
Location Kayseri
Status Unbuilt

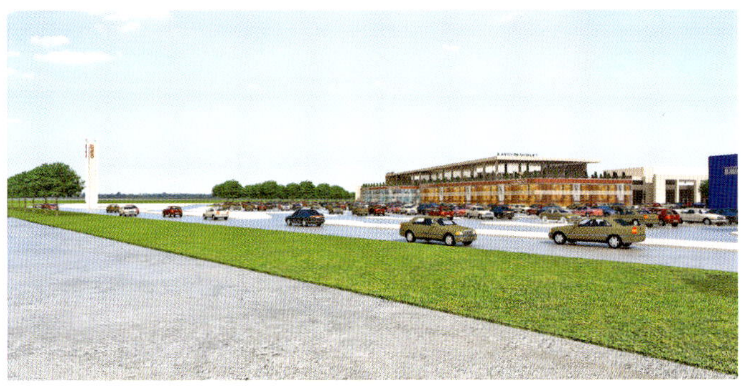

Nata İncek Housing

Client NATA Group and MNM Eurasia Forest Foundation
Project Date 2011
Area 55,000 m²
Location Ankara
Structural Engineer Yüksek Project
Mechanical Engineer Metta Engineering
Electrical Engineer Akay Engineering
Landscape Design Dalokay Design Studio
Fire Consultant Alara Design and Engineering
Contractor NATA Group and MNM Eurasia Forest Foundation
Status Under construction

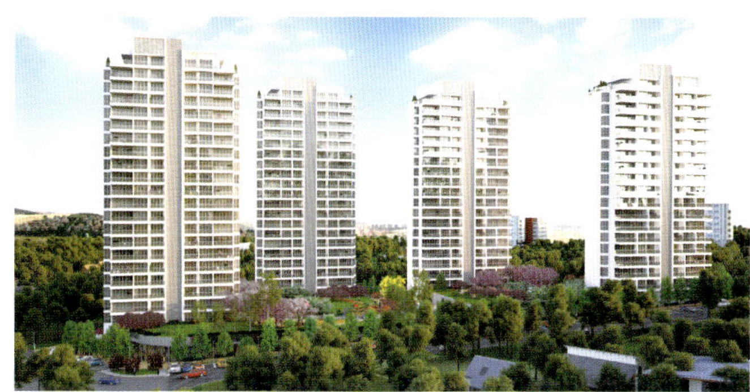

Küçükyalı Business Center

Client Bostancı Real Estate
Project Date 2011
Area 93,090 m²
Location İstanbul
Structural Engineer Yüksek Project
Mechanical Engineer Okutan Engineering
Electrical Engineer RAM Engineering
Landscape Design Dalokay Design Studio
Contractor Renaissance Construction
Status Under construction

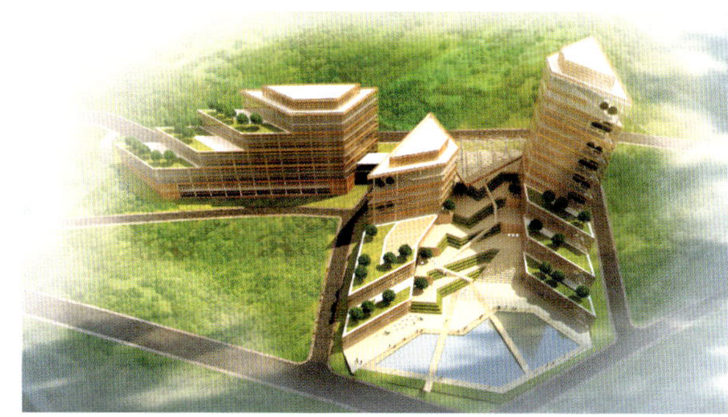

Sipopo Mall

Client SUMMA Inc.
Project Date 2011
Area 12,300 m²
Location Malabo
Structural Engineer Yüksek Project, Meinhardt Engineering
Mechanical Engineer Metta Engineering
Electrical Engineer Yurdakul Engineering
Landscape Design Dalokay Design Studio
Fire Consultant Alara Design and Engineering
Status Ongoing

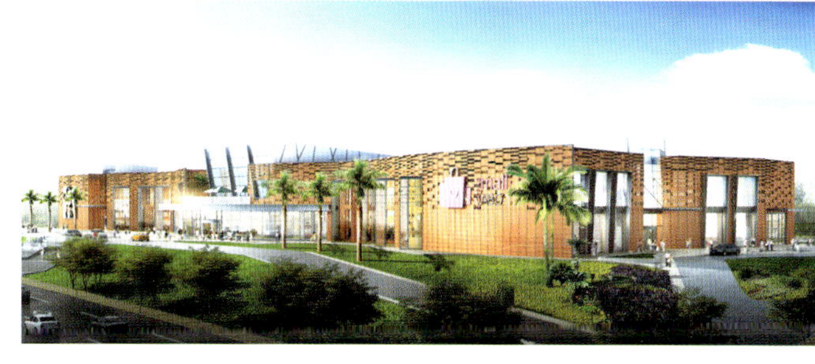

Evo

Client Mutlu Construction and Tokur Construction
Project Date 2011
Area 44,000 m²
Location Ankara
Structural Engineer MN Engineering
Mechanical Engineer Yapıtes Engineering
Electrical Engineer Denge Engineering
Contractor Mutlu Construction and Tokur Construction
Status Under construction

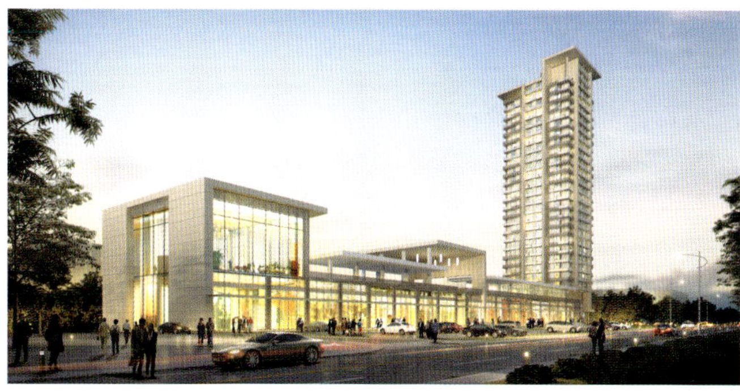

Erdemli Courthouse

Client Republic of Turkey Ministry of Justice
Project Date 2011
Area 12,540 m²
Location Mersin
Structural Engineer Yüksek Project
Mechanical Engineer Metta Engineering
Electrical Engineer Yurdakul Engineering
Fire Consultant Alara Design and Engineering
Status Unbuilt

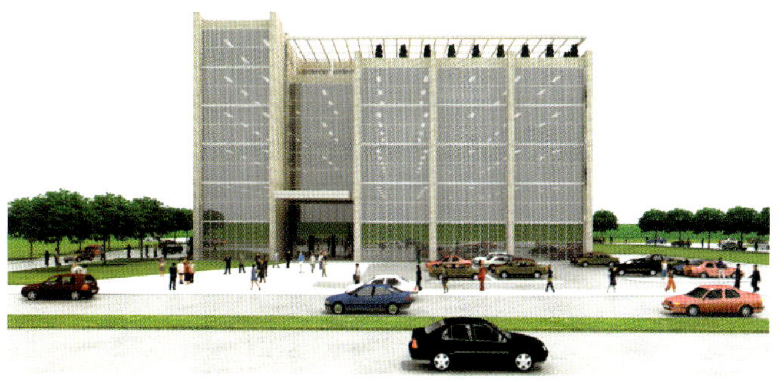

Turan Güneş Boulevard Apartments

Client Tepe Construction Inc.
Project Date 2011
Area 100,000 m²
Location Ankara
Status Unbuilt

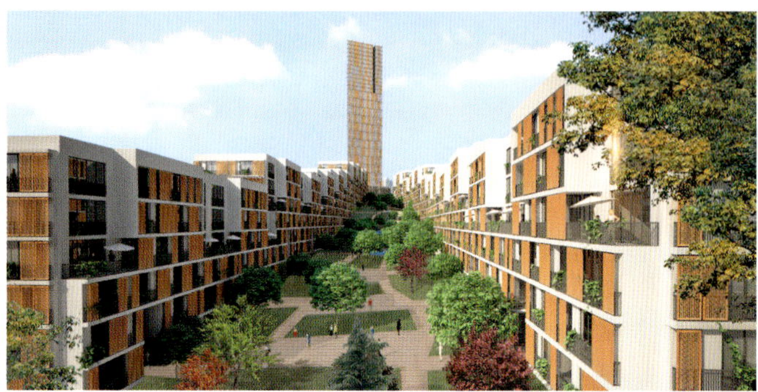

KİPA Shopping Center

Client Tesco Kipa
Project Date 2011
Area 33,000 m²
Location Çanakkale
Structural Engineer Yüksek Project
Mechanical Engineer Mekanik Tesisat
Electrical Engineer Akademi Electrics
Landscape Design Dalokay Design Studio
Status Unbuilt

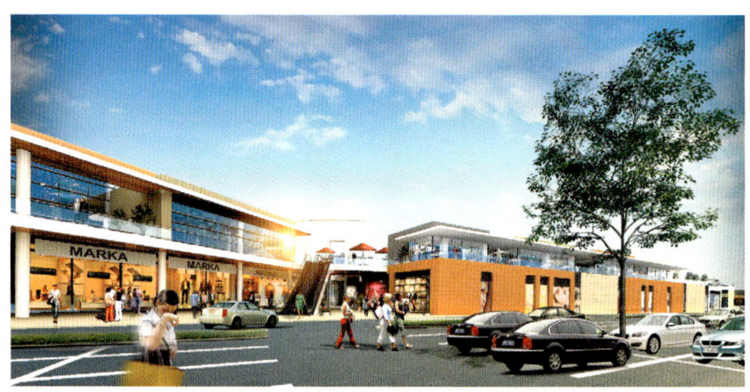

Eskişehir Park

Client Ons Inc.
Project Date 2011
Area 25,645 m²
Location Eskişehir
Structural Engineer Yüksek project
Mechanical Engineer Setes Engineering
Electrical Engineer Akay Engineering
Landscape Design Çevre Landscaping
Status Built

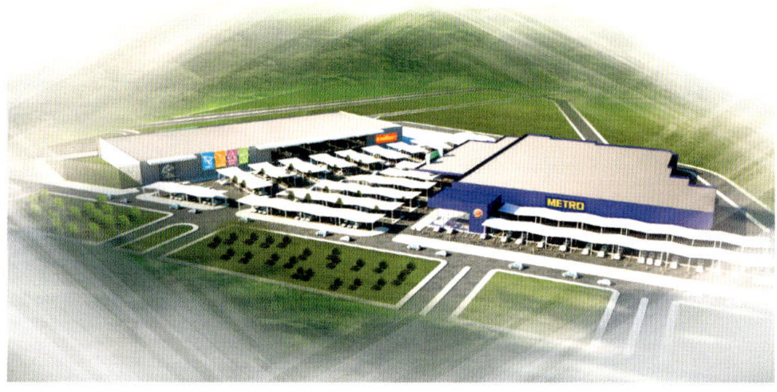

Kazikiçi Bostanları Social and Cultural Facility

Client Ayça Inc., Koza Inc., Aysed Inc., Electricians Inc., Textile Exporters Inc., Building Decorators Inc., Tages Inc., Partnership
Project Date 2012
Area 3,275 m²
Location Ankara
Structural Engineer Yüksek Project
Mechanical Engineer Metta Engineering
Electrical Engineer Akay Engineering
Landscape Design Dalokay Design Studio
Status Built

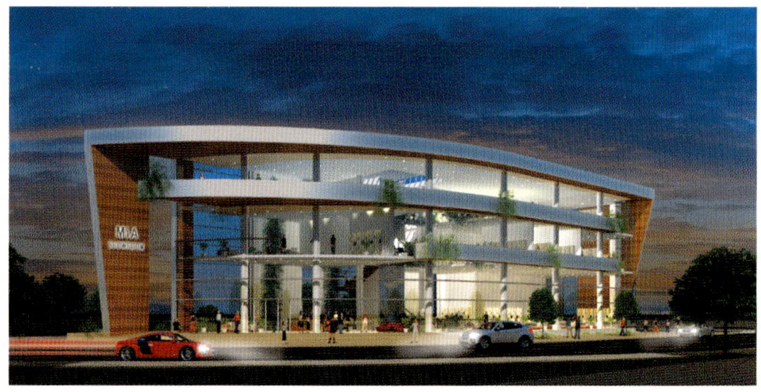

Koza Residence

Client Koza İpek Holding
Project Date 2012
Area 145,415 m²
Location Ankara
Status Unbuilt

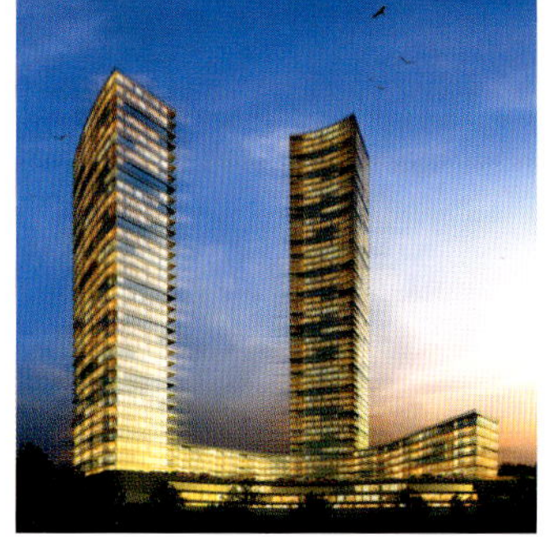
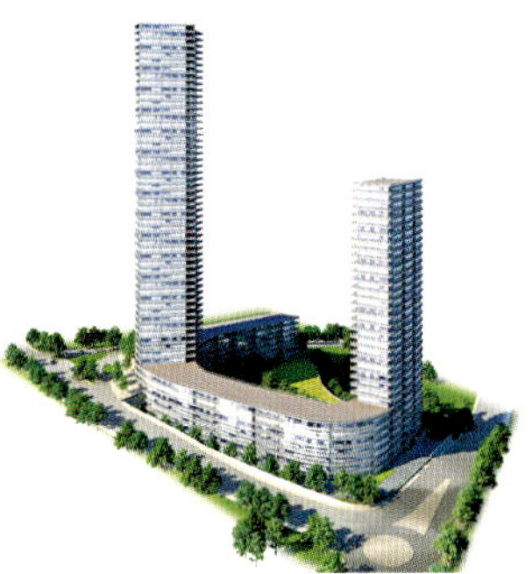

Kayseri Courthouse

Client The Foundation of Justice Organization
Project Date 2012
Area 48,075 m²
Location Kayseri
Structural Engineer Yüksek Project
Mechanical Engineer Metta Engineering
Electrical Engineer Akay Engineering
Landscape Design Dalokay Design Studio
Fire Consultant Alara Design and Engineering
Status Unbuilt

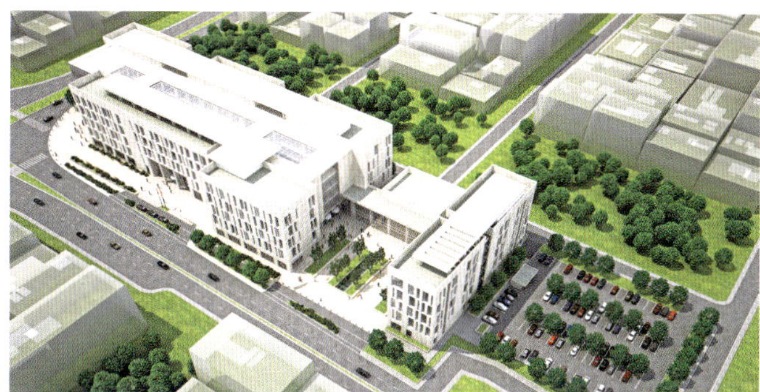

Yaşamkent Housing

Client Tepe Construction Inc., MESA Housing Industries Inc.
Project Date 2012
Area 215,000 m²
Location Ankara
Structural Engineer Yüksek Project
Mechanical Engineer Metta Engineering
Electrical Engineer Yurdakul Engineering
Landscape Design Dalokay Design Studio
Fire Consultant Alara Design and Engineering
Status Ongoing

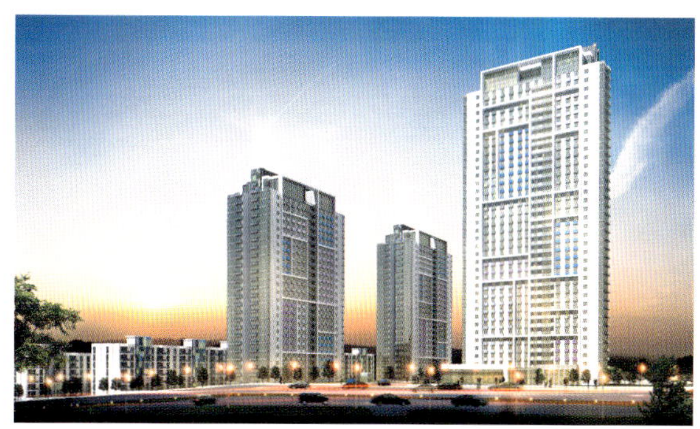

Skopje Mixed-Use Center

Client Limak
Project Date 2012
Area 213,156 m²
Location Skopje, Macedonia
Architectural Design A Architectural Design, CAG Architectural Workshop
Structural Engineer Prota Engineering
Mechanical Engineer Metta Engineering
Electrical Engineer Yurdakul Engineering
Fire Consultant Taru Engineering
Status Ongoing

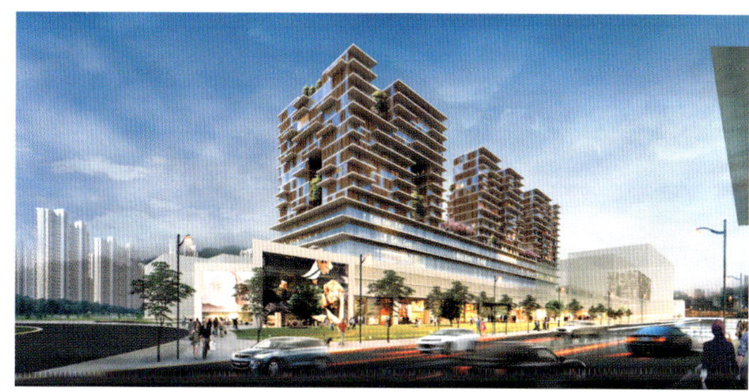

Konya Shopping Center

Client Büyükkaplan Inc.
Project Date 2012
Area 200,000 m²
Location Konya
Status Unbuilt

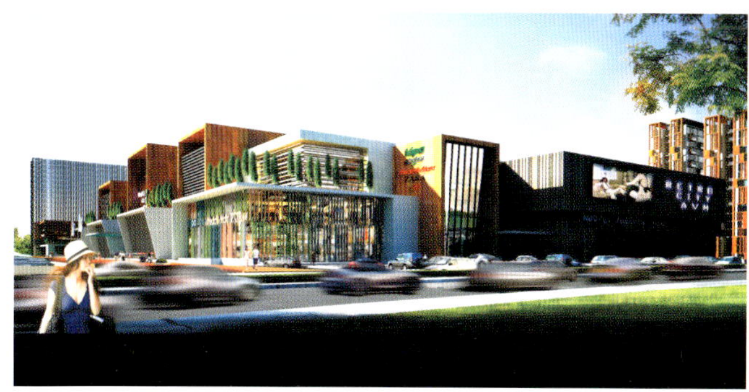

Ankara Stadium

Client Ankara Municipality
Project Date 2012
Area 200,000 m²
Location Ankara
Status Unbuilt

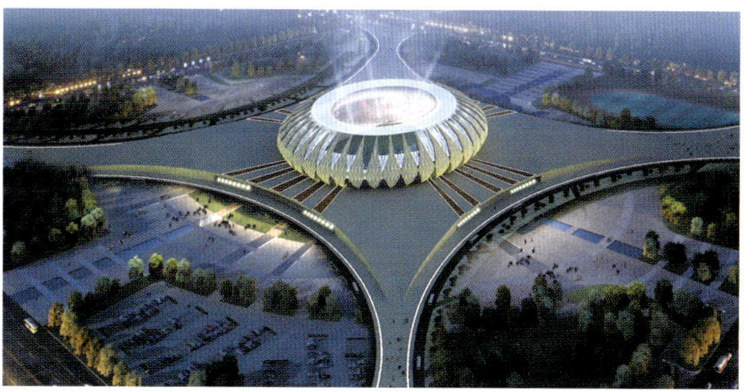

Espinas Hotel

Client Espinas Hotel
Project Date 2012
Area 32,000 m²
Location Tehran, Iran
Status Unbuilt

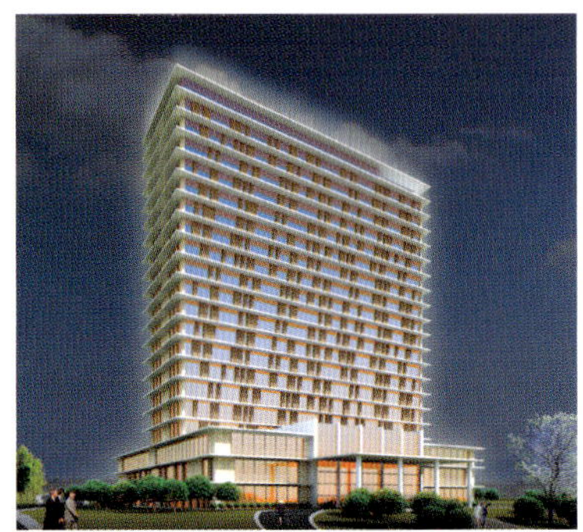

IFC Ziraat Bank

Client T.C Ziraat Bank A.Ş.
Project Date 2013
Area 400,000 m²
Location İstanbul
Architectural Design KPF
Local Architect A Architectural Design
Structural-Mechanical-Electrical Engineer Arup London, Arup İstanbul
Workplace Interior Consultant KKS Strategy
Landscape Design Dalokay Design Studio
Fire Consultancy Arup İstanbul
Acoustics Consultancy Mezzo Studio
LEED Consultancy Altensis
Façade Consultancy ALT
Status Ongoing

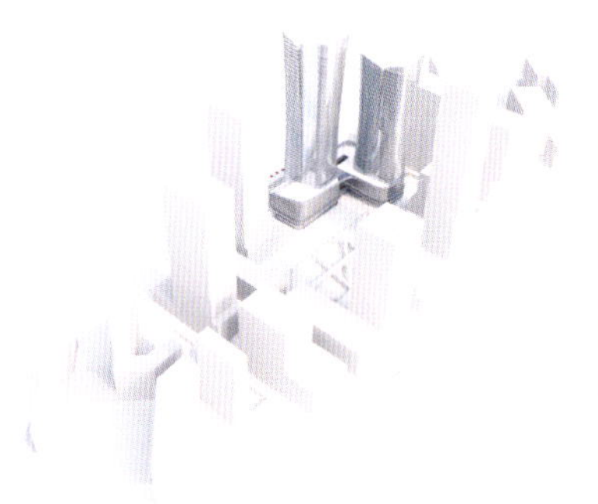

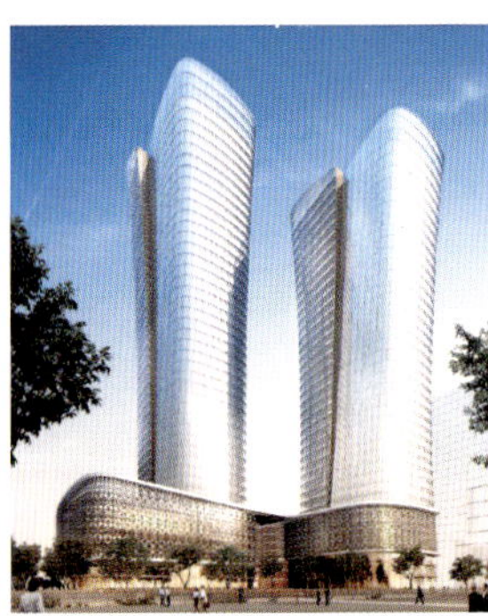

Liva City

Client Liva
Project Date 2013
Area 37,700 m²
Location Ankara
Structural Engineer Yüksek Project
Mechanical Engineer Metta Engineering
Electrical Engineer Akay Engineering
Fire Consultant Alara Project
Status Ongoing

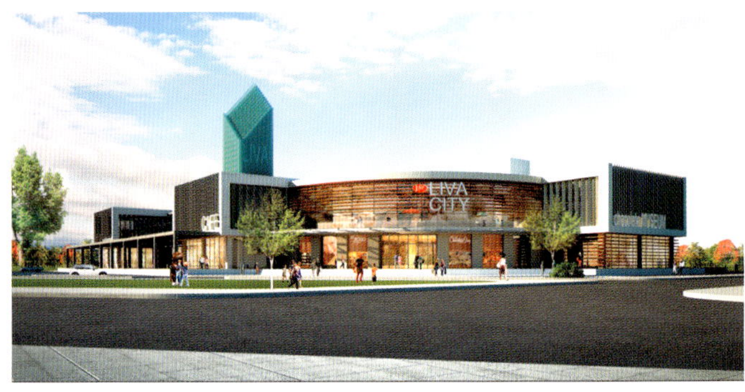

Nata Office

Client Nata Holding Inc.
Project Date 2013
Area 5,600 m²
Location Turkmenistan
Status Unbuilt

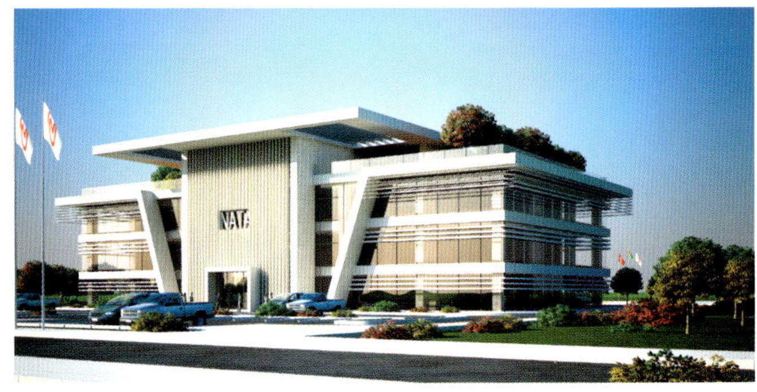

Ankara High Speed Train Station

Client Limak Holding, Kolin Construction, Cengiz Holding
Project Date 2013
Area 175,000 m²
Location Ankara
Status Ongoing

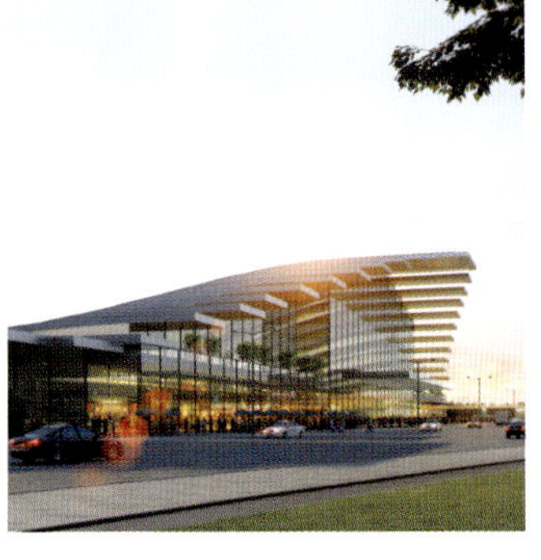

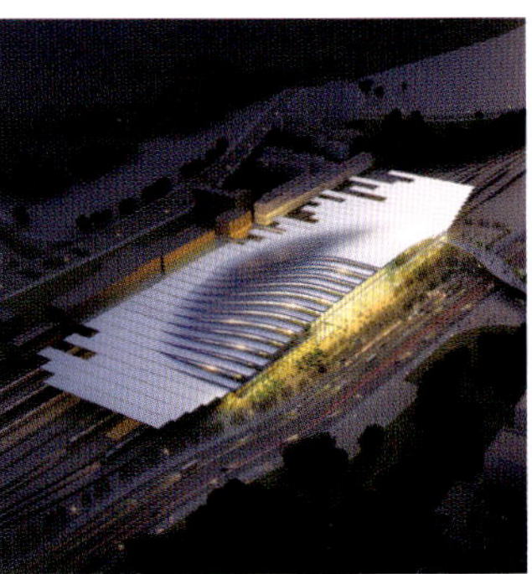

Şahiner Oran

Client Kazova Construction Inc.
Project Date 2013
Area 130,000 m²
Location Ankara
Status Unbuilt

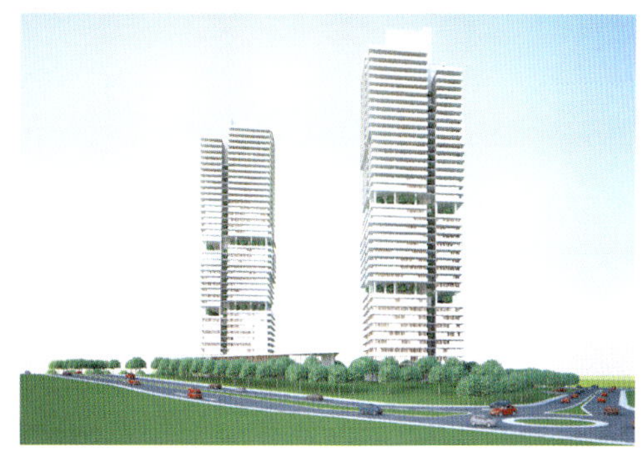

Adnan Beker House

Client Adnan Beker
Project Date 2013
Area 1,410 m²
Location Ankara
Structural Engineer Yüksek Project
Mechanical Engineer Yurdakul Engineering
Electrical Engineer Setes Engineering
Status Unbuilt

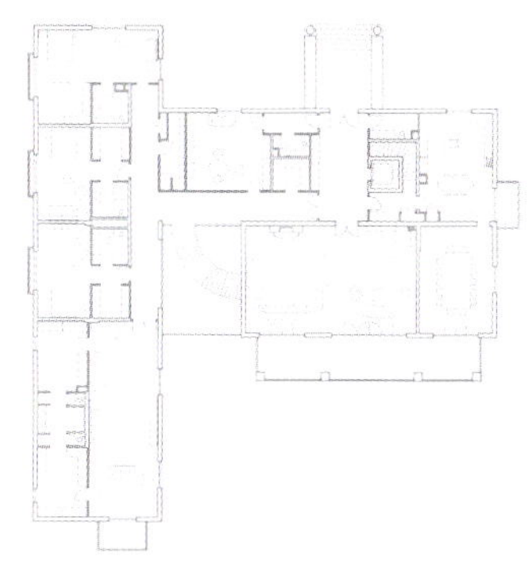

EGE GRUP & BM PLAZA

Client EGE GRUP
Project Date 2013
Area 93,500 m²
Location Ankara
Status Unbuilt

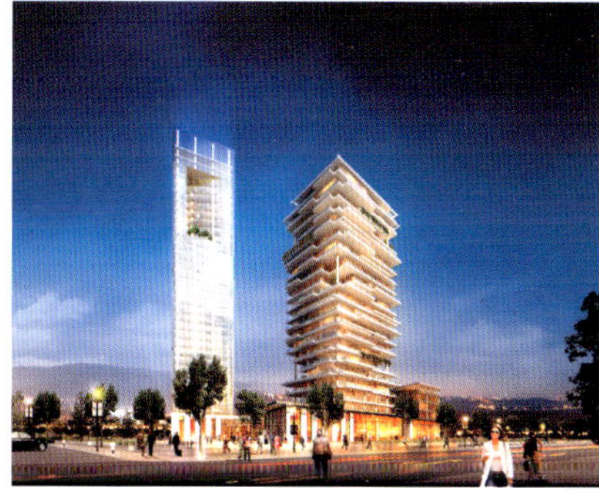

Park View

Client İlci Holding & Salahaddin Holding
Project Date 2013
Area 84,300 m²
Location Iraq
Status Unbuilt

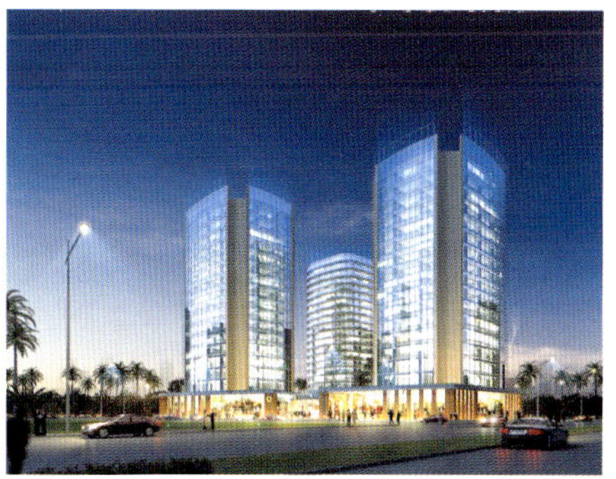

Bibliography

Publications

Chamber of Architects of Turkey, 1988, 1. National Architecture Exhibition and Awards, "TED Campus Student Club," Graphic Presentation Category, p. 176

Özbay, Aslı (ed.), *Turkish Architects 2000*, Association of Turkish Architects in Private Practice, Ankara, 1999, pp. 16–17

Yapı, "Berlinli ve Ankaralı Genç Mimarlar," "Söğütözü İş ve Ticaret Merkezi," February 2000, Issue 219, p. 53

Chamber of Architects of Turkey, 7. National Architecture Exhibition and Awards 2000, The Building Information Centre (YEM) Publications, p. 85

Arredamento Mimarlık, "Söğütözü İş ve Alışveriş Merkezi," 2000/06, pp. 78–79

Savaş, Ayşen (ed.), *METU Architectural Projects 1*, Competition Projects 2000–2008, pp. 132–135, 202, 203

Tasarım 128, 2003/02, pp. 47–59

Beaver, Robyn (ed.), *1000 Architects*, The Images Publishing Group Pty Ltd, 2004, Australia, p. 10

Hindrichs, Dirk U. and Winfried Heusler (eds.), *Birkhauser Façades, Building Envelopes for the 21st Century*, Publishers for Architecture, Basel, Boston, Berlin, 2004, pp. 166–167

Kazmaoğlu, Mine (ed.), *Architecture Almanac 2: Architecture in Turkey*, 2004, Koleksiyon Publications, pp. 164–169

Chamber of Architects of Turkey, 9. National Architecture Exhibition and Awards 2004, "Söğütözü Business and Shopping Centre," Project participation, The Building Information Centre (YEM) Publications, p. 44

Arredamento Mimarlık, "Armada Alışveriş Merkezi," 2004/02, pp. 52–55

Schüco Calendar 2004, Armada Shopping and Business Center

International Architects Association 2005 İstanbul Congress, *Journal 35*, UIA Folder Chamber of Architects, Ankara Office, pp. 26–27

Winning Shopping Center Designs, 28th International Design and Development Awards, *ISCS Catalog Number: 258*, New York 2005, pp. 70–73

XXI Mimarlık Tasarım Mekan, "Yapı Yenileme-Üniversite Kampüsü-Ankara, Rasyonel Bir Dönüşüm," January 2005, Issue 30, pp. 52-55

Yeni Mimar, 3 October–16 October 2005, Issue 29, pp. 6–7

Knauf Alçıpan, October 2005, Issue 19, pp. 8–9

Hürriyet, "Söğütözü Şehir Merkezi, Ankara Ticaret Odası Kongre Merkezi," 20 March 2006, p. 7

İnşaat & Yatırım, May 2006, Issue 22, pp. 126–127

Mitsubishi Chemical Calendar 2006, "TOBB Economy and Technology University"

Yapı, "TOBB ETÜ Kampüsü," January 2007, Issue 302, pp. 70–76

İnşaat & Yatırım, January 2007, Issue 30, p. 164

Winart Proje Kapı-Pencere-Çatı-Cephe Mimari Proje Dergisi, January–February 2007, Issue 2, p. 36

Turkish Architects' Moscow Meeting: 20th Century Turkish Architecture, Şevki Vanlı Architecture Foundation–Architects' Association 1927, Ankara 2008, pp. 158–163

Emine Merdim Yılmaz, Gül Keskin (eds.), *Arkitera Architecture Almanac 2008*, Arkitera Architecture Center, pp. 231, 236–237

Sabah, "Armada'ya 2009'da kardeş gelecek," 1 February 2008, p. 6

Hazır Beton, July–August 2008, pp. 76–78

Ekonomist, 7–13 September, Issue 2008/36, pp. 36–37

Ankara Ekonomist, 2008, "Röportaj," September 21, pp. 32–33

Natura, October 2008, Issue 33, pp. 62–69

Radikal, Kültür/Sanat, "Panora Alışveriş Merkezi," 6 December 2008, p. 20

Architect Vision'08, Ankara 2008, pp. 70–71

Alü & Art, December–January 2009, Issue 2, pp. 66–67

Sabah, "İskitler Merkezi İş Alanı," 25 January 2009, pp. 5

Turkish Buildings & Decoration, March–April 2009, pp. 54–61

Arredamento Mimarlık, 2009/03, p. 93

Concept Plus, March 2009, Issue 01, pp. 124 –154

İnşaat ve Yatırım, "Mimarlık Bir Takım Oyunudur," May 2009, Issue 58, pp. 194–198

Natura, "İstanbul Avrupa Yakası Adalet Sarayı," May–June 2009, pp. 46–50

Çuhadaroğlu, May–August 2009, Issue: 25, pp. 12–13

İnşaat & Yatırım, June 2009, pp. 136–146

Pimeks Group, *Bülten*, June 2009, p. 13

Serbest Mimar, July 2009, 03, p. 14

Turkishtime arasta, July 2009, Issue 46, pp. 46–47

Turkishtime arasta, October 2009, Issue: 49, pp. 44–45

Turkishtime arasta, November 2009, Issue: 50, pp. 45

Yapı, 2010, Issue 348, p.12

Yapı, 2010, Issue 347, pp. 92–96

Kesmez, İlhan and Orçun Ersan (eds.), *Association of Turkish Architects in Private Practice 2010*, Agenda/Housing, pp. 80–81, 92–93, 154–155, 256–257, 341

XXI Mimarlık Tasarım Mekan, June–July 2010, pp. 28–32

Arredamento Mimarlık, 2010/09, pp. 100–121

Radikal Tasarım, 29 September 2010, Issue 20, p. 12

Hürriyet, "İyi mimarlık nedir?," 26 November 2010, p. 11

Projects/Buildings 4: Cultural Buildings, The Building Information Centre (YEM) Publications, 2011, pp. 16–21

Projects/Buildings 3" Educational Buildings, The Building Information Centre (YEM) Publications, 2011, pp. 154–159

Ankara Life, "Ankaralıların Yeni Buluşma Noktası Tepe Prime Açıldı," 10 January 2011, p.14

Tesisat Dergisi, Celal Okutan "Sürdürülebilir Yapılarda Enerji Verimliliği Önerileri," June 2011, Issue 186, p. 8

Ankara Sabah, 30 June 2011, "Ankara havacılığın gözbebeği olacak," p. 5

Başkent Ankara, 30 June 2011, "Ankara IDEF'i geri istiyor," p. 4

Hürriyet Yaşam Emlak, "Tepe Prime'ın açık hava AVM'si açılıyor," 22 September 2011, p. 5

Yapı, 2011, Issue 350, pp. 120–126

XXI Mimarlık Tasarım Mekan, June 2011, pp. 30–32, 34–36, 39, 42, 46

Tasarım, July 2011, Issue 213, pp. 80–85

Ankara Sabah, 26 July 2011, "Bezci: 2013 gelmeden fuar alanına kavuşalım," p. 5

XXI Mimarlık Tasarım Mekan, September 2011, pp. 58–62

Mimar, September 2011, Issue 6–7, pp. 4–5

Ankara Hürriyet, "Başkent'e 250 milyon dolarlık yeni yatırım," 15 September 2011, pp. 1, 5

Başkent Ankara, "Tepe Prime Avenue açıldı," 5 October 2011, p. 4

Konsept Projeler, October 2011, Issue 17, pp. 230–236

İnşaat Dünyası, 9/2011, pp. 103–116, 118–122, 124, 126

Arredamento Mimarlık, October 2011, Issue 250, p. 36

Gayrimenkul Türkiye, November–December 2011, Issue 22, p. 16

Mall Report, 2011, p. 65

Binat, Banu and Neslihan Şık (eds.), *Vitra Contemporary Architecture Series: Commercial Buildings 1*, Vitra, İstanbul, 2012, pp. 76–81, 232–235

Chamber of Architects of Turkey 13: *National Architecture Exhibition and Awards 2012 Catalogue*, pp. 30–31, 73–74

ARKIPARC'12, pp. 42–43

Exclusive Homes, January 2012, Issue 4, p. 86–88

Gayrimenkul Türkiye, January–February 2012, Issue 23, pp. 46–47

Milliyet, 4 February 2012, p. 10

Radikal, 4 February 2012, p. 24

Raf Ürün Dergisi, March 2012, Issue 37, pp. 129–144

G-News, April–June 2012, Issue 1

Haber Türk, 17 June 2012, "Gardenya'da balkona adım attığınızda doğa yanınızda," p. 12

BİMFED Usta, October–November–December 2012, Issue 16, pp. 44–45

Arredamento Mimarlık, November 2012, Issue 262, pp. 99–101

Özgen, Pelin, "Buruk geçen Mimarlık Bieanalleri," *Radikal*, 5 November 2012, p. 41

Yapı, December 2012, Issue 373, pp. 92–97

Mag, December 2012 "Armada Büyülüyor," p. 296

Markalar & Mimarları, pp. 12–17

Yapı, February 2013, Issue 375, p. 46

All Decor, March 2013, p. 116

Şantiye, "Arkiv seçkileri ArkiPARC 2013', 1 May 2013, p.155

Ankara Cumhuriyet "Akyurt kongre merkezi olacak," 6 May 2013, pp. 1–3

Timkoder, July–September 2013, Issue 22, pp. 54–56

Ankara Haber Türk, "Nata İncek'te Mogan Gölü keyfi," 23 June 2013, p. 5

XXI Ek, Yeşil Binalar Referans Rehberi, 2013, p. 62

Yapı, July 2013, Issue 380, p. 169

Ankara Sabah, "Nata İncek'te Mogan Gölü keyfi," 14 July 2013, p. 7

Konsept Projeler, September–October 2013, Issue 36, pp. 176–185

Yapı, October 2013, Issue 383, pp. 122–127

XXI Mimarlık Tasarım Mekan, October 2013, pp. 46–49

Exhibitions

1988 Chamber of Architects of Turkey, 1. National Architecture Exhibition and Awards, "TED Campus Student Club," Graphic Presentation Category

2000 Chamber of Architects of Turkey, 7. National Architecture Exhibition and Awards, "Söğütözü Business and Shopping Centre," Project Participation

2001 Middle East Technical University, Travelling Exhibition

2004 Chamber of Architects of Turkey, 9. National Architecture Exhibition and Awards, "Söğütözü Business and Shopping Centre," Project participation

2006 Association of Turkish Architects in Private Practice, Agenda/Housing Exhibition

2008 Association of Turkish Architects in Private Practice, Educational and Cultural Buildings Exhibition

2009 Turkish Architects' Moscow Meeting: 20th Century Turkish Architecture, Şevki Vanlı Foundation for Architecture – Architects' Association 1927

2010 Chamber of Architects of Turkey, 12. National Architecture Exhibition and Awards, Project Participation

2010 Contemporary, Florence

2011 Architects' Association 1927, Çizgi ile Düşünmek-Çizgi'de Düşünmek, METU Culture and Congress Centre

2011 Koleksiyon/TSMD Hosts Architects-2

2012 Chamber of Architects of Turkey, 13. National Architecture Exhibition and Awards, Project and Building Category Participation

Panels and Workshops

2012 Ankara CBD Urban Transformation and Development Project, ArkiPARC'12

Moderator: Celal Abdi Güzer

Speakers: Özhan Akçalı, Ali Gökşin, Ali Osman Öztürk

28 March 2012

2012 Vitra Contemporary Architecture Series: Zip City, Commercial Buildings Panel Series-2

Moderator: Nil Aynalı

Speakers: Beyhan Bolak, Ertun Hızıroğlu, Ali Osman Öztürk, Atila Yücel

10 April 2012

2012 Vitra Contemporary Architecture Series, ANKARA: The Capital City of Shopping

Commercial Buildings Panel Exhibition-4: "How can shopping centres separate from other real estate investments in the future?"

Moderator: Celal Abdi Güzer

Speakers: Cem Alfar, İhsan Ayrancıoğlu, Bünyamin Mutlu, Enis Öncüoğlu, Ali Osman Öztürk, Nihat Sandıkçıoğlu

2012 Mapic, The International Market for Retail Real Estate, Cannes, France

Speaker: Ali Osman Öztürk, "Prerequisites for retail developments in the city"

17 November 2012

2012 İstanbul Bilgi University, Graduate Program in Architectural Design, Berlin 31 August–7 September 2012, Architectural Excursion with Vitra

2013 TSMD Forum Projects that change Ankara 10/10: 2/10 Kazıkiçi Bostanları Central Business District

CBD as The view of Architect, Corporation and The Planner

Moderator: Enis Öncüoğlu

Speakers: Ali Osman Öztürk (Architect), Ali Gökşin (Vice-President of Ankara Municipality), Prof. Dr. Baykan Günay (METU Faculty of Architecture City and Regional Planning)

2013 İstanbul Bilgi University, Graduate Program in Architectural Design, Paris 7–15 September 2013, Architectural Excursion with Vitra

2013 Hamburg Workshop with gmp Architekten

2013 London Workshop with KPF-Kohn Pedersen Fox Associates

2013 Singapore Workshop with KPF-Kohn Pedersen Fox Associates

Photography Credits

All sketches by **Ali Osman Öztürk**
All drawings by **A Tasarım Mimarlık**

Ali Osman Öztürk: 40(18,19), 41(23,24,25), 205(5), 211(3,4,5)

Kadir Kır: 17(4), 27, 28(2), 29(3,7)

Cemal Emden: Cover photo, 19(12), 20(17,18), 21(20,22), 29(4,5), 93(2), 94, 95, 96(6,8,9,14), 98(16), 103, 104, 105, 106(4,5,6,7), 107 (10,11,12,13), 119, 120(4), 121(3), 121(11), 123, 126(5,7,), 127(8,9,10,11), 129, 130(4), 145(2), 153, 154(5), 156(12,13,14),157(5), 158, 159, 160(19,21), 161 (23,24,25,26), 163(3,4), 167, 168, 169, 170(6), 171(11), 193(2,3,4), 206(1), 207

Fethi Mağara: 17(5), 18(8), 31(3,4,5), 32(7,8,9,10), 35, 36(2,3,6,7), 39(16,17), 41(22), 49(26,27), 65(3,4,5), 89(1,2), 109(2), 144(1,2), 165(4,5,6), 172(1), 173(2), 174(3,4,5,6), 175(7,8), 176(12,13,14,15,16), 177(18,19,20)

Gürkan Akay: 130(4), 131(6)

Oğuzhan Burak: 91(11,13)

Melih Uçar: 20(1), 65(2)

Kerem Şeker-Salih Kılıç: 16(1), 17(6,7), 32(6), 33(11), 38(11), 41(21), 111(8), 220, 226, 227, 228, 229, 230, 231, 232, 233, 236, 237

Ali Cengizkan Archive: 'The Practice' page / Portraits of students and professors in the Middle East Technical University

Via/Port Archive: 124, 125, 126(6), 209(1)